THE AUTHORS

DR CHRISTOPHER PASS, B.Sc. (Econ), M.Sc., M.Phil., Ph.D., is a lecturer in managerial economics at the University of Bradford's Management Centre. He is co-author of the books *Trade and Growth*, *Monopoly*, *The Brewing Industry* and *Savings and Investment*.

DR BRYAN LOWES, B.Sc., M.Phil., Ph.D., Cert.Ed., ACMA, is also a lecturer in managerial Economics at the Management Centre, University of Bradford. He is co-author of the textbooks *Modern Managerial Economics* and *Principles of Modern Management*.

DR LESLIE DAVIES, B.A. (Econ), Ph.D., is a research assistant at the University of Bradford's Management Centre.

COLLINS
REFERENCE

DICTIONARY OF
ECONOMICS

DICTIONARY OF
ECONOMICS

CHRISTOPHER PASS,
BRYAN LOWES AND LESLIE DAVIES

COLLINS
London and Glasgow

First published 1988

© C. Pass, B. Lowes, L. Davies 1988

Diagrams by Gordon Barr

ISBN 0 00 434353 0

British Library Cataloguing in Publication Data

Pass, Christopher
 Collins dictionary of economics.
 1. Economics—Dictionaries
 I. Title II. Lowes, Bryan III. Davies,
 Leslie
 330'.03'21 HB61

Printed in Great Britain by Collins, Glasgow

CONTENTS

PREFACE

This dictionary contains material especially suitable for students reading 'foundation' economics courses at polytechnics and universities, and for students preparing for advanced school economics examinations. The dictionary will be useful also to 'A' and degree-level students reading economics as part of broader-based business studies, commerce or social science courses, as well as to students pursuing professional qualifications in the accountancy and banking areas. Finally, it is expected that the dictionary will be of interest to general readers of the economic and financial press.

The dictionary provides a comprehensive coverage of mainstream economic terms, focusing in particular on theoretical concepts and principles and their practical applications. Key economic terms are given special prominence, including, where appropriate, diagrammatic illustration. In addition, the dictionary includes various business, commercial and accountancy terms, and mathematical and statistical terms which are relevant to an understanding of economic analysis and applications. It is, of course, difficult to draw a precise dividing line between economic and economics-related material and other subject matter. Accordingly, readers are recommended to consult other volumes in this series should they fail to find a particular entry in this dictionary. In the interests of brevity, we have kept institutional minutiae and description, as well as historical preamble, to a minimum.

To cater for a wide-ranging readership with varying degrees of knowledge requirements, dictionary entries have been structured, where appropriate, so as to provide firstly a basic definition and explanation of a particular concept, leading through cross references to related terms and more advanced refinements of the original concept.

Cross references are denoted both in the text and at the end of entries by reproducing the keywords in SMALL CAPITAL LETTERS.

Acknowledgements

We should like to thank Peter Maunder of the Department of Economics, Loughborough University, for invaluable editorial advice on the selection and writing of dictionary entries; and Kate Harris, Ian Crofton and Edwin Moore of Collins for their excellent work in preparing the manuscript for publication. Particular thanks are due to Sylvia Ashdown for her patience and efficiency in typing the manuscript.

Christopher Pass, Bryan Lowes, Leslie Davies

A

ability-to-pay principle of taxation, *n.* the principle that TAXATION should be based on the financial standing of the individual. Thus, persons with high income are more readily placed to pay large amounts of tax than people on low incomes. In practice, the ability-to-pay approach has been adopted by most countries as the basis of their taxation systems (see PROGRESSIVE TAXATION). Unlike the BENEFITS-RECEIVED PRINCIPLE OF TAXATION, the ability-to-pay approach is compatible with most governments' desire to redistribute income from higher income earners to low income earners. See REDISTRIBUTION-OF-INCOME PRINCIPLE OF TAXATION.

above-normal profit or **excess profit,** *n.* a PROFIT greater than that which is just sufficient to ensure that a firm will continue to supply its existing product or service (see NORMAL PROFIT). Short-run (i.e. temporary) above-normal profits resulting from an imbalance of market supply and demand promote an efficient allocation of resources if they encourage new firms to enter the market and increase market supply. By contrast, long-run (i.e. persistent) above-normal profits (MONOPOLY or *supernormal profits*) distort the RESOURCE ALLOCATION process because they reflect the overpricing of a product by monopoly suppliers protected by BARRIERS TO ENTRY. See PERFECT COMPETITION.

above-the-line promotion, *n.* the promotion of goods and services through media ADVERTISING in the press and on television and radio, as distinct from *below-the-line promotion* such as direct mailing and in-store exhibitions and displays. See SALES PROMOTION.

absolute advantage, *n.* an advantage possessed by a country when, using a given resource input, it is able to produce more output than other countries possessing the same resource input. This is illustrated in Fig. 1 on page 2 with respect to two countries (A and B) and two goods (X and Y). Country A's resource input enables it to produce either 100X or 100Y; the same resource input in Country B enables it to produce either 180X or 120Y. It can be seen that Country B is absolutely more efficient than Country A since it can produce more of both goods. Superficially this suggests that there is no basis for trade between the two countries.

However, it is COMPARATIVE ADVANTAGE, not absolute advantage, which determines whether INTERNATIONAL TRADE is beneficial or not, because even if Country B is more efficient at producing both goods it may pay Country B to specialize (see SPECIALIZATION) in producing good X at which it has the greater advantage.

Physical output of X and Y
from a given factor input

Country	Good	
	X	Y
A	100	100
B	180	120

Fig. 1. **Absolute advantage**. The relationship between resource input and output.

absolute concentration measure, see CONCENTRATION MEASURES.

absolute value, *n.* a mathematical term for the magnitude of a number, ignoring its sign. The absolute value of a positive number is the number itself; while the absolute value of a negative number is the number without its minus sign.

In estimating PRICE ELASTICITY OF DEMAND, for example, our interest is in the degree of responsiveness of quantity demanded to changes in price, and the fact that a price *increase* causes a *decrease* in quantity demanded (and vice versa) giving a negative elasticity number is of little interest. Here taking the absolute value of the elasticity number is more appropriate.

absorption, *n.* the allotment of OVERHEADS to units of product by means of OVERHEAD COST RATES. Provided that actual overheads do not exceed BUDGET and that actual output is the same as budgeted output, then the overhead cost rate should allow total product cost to be determined and a selling price set which will recover the overhead costs involved in its production and selling. See STANDARD COST, OVERHEAD COST VARIANCE.

absorption costing, *n.* the management accounting practice of charging all costs (both VARIABLE COSTS and FIXED COSTS) to products.

ACAS, see ADVISORY, CONCILIATION AND ARBITRATION SERVICE.

accelerator, *n.* the relationship between the amount of net or INDUCED INVESTMENT (gross investment less REPLACEMENT INVESTMENT) and the *rate of change* of NATIONAL INCOME. A rapid rise in income and consumption spending will put pressure on existing capacity and encourage businesses to invest not only to replace existing capital as it wears out but also to invest in *new* plant and equipment to meet the increase in demand.

By way of simple illustration, let us suppose a business meets the existing demand for its product utilizing 10 machines, one of which is replaced each year. If demand increases by 20 per cent, it must invest in two new machines to accommodate that demand, in addition to the one replacement machine.

Fig. 2. **Accelerator**. The graph shows how gross national product and the level of investment vary over time. See main entry.

Investment is thus, in part, a function of changes in the level of income: $I = f(\Delta Y)$. A rise in induced investment, in turn, serves to reinforce the MULTIPLIER effect in increasing national income.

The combined effect of accelerator and multiplier forces working through an *investment cycle* has been offered as an explanation for changes in the level of economic activity associated with the BUSINESS CYCLE. Because the *level* of investment depends upon the *rate of change* of GNP, when GNP is rising rapidly then investment will be at a high level, as producers seek to add to their capacity (time t in Fig. 2). This high level of investment will add to AGGREGATE DEMAND and help to maintain a high level of GNP. However, as the rate of growth of GNP slows down from time t onward, businessmen will no longer need to add as rapidly to capacity, and investment will decline towards replacement investment levels. This lower level of investment will reduce aggregate demand and contribute towards the eventual fall in GNP. Once GNP has persisted at a low level for some time, then machines will gradually wear out and businessmen will need to replace some of these machines if they are to maintain sufficient production capacity to meet even the lower level of aggregate demand experienced. This increase in the level of investment

3

at time t_1 will increase aggregate demand and stimulate the growth of GNP.

accepting house, *n.* a MERCHANT BANK or similar organization that underwrites (guarantees to honour) a commercial BILL OF EXCHANGE in return for a fee. See DISCOUNT, REDISCOUNTING.

accounting period, *n.* the time period over which a firm prepares its TRADING AND PROFIT-AND-LOSS ACCOUNT and at the end of which it draws up its BALANCE SHEET. JOINT-STOCK COMPANIES are required by law to prepare ANNUAL REPORTS AND ACCOUNTS and most other firms prepare annual accounts as well, though many firms now prepare quarterly, monthly or even weekly trading accounts to give prompt feedback about performance.

accounting ratio, *n.* a means of placing a firm's accounting or financial figures in context by expressing the figures as ratios of other figures in order to appraise their 'bigness' or 'smallness'. Examples include RETURN ON CAPITAL-EMPLOYED and STOCK-TURNOVER RATIO.

accounts, *n.* the financial statements of an individual or organization prepared from a system of recorded financial transactions. Public limited JOINT-STOCK COMPANIES are required to publish their year- (or period-) end financial statements, which must comprise at least a TRADING AND PROFIT-AND-LOSS ACCOUNT and BALANCE SHEET, to enable SHAREHOLDERS to assess their company's financial performance during the period under review. AUDITORS also require a set of year- (or period-) end accounts to enable them to undertake appropriate tests so as to form and submit their opinion on them to the company's shareholders. Non-incorporated bodies such as sole proprietors and partnerships are not subject to such rigorous legislation but must prepare appropriate financial statements to submit to the INLAND REVENUE as a basis for tax assessments. See LEDGER.

accounts payable, see CREDITORS.

accounts receivable, see DEBTORS.

accruals principle of accounting, *n.* the principle that all a firm's costs and revenues should be counted in the company's accounts from the date when the expenses are legally incurred and when the revenues are receivable, not when the expenses are actually paid or the cash received.

acid test ratio, see CURRENT RATIO.

activity rate, *n.* the proportion of the LABOUR FORCE, or a particular subgroup within the labour force such as women, which is in employment.

actual gross national product (GNP), *n.* the level of real output currently being produced by an economy. Actual GNP may or may not be equal to a country's POTENTIAL GROSS NATIONAL PRODUCT. The level of actual GNP is determined by the interaction of AGGREGATE DEMAND and potential GNP. If aggregate demand falls short of potential GNP at any point in time then actual GNP will be equal to aggregate demand, leaving a DEFLATIONARY GAP (output gap) between actual and potential GNP. However, at high levels of aggregate demand (in excess of potential GNP), potential GNP sets a ceiling on actual output, and any excess of aggregate demand over potential GNP shows up as an INFLATIONARY GAP.

Over time the rate of growth of actual GNP will depend upon the rate of growth of aggregate demand, on the one hand, and the growth of potential GNP, on the other.

actuary, *n.* a statistician who calculates insurance risks and premiums. See RISK AND UNCERTAINTY, INSURANCE COMPANY.

adaptive-expectations hypothesis (of inflation), *n.* the hypothesis that EXPECTATIONS of the future rate of INFLATION are based on the inflationary experience of the recent past. As a result, once under way, inflation feeds upon itself with, for example, trade unions demanding an increase in wages in the current pay round which takes into account the expected future rate of inflation which, in turn, leads to further price rises. See EXPECTATIONS-ADJUSTED AUGMENTED PHILLIPS CURVE, INFLATIONARY-SPIRAL.

'adjustable peg' exchange-rate system, *n.* a form of FIXED EXCHANGE-RATE SYSTEM originally operated by the INTERNATIONAL MONETARY FUND, in which the EXCHANGE RATES between currencies are fixed (pegged) at particular values (for example, £1 = $3); but which can be changed to new fixed values should circumstances require it. For example, £1 = $2, the re-pegging of the pound at a lower value in terms of the dollar (DEVALUATION); or £1 = $4, the re-pegging of the pound at a higher value in terms of the dollar (REVALUATION).

adjustment mechanism, *n.* a means of correcting balance of payments disequilibria. There are three main ways of removing payments deficits or surpluses: (a) external price adjustments; (b) internal price and income adjustments; (c) trade and foreign-exchange restrictions. See BALANCE-OF-PAYMENTS EQUILIBRIUM.

administered price, *n.* **1.** a price for a PRODUCT which is set by an individual producer or group of producers. In PERFECT COMPETITION characterized by many very small producers, the price charged is determined by the interaction of market demand and market supply and the individual producer has no control over this price. By contrast, in an OLIGOPOLY and a MONOPOLY large producers have considerable discretion over the prices they charge and can, for example, use some administrative formula like FULL-COST PRICING to determine the particular price charged. A number of producers may combine to administer the price of a product by operating a CARTEL or price-fixing agreement.

2. a price for a product, or CURRENCY, etc., which is set by the government or an international organization. For example, an individual government or INTERNATIONAL COMMODITY AGREEMENT may fix the prices of agricultural produce or commodities such as tin to support producers' incomes; under an internationally managed FIXED EXCHANGE-RATE SYSTEM member countries establish fixed values for the exchange rates of their currencies.

See PRICE SUPPORT, PRICE CONTROLS.

administration costs, *n.* the COSTS of maintaining an organization within which goods or services can be produced. They include: salaries of managers, accounting, personnel and secretarial staff; rent, heat and light of the offices they occupy; and stationery, postage and equipment costs.

See OVERHEADS.

ad valorem tax, *n.* a TAX which is levied as a percentage of the price of a unit of output.

See SPECIFIC TAX, VALUE-ADDED TAX.

advances, see LOANS.

advertising, *n.* a means of stimulating demand for a product and establishing strong BRAND LOYALTY. Advertising is one of the main forms of PRODUCT DIFFERENTIATION competition, and is used both to inform prospective buyers of a brand's particular attributes and to persuade them that the brand is superior to competitors' offerings.

There are two contrasting views of advertising's effect on MARKET PERFORMANCE. Traditional, 'static' market theory, on the one hand, emphasizes the misallocative effects of advertising. Here advertising is depicted as being solely concerned with brand-switching between competitors within a static overall market demand and serves to increase total supply costs and the price paid by the consumer. This is depicted in Fig. 3a. (See PROFIT MAXIMIZATION).

The alternative view of advertising emphasizes its role as one of expanding market demand and ensuring that firms' demand is maintained at levels which enable them to achieve economies of large-scale production (see ECONOMIES OF SCALE). Thus, advertising may be

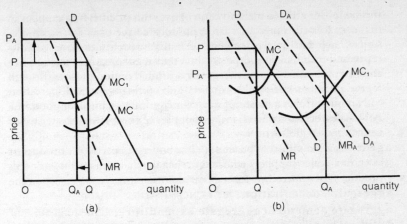

Fig. 3. **Advertising.** (a) The static market effects of advertising on demand (D). The profit maximizing (see PROFIT MAXIMIZATION) price-output combination (PQ) without advertising is shown by the intersection of the marginal revenue curve (MR) and the marginal cost curve (MC). By contrast, the addition of advertising costs serves to shift the marginal cost curve to MC_1, so that the PQ combination (shown by the intersection of MR and MC_1) now results in higher price (P_A) and lower quantity supplied (Q_A). (b) The initial profit-maximizing price-output combination (PQ) without advertising is shown by the intersection of the marginal revenue curve (MR) and the marginal cost curve (MC). The effect of advertising is to expand total market demand from DD to D_AD_A with a new marginal revenue curve (MR_A). This expansion of market demand enables the industry to achieve economies of scale in production which more than offsets the additional advertising cost. Hence, the marginal cost curve in the expended market (MC_1) is lower than the original marginal cost curve. The new profit maximizing price-output combination (determined by the intersection at MR_A and MC_1) results in a lower price (P_A) than before and a larger quantity supplied (Q_A).

See BARRIERS TO ENTRY, MONOPOLISTIC COMPETITION, OLIGOPOLY, DISTRIBUTIVE EFFICIENCY.

associated with a higher market output and lower prices than allowed for in the static model. This is illustrated in Fig. 3b.

Advisory, Conciliation and Arbitration Service (ACAS), *n.* a body established in the UK in 1975 to provide counselling services with regard to INDUSTRIAL RELATIONS and employment policy matters, in particular that of MEDIATION, CONCILIATION and ARBITRATION in cases of INDUSTRIAL DISPUTE.

after-sales service, *n*. the provision of back-up facilities by a supplier or his agent to a customer after he has purchased the product. After-sales service includes the replacement of faulty products or parts and the repair and maintenance of the product on a regular basis. These services are often provided free of charge for a limited period of time through formal guarantees of product quality and performance, and thereafter, for a modest fee, as a means of securing continuing customer goodwill. After-sales service is thus an important part of competitive strategy. See PRODUCT DIFFERENTIATION.

agent, *n*. an individual or business (e.g. a buyer of a particular product or asset, or a dealer/supplier) who acts on behalf of a client and buys or sells products/assets in return for a COMMISSION.

aggregate concentration, see CONCENTRATION MEASURES.

aggregate demand or **aggregate expenditure,** *n*. the total amount of expenditure (in nominal terms) on domestic goods and services. In the CIRCULAR FLOW OF NATIONAL INCOME MODEL aggregate demand is made up of CONSUMPTION expenditure (C) (see CONSUMPTION, sense 1), INVESTMENT EXPENDITURE (I), GOVERNMENT EXPENDITURE (G) and net EXPORTS (exports less imports) (E):

$$\text{aggregate demand} = C + I + G + E$$

Some of the components of aggregate demand are relatively stable and change only slowly over time (e.g., consumption expenditure); others are much more volatile and change rapidly, causing fluctuations in the level of economic activity (e.g., investment expenditure).

Aggregate demand interacts with AGGREGATE SUPPLY to determine the EQUILIBRIUM LEVEL OF NATIONAL INCOME. Governments seek to regulate the level of aggregate demand in order to maintain FULL EMPLOYMENT, avoid INFLATION, promote ECONOMIC GROWTH and secure BALANCE-OF-PAYMENTS EQUILIBRIUM through the use of FISCAL POLICY and MONETARY POLICY.

See AGGREGATE DEMAND SCHEDULE, ACTUAL GROSS NATIONAL PRODUCTS, DEFLATIONARY GAP, INFLATIONARY GAP, BUSINESS CYCLE, STABILIZATION POLICY, POTENTIAL GROSS NATIONAL PRODUCT.

aggregate demand/aggregate supply approach to national income determination, see EQUILIBRIUM LEVEL OF NATIONAL INCOME.

aggregate demand schedule, *n*. a schedule depicting the total amount of spending on domestic goods and services at various levels of NATIONAL INCOME. It is constructed by adding together the CONSUMPTION,

Fig. 4. **Aggregate demand schedule** (a) The graph shows how AGGREGATE DEMAND varies with the level of NATIONAL INCOME. (b) Shifts in the schedule due to determining factor changes. For example, if there is an increase in the PROPENSITY TO CONSUME, the consumption schedule will shift upwards serving to shift the aggregate demand schedule upwards from AD to AD_1; a reduction in government spending will shift the schedule downwards from AD to AD_2.

INVESTMENT, GOVERNMENT EXPENDITURE and EXPORTS schedules, as indicated in Fig. 4a.

A given aggregate demand schedule is drawn up on the usual CETERIS PARIBUS conditions. It will shift upwards or downwards if some determining factor changes. See Fig. 4b.

9

aggregated rebate, *n.* a type of RESTRICTIVE TRADE PRACTICE whereby DISCOUNTS on purchases are related not to customers' individual orders but to their total purchases over a period of time. This can produce anticompetitive effects because it encourages buyers to place the whole of their orders with the one supplier, to the exclusion of competing suppliers. See MONOPOLY POLICY.

aggregate expenditure, see AGGREGATE DEMAND.

aggregate supply, *n.* the total amount of domestic goods and services supplied by businesses, including both consumer products and capital goods. Aggregate supply interacts with AGGREGATE DEMAND to determine the EQUILIBRIUM LEVEL OF NATIONAL INCOME (see AGGREGATE SUPPLY SCHEDULE).

In the short term, aggregate supply will tend to vary with the level of demand for goods and services, though the two need not correspond exactly. For example, businesses could supply more products than are demanded in the short term, the difference showing up as a build-up of unsold STOCKS (unintended INVENTORY INVESTMENT). On the other hand, businesses could supply less products than are demanded in the short term, the difference being met by running down stocks. However, discrepancies between aggregate supply and aggregate demand cannot be very large or persist for long, and generally businesses will only offer to supply output if they expect spending to be sufficient to sell all that output.

Over the long term, aggregate supply can increase as a result of increases in the LABOUR FORCE, increases in CAPITAL STOCK and improvements in labour PRODUCTIVITY.

See ACTUAL GROSS NATIONAL PRODUCT, POTENTIAL GROSS NATIONAL PRODUCT, ECONOMIC GROWTH.

aggregate supply schedule, *n.* a schedule depicting the total amount of domestic goods and services supplied by businesses at various levels of total expenditure. The AGGREGATE SUPPLY schedule is generally drawn as a 45° line because business will offer any particular level of national output only if they expect total spending (AGGREGATE DEMAND) to be just sufficient to sell all of that output. Thus, in Fig. 5 £100 million of expenditure calls forth £100 million of aggregate supply, £200 million of expenditure calls forth £200 million of aggregate supply, and so on. However, this process cannot continue indefinitely, for once an economy's resources are fully employed in supplying products then additional expenditure cannot be met from additional domestic

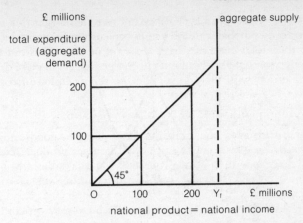

Fig. 5. **Aggregate supply schedule**. See main entry.

resources because the potential output ceiling of the economy has been reached. Consequently beyond the full-employment level of national product, Y_f, the aggregate supply schedule becomes vertical. See POTENTIAL GROSS NATIONAL PRODUCT, ACTUAL GROSS NATIONAL PRODUCT.

Aggregate supply interacts with aggregate demand to determine the EQUILIBRIUM LEVEL OF NATIONAL INCOME.

agricultural policy, *n.* a policy concerned both with protecting the economic interests of the agricultural community by subsidizing farm prices and incomes, and with promoting greater efficiency by encouraging farm consolidation and mechanization. See Fig. 6 on page 12.

The rationale for supporting agriculture partly reflects the 'special case' nature of the industry itself: agriculture, unlike manufacturing industry, is especially vulnerable to events outside its immediate control. Supply tends to fluctuate erratically from year to year depending upon such vagaries as the weather and the incidence of pestilence and disease (S_1, S_2 and S_3 in Fig. 6a), causing wide changes in farm prices and farm incomes. Over the long term, while the demand for many basic foodstuffs and animal produce has grown only slowly (from DD to D_1D_1 in Fig. 6b), significant PRODUCTIVITY improvements associated with farm mechanization, chemical fertilizers and pesticides, etc., have tended to increase supply at a faster rate than demand (from SS to S_1S_1 in Fig. 6b), causing farm prices and incomes to fall.

Farming can thus be very much a hit-and-miss affair, and govern-

Fig. 6. **Agricultural policy.** (a) The short-term shifts in supply (S) and their effects on price (P) and quantity (Q). (b) Long-term shifts caused by the influence of productivity improvement on supply.

ments concerned with the impact of changes in food supplies and prices (on, for example, the level of farm incomes, the balance of payments and inflation rates), may well feel some imperative to regulate the situation. But there are also social and political factors at work; for example, the desire to preserve rural communities and the fact that, even in some advanced industrial countries (for example, the European Community), the agricultural sector often commands a political vote out of all proportion to its economic weight. See ENGEL'S LAW, COBWEB THEOREM, PRICE SUPPORT, INCOME SUPPORT, COMMON AGRICULTURAL POLICY.

allocation, *n.* the breakdown of COSTS (and REVENUES) between different products, functions or company departments where it is possible to attribute costs (and revenues) directly to the departments where the cost (revenue) arises. For example, the depreciation OVERHEADS of factory departments can be allocated precisely between the production departments where the specific fixed assets are located, in analysing costs. See BUDGETING, STANDARD COST, APPORTIONMENT.

allocative efficiency, *n.* an aspect of MARKET PERFORMANCE that denotes the optimum allocation of scarce resources between end uses, in order to produce that combination of goods and services which best accords with the pattern of consumer demand. This is achieved when all market prices and profit levels are consistent with the real resource costs of supplying products. Specifically, consumer welfare is optimized when for each product the price is equal to the lowest real resource cost of supplying that product, including a NORMAL PROFIT reward to suppliers. Fig. 7a on page 14 depicts a normal profit equilibrium under conditions of PERFECT COMPETITION with price being determined by the intersection of the market supply and demand curves and with MARKET ENTRY/MARKET EXIT serving to ensure that price (P) is equal to minimum supply cost in the long run (AC).

By contrast, where some markets are characterized by monopoly elements, then in these markets output will tend to be restricted so that less resources are devoted to producing these products than the pattern of consumer demand warrants. In these markets, prices and profit levels are not consistent with the real resource costs of supplying the products. Specifically, in MONOPOLY markets the consumer is exploited by having to pay a price for a product which exceeds the real resource cost of supplying it, this excess showing up as an ABOVE-NORMAL PROFIT for the monopolist.

Fig. 7b depicts the profit maximizing price-output combination for a monopolist, determined by equating marginal cost and marginal revenue. This involves a smaller output and a higher price than would be the case under perfect competition, with BARRIERS TO ENTRY serving to ensure that the output restriction and excess prices persist over the long run. See PARETO OPTIMALITY.

amalgamation, see MERGER.

amortization, see DEPRECIATION (2).

analysis of variance, *n.* a statistical procedure to test for the statistical

(a)

(b)

Fig. 7. **Allocative efficiency**. (a) A normal profit equilibrium under conditions of perfect competition. (b) The profit maximizing price-output combination for a monopolist.

significance of differences between groups. Such procedures test the null hypothesis (see HYPOTHESIS TESTING) that samples have been drawn from the same POPULATION or from identical populations. Such tests will vary according to whether the samples drawn are related in some way or unrelated. See STATISTICAL INFERENCE.

annual general meeting (AGM), *n.* the yearly meeting of SHARE-HOLDERS which JOINT-STOCK COMPANIES are required by law to convene, in order to allow shareholders to discuss their company's ANNUAL REPORT AND ACCOUNTS, elect DIRECTORS and agree the DIVIDEND payouts suggested by directors. In practice, annual general meetings are usually poorly attended by shareholders and only rarely do directors fail to be re-elected on the strength of PROXY votes cast in favour of the directors.

annual report and accounts, *n.* a yearly report by the directors of a JOINT-STOCK COMPANY to the SHAREHOLDERS. It includes a copy of the company's BALANCE SHEET and a summary TRADING AND PROFIT-AND-LOSS ACCOUNT, along with other information which directors are required by law to disclose to shareholders. A copy of the annual report and accounts is sent to every shareholder prior to the company's ANNUAL GENERAL MEETING.

annuity, *n.* a series of equal payments at fixed intervals from an original lump sum INVESTMENT. Where an annuity has a fixed time span it is termed an *annuity certain* and the periodic receipts comprise both a phased repayment of principal (the original lump sum payment) and interest such that at the end of the fixed term there is a zero balance on the account. An *annuity in perpetuity* does not have a fixed time span but continues indefinitely and receipts can therefore only come from interest earned. Annuities can be obtained from pension funds or life insurance schemes.

anticompetitive practice, *n.* a practice which may have the effect of restricting, distorting or eliminating competition in a market. Examples of anticompetitive practices include EXCLUSIVE DEALING, REFUSAL TO SUPPLY and TIE-IN SALES. The COMPETITION ACT, 1980 provides for the investigation of anti-competitive practices in Britain. See MONOPOLY POLICY.

antimonopoly policy, see MONOPOLY POLICY.

antitrust policy, see MONOPOLY POLICY.

applied economics, *n.* the application of economic analysis to real world economic situations. Applied economics seeks to employ the predictions emanating from ECONOMIC THEORY in offering advice on the formulation of ECONOMIC POLICY. See ECONOMIC MODELS, HYPOTHESIS, HYPOTHESIS TESTING.

apportionment, *n.* the breakdown of COSTS (and REVENUES) between different products, functions or company departments where it is not possible to attribute costs (and revenues) directly to the departments where the cost or revenue concerned arises. For example, it is generally impossible to allocate rent and rates OVERHEADS exactly between departments in a factory and they can only be apportioned on some equitable basis such as the respective floor areas of departments. See BUDGETING, STANDARD COST, ALLOCATION.

appreciation, *n.* **1.** an increase in the value of a CURRENCY against other

15

currencies under a FLOATING EXCHANGE-RATE SYSTEM. An appreciation of a currency's value makes IMPORTS cheaper and EXPORTS more expensive, thereby encouraging additional imports and curbing exports and so assisting in the removal of a BALANCE OF PAYMENTS surplus and the excessive accumulation of INTERNATIONAL RESERVES.

How successful an appreciation is in removing a payments surplus depends on the reactions of export and import volumes to the change in relative prices; that is, the PRICE ELASTICITY OF DEMAND for exports and imports. If these values are low, i.e., demand is inelastic, trade volume will not change very much and the appreciation may in fact make the surplus larger. On the other hand, if export and import demand is elastic then the change in trade volumes will operate to remove the surplus. BALANCE-OF-PAYMENTS EQUILIBRIUM will be restored if the sum of export and import elasticities is greater than unity (the MARSHALL-LERNER CONDITION). See DEPRECIATION (1), INTERNAL–EXTERNAL BALANCE MODEL.

2. *n.* an increase in the price of an ASSET. Also called *capital appreciation*. Assets held for long periods, such as factory buildings, offices or houses, are most likely to appreciate in value because of the effects of INFLATION and increasing site values, though the value of short term assets like STOCKS can also appreciate. Where assets appreciate then their REPLACE-MENT COST will exceed their HISTORIC COST and such assets may need to be revalued periodically to keep their book values in line with their market values. See DEPRECIATION (2), REVALUATION PROVISION, INFLATION ACCOUNTING.

appropriation account, see PROFIT-AND-LOSS APPROPRIATION ACCOUNT.

a priori, *adj.* known to be true independently of the subject under debate. Economists frequently develop their theoretical models by reasoning, deductively, from certain prior assumptions to general predictions.

For example, operating on the assumption that consumers behave rationally in seeking to maximize their utility from a limited income, economists' reasoning leads them to the prediction that consumers will tend to buy more of those products whose relative price has fallen. See ECONOMIC MAN, CONSUMER EQUILIBRIUM.

arbitrage, *n.* the buying or selling of GOODS between two or more MARKETS in order to take profitable advantage of any differences in the prices quoted in these markets. By simultaneously buying in a low-price market and selling in the high-price market a dealer can make a profit from any disparity in prices between them, though in the process of buying and selling the dealer will add to DEMAND in the low-price market and add to SUPPLY in the high-price market and so narrow or eliminate the price disparity.

Arbitrage is practised by dealers in commodity markets and currency markets where their activities serve to iron out price disparities across markets. See SPOT MARKET, FUTURES MARKET.

arbitration, *n.* a procedure for settling disputes, most notably INDUSTRIAL DISPUTES in which a neutral third party or arbitrator, after hearing presentations from all sides in dispute, issues an award binding upon each side. Arbitration is mostly used only as a last resort when normal negotiating proceedings have failed to bring about an agreed settlement.

In the UK the ADVISORY, CONCILIATION AND ARBITRATION SERVICE (ACAS) acts in this capacity. See MEDIATION, COLLECTIVE BARGAINING, INDUSTRIAL RELATIONS.

Fig. 8. **Arc elasticity**. See main entry.

arc elasticity, *n.* a rough measure of the responsiveness of DEMAND or SUPPLY to changes in PRICE, INCOME, etc. In the case of PRICE ELASTICITY OF DEMAND it is the ratio of the percentage change in quantity demanded (Q) to the percentage change in price (P) over a price range such as P_0P_1 in Fig. 8. Arc elasticity of demand is expressed notationally as:

$$e = \frac{Q_1 - Q_0}{P_1 - P_0} \times \frac{P_1 + P_0}{Q_1 + Q_0}$$

where P_0 = original price, Q_0 = original quantity, P_1 = new price, Q_1 = new quantity.

Because arc elasticity measures the elasticity of demand (*e*) over a price range or arc of the demand curve it is only an approximation of demand elasticity at a particular price (POINT ELASTICITY). However, the arc elasticity formula gives a reasonable degree of accuracy in approximating point elasticity when price and/or quantity changes are small. See also ELASTICITY OF DEMAND.

arithmetical progression, *n.* a series of discrete values showing a growth pattern of the form:

$$a + (a + r) + (a + 2r) + (a + 3r), \text{ etc.}$$

where *a* is the original amount at the start and *r* is the amount added each time. Such a progression would show a linear growth trend over time. Arithmetic progressions can be used to analyse many problems in economics such as SIMPLE INTEREST ON LOANS. Compare GEOMETRICAL PROGRESSION.

arithmetic mean, *n.* see MEAN.

articles of association, *n.* the legal constitution of a JOINT-STOCK COMPANY which governs the internal relationship between the company and its members or SHAREHOLDERS. The articles govern the rights and duties of the membership and aspects of administration of the company. They will contain, for instance, the powers of the directors, the conduct of meetings, the dividend and voting rights assigned to separate classes of shareholders, and other miscellaneous rules and regulations. See MEMORANDUM OF ASSOCIATION.

asset, *n.* an item or property owned by an individual or a business which has a money value. Assets are of two main types: (a) physical assets such as plant and equipment, land, consumer durables (cars, washing machines, etc); (b) financial assets such as currency, bank deposits, stocks and shares. See INVESTMENT, LIQUIDITY, BALANCE SHEET, LIABILITY.

asset – growth maximization, *n.* a company objective in the THEORY OF THE FIRM which is used as an alternative to the traditional assumption of PROFIT MAXIMIZATION. Salaried managers of large JOINT-STOCK COMPANIES are assumed to seek to maximize the rate of growth of net assets as a means of increasing their salaries, power, etc, subject to maintaining a minimum share-value, so as to avoid the company being taken over with the possible loss of jobs. In Fig. 9 the rate of growth of assets is shown on the horizontal axis, and the ratio of the market value of company shares to the book value of company net assets (the share-valuation ratio) on the vertical axis. The valuation curve rises at first as increasing asset growth increases share value but beyond growth rate (G) excessive retention of profits to finance growth will reduce dividend payments to shareholders and depress share values. Managers will tend

Fig. 9. **Asset-growth maximization.** The variation of share valuation ratio against the company growth rate.

to choose the fastest growth rate (G★) which does not depress the share valuation below the level (V¹) at which the company risks being taken over. See also MANAGERIAL THEORIES OF THE FIRM, FIRM OBJECTIVES, DIVORCE OF OWNERSHIP FROM CONTROL.

asset–stripper, *n.* a predator firm which takes control of another firm (see TAKEOVER) with a view to selling off that firm's ASSETS, wholly or in part, for financial gain rather than continuing the firm as an on-going business.

The classical recipe for asset-stripping arises when the realizable market value of the firm's assets are much greater than what it would cost the predator to buy the firm; i.e., where there is a marked discrepancy between the asset-backing per share of the target firm and the price per share required to take the firm over. This discrepancy usually results from a combination of two factors: (a) gross under-valuation of the firm's assets in the BALANCE SHEET, (b) mismanagement or bad luck resulting in low profits or losses, both of which serve to depress the firm's share price.

asset structure, *n.* the proportions of various types of ASSET held by a firm as shown in the BALANCE SHEET. For example, a large manufacturing company or public utility is likely to have proportionately large FIXED ASSETS, while retail companies are likely to have proportionately large CURRENT ASSETS, such as DEBTORS and STOCK. A firm's asset structure helps to determine the way in which finance is raised, in particular the balance of long-term LOANS and short-term DEBT. See CAPITAL GEARING.

asset value per share or **break–up value,** *n.* the total value of a firm's tangible book ASSETS less all short and long-term LIABILITIES as shown in the BALANCE SHEET. The net assets figure is divided by the number of

ORDINARY SHARES the company has, to show approximately how much asset value supports each share. In the case of a LIQUIDATION it would be of some use to the SHAREHOLDERS in estimating how much they may reasonably expect to receive from the sale of the firm or of its assets. Book values of assets may be a reasonable estimate of their value to the firm as a going concern but upon break-up they tend to be worth considerably less depending upon the alternative uses to which they can be put. See also ASSET-STRIPPER, SHARE CAPITAL.

asset–value theory (of exchange rate determination), *n.* an explanation of the volatility of EXCHANGE RATE movements under a FLOATING EXCHANGE-RATE SYSTEM. Whereas the PURCHASING–POWER PARITY THEORY suggests that SPECULATION is consistent with the achievement of BALANCE–OF–PAYMENTS EQUILIBRIUM, the asset-value theory emphasizes that in all probability it will not be. In this theory the exchange rate is an asset price, the relative price at which the stock of money, bills and bonds and other financial assets of a country will be willingly held by foreign and domestic asset holders. An actual alteration in the exchange rate or a change in expectations about future rates can cause asset holders to alter their portfolios. The resultant change in demand for holdings of foreign currency relative to domestic currency assets can at times produce sharp fluctuations in exchange rates. In particular, uncertainty about future market rates and the unwillingness of banks and other large financial participants in the foreign exchange markets to take substantial positions in certain currencies, especially SOFT CURRENCIES, may diminish funds for stabilizing speculation that would in turn diminish or avoid erratic exchange rate movements.

If this should prove the case then financial asset-switching is likely to reinforce and *magnify* exchange-rate movements initiated by current account transactions (i.e., changes in imports and exports), and in consequence may produce exchange rates that are inconsistent with effective overall balance-of-payments equilibrium in the longer run.

associated company, *n.* a JOINT-STOCK COMPANY in which another company or group has a significant, but not controlling, shareholding (specifically 20% or more of the voting shares but not more than 50%). In such a situation the investing company can exert influence on the commercial and financial policy decisions of the associated company, though in principle the associated company remains independent under its own management, producing its own annual accounts, and is not a subsidiary of the HOLDING COMPANY.

assurance, see INSURANCE.

asymptote, *n.* a line which continually approaches a given AXIS of a GRAPH but which never quite meets it. The line, in economics, is frequently a curve of the form

$$\gamma = \frac{a}{x},$$

a RECTANGULAR HYPERBOLA, where *a* is a constant.

asymptotic, *adj.* of or relating to an ASYMPTOTE.

atomistic competition, see PERFECT COMPETITION.

auction, *n.* a method of selling GOODS and SERVICES by competitive bidding. The sale will be made to the highest bidder subject to a reserve price being attained.

audit, *n.* the legal requirement for a JOINT-STOCK COMPANY to have its BALANCE SHEET and TRADING AND PROFIT-AND-LOSS ACCOUNT (the financial statements) and underlying accounting system and records examined by a qualified AUDITOR, so as to enable an opinion to be formed as to whether such financial statements show a TRUE AND FAIR VIEW and that they comply with the relevant statutes.

auditor, *n.* a professional accountant appointed to check the accuracy of a JOINT-STOCK COMPANY'S LEDGER accounts and ANNUAL REPORT AND ACCOUNTS, and to present an independent report to SHAREHOLDERS on whether the accounts present a *true and fair view* of the company's affairs.

Austrian school, *n.* a group of late 19th century economists at the University of Vienna who established and developed a particular line of theoretical reasoning. The tradition originated with Professor Carl Menger who argued against the classical theories of value which emphasised PRODUCTION and SUPPLY. Instead, he initiated the 'subjectivist revolution', reasoning that the value of a good was not derived from its cost but from the pleasure, or UTILITY, the CONSUMER can derive from it. This type of reasoning led to the MARGINAL UTILITY theory of value whereby successive increments of a commodity yield DIMINISHING MARGINAL UTILITY.

Friedrich von Wieser developed the tradition further, being credited with introducing the economic concept of OPPORTUNITY COST. Eugen von Böhm-Bawerk helped to develop the theory of INTEREST and CAPITAL, arguing that the price paid for the use of capital is dependent upon consumers' demand for present CONSUMPTION relative to future consumption. Ludwig von Mises and Friedrich von Hayek subsequently continued the tradition established by Carl Menger et al. See also CLASSICAL ECONOMICS.

authorized or **registered** or **nominal share capital,** *n.* the maximum amount of SHARE CAPITAL which a JOINT-STOCK COMPANY can issue at any time. This amount is disclosed in the BALANCE SHEET and may be altered by SHAREHOLDERS at the company ANNUAL GENERAL MEETING. See also ISSUED SHARE CAPITAL.

autocorrelation, *n.* a statistical situation where there is a particular pattern in the residual or error terms after an estimate has been calculated from sample observations of INDEPENDENT VARIABLES and DEPENDENT VARIABLES. If the estimated REGRESSION coefficients are good unbiased estimates of the true population coefficients of the independent variables, then the residual values should be randomly distributed, showing no consistent relationship with each other. If they are not, then the estimated regression equation is an inaccurate fit or has missed out other important independent variables which are affecting the dependent variable. Autocorrelated error terms occur where a series of error terms are related, and they are a frequent problem in TIME-SERIES ANALYSIS, where values of the error terms in consecutive time periods may be correlated. See also DURBIN-WATSON TEST.

automatic (built-in) stabilizers, *n.* elements in FISCAL POLICY which serve to automatically reduce the impact of fluctuations in economic activity. A fall in NATIONAL INCOME and output reduces government TAXATION receipts and increases its unemployment and social security payments. Lower taxation receipts and higher payments increase the government's BUDGET DEFICIT and restore some of the lost income (see CIRCULAR FLOW OF NATIONAL INCOME MODEL). See FISCAL DRAG.

automation, *n.* the application of advanced technology to industrial processes to ensure that all or nearly all of a particular activity (for example, car assembly) is undertaken by machines and not by labour. See PRODUCTIVITY, TECHNOLOGICAL UNEMPLOYMENT, TECHNOLOGICAL PROGRESSIVENESS, CAPITAL-LABOUR RATIO.

autonomous investment, *n.* that part of real INVESTMENT that is independent of the level of, and changes in, NATIONAL INCOME. Autonomous investment is mainly dependent on competitive factors such as plant modernization by businesses in order to cut costs or to take advantages of a new invention.
See INDUCED INVESTMENT, INVESTMENT SCHEDULE.

average, see MEAN.

average collection period, *n.* see DEBTORS–TO–SALES RATIO.

average cost, (long run), *n.* the unit cost (TOTAL COST divided by number of units produced) of producing outputs for plants of *different* sizes. The position of the SHORT-RUN average total cost (ATC) curve depends on its existing size of plant. In the long run a firm can alter the size of its plant. Each plant size corresponds to a different U-shaped short-run ATC curve. As the firm expands its scale of operation it moves from one curve to another. The path along which the firm expands – the LONG-RUN ATC curve – is thus the *envelope curve* of all the possible short-run ATC curves (see Fig. 10a on page 24).

It will be noted that the long-run ATC curve is typically assumed to be a shallow U-shape, with a least-cost point indicated by output level OX. To begin with, average cost falls (reflecting ECONOMIES OF SCALE); eventually, however, the firm may experience DISECONOMIES OF SCALE and average cost begins to rise.

However, empirical studies of companies' long-run average-cost curves suggest that diseconomies of scale are rarely encountered within the typical output ranges over which companies operate, so that most companies' average cost curves are L-shaped as in Fig. 10b. In cases where diseconomies of scale are encountered the MINIMUM EFFICIENT SCALE at which a company will operate corresponds to the minimum point of the long run average cost curve (Fig. 10a). Where diseconomies of scale are not encountered within the typical output range, minimum efficient scale corresponds with the output at which economies of scale are exhausted and constant returns to scale begin (Fig. 10b). Compare AVERAGE COST, (SHORT RUN).

average cost, (short run), *n.* the unit cost (TOTAL COST divided by number of units produced) of producing particular volumes of output in a plant of a given (fixed) size.

Average total cost (ATC) can be split up into average FIXED COST (AFC) and average VARIABLE COST (AVC). AFC declines continuously as output rises as a given total amount of fixed cost is 'spread' over a greater number of units. For example, with fixed costs of £1,000 per year and annual output of 1,000 units, fixed costs per unit would be £1, but if annual output rose to 2,000 units the fixed cost per unit would fall to 50p (see AFC curve in Fig. 11a on page 25).

Over the whole potential output range within which a firm can produce, AVC falls at first (reflecting increasing RETURNS TO THE VARIABLE FACTOR INPUT – output increases faster than costs), but then rises (reflecting DIMINISHING RETURNS to the variable inputs – costs increase

AVERAGE COST, (SHORT RUN)

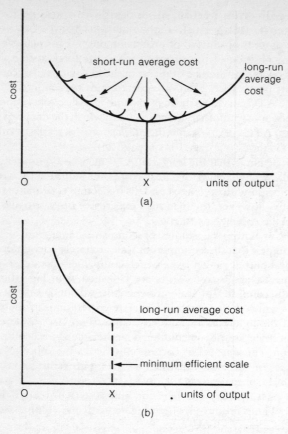

Fig. 10. **Average cost, (long run).** (a) The characteristic U-shape of the long-run average cost curve. (b) The characteristic L-shaped curve that in practice normally results from expansion.

faster than output), as shown by the AVC curve in Fig. 11a. Thus the conventional SHORT-RUN ATC curve is U-shaped.

However, over the more restricted output range in which firms typically operate, constant returns to the variable input are more likely to be experienced, where, as more variable inputs are added to the fixed inputs employed in production, equal increments in output result. In such circumstances AVC will remain constant over the whole output

Fig. 11. **Average cost, (short run).** (a) The characteristic curves of average total cost (ATC), average variable cost (AVC), and average fixed cost (AFC), over the whole output range. (b) The characteristic curves of ATC and AFC and constant line of AVC over the restricted output range.

range (as in Fig. 11b) and as a consequence ATC will decline in parallel with AFC. Compare AVERAGE COST (LONG RUN). See also LOSS.

average cost price, *n.* a selling PRICE for a product or service which is set equal to AVERAGE COST. See FULL-COST PRICING.

average cost pricing, *n.* a pricing principle which argues for setting PRICES equal to the AVERAGE COST of production and distribution, so that prices cover both MARGINAL COSTS and FIXED OVERHEADS costs incurred through past investments. This involves the (sometimes arbitrary) APPORTIONMENT of fixed (overhead) costs to individual units of output, though it does seek to recover in the price charged all the costs which would have been avoided by not producing the product. See also MARGINAL COST PRICING, TWO-PART TARIFF, FULL COST PRICING.

average deviation, *n.* a measure of variation within a group of numerical observations, i.e., the average of the (absolute values of the) deviations of the observations from the group MEAN. For example, if five products had prices of £5, £4, £3, £2 and £1 then the mean price is:

$$£ \frac{5+4+3+2+1}{5} = £ \frac{15}{5} = £3$$

and the distances by which the various prices depart from the mean price is:

		absolute values:	
£5 − 3 =	£2		|2|
£4 − 3 =	£1		|1|
£3 − 3 =	£0		|0|
£2 − 3 =	− £1		|1|
£1 − 3 =	− £2		|2|
	£0		£|6|

Unfortunately, the average of these deviations is always zero because in using a mean for a group of observations, the positive deviations from the mean will always exactly match the negative deviations from the mean. To get around this problem and concentrate upon the magnitude of the deviations rather than their signs the ABSOLUTE VALUES of the deviations can be considered. The sum of the absolute values of the deviations in the example above is £6 and the average of the absolute deviations is therefore £6/5 = £1.2. If the observations are grouped closely around the mean then their dispersion is small and the average of the absolute deviations will be small; if the observations are spread over a considerable distance from the mean then their dispersion is large and the average of the absolute deviations will be large. Compare STANDARD DEVIATION.

average fixed cost, see AVERAGE COST, (SHORT RUN).

average physical product, *n.* the average OUTPUT in the SHORT RUN theory of supply produced by each extra unit of VARIABLE FACTOR INPUT (in conjunction with a given amount of FIXED FACTOR INPUT). See RETURNS TO THE VARIABLE FACTOR INPUT.

average propensity to consume (APC), *n.* the fraction of a given level of DISPOSABLE INCOME which is spent on CONSUMPTION:

$$APC = \frac{\text{consumption}}{\text{income}}$$

See also PROPENSITY TO CONSUME, MARGINAL PROPENSITY TO CONSUME.

average propensity to import (APM), *n.* the fraction of a given level of NATIONAL INCOME which is spent on IMPORTS:

$$APM = \frac{\text{imports}}{\text{income}}$$

See also PROPENSITY TO IMPORT, MARGINAL PROPENSITY TO IMPORT.

average propensity to save (APS), *n.* the fraction of a given level of NATIONAL INCOME which is saved (see SAVINGS):

$$APS = \frac{\text{saving}}{\text{income}}$$

See also PROPENSITY TO SAVE, MARGINAL PROPENSITY TO SAVE.

average propensity to tax (APT), *n.* the fraction of a given level of NATIONAL INCOME which is appropriated by the government in TAXATION:

$$APT = \frac{\text{taxation}}{\text{income}}$$

See also PROPENSITY TO TAX, MARGINAL PROPENSITY TO TAX, AVERAGE RATE OF TAXATION.

average rate of taxation, *n.* the total TAX paid by an individual divided by the total income upon which the tax was based. For example, if an individual earned £10,000 in one year upon which that individual had to pay tax of £2,500, the average rate of taxation would be 25%. See STANDARD RATE OF TAXATION, MARGINAL RATE OF TAXATION, PROPENSITY TO TAX, PROPORTIONAL TAXATION, REGRESSIVE TAXATION, PROGRESSIVE TAXATION.

average revenue, *n.* the total revenue received (price × number of units sold) divided by the number of units. Price and average revenue are in fact equal: i.e., in Fig. 12 on page 28, the price £10 = average revenue (£10 × 10 ÷ 10) = £10. It follows that the DEMAND CURVE is also the average revenue curve facing the firm.

average variable cost, see AVERAGE COST.

Fig. 12. **Average revenue**. The demand curve or average revenue curve.

Fig. 13. **Axis**. See main entry.

axis, *n.* a straight line that intersects with another straight line at right angles to form the reference points of a GRAPH. The axes determine the locus of any point within their bounds by reference to COORDINATES, that is, the measurements along each of the two axes. The vertical axis is referred to as the *y*-axis and is at right angles to the horizontal or x-axis. The axes divide the graph into four quadrants (top right, top left, etc.)

and where the two axes meet is called the origin, denoted by O in Fig. 13. Each point in a two–dimensional plane is referred to as coordinate (X, Y) and each coordinate represents a unique point in that plane. Positive values of a variable such as quantity demanded would lie above the origin on the y-axis or to the right of it on the x-axis. In Fig. 13, point A has positive coordinates OX_1, OY_1.

B

back door, *n.* the informal mechanism whereby the Bank of England purchases TREASURY BILLS and other governmental financial securities from the DISCOUNT MARKET at their market price in order to release money to help the DISCOUNT HOUSES overcome temporary liquidity shortages. Compare FRONT DOOR.

backward integration, *n.* the joining together in one firm of two or more successive stages in a vertically-related production/distribution process, with a later stage (for example, bread making) being combined with an earlier stage (for example, flour milling). Backward integration is undertaken to cut costs and secure supplies of inputs. See VERTICAL INTEGRATION, FORWARD INTEGRATION.

bad debt, *n.* an accounting term for money owed which is unlikely to be paid because, for example, a customer has become insolvent (see INSOLVENCY). Such bad debts are written off against the PROFITS of the trading period as a business cost. See CREDIT CONTROL, DEBTORS–TO–SALES RATIO.

balanced budget, *n.* a situation where GOVERNMENT EXPENDITURE is equal to TAXATION and other receipts. In practice, most governments run unbalanced budgets as a means of regulating the level of economic activity.

Where the government spends more than it receives in taxation then a BUDGET DEFICIT is incurred. Where the government spends less than it receives in taxation then a BUDGET SURPLUS ensues. See BUDGET, FISCAL POLICY, PUBLIC SECTOR BORROWING REQUIREMENT.

balanced budget multiplier, *n.* a change in AGGREGATE DEMAND brought about by a change in GOVERNMENT EXPENDITURE which is exactly matched by a change in revenues received from TAXATION and other sources. The change in government expenditure has an immediate effect on aggregate demand and generates income of an equivalent size. By contrast, the change in taxation does not change aggregate demand by an equivalent amount because some of the increased/reduced DISPOSABLE INCOME will be offset by changes in SAVING. Consequently,

30

an increase in government expenditure and taxation of equal amounts will have a net expansionary effect on aggregate demand and incomes, while a decrease in government expenditure and taxation of equal amounts will have a net contractionary effect. See BUDGET, FISCAL POLICY.

balance of payments, *n.* a statement of a country's trade and financial transactions with the rest of the world over a particular period of time, usually one year. Fig. 14 on page 32 shows a standard presentation of balance of payments. The account is divided up into two main parts: (a) current account, and (b) investment and other capital transactions.

The current account shows the country's profit or loss in day-to-day dealings. It is made up under two headings. The 'visible' trade balance (BALANCE OF TRADE) indicates the difference between the value of EXPORTS and IMPORTS of goods (raw materials and fuels, foodstuffs, semi-processed products and finished manufactures). The second group of transactions make up the 'invisible' balance. These transactions include earnings from and payments for such services as banking, insurance and tourism. It also includes interest and profits on investments and loans, government receipts and spending on defence, overseas administration, etc.

In addition to current account transactions there are also currency flows into and out of the country related to capital items – investment monies spent by companies on new plant and the purchase of assets, borrowing by the government, and interbank dealings in sterling and foreign currency.

The current balance, and the investment and other capital flows, together with the balancing item, result in the *balance for official financing*. This figure shows whether the country has incurred an overall surplus or deficit. If the balance of payments is in surplus the country can add to its INTERNATIONAL RESERVES and, if necessary, repay borrowings; if it is in deficit this has to be covered by running down its international reserves or by borrowing.

A balance-of-payments deficit or surplus can be remedied in a number of ways, including external price adjustments, internal price and income adjustments, and trade and currency restrictions.

See BALANCE-OF-PAYMENTS EQUILIBRIUM.

balance-of-payments disequilibrium, see BALANCE-OF-PAYMENTS EQUILIBRIUM.

balance-of-payments equilibrium, *n.* a situation where, over a run of years, a country spends and invests abroad no more than other

31

Current account	£ million	
Visible balance (Balance of Trade)		
Food, beverages and tobacco	−3,792	
Basic materials	−2,359	
Oil, Lubricants	2,690	
Manufactures	−5,492	
Other items	490	
Invisible balance		−8,463
Services balance	4,990	
Interest, profits and dividends balance	4,686	
Transfers balance – mainly Government		
EEC commitments	−2,193	
		7,483
Current balance		−980

(a)

Transactions in UK assets and liabilities (investment and other capital transactions)*		
UK external assets (increase)	−92,229	
UK external liabilities (increase)	81,482	
Net transactions		−10,747
Balancing item		11,727

*Official financing: these figures include a net addition to UK international reserves of £2,891 million and foreign currency borrowings of £100 million (reflecting an overall balance-of-payments surplus).

(b)

Fig. 14. **Balance of Payments**. The Uk balance of payments for 1986. The balancing item in (b) includes errors and omissions in recording transactions, and leads and lags in currency payments and receipts. Source: *UK Balance of Payments*, CS0 (Pink Book), 1987.

countries spend and invest in it. Thus, the country neither adds to its stock of INTERNATIONAL RESERVES, nor sees them reduced.

In an unregulated world it is highly unlikely that external balance will always prevail. Balance of payments deficits and surpluses will occur, but provided they are small, *balance-of-payments disequilibrium* can be readily accommodated. The main thing to avoid is a FUNDAMENTAL DISEQUILIBRIUM − a situation of chronic imbalance.

There are three main ways of restoring balance-of-payments equilibrium, should an imbalance occur:

UK domestic price of a product	Exchange rate	Price of the UK product exported to US
£1	£1 = $1.60	$1.60
£1	£1 = $1.40	$1.40

(a)

UK domestic price of a product	Exchange rate	Price of the UK product exported to US
£1	£1 = $1.60	$1.60
75p	£1 = $1.60	$1.20

(b)

Fig. 15. **Balance-of-payments equilibrium.** (a) Exchange rate adjustment. (b) Internal price adjustment.

(a) *external price adjustments.* Alterations in the EXCHANGE RATE between currencies involving (depending upon the particular exchange-rate system in operation) the DEVALUATION/DEPRECIATION and REVALU-ATION/APPRECIATION of the currencies concerned to make exports cheaper/more expensive and imports dearer/less expensive in foreign currency terms. For example, with regard to exports, in Fig. 15a if the pound–dollar exchange rate is devalued from $1.60 to $1.40 then this would allow British exporters to reduce their prices by a similar amount, thus increasing their price competitiveness in the American market.

(b) *internal price and income adjustments.* The use of deflationary and reflationary (see DEFLATION, REFLATION) monetary and fiscal policies to alter the prices of domestically produced goods and services vis-a-vis products supplied by other countries so as to make exports relatively cheaper/dearer and imports more expensive/cheaper in foreign currency terms. For example, again with regard to exports, if it were possible to reduce the domestic price of a British product, as shown in Fig. 15b, given an unchanged exchange rate, this would allow the dollar price of the product in the American market to be reduced, thereby improving its price competitiveness vis-a-vis similar American products. The same policies are used to alter the level of domestic income and spending, including expenditure on imports.

(c) *trade and foreign exchange restrictions.* The use of TARIFFS, QUOTAS, EXCHANGE CONTROLS, etc. to affect the price and availability of goods and services, and of the currencies with which to purchase these products.

Under a FIXED EXCHANGE-RATE SYSTEM, minor payments imbalances are corrected by appropriate domestic adjustments (b), but fundamental disequilibriums require, in addition, a devaluation or revaluation of the currency (a). However, it must be emphasized that a number of favourable conditions must be present to ensure the success of devaluations and revaluations (see, especially, DEVALUATION).

In theory, a FLOATING EXCHANGE-RATE SYSTEM provides an 'automatic' mechanism for removing payments imbalances in their incipiency (that is, before they reached 'fundamental' proportions): a deficit results in an immediate exchange-rate depreciation, and a surplus results in an immediate appreciation of the exchange rate. (see PURCHASING-POWER PARITY THEORY) However, again, a number of favourable conditions must be present to ensure the success of depreciations and appreciations. See also J-CURVE, INTERNAL-EXTERNAL BALANCE MODEL, MARSHALL-LERNER CONDITION.

balance of trade, *n.* a statement of a country's trade in GOODS (visibles) with the rest of the world over a particular period of time. The term 'balance of trade' specifically excludes trade in services (invisibles), and concentrates on finished manufactures, intermediate products, and raw materials which can be seen and recorded as they cross national boundaries. See BALANCE OF PAYMENTS.

balance sheet, *n.* an accounting statement of a firm's ASSETS and LIABILITIES on the last day of a trading period. The balance sheet lists the assets which the firm owns and sets against these the balancing obligations or claims of those groups of people who provided the funds to acquire the assets. Assets take the form of FIXED ASSETS and CURRENT ASSETS, while obligations take the form of SHAREHOLDERS' CAPITAL EMPLOYED, long term loans and CURRENT LIABILITIES. The balance sheet is compiled by summarizing information derived from the LEDGER accounts.

A simple balance sheet is illustrated in Fig. 16. Assets include fixed assets (such things as equipment and buildings) and current assets (stocks, debtors and cash); liabilities include money owed to the bank and suppliers of raw materials and components. The difference between assets and liabilities is referred to as the 'net worth', or LONG-TERM CAPITAL, of the company and represents monies subscribed by SHARE-HOLDERS (the owners of the company), together with any profits retained in the business. Thus, fixed assets + (current assets − current liabilities) = long term capital ('net worth').

balances with the Bank of England, *n.* deposits of money by the

Assets employed

Fixed assets	£	£	£
Equipment	500,000		
Factory	300,000		
			800,000
Current assets			
Stock	600,000		
Debtors	175,000		
Cash	25,000		
		800,000	
Current liabilities			
Trade creditors	300,000		
Bank overdraft	200,000		
		500,000	
Net current assets			300,000
Net assets employed			1,100,000
Financed by:			
Ordinary shareholders capital			900,000
Retained profits			200,000
			1,100,000

Fig. 16. **Balance sheet**. An example of a hypothetical firm's balance sheet on the last day of a trading period.

COMMERCIAL BANKS with the Bank of England. The Bank of England acts as the 'bankers' bank' and commercial banks settle indebtedness between themselves by transferring ownership of these balances. Such balances are included as part of the commercial banks' RESERVE ASSET RATIO. In addition to the balances held for settling indebtedness, the banks may be required from time to time to make SPECIAL DEPOSITS with the Bank, which has the effect of reducing their reserve assets.

bank, *n*. an authorized deposit-taking institution which receives deposits of MONEY from the public or other institutions and fulfils its obligation to return that money to the depositor when an instrument (for example, a CHEQUE) is drawn upon it. Banks are commercial institutions which make their profits from lending otherwise unemployed deposits to those wishing to borrow, and charging, usually, for services performed for customers. There are many types of banks ranging from CENTRAL BANKS, (for example, the Bank of England) through to the COMMERCIAL BANKS, MERCHANT BANKS and INVESTMENT BANKS. An institution wishing to operate as a bank in the UK must obtain authorization (a licence) from the Bank of England and cannot call itself a bank until it has such authorization. BUILDING SOCIETIES operate a deposit-taking system and repay monies deposited upon demand but they are not banks because they operate under different specialized legislation. See BANKING SYSTEM.

bank deposit, *n.* a sum of money held on deposit with a COMMERCIAL BANK (or SAVINGS BANK). Bank deposits are of two main types: sight deposits (CURRENT ACCOUNTS) which are withdrawable on demand; time deposits (DEPOSIT ACCOUNTS) which are withdrawable subject usually to some notice being given. Sight deposits represent instant LIQUIDITY – they are used to finance day-to-day transactions and regular payments either in the form of a CURRENCY withdrawal or a CHEQUE transfer. Time deposits are usually held for longer periods of time to meet irregular payments and as a form of savings.

Bank deposits constitute an important component of the MONEY SUPPLY. See BANK DEPOSIT CREATION.

bank deposit creation or **credit creation** or **money multiplier,** *n.* the ability of the COMMERCIAL BANK system to create new bank deposits and hence increase the MONEY SUPPLY. Commercial banks accept deposits of CURRENCY from the general public. Some of this money is retained by the banks to meet day-to-day withdrawals (the RESERVE-ASSET RATIO). The remainder of the money is used to make loans or is invested. When a bank on-lends it creates additional deposits in favour of borrowers. The amount of new deposits the banking system as a whole can create depends on the magnitude of the reserve-asset ratio. In the example set out in Fig. 17 the banks are assumed to operate with a 50% reserve-asset ratio: Bank 1 receives initial deposits of £100 million from the general public. It keeps £50 million for liquidity purposes and on-lends £50 million. This £50 million when spent is redeposited with Bank 2; Bank 2 keeps £25 million as part of its reserve assets and on-lends £25 million; and so on. Thus, as a result of an initial deposit of £100 million, the banking system has been able to 'create' an additional £100 million of new deposits.

Bank for International Settlements (BIS), *n.* an international bank situated in Basle and established in 1930, which originally acted as a coordinating agency for the central banks of Germany, France, Italy, Belgium and the UK in settling BALANCE-OF-PAYMENTS imbalances and for other intercentral bank dealings. Nowadays its membership comprises all West European central banks together with the US, Canada and Japan. Although the INTERNATIONAL MONETARY FUND is the main

Fig. 17. **Bank deposit creation**. Deposit creation operated with a 50% reserve-asset ratio in a multibank system.

institution responsible for the conduct of international monetary affairs, and the EUROPEAN MONETARY SYSTEM specifically for EUROPEAN COMMUNITY members, the BIS is still influential in providing a forum for discussion and surveillance of international banking practices.

banking system, *n.* a network of COMMERCIAL BANKS and other banking institutions engaged in the transmission of money and the provision of loans and credit facilities. Deposits with the banking system are a key element in the money supply and hence the banking system is closely regulated by the monetary authorities. See BANK DEPOSIT CREATION, MONEY SUPPLY, MONETARY POLICY.

bank loan, *n.* CREDIT made available to private and business customers by

COMMERCIAL BANKS. Such loans may be for fixed periods of time at agreed rates of interest, or *overdrafts* where the customer can borrow as much as he requires up to a prearranged total limit and is charged interest on outstanding balances.

bank note, *n.* the paper CURRENCY issued by a CENTRAL BANK which forms part of a country's MONEY SUPPLY. Bank notes in the main constitute the 'high value' part of the money supply.

Bank of England, *n.* the CENTRAL BANK of the UK.

bank rate, *n.* the RATE OF INTEREST charged by a CENTRAL BANK to borrowers, mainly the COMMERCIAL BANKS. Bank rate was formerly used in Britain as an instrument of MONETARY POLICY to control the general level of interest rates in the economy. It was replaced in 1972 by the *minimum lending rate* which itself was abolished in 1984 as part of the government's move towards a more flexible approach to interest rates. The present interest rate charged by the central bank (the BILL DISCOUNTING RATE) is not established administratively by the central bank, like its predecessors, but changes directly in response to changes in the supply and demand for short-term funds, as reflected in the INTER-BANK CLEARING RATE.

bankruptcy, see INSOLVENCY.

barometric forecasts, see FORECASTING.

barometric price leader, see PRICE LEADER.

barriers to entry, *n.* an element of MARKET STRUCTURE which refers to obstacles in the way of potential newcomers to a market. These obstacles operate in a number of ways to discourage entry:

(a) lower cost advantages to established firms arising from the possession of substantial market shares and the realization of ECONOMIES OF LARGE SCALE production and distribution.

(b) strong consumer preferences for the products of established firms resulting from PRODUCT DIFFERENTIATION activities.

(c) the control of essential raw materials, technology and market outlets by established firms either through direct ownership or through PATENTS, FRANCHISES and EXCLUSIVE DEALING CONTRACTS.

(d) large capital outlays required by entrants to set up production and to cover losses during the initial entry phase.

The economic significance of barriers to entry lies in their capacity for blocking MARKET ENTRY, thereby allowing established firms to earn ABOVE–NORMAL PROFIT and affecting the RESOURCE ALLOCATION function of markets.

See also CONDITION OF ENTRY, LIMIT PRICING, POTENTIAL ENTRANT, OLIGOPOLY, MONOPOLY.

barter, *n.* the EXCHANGE of one economic good or service for another. Barter as an exchange mechanism, however, suffers from a number of serious disadvantages (for example, deciding upon an appropriate rate of exchange: how many apples = one orange?) which can be largely overcome by using MONEY. See COUNTERTRADE.

base period, *n.* the initial period from which a system of INDEXATION proceeds. For example, the present British Retail Price Index has as the base period 1974 = 100, with the average price of a typical basket of goods in 1974 being taken as the basis for the index. The 1986 index number was 386 for all items in the basket of goods. Convention dictates that the base period always commences from the number 100. See PRICE INDEX.

base rate, *n.* the RATE OF INTEREST which is used by the COMMERCIAL BANKS to calculate rates of interest to be charged on loans and overdrafts to their customers. For example, a large company might be charged, say, an interest rate of base rate plus 2% on a loan, whereas a smaller borrower might be charged, say, base rate plus 4%. Formerly, base rates were linked directly to BANK RATE, but are now determined by the supply and demand for short-term funds as reflected in the INTERBANK CLEARING RATE.

base-weighted index or **Laspeyres index,** *n.* a weighted index number that uses base-year weights. For example, in calculating a PRICE INDEX the respective quantities of various products bought in the base year would be noted and the prices of these products combined to form a single price index number. At some later time, the new prices of these products would be combined to form a new price index number with no allowance made for changes in the relative quantities of the goods bought over time and their prices change. Compare CURRENT-WEIGHTED INDEX.

batch production, *n.* the manufacture of a product in small quantities using labour-intensive methods of production (see LABOUR-INTENSIVE FIRM/INDUSTRY). Batch production is typically employed in industries where the product supplied is nonstandardized, with consumers demanding a wide variety of product choice. Batch production industries are usually characterized by low levels of SELLER CONCEN-TRATION, easy entry conditions and high unit costs of supply. See MASS PRODUCTION, CONDITION OF ENTRY.

bear, *n.* a person who expects future prices in a STOCK EXCHANGE or

COMMODITY MARKET to fall, and who seeks to make money by selling shares or commodities. By contrast, a *bull* is a person who expects future market prices to rise and seeks to make money by buying shares or commodities. See SPOT MARKET, FUTURES MARKET.

bearer bonds, *n.* FINANCIAL SECURITIES which are not registered under the name of a particular holder but where possession serves as proof of ownership. Such securities are popular in the American financial system, but fairly rare in Britain, where the names of holders of STOCKS and SHARES are recorded in a company's share register.

beggar-my-neighbour policy, *n.* a course of action which is entered into by a country unilaterally in pursuit of its own self interest in INTERNATIONAL TRADE even though this might adversely affect the position of other countries. For example, country A might decide to impose TARIFFS or EXCHANGE CONTROLS, on imports from other countries in order to protect certain domestic industries. The great danger with this type of policy, however, is that it can be self-defeating; that is, other countries may retaliate by imposing tariffs, etc., of their own on country A's exports with the result that everybody's exports suffer. To avoid confrontation of this kind various international organizations have been established to regulate the conduct of international trade and monetary dealings.

See GENERAL AGREEMENT ON TARIFFS AND TRADE, INTERNATIONAL MONETARY FUND, EXPORT INCENTIVES, IMPORT RESTRICTIONS, DIRTY FLOAT, DUMPING.

behavioural theory of the firm, *n.* an alternative to the traditional, profit-maximizing THEORY OF THE FIRM which stresses the nature of large companies as complex organizations, beset by problems of goal conflict and communications. The behavioural theory examines the inherent conflict between the goals of individuals and sub-groups within the organization and suggests that organizational objectives grow out of the interaction among these individuals and sub-groups.

Cyert and March, who helped develop the behavioural theory, suggested five major goals which are relevant to companies' sales, output and pricing strategies: (a) production goal; (b) inventory goal; (c) sales goal; (d) market-share goal; (e) profit goal. Each of these goals will be the primary concern of certain managers in the organization and these managers will press their particular goals. The goals become the subject of 'bargaining' among managers and such overall goals as do emerge will be compromises, often stated as satisfactory-level targets (see SATISFICING THEORY). However, this intergroup conflict rarely threatens the organization's survival because ORGANIZATIONAL SLACK provides a pool of emergency resources which permit managers to meet their goals when the economic environment becomes hostile.

In order to achieve rational decision-making it would be necessary to eradicate inconsistencies between goals and resolve conflicts between objectives. Traditional economic theory suggests that rationality can be achieved, painting a picture of 'ECONOMIC MAN' able to specify his objectives and take actions consistent with their achievement. By contrast, the behavioural theory argues that goals are imperfectly rationalized so that new goals are not always consistent with existing policies; and that goals are stated in the form of aspiration-level targets rather than maximizing goals, targets being raised or lowered in the light of experience. Consequently not all objectives will receive attention at the same time and objectives will change with experience.

The behavioural theory also focuses attention on internal communications problems in large organizations, pointing out that decision-making is distributed throughout the firm rather than concentrated at the apex of the organization pyramid. This happens because lower-level managers do not just execute the orders of those at the top; they exercise initiative (a) in detailed planning within broad limits set by a top management, (b) in summarizing information to be passed upwards as a basis for decision-making by their superiors. These communications problems make it difficult for senior managers to impose their objectives upon the organization.

Though the behavioural theory of the firm is somewhat descriptive, lacking the determinism necessary to generate testable predictions, it has offered many useful insights into the objectives of large companies.

See also MANAGERIAL THEORIES OF THE FIRM, PROFIT MAXIMIZATION.

below-the-line promotion, see ABOVE-THE-LINE PROMOTION.

benefits-received principle of taxation, *n.* the principle that those who benefit most from government-supplied goods and services should pay the TAXES which finance them. The problem with this proposition, apart from the obvious difficulties of quantifying the benefits received by individuals particularly as regards the provision of items such as national defence, fire service, etc., is that it cannot be reconciled with the wider responsibilities accepted by government in providing social services and welfare benefits, i.e. it would make no sense at all to tax an unemployed man in order to finance his unemployment pay. See ABILITY-TO-PAY PRINCIPLE OF TAXATION, REDISTRIBUTION-OF-INCOME PRINCIPLE OF TAXATION.

Benelux, see ECONOMIC UNION.

Bertrand duopoly, see DUOPOLY.

best linear-unbiased estimates (BLUE), *n.* a statistical property of estimates of the regression coefficients in a REGRESSION ANALYSIS. If the estimates of the regression coefficients meet this test then the residual or error terms will be small and randomly distributed.

beta coefficients, *n.* **1.** a statistical term for the estimated coefficients of VARIABLES in a regression equation when INDEPENDENT VARIABLES measured in different units are converted into standard units of measurement. This makes it possible to make direct comparisons between the relative importance of each independent variable in affecting the value of the DEPENDENT VARIABLE, arriving at an estimate of the elasticity of response of the dependent variable to changes in each of the independent variables. See REGRESSION ANALYSIS.

2. a measure of the responsiveness of the expected return of a particular security relative to movements in the average expected return of all other securities in the market. The Financial Times all-share index or the Dow-Jones index are usually taken as proxy measurements for general market movements. In the CAPITAL-ASSET PRICING MODEL, the beta coefficient (β) is taken as a measure of the SYSTEMATIC RISK of a particular security. The beta coefficient is a LINEAR RELATIONSHIP between the return on the security and the return on the market. The slope of the line, called the characteristic line, determines β. The average market risk of all securities is where $\beta = 1$, that is, a 10% increase in market return is reflected as a 10% increase in the return of, say, security A. If the return on, say, security B, is 20%, but there is only a 10% increase in market return, this security has a $\beta = 2$ which indicates a risk greater than the market. If security C has a $\beta = 0.5$, this indicates a security less risky than the market in general. Risk is attached to any security with β greater than zero. See EFFICIENT MARKETS HYPOTHESIS, NONSYSTEMATIC RISK.

bid, *n.* **1.** an offer by one company to purchase all the SHARES of another, so effecting a TAKEOVER by becoming the majority SHAREHOLDER. **2.** an indication of willingness to purchase an item which is for sale at the prevailing selling price. This may occur at auction when many purchasers bid for items on sale, the final sale going to the purchaser offering the highest price unless a predetermined reserve price has been set which was not reached. See AUCTION.

big bang, see STOCK EXCHANGE.

bilateral flows, *n.* movements of money between sectors of the economy to match opposite flows of goods and services. For example, income in return for factor inputs supplied, and consumption expenditure in payment for goods and services consumed. Bilateral flows make it possible to ignore flows of goods and services in the economy and to concentrate on money movements in the CIRCULAR FLOW OF NATIONAL INCOME MODEL.

bilateral monopoly, *n.* a market situation comprising one seller (like MONOPOLY) and one buyer (like MONOPSONY).

bilateral oligopoly, *n.* a market situation with a significant degree of seller concentration (like OLIGOPOLY) and a significant degree of buyer concentration (like OLIGOPSONY). See COUNTERVAILING POWER.

bilateral trade, *n.* the trade between two countries. Bilateral trade is a part of INTERNATIONAL TRADE which is multilateral in scope. See MULTILATERAL TRADE, COUNTERTRADE.

bill-discounting rate of interest, *n.* the RATE OF INTEREST at which the CENTRAL BANK is prepared to lend money to the COMMERCIAL BANKS. This rate is not established administratively by the central bank as it was formerly under BANK RATE, but changes directly in response to changes in the supply and demand for short-term funds.

bill of exchange, *n.* a FINANCIAL SECURITY representing an amount of CREDIT extended by one business to another for a short period of time (usually three months). The lender draws up a bill of exchange for a specified sum of money payable at a given future date and the borrower signifies his agreement to pay the amount indicated by signing (accepting) the bill. Most bills are 'discounted' (i.e., bought from the drawer) by the DISCOUNT MARKET for an amount less than the face value of the bill (the difference between the two constitutes the interest charged). Bills are frequently purchased by the COMMERCIAL BANKS to be held as part of their RESERVE ASSET RATIO. See DISCOUNT, ACCEPTING HOUSE, DISCOUNT HOUSE.

bimodal, *adj.* (of a set of data) possessing two MODES. For example, if five people had weekly incomes of £100, £100, £150, £250 and £250 then there would be two modal incomes of £100 and £250.

binomial distribution, *n.* a special kind of PROBABILITY DISTRIBUTION which applies to DISCRETE VARIABLES. It shows the probability of obtaining a certain number of successes out of a particular number of trials. Binomial distributions can be approximated by NORMAL DISTRIBUTIONS for purposes of statistical analysis.

birth rate, *n.* the number of people born into a POPULATION per thousand per year. In 1986, for example, the UK birth rate was 13 people per 1,000 of the population. The difference between this rate and the DEATH RATE is used to calculate the rate of growth of the population of a country over time. The birth rate tends to decline as a country attains higher levels of economic development. See DEMOGRAPHIC TRANSITION.

black economy, *n.* NONMARKETED ECONOMIC ACTIVITY which is not recorded in the NATIONAL INCOME ACCOUNTS, either because such activity does not pass through the market place or because it is illegal. Illegality is not the same as nonmarketed activity. Illegal economic activity may operate quite efficiently in the usual PRICE SYSTEM which is determined by SUPPLY and DEMAND. Examples may be the purchase and sale of illegal drugs on the street, or alcohol in the US prohibition era of the 1920s, or foodstuffs in Britain during the Second World War when RATIONING was in force. Nonmarketed activity does not have a price determined by demand and supply. Certain nonmarketed activity may be undertaken for altruistic reasons, for example, the services of a housewife on behalf of her family, and the work of charity volunteers. Other nonmarketed activity is done on a BARTER basis, for example, where a mechanic services a motor car of an electrician who in return instals new light fittings in the mechanic's house. Money has not changed hands and the activity is not recorded. Most references to the black economy refer to the illegal situation of people working without declaring their income. See BLACK MARKET.

black knight, see TAKEOVER BID.

black market, *n.* an 'unofficial' market which often arises when the government holds down the price of a product below its equilibrium rate and is then forced to operate a RATIONING system to allocate the available supply between buyers. Given that some buyers are prepared to pay a higher price, some dealers will be tempted to divert supplies away from the 'official' market by creating an under-the-counter secondary market. See BLACK ECONOMY.

board of directors, *n.* the group responsible to the SHAREHOLDERS for running a JOINT-STOCK COMPANY. Often boards of directors are comprised of full-time salaried company executives (the executive directors) and part-time, nonexecutive directors. The board of directors meets periodically under the company chairman to decide on major policy matters within the company and the appointment of key managers. Directors are elected annually at the company ANNUAL GENERAL MEETING.

bond, *n.* a FINANCIAL SECURITY issued by businesses and by the government as a means of BORROWING long-term funds. Bonds are typically issued for periods of several years; they are repayable on maturity and bear a fixed NOMINAL (COUPON) RATE OF INTEREST.

Once a bond has been issued at its nominal value then the market price at which it is sold subsequently will vary in order to keep the EFFECTIVE RATE OF INTEREST on the bond in line with current prevailing interest rates. For example, a £100 bond with a nominal 5% interest rate paying £5 per year would have to be priced at £50 if current market interest rates were 10%, so that a buyer could earn an effective return of £5/50 = 10% on his investment.

In addition to their role as a means of borrowing money, the monetary authorities use government bonds as a means of regulating the MONEY SUPPLY. For example, if the authorities wish to reduce the money supply they can issue bonds to the general public thereby reducing the liquidity of the banking system as customers draw cheques to pay for these bonds.

See also OPEN MARKET OPERATION, BANK DEPOSIT CREATION, PUBLIC SECTOR BORROWING REQUIREMENT, SPECULATIVE DEMAND FOR MONEY, CONSOLS.

bonus shares, n. SHARES issued to existing SHAREHOLDERS in a JOINT–STOCK COMPANY without further payment on their part. See CAPITALIZATION ISSUE.

boom, n. a phase of the BUSINESS CYCLE characterized by FULL EMPLOYMENT levels of output (ACTUAL GROSS NATIONAL PRODUCT) and some upward pressure on the general PRICE LEVEL (see INFLATIONARY GAP). Boom conditions are dependent on there being a high level of AGGREGATE DEMAND which may come about autonomously or be induced by expansionary FISCAL POLICY and MONETARY POLICY. See DEMAND MANAGEMENT, STABILIZATION POLICY.

borrower, n. a person, firm or institution who obtains a LOAN from a LENDER in order to finance CONSUMPTION or INVESTMENT. Borrowers are frequently required to offer some COLLATERAL SECURITY to lenders, for example, property deeds, which lenders may retain in the event of borrowers failing to repay the loan. See DEBT, DEBTOR (ACCOUNTS RECEIVABLE), FINANCIAL SYSTEM.

Boston matrix, n. a matrix (developed by the Boston Consulting Group) for analysing product–development policy within a firm and the cash-flow implications of product development. Fig. 18 on page 46 shows the matrix, which is used to identify products which are cash generators and products which are cash users. One axis of the matrix measures market growth rate; because the faster the growth rate for a

Market share

		High	Low
Market growth rate	High	Star	Problem Child
	Low	Cash Cow	Dog

Fig. 18. **Boston matrix**. The matrix identifies cash generators and cash users.

product the greater will be the capital investment required and cash used. The other axis measures market share; because the larger the market share the greater will be the profit earned and cash generated. The market growth/share matrix encompasses four extreme product types:

(a) star products – those which have a high growth rate (so that they tend to use cash); and a high market share (so that they tend to generate cash). Star products are usually new products in the growth phase of the PRODUCT LIFE CYCLE.

(b) problem child products – those which have a high growth rate (and so tend to use cash); and a low market share (so that they tend to generate little cash). Problem products are frequently a cash drain but they have potential if their market share can be improved.

(c) cash cow products – those which have a low growth rate; and a high market share (so that they tend to generate a lot of cash). Cash cows are usually mature products in the latter phases of the product life cycle.

(d) dog products – those which have a low growth rate; and a low market share which tend to generate cash. Dog products generally have little potential for future development.

It is important for any firm to have a balanced portfolio of mature 'cash cow' products, newer 'stars', etc; and to use the cash generated by cash cows to help the development of problem children if its product development policy is to ensure the firm's long term survival. See PRODUCT PERFORMANCE, DIVERSIFICATION, PRODUCT–MARKET MATRIX.

bottom line, *n.* a FINANCIAL ACCOUNTING term denoting the NET PROFIT from a business operation after all costs have been paid. In financial accounting terms, profit would be net sales revenue less all the costs of production, marketing, finance, etc. and frequently after taxation charges for the period. However, profit would generally be stated before the payment of dividends or appropriation to RESERVES.

Box-Jenkins forecasting method, *n.* a forecasting technique using TIME–SERIES ANALYSIS to EXTRAPOLATE past values of a variable. This method has the particular advantage of allowing the statistician to compile error terms for the data. See FORECASTING.

boycott, *n.* **1.** the withholding of supplies of GOODS from a distributor by a producer or producers in order to force that distributor to resell those goods only on terms specified by the producer. In the past, boycotts were often used as a means of enforcing RESALE PRICE MAINTENANCE. **2.** the prohibition of certain imports or exports, or a complete ban on INTERNATIONAL TRADE with a particular country by other countries.

brand loyalty, *n.* the continuing willingness of consumers to purchase and repurchase the brand of a particular supplier in preference to competitive products. Suppliers cultivate brand loyalty by PRODUCT DIFFERENTIATION strategies aimed at emphasizing real and imaginary differences between competing brands. See ADVERTISING.

brand name, *n.* the name given to a product by a supplier in order to distinguish his offering from that of similar products supplied by competitors. Brand names are used as a focal point of PRODUCT DIFFERENTIATION between suppliers.

In most countries brand names are required to be registered with a central authority so as to ensure that they are uniquely applied to a single, specific product. This makes it easier for consumers to identify the product when making a purchase and also protects suppliers against unscrupulous imitators. See INDUSTRIAL PROPERTY RIGHTS.

brand proliferation, *n.* an increase in the number of brands of a particular product, each additional brand being very similar to those already available. Brand proliferation occurs mainly in oligopolistic markets (see OLIGOPOLY) where competitive rivalry is centred on PRODUCT DIFFERENTIATION strategies, and is especially deployed as a means of MARKET SEGMENTATION. In the THEORY OF MARKETS, 'excessive' brand proliferation is generally considered to be against consumers' interests because it tends to result in higher prices by increasing total ADVERTISING and sales promotional expenses.

break–even, *n.* the short-run rate of output and sales at which a supplier generates just enough revenue to cover his fixed and variable costs, earning neither a PROFIT nor a LOSS. If the selling price of a product exceeds its unit VARIABLE COST then each unit of product sold will earn a CONTRIBUTION towards FIXED COSTS and profits. Once sufficient units are being sold so that their total contributions cover the supplier's fixed costs then the company breaks even. If less than the break–even sales volume is achieved then total contributions will not meet fixed costs and the supplier will make a loss. If the sales volume achieved exceeds the break-

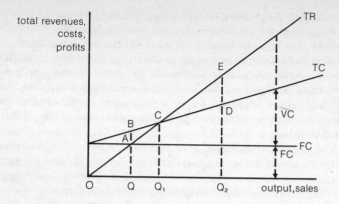

Fig. 19. **Break-even**. A supplier's typical short-run costs and revenues. Fixed costs do not vary with output and so are shown as the horizontal line FC. Total cost comprises both fixed costs and total variable costs and is shown by line TC. Total revenue rises as output and sales are expanded and is depicted by line TR. At low levels of output like Q total costs exceed total revenues and the supplier makes a loss equal to AB. At high levels of output like Q_2 revenues exceed costs and the supplier makes a profit equal to DE. At output Q_1 total revenues exactly match total costs (at C) and the supplier breaks even.

even volume, total contributions will cover the fixed costs and leave a surplus which constitutes profit. See Fig. 19.

break-up value, see ASSET VALUE PER SHARE.

Bretton Woods System, see INTERNATIONAL MONETARY FUND.

British Technology Group, *n.* a UK organization formed in 1981 by the merger of the National Research and Development Corporation and the National Enterprise Board to promote industrial efficiency and innovation by sponsoring and financing industrial investment and re-structuring. See INDUSTRIAL POLICY.

budget, (firm), *n.* a firm's predetermined plan (expressed in quantitative or financial terms) for a given future period. The sales budget is generally compiled with the aid of sales forecasts and shows quantities and values of planned sales broken down by product group, area and type of customer. The linked SELLING COSTS budget shows planned salesforce and advertising costs; while the DISTRIBUTION COSTS budget shows planned distribution activity measured in packages handled, tonnage, etc., and associated warehousing and transport costs. Once the sales budget is complete then the consequences of planned sales can be spelled out in the production budget, after making allowance for any planned changes in finished goods stock. The production budget specifies the quantities of various goods to be produced and the planned DIRECT MATERIALS, DIRECT LABOUR and factory OVERHEADS associated with these production plans, with a purchases budget showing planned purchases of raw materials. The ADMINISTRATION COSTS budget shows the planned cost of personnel, accounts and similar administrative departments.

The capital expenditure budget is concerned with planned expenditure on FIXED ASSETS, itemizing what new or replacement assets are to be required during the forthcoming period and making the necessary finance available. The cash budget shows the overall cash position, with cash inflows resulting from planned sales and cash outflows resulting from planned expenditure on raw materials, wages, capital expenditure etc (so that any anticipated cash surpluses or deficits show up in good time to deal with them). Finally the master budget aggregates all the former budgets to produce a budgeted TRADING, PROFIT-AND-LOSS ACCOUNT and a budgeted BALANCE SHEET, showing what profit will be earned and what the year-end position will be, provided that actual operations go according to plan. See BUDGETING, BUDGETARY CONTROL.

budget, (government), n. a financial statement of the government's planned revenues and expenditures for the fiscal year. The main sources of current revenues as shown in Fig. 20 on page 50 are TAXATION, principally income and expenditure taxes, and NATIONAL INSURANCE CONTRIBUTIONS. The main current outgoings of GOVERNMENT EXPENDITURE, are the provision of goods and services (principally wage payments to health, education, police and other public service employees) and TRANSFER PAYMENTS (old-age pensions, etc.).

The budget has two main uses: (a) it forms the basis of the government's longer-term financial planning of its economic and social commitments; (b) it is an instrument of FISCAL POLICY in regulating the level (and composition) of AGGREGATE DEMAND in the economy. A BUDGET SURPLUS (revenues greater than expenditures) reduces the level of aggregate demand. By contrast, a BUDGET DEFICIT (expenditure greater than revenues) increase aggregate demand. See DEMAND MANAGEMENT.

budgetary control, n. a system for controlling costs and revenues by comparing actual results with BUDGET estimates and then taking corrective action where necessary. See COMPARISON STATEMENT.

budget deficit, n. the excess of GOVERNMENT EXPENDITURE over

BUDGET DEFICIT

	£ million	
Current receipts		153,591
Of which:		
Taxes on income	(52,430)	
Taxes on expenditure	(62,273)	
National insurance	(26,067)	
Current expenditure		155,690
Of which:		
Spending on provision of goods and services	(76,882)	
Transfer payments	(52,778)	
Debt interest	(17,022)	
Capital receipts		2,653
Taxes on capital, etc.		
Capital expenditure		10,517
Of which:		
Capital formation	(7,296)	
Overall budget deficit		9,963

Fig. 20. **Budget, (government)**. The UK budget for 1986–7. Source: *UK National Accounts*, 1987.

government receipts in any one fiscal year. Government receipts are primarily in the form of TAXATION of individuals and institutions but there are other miscellaneous receipts such as the sale of government holdings in private or public enterprises. The operation of a budget deficit (*deficit financing*) is a tool of FISCAL POLICY to enable government to influence the level of AGGREGATE DEMAND and EMPLOYMENT in the economy. Such a policy was advocated by KEYNES in the 1930s to offset the DEPRESSION which occurred at that time. Opinion prior to this was that the government should operate a BALANCED BUDGET policy, allowing the economy to respond in its own way without government intervention. Keynes argued that government should intervene by deliberately imbalancing its budget in order to inject additional aggregate demand into a depressed economy and vice versa.

Since the second world war most western governments have tended to operate a budget deficit to keep employment high and to promote long-term ECONOMIC GROWTH. This has been financed by increasing the PUBLIC SECTOR BORROWING REQUIREMENT (PSBR) through the issue of TREASURY BILLS and long-term gilts. This is acceptable as long as the economy is growing and the interest payments on such borrowings do not become disproportionate to the overall level of government expenditure. Government borrowing in excess of the amount required to promote long term growth and effect counter-cyclical policies will ultimately result in INFLATION. Consequently both the timing and magnitude of the expenditure over and above receipts is of crucial importance.

BUDGET SURPLUS is the opposite of the above whereby there is an excess of government receipts over expenditure.

See AUTOMATIC (BUILT-IN) STABILIZERS, KEYNESIAN ECONOMICS, BUSINESS CYCLE, DEMAND MANAGEMENT, STABILIZATION POLICY.

budgeting, *n.* the process of preparing BUDGETS and exercising BUDGETARY CONTROL. Budgeting encourages forward thinking by managers; serves to help coordinate different functions and departments in the firm; defines the responsibilities of individual managers; provides a framework for delegating responsibility; and provides incentives by setting standards of achievement. Budgeting also provides an instrument for control and a basis for modifying plans, where necessary.

budget line or **consumption possibility line,** *n.* a line showing the alternative combinations of goods that can be purchased by a consumer with a given income facing given prices. See Fig. 21. See also CONSUMER EQUILIBRIUM, REVEALED PREFERENCE THEORY, PRICE EFFECT.

Fig. 21. **Budget line.** If a consumer has an income of £10 and the price of good X is 50 pence and the price of good Y is £1, he can buy 20 units of X or 10 units of Y, or some combination of both, for example 10 units of X and 5 units of Y. The slope of the budget line measures the relative prices of the two goods.

budget surplus, *n.* a surplus of TAXATION receipts over GOVERNMENT EXPENDITURE. Budget surpluses are used as an instrument of FISCAL

POLICY to reduce the level of AGGREGATE DEMAND in the economy. See BUDGET DEFICIT, PUBLIC SECTOR BORROWING REQUIREMENT.

buffer stock, *n.* a stock of a COMMODITY (copper, wheat, etc.) which is held by a trade body or government as a means of regulating the price of that commodity. An 'official' price for the commodity is established and if the open-market price falls below this because there is excess supply at the fixed price, then the authorities will buy the surplus and add it to the buffer stock in order to force the price back up. By contrast, if the open-market price rises above the fixed price because there is an excess demand at the fixed price, then the authorities will sell some of their buffer stock in order to bring the price down. Through this mechanism the price of the commodity can be stabilized over time, avoiding erratic, short-term fluctuations in price.

Thus this mechanism attempts to avoid erratic short-term fluctuations in price. However, if the official price is set at too high a level, this will encourage over-supply in the long term and expensively-accumulating stocks; while if the official price is set at too low a level this will discourage supply in the long term and lead to shortages.

See INTERNATIONAL COMMODITY AGREEMENT, PRICE SUPPORT, COMMON AGRICULTURAL POLICY.

building society, *n.* a financial institution which accepts deposits from savers and which specializes in the lending of money long-term by way of secured mortgages to private individuals for house purchase. Some of the larger building societies also offer depositors limited banking facilities (for example, the use of a cheque book). See also FINANCIAL SYSTEM.

built-in stabilizers, see AUTOMATIC (BUILT-IN) STABILIZERS.

bull, see BEAR.

bullion, *n.* silver and gold coins and bars. Bullion serves as a STORE OF VALUE and govenment holdings of bullion form part of their INTERNATIONAL RESERVES.

Bundesbank, the CENTRAL BANK of West Germany.

burden of debt, *n.* interest charges on DEBT which arise as a result of BORROWING by individuals, firms and governments.

In the case of governments, interest charges on the NATIONAL DEBT are paid for out of TAXATION and other receipts. The term 'burden' would seem to imply that government borrowing is a 'bad' thing in so far as it passes on financial obligations from present (overspending) generations to future generations. However, the fundamental point to emphasize is that the interest paid on the national debt is a TRANSFER PAYMENT and *does not* represent a net reduction in the capacity of the economy to provide goods and services, provided that most of this debt is owed to domestic citizens.

INFLATION has the effect of eroding the real burden of debts which are denominated in NOMINAL VALUES.

See PUBLIC SECTOR BORROWING REQUIREMENT.

burden of taxation, see TAX BURDEN.

business, *n.* a supplier of goods and services. The term can also denote a FIRM. In economic theory businesses perform two roles. On the one hand they enter the market place as producers of goods and services bought by HOUSEHOLDS; on the other hand they buy factor inputs from households in order to produce those goods and services. The term 'businesses' is used primarily in macro (national income) analysis, while the term 'firms' is used in micro (supply and demand) analysis.

See also CIRCULAR FLOW OF NATIONAL INCOME MODEL.

business cycle or **trade cycle,** *n.* fluctuations in the level of economic activity (ACTUAL GROSS NATIONAL PRODUCT) alternating between periods of depression and boom conditions.

The business cycle is characterized by four phases (see Fig. 22 on page 54): (a) DEPRESSION, a period of rapidly falling AGGREGATE DEMAND accompanied by very low levels of output and heavy UNEMPLOYMENT; (b) RECOVERY, an upturn in aggregate demand accompanied by rising output and a reduction in unemployment; (c) BOOM, aggregate demand reaches and then exceeds sustainable output levels (POTENTIAL GROSS NATIONAL PRODUCT). Full employment is reached and the emergence of excess demand causes the general price level to increase (see INFLATION); (d) RECESSION, the boom comes to an end, and is followed by recession. Aggregate demand falls, bringing with it, initially, modest falls in output and employment, but then as demand continues to contract, the onset of depression.

What causes the economy to fluctuate in this way? One prominent factor is the volatility of FIXED INVESTMENT and INVENTORY INVESTMENT expenditures (the investment cycle). At the top of the cycle income begins to level-off and investment in new supply capacity finally 'catches up' with demand (see ACCELERATOR). This causes a reduction in INDUCED INVESTMENT and, via contracting MULTIPLIER effects, leads to a fall in national income which reduces investment even further. At the bottom of the depression investment may rise exogenously (due, for example, to the introduction of new technologies) or through the revival of

BUSINESS EXPANSION SCHEME

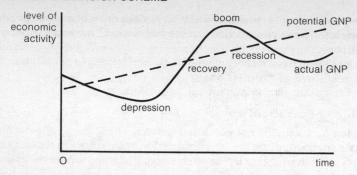

Fig. 22. **Business cycle**. Fluctuations in the level of economic activity.

REPLACEMENT INVESTMENT. In this case, the increase in investment spending will, via expansionary multiplier effects lead to an increase in national income and a greater volume of induced investment.

See also DEMAND MANAGEMENT, STABILIZATION POLICY.

Business Expansion Scheme, *n*. a scheme introduced in the UK in 1981 which is aimed at encouraging small business start-ups by giving ENTREPRENEURS generous tax-relief on their investments. See also INDUSTRIAL POLICY.

buyer, see CONSUMER.

buyer concentration, *n*. an element of MARKET STRUCTURE which refers to the number and size distribution of buyers in a market. In most markets buyers are numerous, each purchasing only a tiny fraction of total supply. In some markets, however, most notably in INTERMEDIATE GOODS industries, a few large buyers purchase a significant proportion of total supply. Such situations are described as OLIGOPSONY, or in the case of a single buyer, MONOPSONY.

Market theory predicts that MARKET PERFORMANCE will differ according to whether there are many buyers in the market, each accounting for only a minute fraction of total purchases, (PERFECT COMPETITION), or only a few buyers, each accounting for a substantial proportion of total purchases (oligopsony), as a single buyer (monopsony).

See COUNTERVAILING POWER.

buyer's market, *n*. a SHORT-RUN market situation in which there is EXCESS SUPPLY of goods or services at current prices which forces prices down to the advantage of the buyer. Compare SELLER'S MARKET.

by-product, *n.* a product which is secondary to the main product emerging from a production process. For example, the refining of crude oil to produce petroleum generates a range of by-products like bitumen, naptha and creosote.

C

calculus, see DIFFERENTIAL CALCULUS.

call money or **money-at-call and short notice,** *n.* CURRENCY (notes and coins) loaned by the COMMERCIAL BANKS to DISCOUNT HOUSES. These can be overnight (24 hour) loans or one-week loans. Call money is included as part of the commercial banks' RESERVE ASSET RATIO.

Cambridge equation, see QUANTITY THEORY OF MONEY.

CAP, see COMMON AGRICULTURAL POLICY.

capacity, *n.* **1.** the maximum amount of output that a firm or industry is physically capable of producing given the fullest and most efficient use of its existing plant. In microeconomic theory, the concept of *full capacity* is specifically related to the cost structures of firms and industries. Industry output is maximized (i.e., full capacity is attained) when all firms produce at the minimum point on their long-run average total cost curves (see PERFECT COMPETITION). If firms fail to produce at this point then the result is EXCESS CAPACITY.

2. in macroeconomics, capacity refers to POTENTIAL GNP. The percentage relationship of actual output in the economy to capacity (i.e. potential national income), shows capacity utilization. See also MONOPOLISTIC COMPETITION.

capital, *n.* the contribution to productive activity made by INVESTMENT in *physical capital* (for example, factories, offices, machinery, tools) and in HUMAN CAPITAL (for example, general education, vocational training). Capital is one of the three main FACTORS OF PRODUCTION, the other two being LABOUR and NATURAL RESOURCES. Physical (and human) capital make a significant contribution towards ECONOMIC GROWTH.

See CAPITAL FORMATION, CAPITAL STOCK, CAPITAL WIDENING, CAPITAL DEEPENING, GROSS FIXED CAPITAL FORMATION, CAPITAL ACCUMULATION.

capital account, *n.* **1.** the section of the NATIONAL INCOME ACCOUNTS which records INVESTMENT expenditure by government on infrastructure such as roads, hospitals and schools; and investment expenditure by the private sector on plant and machinery.

2. the section of the BALANCE OF PAYMENTS accounts which records movements of funds associated with the purchase or sale or long term assets and borrowing or lending by the private sector.

capital accumulation or **capital formation,** *n.* **1.** the process of adding to the net physical CAPITAL STOCK of an economy in an attempt to achieve greater total output. The accumulation of CAPITAL GOODS represents foregone CONSUMPTION which necessitates a reward to capital in the form of INTEREST, greater PROFITS or social benefit derived. The *rate* of accumulation of an economy's physical stock of capital is an important determinant of the rate of growth of an economy and is represented in various PRODUCTION FUNCTIONS and ECONOMIC GROWTH models. A branch of economics, called DEVELOPMENT ECONOMICS, devotes much of its analysis to determining appropriate rates of capital accumulation, type of capital required and types of investment project to maximize 'development' in underdeveloped countries (see DEVELOPING COUNTRY). In developed countries, the RATE OF INTEREST influences SAVINGS and INVESTMENT (capital accumulation) decisions, to a greater or lesser degree, in the private sector (see KEYNESIAN ECONOMICS) and can therefore be indirectly influenced by government. Government itself invests in the economy's INFRASTRUCTURE. This direct control over capital accumulation, and the indirect control over private investment, puts the onus of achieving the economy's optimal growth path on to the government. The nature of capital accumulation (whether CAPITAL WIDENING or CAPITAL DEEPENING) is also of considerable importance. See also CAPITAL CONSUMPTION, INVENTION, INNOVATION, CAPITAL–OUTPUT RATIO.

2. the process of increasing the internally available CAPITAL of a particular firm by retaining earnings to add to RESERVES.

capital allowances, *n.* standard allowances, for TAXATION purposes, against expenditure on FIXED ASSETS by a firm in lieu of DEPRECIATION. A business may choose its own rates of depreciation for fixed assets which may differ from the statutory capital allowances. Capital allowances may also be varied by the government as a tool of FISCAL POLICY to encourage or discourage capital INVESTMENT. See CAPITAL GOODS, DEPRECIATION (2).

capital appreciation, see APPRECIATION (2).

capital-asset pricing model, *n.* a method of computing the cost of a FINANCIAL SECURITY which specifically identifies and measures the single-period RISK factor within a PORTFOLIO holding. In this respect the capital asset pricing model may be viewed as a share-price valuation model in

CAPITAL BUDGETING

Fig. 23. **Capital-asset pricing model.** The model is used to identify the market risk factor for the expected rate of investment. See main entry.

which the major factors of short-term share-price determination are explained. The expected RATE OF RETURN on a particular investment has two constituent components. The first is the risk-free percentage return which could be obtained from, say, short-term TREASURY BILLS. The second component is the risk return associated with an investment. Risk itself can be split into SYSTEMATIC RISK or NONSYSTEMATIC RISK. This relationship between risk and return is shown in Fig. 23.

The total expected return on an investment is Or_m, but risk only attaches to non gilt-edged securities which is why the capital market line intercepts the vertical axis at r_f. The capital market line shows how, in a competitive market, the additional risk premium varies in direct proportion to β, known as the BETA COEFFICIENT. At point M in the figure there is perfect correlation between movements in the market generally, as detailed by an all-share index, and a particular investment. Therefore $\beta = 1$ at point M. Where there is no risk, as in Treasury bills, $\beta = O$. β is a measure of systematic (or market) risk because investors have it within their power to diversify away nonsystematic (or specific) risk to almost zero because of the random nature of such events. Specific risk is sometimes referred to as *diversifiable risk* and market risk as *nondiversifiable risk*. It is possible to estimate the beta coefficient of a security from published information.

See also EFFICIENT MARKETS HYPOTHESIS, RANDOM WALK.

capital budgeting, *n.* the planning and control of CAPITAL expenditure within a firm. Capital budgeting involves the search for suitable investment opportunities; evaluating particular investment projects; raising LONG-TERM CAPITAL to finance investments; assessing the COST OF CAPITAL; dealing with CAPITAL-RATIONING problems; applying suitable expenditure controls to ensure that investment outlays conform with the expenditures authorized; and ensuring that adequate cash is available when required for investments.

See INVESTMENT APPRAISAL, PRESENT VALUE, PAYBACK PERIOD, INVESTMENT, MARGINAL EFFICIENCY OF CAPITAL.

capital consumption, *n.* the reduction in a country's CAPITAL STOCK incurred in producing this year's GROSS NATIONAL PRODUCT (GNP). In order to maintain (or increase) next year's GNP a proportion of new INVESTMENT must be devoted to replacing worn-out and obsolete capital stock. Effectively, capital consumption represents the aggregate of firms' DEPRECIATION charges for the year.

capital deepening, *n.* an increase in the CAPITAL input in the economy (see ECONOMIC GROWTH) at a *faster* rate than the increase in the LABOUR input so that proportionally more capital to labour is used to produce national output. See CAPITAL WIDENING, CAPITAL-LABOUR RATIO, PRODUCTIVITY.

capital employed, see SHAREHOLDER'S CAPITAL EMPLOYED, LONG-TERM CAPITAL EMPLOYED.

capital expenditure, see INVESTMENT.

capital formation, see CAPITAL ACCUMULATION.

capital gain, *n.* the surplus realized when an ASSET (house, SHARE, etc.) is sold at a higher price than was originally paid for it. However because of INFLATION it is important to distinguish between NOMINAL VALUES and REAL VALUES. Thus what appears to be a large nominal gain may, after allowing for the effects of inflation, turn out to be a very small real gain. Furthermore in an ongoing business, provision has to be made for the REPLACEMENT COST of assets which can be much higher than the HISTORIC COST of these assets being sold. See CAPITAL GAINS TAX, CAPITAL LOSS, REVALUATION PROVISION, APPRECIATION (2).

capital gains tax, *n.* a TAX on the surplus obtained from the sale of an ASSET for more than was originally paid for it. Because capital gains tax is generally levied on the nominal CAPITAL GAIN then in a period of rapid INFLATION it can seriously over-tax companies whose real gains (after allowing for the high REPLACEMENT COST of assets) are considerably smaller than their nominal gains.

capital gearing or **leverage,** *n.* the proportion of fixed-interest LOAN

CAPITAL GEARING

	Firm A: ungeared	Firm B: highgeared
Ordinary Shares	£1,000	500
Fixed interest loans	—	500
Total capital employed	1,000	1,000

Year 1 trading profit = 15% on total capital employed

	Firm A: ungeared	Firm B: highgeared
Trading profit	150	150
Less loan interest (at 10%)	—	50
Net profit	150	100
Return to shareholders:	$\frac{150}{1,000} = 15\%$	$\frac{100}{500} = 20\%$

Year 2 trading profit = 7% on total capital employed

	Firm A: ungeared	Firm B: highgeared
Trading profit	70	70
Less loan interest (at 10%)	—	50
Net profit	70	20
Return to shareholders:	$\frac{70}{1,000} = 7\%$	$\frac{20}{500} = 4\%$

Fig. 24. **Capital gearing**. Returns to company A from ungeared long term capital, and to company B from highgeared capital.

CAPITAL TO SHARE CAPITAL employed in financing a company. Where a company raises most of the funds which it requires by issuing shares and uses very few fixed interest loans it has a low capital gearing; where a company raises most of the funds which it needs from fixed interest loans and few funds from SHAREHOLDERS it is highly geared.

Capital gearing is important to company shareholders because fixed interest charges on loans have the effect of gearing up or down the eventual residual return to shareholders from trading profits. When the trading return on total funds invested exceeds the interest rate on loans, any residual surplus accrues to shareholders, enhancing their return. On the other hand when the average return on total funds invested is less than interest rates, then interest still has to be paid and this has the effect of reducing the residual return to shareholders. For example, compare two companies, one financed solely from share capital (*Ungeared*) and another which raises half of its capital from fixed interest loans on which it must pay 10% interest (*Highgeared*). Fig. 24 shows how returns to shareholders vary more violently when highgeared.

The extent to which a company can employ fixed-interest capital as a source of long term funds depends to a large extent upon the stability of its profits over time. For example, large retailing companies whose profits tend to vary little from year to year tend to be more highly geared than, say, mining companies whose profit record is more volatile.

capital goods, *n.* the long-lasting *durable goods* such as machine tools and furnaces which are used as FACTOR INPUTS in the production of other products, as opposed to being sold directly to consumers. See CAPITAL, CONSUMER GOODS, PRODUCER GOODS.

capital inflow, *n.* a movement of funds into the domestic economy from abroad representing either the purchase of domestic FINANCIAL SECURITIES and physical ASSETS by foreigners, or the borrowing (see BORROWER) of foreign funds by domestic residents.

Capital inflows involve the receipt of money by one country, the host, from one or more foreign countries, the source countries. There are many reasons for the transfer of funds between nations:

(a) foreign direct INVESTMENT by MULTINATIONAL FIRMS in physical assets such as the establishment of local manufacturing plant.

(b) the purchase of financial securities in the host country which are considered to be attractive PORTFOLIO investments.

(c) host-government borrowing from other governments or international banks to alleviate short-term BALANCE OF PAYMENTS deficits.

(d) SPECULATION about the future RATE OF EXCHANGE of the host country currency and interest rates, expectation of an appreciation of the currency leading to a capital inflow as speculators hope to make a capital gain after the APPRECIATION of the currency.

By contrast, a CAPITAL OUTFLOW is the payment of money from one country to another for the sort of reasons already outlined. See also FOREIGN INVESTMENT, HOT MONEY.

capital-intensive firm/industry, *n.* a firm or industry which produces its output of goods or services using proportionately large inputs of CAPITAL equipment and relatively small amounts of LABOUR. The proportions of capital and labour which a firm uses in production depends mainly on the relative prices of labour and capital inputs and their relative productivities. This in turn depends upon the degree of standardization of the product. Where standardized products are sold in large quantities it is possible to employ large-scale capital-intensive production methods which facilitate ECONOMIES OF SCALE. Aluminium smelting, oil refining and steelworks are examples of capital-intensive industries. See MASS PRODUCTION; CAPITAL-LABOUR RATIO.

capitalism, see PRIVATE-ENTERPRISE ECONOMY.

capitalization issue or **scrip issue,** *n.* the issue by a JOINT-STOCK

COMPANY of additional SHARES to existing SHAREHOLDERS without any further payment being required. Capitalization issues are usually made where a company has ploughed back profits over several years and so has accumulated substantial RESERVES or has revalued its fixed assets and accumulated capital reserves. If the company wishes to capitalize the reserves it can do so by creating extra shares to match the reserves, and issue them as BONUS SHARES to existing shareholders in proportion to their existing shareholdings. See also RETAINED PROFIT.

capital–labour ratio, *n.* the proportion of CAPITAL to LABOUR inputs in an economy. If capital inputs in the economy increase over time at the same rate as the labour input then the capital-labour ratio remains unchanged (see CAPITAL WIDENING). If capital inputs increase at a faster rate than the labour input then CAPITAL DEEPENING takes place. The capital-labour ratio is one element in the process of ECONOMIC GROWTH. See CAPITAL–INTENSIVE FIRM/INDUSTRY, LABOUR–INTENSIVE FIRM/INDUSTRY, AUTOMATION.

capital loss, *n.* the deficit realized when an ASSET (house, SHARE etc) is sold at a lower price than was originally paid for it. Compare CAPITAL GAIN.

capital market, *n.* the market for long-term company LOAN CAPITAL and SHARE CAPITAL and government BONDS. The capital market together with the MONEY MARKET (which provides short-term funds) are the main sources of external finance to industry and government. The financial institutions involved in the capital market include the CENTRAL BANK, COMMERCIAL BANKS, the saving-investing institutions, (INSURANCE COMPANIES, PENSION FUNDS, UNIT TRUSTS, and INVESTMENT TRUST COMPANIES), ISSUING HOUSES and MERCHANT BANKS.

New share capital is most frequently raised through issuing houses or merchant banks which arrange for the sale of shares on behalf of client companies. Shares can be issued in a variety of ways, including: directly to the general public by way of an 'offer for sale' (or an 'introduction') at a prearranged fixed price; an 'offer for sale by TENDER' where the issue price is determined by averaging out the bid prices offered by prospective purchasers of the share subject to a minimum price bid; a RIGHTS ISSUE of shares to existing shareholders at a fixed price; a placing of the shares at an arranged price with selected investors, often institutional investors. See STOCK EXCHANGE.

capital movements, *n.* the flows of FOREIGN EXCHANGE between countries representing both short-term and long-term INVESTMENT in physical ASSETS and FINANCIAL SECURITIES and BORROWINGS. See CAPITAL INFLOW, CAPITAL OUTFLOW, BALANCE OF PAYMENTS, FOREIGN INVESTMENT.

capital outflow, *n.* a movement of domestic funds abroad representing either the purchase of foreign FINANCIAL SECURITIES and physical ASSETS by domestic residents, or the BORROWING of domestic funds by foreigners. See CAPITAL INFLOW, BALANCE OF PAYMENTS, FOREIGN INVESTMENT, HOT MONEY.

capital–output ratio, *n.* a measure of how much additional CAPITAL is required to produce each extra unit of OUTPUT, or put the other way round, the amount of extra output produced by each unit of added capital. The capital–output ratio indicates how 'efficient' new INVESTMENT is in contributing to ECONOMIC GROWTH. Assuming, for example, a 4:1 capital–output ratio each four units of extra investment enables national output to grow by one unit. If the capital–output ratio is 2:1, however, then each two units of extra investment expands national income by one unit. See CAPITAL ACCUMULATION, PRODUCTIVITY.

capital rationing, *n.* a situation where a firm selects an annual capital budget which is less than the amount required to undertake all INVESTMENTS which promise a rate of return in excess of the cost of capital. For example, if a firm requires a minimum 20% return on any investment then *all* of the appropriate investment opportunities available to the firm which promise a return of 20% or more may involve a total expenditure of, say, £10 million. However, if the firm decides that it is willing to spend only £6 million, then it must rank investment opportunities in descending order of rate of return, undertaking those with the highest promised return and rejecting others even though the latter opportunities promise a return greater than the 20% cost of capital. The firm is said to be in a situation of capital rationing because it is investing less than the amount dictated by usual PROFIT MAXIMIZING criteria. See MARGINAL EFFICIENCY OF CAPITAL; CAPITAL BUDGETING.

capital stock, *n.* the net accumulation of a physical STOCK of CAPITAL GOODS (buildings, plant, machinery, etc.) by a firm, industry or economy at any one point in time (see POTENTIAL GROSS NATIONAL PRODUCT).

The measurements most frequently used for the value of a country's capital stock are from the NATIONAL INCOME and expenditure statistics. These statistics take private and public expenditure on capital goods and deduct CAPITAL CONSUMPTION (see DEPRECIATION sense 2) to arrive at net accumulation (which may be positive or negative). The more relevant value of capital stock, from the economist's point of view, is the present value of the stream of income such stock can generate. More broadly, the size of a country's capital stock has an important influence on its rate of ECONOMIC GROWTH.

See CAPITAL ACCUMULATION, CAPITAL WIDENING, CAPITAL DEEPENING, DEPRECIATION METHODS, PRODUCTIVITY, CAPITAL–OUTPUT RATIO.

capital structure, *n.* the composition of a JOINT-STOCK COMPANY's long-term capital which reflects the sources of that capital, for example, SHARE CAPITAL and long-term LOAN CAPITAL. See CAPITAL GEARING.

capital transfer tax, see WEALTH TAX.

capital widening, *n.* an increase in the CAPITAL input in the economy (see ECONOMIC GROWTH) at the same rate as the increase in the LABOUR input so that the proportion in which capital and labour are combined to produce national output remains unchanged. See CAPITAL DEEPENING, CAPITAL–LABOUR RATIO, PRODUCTIVITY.

cardinal utility, *n.* the measurement of (subjective) UTILITY on an absolute scale. Early economists coined the term UTIL to refer to the satisfaction derived from consuming a product. However, because it proved impossible to construct an accurate measure of cardinal utility, ORDINAL UTILITY measures replaced the idea of cardinal utility in the theory of CONSUMER EQUILIBRIUM. See DIMINISHING MARGINAL UTILITY.

cartel, *n.* an extreme form of COLLUSION, particularly associated with the desire of PROFIT-MAXIMIZING OLIGOPOLISTIC suppliers to secure JOINT-PROFIT MAXIMIZATION. Under a full cartel arrangement, a central administration agency could determine the price and output of the industry, and the output quotas of each of the separate member firms in such a way as to restrict total industry output and maximize the joint-profits of the group. Price and output will thus tend to approximate those of a profit-maximizing monopolist. See Fig. 25.

cash, see CURRENCY.

cash discount, see DISCOUNT.

cash drain, *n.* a constraint on the expansion of the MONEY SUPPLY through BANK DEPOSIT CREATION caused by individuals retaining larger amounts of cash than usual. This means that not all of the increase in cash calculated by using the reciprocal of the RESERVE ASSET RATIO is passed on from the public back into the banking system. For example, a new deposit of £100 is made into the banking system. Assuming a 10% reserve asset ratio, the average fraction of money held in cash form is one-tenth and the reciprocal 10. Thus ultimately a £1,000 increase in money supply is theoretically possible. However if the public's demand for cash grows then the increase in the money supply will not be 10 times the initial deposit, but something less.

Fig. 25. **Cartel.** D is the industry demand curve, showing the aggregate quantity which the combined group may sell over a range of possible prices and MR is the industry marginal revenue curve. The industry marginal cost curve $\sum$MC is constructed from the marginal cost curves of the individual firms making up the cartel. For any given level of industry output the cartel is required to calculate the allocation of the output among member firms on the basis of their individual marginal costs to obtain the lowest possible aggregate cost of producing their output.

To maximize industry profit the cartel will set price OP and produce output OQ. Quotas of Q_A and Q_B are given to firms A and B respectively where a horizontal line drawn from the intersection of MR and $\sum$MC (the line of aggregate marginal costs) intersects MC_A and MC_B.

Profit contributed by each firm is computed by multiplying the number of units produced by the difference between industry price and the firm's average cost at that level of output.

The aggregate profit is then divided among the member firms in some agreed manner, not necessarily, it is to be noted, in the same proportion as actually contributed by each of the individual firms. Disputes over the sharing of aggregate profit frequently lead to the break-up of cartels.

Other, looser, forms of cartel like the ORGANIZATION OF PETROLEUM EXPORTING COUNTRIES, merely jointly determine industry price but not output quotas.

cash flow, *n.* the money coming into a business from sales and other receipts and going out of the business in the form of cash payments to suppliers, workers, etc. See SOURCES AND USES OF FUNDS STATEMENT.

cash ratio, *n.* the proportion of a bank's total liabilities which it holds in the form of CURRENCY (notes and coins) to meet the demands of its customers for *immediate* currency withdrawals. In some countries the size of the cash ratio is determined by the banks themselves in accordance with some enshrined principle of 'sound banking practice'; in others, the government prescribes the size of the cash ratio.

It is to be noted, however, that this cash ratio can form part of a bank's wider liquidity 'safety net', the RESERVE ASSET RATIO, and it is usually this latter ratio which forms the basis for monetary control by the authorities.

See MONETARY POLICY, BANK DEPOSIT CREATION.

caveat emptor, *n*. a Latin phrase meaning 'let the buyer beware'. Put simply this means that the supplier has no legal obligation to inform buyers about any defects in his goods or services. The onus is on the buyer to determine for himself that the good or service is satisfactory. Compare CAVEAT VENDOR.

caveat vendor, *n*. a Latin phrase meaning 'let the seller beware'. In brief this means that the supplier may be legally obliged to inform buyers of any defects in his goods or services. Compare CAVEAT EMPTOR.

census, *n*. a comprehensive official survey of households or businesses undertaken at regular intervals in order to obtain socio-economic information. In the UK, a *population census* has been carried out every 10 years since 1891 to provide information on demographic trends. This data is useful to the government in the planning of housing, education and welfare services. A *production census* is carried out annually to provide details of industrial production, employment, investment, etc. A *distribution census* provides data about wholesaling and retailing. This information can be used by the government in formulating its economic and industrial policies.

central bank, *n*. the primary banking institution of a nation under the direct or indirect control of government to facilitate the normal banking services required by government and to act as an instrument of MONETARY POLICY. The central bank typically acts as banker to the commercial banking system; controls the MONEY SUPPLY according to government instruction; influences the RATE OF INTEREST prevailing in an economy; holds the nation's INTERNATIONAL RESERVES; issues bank notes; intervenes on occasions to stabilize EXCHANGE RATE fluctuations; manages the PUBLIC DEBT; acts as a LENDER OF LAST RESORT; and generally acts as a monetary tool of government macro-economic policy.

The Bank of England, Federal Reserve System, Banque de France and Deutsche Bundesbank are the central banks of Britain, USA, France and West Germany respectively.

See BANK DEPOSIT CREATION, COMMERCIAL BANK, DISCOUNT MARKET, OPEN MARKET OPERATIONS.

centrally planned economy or **state economy** or **collectivism,** *n.* a method of organizing the economy to produce goods and services. Under this ECONOMIC SYSTEM economic decision-making is centralized in the hands of the state with collective ownership of the means of production, (except labour). It is the state which decides what goods and services are to be produced in accordance with its centralized NATIONAL PLAN. Resources are allocated between producing units, and final outputs between customers by the use of physical quotas. See PRIVATE-ENTERPRISE ECONOMY, MIXED ECONOMY, NATIONALIZATION, COMMUNISM.

Central Statistical Office (CSO), *n.* a UK government department responsible for the collection, analysis and publication of national economic statistics such as the NATIONAL INCOME ACCOUNTS and BALANCE-OF-PAYMENTS accounts.

certainty equivalent, see DECISION TREE.

certificate of incorporation, *n.* a certificate issued by the COMPANY REGISTRAR to a new JOINT-STOCK COMPANY whose MEMORANDUM OF ASSOCIATION and ARTICLES OF ASSOCIATION are acceptable to the Registrar. A company starts its legal existence from the date of its incorporation and thereafter is able to enter into contracts, etc. in its own name.

ceteris paribus, *n.* a Latin term meaning 'other things being equal' which is widely used in economic analysis as an expository technique. It allows us to isolate the relationship between two variables. For example, in demand analysis, the DEMAND CURVE shows the effect of a change in the price of a product on the quantity demanded on the assumption that all of the 'other things' (incomes, tastes, etc.) influencing the demand for that product remain unchanged. See PARTIAL CORRELATION COEFFICIENT, DIFFERENTIAL CALCULUS.

chain store, *n.* a multibranch retail firm. All types of retailer, ranging from SPECIALIST SHOPS to DEPARTMENT STORES, can be organized to take advantage of the economies of HORIZONTAL INTEGRATION. Unlike single-shop concerns, chain stores are able to maximize their sales potential through geographical spread and maximize their competitive advantage by being able to secure bulk-buying price concessions from manufacturers. See SUPERMARKETS, DISCOUNT STORES, COOPERATIVES, DO-IT-YOURSELF STORES, RETAILING.

Chamberlin, Edward (1899–1967) American economist who helped develop the theory of MONOPOLISTIC COMPETITION in his book *The Theory of Monopolistic Competition.* Prior to Chamberlin's work economists classified markets into two groups: (a) perfect competition where firm's products are perfect substitutes; (b) monopoly, where a firm's product has no substitutes. Chamberlin argued that in real markets goods are often partial substitutes for other goods, so that even in markets with many sellers the individual firm's demand curve might be downward sloping. He then proceeded to analyse the firm's price and output decisions under such conditions and derive the implications for market supply and price. See also ROBINSON.

cheap money, *n.* a government policy whereby the CENTRAL BANK is authorized to purchase government BONDS on the open market to facilitate an increase in the MONEY SUPPLY.

The increase in money supply serves to reduce interest rates which encourages INVESTMENT because previously unprofitable investments now become profitable due to the reduced cost of borrowing (see MARGINAL EFFICIENCY OF CAPITAL/INVESTMENT).

Cheap money policy, when supplemented by government investment, is essentially the Keynesian TRANSMISSION MECHANISM for increasing AGGREGATE DEMAND. See MONEY SUPPLY–SPENDING LINKAGES, TIGHT MONEY.

cheque, *n.* a BILL OF EXCHANGE drawn on a bank by the holder of a CURRENT ACCOUNT with that bank, and payable upon demand. A cheque may be drawn upon either COMMERCIAL BANKS or the CENTRAL BANK but the latter is not concerned with private individuals' accounts except in special circumstances; it holds accounts primarily on behalf of other banking establishments and the government.

Chicago school, *n.* a prominent group of economists at Chicago University, most notable of whom is Milton FRIEDMAN, who have adopted and refined the QUANTITY THEORY OF MONEY, arguing the need for governments to control the growth of the MONEY SUPPLY over the long term. Within the broad parameters set by stable money growth the Chicago school stresses the importance of the market system as an allocative mechanism, leaving consumers free to make economic decisions with minimal government interference. See MONETARISM.

Chinese wall, *n.* the segregation of the stockbroking, jobbing (see STOCKBROKER, JOBBER), fund management, etc., activities of a financial institution in order to protect the interest of its clients. For example, the same institution could be responsible for making a market in a particular financial security (jobbing), while at the same time offering investment advice to clients to purchase this security, with the danger that the advice given will not be impartial. See CITY CODE.

chi-square distribution, *n.* a special kind of PROBABILITY DISTRIBUTION which is used in formulating tests of significance for HYPOTHESIS TESTING when we wish to decide whether observed *proportions* in SAMPLES may reasonably be attributed to chance. Areas under the chi-square distribution curve indicate the criterion probabilities concerned. Where the observed frequencies in different samples diverge greatly from the frequencies we could have expected (embodied in a null hypothesis) then we can conclude that the null hypothesis must be false.

The chi-square criterion may be used to test whether it is justifiable to approximate an observed distribution with a normal curve.

choice, *n.* the necessity for CENTRALLY PLANNED ECONOMIES and PRIVATE ENTERPRISE ECONOMIES to have to choose which goods and services to produce and in what quantities, arising from the relative SCARCITY of economic resources (FACTORS OF PRODUCTION) available to produce those goods and services. See ECONOMICS.

c.i.f., *abbrev. for* 'cost-insurance-freight', i.e. charges which are incurred in transporting imports and exports of goods from one country to another. In BALANCE OF PAYMENTS terms c.i.f. charges are added to the basic prices of imports and exports of goods in order to compute the total foreign currency flows involved. See F.O.B.

circular flow of national income model, *n.* a simplified exposition of money and physical or real flows through the economy which serves as the basis for macroeconomic analysis. In Fig. 26a on page 70, the solid lines show how, in monetary terms, HOUSEHOLDS purchase goods and services from BUSINESSES using income received from supplying factor inputs to businesses. In physical terms (shown by the broken lines), businesses produce goods and services using factor inputs supplied to them by households.

The basic model can be developed to incorporate a number of 'INJECTIONS' to, and 'WITHDRAWALS' from, the income flow. In Fig. 26b, not all of the income received by households is spent – some is saved. SAVINGS is a 'withdrawal' from the income flow. INVESTMENT expenditure 'injects' funds into the income flow. Part of the income accruing to households is taxed by the government and serves to reduce disposable income available for consumption expenditure. TAXATION is a 'withdrawal' from the income flow. GOVERNMENT EXPENDITURE on products and factor inputs 'injects' funds into the income flow. Households spend some of their income on imported goods and services. IMPORTS are a 'withdrawal' from the income flow. On the other hand, some output is sold to overseas customers. EXPORTS represent a demand for domestically produced goods and services and hence constitute an

CIRCULAR FLOW OF NATIONAL INCOME MODEL

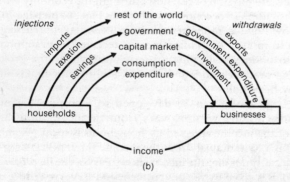

Fig. 26. **Circular flow of national income model.** (a) The basic model of the relationship between money flows and physical flows. (b) A more complex model, incorporating injections to and withdrawals from the income flow.

'injection' into the income flow. See also AGGREGATE DEMAND, EQUILIB-RIUM LEVEL OF NATIONAL INCOME MODEL.

City code, *n.* a regulatory system operated voluntarily by interested parties to the UK STOCK EXCHANGE that lays down 'rules of good conduct' governing the tactics and procedures used in TAKEOVER BIDS and MERGERS. The general purpose of the code is to ensure that all SHAREHOLDERS (both the shareholders of the firm planning the takeover and those of the target firm) are treated equitably, and that the parties involved in arranging a takeover bid do not abuse privileged 'insider' information, or misuse such tactics as CONCERT PARTIES, DAWN RAIDS and CHINESE WALLS.

The City code is administered by the *City Panel on Takeovers and Mergers*, which is responsible for formulating rules of practice and for investigating suspected cases of malpractice.

See also INSIDER TRADING.

City (of London), *n.* the centre of the UK's FINANCIAL SYSTEM, embracing the MONEY MARKETS (commercial banks, etc.) CAPITAL MARKET (STOCK EXCHANGE), FOREIGN EXCHANGE MARKET, COMMODITY MARKETS and INSURANCE MARKETS. The City of London is also a major international financial centre and earns Britain substantial amounts of foreign exchange on exports of financial services.

City Panel on Takeovers and Mergers, see CITY CODE.

classical economics, *n.* a school of thought or a set of economic ideas based on the writings of SMITH, RICARDO, MILL, etc., which dominated economic thinking until about 1870, when the 'marginalist revolution' occurred.

The classical economists saw the essence of the economic problem as one of producing and distributing the economic wealth created between landowners, labour and capitalists; and were concerned to show how the interplay of separate decisions by workers and capitalists could be harmonized through the market system to generate economic wealth. Their belief in the power of market forces led them to support LAISSEZ-FAIRE and they also supported the idea of FREE TRADE between nations. After about 1870 classical economic ideas receded as the emphasis shifted to what has become known as NEOCLASSICAL ECONOMIC ANALYSIS, embodying marginalist concepts.

Classical economists denied any possibility of UNEMPLOYMENT caused by deficient AGGREGATE DEMAND, arguing that market forces would operate to keep aggregate demand and POTENTIAL GROSS NATIONAL PRODUCT in balance (SAY'S LAW). Specifically they argued that business recessions would cause interest rates to fall under the pressure of accumulating savings, so encouraging businesses to borrow and invest more; and would cause wage rates to fall under the pressure of rising unemployment, so encouraging businessmen to employ more workers.

See LABOUR THEORY OF VALUE, KEYNES, PRIVATE ENTERPRISE ECONOMY.

clearing house system, *n*. a centralized mechanism for settling indebtedness between COMMERCIAL BANKS. For example, when a customer of bank A draws a cheque in favour of a customer of bank B, and the second customer pays in the cheque to bank B, then bank A is indebted to bank B for the amount of that cheque. There will be many thousands of similar transactions going on day-by-day, creating indebtedness between all banks. The role of the clearing system is to bring together all of these cheques, crosscancel them and determine at the end of each day any net indebtedness between the banks. This net indebtedness is then settled by transferring balances held by the commercial banks at the CENTRAL BANK.

close company, *n*. a JOINT-STOCK COMPANY which is under the control of five or fewer large SHAREHOLDERS or directors.

closed economy, *n*. an economy that is not influenced by any form of INTERNATIONAL TRADE, that is, there are no EXPORTS or IMPORTS of any kind. By concentrating on a closed economy it is possible to simplify the CIRCULAR FLOW OF NATIONAL INCOME MODEL and focus upon income and expenditure within an economy.

In terms of the circular flow, AGGREGATE DEMAND in a closed economy is represented by:

$$Y = C + I + G$$

where Y = national income
C = consumption expenditure
I = investment expenditure
G = government expenditure

By contrast, the OPEN ECONOMY allows for the influence of imports and exports and here aggregate demand is represented in the circular flow as:

$$Y = C + I + G + (X - M)$$

where X = exports
M = imports

club principle, *n*. a means of allocating the common overhead costs incurred in providing a good or service to each individual consumer. For example, residents may create a club to arrange for the resurfacing of a private road. See COLLECTIVE PRODUCTS, FREE-RIDER.

Cobb-Douglas production function, *n*. a particular physical relationship between OUTPUT of products and FACTOR INPUTS (LABOUR and

CAPITAL) used to produce these outputs. This particular form of the PRODUCTION FUNCTION suggests that where there is effective competition in factor markets the ELASTICITY OF TECHNICAL SUBSTITUTION between labour and capital will be equal to one; that is, labour can be substituted for capital in any given proportions and vice versa, without affecting output.

The Cobb-Douglas production function suggests that the share of labour input and the share of capital input are relative constants in an economy, so that although labour and capital inputs may change in absolute terms, the *relative* share between the two inputs remains constant.

See PRODUCTION POSSIBILITY BOUNDARY, CAPITAL–LABOUR RATIO, PRODUCTION FUNCTION, CAPITAL–INTENSIVE FIRM/INDUSTRY, LABOUR–INTENSIVE FIRM/INDUSTRY, ISOQUANT CURVE, ISOQUANT MAP.

cobweb theorem, *n.* a theory designed to explain the path followed in moving toward an equilibrium situation when there are lags in the adjustment of either SUPPLY or DEMAND to changes in prices. COMPARATIVE STATIC EQUILIBRIUM ANALYSIS predicts the effect of demand or supply changes by comparing the original equilibrium price and quantity with the new equilibrium which results. The cobweb theorem focuses upon the dynamic process of adjustment in markets by tracing the path of adjustment of prices and output in moving from one equilibrium situation toward another (see DYNAMIC ANALYSIS).

The cobweb theorem is generally used to describe oscillations in prices in agricultural markets where the delay between, for example, planting and harvesting means that supply reacts to prices with a time lag. The simplest case where current quantity demanded responds to current price while current quantity supplied depends upon price in the previous period is depicted in Fig. 27 on page 74. In the Fig., D_t denotes quantity demanded in the current period, S_t denotes quantity supplied, while price is denoted by Pt, and price in the previous period is denoted by P_{t-1}. If demand were to fall rapidly such that the demand curve shifted left from D_t to D^1_t then comparative static analysis suggest that the market will eventually move from equilibrium point E (with price OP_1 and quantity OQ_1). to equilibrium point E^1 (with price OP_4 and quantity OQ_4). Dynamic analysis suggest that the path followed will be less direct than this.

Starting from the original equilibrium price OP_1, which has prevailed in years $t-1$ and t, farmers will have planned to produce quantity OQ_1. However, after the contraction in demand in year t, supply will exceed

Fig. 27. **Cobweb theorem**. See main entry.

demand by QQ_1, and in order to sell all the quantity OQ_1 coming onto the market, price has to fall to OP_2. The lower price OP_2 which prevails in year t will discourage farmers from producing and they will reduce acreage devoted to this crop so that in the next year $t+1$ a much smaller quantity OQ_2 is supplied.

In year $t+1$, and at price OP_2, demand now exceeds supply by the amount $Q_1 Q_2$, and in order to ration the limited supply OQ_2 which is available price will rise to OP_3. This higher price in year $t+1$ will encourage farmers to increase their acreage planted so that in the following year $t+2$, a larger quantity OQ_3 will be supplied which means that in year $t+2$ supply exceeds demand and price will fall below OP_3 which will discourage planting for the following year, and so on. The eventual result of this process of adjustment is that a new equilibrium is achieved at E^1 but only after a series of fluctuating prices in intermediate periods are experienced. See AGRICULTURAL POLICY.

coefficient, see PARAMETER.

coefficient of determination, *n.* a statistical term (usually denoted r^2) which measures the proportion of the variance of a DEPENDENT VARIABLE (such as consumption expenditure) explained by the linear influence of an INDEPENDENT VARIABLE (like disposable income). If two variables are strongly related with a CORRELATION COEFFICIENT (r) of, say, 0.9 then the coefficient of determination is 0.81. The values of r^2 lie between 0 and 1. It is frequently used in economics to assess the estimated relationship between variables like disposable income and consumption expenditure (see Fig. 28).

Fig. 28. **Coefficient of determination**. The scatter diagram displays the line of estimated consumption function. This is the line which best fits the consumption/income observations recorded. Where all the observations lie exactly on the line, r^2 is equal to 1.

coefficient of variation, *n.* a measure of relative variation which expresses the magnitude of the variation within a group of numerical observations in relation to the group mean (specifically, the STANDARD DEVIATION expressed as a percentage of the MEAN). For example, if five products had prices of £5, £4, £3, £2 and £1, so that their mean price was £3 and their standard deviation was £1.41, then the coefficient of variation would be:

$$\frac{1.41}{3.00} \times 100 = 47\%$$

By using the coefficient of variation it is possible to compare the variability of several groups of observations, each of which is measured in different units (pounds, dollars, etc.) since all the group dispersion measures will be expressed in common percentage terms.

coinage, *n.* the metallic CURRENCY issued by a CENTRAL BANK which forms part of a country's MONEY SUPPLY. Various metals have been used for coinage purposes. Formerly, gold and silver were commonly used but these have now been replaced in most countries by copper, brass and nickel. Coins in the main constitute the 'low value' part of the money supply.

collateral security, *n.* the ASSETS pledged by a BORROWER as security for a LOAN, for example, the title deeds of a house. In the event of the borrower defaulting on the loan the LENDER can claim these assets in lieu of the sum owed. See DEBT, DEBTOR.

collective bargaining, *n.* the negotiation of WAGE RATES, conditions of employment, etc. by representatives of the labour force (usually trade union officials) and management. Collective bargaining agreements are negotiated at a number of different levels ranging from local union branches and a single factory to general unions and an entire industry.
See TRADE UNION, INDUSTRIAL RELATIONS, INDUSTRIAL DISPUTE.

collective products, *n.* any goods or services that cannot be provided other than on a group basis because the quantity supplied to any one individual cannot be independently varied. It is virtually impossible to get consumers to reveal their preferences regarding collective goods because rational consumers will attempt to become FREE-RIDERS, each understating his demand in the hope of avoiding his share of the cost without affecting the quantity he obtains. Consequently such products cannot be marketed in the conventional way and we cannot use market prices to value them. Many goods and services supplied by government are of a collective nature, for example, national defence and police protection, and here government decides on the amounts of such products to provide and compels individuals to pay for them through taxation. See CLUB PRINCIPLE, SOCIAL PRODUCTS.

collectivism, see CENTRALLY PLANNED ECONOMY.

collusion, *n.* a form of INTER-FIRM CONDUCT pattern in which firms arrive at an agreement or 'understanding' covering their market actions. Successful collusion requires the acceptance of a common objective for all firms (for example, JOINT-PROFIT MAXIMIZATION) and the suppression of behaviour inconsistent with the achievement of this goal (for example, price competition). Collusion may be either overt or tacit. Overt collusion usually takes the form of either an express agreement in writing or an express oral agreement arrived at through direct consultation between the firms concerned. Alternatively, collusion may take the form of an 'unspoken understanding' arrived at through firms' repeated experiences with each other's behaviour over time.
See CARTEL, RESTRICTIVE TRADE AGREEMENTS, MONOPOLY POLICY, OLIGOPOLY, DUOPOLY, INFORMATION AGREEMENT.

collusive duopoly, see DUOPOLY.

comecon, *n.* see COUNCIL FOR MUTUAL ECONOMIC ASSISTANCE.

commercial bank or **clearing bank,** *n.* a bank which accepts deposits of money from customers and provides them with a payments transmission service (CHEQUES), together with saving and loan facilities.

A commercial bank has the dual objective of being able to meet currency withdrawals on demand and of putting its funds to profitable use. This influences the pattern of its asset holdings; a proportion of its funds are held in a highly liquid form (the RESERVE ASSET RATIO), including TILL MONEY, BALANCES WITH THE BANK OF ENGLAND, CALL MONEY with the DISCOUNT MARKET, BILLS OF EXCHANGE and TREASURY BILLS. These liquid assets enable the bank to meet any immediate cash requirements that its customers might make, thereby preserving public confidence in the bank as a safe repository for deposits. The remainder of the bank's funds are used to earn profits from portfolio investments in public sector securities and fixed-interest corporate securities, together with loans and overdrafts.

BANK DEPOSITS are a key element in the MONEY SUPPLY. See BANK DEPOSIT CREATION, MONETARY POLICY, CLEARING HOUSE SYSTEM.

commission, *n.* payments to AGENTS for performing services on behalf of a seller or buyer. Commissions are usually based on the value of the product being sold or bought. Examples of commissions include salespersons' commissions, estate agents' fees and insurance brokers' commissions.

commodity, *n.* **1.** see GOODS. **2.** raw materials rather than goods in general: for example, tea, coffee, iron ore, aluminium, etc.

commodity broker, *n.* a dealer in raw materials. See COMMODITY MARKET.

commodity market, *n.* a market for the buying and selling of raw materials such as tea, coffee, iron ore, aluminium etc. Many of the main commodity markets are based in the City of London, e.g., the London Metal Exchange. See SPOT MARKET, FUTURES MARKET.

Common Agricultural Policy (CAP), *n.* the policy of the EUROPEAN COMMUNITY (EC) for assisting the farm sector. The main aims of the CAP are fair living standards for farmers and an improvement in agricultural efficiency (see AGRICULTURAL POLICY).

The CAP is administered by the European Agricultural Guidance and Guarantee Fund, with major policy and operational decisions (e.g., the fixing of annual farm prices) residing in the hands of the Council of Ministers of the EC. The farm sector is assisted in four main ways:

(a) around 70–75% of EC farm produce benefits directly from the operation of a PRICE SUPPORT system which maintains EC farm prices at levels in excess of world market prices. The prices of milk, cereals, butter, sugar, pork, beef, veal, certain fruits and vegetables and table wine are fixed annually, and once determined are then maintained at this

77

level by support buying of output which is not bought in the market. MONETARY COMPENSATION AMOUNTS are used to convert the common price for each product into national currencies and to realign prices when the exchange rates of member's currencies change.

(b) Variable TARIFF rates are used to increase import prices to internal price-support levels in the cases of the products referred to above, thus ensuring that EC output is fully competitive. The 25% of EC farm produce which is not subject to direct price-support relies entirely on tariff protection to maintain high domestic prices.

(c) EXPORT SUBSIDIES are used to enable EC farmers to lower their export prices and thus compete successfully in world markets.

(d) Grants are given to facilitate farm modernization and improvements as a means of improving agricultural efficiency.

The CAP is the largest single component of the EC's total budget. In 1986 it accounted for 65% of total EC spending. Over 90% of the CAP's budget in recent years has been spent on price-support and export subsidies.

Although the CAP can claim a number of successes, most notably the attainment of EC self-sufficiency in many food products, critics complain it has many drawbacks: consumers lose out because they are required to pay unnecessarily high prices for food products; resources are misallocated because inefficient, high cost farmers are over protected, and too little of the CAP's resources are devoted to long-term structural reform and modernization of the sector; artificially high prices supported by intervention buying encourages gross overproduction and results in large surpluses ('mountains') of produce which is expensive to stockpile and difficult to sell off; subsidized exports from the EC can depress world farm prices making life even more difficult for the less-developed countries, many of whom (specifically non-LOMÉ AGREEMENT countries) had already been hard hit by the trade diversionary effects of the EC (see TRADE DIVERSION). See INCOME SUPPORT.

common external tariff, see CUSTOMS UNION, COMMON MARKET.

common law, *n.* the body of law built-up over many years as a result of previous court decisions interpreting legislation. These establish legal precedents which then need to be followed consistently in subsequent court cases. Compare STATUTE LAW.

common market, *n.* a form of TRADE INTEGRATION between a number of countries in which members eliminate all trade barriers (TARIFFS, etc.) amongst themselves on goods and services and establish a uniform set of barriers against trade with the rest of the world, in particular, a common external tariff (see CUSTOMS UNION). In addition, a common market provides for the free movement of labour and capital across national boundaries. The aim of a common market is to secure the benefits of international SPECIALIZATION, thereby improving members' real living standards.

The short and medium-term impact of the formation of a common market is mainly felt through an increase in trade between member countries. TRADE CREATION is typically associated with a reallocation of resources within the market favouring least-cost supply locations and a reduction in prices resulting from the elimination of tariffs and lower production costs. (See GAINS FROM TRADE.)

In addition, a common market can be expected to promote longer-term (dynamic) changes conducive to economic efficiency through:

(a) COMPETITION. The removal of tariffs, etc., can be expected to widen the area of effective competition; high-cost producers are eliminated, while efficient and progressive suppliers are able to exploit new market opportunities.

(b) ECONOMIES OF SCALE. A larger 'home' market enables firms to take advantage of economies of large scale production and distribution, thereby lowering supply costs and enhancing COMPARATIVE ADVANTAGE.

(c) TECHNOLOGICAL PROGRESSIVENESS. Wider market opportunities and exposure to greater competition can be expected to encourage firms to invest and innovate new techniques and products.

(d) INVESTMENT and ECONOMIC GROWTH. Finally, the 'virtuous' circle of rising income per head, growing trade, increased productive efficiency and investment may be expected to combine to produce higher growth rates and real standards of living.

The EUROPEAN COMMUNITY is one example of a common market.

communism, *n.* a political and economic doctrine which advocates that the state should own all property and organize all the functions of PRODUCTION and EXCHANGE, including LABOUR. Karl MARX succinctly stated his idea of communism as 'from each according to his ability, to each according to his needs'. Communism involves a CENTRALLY PLANNED ECONOMY where strategic decisions concerning production and distribution are taken by government as opposed to being determined by the PRICE SYSTEM as in a market based PRIVATE ENTERPRISE ECONOMY. Countries which have adopted forms of communism include the Soviet Union and its East European satellites, and China.

company, see FIRM.

company formation, *n.* the process of forming a JOINT-STOCK

COMPANY, which involves a number of steps: (a) the drawing up of a MEMORANDUM OF ASSOCIATION; (b) the preparation of ARTICLES OF ASSOCIATION; (c) application to the COMPANY REGISTRAR for a CERTIFICATE OF INCORPORATION; (d) issue SHARE CAPITAL; (e) the commencement of trading.

company laws, *n.* a body of legislation providing for the regulation of JOINT-STOCK COMPANIES. British company law encouraged the development of joint-stock companies by establishing the principle of LIMITED LIABILITY and provides for the protection of SHAREHOLDERS' interests by controlling the formation and financing of companies. The major provisions of UK company law are the 1948, 1967 and 1976 Companies Acts. See ARTICLES OF ASSOCIATION, MEMORANDUM OF ASSOCIATION.

Company Registrar, *n.* a government official who maintains a record of all JOINT-STOCK COMPANIES operating in the UK. All joint-stock companies must lodge a copy of their MEMORANDUM OF ASSOCIATION and ARTICLES OF ASSOCIATION with the Registrar when they are first formed, and larger companies must continue to file their ANNUAL REPORT AND ACCOUNTS with the Registrar each year. Any potential lender or investor can inspect the company register to gain background information about a particular company.

comparative advantage, *n.* the advantage possessed by a country engaged in INTERNATIONAL TRADE if it can produce a given good at a lower resource input cost than other countries. Also called *comparative cost principle*. This proposition is illustrated in Fig. 29 with respect to two countries (A and B) and two GOODS (X and Y).

The same given resource input in both countries enables them to produce either the quantity of good X or the quantity of good Y indicated in Fig. 29. It can be seen that country B is absolutely more efficient than country A since it can produce more of both goods. However, it is comparative advantage not ABSOLUTE ADVANTAGE which determines whether trade is beneficial or not. Comparative advantage arises because the marginal OPPORTUNITY COSTS of one good in terms of the other differ as between countries (see HECKSCHER–OHLIN FACTOR PROPORTIONS THEORY).

It can be seen that country B has a comparative advantage in the production of good X for it is able to produce it at a lower factor cost than country A; the resource or opportunity cost of producing an additional unit of X is only 2/3Y in country B, whereas in country A it is 1Y.

Country A has a comparative advantage in the production of good Y

Country	Output of good		Opportunity cost ratio	
	X	Y	X	Y
A	100	100	1	: 1
B	180	120	1	: $\frac{2}{3}$ (or 1$\frac{1}{2}$:1)

Fig. 29. **Comparative advantage**. The physical output of X and Y from a given factor input, and the opportunity cost of X in terms of Y. The opportunity cost of producing one more unit of X is 1Y in country A, and $\frac{2}{3}$Y in country B. The opportunity cost of producing one more unit of Y is 1X in country A, and 1$\frac{1}{2}$X in country B.

for it is able to produce it at lower factor cost than country B; the resource or opportunity cost of producing an additional unit of Y is only 1X, whereas in country B it is 1$\frac{1}{2}$X.

Both countries, therefore, stand to increase their economic welfare if they specialize (see SPECIALIZATION) in the production of the good in which they have a comparative advantage (see GAINS FROM TRADE entry for an illustration of this important proposition). The extent to which each will benefit from trade will depend upon the real terms of trade at which they agree to exchange X and Y.

comparative cost principle, see COMPARATIVE ADVANTAGE.

Fig. 30. **Comparative static equilibrium analysis**. The initial level of national income is Y₁ (at point A) where the AGGREGATE DEMAND SCHEDULE (AD₁) intersects the AGGREGATE SUPPLY SCHEDULE (AS).

comparative static equilibrium analysis, *n.* a method of economic analysis which compares the differences between two or more equilibrium states which result from changes in EXOGENEOUS VARIABLES. Consider, for example, the effect of a change in export demand on the EQUILIBRIUM LEVEL OF NATIONAL INCOME as shown in Fig. 30. Assume that foreigners demand more of the country's products. Exports rise and the aggregate demand schedule shifts upwards to a new level (AD_2) resulting in the establishment of a new equilibrium level of national income Y_2 (at point H). The effect of the increase in exports can then be measured by comparing the original level of national income with that of the new level of national income. See DYNAMIC ANALYSIS, EQUILIBRIUM MARKET PRICE (CHANGES IN).

comparison statement, *n.* a management accounting statement which sets out budgeted revenues and costs alongside actual revenues and costs, in order to facilitate comparisons between the two. See BUDGET, BUDGETARY CONTROL, STANDARD COST.

compensation principle, see WELFARE ECONOMICS.

competition, *n.* **1.** a form of MARKET STRUCTURE in which the number of firms supplying the market is used to indicate the type of market it is, e.g. PERFECT COMPETITION (many small competitors), OLIGOPOLY (a few large competitors). **2.** a process whereby firms strive against each other to secure customers for their products, i.e., the active rivalry of firms for customers using price variations, PRODUCT DIFFERENTIATION strategies, etc. See METHODS OF COMPETITION, MONOPOLISTIC COMPETITION, MONOPOLY.

Competition Act of 1980, *n.* a Parliamentary Act which extended UK monopoly law by giving the OFFICE OF FAIR TRADING wider powers to deal with restraints on competition such as EXCLUSIVE DEALING, REFUSAL TO SUPPLY, TIE-IN SALES, etc. Previously these practices could only be dealt with in the context of a full-scale and lengthy monopoly probe, whereas the Act now allows the OFT to deal with them on a separate one-off basis. See MONOPOLY POLICY.

competition policy, *n.* a policy concerned with promoting effective competition between suppliers by regulating for example, MERGERS, RESTRICTIVE TRADE AGREEMENTS and ANTICOMPETITIVE PRACTICES which restrict, distort or eliminate competition in a market. See MONOPOLY POLICY.

complementary products, *n.* GOODS or SERVICES whose demands are interrelated (a *joint demand*), so that an increase in the price of one of the goods results in a fall in the demand for the other. For example, if the price of tennis rackets goes up, this results not only in a decrease in the demand for rackets but, because less tennis is now played, a fall also in the demand for tennis balls. See SUBSTITUTE PRODUCTS, CROSS–ELASTICITY OF DEMAND.

complex monopoly, *n.* a situation defined under UK MONOPOLY

POLICY as one where a number of independent suppliers of a particular good or service follow a common course of conduct which has the effect of restricting competition between themselves. See OFFICE OF FAIR TRADING.

compound interest, *n.* the INTEREST on a LOAN which is based not only on the original amount of the loan but the amount of the loan plus previous accumulated interest. This means that over time interest charges grow exponentially, for example, a £100 loan earning compound interest at 10% per annum would accumulate to £110 at the end of the first year and £121 at the end of the second year, etc., based on the formula:

$$\text{compound sum} = \text{principal } (1 + \text{interest rate})^{\text{number of periods}}$$

i.e. $121 = 100(1 + 0.1)^2$. Compare SIMPLE INTEREST.

Fig. 31. **Concave.** The characteristic shape of a concave line.

concave, *adj.* (of a line on a GRAPH) bulging away from the origin, as in Fig. 31. Concavity is encountered in various areas of economic analysis, most notably in OPPORTUNITY COST analysis (PRODUCTION POSSIBILITY BOUNDARY). Compare CONVEX.

concealed unemployment, see DISGUISED UNEMPLOYMENT.

concentration measures, *n.* the measures of the size distribution of firms engaged in economic activities.

The broadest concentration measure is the *aggregate concentration* measure which looks at the share of total activity in an economy accounted for by the larger firms, for example, the proportion of total industrial output accounted for by the largest 200 firms; or the share of total manufacturing output produced by the 100 largest companies. Various size criteria may be used for this measure, in particular, sales, output, numbers employed and capital employed, each of which can give slightly different results because of differences in capital intensity. Such measures serve to give an overall national view of concentration and how it is changing over time.

Though aggregate concentration measures are useful they are generally too broad for purposes of economic analysis where interest focuses upon markets and performance in these markets. Consequently economists have developed several measures of MARKET concentration which seek to measure SELLER or BUYER CONCENTRATION. The most common of these measures is the CONCENTRATION RATIO, which records the percentage of a market's sales accounted for by a given number of the largest firms in that market. In the UK it has been usual to estimate the concentration ratio for the three or (more recently) five largest firms; whereas in the US the four-firm concentration ratio tends to be employed.

However, the concentration ratio only records seller concentration at one point along the cumulative concentration curve, as Fig. 32a indicates. This makes it difficult to compare concentration curves for two different markets, like A and B in the figure, where their concentration curves intersect. For example, using a three-firm concentration ratio, market A is more concentrated while using a five-firm ratio shows market B to be more concentrated. An alternative concentration index called the HERFINDAHL INDEX gets around this problem by taking into account the number and market shares of all firms in the market. The Herfindahl index is calculated by summing the squared market shares of all firms. The index can vary between a value of zero (where there are a large number of equally-sized firms) and one (where there is just one firm).

Concentration measures like the concentration ratio and the Herfindahl index are known as *absolute concentration* measures since they are concerned with the market shares of a given (absolute) number of firms. By contrast, *relative concentration measures* are concerned with inequalities in the share of total firms producing for the market. Such irregularities can be recorded in the form of a Lorenz curve as in Fig. 32b. The diagonal straight line shows what a distribution of complete equality in firm shares would look like, so the extent to which the Lorenz curve deviates from this line gives an indication of relative seller concentration. For example, the diagonal line shows how we might expect 50% of market sales to be accounted for by 50% of the total firms, whilst in fact 50% of market sales are accounted for by the largest 25% of

(a)

(b)

Fig. 32. **Concentration measures**. (a) Cumulative concentration curves, showing the cumulative share of market size accounted for by various (cumulative) *numbers* of firms. (b) The Lorenz curve shows the cumulative share of market size on one axis accounted for by various (cumulative) *percentages* of the number of firms in the market.

total firms, as the Lorenz curve indicates. The *Gini coefficient* provides a summary measure of the extent to which the Lorenz curve for a particular market deviates from the linear diagonal. It indicates the extent of the bow-shaped area in the Fig. by dividing the area above the

85

Lorenz curve by the area above the line of equality. The value of the Gini coefficient ranges from zero (complete equality) to one (complete inequality).

In practice, most market concentration studies use concentration ratios calculated from data derived from the census of production.

concentration ratio, *n.* a measure of the degree of SELLER CONCENTRATION in a MARKET. The concentration ratio shows the percentage of market sales accounted for by, for example, the largest four firms or largest eight firms. The concentration ratio is derived from the market concentration curve, which can be plotted on a graph with the horizontal scale showing the number of firms cumulated from the largest size and the vertical scale showing the cumulative percentage of market sales accounted for by particular numbers of firms. See Fig. 33. See CONCENTRATION MEASURES, MARKET STRUCTURE.

Fig. 33. **Concentration ratio.** Market A is here highly concentrated, with the four largest firms accounting for 80% of market sales, while market B has a relatively low level of concentration.

concert party, *n.* a group of individuals or firms that acts 'in concert', pooling its various resources in order to effect the TAKEOVER of a company. See TAKEOVER BID, CITY CODE.

conciliation, *n.* a procedure for settling disputes, most notably INDUSTRIAL DISPUTES, in which a neutral third party meets with the disputants and endeavours to help them resolve their differences and reach agreement through continued negotiation. In the UK the ADVISORY, CONCILIATION AND ARBITRATION SERVICE acts in this capacity. See MEDIATION, ARBITRATION, INDUSTRIAL RELATIONS, COLLECTIVE BARGAINING.

Fig. 34. **Conditional distribution**. The three-dimensional curves show two conditional distributions for consumption expenditure (C), corresponding to two specific levels of disposable income, Y_1 and Y_2 based on the regression equation: $C = a + bY$.

conditional distribution, *n.* a special kind of PROBABILITY DISTRIBUTION showing likely values of the DEPENDENT VARIABLE predicted by a regression equation for a given fixed value of the INDEPENDENT VARIABLE. See Fig. 34.

Conditional distributions arise because we cannot expect predictions of the dependent variable based on a regression equation to always give an identical, accurate prediction; since we are merely predicting what, *on average* consumption expenditure will be for a given level of disposable income. Consequently it is useful to construct a CONFIDENCE INTERVAL for the true underlying consumption spending which corresponds to a given level of disposable income like Y_1. The STANDARD DEVIATION of these conditional distributions forms the basis for calculating the STANDARD ERROR of the estimates which establishes a confidence interval (see REGRESSION ANALYSIS).

condition of entry, *n.* an element of MARKET STRUCTURE which refers to the ease or difficulty new suppliers face in entering a market. Market theory indicates that at one extreme, entry may be entirely 'free', with, as in PERFECT COMPETITION, new suppliers being able to enter the market and compete immediately on equal terms with established firms; at the other extreme, in OLIGOPOLY and MONOPOLY markets, BARRIERS TO ENTRY operate which severely limit the opportunity for new entry. The significance of barriers to entry in market theory is that they allow established firms to secure a long-term profit return in excess of the

NORMAL PROFIT equilibrium attained under fully competitive ('free' entry) conditions.

See MARKET ENTRY, POTENTIAL ENTRANT, LIMIT PRICING.

Confederation of British Industry (CBI), *n.* a UK organization that represents the collective interests of member companies in dealings with government and TRADE UNIONS.

confidence interval, *n.* the range of values or interval within which we can assert (with a suitable probability) that the true POPULATION mean will lie. For example, with a 95% confidence interval there is a 0.95 probability that this interval contains the true MEAN of the population. The limits of the numerical interval within which we would be 95% confident of finding the population mean can be calculated by means of a formula linking the mean of a random sample, the sample STANDARD DEVIATION, and sample size. If we increase the degree of certainty required from, say, 95% to 99% then the numerical limits arising from the formula become wider. On the other hand, if we decrease the degree of certainty required and calculate 90% confidence intervals, then the limits will be narrower.

Confidence intervals of the above type are generally applicable only to large samples; for small samples, confidence intervals are established by means of the T DISTRIBUTION.

conglomerate firm, *n.* see FIRM.

consolidated accounts, *n.* the aggregate accounts of a group of companies. A consolidated BALANCE SHEET is compiled by adding the ASSETS and LIABILITIES of all companies in the group, after making allowance for any amounts that companies in the group owe to one another. A consolidated TRADING AND PROFIT-AND-LOSS ACCOUNT is prepared by adding the SALES REVENUES and COSTS of all companies in the group, after deducting the effects of any sales between companies within the group. The claims of any MINORITY INTERESTS in group assets and profits must also be allowed for. See HOLDING COMPANY.

consolidated fund, *n.* the UK government's account at the Bank of England into which it pays its TAXATION and other receipts, and which it uses to make payments.

consols, *n.* government BONDS which have an indefinite life rather than a specific maturity date. People acquire consols in order to buy a future nominal annual income without any expectation of repayment of the issue, though they can be bought and sold on the STOCK EXCHANGE. Because they are never redeemed by the government the market value of consols can vary greatly in order to bring their EFFECTIVE RATE OF

INTEREST in line with their NOMINAL RATE OF INTEREST. For example, a £100 consul with a nominal rate of interest of 5% would yield a return of £5 per year. If current market interest rates were 10%, then the market price of the consol would need to fall to £50 so that a buyer would earn an effective return on it of £5/£50 = 10%.

consortium, *n.* a temporary grouping of independent firms, organizations and governments, brought together to pool their resources and skills in order to undertake a particular project such as a major construction programme or the building of an aircraft, or to combine their buying power in bulk-buying factor inputs.

conspicuous consumption *n.*, the CONSUMPTION of goods and services not for the UTILITY derived from their use but for the utility derived from the ostentatious exhibition of such goods and services.

A person may buy and run a Rolls-Royce motor car not just as a vehicle for transportation but because it suggests to the outside world something about the owner. That person may wish to be seen as affluent or a person of taste. This phenomenon (known as the VEBLEN EFFECT) can be viewed as an alternative to the more usual consumption theories where the quantity of a particular good varies inversely with its price (a downward-sloping DEMAND CURVE). A conspicuous consumption good may well have an UPWARD-SLOPING DEMAND CURVE so that the quantity demanded increases with its price.

constant, *n.* a term which takes only a single numerical value, as opposed to a VARIABLE which can take a range of numerical values. Variables and constants are used in constructing ECONOMIC MODELS. See ECONOMETRICS, HYPOTHESIS TESTING.

constant returns, *n.* **1.** (in the SHORT RUN) constant returns to the VARIABLE FACTOR INPUT that occur when additional units of variable input added to a given quantity of FIXED FACTOR INPUT generate equal increments in output. With an unchanged price for variable factor inputs, constant returns will cause the short-run unit variable cost of output to stay the same over an output range. See RETURNS TO THE VARIABLE FACTOR INPUT. **2.** (in the LONG RUN) constant returns that occur when successive increases in all factor inputs generate equal increments in output. In cost terms this means the long run unit cost of output remains constant so long as factor input prices stay the same. See MINIMUM EFFICIENT SCALE, ECONOMIES OF SCALE.

consumer or **buyer,** *n.* the basic consuming/demanding unit of economic theory. In economic theory, a consuming unit can be either an individual purchaser of a good or service, a HOUSEHOLD (a group of individuals who make joint purchasing decisions), or a government.

consumer credit, *n.* LOANS made available to buyers of products to assist them in financing purchases. Consumer credit facilities include HIRE PURCHASE, BANK LOANS and CREDIT CARDS.

consumer durables, *n.* CONSUMER GOODS such as houses, cars, televisions which are 'consumed' over relatively long periods of time rather than immediately. Compare CONSUMER NONDURABLES.

consumer equilibrium, *n.* the point at which the consumer maximizes his TOTAL UTILITY or satisfaction from the spending of a limited (fixed) income. The economic 'problem' of the consumer is that he has only a limited amount of income to spend and therefore cannot buy all the goods and services he would like to have. Faced with this constraint, demand theory assumes that the goal of the consumer is to select that combination of goods, in line with his preferences, which will maximize his total utility or satisfaction. Total utility is maximized when the MARGINAL UTILITY of a penny's worth of good X is exactly equal to the marginal utility of a penny's worth of all of the other goods purchased; or, restated, when the prices of goods are different, the marginal utilities are proportional to their respective prices. For two goods X and Y total utility is maximized when:

$$\frac{\text{marginal utility of X}}{\text{price of X}} = \frac{\text{marginal utility of Y}}{\text{price of Y}}$$

Consumer equilibrium can also be depicted graphically using INDIFFERENCE CURVE analysis. See Fig. 35. See also REVEALED PREFERENCE THEORY, PRICE EFFECT, INCOME EFFECT, SUBSTITUTION EFFECT, ECONOMIC MAN, CONSUMER RATIONALITY.

consumer goods, *n.* any products such as washing machines, beer, toys, that are purchased by consumers as opposed to businesses. Compare CAPITAL GOODS, PRODUCER GOODS.

consumerism, *n.* an organized movement to protect the economic interests of CONSUMERS. The movement developed in response to the growing market power of large companies and the increasing technical complexity of products. It embraces bodies such as the Consumers Association in the UK, which is concerned with product testing and informing consumers through publications such as *Which?*. Consumerism has been officially incorporated into British MONOPOLY POLICY since the 1973 FAIR TRADING ACT.

consumer nondurables, *n.* CONSUMER GOODS which yield up all their

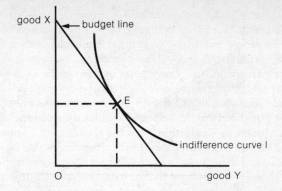

Fig. 35. **Consumer equilibrium**. The optimal combination of Good X and Good Y is at point E when the BUDGET LINE is tangential to indifference curve I. At this point the slope of the budget line (the ratio of prices) is equal to the slope of the indifference curve (the ratio of marginal utilities), so the goods' marginal utilities are proportional to their prices.

UTILITY at the point of consumption. They include such items as beer, steak or cigarettes. Compare CONSUMER DURABLES.

consumer rationality or **economic rationality,** *n.* the assumption, in demand theory, that CONSUMERS attempt to obtain the greatest possible satisfaction from the money resources they have available when making purchases. Because economic theory tends to sum household demands in constructing market DEMAND CURVES, it is not important if a few households do not conform to rational behaviour as long as the majority of consumers or households act rationally.

See ECONOMIC MAN.

consumer sovereignty, *n.* the power of CONSUMERS to determine what is produced since they are the ultimate purchasers of goods and services. In general terms, if consumers demand more of a good then more of it will be supplied. This implies that PRODUCERS are 'passive agents' in the PRICE SYSTEM, simply responding to what consumers want. However, in certain kinds of market (notably, OLIGOPOLY and MONOPOLY), producers are so powerful vis-à-vis consumers that it is they who effectively determine the range of choice open to the consumer. See REVISED SEQUENCE.

consumers' surplus, *n.* the extra satisfaction or UTILITY gained by consumers from paying an actual price for a good which is *lower* than

Fig. 36. **Consumers' surplus.** (a) At the EQUILIBRIUM PRICE OP utility from the marginal unit of the good is just equal to its price; all previous units yield an amount of utility which is greater than the amount paid by the consumer, insofar as consumers would have been prepared to pay more for these intramarginal units than the market price. The total consumer surplus is represented by the shaded area PEP$_1$. (b) The loss of consumers' surplus due to monopoly.

that which they would have been prepared to pay. See Fig. 36a. The consumers' surplus is maximized only in PERFECT COMPETITION, where price is determined by the free play of market demand and supply forces.

Where market price is not determined by demand and supply forces in competitive market conditions, but is instead determined administratively by a profit-maximizing MONOPOLIST, then the resulting restriction in market output and the increase in market price causes a loss of consumer surplus, indicated by the shaded area PP_mXE in Fig. 36b. See DIMINISHING MARGINAL UTILITY.

consumption, *n.* **1.** the satisfaction obtained by CONSUMERS from the use of goods and services. Certain CONSUMER DURABLE products like washing machines are consumed over a longish period of time, while other products like cakes are consumed immediately after purchase. The DEMAND CURVE for a particular product reflects consumers' satisfactions from consuming it. See WANTS, DEMAND.

2. the proportion of NATIONAL INCOME spent by HOUSEHOLDS and public authorities on final goods and services. Consumption is the largest component of AGGREGATE DEMAND and spending in the CIRCULAR FLOW OF NATIONAL INCOME. It is one of the most stable components of aggregate demand, showing little fluctuation from period to period. See CONSUMPTION SCHEDULE, VEBLEN EFFECT.

consumption function, *n.* a statement of the general relationship between the dependent variable, CONSUMPTION expenditure, and the various independent variables which determine consumption such as current DISPOSABLE INCOME and income from previous periods. See CONSUMPTION SCHEDULE, LIFE–CYCLE HYPOTHESIS, PERMANENT INCOME HYPOTHESIS.

consumption possibility line, see BUDGET LINE.

consumption schedule, *n.* a schedule depicting the relationship between CONSUMPTION and the level of INCOME. Also called *consumption function*. At low levels of DISPOSABLE INCOME households consume more than their current income (see DISSAVINGS), drawing on past savings, borrowing, or selling assets in order to maintain consumption. At higher levels of disposable income they consume only a part of their current income and save the rest (see SAVINGS). See Fig. 37 on page 94.

contestable market, *n.* a MARKET where new entrants face costs similar to those of established firms and where, on leaving, firms are able to recoup their capital costs, less depreciation. Consequently, it is not possible for established firms to earn ABOVE–NORMAL PROFIT as this will be eroded by the entry of new firms, or, alternatively, the mere threat of such new entry may be sufficient to ensure that established firms set prices which yield them only a NORMAL PROFIT return. See WORKABLE COMPETITION, CONDITION OF ENTRY, BARRIERS TO ENTRY.

CONTINGENCY TABLE

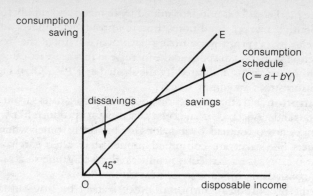

Fig. 37. **Consumption schedule**. A simple consumption schedule which takes the linear form $C = a + bY$, where C is consumption, a is the minimum level of consumption expenditure at zero disposable income, and b is the proportion of each extra £ (pound) of disposable income which is spent. The 45° line OE shows what consumption expenditure would have been had it exactly matched disposable income. The difference between OE and the consumption schedule indicates the extent of dissavings or SAVINGS at various income levels. The slope of the consumption schedule is equal to the MARGINAL PROPENSITY TO CONSUME. See SAVINGS SCHEDULE, LIFE-CYCLE HYPOTHESIS, PERMANENT-INCOME HYPOTHESIS.

contingency table, *n.* a table that sets out in matrix form the interrelations between two quantitative or qualitative VARIABLES. This matrix can then be used to test the strength of any relationship which exists between the variables. For example, if we wished to determine whether there is any relationship between a family's disposable income and the family's means of transport, then we would choose appropriate classifications for income and means of transport, and set up a contingency table like Fig. 38.

If we formulate the null hypothesis that there is no relationship between family income and means of transport, then we would expect the proportions of families using cars and buses to be the same for each individual group. These expected cell frequencies can be calculated by multiplying each cell's row total by its column total and then dividing by the grand total, which generates the bracketed figures in the table. These expected cell frequencies can be compared with the observed sample cell frequencies and a HYPOTHESIS TEST can be carried out, using

		Car	**Bus**	
Disposable income	High	70 (50)	30 (50)	100
	Low	30 (50)	70 (50)	100
		100	100	grand total = 200

Fig. 38. **Contingency table**. The cells of the table report the distribution of results from a random sample of 200 families' choice of transport.

the CHI–SQUARE DISTRIBUTION. If the test value for chi–square is sufficiently large then the null hypothesis is rejected and we can conclude that there is a significant correlation between the two variables. The strength of this relationship can be assessed by a measure called the *contingency coefficient*.

In this particular case the figures suggest that there is a valid relationship between income and transport mode with high-income consumers favouring car transport and low income consumers favouring buses.

continuous distribution, *n*. a graphical presentation of a FREQUENCY DISTRIBUTION in which the frequency or probability of each category or numerical value is portrayed by means of the height of a smooth curve. For example, in the continuous distribution graph in Fig. 39 on page 96 the variable 'weekly income' is depicted on the horizontal axis and frequencies or probabilities on the vertical axis. As with HISTOGRAMS, the frequencies or probabilities associated with particular categories or numerical values are represented by the corresponding area under the curve.

continuous variable, *n*. a VARIABLE which can take an infinite variety of values, increasing or decreasing in tiny increments along a continuous scale. Compare DISCRETE VARIABLE.

contract, *n*. a legally enforceable agreement between two or more parties. A contract involves obligations on the part of the contractors which may be expressed verbally or in writing. For example, one company may enter into an agreement to supply a product to another company at a given future date and on specified terms. Both parties would then be legally bound to honour their agreement to sell and to buy the product.

contract curve, SEE EDGEWORTH BOX.

Fig. 39. **Continuous distribution.** The total area under the curve represents all the categories or numerical values (100%) and the frequency or probability of any class such as the income band from £100 to £200 is equivalent to the shaded area expressed as a proportion of the total area under the curve.

contribution, *n.* the difference between a product's SALES REVENUE and its VARIABLE COSTS. If total contributions are just large enough to cover FIXED COSTS then the producer BREAKS-EVEN; if contributions are less than fixed costs the producer makes a LOSS; while if contributions exceed fixed costs then the producer makes a PROFIT. See LOSS MINIMIZATION, MARGINAL COSTING.

convertibility, *n.* the extent to which one foreign currency or INTERNATIONAL RESERVE ASSET can be exchanged for some other foreign currency or international reserve asset.

International trade and investment opportunities are maximized when the currencies used to finance them are fully convertible, i.e. free of EXCHANGE CONTROL restrictions.

convertible loans, *n.* long-term LOANS to a JOINT-STOCK COMPANY which may be converted at the option of the lender into ORDINARY SHARES at a predetermined share price.

convex, *adj.* (of a line on a GRAPH) bulging towards the origin, as in Fig. 40. Convexity is encountered in various areas of economic analysis, most notably in the theory of CONSUMER EQUILIBRIUM (INDIFFERENCE CURVES) and the theory of production (ISOQUANTS). Compare CONCAVE.

cooperative, *n.* a form of business FIRM which is owned and run by a group of individuals for their mutual benefit. Examples of cooperatives

Fig. 40. **Convex**. The characteristic shape of a convex line.

include:

(a) *worker* or *producer cooperatives* – businesses that are owned and managed by their employees, who share in the net profit of the business.

(b) *retail cooperatives* – businesses whose membership comprises a multitude of small independent retailers. The prime objective of such a group is to use its combined bulk-buying power to obtain discounts and concessions from manufacturers similar to those achieved by larger SUPERMARKET chains.

(c) *consumer cooperatives* – businesses that are run in the interest of customers holding membership rights which entitle them, for instance, to receive an annual dividend or refund in proportion to their spending at the cooperative's shops.

See RETAILING, CHAIN STORE.

coordinates, *n.* the specific magnitudes used to locate the position of a point or plane within a GRAPH defined by the axes, as in Fig. 41 on page 98. The vertical AXIS, axis-y, for example, we may call price (P). The horizontal axis, axis-x (at right angles to the vertical axis), we may call quantity. The point O, where the axes intersect, is called the origin. Point A in Fig. 41 has the coordinates OP_1 and OQ_1.

Coordinates may have negative magnitudes as well as positive ones. Negative values of a variable such as quantity demanded would lie below the origin on the y-axis or to the left of the origin on the x-axis; while positive values would lie above the origin on the y-axis or to the right of it on the x-axis, as shown by the minus and plus signs in Fig. 41.

copyright, *n.* the ownership of the rights to a publication of a book, manual, newspaper, etc., giving legal entitlement and powers of redress

Fig. 41. **Coordinates**. See main entry.

against theft and unauthorized publication or copying. See INDUSTRIAL PROPERTY RIGHTS.

corner, *vb.* to buy or attempt to buy up all of the supplies of a particular product on the MARKET, thereby creating a temporary MONOPOLY situation with the aim of exploiting the market.

corporate planning, *n.* the process of formulating and implementing long-term plans for an organization which integrate the individual plans of different functions and departments of the business into a comprehensive company plan.

Planning starts with the setting of long-term objectives (profit, growth, etc) directed at the kind of businesses the firm should be in, and proceeds towards the formulation of long-range policies and strategies which will achieve these objectives. This involves an appraisal of the organization's broad economic, technological, social and political environment, and its more immediate market environment, in order to appraise the threats and opportunities presented by that environment. It also involves an internal analysis of the organization in order to identify the organization's major strengths and weaknesses. On the basis of these analyses, companies can then plan product-development policies, market-development policies, or DIVERSIFICATION strategies which generate synergy. Corporate planning is a continuous process and once plans are implemented, then feedback can be used to modify plans in the light of changing circumstances.

See BOSTON MATRIX, BUDGETING, PLANNING, PROGRAMMING, BUDGET-
ING SYSTEM.

corporate sector, *n.* that part of the ECONOMY concerned with the
transactions of BUSINESSES. Businesses receive income from supplying
goods and services and influence the workings of the economy through
their use of, and payment for, factor inputs and INVESTMENT decisions.
The corporate sector, together with the PERSONAL SECTOR and FINANCIAL
SECTOR, constitute the PRIVATE SECTOR. The private sector, PUBLIC
(GOVERNMENT) SECTOR and FOREIGN SECTOR make up the national
economy.

See CIRCULAR FLOW OF NATIONAL INCOME MODEL.

corporation, *n.* **1.** a private enterprise FIRM incorporated in the form of a
JOINT-STOCK COMPANY. **2.** a publicly-owned business such as a nationalized industry.

corporation tax, *n.* a DIRECT TAX levied by the government on the
PROFITS accruing to businesses.

See TAXATION, FISCAL POLICY.

correlation, *n.* a statistical term that describes the degree of association
between two VARIABLES. When two variables tend to change together
then they are said to be correlated, and the extent to which they are
correlated is measured by means of the CORRELATION COEFFICIENT.

correlation coefficient, *n.* a statistical term (usually denoted by r) that
measures the strength of the association between two VARIABLES. Where
two variables are completely unrelated then their correlation coefficient
will be zero; where two variables are perfectly related then their
correlation would be one. A high correlation coefficient between two
variables merely indicates that the two generally vary together – it does
not imply causality in the sense of changes in one variable causing
changes in the other.

Where high values of one variable are associated with high values of
the other (and vice versa), then they are said to be *positively correlated*.
Where high values of one variable are associated with low values of the
other (and vice versa), then they are said to be *negatively correlated*. Thus
correlation coefficients can range from $+1$ for perfect positive
association to -1 for perfect negative association, with zero representing the case where there is no association between the two.

The correlation coefficient also serves to measure the *goodness of fit* of a
regression line (see REGRESSION ANALYSIS) which has been fitted to a set of
sample observations by the technique of ordinary least squares. A large
positive correlation coefficient will be found when the regression line

slopes upward from left to right and fits closely with the observations; a large negative correlation coefficient will be found when the regression line slopes downward from left to right and closely matches the observations. Where the regression equation contains two (or more) independent variables a multiple correlation coefficient can be used to measure how closely the three-dimensional plane, representing the multiple regression equation, fits the set of data points.

corset, see SPECIAL DEPOSITS.

cost-benefit analysis, *n.* a technique for enumerating and evaluating the total SOCIAL COSTS and total social benefits associated with an economic project. Cost-benefit analysis is generally used by public agencies when evaluating large-scale public INVESTMENT projects such as major new motorways or rail lines, in order to assess the welfare or net social benefits which will accrue to the nation from these projects. This generally involves the sponsoring bodies taking a broader and longer-term view of a project than would a commercial organization concentrating on project profitability alone.

The main principles of cost-benefit are encompassed within four key questions:

(a) which costs and which benefits are to be included. All costs and benefits should be enumerated and ranked according to their remoteness from the main purpose of the project so that more remote costs and benefits might be excluded. This requires careful definition of the project and estimation of project life, and consideration of EXTERNALITIES and SECONDARY BENEFITS.

(b) how these costs and benefits are to be valued. The values placed on costs and benefits should pay attention to likely changes in relative prices but not the general price level, since the general price level prevailing in the initial year should be taken as the base level. Though market prices are normally used to value costs and benefits, difficulties arise when investment projects are so large that they significantly affect prices; where monopoly elements distort relative prices; where taxes artificially inflate the resource costs of inputs; and where significant unemployment of labour or other resources means that labour or other resource prices overstate the social costs of using these inputs which are in excess supply. In such cases SHADOW PRICES may be needed for costs and benefits. In addition, there are particular problems of establishing prices for INTANGIBLE PRODUCTS and COLLECTIVE PRODUCTS.

(c) the interest rate at which costs and benefits are to be discounted. This requires consideration of the extent to which social time preference will dictate a lower DISCOUNT RATE than private time preference because social time preference discounts the future less heavily; and OPPORTUNITY COST considerations which mitigate against using a lower discount rate for public projects for fear that mediocre public projects may displace good private sector projects if the former have an easier criterion to meet.

(d) the relevant constraints. This group includes legal, administrative and budgetary constraints, and constraints on the redistribution of income. Essentially, cost-benefit analysis concentrates on the economic efficiency benefits from a project and providing the benefits exceed the costs recommends acceptance of the project, regardless of who benefits and who bears the costs. However, where the decision-maker feels that the redistribution of income associated with a project is unacceptable, he may reject that project despite its net benefits.

There is always uncertainty surrounding the estimates of future costs and benefits associated with a public investment project, and cost-benefit analysis needs to allow for this uncertainty by testing the sensitivity of the net benefits to changes in such factors as project life and interest rates.

See WELFARE ECONOMICS, COST EFFECTIVENESS.

cost centre, *n.* a group of machines or factory department under the control of a manager, for which costs can be ascertained and used for purposes of cost control. See also STANDARD COST, PROFIT CENTRE.

cost effectiveness, *n.* the achievement of maximum provision of a good or service from *given* quantities of resource inputs. Cost effectiveness is often established as an objective when organizations have a given level of expenditure available to them and are seeking to provide the maximum amount of service, in a situation where service outputs cannot be valued in money terms (e.g., the UK National Health Service). Where it is possible to estimate the money value of outputs as well as the money value of inputs then COST-BENEFIT techniques can be applied.

cost function, *n.* a function that depicts the general relationship between the COSTS of FACTOR INPUTS and the cost of OUTPUT in a firm. In order to determine the cost of producing a particular output it is necessary to know not only the required quantities of the various inputs but also their prices. The cost function can be derived from the PRODUCTION FUNCTION by adding the information about factor prices. It would take the general form:

$$Qc = f\,(p1\ I1,\ p2\ I2 \ \underline{\quad\quad}\ pn\ In)$$

where Qc is the cost of producing a particular output Q, and $p1$, $p2$, etc., are the prices of the various factors used, while $I1$, $I2$, etc., are the quantities of factors 1,2, etc., required. The factor prices $p1$, $p2$ etc., which a firm must pay in order to attract units of these factors will depend upon the interaction of the forces of demand and supply in factor markets. See EFFICIENCY.

cost minimization, *n.* production of a given OUTPUT at minimum cost by combining FACTOR INPUTS with due regard to their relative prices. See COST FUNCTION, ISOQUANT CURVE.

cost of capital, *n.* the payments made by a firm for the use of long-term capital employed in its business. The average cost of capital to a firm which uses several sources of long-term funds (e.g., LOANS, SHARE CAPITAL (EQUITY), to finance its investments will depend upon the individual cost of each separate source of capital (for example, INTEREST on loans) weighted in accordance with the proportions of each source used. See CAPITAL GEARING, DISCOUNT RATE.

cost of goods sold or **cost of sales,** *n.* the relevant cost that is compared with sales revenue in order to determine GROSS PROFIT in the TRADING AND PROFIT–AND–LOSS ACCOUNT. Where a trading company has STOCKS of finished goods, the cost of goods sold is not the same as purchases of finished goods. Rather, purchases of goods must be added to stocks at the start of the trading period to determine the goods available for sale, then the stocks left at the end of the trading period must be deducted from this to determine the cost of the goods which have been sold during the period. See STOCK VALUATION.

cost of living, *n.* the general level of prices of goods and services measured in terms of a PRICE INDEX. To protect peoples' living standards from being eroded by price increases (INFLATION), wage contracts, old age pensions, etc., sometimes contain cost-of-living adjustment provisions which automatically operate to increase wages, pensions, etc., in proportion to price increases. See INDEXATION.

cost–plus pricing, *n.* a method of arriving at a final SELLING PRICE for a product by taking the actual COSTS incurred in producing and distributing it and adding to them a PROFIT MARGIN. The profit margin is frequently calculated by taking a percentage of actual cost so that the selling price becomes actual cost plus percentage added, or the agreement between purchaser and seller may state that selling price is actual costs plus an agreed fixed amount of profit per unit. Such pricing methods may be found in large capital projects, or in defence contracts where the length of time of construction or changing technical specifications leads to a high degree of uncertainty in the costing exercise. Cost-plus pricing is frequently criticized for failing to give the supplier an incentive to keep costs down (and sometimes an incentive to raise them).

See also COST PRICE, FULL–COST PRICING.

cost price, *n*. a PRICE for a product which just covers its production and distribution COSTS with no PROFIT MARGIN added.

cost-push inflation, *n*. a general increase in PRICES caused by increases in FACTOR INPUT costs. Factor input costs may rise because WAGE RATES in the economy increase at a faster rate than output per man (PRODUCTIVITY), or because raw materials and energy costs increase due to world-wide shortages or the operation of CARTELS (oil for example). Faced with increased input costs producers try to 'pass-on' increased costs by charging higher prices. In order to maintain profit margins, producers would need to pass on the full increased costs in the form of higher prices, but whether they are able to depends upon PRICE ELASTICITY OF DEMAND for their products. See INFLATION.

costs, *n*. the payments (both EXPLICIT COSTS and IMPLICIT COSTS) incurred by a firm in producing its output. See TOTAL COST, AVERAGE COST, MARGINAL COST, PRODUCTION COST, SELLING COST.

Council for Mutual Economic Assistance (COMECON), *n*. an organization established in 1949 by the Soviet-Union dominated bloc to coordinate the central planning of member countries, and to promote greater trade between members. Membership of COMECON currently includes the Soviet Union, Bulgaria, Czechoslovakia, Hungary, Poland, Romania, E. Germany, Mongolia and Cuba.

The physical planning procedures, however, of most socialist states which specify a 'shopping list' of import requirements and a limited range of export products, mitigate against widespread multilateral trade and have tended to favour bilateral deals between countries, often on a BARTER basis, or using Western prices as reference points. In recent years there has been an increase in East-West trade which has forced COMECON to place a greater reliance on the FOREIGN EXCHANGE MARKETS, and this, in turn, has given intra-COMECON trade as well as internal planning mechanisms, much greater price consciousness.

countertrade, *n*. a form of INTERNATIONAL TRADE which is based on the physical exchange of one product or commodity for some other product or commodity (BARTER) as opposed to the use of foreign currencies.

Companies and dealers resort to countertrade when particular foreign currencies are in short supply, or when, because of balance of payments difficulties, countries apply EXCHANGE CONTROLS.

countervailing duty, *n.* a TAX levied on an imported product (see IMPORTS) which raises the price in the domestic market as a means of counteracting 'unfair' trading practices by other countries. Countervailing duties are frequently employed against imported products which are deliberately 'dumped' (see DUMPING) or subsidized by EXPORT INCENTIVES.

See TARIFF, IMPORT DUTY, BEGGAR-MY-NEIGHBOUR POLICY.

countervailing power, *n.* the ability of large buyers to offset the market power of large suppliers as in BILATERAL OLIGOPOLY. Large buyers usually have the upper hand in a vertical market chain (for example, multiple retailers buying from food manufacturers) because, unless suppliers collude (see COLLUSION), a large buyer is able to play one supplier off against another and obtain favourable discounts on bulk purchases. Provided that competition is strong in final selling markets countervailing power can play an important rôle in checking monopolistic abuse.

GALBRAITH uses the phrase 'countervailing power' in a slightly different way to refer to the growth of trade unions and consumer groups in response to the growth of large firms.

coupon, *n.* **1.** a document that shows proof of legal ownership of a FINANCIAL SECURITY and entitlement to payments thereon. For example, a SHARE certificate or BEARER BOND certificate. **2.** a means of promoting the sale of a product by offering coupons to buyers of the product which can be redeemed for cash, gifts or other goods.

coupon rate of interest, see NOMINAL (COUPON) RATE OF INTEREST.

Cournot, Augustin (1801–77) French economist who explored the problems of price in conditions of competition and monopoly in his book: *The Mathematical Principles of the Theory of Wealth* (1838).

Cournot concentrated attention on the exchange values of products rather than their utilities; and he used mathematics to explore the relationship between the sale price of products and their costs, developing the idea of a MONOPOLY price. Cournot is also known for his work on DUOPOLY, his analysis showing that two firms would react to one another's output changes until they eventually reached a stable output position from which neither would wish to depart.

Cournot duopoly, see DUOPOLY.

covenant, *n.* a specific condition in a legal agreement or CONTRACT. For instance, a formal agreement between a COMMERCIAL BANK and a JOINT-STOCK COMPANY to which it is loaning money might contain a covenant stipulating a limit on dividend distributions from profits.

crawling-peg exchange rate system, *n*. a form of FIXED EXCHANGE RATE SYSTEM in which the EXCHANGE RATES between currencies are fixed (pegged) at particular values (for example £1 = $2), but which are changed frequently (weekly or monthly) by small amounts to new fixed values to reflect underlying changes in the FOREIGN EXCHANGE MARKETS. For example, £1 = $1.90 cents, the repegging of the pound at a lower dollar value (DEVALUATION), or £1 = $2.10 cents, the repegging of the pound at a higher dollar value (REVALUATION).

credit, *n*. LOANS and other deferred payment methods made available to consumers and firms to enable them to purchase goods and services, and raw materials and components. See HIRE PURCHASE, BANK LOANS, CREDIT CARDS, CREDIT CONTROLS, TRADE CREDIT, CREDITORS, LENDER.

credit card, *n*. a plastic card or token used to finance the purchase of products by gaining point-of-sale CREDIT. Credit cards are issued by commercial banks, hotel chains, and larger retailers.

credit controls, *n*. **1.** the regulation of borrowing from the FINANCIAL SYSTEM as part of MONETARY POLICY. OPEN MARKET OPERATIONS are one general means of limiting the expansion of credit. A more selective form of control is consumer instalment credit regulation (HIRE PURCHASE). Under this arrangement the purchase of certain goods is regulated by the authorities stipulating the minimum down-payment and the maximum period of repayment.

   2. the control which a firm exercises over its TRADE DEBTORS in order to ensure that customers pay their DEBTS promptly and to minimize the risk of bad debts. Credit control involves: (a) assessing the creditworthiness of new and established customers; (b) persuading tardy customers to pay quickly (through cash discounts for prompt payment, reminder letters, etc.); (c) seeking to recover bad debts. The purpose of credit control is to minimize the funds which a firm has to tie up in debtors so improving profitability and LIQUIDITY. See FACTORING, DEBTORS-TO-SALES RATIO, WORKING CAPITAL, WORKING CAPITAL RATIO.

credit creation, see BANK-DEPOSIT CREATION.

creditors (accounts payable), *n*. the money owed to individuals or firms because they have supplied goods, services or raw materials for which they have not yet been paid (trade creditors), or because they have made LOANS. See DEBTORS (ACCOUNTS RECEIVABLE), CREDIT, CREDITORS RATIO.

creditors ratio, *n*. an accounting measure of a firm's average period of

CREDIT taken from suppliers, which expresses the firm's period-end CREDITORS as a ratio of its average daily purchases (or sales). The resulting figure shows how many days on average the firm took to pay its creditors.

Compare DEBTORS–TO–SALES RATIO.

credit squeeze, *n.* any action taken by the monetary authorities to reduce the amount of CREDIT granted by COMMERCIAL BANKS, FINANCE HOUSES, etc. Such action forms part of the government's MONETARY POLICY directed towards reducing AGGREGATE DEMAND by making less credit available and forcing up RATES OF INTEREST.

creeping inflation, *n.* the small increases in the general level of prices in an economy. See INFLATION, HYPERINFLATION.

critical path analysis or **network analysis,** *n.* a framework for establishing the shortest time in which a project can be completed. At each stage of PRODUCTION of a commodity, be it a bicycle or a nuclear power station, certain activities have to be performed before the next stage of production can be embarked upon. By making a schematic diagram of these operations it is possible to plan production so that the time taken is reduced to an absolute minimum.

The whole diagram is referred to as a network and the *sequential path* which takes least time to achieve the goal is called the 'critical path'. Such an analysis can help identify problem areas where perhaps bottlenecks may occur and action can be taken to remove them before the operation is underway.

cross–elasticity of demand, *n.* a measure of the degree of responsiveness of the DEMAND for one good to a given change in the PRICE of some other good.

$$\frac{\text{cross elasticity}}{\text{of demand}} = \frac{\text{\% change in quantity demanded of good A}}{\text{\% change in price of good B}}$$

If a given change in the price of good B (tea, for example) results in some change in the quantity demanded of good A (coffee, for example), then the two goods are SUBSTITUTE PRODUCTS. The degree of suitability is reflected in the cross–elasticity measure. If a small change in the price of good B results in a large change in the quantity of good A (highly cross-elastic), then goods A and B are close substitutes.

Cross–elasticities provide a useful indication of the substitutability of products and so help to indicate the boundaries between markets. A group of products with high cross–elasticities of demand constitutes a distinct market whether or not they share common technical characteristics; for example, mechanical and electronic watches are regarded by consumers as close substitutes.

Cross-elasticities are also helpful in analysing relationships between COMPLEMENTARY PRODUCTS where interdependence means that a rise in the price of good B will tend to reduce the quantity of good A demanded.

See MARKET.

cross-sectional, *adj.* of or referring to SAMPLE observations collected at a particular point in time. For example, we could collect data on company size and the remuneration of chief executives in the current year, embracing a wide range of different sized firms, as a basis for investigating the relationship between executive remuneration and company size. Compare LONGITUDINAL.

crowding-out effect, *n.* an increase in GOVERNMENT EXPENDITURE that has the effect of reducing the level of private sector spending. Financial crowding-out of the type described in the caption to Fig. 42 on page 108 would only occur to the extent that the MONEY SUPPLY is fixed, so that additional loanable funds are not forthcoming to finance the government's additional expenditure. If money supply is fixed then increases in the PUBLIC SECTOR BORROWING REQUIREMENT associated with additional government expenditure will tend to increase interest rates as the government borrows more, these higher interest rates serving to discourage private sector investment. On the other hand, if additional loanable funds were obtainable from, say, abroad, then additional government borrowing could be financed with little increase in interest rates or effect on private investment.

The term 'crowding-out' is also used in a broader sense to denote the effect of larger government expenditure in pre-empting national resources, leaving less for private consumption spending, private sector investment and for exports. Such real crowding out would only occur to the extent that total national resources are fixed and fully employed so that expansion in public sector claims on resources contract the amount left for the private sector. Where unemployed resources can be brought into use additional claims by both the public and private sectors can be met. See MONEY-SUPPLY/SPENDING LINKAGES, MARGINAL EFFICIENCY OF CAPITAL/INVESTMENT.

CSO, see CENTRAL STATISTICAL OFFICE.

cum-dividend, *adj.* (of a particular SHARE) including the right to receive the DIVIDEND which attaches to the share. If shares are purchased on the STOCK EXCHANGE 'cum. div.', the purchaser would be entitled to the

(a)

(b)

Fig. 42. 'Crowding out' effect. (a) An increase in government expenditure raises real NATIONAL INCOME and output (see EQUILIBRIUM LEVEL OF NATIONAL INCOME) which in turn increases the demand for money from D_m to $D_m{}^1$, with which to purchase the greater volume of goods and services being produced. (b) This causes the equilibrium RATE OF INTEREST to rise (from r to r^1) which then reduces – 'crowds out' – an amount of private INVESTMENT (ΔI). (c) An increase in government expenditure by itself would increase AGGREGATE DEMAND from AD to AD¹, but, allowing for the fall in private investment, the net result is to increase aggregate demand to only AD².

(c)

dividend accruing to that share when the dividend is next paid. Compare EX–DIVIDEND.

currency, *n.* the BANK NOTES and coins issued by the monetary authorities which form part of an economy's MONEY SUPPLY. The term 'currency' is often used interchangeably with the term *cash* in economic analysis and monetary policy.

currency appreciation, see APPRECIATION (1).

currency depreciation, see DEPRECIATION (1).

current account, *n.* **1.** a statement of a country's trade in goods (visibles) and services (invisibles) with the rest of the world over a particular period of time. See BALANCE OF PAYMENTS. **2.** a form of BANK DEPOSIT.

current assets, *n.* ASSETS such as STOCKS, money owed by DEBTORS, and cash, which are held for short-term conversion within a firm as raw materials are bought, made up, sold as finished goods and eventually paid for. See FIXED ASSETS, WORKING CAPITAL, WORKING–CAPITAL RATIO.

current liabilities, *n.* all obligations to pay out cash at some date in the near future, including amounts which a firm owes to trade CREDITORS and BANK LOANS/overdrafts. See WORKING CAPITAL, WORKING–CAPITAL RATIO.

current ratio or **acid–test ratio,** *n.* an accounting measure of a firm's ability to pay its short-term liabilities out of its quickly-realizable CURRENT ASSETS, which expresses the firm's liquid current assets (DEBTORS plus cash) as a ratio of CURRENT LIABILITIES. See WORKING CAPITAL RATIO.

current-weighted index or **Paasch index,** *n.* a weighted index number that uses current-year weights. For example, in calculating a

PRICE INDEX the respective quantities of various products bought in the base year would be noted and the prices of products combined to form a single price index number. At some later time the new prices of these products would be combined to form a new price index number, making allowance for changes in the relative quantities of the products bought over time as their prices change. Compare BASE-WEIGHTED INDEX.

Customs and Excise, *n.* a governmental agency for the collection of INDIRECT TAXES levied in accordance with appropriate rates, rules and regulations. In the UK, Her Majesty's Customs and Excise typically collects revenue from VALUE ADDED TAX and EXCISE DUTY payable on alcoholic drink, tobacco and betting. The agency also enforces the laws regarding the import and export of certain goods, collects IMPORT DUTIES, and seeks to prevent attempts to avoid paying import duties by smuggling. See also INLAND REVENUE.

customs duty, *n.* a TAX levied on imported products (see IMPORTS). Unlike TARIFFS, customs duties are used primarily as a means of raising revenue for the government rather than as a means of protecting domestic producers from foreign competition. See TAXATION.

customs union, *n.* a form of TRADE INTEGRATION between a number of countries, in which members eliminate all trade barriers (TARIFFS, etc.) amongst themselves on goods and services, and establish a uniform set of barriers against trade with the rest of the world, in particular a *common*

Fig. 43. **Cyclical fluctuation.** The pronounced short-term swings in output growth rates over the course of the BUSINESS CYCLE, around a rising long-term trend growth line for the country's GROSS NATIONAL PRODUCT.

external tariff. The aim of a customs union is to secure the benefits of international SPECIALIZATION, thereby improving members' real living standards. See GAINS FROM TRADE, TRADE CREATION, EUROPEAN COMMUNITY.

cyclical fluctuation, *n.* the short-term movements, both upwards and downwards in some economic variable around a long-term SECULAR TREND line. See Fig. 43. See STABILIZATION POLICY, DEMAND MANAGEMENT.

cyclically-adjusted public-sector borrowing requirement, see PUBLIC-SECTOR BORROWING REQUIREMENT.

cyclical unemployment, *n.* the UNEMPLOYMENT that occurs as a result of a fall in the level of business activity during the RECESSION and DEPRESSION phases of the BUSINESS CYCLE.

cyclical variation, see TIME-SERIES ANALYSIS.

D

dawn raid, *n.* a situation in which a potential TAKEOVER bidder for a company buys a substantial shareholding in the target company at current market prices, often through intermediaries (to disguise the identity of the bidder). This shareholding can then be used as a platform for a full takeover bid for all the shares at a stated offer price.

See TAKEOVER BID, CITY CODE.

DE, see DEPARTMENT OF EMPLOYMENT.

dear money, see TIGHT MONEY.

death rate, *n.* the number of people in a POPULATION who die per thousand per year. In 1986, for example, the UK death rate was 12 people per 1,000 of the population. The difference between this rate and the BIRTH RATE is used to calculate the rate of growth of the population of a country over time. The death rate tends to decline as a country attains higher levels of economic development. See DEMOGRAPHIC TRANSITION.

debentures, *n.* a means of financing companies through fixed-interest LOANS secured against company ASSETS.

In some cases the company may offer a specific asset such as a particular machine as security for the loan; in other cases lenders are offered security by means of a general claim against all company assets in the event of default. See LOAN CAPITAL.

debt, *n.* an amount of money owed by one person, company, etc., to another. Debts result from borrowing money to purchase a product, service or financial asset (e.g. HIRE PURCHASE). Debt contracts provide for the eventual repayment of the sum borrowed and include INTEREST charges for the duration of the LOAN. See DEBTORS, BORROWER.

debt capital, see LOAN CAPITAL.

debtors (accounts receivable), *n.* the money owed by individuals or firms because they have bought goods, services or raw materials for which they have not yet paid (trade DEBTORS), or because they have borrowed money. See CREDITORS (ACCOUNTS PAYABLE), DEBT, DEBTORS-TO-SALES RATIO, CREDIT CONTROL, WORKING CAPITAL, BAD DEBT.

debtors-to-sales ratio or **average collection period** or **debtor**

days ratio, *n.* an accounting measure of a firm's average collection period for DEBTS, which expresses the firm's period-end DEBTORS as a ratio of its average daily sales. The resulting figure shows the average period that customers took to pay their debts, expressed in days. See CREDITORS RATIO, CREDIT CONTROL, BAD DEBT, FACTORING.

debt servicing, *n.* the cost of meeting INTEREST payments and regular contractual repayments of principal on a LOAN along with any administration charges borne by the BORROWER.

deciles, *n.* the numerical values that divide a group of numerical observations into 10 parts, each containing an equal number of observations. Deciles are frequently applied to data arranged in decreasing numerical order. Consequently one-tenth of the observations will exceed the first decile, two-tenths will exceed the second decile, etc. Compare QUARTILES, PERCENTILES.

decision tree, *n.* an aid to decision-making in uncertain conditions, that sets out alternative courses of action and the economic consequences of each alternative, and assigns subjective statistical probabilities to the likelihood of future events occurring. For example, a businessman thinking of opening a shop whose success will depend upon consumer spending (and thus the state of the economy) would have a decision tree like Fig. 44 on page 114.

In order to make a decision, the businessman needs a decision criterion to enable him to choose which he regards as the best of the eligible acts, and since these choices involve an element of risk then we need to know something about his attitudes to risk. If the businessman were neutral in his attitude to risk then we could calculate the *certainty equivalent* of the 'open shop' act using the expected money value criterion which takes the financial consequence of each outcome and weights it by the probability of its occurence, thus:

$$0.5 \times + £40,000 = + £20,000$$
$$0.5 \times - £30,000 = - £15,000$$
$$\overline{+ £\ 5,000}$$

which being greater than the £0 for certain of not opening the shop, would justify going ahead with the shop project.

However if the businessman were averse to risk then he might not regard the expected money value criterion as being appropriate, for he might require a risk premium to induce him to take the risk. Application of a more cautious certainty equivalent criterion would reduce the

DECREASING RETURNS

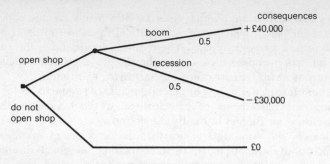

Fig. 44. **Decision tree**. The businessman has two options: open shop or do not open shop; and has to consider two states of nature or events which can occur: economic boom or recession. The businessman must assess the likelihood of each of these events occurring, and in this case, based on his knowledge and experience, he estimates that there is a one-in-two chance of a boom and a 0.5 PROBABILITY of a recession. Finally, the businessman estimates the financial consequences as a £40,000 profit for the shop if there is a boom, and a £30,000 loss if there is a recession.

certainty equivalent of the 'open shop' branch and might even tip the decision against going ahead. See RISK AND UNCERTAINTY, UTILITY INDEX, RISK PROFILE.

decreasing returns, see DIMINISHING RETURNS.

deficiency payment, see INCOME SUPPORT.

deficit financing, see BUDGET DEFICIT, PUBLIC SECTOR BORROWING REQUIREMENT.

deflation, *n.* a reduction in the level of NATIONAL INCOME and output, usually accompanied by a fall in the general price level (DISINFLATION).

A deflation is often deliberately brought about by the authorities in order to reduce INFLATION and to improve the BALANCE OF PAYMENTS by reducing import demand. Instruments of deflationary policy include fiscal measures (e.g., tax increases) and monetary measures (e.g., high interest rates). See MONETARY POLICY, FISCAL POLICY.

deflationary gap, *n.* the shortfall in total spending (AGGREGATE DEMAND) at the FULL EMPLOYMENT level of national income (POTENTIAL GNP) in KEYNSIAN ECONOMICS. Because of a deficiency in spending some of the economy's resources lie idle and ACTUAL GNP is below that of potential GNP. To counteract this deficiency in spending, the authorities can use FISCAL and MONETARY POLICY to expand aggregate demand.

Fig. 45. **Deflationary gap**. The AGGREGATE SUPPLY SCHEDULE is drawn as a 45° line because businesses will offer any particular level of national output only if they expect total spending (aggregate demand) to be just sufficient to sell all of that output. However, once the economy reaches the full employment level of GNP, then actual output cannot expand further and at this level of output the aggregate supply schedule becomes vertical.

If aggregate demand is at a low level (AD₁) then actual output will be determined by the intersection of AD₁ and the aggregate supply schedule at point A; this output is less than potential output, leaving an output gap. An output gap can be removed by the authorities by expanding aggregate demand to the full employment level of aggregate demand (AD₂) where actual output (determined by the intersection of AD₂ and the aggregate supply schedule at point B) corresponds with potential GNP.

See Fig. 45. See also DEFLATION, REFLATION, INFLATIONARY GAP.

degrees of freedom, *n*. the quantity n–1, when using a SAMPLE of size n to estimate the MEAN and STANDARD DEVIATION of a population. The sum of the deviations from the mean is always equal to zero, because positive deviations from the mean always exactly offset negative deviations from the mean (see AVERAGE DEVIATION). Consequently if we already know n–1 deviations from the mean then the nth is automatically determined. For example, if five products have prices of £5, £4, £3, £2 and £1 then the mean price is:

$$£ \frac{5+4+3+2+1}{5} = £3$$

and the deviations of these prices from the mean price are £2, £1, £0,

$-£1$, $-£2$ respectively. If we knew any four of these deviations from the mean, then the 5th deviation from the mean would be determined. In the above example, if the first four deviations were known, then by summing the first four we can determine what the offsetting final deviation must be:

$$(£2 + £1 + £0 - £1) - £2 = £0$$

Since n-1 of the deviations determine the nth, then effectively the standard deviation is based on n-1 independent quantities, denoted by the term n-1 degrees of freedom.

deindustrialization, *n.* a sustained fall in the proportion of national output accounted for by the industrial and manufacturing sectors of the economy, a process which is often accompanied by a decline in the number of people employed in industry (compare INDUSTRIALIZATION).

There is a well-established trend in advanced economies for the industrial sector to grow more slowly than the service sector, as shown in Fig. 46. For the UK the share of industry in GDP fell from 43% in 1960 to 32% in 1984, while the share of services increased from 54% to 66%. Over the same period employment in industry in the UK fell from 11.8 million in 1960 to 7.8 million in 1984.

Changes in sector shares may simply reflect changes in the pattern of final demand for goods and services over time, and as such may be considered a 'natural' development associated with a maturing economy. On the other hand, deindustrialization which stems from supply-side deficiencies (high costs, an over-valued exchange rate, lack of investment and innovation) which put a country at a competitive disadvantage in international trade (see IMPORT PENETRATION) is a more serious matter. In this case, deindustrialization often brings with it a fall in national output, rising unemployment and balance of payments difficulties.

The extent of deindustrialization in the UK was even more marked in the early 1980s because of Britain's artificially high exchange rate, bolstered by UK oil exports, which caused Britain to lose overseas markets. See STRUCTURE OF INDUSTRY, STRUCTURAL UNEMPLOYMENT.

delivered pricing, *n.* the charging of a PRICE for a product that includes the cost of transporting the product from the manufacturer to the customer. The delivered prices quoted by a manufacturer might accurately reflect the actual costs of transportation to different areas, or alternatively, discriminatory prices might be used to cross-subsidize areas in order to maximize sales across the country.

	Agriculture		Industry		Manufacturing		Services	
	1960	1984	1960	1984	1960	1984	1960	1984
UK	3	2	43	32	32	18	54	66
US	4	2	38	32	29	21	58	66
Japan	13	4	45	42	34	30	42	54
W. Germany	6	2	53	46	40	35	41	52

Fig. 46. **Deindustrialization**. The distribution of gross domestic product shows how the industrial sector in advanced economies grows more slowly than the service sector. The figures for industry include those for manufacturing. Source: *World Development Report*, World Bank, 1984.

delivery note, *n.* a document sent by a supplier to a customer at the time when products are supplied that itemizes the physical quantities of product supplied. Thereafter an INVOICE is usually sent to the customer showing the money value of products supplied. Compare STATEMENT OF ACCOUNT.

demand or **effective demand,** *n.* the WANT, need or desire for a product backed by the money to purchase it. In economic analysis, demand is always based on 'willingness and ability to pay' for a product, not merely want or need for the product. CONSUMERS' total demand for a product is reflected in the DEMAND CURVE. Compare SUPPLY.

demand curve, *n.* a line showing the relationship between the PRICE of a PRODUCT and the quantity DEMANDED per time period, as in Fig. 47 on page 118.

Most demand curves slope downwards because (a) as the price of the product falls, consumers will tend to substitute this (now relatively cheaper) product for others in their purchases; (b) as the price of the product falls, this serves to increase their real income allowing them to buy more products (see PRICE EFFECT, INCOME EFFECT, SUBSTITUTION EFFECT). However in a small minority of cases products can have an UPWARD–SLOPING DEMAND CURVE.

The slope of the demand curve reflects the degree of responsiveness of quantity demanded to changes in the products price. For example, if a large reduction in price results in only a small increase in quantity demanded (as would be the case where the demand curve has a steep slope) then demand is said to be *price inelastic* (see PRICE–ELASTICITY OF DEMAND).

The demand curve interacts with the SUPPLY CURVE to determine the EQUILIBRIUM MARKET PRICE. See DEMAND FUNCTION, DEMAND CURVE (SHIFTS IN), DIMINISHING MARGINAL UTILITY.

DEMAND CURVE, (SHIFT IN)

Fig. 47. **Demand curve**. Demand is the total quantity of a good or service which buyers are prepared to purchase at a given price. Demand is always taken to be *effective demand*, backed by the ability to pay, and not just based on want or need. The typical market demand curve slopes downwards from left to right, indicating that as price falls more is demanded. Thus, if price falls from OP_1 to OP_2, the quantity demanded will increase from OQ_1 to OQ_2.

demand curve, (shift in), *n*. a movement of the DEMAND CURVE from one position to another (either left or right) as a result of some economic change other than price. A given demand curve is always drawn on the CETERIS PARIBUS assumption that all of the other factors affecting demand (income, tastes, etc.) are held constant. If any of these change, however, then this will bring about a shift in the demand curve. For example, if income increases, the demand curve will shift to the right, so that more is now demanded at each price than formerly. See Fig. 48. See also DEMAND FUNCTION, INCOME–ELASTICITY OF DEMAND.

demand elasticity, see ELASTICITY OF DEMAND.

demand function, *n*. a form of notation which links the DEPENDENT VARIABLE, quantity demanded (Qd), with various INDEPENDENT VARIABLES which determine quantity demanded such as product price (P), income (Y), prices of substitute products (Ps), advertising (A), etc:

$$Qd = f(P, Y, Ps, A, \text{ etc})$$

Changes in any of these independent variables will affect quantity demanded, and if we wish to investigate the particular effect of any one of these variables upon quantity demanded, then we could (conceptually) hold the influence of the other independent variables constant (CETERIS PARIBUS), whilst we focus upon the particular effects of that

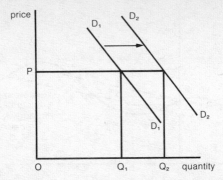

Fig. 48. **Demand curve, (shift in)**. An increase in income shifts the demand curve D,D, to D₂D₂, increasing the quantity demanded from OQ₁ to OQ₂. The magnitude of this shift depends upon the INCOME ELASTICITY OF DEMAND for the product.

independent variable. See DEMAND CURVE, DEMAND CURVE (SHIFTS IN).

demand management, *n.* the control of the level of AGGREGATE DEMAND in an economy, using FISCAL POLICY and MONETARY POLICY to moderate or eliminate fluctuations in the level of economic activity (see BUSINESS CYCLE). The general objective of demand management is to ensure that aggregate demand is neither deficient relative to POTENTIAL GROSS NATIONAL PRODUCT (thereby avoiding a loss of output and UNEMPLOYMENT) nor overfull (thereby avoiding INFLATION). See Fig. 49 on page 120.

See DEFLATIONARY GAP, INFLATIONARY GAP, EQUILIBRIUM LEVEL OF NATIONAL INCOME, MACROECONOMIC POLICY, STABILIZATION POLICY, AUTOMATIC (BUILT-IN) STABLIZERS, INTERNAL–EXTERNAL BALANCE MODEL.

demand-pull inflation, *n.* a general increase in prices caused by a level of AGGREGATE DEMAND in excess of the supply potential of the economy. At full employment levels of output (POTENTIAL GROSS NATIONAL PRODUCT) excess demand bids up the price of a fixed real output (see INFLATIONARY GAP). According to MONETARISM, excess demand results from too rapid an increase in the MONEY SUPPLY.

See INFLATION, QUANTITY THEORY OF MONEY, COST-PUSH INFLATION.

demand schedule, *n.* a table listing various prices of a product and the specific quantities demanded at each of these prices. The information provided by a demand schedule can be used to construct a DEMAND CURVE showing the price-quantity demanded relationship in graphical form.

Fig. 49. **Demand management**. The management of aggregate demand in an economy.

demand theory, see THEORY OF DEMAND.

demographic transition, *n.* a POPULATION cycle which is associated with the ECONOMIC DEVELOPMENT of a country. In underdeveloped countries (i.e., subsistence agrarian economies) BIRTH RATES and DEATH RATES are both high, so there is very little change in the overall size of the population. With economic development (i.e., INDUSTRIALIZATION), INCOME PER HEAD begins to rise and there is a fall in the death rate (through better nutrition, sanitation, medical care, etc.,), which brings about a period of rapid population growth. Provided ECONOMIC GROWTH is consistently greater than the increase in population, income per head continues to expand and eventually serves to reduce the birth rate (small families become the 'norm' in society as people seek to preserve their growing affluence). At this point population growth slows down and may eventually level-off. See Fig. 50 on page 121. See POPULATION TRAP, DEVELOPING COUNTRY.

Most advanced industrial countries have gone through a demographic transition of the kind described above and are today characterized by both low birth and death rates and slow-growing populations.

demography, *n.* the study of human POPULATIONS including their total size, population changes over time as determined by changes in BIRTH RATES, DEATH RATES and MIGRATION; the age and sex distribution of populations and their geographical and occupational distributions. Statistical data on populations is compiled from CENSUSES of population, and records of births, deaths, etc. See DEMOGRAPHIC TRANSITION.

Department of Employment (DE), *n.* the UK government

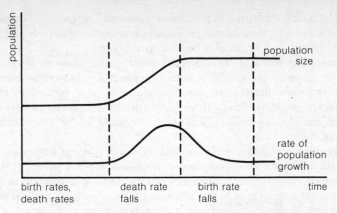

Fig. 50. **Demographic transition.** The levelling-off of the rate of population growth during a country's economic development.

department responsible for administering the government's EMPLOYMENT LAWS and policies. The DE seeks to promote the efficient use of labour resources by running local employment offices, which help workers seeking employment to find jobs, and industrial training schemes designed to improve job skills.

Department of Health and Social Security (DHSS), *n.* the UK government department responsible for administering the government's social security programmes. The DHSS pays SOCIAL SECURITY BENEFITS such as state pensions, unemployment and sickness benefit, runs the national health service, and collects NATIONAL INSURANCE CONTRIBUTIONS to help finance these payments and services.

Department of the Environment (DOE), *n.* the UK government department responsible for monitoring and controlling environmental pollution and for the regulation of local authorities.

Department of Trade and Industry (DTI), *n.* the UK government department responsible for administering the government's industrial and trade laws and policies. The DTI seeks to promote industrial efficiency and trade by encouraging new business start-ups and the expansion of existing firms on the one hand, and assisting in the rationalization of declining industries on the other hand, as part of INDUSTRIAL POLICY. The DTI is also concerned with promoting a balanced distribution of industrial activities through REGIONAL POLICY; regulating the formation of companies and their conduct through the

121

Registrar of Companies; protecting consumer interests through the OFFICE OF FAIR TRADING; and promoting international trade by offering information and financial assistance to exporters.

department store, *n.* a large retail outlet. Department stores may be under single-shop ownership, or run as a multiple CHAIN STORE business. Unlike most other retailers who tend to specialize in relatively narrow ranges of products, the essential characteristic of a department store is the great variety of products it stocks: 'everything under one roof'. See RETAILING.

dependent variable, *n.* a VARIABLE which is affected by some other variable in a model. For example, the demand for a product will be influenced by its price. It is conventional to place the dependent variable on the left-hand side of an EQUATION and to show it on the vertical axis of a GRAPH. If, therefore, demand is a function of price of a good, P (the INDEPENDENT VARIABLE), demand D is dependent upon P. Notationally this is written:

$$D = f(P)$$

See FUNCTIONAL NOTATION.

deposit account or **time account** or **savings account,** *n.* a bank account which pays interest on the balance in the account. The account holder is generally obliged to give notice to withdraw cash from such an account though this requirement may be waived at the particular institution's discretion. Unlike a CURRENT ACCOUNT, cheques cannot generally be drawn upon deposit accounts.

See BANK DEPOSITS.

depreciation, *n.* **1.** a fall in the value of a CURRENCY against other currencies under a FLOATING EXCHANGE RATE SYSTEM, as shown in Fig. 51a on page 123. A depreciation of a currency's value makes IMPORTS more expensive and EXPORTS cheaper, thereby reducing imports and increasing exports, and so assisting in the removal of a BALANCE OF PAYMENTS deficit. For example, as shown in Fig. 51b, if the pound–dollar exchange rate depreciates from £1.60 to £1.40, then this would allow British exporters to reduce their prices by a similar amount, thus increasing their price competitiveness in the American market (though they may choose not to reduce their prices by the full amount of the depreciation in order to boost profitability, or devote more funds to sales promotion, etc.) By the same token, the depreciation serves to raise the sterling price of American products imported into Britain, thereby making them less price-competitive than British products in the home market.

Exchange rate	UK domestic price of a product	Price of the UK product exported to US	US domestic price of a product	Price of the US product imported into UK
£1 = $1.60	£1	$1.60	$1	62p
£1 = $1.40	£1	$1.40	$1	71p

(b)

Fig. 51. **Depreciation 1.** (a) A depreciation of the pound against the dollar. (b) The effect of depreciation on export and import prices.

In order for a currency depreciation to 'work' three basic conditions must be satisfied:

(a) how successful the depreciation is depends on the reactions of export and import volumes to the change in relative prices, i.e., the PRICE ELASTICITY OF DEMAND for exports and imports. If these volumes are low, i.e., demand is inelastic, trade volumes will not change much and the depreciation may in fact worsen the situation. On the other hand, if export and import demand is elastic then the change in trade volume will improve the payments position. Balance-of-payments equilibrium will be restored if the sum of export and import elasticities is greater than unity (the MARSHALL-LERNER CONDITION).

(b) on the supply side, resources must be available, and sufficiently mobile, to be switched from other sectors of the economy into industries producing exports and products which will substitute for imports. If the economy is fully employed already, domestic demand will have to be reduced and/or switched by deflationary policies to accommodate the required resource transference.

(c) over the longer term, 'offsetting' domestic price, rises must be contained. A depreciation increases the cost of essential imports of raw materials and foodstuffs which can push up domestic manufacturing costs and the cost of living. This in turn can serve to increase domestic prices and money wages thereby necessitating further depreciations to maintain price competitiveness.

See BALANCE-OF-PAYMENTS EQUILIBRIUM, INTERNAL-EXTERNAL BALANCE MODEL, PRICE ELASTICITY OF SUPPLY, APPRECIATION(1).

2. the fall in the value of an ASSET during the course of its working life. Also called *amortization*. The condition of plant and equipment used in production deteriorates over time and these items will eventually have to be replaced. Accordingly, a firm is required to make financial provision for the depreciation of its assets.

Depreciation is an accounting means of dividing up the historic cost of a FIXED ASSET over a number of accounting periods which correspond with the asset's estimated life. The depreciation charged against the revenue of successive time periods in the TRADING AND PROFIT-AND-LOSS ACCOUNT serves to spread the original cost of a fixed asset which yields benefits to the firm over several trading periods. In the period-end BALANCE SHEET such an asset would be included at its cost less depreciation deducted to date. This depreciation charge does not attempt to calculate the reducing market value of fixed assets, so that balance sheets do not show realization values.

Different formulas used to calculate depreciation can lead to variations in the balance sheet 'value' of a fixed asset and in the charge against GROSS PROFIT for depreciation. The formula in Fig. 52 on page 125 gives a large depreciation charge in the early periods of the fixed asset's life and a small charge in the later years. In the interests of consistency, firms generally do not change the depreciation formula used for their fixed assets but stick to the same formula indefinitely.

All these depreciation formulas base the depreciation charge of the HISTORIC COST of fixed assets. However, during a period of INFLATION it is likely that the REPLACEMENT COST of an asset is likely to be higher than its original cost. Thus, prudent companies need to make PROVISION for higher replacement costs in the form of a REVALUATION RESERVE.

See INFLATION ACCOUNTING, CAPITAL CONSUMPTION, APPRECIATION (2).

depressed area, *n.* a region of an economy which is characterized by

Straight-line method

	Opening book value	Depreciation (£21,000 ÷ 3)	closing book value
Year 1	£24,000	£7,000	£17,000
Year 2	17,000	7,000	10,000
Year 3	10,000	7,000	3,000

(a)

Reducing-balance method

	Opening book value	Depreciation (50%)	Closing book value
Year 1	£24,000	£12,000	£12,000
Year 2	12,000	6,000	6,000
Year 3	6,000	3,000	3,000

(b)

Fig. 52. **Depreciation 2.** (a) In this example, the *straight-line method* divides the original cost of a fixed asset (£24,000) by its estimated life (three years), giving equal depreciation charges each trading period. (b) The *reducing-balance method* writes off, each period, a fixed percentage of the net book value of the fixed asset at the beginning of the period.

significantly higher rates of UNEMPLOYMENT and lower levels of INCOME PER HEAD compared to the national average. See REGIONAL POLICY.

depression, *n.* a phase of the BUSINESS CYCLE characterized by a severe decline (*slump*) in the level of economic activity (ACTUAL GROSS NATIONAL PRODUCT). Real output and INVESTMENT are at very low levels and there is a high rate of UNEMPLOYMENT. A depression is caused mainly by a fall in AGGREGATE DEMAND, and can be reversed provided that the authorities evoke expansionary FISCAL POLICY and MONETARY POLICY. See DEFLATIONARY GAP, DEMAND MANAGEMENT, STABILIZATION POLICY.

derivative, see DIFFERENTIAL CALCULUS.

derived demand, *n.* the DEMAND for a particular FACTOR INPUT or PRODUCT that is dependent on there being a demand for some other product. For example, the demand for labour to produce motor cars is dependent on there being a demand for motor cars in the first place; the demand for teacups is dependent on there being a demand for tea. See MARGINAL REVENUE PRODUCT, FACTOR MARKETS, COMPLEMENTARY PRODUCTS.

deseasonalized data, see TIME SERIES ANALYSIS.

Fig. 53. **Devaluation**. A devaluation of the pound against the dollar.

devaluation, *n*. an administered reduction in the value of a CURRENCY against other currencies under a FIXED EXCHANGE RATE SYSTEM, as shown in Fig. 53. The objective of a devaluation is to assist in the removal of a deficit in a country's BALANCE OF PAYMENTS. See DEPRECIATION (1) and Fig. 51b.

developed country, *n*. an economically advanced country whose economy is characterized by large industrial and service sectors and high levels of INCOME PER HEAD. See STRUCTURE OF INDUSTRY, DEVELOPING COUNTRY, ECONOMIC DEVELOPMENT.

developing country or **underdeveloped country** or **Third World country,** *n*. a country in which the level of GROSS DOMESTIC PRODUCT and INCOME PER HEAD is presently inadequate to generate the SAVINGS necessary to embark upon substantial agricultural and industrial INVESTMENT programmes. Such countries are typically characterized by a large PRIMARY SECTOR (usually agriculture) in which the majority of the POPULATION exists at or near subsistence levels, producing barely enough for their immediate needs, and thus being unable to release the amounts required to support a large urbanized industrial population. To facilitate an increase in urban population necessary for INDUSTRIALIZATION, a nation may either IMPORT the necessary commodities from abroad with the FOREIGN EXCHANGE earned from the EXPORT of (predominantly) primary goods, or it can attempt to improve its own agriculture. Originally the belief was held that industrialization would provide the much needed impetus to achieve the breakthrough, or take-off, into sustained ECONOMIC GROWTH. The present emphasis has shifted to increasing PRODUCTIVITY from an indigenous agricultural sector, thereby releasing both LABOUR and goods, to assist the INDUSTRIAL SECTOR. With appropriate ECONOMIC AID from industrialized countries and the ability and willingness on the part of a developing country, the transition into a NEWLY-INDUSTRIALIZED COUNTRY, could be made.

However, certain problems do exist. For instance, increases in real income which are achieved need to be maintained, which means keeping the population number in check. The illiteracy and social customs for large families tend to work against governmental efforts to increase the STANDARD OF LIVING of its citizens. Also, most of the foreign exchange earned by such countries is by exporting, mainly COMMODITIES but increasingly augmented by manufactures as their industrialization programmes progress. In both these areas, however, the developing countries have been up against adverse developments in the world economy, particularly since the oil price increases of 1973 and the advent of recessionary conditions and the spread of PROTECTIONISM.

See ECONOMIC DEVELOPMENT, STRUCTURE OF INDUSTRY, DEMOGRAPHIC TRANSITION, POPULATION TRAP, INTERNATIONAL COMMODITY AGREEMENTS, UNITED NATIONS CONFERENCE ON TRADE AND DEVELOPMENT.

development area, *n.* a severely DEPRESSED AREA which is formally recognized by a country's REGIONAL POLICY as in need of industrial regeneration. The usual practice is to encourage the establishment of new firms, the expansion of existing firms, and the establishment of new industries by offering a variety of investment incentives: investment grants and allowances, tax write-offs, rent and rate free (or reduced) factories, etc.

In the UK, firms investing in development areas are offered two main forms of financial assistance: (a) regional development grants, which are given automatically to cover part of the capital cost of new buildings and works, plant and machinery; (b) regional selective assistance which is given on a discretionary basis to cover capital and training costs for projects which meet specified job-creation criteria.

development economics, *n.* the branch of economics that seeks to explain the processes by which a DEVELOPING COUNTRY increases its productive capacity, both agricultural and industrial, in order to achieve sustained ECONOMIC GROWTH. Economic growth is frequently measured in terms of INCOME PER HEAD which raises problems associated with measuring economic welfare in terms of GROSS NATIONAL PRODUCT, and creates difficulties in making international comparisons of GNP figures.

Much work in development economics has focused upon the way in which such growth can be achieved, and how to arrive at the optimal balance of contributing factors. For instance, the question of whether agriculture ought to be developed in tandem with industry, or whether leading industries should be allowed to move forward independently, so encouraging all other sectors of society. Another controversial question is whether less-developed countries are utilizing the most appropriate technology. Many economists argue for intermediate technology as most appropriate rather than very modern plants initially requiring Western technologists and managers to run them. Socio-cultural factors are also influential in attempting to achieve take-off into sustained economic growth.

DHSS, see DEPARTMENT OF HEALTH AND SOCIAL SECURITY.

differential calculus, *n.* a set of mathematical techniques that focuses on the slope of a line, investigating how a DEPENDENT VARIABLE changes when there is an infinitesimally small change in an INDEPENDENT VARIABLE. For example, if we wish to know how consumption expenditure (C) changes when disposable income (Y) changes, we use the symbol Δ to indicate a change in a variable, and can express the relationship in the ratio: $\Delta C/\Delta Y$ which tells us how C changes as Y changes. For a LINEAR EQUATION (of the form $C = a + b.Y$) this ratio will always be constant and equal to b (the slope of the line).

However, for nonlinear equations containing squares or cubes of the variables, such as:

$$C = a + bY - cY^2$$

the slope of the line will not remain constant, so that it becomes important to state over what income range we are measuring the slope of the equation. Fig. 54 on page 129 shows a typical nonlinear relationship based on the above equation. The slope of this line varies considerably, being very steep for the low income range (OY_1) and less steep for higher income ranges (Y_1Y_2), until at income Y_2 the line reaches a maximum where its slope is zero. Indeed, the fact that the line has a zero slope tells us that it has reached a maximum (or minimum).

If we wanted to measure the sensitivity of consumption to small changes in income at a particular level of income such as OY_1, then we could reduce the income range over which we measure $\Delta C/\Delta Y$ in the vicinity of income level OY_1, until ΔY is a minute change. Then the ratio $\Delta C/\Delta Y$ would effectively measure the slope of the tangent to the curve at this income level OY_1. This measure is called the first *derivative* of consumption with respect to income, labelled dC/dY (technically

Fig. 54. **Differential calculus.** The characteristic slope of a nonlinear equation. See main entry.

dC/dY is the limiting value of $\Delta C/\Delta Y$ as ΔY tends to zero). Derivatives are used in many areas of economics where we are concerned with the slopes of functions: for example, MARGINAL REVENUE is the first derivative of TOTAL REVENUE (with respect to quantity); MARGINAL COST is the first derivative of TOTAL COST (with respect to quantity). Derivatives are used to measure ELASTICITY OF DEMAND/SUPPLY.

Where a dependent variable is influenced by two (or more) independent variables then the relationship could only be visualized as a curved surface on a multidimensional graph. However, even here techniques of differentiation can be used to measure the slope of the surface of the plane at a particular point, by calculating a *partial derivative*. For example, if consumption expenditure (C) is affected by both disposable income (Y) and consumer credit terms (I) then it is possible to calculate the partial derivative of consumption with respect to income: dC/dY, which shows how consumption changes as income varies, holding constant the influence of consumer credit terms upon consumption. Thus partial derivatives serve to hold other things equal (CETERIS PARIBUS), allowing examination of the influence of just one independent variable upon the dependent variable. See PARTIAL CORRELATION COEFFICIENT, BETA COEFFICIENTS.

differentiated product, see PRODUCT DIFFERENTIATION.

diminishing average returns, see DIMINISHING RETURNS.

diminishing marginal returns, see DIMINISHING RETURNS.

diminishing marginal utility, *n*. a principle which states that as a

Fig. 55. **Diminishing marginal utility**. To a hungry man the utility of the first slice of bread consumed will be high (O_a) but as his appetite becomes satiated, successive slices of bread yield smaller and smaller amounts of satisfaction, for example, the fifth slice of bread yields only O_b of additional utility.

person consumes a greater quantity of a good or service, the extra satisfaction obtained from each additional unit will progressively fall. See Fig. 55.

The principle of diminishing MARGINAL UTILITY, together with the concept of CONSUMER EQUILIBRIUM, can be used to explain why DEMAND CURVES are downward-sloping. For two goods, X and Y, the condition for consumer equilibrium is:

$$\frac{\text{marginal utility of X}}{\text{price of X}} = \frac{\text{marginal utility of Y}}{\text{price of Y}}$$

Assume now that this situation is 'disturbed', as a result of a fall in the price of good X. To restore equilibrium (i.e., make the two ratios equal again), the marginal utility of X has to fall (and that of Y to increase), which, according to diminishing marginal utility theory, will occur if the consumer purchases more of X (and less of Y). Hence, a fall in the price of a good induces an increase in the quantity demanded.

However, analysis can only be undertaken in this form if CARDINAL UTILITY measurement is possible, i.e., measurement of an individual's subjective UTILITY FUNCTION to quantify the distances O_a and O_b in Fig. 55. In practice, it is not possible to measure utility with this degree of precision and so cardinal utility analysis was superseded by the concept of ORDINAL UTILITY.

Demand curves are now generally constructed from INDIFFERENCE CURVES which are based upon ordinal utility, and sometimes based upon the similar concept of REVEALED PREFERENCE. See TOTAL UTILITY, UTIL.

Fig. 56. **Diminishing returns**. The rise and fall of units of output as units of variable factor input are added to the production function.

diminishing returns, *n*. the law in the SHORT RUN theory of supply of diminishing marginal returns or *variable factor proportions* that states that as equal quantities of one VARIABLE FACTOR INPUT are added into the production function (the quantities of all other factor inputs remaining fixed), a point will be reached beyond which the resulting addition to output (that is, the MARGINAL PHYSICAL PRODUCT of the variable input) will begin to decrease as shown in Fig. 56. As the marginal physical product declines, this will eventually cause AVERAGE PHYSICAL PRODUCT to decline as well (*diminishing average returns*).

The marginal physical product changes because additional units of the variable factor input do not add equally readily to units of the fixed factor input. At low level of output, marginal physical product rises with the addition of more variable inputs to the (underworked) fixed input, the extra variable inputs bringing about a more intensive use of the fixed input. Eventually, as output is increased an optimal factor combination is attained at which the variable and fixed inputs are mixed in the most appropriate proportions to maximize marginal physical product. Thereafter, further additions of variable inputs to the (now overworked) fixed input leads to a less than proportionate increase in output so that marginal physical product declines. See RETURNS TO THE VARIABLE FACTOR INPUT.

direct cost, see PRIME COST.

direct investment, *n.* any expenditure on physical ASSETS such as plant, machinery and stocks. See INVESTMENT.

directive (bank), *n.* an instrument of MONETARY POLICY involving the control of bank lending as a means of regulating the MONEY SUPPLY. If, for example, the monetary authorities wish to lower the money supply, they can 'direct' the banks to reduce the total amount of loan finance made available to personal and corporate borrowers. A reduction in bank lending can be expected to lead to a multiple contraction of bank deposits, and, hence, a fall in the money supply. See BANK DEPOSIT CREATION.

direct labour, *n.* **1.** that part of the labour force in a firm which is directly concerned with the manufacture of a good or the provision of a service. Direct labour cost depends on the hours of labour worked by factory operatives engaged directly in making a product. Provided that wage rates remain constant then direct labour cost will tend to vary exactly with output.
2. workers employed directly by local or central government to perform tasks rather than contracting out such tasks to private-sector companies. For example, a local authority might employ its own permanent construction workers to repair council houses rather than putting such repair work out to local firms.
See INDIRECT LABOUR, VARIABLE COST, STANDARD COST, PRIVATIZATION.

direct labour cost variance, *n.* the difference between the standard DIRECT LABOUR cost of a product (standard labour time × standard wage rate) and its actual direct labour cost (actual labour time × actual wage rate). This difference can be broken down into two parts: (a) *labour efficiency variance*, which involves calculating the difference between the standard labour time specified and the actual labour time, converted into money terms by multiplying by the standard wage rate; (b) *labour rate variance*, which involves calculating the difference between the predetermined standard wage rate and the actual wage rate, multiplied by the actual labour time. With this distinction it is possible to trace whether an adverse direct labour cost variance is due to lower labour efficiency or higher wage rates. See STANDARD COST.

direct materials, *n.* raw materials which are incorporated in a product. Provided that materials prices remain constant, then direct materials cost will tend to vary exactly with output. See INDIRECT MATERIALS, VARIABLE COST.

direct materials cost variance, *n.* the difference between the standard DIRECT MATERIALS cost of a product (standard materials usage × standard materials price) and its actual direct materials cost (actual materials usage × actual materials price). This difference can be broken down into two parts: (a) *materials quantity variance*, which involves calculating the difference between the standard quantity of materials specified and the actual quantity used, converted into money terms by multiplying by the standard materials price; (b) *materials price variance*, which involves calculating the difference between the standard price of materials specified and the actual price paid, multiplied by the actual quantity of materials used. With this distinction it is possible to trace whether an adverse direct materials cost variance is due to excess usage of materials or higher materials prices. See STANDARD COST.

direct tax, *n.* a TAX levied by the government on the income and wealth received by households and businesses in order to raise revenue and as an instrument of FISCAL POLICY. Examples of a direct tax are INCOME TAX, CORPORATION TAX and WEALTH TAX. Direct taxes are progressive in so far as the amount paid varies according to the income and wealth of the taxpayer. By contrast, INDIRECT TAX is regressive in so far as the same amount is paid by each tax paying consumer regardless of their income. See TAXATION, PROGRESSIVE TAXATION, REGRESSIVE TAXATION.

dirty float, *n.* the manipulation by the monetary authorities of a country's EXCHANGE RATE under a FLOATING EXCHANGE RATE SYSTEM primarily in order to gain a competitive advantage over trade partners. Thus, the authorities could intervene in the FOREIGN EXCHANGE MARKET to stop the exchange rate from otherwise appreciating (see APPRECIATION 1) in the face of market forces, or, alternatively they could deliberately engineer a DEPRECIATION of the exchange rate. See BEGGAR-MY-NEIGHBOUR POLICY.

discount, *n.* **1.** a deduction from the published LIST PRICE of a good or service allowed by a supplier to a customer. The discount could be offered for prompt payment in cash (*cash discount*) or for bulk purchases (*trade discount*).

2. the sale of new STOCKS and SHARES at a reduced price. In the UK this involves the issue of a new share at a price below its nominal value. In other countries where shares have no nominal value it involves the sale of new shares below their current market price.

3. the purchase of a particular company's issued stock or share at a price below the average market price of those of other companies operating in the same field. The price is lower because investors feel less optimistic about that company's prospects.

4. a fall in the prices of all stocks and shares in anticipation of a downturn in the economy.

5. the purchase of a BILL OF EXCHANGE or BOND for less than its nominal value. Bills and bonds are redeemable at a specific future date for a specific sum of money. The original purchaser will buy the bill or bond for less than its nominal value (at a discount). The discount between the price which he pays and the nominal value of the bill or bond represents interest received on the loan made against the security of the bill or bond. If the owner of the bill or bond then wishes to sell it prior to maturity (rediscount it) then he will have to accept less than its nominal value (though more than he paid for it). The difference between the original price which he paid and the price received will depend largely upon the length of time before maturity. For example, if a bond with a nominal value of £1,000 redeemable in one year's time were bought for £900, then the £100 discount on redemption value represents an interest rate of £100/900 = 11.1% on the loan.

6. the extent to which a foreign currency's market EXCHANGE RATE falls below its 'official' exchange rate under a FIXED EXCHANGE RATE SYSTEM.

discounted cash flow, *n.* a cash flow associated with economic projects that are adjusted to allow for the timing of the cash flow and the potential interest on the funds involved. Such an allowance for timing is important for most INVESTMENT projects have their main costs or cash outflows in the first year or so, while their revenues or cash inflows are spread over many future years.

For example, with interest rates at 10% a company could invest £100 now and have it accumulate at compound interest of £110 at the end of one year and £121 at the end of two years. So £100 in the hands of the company now is worth the same as £110 in a year's time or £121 in two years' time. Looking at this cash flow the other way round, the company would regard £110 receivable in one year's time or £121 receivable in two year's time as having a present value of £100. Following this principle, it is possible to calculate the present value of the estimated stream of future cash outflows associated with an investment project, *and* the *present value* of the estimated stream of future cash inflows from the project and compare the two. If the present value of the cash inflows from the project exceeds the present value of outflows when both are discounted at, say 10% then the *net present value* is positive. This suggests that it would be worthwhile for a company to use its own money or borrow money at 10% and undertake the project, for it will earn a return in excess of its financing costs.

Alternatively, it is possible to calculate the percentage internal rate of return which will equate the present value of the stream of cash outflows associated with an investment project with the present value of the stream of cash inflows from the project, so as to give a zero net present value. This calculated internal rate of return can then be compared with a predetermined DISCOUNT RATE which is usually based on market rates of interest. If the calculated internal rate of return (say, 15%) exceeds the discount rate (say, 12%) then the project is worthwhile, otherwise not.

discount house, *n.* a financial institution, unique to the UK financial market, that operates in the DISCOUNT MARKET. Discount houses are engaged in the buying and selling of short-dated BILLS OF EXCHANGE and TREASURY BILLS. They make their profit from borrowing short from COMMERCIAL BANKS (CALL MONEY) and lending for longer periods (usually three months). The differential in interest rates between short and long, which is usually a fraction of a percent, earns their profit.

When discount houses find themselves temporarily unable to match their borrowings and loans, it is possible for them to go to the Bank of England as the LENDER OF LAST RESORT, for additional funds.

See BACK DOOR, TAP ISSUE, TENDER ISSUE.

discount market, *n.* a market that deals in the buying and selling of short-dated BILLS OF EXCHANGE, TREASURY BILLS, BONDS and other financial securities. Bill brokers use money borrowed in the main from the COMMERCIAL BANKS (CALL MONEY) to 'discount' (i.e., purchase bills) which are then either held until maturity, or, more commonly sold later to the commercial banks. See DISCOUNT HOUSE, LENDER OF LAST RESORT, TAP ISSUE, TENDER ISSUE.

discount rate, *n.* the RATE OF INTEREST at which the streams of cash inflows and outflows associated with an INVESTMENT project are to be discounted. For private-sector projects the discount rate is frequently based upon the weighted-average COST OF CAPITAL to the firm, with the interest cost of each form of finance (long term loans, overdrafts, equity, etc.) being weighted by the proportion which each form of finance contributes to total company finances.

The discount rate for public-sector investment projects involves more complex considerations. It can be argued that while individuals have a limited lifespan and so will not look too many years ahead in looking for returns on investment, society continues indefinitely as some individuals die and are replaced by others being born, so that society will tend to look further ahead in looking for returns. This disparity between *private time preference* and *social time preference* means that society will tend to discount the future less heavily than the individual and would favour a lower discount rate. On the other hand, opportunity cost considerations may make it difficult for society to apply a lower, less stringent, discount rate to public sector projects than is applied in the private sector, otherwise inferior projects in the public sector could divert funds away from superior projects in the private sector. The social opportunity cost discount rate may well therefore need to be similar to the private sector rate. Finally, the government borrowing rate is a risk-free interest rate since it entails little risk of default in repaying the loan, while private sector rates entail a risk premium, so that the government borrowing rate may be too low in opportunity-cost terms.

In most public investment appraisals the discount rate applied has tended to follow current prevailing private-sector interest rates. See DISCOUNTED CASH FLOW, COST–BENEFIT ANALYSIS, TIME PREFERENCE THEORY.

discount store, *n.* a self-service retail outlet which tends to specialize in a narrow range of products and which uses aggressive cut-pricing techniques to maximize store sales. Discount stores are usually run as part of a multiple CHAIN STORE business which is able to derive considerable benefits from concentrated bulk-buying from manufacturers. See RETAILING.

discrete variable, *n.* a VARIABLE which can take only a limited number of values, increasing or decreasing in large increments. Compare CONTINUOUS VARIABLE.

discretionary monopoly policy, *n.* an approach to the control of MONOPOLY which involves the individual examination of, for example, MERGERS, RESTRICTIVE TRADE AGREEMENTS and practices, etc., in terms of their advantages and disadvantages in order to determine whether or not their economic effects are, on balance, beneficial or harmful. See MONOPOLY POLICY, WILLIAMSON TRADE–OFF MODEL, PUBLIC INTEREST.

discriminating monopolist, *n.* a monopolist (see MONOPOLY) who is sometimes able to increase his or her profit by dividing his or her market and charging discriminating prices. Apart from the requirement that the two markets are in some way distinct such that buyers in one market cannot resell to those being asked a higher price in another market, price discrimination is only worthwhile when the PRICE ELASTICITY OF DEMAND

Fig. 57. **Discriminating monopolist**. A price-discriminating model, involving two markets. The demand curve facing the monopolist in market A (D_a) is less elastic than that in market B (D_b). The horizontal addition of D_a and D_b gives D_t, and the horizontal addition of MARGINAL REVENUE curves MR_a and MR_b gives MR_t. MC is the monopolist's MARGINAL COST curve. The profit maximizing output (see PROFIT MAXIMIZATION) for the monopolist is determined by the intersection of the MC curve for his total output and the aggregated MR_t curve. The broken horizontal line connects the two diagrams at the level where the MR of the monopolist in market A is equal to the MR in market B, and this aggregate MR_t is equal to the MC of the total output. It follows that the profit maximizing output in market A is OA and in market B, OB. At these respective outputs, the discriminating monopolist will charge OP_a in market A and the lower price OP_b in market B.

in each market is different. See Fig. 57.

discriminatory tariff, *n.* a TARIFF that is applied on an imported product at different rates depending upon the country of origin of those IMPORTS. Discriminating tariffs distort the pattern of international trade and are generally prohibited by the GENERAL AGREEMENT ON TARIFFS AND TRADE (GATT) unless practised within a CUSTOMS UNION.

diseconomies of scale, *n.* the possible increase in long-run unit or AVERAGE COST which may occur as the scale of the firms' output is increased beyond some critical point.

Initially, as output is increased long-run average costs may at first decline, reflecting the presence of ECONOMIES OF SCALE, but after a certain point long-run average costs may start the rise. See Fig. 58 on page 138.

The most frequently cited sources of such diseconomies are the managerial and administration problems of controlling and coordinating large-scale operations and labour relations problems in large plants. See MINIMUM EFFICIENT SCALE.

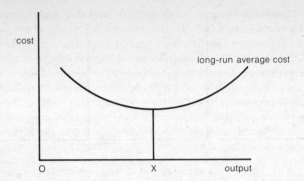

Fig. 58. **Diseconomies of scale.** In the range of output beyond point X, the firm is experiencing diseconomies of scale with costs increasing as output increases.

disequilibrium, *n.* a situation where a state of EQUILIBRIUM has not been attained, or having been attained, ceases to be maintained. If there is a natural tendency towards equilibrium the system is said to be *stable*. If the reverse is true, the system is said to be *unstable*. See COBWEB THEOREM, DYNAMIC ANALYSIS.

disguised (concealed) unemployment, *n.* a form of UNEMPLOYMENT in which people able and willing to work do not register as unemployed and seeking work, which results in their absence from the official unemployment figures. Unless there are clear incentives for people to register as unemployed (by, for example, linking registration with entitlement to unemployment payments) then the official unemployment figure may considerably understate the actual level of unemployment.

disinflation, *n.* a fall in the general price level, frequently accompanied by a reduction in the level of national income (DEFLATION). A disinflation is often deliberately brought about by the authorities in order to combat INFLATION and to eliminate a BALANCE OF PAYMENTS deficit. Instruments of disinflationary policy include fiscal measures (e.g., tax increases), monetary measures (e.g., higher interest rates), and prices and income controls. See FISCAL POLICY, MONETARY POLICY, PRICES AND INCOME POLICY, INFLATIONARY GAP, INTERNAL–EXTERNAL BALANCE MODEL.

disintermediation, *n.* a situation where a FINANCIAL INTERMEDIARY such as a BUILDING SOCIETY is forced to reduce its lending operations because of the withdrawal of deposits from it, and because it is unable to attract new funds. Disintermediation usually occurs (and then only temporarily) when an intermediary (see INTERMEDIATION) fails to adjust its borrowing rates on deposits promptly when interest rates rise, so that its rates are insufficiently competitive vis-a-vis other deposit-taking institutions.

disinvestment, *n*. **1.** a decrease in a country's CAPITAL STOCK that occurs when there is insufficient new INVESTMENT to cover CAPITAL CONSUMPTION/DEPRECIATION (capital lost due to wear and tear). **2.** also called *divestment*, the sale or closure by a firm of part of its business. For example, a diversified firm may decide to pull out altogether from a particular activity by selling the subsidiary involved to another firm or the subsidiary's management (see MANAGEMENT BUY-OUT).

dispersion, *n*. see VARIANCE (2).

disposable income, *n*. the amount of income available to HOUSEHOLDS after payment of personal INCOME TAXES and NATIONAL INSURANCE CONTRIBUTIONS. Disposable income is an important determinant of the level of CONSUMPTION expenditure and SAVINGS in the economy. See CONSUMPTION SCHEDULE, SAVINGS SCHEDULE.

dissavings, *n*. the excess of current CONSUMPTION expenditure over current DISPOSABLE INCOME, the difference being met by HOUSEHOLDS drawing on their past SAVINGS. See SAVINGS SCHEDULE.

distribution, *n*. see FREQUENCY DISTRIBUTION.

distribution census, see CENSUS.

distribution costs, *n*. the COSTS involved in the physical distribution of products. They include packaging and transport costs, and warehousing costs. See OVERHEADS.

distribution of income, see INCOME DISTRIBUTION.

distributive efficiency, *n*. an aspect of MARKET PERFORMANCE that denotes the EFFICIENCY of a market in distributing its outputs from suppliers to consumers. The costs of distribution include transportation, storage and handling expenses, together with the distributor's profit margins. In addition, suppliers incur SELLING COSTS (ADVERTISING and other PRODUCT DIFFERENTIATION expenditures) in creating and sustaining a demand for their products. Optimal distributive efficiency is achieved when physical distribution costs are minimized and selling costs are maintained at the minimum level to sustain total market demand.

disutility, *n*. the dissatisfaction or pain that an individual encounters in consuming a product or in working. Compare UTILITY.

diversification or **conglomerate integration,** *n*. the process whereby a firm expands by supplying a range of different products and as such operates in a number of markets rather than a single market. There may be links between the products based on complementary research, production or marketing functions (e.g., two products which utilize a common technological base – steel razor blades and garden spades – and which are sold through the same outlets – supermarkets), or the products may be entirely unrelated (for example, cigarettes and banking services).

From the firm's point of view the main attractions of diversification are:

(a) the ability to spread risks, thereby avoiding the failure of a division of the firm because of 'gambler's ruin' – the possibility that while the average return of the division may be satisfactory, fluctuations in the average return may give rise to a series of losses causing bankruptcy of the division. A one-product firm is extremely vulnerable to cyclical fluctuations in sales over a business cycle.

(b) (from a longer-term strategic perspective), the ability to reorientate its activities away from mature and declining markets into new areas of higher growth and profit potential. A one-product firm is especially vulnerable to both product and market obsolescence in a world of increasing technical complexity and change as new products are invented and new consumer demands created (see PRODUCT-MARKET MATRIX; BOSTON MATRIX).

Diversification is especially associated with the expansion of large, oligopolistic firms (see OLIGOPOLY) controlled in the main by professional managers rather than the firms' shareholders (see DIVORCE OF OWNERSHIP FROM CONTROL) who pursue growth and long-run profit maximization objectives rather than the goal of static (short-run) profit maximization as portrayed in the traditional THEORY OF THE FIRM (see MANAGERIAL THEORIES OF THE FIRM).

The growing importance of large diversified firms raises some fundamental issues with regard to resource allocation processes. Specifically, RESOURCE ALLOCATION decisions are determined less by competition in markets and have come to depend more on the planning of activities within firms. Competition for investment funds in the market is replaced by competition for funds between various branches within the company, with retained profits providing the finance and senior head office staff acting as an internal capital market, channelling funds from low profit to high profit areas. Managers rather than markets become the main arbiters in the resource allocation process. Yet this can be compatible with a diversified firm having only a small market share in each of its many markets, and so no measurable market power of the conventional kind.

In terms of its wider impact on resource allocation, diversification may, on the one hand, promote greater efficiency and stimulate competition, thereby improving resource allocation, or, on the other hand, by limiting competition, it may lead to a less efficient use of resources.

Diversification may produce *synergy* (i.e., the $2+2=$ more than 4 effect). Synergy results from complementary activities or from the carry-over of management capabilities. For example, in the case of a diversified merger, one firm may have a strong production organization, while the other excels in marketing – joining the two renders both firms more effective. Similarly, a high degree of carry-over of management expertise may make it possible to reduce production costs and improve product quality of the combined group.

Diversification can serve to increase the degree of competition by facilitating entry into industries where entry barriers are too high for smaller, more specialized firms without the financial resources of the conglomerate, i.e., the alternative profit sources to withstand initial losses in new markets whilst getting established.

Diversification can, however, produce various anticompetitive effects. For example, diversified firms are in a position to cross-subsidize temporary losses in a particular market with profits earned elsewhere. This allows the diversified firm to practise predatory pricing in the market to drive out competitors or discipline them, so raising prices to monopoly levels in the long run. The same financial power and cross-subsidizing capabilities of the diversified firm can be used to bear the short-run costs of deterring new entrants into one of its markets, thereby raising entry barriers.

Where diversified firms face each other in a number of markets then they may adopt a less competitive stance, each firm avoiding taking competitive action in markets where it is strong, for fear of risking retaliatory action by diversified rivals in other markets where it is weak. Here firms may develop 'spheres of influence', adopting live-and-let-live policies by dominating in certain of their markets and recognizing the domination of rivals in other markets. The result of such behaviour is a lack of vigorous competition with higher prices to the detriment of consumers.

The interdependence of diversified firms as buyers and sellers may also distort competition. Where firm A is both an important supplier to firm B for one product, and an important customer of firm B for another product, they may engage in reciprocal dealing, buying from firms that are good customers rather than alternative suppliers. The practice allows diversified firms to increase their market shares and increase obstacles to new entry.

Thus, diversification may produce, simultaneously, both beneficial or detrimental results. Under UK MONOPOLY POLICY a proposed MERGER (TAKEOVER) between two firms supplying unrelated products, involving assets in excess of £30 million can be referred to the MONOPOLIES AND MERGERS COMMISSION to determine whether or not it operates against the public interest. See OFFICE OF FAIR TRADING, VERTICAL INTEGRATION, HORIZONTAL INTEGRATION.

divestment, see DISINVESTMENT.

dividend, *n.* a payment made by a JOINT-STOCK COMPANY to its SHAREHOLDERS for providing SHARE CAPITAL. Dividends are a distribution of the PROFITS of the company.

dividend cover ratio or **times covered ratio,** *n.* an accounting measure of the extent to which a firm's earnings cover DIVIDEND payments on SHARES, that expresses PROFIT after tax and interest charges as a ratio of total dividend payments.

dividend yield, *n.* the DIVIDEND paid by a JOINT-STOCK COMPANY for a given ACCOUNTING PERIOD (usually one year) as a proportion of the current market price of its share. For example, if Company X declared a dividend of £1 per ORDINARY SHARE for the twelve month accounting period ended 31st December, and the current market price of one ordinary share in Company X was £8, the dividend yield would be:

$$\frac{\text{Dividend per share}}{\text{Price per share}} = \frac{£1}{£8} = 12\tfrac{1}{2}\%$$

division of labour, see SPECIALIZATION.

divorce of ownership from control, *n.* a situation where although a firm is owned by its SHAREHOLDERS it is actually controlled by the firm's management (the board of directors, appointed by the shareholders at the annual general meeting to run the business on their behalf). Because the average size of individual shareholding tends to be small and shareholders are remote from day-to-day decision making, it is the firm's management which effectively determines the policies of the firm. Recognition of the control power exercised by management has led economists to develop theories of the firm which substitute managerial objective for the traditional hypothesis of PROFIT MAXIMIZATION. See MANAGERIAL THEORIES OF THE FIRM.

DOE, *n.* DEPARTMENT OF THE ENVIRONMENT.

do-it-yourself store, *n*. a retail outlet that specializes in the sale of equipment and materials primarily for home improvement purposes. See RETAILING.

dollar, *n*. the domestic CURRENCY of the USA. The dollar also performs various international roles, in particular, as an INTERNATIONAL RESERVE asset, and as the numeraire of the international oil trade. See also EUROCURRENCY MARKET.

Domar economic growth model, *n*. a theoretical construct which examines the dual role of INVESTMENT in both expanding AGGREGATE DEMAND and the economy's AGGREGATE SUPPLY capacity (POTENTIAL GROSS NATIONAL PRODUCT) over time.

As one of the components of aggregate demand, investment expenditure has the effect of adding to total demand. According to the Keynesian theory of income determination, income will increase until the saving generated by the additional income offsets the higher level of investment (see EQUILIBRIUM LEVEL OF NATIONAL INCOME). Thus, if we designate the increase in investment as ΔI, income (Y) will increase by the amount:

$$\Delta Y = \frac{\Delta I}{\propto}$$

where $\propto$ is the MARGINAL PROPENSITY TO SAVE.

This short-term theory of income determination ignores the other effect of investment spending, i.e., that it adds to productive capacity. This capacity-creating effect is negligible in the short term, but ECONOMIC GROWTH has to do with the long term, and in the long term the role of investment in adding to productive capacity needs to be considered along with its demand-creating effect.

The question posed by Domar was: 'if investment increases productive capacity and also creates income, at what rate should investment grow in order to make the increase in income equal to that of productive capacity?' To answer this question, Domar set up an equation, one side of which represented the rate of increase of productive capacity, the other the rate of increase of income, and the solution of which gave the required rate of growth.

Let each pound of investment, *I*, add to productive capacity by the amount £θ per year. For example, if it requires £3,000 of capital to produce £1,000 of output per year, θ will be one-third or 33% per year. The symbol θ represents the CAPITAL-OUTPUT RATIO, which is the relationship between increments of investment and the resulting increments of output. The productive capacity of the economy has therefore increased by $I\theta$, which is the capacity-creating effect of investment and the supply side of our equation.

To utilize this additional capacity, demand must increase by an equal amount. Turning to the demand side of the equation, MULTIPLIER theory tells us that with any given marginal propensity to save, $\propto$, an increase in national income is a function not of I but of the increment in investment, $\varDelta I$, that is, the absolute annual increase in investment. The corresponding absolute annual increase in income is then:

$$\varDelta Y = \varDelta I . \frac{I}{\propto}$$

where $1/\propto$ is the multiplier. To fulfil the condition that income and capacity should increase at the same rate requires that

$$\varDelta I . \frac{1}{\propto} = I\theta$$

which is the fundamental equation set up by Domar. To solve the equation we multiply both sides by $\propto$ and divide by I to get

$$\frac{\varDelta I}{I} = \propto \theta$$

The left-hand side expression is the annual percentage rate of growth of investment which, to maintain an assumed full employment with growing productive capacity, must grow at the annual percentage rate $\propto \theta$. Income must also grow at the same annual percentage rate.

See SOLOW ECONOMIC GROWTH MODEL, HARROD ECONOMIC GROWTH MODEL.

domestic credit expansion (DCE), *n*. a monetary aggregate that is sometimes used by the INTERNATIONAL MONETARY FUND in requiring monetary restraint on the part of a member country with a balance of payments deficit as a condition of access to the Fund's resources. The main elements of DCE are made up primarily of the annual rate of change of the domestic MONEY SUPPLY (defined in a number of possible ways) and annual rate of change of external borrowing by the private and public sectors. Under a FIXED EXCHANGE-RATE SYSTEM excessive monetary expansion either by an increase in the money supply or overseas financing can lead to domestic price levels rising at a faster rate than trade partners, resulting in a balance-of-payments deficit. It follows, therefore, that monetary restraint (or, in the last resort, a currency DEVALUATION) is necessary to restore balance-of-payments equilibrium. Under a FLOATING-EXCHANGE-RATE SYSTEM, tight control of monetary expansion is less urgent, it is argued, because divergences in domestic price levels between countries will be offset by exchange rate movements.

See PURCHASING POWER PARITY THEORY.

dominant firm, *n*. a firm that accounts for a significant proportion of the supply of a particular good or service. Such a firm exercises a considerable degree of power in determining the supply terms of the product (see PRICE LEADERSHIP) and may be tempted to further its own interests at the expense of consumers. A *monopoly firm* is one that controls the entire supply of a particular product (a *monopoly of scale*).

Under UK MONOPOLY POLICY a dominant firm is defined as a firm which supplies one-quarter or more of a specified good or service. See OFFICE OF FAIR TRADING, MONOPOLIES AND MERGERS COMMISSION.

dominant firm-price leader, see PRICE LEADERSHIP.

double-entry accounts, *n*. the accounting records of a firm's day to day financial transactions with outside parties which record both aspects of each transaction, namely, what is 'given' and what is received in return. By making a double entry in the accounts the firm can record both aspects of the exchange, e.g., the exchange of cash for raw materials purchased, or the exchange for cash of goods or services sold. See LEDGER.

double taxation, *n*. the TAXATION of INCOMES and PROFITS in both the country where they arise, and again where these incomes and profits are remitted to the income earner's home country. Such double taxation can be a significant deterrent to international labour and capital movements. For this reason many countries have negotiated double taxation agreements which limit taxation liability to the country in which the income is earned.

Compare UNITARY TAXATION.

Dow-Jones Index, see SHARE-PRICE INDEX.

drawing right, see INTERNATIONAL MONETARY FUND.

DTI, *n*. see DEPARTMENT OF TRADE AND INDUSTRY.

dual economy, *n*. an economy in which capital-intensive and techno-logically-advanced sectors exist in mutual cohabitation with labour-intensive and technologically-primitive sectors. An area of study within DEVELOPMENT ECONOMICS, the problem is whether to achieve ECONOMIC GROWTH through leading technological sectors or to attempt to spread an economy's resources more thinly across all sectors to achieve balanced growth. The concept is mainly applied within the context of a DEVELOPING COUNTRY.

See INDUSTRIALIZATION.

dummy variable, *n.* an additional INDEPENDENT VARIABLE introduced into an estimated regression equation in a simple binary (0/1) form to test whether the presence of the variable (1) helps improve the fit of the estimated equation to the available data, compared with when the variable is absent (0).

See REGRESSION ANALYSIS.

dumping, *n.* the EXPORT of a good at a price below the full cost of producing it. Dumping may occur as a short-term response to a domestic recession (i.e., surplus output is sold abroad at a cut-price simply to off-load it), or as a longer-term strategic means of penetrating export markets (once a foothold has been gained prices would then be increased to generate profits). Either way, dumping is viewed as 'unfair' trade, and is outlawed by international trade pacts such as the GENERAL AGREEMENT ON TARIFFS AND TRADE. See BEGGAR-MY-NEIGHBOUR POLICY, COUNTERVAILING DUTY.

duopoly, *n.* a subset of OLIGOPOLY describing a MARKET situation in which there are only two suppliers. There are a number of models of duopoly markets which fall into two main categories:

(a) nonreactive models that do not allow for any anticipation by one firm of his competitor's reaction to either a price or quantity change. For example, in the *Bertrand duopoly* model, each supplier assumes that his rival will not change price in response to his own initial price cut, and this assumption will encourage him to cut his price in order to increase his sales. Since both firms reason in this way the price will eventually be driven down to the competitive level (i.e., a NORMAL PROFIT equilibrium). In the *Cournot duopoly* model it is quantity not price which is adjusted, with one firm altering its output on the assumption that his rival's output will remain unchanged. Since both firms reason in this way output will eventually be expanded to the point where the firms share the market equally and both secure only normal profits.

(b) reactive models that explicitly assume that the two firms recognize that their actions are interdependent and hence will attempt to avoid mutually ruinous forms of rivalry. Also called *collusive duopoly*. Specifically, firms will attempt to maximize their joint profits by establishing agreed prices above the competitive equilibrium price. This can be achieved by informal means such as the acceptance by both duopolists that one of them acts as price leader (see PRICE LEADERSHIP model) or by means of formal COLLUSION between the two duopolists (see CARTEL).

duopsony, *n.* a MARKET situation in which there are only two buyers, but many sellers.

Compare DUOPOLY.

durable goods, see CAPITAL GOODS.

Durbin–Watson test, *n.* a statistical test that checks for the presence of a pattern in the residuals or error terms, after an estimated regression equation has been calculated from observations of INDEPENDENT VARIABLES and DEPENDENT VARIABLES. See AUTOCORRELATION, REGRESSION ANALYSIS.

dynamic analysis, *n.* a method of economic analysis which traces out the path of adjustment from one state of EQUILIBRIUM to another. Consider, for example, the effects of a change of the export demand on the EQUILIBRIUM LEVEL OF NATIONAL INCOME.

See Fig. 59. See COMPARATIVE STATIC EQUILIBRIUM ANALYSIS, DISEQUILIBRIUM.

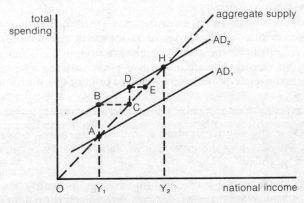

Fig. 59. **Dynamic analysis.** An increase in export demand raises AGGREGATE DEMAND from AD_1 to AD_2 and results in an increase in the equilibrium level of national income from Y_1 to Y_2. In moving from Y_1 to Y_2, a number of steps are involved. The initial increase in exports raises aggregate demand from A to B and produces an increase in real output from B to C. This extra output creates, via the MULTIPLIER EFFECT, additional income and expands aggregate demand further from C to D. The extra spending in turn produces an increase in real output from D to E. These movements continue until a new equilibrium position is reached at point H.

E

earned income, *n*. the return accruing to LABOUR for work done. The distinction between earned and unearned INCOME is made by the INLAND REVENUE for ease of assessment and collection of INCOME TAX. Earned income comprises WAGES, SALARIES, FEES, COMMISSION and PROFITS attributable to sole proprietors and partners within partnerships. *Unearned income*, by contrast, is primarily the return accruing to NATURAL RESOURCES and CAPITAL in the form of rental income, DIVIDENDS or INTEREST received. Earned income is generally taxed progressively, commencing with a tax-free income band and progressively increasing the rate of TAXATION in predetermined bands of income as income increases.

The distinction between earned and unearned income is not a valid one in economics as all FACTORS OF PRODUCTION can be said to 'earn' income. Even from the taxation authorities' view the distinction has been controversial, the argument being put forward that unearned income is the result of investing from the SAVINGS of income previously earned.

See INCIDENCE OF TAXATION, PROGRESSIVE TAXATION.

earnings, *n*. the returns accruing to FACTORS OF PRODUCTION, such as WAGES, SALARIES, FEES and COMMISSIONS, PROFITS, RENTS, DIVIDENDS and INTEREST payments.

earnings drift, *n*. the propensity for earnings, primarily WAGES and SALARIES, to increase at a rate faster than agreed rates per unit of LABOUR. Many factors contribute towards an earnings drift such as OVERTIME, bonuses, special agreements, restructuring of PIECEWORK agreements and so forth. Areas where a particular skill is in demand will pay higher rates than areas where shortages do not exist. The ability to negotiate such terms and conditions, sometimes informally, between employer and employee, leads to a significant weakening in the case for an incomes policy as a tool of economic management due to the ease by which it can be circumvented. Earnings drift tends to be associated with conditions of

148

full employment where employers are more readily prepared to concede wage increases to retain their labour force.

See INFLATION, PRICES AND INCOMES POLICY.

earnings per share, *n.* NET PROFIT after tax accruing to the ordinary shareholders in a JOINT-STOCK COMPANY, divided by the number of ORDINARY SHARES.

EC, see EUROPEAN COMMUNITY.

econometrics, *n.* the discipline within economics that attempts to measure and estimate statistically the relationship between two or more economic VARIABLES. For example, economic theory suggests that consumption expenditure is a function of disposable income $(C = f(Y))$ or, more precisely, that consumption expenditure is linked to disposable income through the equation: $C = a + b.Y$. For each level of disposable income, consumption can be measured and a statistical relationship established between the two variables by making numerical estimates of the PARAMETERS, a and b in the equation. Because consumption is dependent upon income it is termed the DEPENDENT VARIABLE, whilst disposable income is termed the INDEPENDENT VARIABLE. Econometric models can have many hundreds of measured variables, linked by several hundred estimated equations, not just one, as is the case when models are constructed for macroeconomic FORECASTING purposes.

See REGRESSION ANALYSIS.

economic aid, *n.* the provision of financial and physical forms of assistance to (mainly) the DEVELOPING COUNTRIES as a means of strengthening their economies. Economic aid is provided both on a bilateral basis by individual governments and private institutions (commercial banks, for example), and on a multilateral basis through the WORLD BANK and other international organizations, for example, the European Community's Overseas Development Fund. Such assistance 'tops-up' the foreign exchange earnings and domestic savings of recipient countries, as well as providing techniques and managerial resources and expertise which would otherwise be unobtainable locally.

See ECONOMIC DEVELOPMENT.

economic cost, see OPPORTUNITY COST.

economic development, *n.* a process of economic transition involving the structural transformation of an economy through INDUSTRIALIZATION and a raising of gross domestic product and INCOME PER HEAD. Generally speaking DEVELOPING COUNTRIES are characterized by subsistence primary production (mainly agriculture) and low levels of income per head; DEVELOPED COUNTRIES are characterized by large manufacturing and service sectors and high levels of income per head.

Capital INVESTMENT is a significant factor in the transformation process. Investment not only enlarges an economy's capacity to produce goods and service and raise the PRODUCTIVITY of resources, but also, via multiplier effects, increases aggregate demand and national income. An increase in national income raises the level of savings, thereby providing the finance for further capital accumulation. See Fig. 60.

See DEMOGRAPHIC TRANSITION, STRUCTURE OF INDUSTRY.

	Income per head	Economic structure		
	$ dollars	Agriculture	Industry	Services
Developing countries				
Chad	80	64	7	29
Burkina Faso	210	41	16	43
Uganda	230	82	4	14
Tanzania	280	52	15	33
Developed countries				
UK	9,660	2	33	65
Japan	10,080	4	42	54
US	13,160	3	33	64

Fig. 60. **Economic development**. The income per head and economic structure for selected countries. Source: *World Development Report*, World Bank, 1984.

economic efficiency, *n.* an aspect of PRODUCTION which seeks to identify for a given level of OUTPUT, that combination of FACTOR INPUTS which minimizes the COST of producing that output. See EFFICIENCY, COST FUNCTION.

economic forecasts, see FORECASTING.

economic goods, see GOODS.

economic growth, *n.* the growth of the real OUTPUT of an economy over time. The physical ability of an economy to produce more goods and services is dependent on a number of things:

(a) an increase in the stock and quality of its capital goods (CAPITAL ACCUMULATION).

(b) an increase in the quantity and quality of its LABOUR FORCE.

(c) an increase in the quantity and quality of its NATURAL RESOURCES.

(d) an efficient use of these factor inputs so as to maximize their contribution to the expansion of output, through improved PRODUCTIVITY.

(e) The development and introduction of innovative techniques and new products (TECHNOLOGICAL PROGRESSIVENESS).

Whether or not an economy actually realizes its growth potential is dependent on one further consideration:

(f) the level of AGGREGATE DEMAND. The level of demand needs to be high enough to ensure the full utilization of the increased productive capabilities of the economy.

The achievement of a high rate of economy growth is one of the four main objectives of MACROECONOMIC POLICY. The significance of economic growth lies in its contribution to the general prosperity of the community. Growth is desirable because it enables the community to consume more private goods and services, and it also contributes to the provision of a greater quantity of social goods and services (health, education, etc.), thereby improving real living standards.

Economic growth is usually measured in terms of an increase in real GROSS DOMESTIC PRODUCT (GDP) over time (see Fig. 61) or an increase in GDP per head over time. The latter measure relates increases in total output to changes in the population. Therefore, if total output rises only a little faster than the increase in population then there will be only a small improvement in average living standards. See CAPITAL-LABOUR RATIO, CAPITAL-OUTPUT RATIO, CAPITAL WIDENING, CAPITAL-DEEPENING, POTENTIAL GROSS NATIONAL PRODUCT, DOMAR ECONOMIC GROWTH MODEL, HARROD ECONOMIC GROWTH MODEL, SOLOW ECONOMIC GROWTH MODEL.

Average annual % increases

Japan	3.8
US	2.6
W. Germany	1.8
UK	1.3

Fig. 61. **Economic growth**. The increase in gross domestic product from 1974 to 1985. Source: OECD *Economic Outlook*, 1986.

economic growth models, see DOMAR ECONOMIC GROWTH MODEL, HARROD ECONOMIC GROWTH MODEL, SOLOW ECONOMIC GROWTH MODEL.

economic man, *n.* an assumption in economic theory that individuals act rationally in specifying their objectives and then take decisions which are consistent with those objectives. Thus, the ENTREPRENEUR will set a goal of PROFIT MAXIMIZATION and will adjust his output and price to

Fig. 62. **Economic man**. The graph demonstrates why, if the assumption of rational consumer behaviour holds, a consumer's INDIFFERENCE CURVES cannot cross. Indifference curves II and I_1I_1 show a consumer's preference between two products, X and Y. Point A on indifference curve II represents a higher level of satisfaction to the consumer than point B on indifference curve I_1I_1, because point A represents more of both products than point B. Yet point C lies on both curves. This suggests that the consumer, having preferred the combination of goods indicated by point A to the combination represented by point B, now regards them as equal at point C. If the consumer is rational, such an inconsistent or intransitive set of preferences would not arise; hence indifference curves do not intersect.

achieve this goal. Again, the CONSUMER will seek to maximize his UTILITY or satisfaction and will determine his purchases in the light of his tastes for products and the relative prices of those products. See Fig. 62 for an illustration of rational consumer choice. See CONSUMER RATIONALITY, CONSUMER EQUILIBRIUM, BEHAVIOURAL THEORY OF THE FIRM.

economic model, *n.* a construct or model incorporating two or more VARIABLES that: (a) describes the relationship that exists between the variables; (b) depicts the economic outcome of their relationships; (c) predicts the effects of changes in the variables on the economic outcome.

There are numerous economic models portrayed in this book; for example, EQUILIBRIUM MARKET PRICE, EQUILIBRIUM MARKET PRICE (CHANGES IN), EQUILIBRIUM LEVEL OF NATIONAL INCOME, MULTIPLIER. See also ECONOMETRICS, HYPOTHESIS TESTING.

economic order quantity, see STOCKHOLDING (INVENTORY) COSTS.

economic planning, see INDICATIVE PLANNING, CENTRALLY PLANNED ECONOMY, NATIONAL PLAN.

economic policy, *n.* a strategy decided upon collectively by a government to achieve its economic objectives.

The objectives a community sets for itself in a democracy are reflected through the ballot box in voting for a particular party with a given mandate. The goals an elected government sets itself are political and of a normative nature, since they invariably involve views about the most appropriate INCOME DISTRIBUTION (i.e., value judgements are made about the relative effects of policies upon particular subgroups within the community, and the desirability of helping some groups at the expense of others).

Consequently these objectives are the subject of debate between different political parties. Even if political parties had the *same* objectives, such as achieving ECONOMIC GROWTH, reducing UNEMPLOYMENT, controlling INFLATION and achieving BALANCE OF PAYMENTS surplus, the *degree* of importance attached to each would vary according to the government in power and the time period in which the decision was taken.

The welfare of an economy is frequently associated with the consumption and use of material goods. This is not the whole story. The psychological effect of being unemployed or of pollution from a production unit may decrease welfare. This is something which governments take into account, to a greater or lesser extent, when determining economic policy.

The government attains its policy objectives through the use of policy instruments. Such instruments may take the form of increasing or decreasing the MONEY SUPPLY through OPEN MARKET OPERATIONS (monetary instrument) or increasing or decreasing the rate of TAXATION (fiscal instrument).

See FISCAL POLICY, NORMATIVE ECONOMICS, MONETARY POLICY, WELFARE ECONOMICS, MACRO–ECONOMIC POLICY.

economic rent, *n.* a payment made for the use of a FACTOR OF PRODUCTION, such as land, which is in fixed supply both in the short run and in the long run. Because such FACTOR INPUTS cannot be transferred to other uses their TRANSFER EARNINGS are zero, and any payments made for them represent economic rent. The equilibrium rent is determined by the demand for, and supply of, land. See Fig. 63. See also QUASI–RENT.

economics, *n.* the study of the problem of using available FACTORS OF PRODUCTION as efficiently as possible so as to attain the maximum fulfilment of society's unlimited demands for GOODS and SERVICES. The ultimate purpose of economic endeavour is to satisfy human wants for

Fig. 63. **Economic rent**. The demand curve (D) for land as a factor input is downward-sloping, reflecting a fall in the marginal productivity of land as more land is used (SEE MARGINAL PHYSICAL PRODUCT and MARGINAL REVENUE PRODUCT). The supply of land, by definition, is completely fixed and hence the supply curve is perfectly inelastic (S). The equilibrium rate of rent is R_e where the two curves intersect.

goods and services. The problem is that whereas wants are virtually without limit, the resources – NATURAL RESOURCES, LABOUR and CAPITAL – available at any one time to produce goods and services, are limited in supply; i.e., resources are scarce (see SCARCITY) relative to the demands they are called upon to satisfy. The fact of scarcity means that we must always be making CHOICES. If, to take a simple example, more resources are devoted to producing motor cars, fewer resources are then available for providing hospitals and other goods.

See OPPORTUNITY COSTS, PRODUCTION POSSIBILITY BOUNDARY, EFFICIENCY.

economic sanctions, *n.* bilateral or multinational prohibitions (embargoes) on the EXPORT and IMPORT of goods, services and capital to and from a particular country. Economic sanctions are applied as an adjunct to political pressure being brought to bear on a country by the international community for that country to change its political/economic policies (For example, the abolition of the system of apartheid in South Africa).

economic statistics, *n.* the statistics collected by government and other bodies, to show where an economy is at the time of collecting the data and to facilitate comparisons and analyses with other data and indices of previous time periods. Data is shown in government publications, e.g., in the UK, *UK National Accounts* (Blue Book), *UK Balance of Payments*

(Pink Book), and the *Department of Employment Gazette*. International Statistics appear in such publications as the *United Nations Yearbook*; *OECD Main Economic Indicators*; and *EC Statistical Digest*.

Such data may be analysed by conventional statistical methods or by ECONOMETRICS to establish significant relationships between the indices of the variables involved.

economic system, *n*. a mechanism for tackling the twin problems of SCARCITY and CHOICE. Because economic resources are limited relative to society's demand for goods and services, some means of allocating resources between alternative ends is required. In the modern world three basic allocative mechanisms perform this function: PRIVATE ENTERPRISE ECONOMY in which resources are allocated through markets; CENTRALLY PLANNED ECONOMY in which resources are allocated by the State; MIXED ECONOMY in which resources are allocated both by the market and by the State.

economic theory, *n*. the formulation of ECONOMIC MODELS about the relationships between economic VARIABLES in order to generate testable hypotheses from these models and the testing of these hypotheses against empirical data. Where a HYPOTHESIS conflicts with real world data then the hypothesis will be amended or abandoned in favour of a better one; where the hypothesis is confirmed by the data then it can form a valuable guide in the specification of ECONOMIC POLICY. See HYPOTHESIS TESTING.

economic union, *n*. a form of TRADE INTEGRATION between a number of countries, that provides not only the COMMON MARKET features of free trade and factor movements but also the unification of members' general economic objectives in respect of economic growth, employment, etc., and the harmonization of monetary, fiscal and other policies.

Benelux (the alliance of Belgium, the Netherlands, and Luxembourg) formed in 1921, is one example of an economic union, although, politically, they remain separate sovereign states. By definition, of course, all of the regions making up the nation (political) state constitute an economic union. Economic union is one of the long-term objectives of the EUROPEAN COMMUNITY.

economies of scale, *n*. the LONG RUN reduction in AVERAGE (or unit) COSTS that occurs as the scale of the firm's output is increased (all FACTOR INPUTS being variable). There are available in most industries 'economies of scale', so that when producing a greater quantity of a product, average or unit costs are reduced. See Fig. 64 on page 156.

Economies of scale may operate both at the level of the individual plant and the firm (operating a number of plants) and arise due to:

ECONOMIES OF SCALE

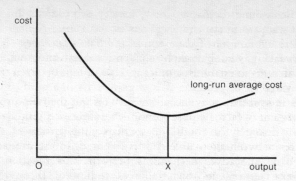

Fig. 64. **Economies of scale**. A typical U-shaped long-run average cost curve for a plant. OX is the scale of output at which average cost is minimized and economies of scale exhausted. Thereafter DISECONOMIES OF SCALE may set in, although this is not always the case (see MINIMUM EFFICIENT SCALE).

(a) indivisibilities in machinery and equipment especially where a number of processes are linked together; (b) economies of increased dimensions – for many types of capital equipment (tankers, boilers) both set-up and operating costs increase less rapidly than capacity; (c) economies of SPECIALIZATION – at larger outputs there is more scope for using specialist labour and capital equipment; (d) superior techniques or organization of production – as scale is increased automatic machinery may be used instead of manually operated items, or it may be possible to substitute continuous MASS PRODUCTION for BATCH PRODUCTION; (e) economies of bulk-buying of raw materials and supplies; (f) marketing economies resulting from the use of mass advertising media and greater density of deployment of sales forces; (g) financial economies which arise from the ability of large firms to raise capital on more advantageous terms; (h) managerial economies from the use of specialist management techniques like work study, operational research and critical path analysis.

The potential to realize economies of scale can be limited for a variety of reasons. In some industries the nature of the product and the processes of manufacture, or technology, may be such that DISECONOMIES OF SCALE are encountered at modest output levels. On the demand side, total market demand may be insufficient to permit firms to attain minimal efficient scale, or firms' individual market shares may be too small.

Where consumers demand a wide variety of products this mitigates against standardization and long production runs.

Where economies of scale are substantial, SELLER CONCENTRATION tends to be high, as for example in petro-chemicals and motor vehicles. See EXTERNAL ECONOMIES OF SCALE, NATURAL MONOPOLY.

economize, *vb.* to produce: (a) a *given* OUTPUT of a product using less FACTOR INPUTS than previously; (b) *more* output than before from the *same* amount of factor inputs; (c) a given output of a product at lower cost than before by substituting cheaper factor inputs for more expensive ones in the production process (the 'ideal' or optimum position is attained when the largest possible output is produced from a given volume of factor inputs using available technology); (d) a given output at the least possible factor cost.

See PRODUCTIVITY, EFFICIENCY, ECONOMICS, PRODUCTION POSSIBILITY BOUNDARY.

economy, *n.* a country defined in terms of the total and composition of its economic activities. The total value of goods and services produced in an economy in any one year is called GROSS DOMESTIC PRODUCT (GDP). The contribution made to GDP by the various subdivisions of the economy can be viewed in a variety of ways: for example, either by broad sectors (the PERSONAL or household SECTOR, the CORPORATE or business SECTOR, the FINANCIAL SECTOR, PUBLIC (GOVERNMENT) SECTOR, the FOREIGN SECTOR), or by individual industries.

Edgeworth box, *n.* a conceptual device for analysing possible trading relationships between two individuals or countries, using INDIFFERENCE CURVES. It is constructed by taking the indifference map of one individual (B) for two goods (X and Y) and inverting it to face the indifference map of a second individual (A) for the same two goods, as in Fig. 65 on page 158. Individual A's preferences are depicted by the three indifference curves A_1, A_2 and A_3, corresponding to higher levels of satisfaction as we move outward from origin OA. Individuals B's preferences are depicted by the three indifference curves B_1, B_2 and B_3, corresponding to higher levels of satisfaction as we move outward from origin OB. Both consumers' preferences as between the two products X and Y are reflected in the slopes of their indifference curves, with the slope of a curve at any point reflecting the MARGINAL RATE OF SUBSTITUTION of X for Y.

Only where individual A's indifference curves are tangential to individual B's indifference curves (points E, F and G in Fig. 65), will A's marginal rate of substitution of product X for product Y be the same as

Fig. 65. **Edgeworth box**. See main entry.

B's marginal rate of substitution of X for Y, so that their relative valuations of the two products are the same. Starting from any other point, say Z, the two can gain by trading with one another. At point Z individual A has a lot of product X and little of product Y; consequently he values product Y more highly than product X, being prepared to give up a lot of product X ($X_1 X_3$) to gain just a little of product Y ($Y_1 Y_2$). This is why his indifference curve A_1 is relatively flat at point Z. On the other hand, at point Z individual B has a lot of product Y and little product X; consequently he values product X more highly than product Y, being prepared to give up a lot of product Y ($Y_1 Y_3$) to gain just a little of product X ($X_2 X_3$). This is why his indifference curve B_2 is relatively steep at point Z.

These two sets of relative valuations of product X and product Y offer the promise of mutually beneficial exchange. If individual A offers some of his plentiful and low-valued product X in exchange for extra units of scarce and high-valued product Y he can gain from trade. Similarly if individual B offers some of his plentiful and low-valued product Y in exchange for extra units of scarce and high-valued product X he can also gain from trade. The two will continue to exchange product X in return for product Y (individual A) and product Y in return for product X (individual B), until they reach a point such as E or F where the indifference curves have the same slope, so that their marginal rates of substitution of the two products are the same.

The *contract curve* or *offer curve* in Fig. 65 traces out the path of all the points such as E, F and G, where the indifference curves are tangential, and if individuals A and B start with any combination of products X and Y other than ones lying along the contract curve, then they have an incentive to redistribute products X and Y between themselves through exchange. Where they come to lie along the contract curve will depend upon their relative bargaining strength and skills. If individual A is the stronger they may end up at a point like G far from A's origin OA and putting individual A on a high indifference curve A_3; while individual B ends up on a low indifference curve B_1 near his origin OB. On the other hand, if individual B is the stronger, they may end up at a point like E far from B's origin OB and putting individual B on a high indifference curve B_3; while individual A ends up on a low indifference curve A_1 near his origin OA. See also PARETO OPTIMALITY, THEORY OF CONSUMER BEHAVIOUR, THEORY OF INTERNATIONAL TRADE.

EEC, see ECONOMIC COMMUNITY.

effective demand, see DEMAND.

effective rate of interest or **yield,** *n.* the RATE OF INTEREST payable on the purchase price of a BOND. For example, a bond with a face value of £100 and a NOMINAL (COUPON) RATE OF INTEREST of 5% generates a nominal return of £5 per year. If, however, the bond can be purchased for £50 on the open market, then the effective interest rate now rises to 10% representing a 10% return on the £50 invested. The lower the purchase price of a bond with a given nominal rate of interest the higher its effective rate of interest will be, and vice-versa. There is thus an inverse relationship between the price paid for a bond and its effective rate of interest.

effective rate of protection, *n.* the real amount of PROTECTION accorded to domestic suppliers of a final product when a TARIFF is applied to a competing imported final product (see IMPORTS) but either no tariff, or a lower rate of tariff, is applied on FACTOR INPUTS which are imported to produce that product. For example, assume that initially the same domestic final product and imported final product are both priced at £100. Assume further that the price of the domestic product is made up of 50% value added by *domestic inputs* and 50% by *imported raw materials*. If an *ad valorem* tariff of 10% is now applied to the imported final product, its price will increase to £110. If no tariff, however, is applied to imported raw materials then the import price of these will remain at £50. This allows domestic VALUE ADDED (and prices) to increase by up to £10 with the domestic final product still remaining fully competitive with the imported final product. The effective rate of protection accorded to domestic suppliers is thus 20% (that is, £10 additional value added/£50 existing value added). See NOMINAL RATE OF PROTECTION.

efficiency, *n.* the relationship between scarce FACTOR INPUTS and OUTPUTS of goods and services. This relationship can be measured in physical terms (TECHNOLOGICAL EFFICIENCY) or cost terms (ECONOMIC EFFICIENCY). The concept of efficiency is used as a criterion in judging how well MARKETS have allocated resources. See MARKET PERFORMANCE, RESOURCE ALLOCATION, ECONOMIZE.

efficient–markets hypothesis, *n.* a hypothesis which suggests that an efficient financial market exists where all available information which may influence the price of a FINANCIAL SECURITY is reflected in that price. This implies that there exists PERFECT COMPETITION within such a market, so that changes in the price of securities would only be affected by the acquisition of new information. The hypothesis suggests that due to the rapid assimilation of this new information by the market, expectations of future price changes are revised randomly about the security's intrinsic value. Statisticians term such occurrences a *random walk*. For example, if a SHARE has an initial price of £1, the next change in price has an equal chance of being an increase or a decrease in value. If it goes up to, say, £1.10p, the next change in price has an equal chance of going up or down. The implication that STOCK and share prices follow a random walk implies that price changes are independent of one another.

Empirical tests of the efficient–markets hypothesis have been classified into weak–form tests, semistrong–form tests and strong–form tests. The weak–form tests suggest that future prices cannot be predicted from past prices, which is supported by the random–walk hypothesis. The semistrong form tests suggest that share prices reflect all publicly available information, and the strong form tests suggest share prices reflect *all* information. It is unlikely that the efficient–markets hypothesis holds in its strong form as it is clearly most difficult to be in possession of *all* necessary information.

See CAPITAL–ASSET PRICING MODEL, STOCK EXCHANGE.

EFTA, see EUROPEAN FREE TRADE ASSOCIATION.

elastic, *adj.* relatively responsive to change. See PRICE–ELASTICITY OF DEMAND, PRICE–ELASTICITY OF SUPPLY, INCOME–ELASTICITY OF DEMAND, CROSS–ELASTICITY OF DEMAND.

elasticity of demand or **demand elasticity,** *n.* a measure of the degree of responsiveness of quantity demanded of a particular product (see DEMAND) to a given change in one of the INDEPENDENT VARIABLES which affect demand for that product. The responsiveness of demand to a change in price is referred to as PRICE-ELASTICITY OF DEMAND; the responsiveness of demand to a change in income is known as INCOME-ELASTICITY OF DEMAND; and the responsiveness of demand for a particular product to changes in the prices of other related products is called CROSS-ELASTICITY OF DEMAND.

elasticity of supply, *n.* the degree of responsiveness of quantity supplied of a particular product (see SUPPLY) to changes in the product's PRICE (PRICE ELASTICITY OF SUPPLY).

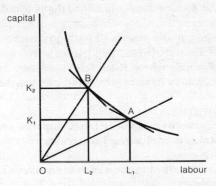

Fig. 66. **Elasticity of technical substitution**. The numerator of the expression is the percentage change in factors employed when moving from process ray OA to process ray OB. The denominator is the change in each factor's relative MARGINAL PHYSICAL PRODUCT, given by the slope of the isoquent curve at the points of tangency A and B.

elasticity of technical substitution, *n.* the rate at which one FACTOR INPUT can be substituted for another with OUTPUT remaining constant. For example, the rate of substitution between CAPITAL and LABOUR may be expressed as:

$$e = \frac{\% \text{ change in the ratio of amounts of factors of production employed}}{\% \text{ change in the ratio of their marginal physical products}}$$

The denominator in the above expression is known as the MARGINAL RATE OF TECHNICAL SUBSTITUTION. Essentially, the elasticity of substitution is the change in factor proportions used (the numerator) in relation to their substitutability (the denominator). The above expressions may be illustrated graphically using ISOQUANT CURVES (equal product curves) and PROCESS RAYS (see Fig. 66).

The elasticity of substitution between factor inputs is not infinite. Where no substitution is possible (e = 0) inputs must be used in fixed proportions; where factors are perfect substitutes e = ∞. The actual measure will lie somewhere between the two. Where it is one (as exhibited in the COBB-DOUGLAS PRODUCTION FUNCTION) there exists constant returns to scale, i.e., labour can be substituted for capital in any given proportions and vice versa, without affecting output.

embargo, *n.* the prohibition of the IMPORT and EXPORT of particular types of product (for example, military equipment) or a complete ban on trade with a particular country as an adjunct to the political policies pursued by the government.

empirical testing, *n.* the process of testing economic theories against empirical data. See HYPOTHESIS, HYPOTHESIS TESTING.

employee, *n.* a person who is hired (employed) by another person or FIRM to provide LABOUR services as a FACTOR INPUT in the production of a good or service.

Compare EMPLOYER.

employer, *n.* a person or FIRM which hires (employs) LABOUR as a FACTOR INPUT in the production of a good or service.

Compare EMPLOYEE.

employment, *n.* the use of LABOUR as a FACTOR INPUT in the production of a good or service.

employment contract, *n.* a contract between an EMPLOYEE and the company for which he works, specifying the terms and conditions governing his employment. Employment contracts of directors and senior executives are called *service contracts*, and these often contain provision for generous severance payments in the event of early dismissal.

employment laws, *n.* the body of legislation providing for the regulation of relations between employers and employees and the conduct of INDUSTRIAL DISPUTES. UK employment law provides for the protection of individual employees' rights such as the right to protection from unfair dismissal, the right to statutory redundancy payments, etc. UK employment law embodies ARBITRATION and CONCILIATION mechanisms for settling industrial disputes, and proscribes certain courses of action which parties might employ in furtherance of an industrial dispute, such as certain forms of PICKETING.

endogenous money or **inside money,** *n.* that part of the MONEY SUPPLY which is created inside the economic system by the banking sector, as opposed to being 'put into' the system from outside by the government (EXOGENOUS MONEY). See BANK DEPOSIT CREATION, MONEY SUPPLY SCHEDULE.

endogenous variable, *n.* a VARIABLE in an ECONOMIC MODEL which both affects and is itself affected by the relationship depicted in the model. For example, in the EQUILIBRIUM LEVEL OF NATIONAL INCOME model an increase in consumption spending increases aggregate demand and raises the level of national income. By the same token, an increase in the level of national income (which results, say, from an increase in investment) will induce an increase in consumption spending. Compare EXOGENOUS VARIABLE.

Engel's law, *n.* a principle that states that consumers will tend to spend an increasing proportion of any additional income upon LUXURY GOODS and a smaller proportion on STAPLE GOODS; so that a rise in income will lower the overall share of consumer expenditures spent on staple goods (such as basic foodstuffs) and increase the share of consumer expenditures on luxury goods (such as motor cars).

See INFERIOR PRODUCTS, INCOME ELASTICITY OF DEMAND, INCOME CONSUMPTION CURVE, AGRICULTURAL POLICY.

enterprise zone, *n.* a small area scheduled by the British authorities for special financial assistance (for example, 100% capital allowance, exemption from rates, etc, for investing firms) and other forms of assistance to encourage industrial expansion.

Although not formally part of REGIONAL POLICY, enterprise zones like their larger brethren the DEVELOPMENT AREAS are clearly intended to act as a magnet for new investment and job creation.

entrepôt trade, *n.* a commercial operation whereby goods are imported into a country and re-exported without distribution within the importing country (see IMPORTS, EXPORTS).

Entrepôt transactions are confined in the main to COMMODITIES such as tea and tin, where a MIDDLEMAN located in a particular commodity centre (London, for example, in the case of tea and tin), can arrange for the sale of the commodity and its world-wide shipment to customer countries.

entrepreneur, *n.* an individual who assembles and organizes FACTORS OF PRODUCTION to undertake a venture with a view to PROFIT. The individual may supply one or more of the three factors of production (NATURAL RESOURCES, LABOUR, CAPITAL) himself, or may hire or buy any or all factors in the expectation of future profits. The entrepreneurial function is sometimes called a *fourth factor of production*.

The entrepreneur was seen in the 19th century as an individual proprietor who supplied most or all of the factors of production but especially managerial expertise. The advent of the JOINT-STOCK COMPANY led to the division of management and the supply of capital, so that the term entrepreneur became a more hypothetical abstract term attached to any individual or group who performs the risk-bearing and organizing functions above. The traditional THEORY OF THE FIRM suggests that entrepreneurs attempt to maximize profit, but since the 1930s there has been growing awareness that the DIVORCE OF OWNERSHIP FROM CONTROL in large joint-stock companies influences the behavioural attitudes of groups of individuals within organizations, which may lead to corporations following objectives other than PROFIT MAXIMIZATION.

See BEHAVIOURAL THEORY OF THE FIRM, MANAGERIAL THEORIES OF THE FIRM, RISK AND UNCERTAINTY.

entry, see MARKET ENTRY, CONDITION OF ENTRY, BARRIERS TO ENTRY, POTENTIAL ENTRANT.

entry-forestalling price, see LIMIT PRICING.

envelope curve, see AVERAGE COST (LONG-RUN).

equation, *n*. a means of portraying arithmetically the relationship between VARIABLES. For example, the equation: $C = 1,000 + 0.9Y$ suggests a particular relationship between consumer expenditure (C) and disposable income (Y), which would be true for certain values of C and Y (such as 10,000 and 10,000 respectively), but not true of other values of C and Y (such as 6,000 and 10,000 respectively). Equations are generally written with a two-bar equals sign ($=$) with the value to the left of the sign being equal to the value to the right of the sign. The validity of an equation can be tested statistically by collecting paired observations of the variables involved and testing whether or not these observations conform with the equation formulated. See IDENTITY, INEQUALITY.

equilibrium, *n*. a state of balance with no tendency to change. See EQUILIBRIUM MARKET PRICE, EQUILIBRIUM LEVEL OF NATIONAL INCOME.

equilibrium level of national income, *n*. **1.** the level of NATIONAL INCOME at which the purchasing and production plans of the economy are synchronized. This occurs at the point of intersection of the AGGREGATE DEMAND SCHEDULE with the AGGREGATE SUPPLY SCHEDULE, which is Point E in Fig. 67a on page 165. Equilibrium income is not necessarily the level of income at which FULL EMPLOYMENT is attained, for an equilibrium level of income can occur at any level of economic activity. Full employment equilibrium is a special case where aggregate demand exactly corresponds with POTENTIAL GROSS NATIONAL PRODUCT,

EQUILIBRIUM LEVEL OF NATIONAL INCOME

(a)

(b)

Fig. 67. **Equilibrium level of national income.** (a) Income levels above point E are not sustainable because total spending is insufficient to buy up all of the output being produced. Businesses find themselves with unplanned stocks on their hands and thus cut back production. Conversely, at income levels below point E aggregate demand exceeds aggregate supply. Businesses find that they can sell all of their current output and are encouraged to expand production. (b) The equilibrium level of national income will change if there is a shift in the aggregate demand schedule. For example, if aggregate demand rises from AD to AD_1 this results in an increase in the equilibrium income level from E to E_1. (See MULTIPLIER).

EQUILIBRIUM LEVEL OF NATIONAL INCOME

(c)

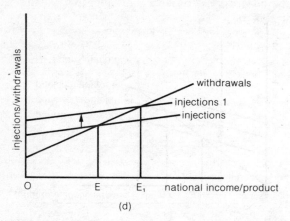

(d)

(c) Equilibrium is achieved where withdrawals = injections, i.e. point E, which is the same as point E in the aggregate demand/aggregate supply schedules in (b). If withdrawals exceed injections then total expenditure will fall, resulting in a contraction of income and output. Conversely, if injections exceed withdrawals then total expenditure will rise, resulting in an increase in income and output. Only when injections and withdrawals are equal will income and output remain unchanged. (d) The equilibrium level of national income will change if there is a shift in either the injections or withdrawals schedules. For example, an increase in investment spending will shift the injections schedule from I to I_1 resulting in an increase in the equilibrium income level from E to E_1 (see also PARADOX OF THRIFT).

leaving no INFLATIONARY GAP or DEFLATIONARY GAP. For example, aggregate demand 2 in Fig. 67b on page 165 represents a full employment equilibrium where E_2 corresponds with full employment output.

2. the level of national income at which total INJECTIONS (investment + government expenditure + exports) is exactly equal to WITHDRAWALS (saving + taxes + imports). Also called *injections-with-drawals approach to national income determination*. In the CIRCULAR FLOW OF NATIONAL INCOME MODEL, income = consumption + withdrawals, spending = consumption + injections. See Fig. 67c, d, on page 166.

equilibrium market price, *n.* the PRICE at which the quantity demanded of a good is exactly equal to the quantity supplied (see DEMAND, SUPPLY). The DEMAND CURVE depicts the quantity that consumers are prepared to buy at particular prices; the SUPPLY CURVE depicts the quantity that producers are prepared to sell at particular prices. See Fig. 68.

Fig. 68. **Equilibrium market price.** The equilibrium market price, OP, is generated by the intersection of the demand and supply curves. A higher initial price such as OP₁ results in EXCESS SUPPLY which forces price down; a lower initial price such as OP₂ results in EXCESS DEMAND which forces the price up. Only at price OP are buying and supply intentions fully synchronized.

equilibrium market price, (changes in), *n.* an increase or decrease in PRICE resulting from a shift in the DEMAND CURVE or SUPPLY CURVE. See Fig. 69 on page 169. See DEMAND CURVE, (SHIFT IN), SUPPLY CURVE, (SHIFT IN).

equilibrium market quantity, see EQUILIBRIUM MARKET PRICE.

equity capital, see ORDINARY SHARES.

error term, see REGRESSION ANALYSIS.

estate agent, *n*. an AGENT who acts on behalf of clients in selling houses, industrial property and land.

estate duty, see WEALTH TAX.

Eurobond market, see EUROCURRENCY MARKET.

Eurocurrency market or **Eurobond market,** *n*. a market based primarily in Europe that is engaged in the lending and borrowing of US DOLLARS and other major foreign currencies outside their countries of origin to finance international trade and investment.

The main financial instrument used in the Eurocurrency market for long-term investment purposes is the Eurobond (see BOND), a form of fixed-interest security denominated in a particular currency or currencies. Depositers in the eurocurrency market include commercial banks, industrial companies and central banks. Borrowers for the most part are companies, who have resorted to Eurofinance during times of domestic credit restrictions and/or when domestic interest rates have been high in comparison to those prevailing in the Eurocurrency market. See FOREIGN EXCHANGE MARKET.

Eurodollar, see EUROCURRENCY MARKET.

European Atomic Energy Community (Euratom), *n*. an organization established by member countries of the EUROPEAN COMMUNITY to develop the Community's nuclear energy capabilities for industrial and commercial purposes.

European Coal and Steel Community (ECSC), *n*. a regional alliance established in 1951 to promote free trade in coal and steel. Its founding members were West Germany, France, Italy, Belgium and Luxembourg, five of the six countries who later went on to build on the spirit of cooperation kindled by the ECSC to establish the broader-based EUROPEAN COMMUNITY. One of the main roles of the ECSC is the regulation of the industry's capacity to ensure that long-run supply is kept in line with demand potential, and that individual suppliers, including nationalized concerns, are prevented from dominating the market.

European Commission, *n*. the central body which is responsible for the day-to-day administration and coordination of the affairs of the EUROPEAN COMMUNITY (EC), the control of the EC's general budget finances, and which, together with the various specialist agencies set up to run particular programmes (for example, the Common Agricultural

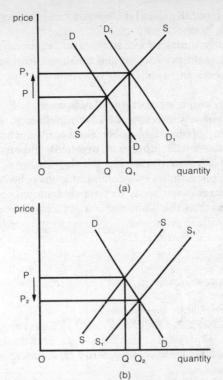

Fig. 69. **Equilibrium market price, (changes in)**, (a) If there is a shift in the demand curve from DD to D_1D_1, with supply unchanged, the equilibrium price will rise from OP to OP_1. (b) If there is a shift in the supply curve from SS to S_1S_1, with demand unchanged, the equilibrium price will fall from OP to OP_2.

Policy), is involved in the detailed implementation of Community policies.

European Community (EC) or (formerly) **European Economic Community (EEC),** *n.* a regional alliance established by the Treaty of Rome in 1958 with the general objective of integrating the economies of member countries. There were six founding countries of the EC: West Germany, France, Italy, Netherlands, Belgium and Luxembourg, who had previously cooperated (with the exception of the Netherlands) in the EUROPEAN COAL AND STEEL COMMUNITY. Further countries have since joined the EC: the UK, Eire and Denmark in 1973, Greece (1981), Spain and Portugal (1986).

The EC is now a major force in the world economy, accounting for over 40% of world production and trade in 1985, while, in political terms, the EC is seen as the third 'superpower' alongside the US and Russia.

The strategic and main operational policies of the EC are formulated by member country governments acting through the Council of Ministers (one appointed member per country, one vote) and the European Parliament (democratically elected). The EUROPEAN COMMISSION is responsible for overseeing the day-to-day administration of Community policy and in controlling its general budget finances (see Fig.70), while various other bodies are charged with running specific programmes such as the Common Agricultural Policy.

	European currency units (in millions)
Farm price support	21,012
Structural policies (social, regional and farm)	5,606
Repayments and reserves	3,159
Administration	1,604
Aid and development	1,172
Research, energy and industry	762
	33,315

Fig. 70. **European Community**. The EC budget for 1986.

The primary economic developments within the EC to date include:

(a) the creation of a COMMON MARKET providing for free trade in goods and services and the free movement of labour and capital resources across national boundaries. Member countries are committed to removing TARIFFS, QUOTAS and other obstacles to trade within the Community and to maintaining the EC's common external tariff against nonmember countries. Import restrictions by the six original members against each other were dismantled and their external barriers harmonized, in stages between 1958 and 1968. The EC has concluded a number of trade preference agreements with nonmember countries, including the multilateral LOMÉ AGREEMENT with over 40 less-developed countries, most of them former colonies of EC members, and bilateral pacts with members of the EUROPEAN FREE TRADE ASSOCIATION (see GAINS FROM TRADE, TRADE CREATION, TRADE DIVERSION).

(b) a *competition policy* providing for the prohibition of price-fixing and market-sharing agreements between firms, etc., and the abuse of a dominant market position, which have the effect of reducing or eliminating intra-EC trade (see MONOPOLY POLICY).

(c) a *common agricultural policy* providing for the subsidization and protection of the farm sector (see COMMON AGRICULTURAL POLICY).

(d) a *regional policy* providing financial assistance for the removal of regional imbalances both within and between member countries (see EUROPEAN REGIONAL DEVELOPMENT FUND, EUROPEAN INVESTMENT BANK).

(e) the establishment of the EUROPEAN MONETARY SYSTEM to provide a closer coordination of member countries' exchange rates and settlement of payments imbalances.

(f) the creation of a special monetary unit, the EUROPEAN CURRENCY UNIT to provide a common basis for intercountry settlements under the Common Agricultural Policy, European Monetary System, etc.

Over the longer-term it is hoped to work towards a full ECONOMIC UNION, involving a closer harmonization of member countries' general economic policies and the centralization of fiscal and monetary control procedures. Whether or not this can be achieved within a supranational framework given different vested national (political as well as economic) interests remains a moot question. Does economic unification first of all require political unification, or does economic unification itself eventually provide the basis for political unification?

European Currency Unit (ECU), *n.* a monetary asset held by member countries of the EUROPEAN MONETARY SYSTEM (EMS) as part of their INTERNATIONAL RESERVES. Unlike other reserve assets such as gold, ECUs have no tangible life of their own. They are 'created' by the EMS's European Monetary Cooperation Fund in exchange for the in-payment of GOLD and other reserve assets by members and take the form of bookkeeping entries in a special account managed by the Fund. The value at the ECU is based on a weighted basket of members' national currencies. See EUROPEAN COMMUNITY.

European Economic Community, see EUROPEAN COMMUNITY.

European Free Trade Association (EFTA), *n.* a regional alliance established by the Stockholm Treaty, 1959, with the general objective of securing the benefits of FREE TRADE for its member countries. EFTA came about following the breakdown of attempts in the latter half of the 1950s to create a large European-based CUSTOMS UNION. Those countries in favour of the customs union approach, with its detailed commitment to long-term economic integration duly formed the EUROPEAN COMMUNITY (EC) in 1958. The remainder, for a variety of reasons such as colonial

171

connections and a political preference for neutrality, chose the FREE TRADE AREA route and formed EFTA.

There were seven original members of EFTA: Austria, the UK, Denmark, Norway, Portugal, Sweden and Switzerland. Finland joined in 1961 and Iceland in 1970. In 1973, however, the UK and Denmark left and joined the EC.

Import restrictions on trade between member countries, were abolished in stages over the period 1960–66, while each country continued to operate its own separate TARIFFS, etc., against nonmember countries. EFTA members have, however, negotiated bilateral trade preference agreements with the EC. See GAINS FROM TRADE.

European Investment Bank, *n.* an institution established in 1958 with the formation of the EUROPEAN COMMUNITY to provide financial assistance for the schemes and projects considered to be beneficial in promoting the economic integration of the Community. Together with the EUROPEAN REGIONAL DEVELOPMENT FUND, the Bank is an important source of funds for the development of the more impoverished areas of the Community. The Bank also makes finance available to less developed countries. See REGIONAL POLICY.

European Monetary Cooperation Fund, see EUROPEAN MONETARY SYSTEM.

European Monetary System (EMS), *n.* the monetary system established by the EUROPEAN COMMUNITY (EC) in 1979 to coordinate and stabilize the EXCHANGE RATES of member countries. The EMS is based on a FIXED EXCHANGE RATE mechanism, a pool of FOREIGN EXCHANGE and GOLD reserves for settling payments imbalance, and the ECU, a monetary unit which is used to value, on a common basis, exchange rates and reserves.

The EMS is managed by the *European Monetary Cooperation Fund*. Membership of the EMS is voluntary and two countries, the UK and Greece, have (as at August 1987), decided not to participate in the exchange rate arrangements of the EMS, although they are fully involved in the operation of the reserve pool.

The exchange rate system used by the EMS is a variant of the ADJUSTABLE PEG FIXED EXCHANGE SYSTEM formerly used by the INTERNATIONAL MONETARY FUND. Exchange rate movements are controlled by a parity grid. Each currency is given a central par value expressed in terms of the ECU. A currency may move to a limit of 2.25% either side of its central rate (the Italian lira is allowed a 6% range either side). If a currency reaches its outer limit the country's central bank must intervene either directly in the foreign exchange market and/or by adjusting domestic interest rates to stabilize the rate.

Should the central rate itself prove to be overvalued or undervalued against other members' currencies, then, with the approval of the European Monetary Corporation Fund, a member may devalue or revalue its currency, re-pegging at a new fixed central parity rate (see DEVALUATION, REVALUATION). See EUROPEAN CURRENCY UNIT.

European Regional Development Fund, *n.* an organization established by the EUROPEAN COMMUNITY in 1975 to provide financial assistance for the removal of intra and interregional imbalances.

Financial assistance is made available in two ways: (a) on a national quota basis with the Fund contributing towards job-creation investments and infrastructure projects under the national policies of each member country. This accounts for around 85% of Fund disbursements. (b) on a discretionary basis with the Fund contributing to schemes aimed at tackling especially urgent regional problems, or those that are of a Community-wide nature. See REGIONAL POLICY.

ex ante, *adj.* being applied from before an action. The concept of an 'ex ante' approach to economics, together with that of *ex post* (from after) is widely employed in economic analysis to examine the change in some economic phenomenon as it moves from a state of DISEQUILIBRIUM to a position of EQUILIBRIUM. For example, 'ex ante' in the Keynsian model of national income determination planned investment may be greater than planned saving so that the economic system is in a state of disequilibrium. The excess of investment, however, serves to inject additional income into the economy and, via the MULTIPLIER effect, increases both income and saving, bringing about an eventual 'ex post' equilibrium where realized investment equals realized savings.

See EQUILIBRIUM LEVEL OF NATIONAL INCOME.

excess capacity, *n.* **1.** a situation where a firm or industry has more than enough plant on hand to supply a product than is currently being demanded. As a result a proportion of the firm or industry's CAPACITY is left idle. Excess capacity can result from a temporary (short-run) downturn in demand, a secular (long-run) fall in demand, or from the industry having overinvested in new plant relative to long-run demand potential. In the latter two instances, excess capacity may be eliminated by an intensification of competitive pressures (see EXCESS SUPPLY) which forces the more inefficient suppliers to exit the industry, or by RATIONALIZATION schemes.

2. in economic theory, the cost structures of firms operating in

Fig. 71. **Excess capacity**. Under the imperfect market conditions of monopolistic competition, the equilibrium (PROFIT MAXIMIZING) position for the firm is at a point (Q_e) to the left of the cost-minimizing point (Q_c) on the long-run average total cost curve; industry output is less, and costs are higher than the optimum position. Thus 'excess capacity' is measured as the difference between actual industry output and the cost-minimizing level of industry output (distance AB).

imperfect markets. Industry output is maximized (that is, full capacity attained) when all firms produce at the minimum point on their long-run average total cost curves (see PERFECT COMPETITION). See Fig. 71 for the effect of MONOPOLISTIC COMPETITION.

excess demand or **shortages,** *n.* a situation in which the quantity demanded (see DEMAND) of a product (OQ_2 in Fig. 72 on page 175) exceeds the quantity supplied (see SUPPLY) (OQ_1) at the *existing* market price (OP). In competitive markets there will be an upward pressure on price reflecting a shortage of the product, but where the price is controlled the excess could persist. See EQUILIBRIUM MARKET PRICE, EXCESS SUPPLY, PRICE CONTROLS.

excess profit, see ABOVE-NORMAL PROFIT.

excess supply, *n.* a situation in which the quantity supplied (see SUPPLY) of a product (OQ_2 in Fig. 73 on page 175) exceeds the quantity demanded (see DEMAND) of the product (OQ_1) at the *existing* market-price (OP). In a competitive market there will be a downward pressure on price as suppliers compete to dispose of surpluses, but where there is government intervention the situation could persist. See EQUILIBRIUM MARKET PRICE, EXCESS DEMAND, PRICE CONTROLS, PRICE SUPPORT, COMMON AGRICULTURAL POLICY.

Fig. 72. **Excess demand**. See main entry.

Fig. 73. **Excess supply**. See main entry.

exchange, *n.* **1.** the act of buying and selling goods and services either in the form of BARTER or through a MARKET. **2.** the means of financing the purchase of goods and services in a market. See MONEY, FOREIGN EXCHANGE.

exchange controls, *n.* a means of limiting the extent to which a country's CURRENCY can be freely exchanged for foreign currencies. They are applied in order to assist in the removal of a BALANCE OF PAYMENTS deficit and to protect a FIXED EXCHANGE RATE against HOT-MONEY currency inflows and outflows. Exchange-control systems place an overall ceiling on the amount of currency available for overseas trade and investment purposes and often discriminate against particular items, for example, 'nonessential' imports. See BALANCE-OF-PAYMENTS EQUILIBRIUM.

exchange equalization account, *n.* a pool of foreign currencies held by a country's CENTRAL BANK for purposes of intervention in the FOREIGN EXCHANGE MARKET in order to control the EXCHANGE RATE of that country's currency. See FIXED EXCHANGE RATE SYSTEM, EUROPEAN MONETARY SYSTEM, INTERNATIONAL MONETARY FUND.

exchange rate, *n.* the price of one CURRENCY expressed in terms of some other currency. Fig. 74a on page 177 shows the rate, or price, at which dollars ($s) might be exchanged for pounds (£s). The demand curve (D) for £s is downwards-sloping, reflecting the fact that if £s become less expensive to Americans, British goods, services and assets will become cheaper to them. This causes Americans to demand greater quantities of British goods, etc. and therefore greater amounts of £s with which to buy those items. The supply curve (S) of £s is upwards-sloping, reflecting the fact that as the dollar price of £s rises, American goods, services and assets become cheaper to the British. This causes the British to demand greater quantities of American goods, etc. and hence the greater the supply of £s offered in exchange for $s with which to purchase those items. The equilibrium rate of exchange between the two currencies is determined by the intersection of the demand and supply schedules ($2 = £1, in Fig. 74a).

Under a FIXED EXCHANGE-RATE SYSTEM the exchange rate, once established, will remain unchanged for longish periods. If the exchange rate gets too much out of line with underlying market conditions, however, and becomes overvalued, resulting in a country being persistently in BALANCE OF PAYMENTS deficit, the exchange rate can be DEVALUED; i.e., refixed at a new lower value, which makes IMPORTS more expensive and its EXPORTS cheaper. By the same token, if the exchange rate becomes undervalued, resulting in a country being persistently in balance of payments surplus the exchange rate can be revalued; i.e., refixed at a new higher value, which makes imports cheaper and its exports more expensive (see REVALUATION).

Under a FLOATING EXCHANGE-RATE SYSTEM the exchange rate is free to fluctuate day-by-day and will fall (see DEPRECIATION sense 1) or rise (see APPRECIATION sense 1) in line with changing market conditions, serving to keep a country's balance of payments more or less in equilibrium on a continuous basis.

The *effective exchange rate* is a given currency's value in terms of a WEIGHTED AVERAGE of a 'basket' of other currencies. Fig. 74b depicts the

Fig. 74. **Exchange rate**. (a) The graph shows the interaction of demand (D) and supply (S) in determining the exchange rate between pounds and dollars. (b) The effective exchange rate of sterling. The graph shows the monthly average of daily rates, with 1975 = 100.

'effective exchange rate' over time of the UK pound against other major trading countries' currencies, for example, the US dollar, Japanese yen, etc.

A fall (depreciation) in the effective exchange rate indicates an improvement in the price competitiveness of a country's products vis-a-vis trade partners. See also PURCHASING-POWER PARITY THEORY, ASSET VALUE THEORY, BALANCE OF PAYMENTS EQUILIBRIUM, INTERNATIONAL FISHER EFFECT.

Exchequer, *n.* a UK government office within the TREASURY responsible for the receipt, custody and issue of government funds.

excise duty, *n.* an INDIRECT TAX levied by the government on certain goods, most notably tobacco, oil and alcoholic drink. Demand for these goods is price inelastic (see PRICE ELASTICITY OF DEMAND) so that duty increases, implemented as part of FISCAL POLICY, will not only raise government revenue but also leave customers with less money to spend on other goods. See TAXATION.

exclusive dealing, *n.* a practice whereby a supplier contracts distributors to deal only in his products to the exclusion of competitors' products. Exclusive dealing may be beneficial in some cases by allowing distribution costs to be lowered but, if exclusive dealing is pursued by several large firms in a market, the access of smaller suppliers and potential entrants to established distributive outlets may be severely restricted. See RESTRICTIVE TRADE PRACTICE, MONOPOLY POLICY, OFFICE OF FAIR TRADING.

ex-dividend, *adj.* (of a particular SHARE) excluding entitlement to the DIVIDEND which attaches to the share. If shares are purchased on the STOCK EXCHANGE 'ex. div.', the purchaser would not be entitled to the dividend accruing to that share when the dividend is next paid. Compare CUM-DIVIDEND.

exit, see MARKET EXIT.

exogenous money, *n.* that part of the MONEY SUPPLY which is 'put into' the economic system from outside by the government, as opposed to being created inside the system by the banking sector (ENDOGENOUS MONEY). See MONEY SUPPLY SCHEDULE.

exogenous variable, *n.* a VARIABLE that affects the operation of an ECONOMIC MODEL but which itself is not affected by any of the relationships depicted in the model. For example, in the EQUILIBRIUM LEVEL OF NATIONAL INCOME model, an increase in exports will increase AGGREGATE DEMAND and induce an increase in the level of national income, but the volume of exports itself is determined by any other country's propensity to import and not by the level of its own national income. Compare ENDOGENOUS VARIABLE.

expectations, *n.* anticipations of future events in order to guide present economic acts. A major unresolved problem in economics is how to deal with the uncertainty the future holds, especially when each individual has a different subjective perception of that future.

Consequently much economic analysis incorporates expectations into the various models as a given variable, usually under the heading CETERIS PARIBUS, or by assuming that an individual acts in accordance with the RATIONAL EXPECTATIONS HYPOTHESIS. A further problem is that expectations involve a time period and much economic analysis is static, i.e., points of equilibrium may be observed but the route between them is considered irrelevant. A simple and instructive demonstration of expectations is given in the COBWEB THEOREM.

Nevertheless, expectations have played a significant part in economic theory, most notably in the work of Keynes. Expectations are a major variable, it is argued, in determining business cycles, and affecting the SPECULATIVE DEMAND for money. Expectations are also influential when dealing with the TERM STRUCTURE OF INTEREST RATES.

To incorporate expectations into economic theory it is possible to treat individual behaviour as adaptive, as illustrated in the ADAPATIVE EXPECTATIONS HYPOTHESIS. Although the concept is straightforward, future expectations being adapted from past and present experiences, the attempts to reflect reality have led to complex structures being formulated.

See KEYNESIAN ECONOMICS, EXPECTATIONS–ADJUSTED AUGMENTED PHILLIPS CURVE, SPECULATOR.

expectations–adjusted/augmented Phillips curve, *n*. a reformulated PHILLIPS CURVE that allows for the effects of price EXPECTATIONS on money wage increases. In the expectations-adjusted Phillips curve (see Fig. 75 on page 180) $U^\star$ is the 'natural' rate of unemployment or NON–ACCELERATING INFLATION RATE OF UNEMPLOYMENT (NAIRU) (i.e., the rate of UNEMPLOYMENT at which INFLATION is neither accelerating nor decelerating). If the authorities attempt to reduce unemployment below the 'natural' rate to, say, U_1 the inflation rate rises from point A to point B on Phillips curve PC_1.

Assuming that the increase in money wages exceeds the growth of output per man then labour 'prices itself out of jobs', and unemployment reverts to its 'natural level' (point C) on a 'new' Phillips curve (PC_2) which is based on a higher 'expected' rate of inflation. Starting now at point C, if the authorities again attempt to reduce unemployment (to U_1), this will produce an acceleration in the inflation rate to point D, but again the higher rate of money wages will cause unemployment to

Fig. 75. **Expectations-adjusted/augmented Philips curve.** See main entry.

revert back to its natural level (point E) on a 'new' Phillips curve (PC_3) which is based on a yet higher 'expected' rate of inflation.

To get the inflation rate down the authorities need to force unemployment above the 'natural' rate temporarily (from point E to point F on Phillips curve PC_3) so as to reduce public expectations about the expected rate of inflation. As money wage rates fall people are 'priced back into jobs' and unemployment falls to its 'natural' level (at point C) on PC_2. See also INFLATIONARY SPIRAL.

expected value, *n.* the quantitative results of uncertain events weighted by the PROBABILITY of their occurrence. See DECISION TREE, RISK PROFILE, UTILITY INDEX.

expenditure approach to GDP, *n.* see NATIONAL INCOME ACCOUNTS.

expenditure tax, *n.* a form of INDIRECT TAX that is incorporated into the selling price of a product and which is borne by the consumer.

In raising revenue and in applying FISCAL POLICY governments have two broad choices: the use of taxes on expenditure and the use of taxes on INCOME (DIRECT TAXES). Taxes on income, such as INCOME TAX, deduct tax at source whereas taxes on expenditure are levied at the point of sale. Direct taxes tend to be PROGRESSIVE TAXES in so far as the amount of tax paid is related to a person's income, whereas expenditure taxes are REGRESSIVE TAXES in so far as consumers pay tax in proportion to their spending regardless of income.

In the UK, VALUE ADDED TAX, EXCISE DUTIES and CUSTOMS DUTIES are the main types of expenditure tax. See TAXATION, BUDGET (GOVERNMENT).

experience curve or **learning curve,** *n.* the process whereby managers and operators learn from experience how to operate new technologies more effectively over time such that a growing familiarity with, and the repetitive operation of, a new technology enables unit costs of production to be progressively reduced. See Fig. 76. See PRODUCTIVITY.

Fig. 76. **Experience curve.** The estimated reduction in total cost per square foot accruing from accumulated increases in the production of float glass using the revolutionary 'float glass' process. Source: Monopolies Commission, *Float Glass* report, HMSO, 1968.

explicit cost, *n.* a payment made by a firm for the use of FACTOR INPUTS (labour, capital) not owned by the firm. Unlike IMPLICIT COSTS (which represent payments for the use of factor inputs owned by the firm itself), explicit costs involve the firm in purchasing inputs from outside FACTOR MARKETS.

exponential function, *n.* a function in which a variable quantity is the power of a fixed number. Thus a^x, or $(a+b)^x$ are exponential functions where x is the exponent. This can also be read "a to the power of x" and means that a is multiplied by itself the number of times the exponent states. In the exponential function: $y = a^x$, if $a = 2$ and $x = 3$, then $y = 8$ (that is, $2 \times 2 \times 2$). Exponential functions transform into logarithms and vice versa. See LOGARITHMIC FUNCTION, LOG–LINEAR FUNCTION.

exponential smoothing, see TIME SERIES ANALYSIS.

Export Credit Guarantee Department (ECGD), a UK government office which provides insurance cover for British exporters against the risk of nonpayment by overseas customers as a means of encouraging exports.

export incentives, *n.* the financial assistance given to domestic firms by the government as a means of promoting EXPORTS and assisting the country's balance of payments. Export incentives include direct subsidies to lower export prices (EXPORT SUBSIDY), tax concessions (remission of profits earned on exports), credit facilities (cheap export finance) and financial guarantees (provision for bad debts, etc).

Export incentives are often viewed as an 'unfair' trade practice by other countries and frequently result in retaliatory action being taken by them.

See COUNTERVAILING DUTY, BEGGAR–MY–NEIGHBOUR POLICY.

export-led growth, *n.* an expansion of the economy with EXPORTS serving as a 'leading sector'. As exports rise they inject additional income into the domestic economy and increase total demand for domestically-produced output (see EXPORT MULTIPLIER). Equally importantly, the increase in exports enables a higher level of import absorption to be accommodated so that there is no BALANCE OF PAYMENTS contraint on the achievement of sustained ECONOMIC GROWTH. See CIRCULAR FLOW OF NATIONAL INCOME MODEL.

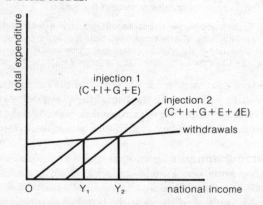

Fig. 77. **Export multiplier**. The effect of an increase in exports on national income. The additional exports (ΔE) serve to increase total injections and shift the injection schedule to the right, increasing national income by $Y_1 Y_2$.

export multiplier, *n.* the ratio of the increase in a country's NATIONAL INCOME to the increase in the demand for the country's EXPORTS that brought it about. The INJECTION of increased exports into the CIRCULAR FLOW OF NATIONAL INCOME raises national income by some multiple of the original increase in exports. The value of the export multiplier depends on the country's MARGINAL PROPENSITY TO SAVE, MARGINAL PROPENSITY TO IMPORT and MARGINAL PROPENSITY TO TAXATION. The larger these propensities – the larger, that is, the 'WITHDRAWALS' from the income flow – the smaller will be the value of the export multiplier. See Fig. 77. See also MULTIPLIER, FOREIGN TRADE MULTIPLIER, EXPORT-LED GROWTH.

export restraint agreement, *n.* an arrangement between an exporting country and an importing country that limits the volume of trade in a particular product (or products). Specifically, EXPORTS/IMPORTS between the two countries are limited to an agreed number of units, or percentage share of the importing country's domestic sales. An export restraint agreement is thus a protectionist measure (see PROTECTIONISM) designed to shield domestic producers in the importing country from foreign competition and assist that country's balance of payments. See MULTI-FIBRE ARRANGEMENT.

exports, *n.* goods, services and capital assets that are sold to foreign countries. Exports are important in two main respects: (a) together with IMPORTS they make up a country's BALANCE OF PAYMENTS (a country must export in order to finance ('pay for' in foreign currency terms) its imports); (b) they represent an 'injection' into the CIRCULAR FLOW OF NATIONAL INCOME, serving to raise real income and output. See EXPORT MULTIPLIER.

export subsidy, *n.* a direct payment, or tax concession, made by the government to domestic firms to enable them to reduce their EXPORT prices. Although the widespread use of export subsidies by a country can increase its exports and assist its balance of payments, such subsidies are viewed as an 'unfair' trade practice by the GENERAL AGREEMENT ON TARIFFS AND TRADE, and are likely to lead to retaliatory action by other countries. See COUNTERVAILING DUTY, BEGGAR-MY-NEIGHBOUR POLICY.

ex post, see EX ANTE.

external balance, *n.* a situation of BALANCE-OF PAYMENTS EQUILIBRIUM that, over a number of years, results in a country spending and investing abroad no more than other countries spend and invest in it. The achievement of external balance is one of the macroeconomic objectives of the government. Compare INTERNAL BALANCE. See also DEMAND MANAGEMENT, EXCHANGE RATES, MACROECONOMIC POLICY, INTERNAL-EXTERNAL BALANCE MODEL.

external diseconomies of scale, *n.* the factors outside the influence of a single firm that lead to increasing long run AVERAGE COSTS for firms within an industry as a whole. For example, if a large number of firms settle in a particular area then the additional road congestion which they cause could slow up deliveries for any particular firm, increasing its own (internal) transport costs. See EXTERNAL ECONOMIES OF SCALE, DISECONOMIES OF SCALE.

external economies of scale, *n.* the factors outside the influence of a single firm that lead to decreasing long run AVERAGE COSTS for firms within an industry as a whole. For example, if a college concentrated on training large numbers of, say, computer programmers to serve the needs of local computer businesses nearby, then the individual employer would have a supply of trained programmers available with a resulting reduction in the firm's own (internal) training costs.

See EXTERNAL DISECONOMIES OF SCALE, ECONOMIES OF SCALE, INTERNAL ECONOMIES OF SCALE.

externalities, *n.* factors that are not included in GROSS NATIONAL PRODUCT but which have an effect on human welfare. POLLUTION is a prime example of an external cost imposed on society: national output may only be maintained by allowing a certain degree of pollution which detracts from the quality of life. A firm will include the PRIVATE COSTS of materials, labour and capital used in producing goods and services but will not count the SOCIAL COSTS of pollution involved. On the other hand, positive externalities such as the social benefits conferred by firms in training workers who become available for employment elsewhere, are again not counted in national output.

See WELFARE ECONOMICS, COST–BENEFIT ANALYSIS.

extrapolate, *vb.* to estimate an unknown (future) value by projecting from known (past) values (in TIME–SERIES ANALYSIS). This involves predicting a value for the DEPENDENT VARIABLE from a value of the INDEPENDENT VARIABLE which is beyond the range of observed independent variables, and outside the range the trend line may be inaccurate because the underlying relationship may be different over the broader range. By contrast, if we *interpolate*, i.e., predict a value for the dependent variable from a value of the independent variable which lies within the range of observed independent variables, then the prediction is likely to be more reliable. See FORECASTING.

F

factor, *n.* **1.** a FACTOR INPUT which is used in production (see NATURAL RESOURCES, LABOUR, CAPITAL). **2.** a business that buys in bulk and performs a WHOLESALING function. **3.** a business that buys trade debts from client firms (at some agreed price below the nominal value of the debts) and then arranges to recover them for itself.

See FACTOR MARKET, FACTORING.

factor cost, *n.* the value of goods and services produced measured in terms of the cost of the FACTOR INPUTS (materials, labour, etc.) used to produce them, that is, excluding any indirect taxes levied on products and any subsidies offered on products. For example, a product costing £10 to produce (including profit) and with a £1 indirect tax levied on it would have a market price of £11 and a factor cost of £10. See FACTORS OF PRODUCTION.

factor income, see NATIONAL INCOME.

factoring, *n.* a financial undertaking whereby a specialist finance company (the factor) purchases a firm's TRADE DEBTORS (ACCOUNTS RECEIVABLE) (generally) for an amount less than the book value of those debts. The factor's profit derives from the difference between monies collected from the DEBTS purchased and the actual purchase price of those debts. The firm benefits by receiving immediate cash from the factor rather than having to wait until trade debtors eventually pay their debts, and avoids the trouble and expense of pursuing tardy debtors. For example, if a firm had £100,000 of debtors on its books, it may sell them to a factoring company for £80,000 cash, giving the factoring company a discount of 20% and a potential profit of £20,000 if it collects all the debts. Factoring companies may also advise on credit ratings of individuals and firms, for which a fee is charged.

See DEBTORS, CREDIT CONTROL.

factor inputs, *n.* FACTORS OF PRODUCTION (labour, capital, etc.) which are combined to produce OUTPUT of goods and services. See PRODUCTION FUNCTION, COST FUNCTION.

factor markets, *n.* markets in which FACTORS OF PRODUCTION are bought and sold, and in which the prices of labour and other FACTOR INPUTS are determined by the interplay of demand and supply forces. See LABOUR MARKET, CAPITAL MARKET, COMMODITY MARKET, DERIVED DEMAND, MARGINAL PHYSICAL PRODUCT, MARGINAL REVENUE PRODUCT.

factors of production, *n*. the resources that are used by firms as FACTOR INPUTS in producing a good or service. There are three main groups of factor inputs: NATURAL RESOURCES, LABOUR and CAPITAL. Factors of production can be combined together in different proportions to produce a given output (see PRODUCTION FUNCTION); it is assumed in the THEORY OF THE FIRM that firms will select that combination of inputs for any given level of output which minimizes the cost of producing that output (see COST FUNCTION). See ENTREPRENEUR, MOBILITY.

factory cost or **works cost,** *n*. the ex-factory cost of products. See PRODUCTION COSTS.

Fair Trading Act, *n*. a UK Act of 1973 that consolidated and extended previous British monopoly law for controlling MONOPOLIES, MERGERS, RESTRICTIVE TRADE AGREEMENTS and ANTICOMPETITIVE PRACTICES, and established a new authority, the Director-General of Fair Trading and the Office of Fair Trading, to administer all aspects of MONOPOLY POLICY. The Act also established a new body, the Consumer Protection Advisory Committee to deal with matters relating to consumers' interests in general.

See OFFICE OF FAIR TRADING, MONOPOLIES AND MERGERS COMMISSION, RESTRICTIVE PRACTICES COURT, for details of the legal and institutional framework of monopoly control in Britain.

fallacy of composition, *n*. an error in economic thinking that often arises when it is assumed that what holds true for an individual or part must also hold true for a group or whole. For example, if a small number of people save more of their income, this might be considered to be a 'good thing' because more funds can be made available to finance investment. But if everybody attempts to save more this will reduce total spending and income and result in a fall in total saving. See PARADOX OF THRIFT.

feasible region, *n*. see LINEAR PROGRAMMING.

Federal Reserve Bank, *n*. the CENTRAL BANK of the US.

fees, *n*. the payments to professional persons such as lawyers and accountants for performing services on behalf of clients.

fiat currency, see FIDUCIARY ISSUE.

fiduciary issue or **fiat currency,** *n*. CURRENCY issued by a government that is not matched by government holdings of GOLD or other securities.

In the 19th century most currency issues were backed by gold, and people could exchange their banknotes for gold on demand. Nowadays most governments have only minimal holdings of gold and other securities to redeem their currency so that most of their currency issues are fiduciary. See MONEY SUPPLY.

final products, *n.* GOODS and SERVICES which are consumed by end-users, as opposed to INTERMEDIATE PRODUCTS which are used as FACTOR INPUTS in producing other goods and services. Thus purchases of bread count as part of final demand but not the flour used to make this bread.

The total market value of all final products (which corresponds with total expenditure in the NATIONAL INCOME ACCOUNTS) corresponds with the total VALUE ADDED at each product stage for all products in the economy.

Finance Corporation for Industry, see INVESTORS IN INDUSTRY.

finance house, *n.* a financial institution that accepts deposits from savers and which specializes in the lending of money by way of instalment credit (HIRE PURCHASE loans) and LEASING for private consumption and business investment purposes. See FINANCIAL SYSTEM.

financial accounting, *n.* the accounting activities directed towards the preparation of annual TRADING, PROFIT-AND-LOSS ACCOUNTS and BALANCE SHEETS in order to report to shareholders on their company's overall (profit) performance. See MANAGEMENT ACCOUNTING.

financial institution, *n.* an institution that acts primarily as a FINANCIAL INTERMEDIARY in channelling funds from LENDERS to BORROWERS (e.g., COMMERCIAL BANKS, BUILDING SOCIETIES), or from SAVERS to INVESTORS (e.g., PENSION FUNDS, INSURANCE COMPANIES). See FINANCIAL SYSTEM.

financial intermediary, *n.* an organization that operates in financial markets linking LENDERS and BORROWERS or SAVERS and INVESTORS. See FINANCIAL SYSTEM, COMMERCIAL BANK, SAVINGS BANK, BUILDING SOCIETY, PENSION FUND, INSURANCE COMPANY, UNIT TRUST, INVESTMENT TRUST COMPANY, INTERMEDIATION.

financial ratio, see ACCOUNTING RATIO.

financial sector, *n.* that part of the ECONOMY concerned with the transactions of FINANCIAL INSTITUTIONS. Financial institutions provide money transmission services and loan facilities, and influence the workings of the 'real' economy by acting as intermediaries in channelling SAVINGS and other funds into INVESTMENT uses. The financial sector, together with the CORPORATE SECTOR and PERSONAL SECTOR constitute the PRIVATE SECTOR. The private sector, PUBLIC (GOVERNMENT) SECTOR and FOREIGN SECTOR make up the national economy. See FINANCIAL SYSTEM.

financial security, *n.* the financial instruments issued by firms, financial institutions and government. Financial securities include: SHARES, STOCKS, DEBENTURES, BILLS OF EXCHANGE, TREASURY BILLS, BONDS.

financial system, *n.* a network of financial institutions (BANKS, COMMERCIAL BANKS, BUILDING SOCIETIES, etc.) and markets (MONEY MARKET, STOCK EXCHANGE) dealing in a variety of financial instruments (BANK DEPOSITS, TREASURY BILLS, STOCKS and SHARES etc.) that are engaged in money transmission and the lending and borrowing of funds.

The financial institutions and markets occupy a key position in the economy as intermediaries in channelling SAVINGS and other funds to BORROWERS. In so doing one of their principal tasks is to reconcile the different requirements of savers and borrowers, thereby facilitating a higher level of saving and INVESTMENT than would otherwise be the case. Savers in general are looking for a safe and relatively risk-free repository for their monies, which combines some degree of liquidity (i.e., ready access to their money) with a longer-term investment return which protects the real value of their wealth as well as providing current income. Borrowers, in general, require access to funds of varying amounts to finance current, medium-term and long-term financial and capital commitments often, as is especially the case with business investments, under conditions of unavoidable uncertainty and high degrees of risk. The financial institutions help to reconcile these different requirements in the following three main ways:

(a) by pooling together the savings of a large number of individuals, so making it possible in turn to make single loans running into millions of pounds;

(b) by holding a diversified portfolio of assets and lending for a variety of purposes to gain economies of scale by spreading their risks while still keeping profitability high;

(c) by combining the resources of a large number of savers to provide both for an individual to remove his funds at short notice, and for their own deposits to remain stable as a base for long-term lending.

Financial Times All-Share Index, see SHARE PRICE INDEX.

fine-tuning, *n.* a short-run interventionist approach to the economy that uses monetary and fiscal measures to control fluctuations in the level of AGGREGATE DEMAND, with the aim of minimizing deviations from MACROECONOMIC POLICY objectives. The application of 'fine-tuning', however, is beset with problems of accurately FORECASTING fluctuations in economic activity and in gauging the magnitude and timing of counter-cyclical measures.

See DEMAND MANAGEMENT, STABLIZATION POLICY, MONETARY POLICY, FISCAL POLICY.

firm or **company** or **supplier,** *n.* a transformation unit concerned with converting FACTOR INPUTS into higher-valued intermediate and final GOODS or SERVICES. The firm or BUSINESS is the basic producing/supplying unit and is a vital building block in constructing a theory of the market to explain how firms interact and how their pricing and output decisions influence market supply and price (see THEORY OF THE FIRM, THEORY OF MARKETS).

The legal form of a firm consists of:

(a) a *sole proprietorship*, a firm owned and controlled (managed) by a single person, i.e., the type of firm that most closely approximates to that of the 'firm' in economic theory.

(b) a *partnership*, a firm owned and controlled by two or more persons who are parties to a partnership agreement.

(c) a JOINT-STOCK COMPANY, a firm owned by a group of ordinary shareholders and whose capital is divided-up into a number of SHARES. See COOPERATIVE.

The economic form of a firm consists of:

(a) a *horizontal firm*, a firm that is engaged in a single productive activity; e.g., motor-car assembly.

(b) a *vertical firm*, a firm that undertakes two or more vertically-linked productive activities; e.g., the production of car components (clutches, steel body shells) and car assembly.

(c) a *diversified* or *conglomerate firm*, a firm that is engaged in a number of unrelated productive activities; e.g., car assembly and the production of bread.

See HORIZONTAL INTEGRATION, VERTICAL INTEGRATION, DIVERSIFICATION.

firm location, *n.* the area where a firm chooses to locate its business. In principle a profit-maximizing firm will locate where its production and distribution costs are minimized relative to revenues earned. Often firms are faced with competing pulls of nearness to their market (to reduce product distribution costs), and nearness to their raw material supplies (to reduce materials transport costs), and must seek to balance these costs. Some firms have little choice in this regard, service companies being forced to locate near customers, and mineral extraction companies having to locate near materials sources. Many firms are relatively footloose, though, and are free to locate anywhere, influenced by the general attractiveness of an area; the quality of its transport, communications and education infrastructure; skills and reputation of its workforce, etc. See REGIONAL POLICY.

firm objectives, *n.* an element of MARKET CONDUCT that denotes the goals of the firm in supplying GOODS and SERVICES. In the traditional THEORY OF THE FIRM and the THEORY OF MARKETS, in order to facilitate intermarket comparisons of performance, *all* firms, whether operating under conditions of PERFECT COMPETITION, MONOPOLISTIC COMPETITION, OLIGOPOLY or MONOPOLY, are assumed to be seeking PROFIT MAXIMIZATION. More recent contributions to this body of theory have postulated a number of alternative firm objectives, including SALES-REVENUE MAXIMIZATION and ASSET–GROWTH MAXIMIZATION. In these formulations profits are seen as contributing to the attainment of some other objective rather than as an end in themselves.

See MANAGERIAL THEORIES OF THE FIRM, DIVORCE OF OWNERSHIP FROM CONTROL, BEHAVIOURAL THEORY OF THE FIRM, SATISFICING THEORY, MANAGEMENT UTILITY MAXIMIZATION.

first–in first–out (FIFO), see STOCK VALUATION.

fiscal drag, *n.* the restraining effect of PROGRESSIVE TAXATION on economic expansion. As NATIONAL INCOME rises, people move from lower to higher tax brackets, thereby increasing government TAXATION receipts. The increase in taxation constitutes a 'leakage' (from the CIRCULAR FLOW OF NATIONAL INCOME) which will reduce the rate of expansion of AGGREGATE DEMAND below that which would otherwise be the case. Governments may choose as part of FISCAL POLICY to adjust for the effects of fiscal drag by regularly increasing personal tax allowances.

Fiscal drag can also serve to automatically constrain the effect of the pressure of INFLATION in the economy, for with a high rate of inflation people will tend to move into higher tax brackets thereby increasing their total taxation payments, decreasing their disposable income, and reducing aggregate demand. This has the effect of reducing the pressure of DEMAND–PULL INFLATION. See AUTOMATIC (BUILT–IN) STABILIZERS.

fiscal policy, *n.* a tool of general MACROECONOMIC POLICY that seeks to influence the level of economic activity through the control of GOVERNMENT EXPENDITURE and TAXATION.

The use of deficit financing (that is, a BUDGET DEFICIT where the government spends more than its income from taxation) was advocated by KEYNES in the 1930s to effect a transition from a situation of mass UNEMPLOYMENT to one approaching FULL EMPLOYMENT. Theoretically, an increase in government spending or reduction in taxes (an INJECTION into the economy) stimulates AGGREGATE DEMAND via the MULTIPLIER

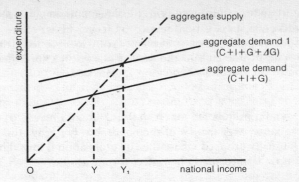

Fig. 78. **Fiscal Policy**. The effect of an increase in government expenditure on aggregate demand and national income.

effect, thus creating jobs to satisfy that demand, raising national income (from Y to Y_1 in Fig. 78). If the level of economic activity is too high, that is, the economy is 'overheating', the government has the option of running a BUDGET SURPLUS, decreasing its expenditure or increasing taxes (a WITHDRAWAL from the economy) to decrease aggregate demand.

The main aim of fiscal policy is to effect a countercyclical policy so that BOOMS and DEPRESSIONS during the course of the BUSINESS CYCLE are offset to their full extent. This leads fiscal policy to be used for the FINE-TUNING of an economy. Many economists believe that fiscal policy as a panacea for economic ills was misplaced, that it is more suited to the conditions of depression that existed when Keynes wrote his *General Theory of Employment, Interest and Money* in 1936 than to inflationary economies. Consequently, in the late 1970s during periods of high inflation it fell from favour and was replaced by a faith in MONETARY POLICY to achieve the government's objectives. Recently, fiscal policies have re-emerged and are now being received with more credibility than was given to them in the late 1970s. However, the debate still continues as to the most effective fine-tuning instruments to use.

See also CIRCULAR FLOW OF NATIONAL INCOME MODEL, DEFLATIONARY GAP, ECONOMIC POLICY, EQUILIBRIUM LEVEL OF NATIONAL INCOME, KEYNESIAN ECONOMICS, STABILIZATION POLICY, INFLATIONARY GAP, DEMAND MANAGEMENT.

fiscal year, *n.* the government's accounting year which, in the UK, runs from 6th April to 5th April the following year. Different countries frequently have a fiscal year different to the normal calendar year. In the

US the fiscal year runs up to 30th June. See BUDGET (GOVERNMENT).

Fisher effect, *n.* an equation devised by Irving Fisher (1867–1947) in which the NOMINAL RATE OF INTEREST on a BOND is expressed as the sum of the *real* rate of interest and the rate of INFLATION expected over the duration of the bond. The equation is expressed as:

$$r = R + \infty + R\infty$$

where r = nominal rate of interest, R = real rate of interest, ∞ = rate of annual inflation over the life of the bond. $R\infty$ is a crossproduct term which is usually dropped where the rate of inflation is low. This leaves what is now termed the Fisher effect formulation of:

$$r = R + \infty$$

Put another way, the interest rate must include an element to compensate lenders for the reduced value of present currency loaned when it is returned by the borrower (termed the inflation premium). For example, if inflation is 5% in one year, then nominal interest rates will rise by 5%, the real rate being unchanged. The Fisher effect suggests a one-to-one ratio between inflation and nominal interest rates. See INTERNATIONAL FISHER EFFECT.

Fisher equation, see QUANTITY THEORY OF MONEY.

fixed assets, *n.* the ASSETS such as buildings and machinery that are bought for long-term use in a firm rather than for resale. Fixed assets are retained in the business for long periods and generally each year a proportion of their original cost will be written off against PROFITS for amortization (see DEPRECIATION 2) to reflect the diminishing value of the asset. In a BALANCE SHEET fixed assets are usually shown at cost less depreciation charged to date. Certain fixed assets such as property tend to appreciate in value (see APPRECIATION 2) and need to be revalued periodically to help keep their BALANCE SHEET values in line with market values. See CURRENT ASSETS, REVALUATION RESERVE.

fixed costs or **overhead costs,** *n.* any COSTS that, in the SHORT RUN, do not vary with the level of output. See Fig. 79.

In the THEORY OF MARKETS, a firm will leave a product market if in the LONG RUN it cannot earn sufficient TOTAL REVENUE to cover both total fixed costs and total VARIABLE COSTS. However, it will remain in a market in the short run as long as it can generate sufficient total revenue to cover total variable cost and make some CONTRIBUTION towards total fixed costs even though it is still making a loss, on the assumption that this loss-making situation is merely a temporary one. See MARKET EXIT.

Fig. 79. **Fixed costs**. (a) The graph represents payments made for the use of FIXED FACTOR INPUTS (plant and equipment, etc.) which must be met irrespective of whether output is high or low. (b) The graph represents the continuous decline in average fixed cost (AFC) as output rises as a given amount of fixed cost is spread over a greater number of units.

fixed exchange-rate system, *n.* a method of regulating the EXCHANGE RATES between CURRENCIES. Under this system, currencies are assigned a fixed par value in terms of other currencies and countries are committed to maintaining this value by support buying and selling. For example, between 1949 and 1967, under the INTERNATIONAL MONETARY FUND's (IMF) fixed exchange rate regime, the UK maintained a rate of exchange of £1 = $2.80 with the US dollar. If the price of the £ rose (appreciated) in the FOREIGN EXCHANGE MARKET the UK authorities bought dollars and sold pounds; if the price of the £ fell (depreciated) the authorities sold dollars and bought pounds. See Fig. 80 on page 194.

Fixed exchange rates have the advantage that trade and financial deals can be concluded in terms of known values but the disadvantage is that they often get out of line with underlying market trends and commit countries with serious balance of payments difficulties to defend unrealistic parities. For this reason the IMF system allowed for periodic DEVALUATIONS or REVALUATIONS of par values.

See BALANCE OF PAYMENTS EQUILIBRIUM, ADJUSTABLE PEG EXCHANGE RATE SYSTEM, CRAWLING PEG EXCHANGE RATE SYSTEM, GOLD STANDARD, EUROPEAN MONETARY SYSTEM; also FLOATING EXCHANGE RATE SYSTEM; EXCHANGE EQUILIZATION ACCOUNT.

fixed factor input, *n.* a FACTOR INPUT to the production process that cannot be increased or reduced in the SHORT RUN. This applies particularly to capital inputs such as (given) plant and equipment. See

Fig. 80. **Fixed exchange-rate system**. The exchange rate between the pound and the dollar between 1949 and 1967.

VARIABLE FACTOR INPUT, RETURNS TO THE VARIABLE FACTOR INPUT, FIXED COSTS.

fixed-interest financial securities, *n*. any FINANCIAL SECURITIES that have a predetermined fixed RATE OF INTEREST attached to their PAR VALUE. For example, TREASURY BILLS, DEBENTURES and PREFERENCE SHARES. A debenture with a par value of £100 at 5% will pay out a fixed rate of interest of £5 per annum until the expiry of the debenture, that is, the date of redemption. See BONDS.

fixed investment, *n*. any INVESTMENT in plant, machinery, equipment and other durable CAPITAL GOODS.

Fixed investment in the provision of social products like roads, hospitals and schools is undertaken by central and local government as part of government expenditure. Fixed investment in plant, equipment and machinery in the private sector will be influenced by the expected returns on such investments and the cost of capital needed to finance planned investments.

Investment is a component of AGGREGATE DEMAND and so affects the level of economic activity in the short-run, while fixed investment serves to add to the economic INFRASTRUCTURE and raise POTENTIAL GROSS NATIONAL PRODUCT over the longer term. See INVENTORY INVESTMENT.

fixed overheads, *n*. any indirect COSTS that do not vary with the level of output of a product. They include such items as rents and depreciation of fixed assets, whose total cost remains unchanged regardless of changes in the level of activity. Consequently, fixed overhead cost per unit of product will tend to fall as output increases (as OVERHEADS are spread over a larger output). See VARIABLE OVERHEADS, SEMI-VARIABLE OVERHEADS, STANDARD COST.

fixed targets, *n.* an approach to macroeconomic policy that sets specific target values in respect of the objectives of FULL EMPLOYMENT, PRICE STABILITY, ECONOMIC GROWTH and BALANCE OF PAYMENTS EQUILIBRIUM.

The essence of this approach can be illustrated, to simplify matters, by reference to the PHILLIPS CURVE 'trade-off' between unemployment and inflation illustrated in Fig. 81. See MACROECONOMIC POLICY, OPTIMIZING.

Fig. 81. **Fixed targets**. The Phillips curve shows that as unemployment (U) falls, inflation (I) increases, and vice-versa. The Phillips curve is drawn as P. Ideally, the authorities would like the economy to be at the origin, point O, for here full employment and complete price stability are simultaneously attained. The Phillips curve, however, sets a limit to the combinations of U and I which can be achieved in practice. Given this constraint, the task of the authorities is to specify 'acceptable' target values for the two objectives. They could, for example, set a fixed target value on unemployment at 6% and a target value for inflation at 8%, or, alternatively a lower value for I and a higher value for U.

flexible budget, *n.* a BUDGET that allows for the variation in COSTS associated with changes in output volume. The costs associated with running a manufacturing plant, for instance, at 50% of capacity are different from running it at 70% or 100% capacity. The budget must allow for the variation in plant utilization by distinguishing between FIXED COSTS, VARIABLE COSTS and SEMIVARIABLE COSTS and their relationship to output. See BUDGETARY CONTROL, BUDGETING.

floating debt, *n.* any short-term FIXED-INTEREST FINANCIAL SECURITIES. Government floating debt is characterized by TREASURY BILLS or Exchequer stock nearing maturity, and company floating debt by short-term bank loans. By means of a FUNDING operation it is possible to convert short-term fixed interest debt into long-term fixed interest debt. See FUNDED DEBT.

floating exchange-rate system, *n.* a system for determining the EXCHANGE RATES between CURRENCIES by the inter-play of market forces. Under a 'free' float system, the exchange rates between currencies are left to be determined entirely by market forces. Over time, the exchange rate between two currencies will alter in accordance with changes in the demand for and supply of, the currencies concerned, as shown in Fig. 82a. In theory, this should always result in an equilibrium-exchange rate (i.e., a rate which ensures that a country achieves a BALANCE-OF-PAYMENTS EQUILIBRIUM), leaving the country free to pursue desirable domestic policies without external constraints. In practice, however, the uncertainties associated with free floats tend to produce erratic and random exchange rate movements which tend to inhibit trade as well as producing de-stabilizing domestic effects. For these reasons countries prefer to 'manage' their exchange rates, as shown in Fig. 82b. See PURCHASING-POWER PARITY THEORY, ASSET VALUE THEORY, EXCHANGE EQUALIZATION ACCOUNT, INTERNATIONAL MONETARY FUND, DIRTY FLOAT, HOT MONEY.

flow, *n.* a measurement of quantity over a specified period of time. Unlike a STOCK, which is not a function of time, a flow measures quantity passing per minute, hour, day or whatever. A common analogy is to a reservoir. The water entering and leaving the reservoir is a flow, but that water actually in the reservoir at any one point in time is a stock. INCOME is a flow but WEALTH is a stock.

f.o.b, *abbrev. for* free-on-board. In BALANCE OF PAYMENTS terms, f.o.b means that only the basic prices of imports and exports of goods (plus loading charges) are counted while the 'cost-insurance-freight' (C.I.F) charges incurred in transporting the goods from one country to another are excluded.

Food and Agricultural Organization (FAO), *n.* an international agency of the UNITED NATIONS, established in 1945. Its primary objective is to improve agricultural productivity and hence the nutritional standards of agrarian countries throughout the world. It achieves this objective through undertaking research on all aspects of farming, fishing and forestry and by offering technical assistance to those countries which

Fig. 82. **Floating exchange-rate system**. (a) If the UK's imports from the US rise faster than the UK's exports to the US, then, in currency terms, the UK's demand for dollars will increase relative to the demand in the US for pounds. This will cause the pound to fall (see DEPRECIATION 1) against the dollar, making imports from the US to the UK more expensive and exports from the UK to the US cheaper. By contrast, if the UK's imports from the US rise more slowly than its exports to the US, then, in currency terms, its demand for dollars will be relatively smaller than the US demand for pounds. This will cause the pound to rise (see APPRECIATION sense 1), making imports from the US to the UK cheaper and exports from the UK to the US more expensive. (b) The graph shows how nations can manage the float by intervening in the currency market to buy and sell currencies, using their national currency reserves to moderate the degree of short-term fluctuation and smooth out the long-term trend line.

require it. In addition, the FAO continually surveys world agricultural conditions, collects and issues statistics on human nutritional requirements and statistics on farming, fishing, forestry and related topics.

forced saving or **involuntary saving,** *n.* the enforced reduction of CONSUMPTION in an economy. This can be achieved directly by the government increasing TAXATION so that consumers' DISPOSABLE INCOME is reduced or it may occur indirectly as a consequence of INFLATION which increases the price of goods and services at a faster rate than consumers' money incomes increase.

Governments may deliberately increase taxes so as to secure a higher level of SAVING in order to obtain additional resources for INVESTMENT in the public sector. A 'forced saving' policy is often attractive for a DEVELOPING COUNTRY whose ECONOMIC DEVELOPMENT is being held back by a shortage of savings.

forecasting, *n.* the process of making predictions about future general economic and market conditions as a basis for decision-making by government and business. Various forecasting methods can be used to estimate future economic conditions, varying greatly in terms of their subjectivity, sophistication, data requirements and cost:

(a) survey techniques involving the use of interviews or mailed questionnaires asking consumers or industrial buyers about their future (buying) intentions. Alternatively, members of the sales force may provide estimates of future market sales; or industry experts can offer scenario-type forecasts about future market developments.

(b) experimental methods providing demand forecasts for new products, etc, based on either the buying responses of small samples of panel consumers, or large samples in test markets.

(c) EXTRAPOLATION methods employing TIME-SERIES ANALYSIS, using past economic data to predict future economic trends. These methods implicitly assume that the historical relationships which have held in the past will continue to hold in the future, without examining causal relationships between the variables involved. Time-series data usually comprises: a long run secular trend, with certain medium-term cyclical fluctuations; and short-term seasonal variations, affected by irregular, random influences. Techniques such as moving averages or exponential smoothing can be used to analyse and project such time series, though they are generally unable to predict sharp upturns or downturns in economic variables.

(d) *Barometric forecasts* to predict the future value of economic variables from the present values of particular statistical indicators which have a consistent relationship with these economic variables. Such LEADING INDICATORS as business capital investment plans and new housebuilding starts can be used as a barometer for forecasting values like economic activity levels or product demand, and they can be useful for predicting sharp changes in these values.

(e) INPUT-OUTPUT methods using input-output tables to show interrelationships between industries, and to analyse how changes in demand conditions in one industry will be affected by changes in demand and supply conditions in other industries related to it. For example, car component manufacturers will need to estimate the future demand for cars and the future production plans of motor car manufacturers who are their major customers.

(f) ECONOMETRIC methods predicting future values of economic variables by examining other variables which are causally related to it. Econometric models link variables in the form of equations which can be

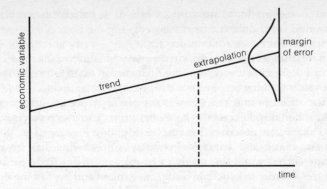

Fig. 83. **Forecasting**. The margin of error expected in economic forecasts.

estimated statistically and then used as a basis for forecasting. Judgement has to be exercised in identifying the INDEPENDENT VARIABLES which causally affect the DEPENDENT VARIABLE to be forecast. For example, in order to predict future quantity of a product demanded (Qd) we would formulate an equation linking it to product price (P) and disposable income (Y):

$$Qd = a + bP + cY$$

then use past data to estimate the regression coefficients a, b and c (see REGRESSION ANALYSIS). Econometric models may consist of just one equation like this, but often in complex economic situations the independent variables in one equation are themselves influenced by other variables, so that many equations may be necessary to represent all the causal relationships involved. For example, the macroeconomic forecasting model used by the British Treasury to predict future economic activity levels has over 600 equations.

No forecasting method will generate completely accurate predictions, so when making any forecast we must allow for a *margin of error* in that forecast. In the situation illustrated in Fig. 83, we cannot make a precise estimate of the future value of an economic variable, rather we must allow that there is a PROBABILITY DISTRIBUTION of possible future outcomes centred around the forecast value, showing a range of values with their associated probability distribution. Consequently forecasters need to exercise judgement in predicting future economic conditions both in choosing which forecasting methods to use and in combining information from different forecasts.

foreign currency, see FOREIGN EXCHANGE.

foreign exchange, *n.* foreign currencies which are exchanged for a country's domestic CURRENCY in the financing of INTERNATIONAL TRADE and FOREIGN INVESTMENT. See FOREIGN EXCHANGE MARKET.

foreign exchange market, *n.* a MARKET in which foreign currencies are bought and sold and EXCHANGE RATES between CURRENCIES determined. Such a market is necessary because each country engaged in INTERNATIONAL TRADE and FOREIGN INVESTMENT/borrowing has its own domestic currency and this needs to be exchanged for trade partners' currencies in order to conclude trade, investment and borrowing deals.

Currencies may be freely bought and sold (see FLOATING-EXCHANGE-RATE SYSTEM), or subjected to government support buying and selling (FIXED EXCHANGE-RATE SYSTEM) and EXCHANGE CONTROLS.

The main centres for foreign exchange dealings are London, New York, Paris, Basle, Hong Kong and Tokyo. See INTERNATIONAL DEBT.

foreign exchange reserves, see INTERNATIONAL RESERVES.

foreign investment, *n.* an INVESTMENT by domestic residents (individuals, companies and financial institutions) in the acquisition of overseas physical ASSETS and FINANCIAL SECURITIES. Thus, for example, a MULTINATIONAL FIRM may invest abroad by building a new overseas factory, or by acquiring an established overseas company. Interest, profits and dividends gained on these foreign investments may be repatriated or reinvested overseas. See CAPITAL MOVEMENTS, BALANCE OF PAYMENTS, CAPITAL INFLOW, CAPITAL OUTFLOW.

foreign sector, *n.* that part of the ECONOMY concerned with transactions with overseas countries. The foreign sector includes IMPORTS and EXPORTS of goods and services as well as CAPITAL MOVEMENTS in connection with investment and banking transactions. The net balance of foreign transactions influences the level and composition of domestic economic activity and the state of the country's BALANCE OF PAYMENTS. The foreign sector, together with the PERSONAL SECTOR, CORPORATE SECTOR, FINANCIAL SECTOR, PUBLIC (GOVERNMENT) SECTOR make up the national economy. See also CIRCULAR FLOW OF NATIONAL INCOME MODEL.

foreign trade multiplier, *n.* the increase in a country's foreign trade resulting from an expansion of domestic demand. The increase in domestic demand has a twofold effect. As well as directly increasing the demand for domestic products it will also (a) *directly* increase the demand for IMPORTS by an amount determined by the country's MARGINAL

PROPENSITY TO IMPORT, (b) *indirectly* it may also increase overseas demand for the country's EXPORTS by those countries whose own incomes have now been increased by being able to export more to the country concerned.

The latter effect, however, is usually much less than the former so that the overall effect is to 'dampen' down the value of the domestic MULTIPLIER; i.e., the increase in net imports serves to partially offset the extra income created by increased spending on domestic products. See CIRCULAR FLOW OF NATIONAL INCOME MODEL.

forward exchange market, see FUTURES MARKET.

forward integration, *n.* the joining together in one FIRM of two or more successive stages in a vertically-related production/distribution process, for example, flour millers acquiring their own outlets for flour, such as bakeries. The main motives for forward integration by a firm are to secure the market for the firm's output and to obtain cost savings. See VERTICAL INTEGRATION, BACKWARD INTEGRATION.

franchise, *n.* the assignment by one FIRM to another firm (*exclusive franchise*) or others (*nonexclusive franchise*) of the right/s to supply its product. A franchise is a contractual arrangement (see CONTRACT) which is entered into for a specified period of time, with the franchisee paying a ROYALTY to the franchisor for the rights assigned. Examples of franchises include the Kentucky Fried Chicken and McDonald Burger diner and 'take-away' chains. Individual franchisees are usually required to put up a large capital stake with the franchisor providing back-up technical assistance, specialized equipment and advertising and promotion. Franchises allow the franchisor to develop his business without having to raise large amounts of capital.

F ratio or **F statistic,** *n.* the ratio of the variation *between* SAMPLE means and the variation *within* the samples. It is used in HYPOTHESIS TESTING when deciding whether observed differences between the means of several samples may reasonably be attributed to chance. Where the variation between sample means is much larger than the variation within the samples, then the variation between the means is too large to be accounted for by chance (since the variation within the samples provides a measure of chance variation). Under these circumstances the null hypothesis that the sample means are not significantly different, would be rejected.

It is possible to construct a PROBABILITY DISTRIBUTION for the F ratio (called the *F distribution*) to establish a level of significance for hypothesis testing. Customarily, the values chosen as significance criteria are the areas under the F distribution curve to one side of the 0.01 and 0.05 probabilities.

F ratios are used in formulating and testing hypothesis against sample data because of their value in analysing variance. They enable us to analyse the total variation in data into two components: (a) variation between means or explicable variation; (b) chance variation.

freedom of entry, see CONDITION OF ENTRY.

free enterprise economy, see PRIVATE ENTERPRISE ECONOMY.

free market economy, see PRIVATE ENTERPRISE ECONOMY.

free port, see FREE TRADE ZONE.

free rider, *n.* a CONSUMER who deliberately understates his preference for a COLLECTIVE PRODUCT in the hope of being able to consume the product without having to pay the full economic price for it.

For example, where a number of householders seek to resurface their common private road, an individual householder might deliberately understate the value of the resurfaced road to himself, on the grounds that the other householders will pay to have all the road resurfaced anyhow, and that he will therefore enjoy the benefit of it without having to pay towards its resurfacing. See CLUB PRINCIPLE.

free trade, *n.* the INTERNATIONAL TRADE that takes place without barriers such as TARIFFS, QUOTAS and EXCHANGE CONTROLS, being placed on the free movement of goods and services between countries. The aim of free trade is to secure the benefits of international SPECIALIZATION. Free trade as a policy objective of the international community has been fostered both generally by the GENERAL AGREEMENT ON TARIFFS AND TRADE (GATT), and on a more limited regional basis by the establishment of various FREE TRADE AREAS, CUSTOM UNIONS and COMMON MARKETS. See GAINS FROM TRADE, EUROPEAN COMMUNITY, EUROPEAN FREE TRADE ASSOCIATION, TRADE INTEGRATION.

free trade area, *n.* a form of TRADE INTEGRATION between a number of countries, in which members eliminate all trade barriers (TARIFFS, etc.) among themselves on goods and services, but each continues to operate its own particular barriers against trade with the rest of the world. The aim of a free trade area is to secure the benefits of international SPECIALIZATION, thereby improving members' real living standards. The EUROPEAN FREE TRADE AREA is one example of a free trade area. See GAINS FROM TRADE, LATIN AMERICAN FREE TRADE AREA.

free trade zone or **freeport,** *n.* a designated area within the immediate hinterland of an air or shipping port into which IMPORTS are allowed without payment of IMPORT DUTY (TARIFFS), provided the goods are to be subsequently exported (see EXPORTS) either in their original form or as intermediate products within a final good. See ENTREPÔT TRADE.

frequency distribution, *n.* a means of summarizing large amounts of data by grouping statistical observations into convenient classes then showing how these observations are distributed among the different classes. Often shortened to *distribution*. A numerical frequency distribution groups data according to numerical size, for example, income bands as in Fig. 84a. A qualitative frequency distribution sorts data into categories according to some qualitative description such as industry group, as in Fig. 84c.

For certain purposes it is useful to have a numerical frequency distribution which groups observations in terms of cumulative ascending (or descending) size. This shows how many cases fall above (more than) or below (less than) certain values. For example, Fig. 84b shows how a distribution, with cases falling into income classes, can be converted into a cumulate 'less than' distribution. See HISTOGRAM.

Numerical distribution		Cumulative numerical distribution	
Weekly income (£)	number	Weekly income (£)	number
0–100	400	less than 100	400
101–200	300	less than 200	700
201–300	200	less than 300	900
301–400	100	less than 400	1,000
	1,000		
(a)		(b)	

Qualitative distribution	
Industry	Numbers employed
Agriculture/Mining	100
Manufacturing	300
Construction/Building	200
Services/Retail	400
(c)	

Fig. 84. **Frequency distribution.** See main entry.

frictional unemployment or **transitional unemployment,** *n.* the UNEMPLOYMENT experienced where people are changing jobs and are unemployed for a short period between jobs. Often people do not cease work, for whatever reason, and find another job immediately. The period of time between jobs, be it several days or even months, is seasonal *unemployment* of a 'frictional' nature, i.e., the markets do not operate smoothly. Frictional unemployment is only temporary and is thus usually ignored in estimating FULL EMPLOYMENT equilibrium.

Friedman, Milton (b. 1912) American economist at Chicago University who advocates the virtues of the free market system and the need to minimize government regulations of markets in his book, *Capitalism and Freedom* (1962).

Friedman has attacked Keynesian policies of government fine tuning of aggregate demand, arguing that such policies accentuate business uncertainty and can destabilize the economy. Instead he suggests that governments should gradually expand the MONEY SUPPLY at a rate equal to the long-run increase in national output, in order to eliminate inflationary tendencies in the economy. In an economy experiencing a high inflation rate Friedman acknowledges that a sharp reduction in the rate of growth of money supply would deflate demand and cause unemployment to rise. However, he argues that such a rise in unemployment would be temporary, for once people lower their expectations about future inflation rates full employment can be restored. Friedman's monetarist ideas have had considerable influence among governments in the 1980s.

Friedman also looked at the relationship between consumption and income, rejecting the Keynesian idea that as peoples' incomes rise they will spend a smaller proportion of them and save a larger share. Instead he argued that consumption is a constant fraction of the consumer's PERMANENT INCOME, and that as long-term income rises the proportion of it spent remains the same. See MONETARISM.

friendly society, *n.* an association of individuals (members) who made regular voluntary contributions into a fund upon which they could draw in times of need or to provide themselves with houses. These friendly societies were the forerunner of the modern INSURANCE COMPANIES and BUILDING SOCIETIES whose operations are now overseen in Britain by the Registrar of Friendly Societies.

fringe benefits, *n.* any additional benefits offered to employees such as the use of a company car, free meals or luncheon vouchers, interest-free or low-interest loans, private health care subscriptions, subsidized holidays and share purchase schemes. In the case of senior managers such benefits or perquisites (perks) can be quite substantial in relation to wages and salaries. Companies offer fringe benefits to attract employees and because such benefits provide a low tax or no-tax means of rewarding employees compared with normally-taxed salaries.

front door, *n.* the formal mechanism whereby the Bank of England makes loans to the DISCOUNT HOUSES when the discount houses experience temporary liquidity shortages. In this capacity as LENDER OF LAST RESORT the Bank of England charges a penal interest rate on the loans which it makes (called BILL DISCOUNTING rate). Compare BACK DOOR.

full capacity, see CAPACITY.

Fig. 85. **Full-cost pricing.** The price (OP) is made up of three elements: a contribution to cover part of the firm's overhead costs (average FIXED COST) – AB; the actual unit cost (average VARIABLE COST) of producing a planned output of OQ units – BC; a PROFIT MARGIN expressed as a fixed percentage of total unit costs (average variable cost plus average fixed cost) – CD.

full-cost pricing, *n.* a method used by firms to price goods and services. See Fig. 85. The problem with this pricing method is that it takes no account of demand and hence the revenue implications of the selected price. Compare the marginal pricing method (see PROFIT MAXIMIZATION). See also COST-PLUS PRICING.

full employment, *n.* the full utilization of all available labour (and capital) resources that the economy is able to produce at the limits of its POTENTIAL GROSS NATIONAL PRODUCT. Full employment is one of the main objectives of MACROECONOMIC POLICY.

FULL EMPLOYMENT EQUILIBRIUM

In practice, of course, 100% employment cannot be achieved. Inevitably there will always be some unemployment present due to labour turnover and people spending time in searching for and selecting new jobs; and because of structural changes in the economy – job losses in declining trades which require people to transfer to new jobs created in expanding sectors. Accordingly, a more realistic interpretation of full employment suggests itself: full employment is achieved when the number of registered unemployed is equal to the number of job vacancies. However, even this measure does not give an accurate estimate because many groups like housewives and older workers may fail to register as unemployed when job prospects are bleak even though they wish to work (DISGUISED UNEMPLOYMENT).

For macroeconomic purposes, however, most governments tend to specify their full employment objectives in terms of some 'targeted' level of unemployment (for example, 3% of the total labour force), though the exact target level is rarely publicly disclosed.

See UNEMPLOYMENT, FIXED TARGETS (APPROACH TO MACROECONOMIC POLICY).

full employment equilibrium, see EQUILIBRIUM LEVEL OF NATIONAL INCOME, POTENTIAL GROSS NATIONAL PRODUCT.

full line forcing, *n.* a type of RESTRICTIVE TRADE PRACTICE whereby a supplier requires a retailer to take all of the items making up a particular product line, thereby restricting the freedom of the retailer to select the product mix, including items from competing suppliers, which best suits his own requirements. See MONOPOLY POLICY, OFFICE OF FAIR TRADING.

functional distribution of income, *n.* the distribution of NATIONAL INCOME classified according to type of FACTOR INPUT: LABOUR, CAPITAL, etc. Here income is seen as a payment for the various factor inputs in contributing to the output of the economy. WAGES constitute the largest single element in factor payments, as Fig. 86 shows. See PERSONAL DISTRIBUTION OF INCOME.

	Percentage
Wages	72.7
Profits	19.8
Rent	7.5
	100.0

Fig. 86. **Functional distribution of income.** The functional distribution of national income for the UK, 1986. Source: *National Income and Expenditure* (Blue Book), CSO 1987.

functional notation, *n*. a mathematical shorthand for expressing a relationship between two or more VARIABLES. To express the causality of relationship between the DEPENDENT VARIABLE (on the left hand side of the equation) and the INDEPENDENT VARIABLE(s) (on the right hand side of the equation), the usual terminology says one is a function of the other. For example, economists would suggest that demand for a product (D) is a function (f) of the price of that product (P), i.e:

$$D = f(P)$$

fundamental disequilibrium, *n*. a situation under a FIXED-EXCHANGE-RATE SYSTEM (originally that operated by the INTERNATIONAL MONETARY FUND), where a country is in a position of *persistent* (long-run) BALANCE OF PAYMENTS deficit or surplus at a particular (fixed) exchange rate against other countries. The only practical course of action, given the inadequacy of internal measures such as DEFLATION and REFLATION to remedy the situation, is a DEVALUATION to a lower exchange rate value to eliminate a deficit, and a REVALUATION to a higher exchange rate value to eliminate a surplus. See BALANCE-OF-PAYMENTS EQUILIBRIUM, INTERNAL-EXTERNAL BALANCE MODEL.

funded debt, see FUNDING.

funding, *n*. the process by which a government or company converts its short-term, fixed-interest DEBTS into long-term, fixed-interest debts (*funded debts*). This involves persuading holders of short-term FIXED-INTEREST FINANCIAL SECURITIES to relinquish these in return for an equivalent amount of long-term, fixed-interest financial securities and this usually can only be done by offering a more attractive rate of interest on the latter.

Funding is undertaken by the monetary authorities as a means of reducing the liquidity of the banking system, and by companies as a means of improving their short-term liquidity. See FLOATING DEBT, PUBLIC SECTOR BORROWING REQUIREMENT.

futures market or **forward market** or **forward exchange market,** *n*. a MARKET for the purchase and sale of COMMODITIES (tea, rubber, etc.) and financial instruments (foreign currencies, stocks and shares) for delivery at some future point in time, as opposed to a SPOT MARKET which provides for immediate delivery. Forward positions are taken by traders dealing in a particular commodity or financial instrument whose price can fluctuate greatly over time, in order to minimize the uncertainty and risk surrounding their business dealings on a long-term basis.

Traders minimize uncertainty about future prices by buying and selling *futures*, i.e., contracts that promise to sell or buy a commodity or financial instrument at a specified future date at a price agreed upon now. Unlike the spot market, where commodities are traded in the physical sense, in the futures market it is only these contracts which are bought and sold. A dealer can enter into a contract agreeing to deliver a commodity at the agreed price (take a short position), or enter into a contract agreeing to accept the commodity and pay the agreed price on delivery (take a long position). Producers can contract to sell a commodity at a certain price at some time in the future in order to protect themselves against the risk of future adverse price changes. Buyers similarly can contract to buy a commodity at a certain price at some time in the future in order to protect themselves against the risk of future adverse price changes. Between the buyers and producers using futures as a hedge to minimize risk are dealers and SPECULATORS who buy and sell futures, hoping to earn windfall profits by taking the risk of future price changes.

Many futures contracts take the form of OPTIONS which are used to hedge against uncertainty about future prices. An option offers the right to sell or buy a commodity at an agreed price within some specified future time period and once the option has been purchased then it is exercisable at the discretion of the option holder.

G

gains from trade, *n.* the extra production and consumption benefits that countries can achieve through INTERNATIONAL TRADE. Countries trade with one another basically for the same reasons that individuals, firms and regions engaged in the exchange of goods and services – to obtain the benefits of SPECIALIZATION. By exchanging some of its own products for those of other nations, a country can enjoy a much wider range of commodities, and obtain them more cheaply than would otherwise be the case. International division of labour, with each country specializing in the production of only some of the commodities that it is capable of producing, enables total world output to be increased and raises countries' real standards of living.

A country's choice of which commodities to specialize in will be determined in large measure by the advantages it possesses over others in the production of these things. Such advantages can arise because the country can produce particular commodities more efficiently, at lower cost, than can others. The static, or 'pure' theory of international trade emphasizes that opportunities for mutually beneficial trade occur as the result of differences in comparative costs or COMPARATIVE ADVANTAGE. Countries will gain from trade if each country EXPORTS those commodities in which its costs of production are comparatively lower, and IMPORTS commodities in which its costs are comparatively higher.

This proposition is demonstrated in Fig. 87a on page 210 for a simple two country (A and B) and two product (X and Y) world economy. The same given resource input in both countries enables them to produce either the quantity of X or the quantity of Y. In the absence of trade between the two, X and Y exchange in country A is in the ratio 1X/1Y, and, in country B in the ratio 1X/3Y. These exchange ratios indicate the marginal OPPORTUNITY COST of one commodity in terms of the other. Thus, in country A the opportunity cost of producing one more unit of X is 1Y.

It can be seen that country B is absolutely more efficient than country A in the production of Y and just as efficient in the production of X.

Country	Commodity		Opportunity cost ratios		
	X	Y	X	:	Y
A	200	200	1	:	1
B	200	600	1	:	3

(a)

	Country B	Country A
Production	600Y	200X
Consumption with trade	400Y	200Y
	100X	100X
Consumption without trade	400Y	100Y
	66⅔X	100X

(b)

Fig. 87. **Gains from trade.** (a) The physical output of commodity X and commodity Y from a given factor input. (b) Production and consumption possibilities with and without trade (internal exchange rates are 1X/1Y in A, 1X/3Y in B, and the international exchange 1X/2Y).

However, it is *comparative advantage*, not ABSOLUTE ADVANTAGE, which determines whether trade is advantageous or not. Country B's comparative advantage is greatest in the production of commodity Y of which it can produce three times as much as country A. Alternatively, we can say that country B's relative efficiency is greatest in producing commodity Y because the resource or opportunity cost of producing an additional unit of Y is one-third of one unit of X in country B, but 1X in country A. Country A, by concentrating on the commodity it can produce with least relative inefficiency, has a comparative advantage in the production of X; i.e., the resource or opportunity cost of producing an additional unit of X in country A is only 1Y, while in country B it is 3Y. Thus, in terms of real factor costs commodity X can be produced more cheaply in country A, and commodity Y can be produced more cheaply in country B.

This combination of comparative advantages opens up the possibility of mutually beneficial trade. Domestically, in country A, 1X can be exchanged for 1Y, but abroad it can be exchanged for anything up to 3Y. Trade will be advantageous to it if it can obtain more than 1Y for 1X. Domestically, in country B, 1Y can be exchanged for one-third of 1X, but abroad it can be exchanged for anything up to 1X. It will be to B's advantage if it can obtain through trade more than one-third of X for 1Y.

The limits to mutually beneficial trade are set by the opportunity cost ratios. Within these limits, specialization and trade on the basis of comparative advantage will enable both countries to attain higher consumption levels. This possibility is indicated in Fig. 87b assuming the exchange ratio to be $1X = 2Y$. Using its entire resources, country B can produce 600Y, of which it consumes, say, 400 and exports 200. Country A can produce 200X, of which it consumes 100 and exports 100. With trade, the 200Y can be exchanged for 100X, enabling country B to consume 400Y and 100X, and country A to consume 200Y and 100X. Without trade, country B can transform (at an internal exchange ratio of $1X/3Y$) 200Y into only $66\frac{2}{3}X$, while country A can transform (at an internal exchange ratio of $1X/1Y$) 100X into only 100Y. Thus both countries gain by specialization and trade. How the gain is shared between countries A and B depends essentially upon the strength of demand in the two countries for the goods they import. If country A's demand for commodity Y increases, the trading ratio of 1X to 2Y would be likely to move against country A. Thus it might require $2\frac{1}{2}Y$ exports to obtain 1X imports, pushing country B nearer to the limit to mutually beneficial trade.

Obviously, in a more complex multicountry, multiproduct 'real' world situation it is less easy to be categorical about who gains from international trade and by how much. Some countries may possess a comparative advantage in a large number of products, others may possess few such advantages; countries differ in the quantity and quality of their factor endowments, and are at different stages of ECONOMIC DEVELOPMENT. DEVELOPING COUNTRIES, in particular, may find themselves at a disadvantage in international trade, especially those that are over-reliant on a narrow range of volatile commodity exports.

See THEORY OF INTERNATIONAL TRADE, TRADE INTEGRATION, TRADE CREATION.

Galbraith, John Kenneth (b.1908) Canadian professor of economics at Harvard University whose radical views about the workings of the market economy have been expressed in a series of books such as *The Affluent Society* (1958) and *The New Industrial State* (1967). Galbraith suggests that advanced industrial economies comprise a competitive sector of small owner-managed businesses and a monopoly sector of large industrial companies managed by salaried technocrats and he concentrates on the workings of the latter.

Galbraith argues that large companies plan their activities so as to minimize market uncertainty and that they seek through advertising to create demand for new products before manufacturing them: a REVISED SEQUENCE, compared with the conventional economic view that consumers express innate wants then see resources allocated to satisfying these wants. Nevertheless, Galbraith acknowledges that such large firms help to foster technical innovation and scale-economies which have yielded large gains in incomes. Furthermore he sees the growth of large companies leading to the growth of trade unions as a COUNTERVAILING POWER to secure a share of efficiency gains for workers. Consequently, Galbraith argues that large companies should not be broken up but controlled by government to prevent abuse of their monopoly power, with attempts to increase the countervailing power of consumers and small businesses.

Galbraith also attacked the American market economy for devoting too few resources to the public sector whilst allowing private sector activities to dominate, creating a situation of private affluence and public squalor.

game theory, *n.* a technique that uses logical deduction to explore the consequences of various strategies which might be adopted by competing game players. Game theory can be used in economics to represent the problems involved in formulating marketing strategy by small numbers of interdependent competitors.

An oligopolist (see OLIGOPOLY) needs to assess competitors' reactions to his own marketing policies to ensure that the 'payoff' from any particular marketing strategy may be estimated. For example, consider a struggle for market share between two firms (X and Y) where total market-size is fixed, so that every percentage increase in the market share of one firm is necessarily lost to the other (that is, a ZERO-SUM GAME situation). Suppose company X has two strategy choices available, a price reduction (P) or a new advertising campaign (A), and that company Y has the same two strategies available. Any pair of strategies open to the two firms would result in a particular division of the market between them: if firm X were to adopt strategy P, and firm Y were to adopt its strategy P, then firm X would gain 50% of the market leaving 50% for firm Y. This 50% market share is firm X's payoff and all such market share information can be summarized in the form of a *payoff matrix* as in Fig. 88.

Each firm must decide on its own best strategy, using the information in the table. If firm X adopts a cautious approach then it would assume that in response to its strategy P, firm Y would counter with strategy A, reducing firm X's payoff from its strategy P to its minimum value 40% (underlined). Similarly the fatalistic view of firm X's strategy A is that firm Y will counter with strategy P, reducing firm X's payoff from strategy A to its minimum value 55% (underlined). Following this pessimistic view firm X can make the best of the situation by aiming at the highest of these (underlined) minimum payoffs, in this case 55% yielded by strategy A (a *maximum strategy*).

Firm Y could employ a similar strategy, though for Y to assume the worst means that firm X receives a large market share so that firm Y, residually, receives very little. Thus, if firm Y employs its strategy P, its worst possible payoff is 45% of the market (55% going to firm X) and this is marked by circling 55% on the matrix. If firm Y were to employ its strategy A, its worst possible payoff would be 40% of the market (60% going to firm X) and this 60% is similarly marked by a circle. The best of these pessimistic payoffs for firm Y is the smallest of these circled figures, in this case 55% of the market going to firm X (a *minimax strategy*).

The outcome of this situation is that firm X will choose its strategy A and firm Y its strategy P and neither would be inclined to alter its choice of strategy.

Firm Y's strategy

		P	A
Firm X's strategy	P	50	40
	A	⊙55	⊙60

Fig. 88. **Game theory**. The payoff matrix between firm X and firm Y.

GATT, see GENERAL AGREEMENT ON TARIFFS AND TRADE.

GDP, see GROSS DOMESTIC PRODUCT.

gearing, see CAPITAL GEARING.

General Agreement on Tariffs and Trade (GATT), *n.* a multinational institution set up in 1947 to promote the expansion of INTERNATIONAL TRADE through a coordinated programme of trade liberalization. A major part of GATT's work has centred on the negotiation of multilateral TARIFF reductions and the elimination of QUOTAS and other nontariff barriers to trade. GATT has supervised ten conferences on tariff reductions, including the 'Kennedy Round' of 1962–67 which secured an average cut in tariff rates of 35%, and more recently the 'Tokyo Round' of 1973–79, which 'committed' the main industrial countries to cut tariff rates by a further one-third over an eight-year period commencing in 1980.

These GATT initiatives, together with the operations of the INTERNATIONAL MONETARY FUND and sustained economic growth in the developed countries combined to bring about a record expansion of world trade down to the end of the 1960s. Since the onset of recessionary conditions in 1973, however, much of the work of GATT has been undermined by the resurgence of PROTECTIONISM. The 'new protectionism', as it is commonly referred to, is based not on tariffs but on devices which are much less visible and hence more difficult to detect and control, for example, EXPORT RESTRAINT AGREEMENTS, import licencing procedures, local-content requirements, SUBSIDIZATION of domestic industries, etc. See GAINS FROM TRADE, MOST–FAVOURED–NATION CLAUSE, MULTI–FIBRE ARRANGEMENT.

Fig. 89. **General equilibrium analysis.** An increase in the price of oil is likely to increase the cost structures of many other industrial sectors, and hence serve to raise the general price level and related wage rates. This increase in prices and wages, in turn, increases input costs to the oil industry.

general equilibrium analysis, *n.* the analysis of the interrelationships that exist between subsectors of an ECONOMY. General equilibrium analysis proceeds on the basis that events in one sector can have such a significant impact on other sectors that feed-back effects, in turn, are likely to affect the functioning of the first. See Fig. 89.

Thus, in general equilibrium analysis, an attempt is made to determine the nature and strength of intersectoral linkages using, for example, INPUT–OUTPUT analysis. See PARTIAL EQUILIBRIUM ANALYSIS.

geometrical progression, *n.* a series of discrete values showing a growth pattern of the form:

$$a + ar + ar^2 + ar^3, \text{ etc.}$$

where *a* is the original amount at the start and *r* is the amount added each time. Such a progression would show an accelerating growth trend over time. Geometrical progressions can be used to analyse many problems in economics such as COMPOUND INTEREST on loans, where *a* is the principal and *r* the interest rate, investment appraisal and the MULTIPLIER. Compare ARITHMETICAL PROGRESSION.

Giffen good, *n.* a GOOD for which quantity demanded increases as its PRICE increases, rather than falls, as predicted by the general theory of DEMAND. It only applies in the highly exceptional case of a good (see INFERIOR PRODUCT) which accounts for such a high proportion of households' budgets that an increase in price produces a large negative INCOME EFFECT which completely overcomes the normal SUBSTITUTION EFFECT. See PRICE EFFECT, UPWARD–SLOPING DEMAND CURVE.

gilt–edged security or **government bond,** *n.* a financial security (see BOND) issued by the government as a means of borrowing money. The term 'gilt-edged' denotes the fact that such securities are a very safe ASSET for people to hold in so far as governments are usually able to honour their debts. In addition, the monetary authorities use gilt-edged securities as a means of regulating the MONEY SUPPLY. See OPEN MARKET OPERATION.

Gini coefficient, *n.* see CONCENTRATION MEASURES.

GNP, *n.* see GROSS NATIONAL PRODUCT.

GNP deflator, *n.* a PRICE INDEX that is used as a means of adjusting money GROSS NATIONAL PRODUCT values to obtain *real* GNP values (see REAL VALUES). Real GNP is important because this represents output of physical goods and services not their money values. An economy may appear to produce more goods and services (ECONOMIC GROWTH) because money GNP has increased, but this may simply reflect price increases (INFLATION) without any increase in physical output. The GNP deflator is thus designed to remove the influence of price changes and record only real changes.

gold, *n.* a monetary ASSET that is held by countries as part of their INTERNATIONAL RESERVES and used to finance BALANCE OF PAYMENTS deficits.

Formerly, many countries operated a GOLD STANDARD system under which gold was used as the basis of a country's domestic MONEY

SUPPLY, as well as being used to finance payments deficits. Gradually, however, the 'pure' gold standard gave way to domestic monetary systems based on paper money and other metallic coins and, internationally, the gold–exchange standard in which foreign currencies such as sterling and the American dollar were used alongside gold as reserve assets.

In 1935 the price of gold was 'fixed' at $35 per fine ounce by America, Britain and France as part of a monetary pact between the three countries. This price was then 'officially' adopted by member countries of the INTERNATIONAL MONETARY FUND on its formation in 1947; gold was used as the numeraire of the Fund's fixed exchange rate system in setting par values for members' currencies, and members were required to pay one quarter of their 'quota' subscriptions to the Fund in gold. Gold continued to serve as the linchpin of the IMF system, and its 'official' price remained pegged at $35 per ounce, down to 1971, when the Fund's fixed exchange-rate system gave way to floating exchange rates. Countries had, however, found it increasingly difficult to hold the price of gold at the $35 per ounce level as world demand for gold as an industrial metal and for ornamental purposes continued to expand. In 1961 a 'gold pool' was set up to regulate dealings in the metal, but in 1968 Fund members bowed to the inevitable and a 'two-tier' price structure was established: gold continued to be priced at $35 per ounce for 'official' transactions between countries' central banks and the Fund, while the 'free' market price of gold was left to be determined by market forces.

In 1972, gold was dropped as the numeraire of the Fund and replaced by the SPECIAL DRAWING RIGHT unit; the Fund's existing gold holdings were sold off and members were required to subscribe their quotas in a nongold form.

Outside the Fund, however, gold has continued to hold on to its status as the single most important component of international reserves. The attractiveness of gold as a reserve asset is underpinned by the fact that unlike national paper currencies (which are intrinsically worthless) it has a value in exchange as a commodity related to its use as an industrial base metal and for ornamental purposes. Gold holdings, however, suffer from the disadvantage that compared with other assets such as STOCKS and SHARES they yield no interest return.

golden handshake, *n.* a generous severance payment made to a director or worker of a company who is dismissed prior to the expiry of his service contract.

golden hello, *n.* a large lump-sum payment made to a new director or worker of a company to attract him to join that company.

golden parachute, see TAKEOVER BID.

gold-exchange standard, *n.* a modified version of the 'pure' GOLD STANDARD in which CURRENCIES such as the US DOLLAR are used by countries in addition to GOLD to settle BALANCE OF PAYMENTS deficits. See INTERNATIONAL RESERVES.

gold standard, *n.* an INTERNATIONAL MONETARY SYSTEM in which GOLD forms the basis of countries' domestic MONEY SUPPLY and is used to finance INTERNATIONAL TRADE and BALANCE OF PAYMENTS deficits.

Under the gold standard EXCHANGE RATES were rigidly fixed in terms of gold. (The gold standard was widely adopted in the 19th century and operated down to the early 1930s). In theory, the gold standard provided an 'automatic' ADJUSTMENT MECHANISM for eliminating payments imbalances between countries: deficits were financed by outward gold transfers which reduced the domestic MONEY SUPPLY. This in turn deflated (see DEFLATION) the domestic price level, making IMPORTS relatively more expensive and EXPORTS relatively cheaper, thereby reducing the volume of imports and increasing the volume of exports. Surpluses were financed by inward gold transfers which increased the domestic money supply. This in turn inflated (see INFLATION) the domestic price level making imports relatively cheaper and exports relatively more expensive, resulting in a fall in the volume of exports and an increase in the volume of imports. In this way both deficits and surpluses were removed and BALANCE-OF PAYMENTS EQUILIBRIUM restored. In practice, however, countries found that a combination of rigidly fixed exchange rates and the complete subordination of domestic economic policy to the external situation was too onerous and opted for more flexible arrangements.

See FIXED EXCHANGE RATE SYSTEM, INTERNATIONAL MONETARY FUND.

goodness of fit, see REGRESSION ANALYSIS.

goods or **commodities,** *n.* any tangible economic products (cars, soap powders, tools, machines, etc.) that contribute directly (see FINAL PRODUCTS) or indirectly (see INTERMEDIATE PRODUCTS) to the satisfaction of human wants. CONSUMER GOODS and PRODUCERS' GOODS are an important component of GROSS NATIONAL PRODUCT.

goodwill, *n.* the difference at a particular point in time between the market valuation of a FIRM and the sum of its (net) ASSETS recorded in a BALANCE SHEET. If another firm wishes to acquire this firm, goodwill represents the premium which the buyer must be prepared to pay for the firm, over and above its asset value, because of the firm's trade contacts, reputation, management expertise and general 'know-how'. Where a firm has a poor trading record its market value as a going concern to a potential buyer may be less than the BALANCE SHEET value of its assets, in which case goodwill is negative.

government bonds, see GILT-EDGED SECURITY.

government broker, *n.* the firm formerly appointed by the government to handle issues of government securities. In 1986 the Bank of England itself undertook the sale of such securities through a network of 'approved' dealing firms.

See CAPITAL MARKET, STOCK EXCHANGE.

government debt, see NATIONAL DEBT.

government (public) expenditure, *n.* the current spending and INVESTMENT by central government and local authorities on the provision of SOCIAL GOODS and services (health, education, defence, roads, etc.), marketed goods and services (water, electricity etc.) and TRANSFER PAYMENTS (unemployment benefit, state pensions, etc.). In the CIRCULAR FLOW OF INCOME MODEL, transfer payments are excluded from government spending because these are not made in return for productive services (that is, add to total output) but merely transfer taxation receipts from one household to another.

Government expenditure is financed by TAXATION and by borrowing (see PUBLIC SECTOR BORROWING REQUIREMENT).

Government expenditure is an important component of AGGREGATE DEMAND in the circular flow of income/expenditure, and is used as an instrument of FISCAL POLICY in regulating the level of spending in the economy. However, short-term changes in government expenditure may be difficult to achieve because of administrative and political difficulties, especially where cuts in expenditure are being made with a view to contracting aggregate demand. For example, short-term cuts can be difficult to achieve in health, education, etc. expenditures, given the labour-intensive nature of these activities, without heavy redundancies and disruption of public services; whilst cuts in transfer payments to poorer members of the community are politically unpopular. Furthermore, where the brunt of changes fall upon public investment expenditures this can severely disrupt long-term investment projects, while cuts serve to deplete the social infrastructure. In addition, where government expenditure includes spending on goods and services bought in from businesses, changes can have dramatic effects on the prosperity of the private sector.

See SOCIAL PRODUCTS, BUDGET (GOVERNMENT), COLLECTIVE PRODUCTS.

government sector, see PUBLIC SECTOR.

graph, *n*. a means of portraying data in pictorial form that shows the relationship between an INDEPENDENT VARIABLE and a DEPENDENT VARIABLE by labelling and scaling the two axis of the graph (see AXIS) to represent the two variables, plotting joint values of the two in the space between the axes, and joining these values with a line. Frequently graphs show time as the independent variable, depicting by means of a line how the dependent variable has changed over time.

greenfield venture, *n*. a company which starts up from scratch, or, in the case of an established MULTINATIONAL FIRM, enters a foreign market by building a new factory as opposed to taking over or merging with an established firm. See TAKEOVER, MERGER.

greenmail, see TAKEOVER BID.

green money, *n*. see MONETARY COMPENSATION AMOUNTS.

Gresham's law, *n*. the economic hypothesis that 'bad' MONEY forces 'good' money out of circulation. The principle applies only to precious metal coinage where people are tempted to hoard the coins for the commodity value of their metal content rather than leaving them to circulate as currency.

gross domestic–fixed-capital formation, *n*. the total spending on FIXED INVESTMENT (plant, equipment, etc.) in an economy over a one-year period. Gross domestic–fixed-capital formation is one component of GROSS NATIONAL PRODUCT. However, because of CAPITAL CONSUMPTION (fixed capital lost due to wear and tear) *net domestic-fixed-capital formation* may be considerably less than gross investment. In this case the net addition to the CAPITAL STOCK would be much smaller than the total figure unadjusted for capital DEPRECIATION. See NET NATIONAL PRODUCT.

gross domestic product (GDP), *n*. the total money value of all final GOODS and SERVICES produced in an economy over a one-year period. Gross domestic product can be measured in three ways:

(a) the sum of the value added by each industry in producing the year's output (the output method).

(b) the sum of factor incomes received from producing the year's output (the income method).

(c) the sum of expenditures on the year's domestic output of goods and services (the expenditure method).

See NATIONAL INCOME ACCOUNTS.

gross national product, *n*. the total money value of all final goods and services produced in an economy over a one-year period (GROSS

DOMESTIC PRODUCT) plus net property income from abroad. See ACTUAL GROSS NATIONAL PRODUCT, NATIONAL INCOME ACCOUNTS.

gross profit, *n.* the difference between SALES REVENUE and the COST OF GOODS SOLD. Gross profit less the operating expenses of the business equals NET PROFIT.

growth, see ECONOMIC GROWTH.

H

hard currency, *n.* a foreign CURRENCY that is in strong demand, but in short supply on the foreign exchange market. Hard-currency status is usually associated with an economically-strong country which is running a large surplus on its balance of payments; demand for the currency is high to finance purchases of its exports, but the supply of the currency is relatively limited because the amount of it being made available for the purchase of imports is much lower. However, under a FLOATING-EXCHANGE-RATE SYSTEM, the demand for, and supply of, the currency should be, in theory, brought into balance by an APPRECIATION of its EXCHANGE RATE value. Compare SOFT CURRENCY.

Harrod economic-growth model, *n.* a theoretical construct that examines the growth path of the economy. Specifically, the model is concerned with the rate at which NATIONAL INCOME (Y) must grow in order to satisfy the Keynesian EQUILIBRIUM NATIONAL INCOME condition:

$$\text{saving } (S_t) = \text{investment } (I_t) \tag{1}$$

where t denotes a time period.

In the model, S_t depends on national income:

$$S_t = sY_t \tag{2}$$

i.e., saving in each period depends on the income of the same period; s represents the AVERAGE PROPENSITY TO SAVE and MARGINAL PROPENSITY TO SAVE.

I_t depends on the *rate of change of income* from one period to the next, notationally Y_t (income in current time period), Y_{t-1} (income in previous time period), i.e:

$$I_t = \propto (Y_t - Y_{t-1}) \tag{3}$$

i.e., investment is INDUCED INVESTMENT with the symbol '$\propto$' representing the ACCELERATOR.

Given this assumed saving and investment behaviour, what will the equilibrium condition represented in equation (1) require? By substituting equations (2) and (3) into equation (1) we obtain:

$$sY_t = \propto (Y_t - Y_{t-1}) \qquad (4)$$

and by dividing both sides of equation (4) by $\propto Y_t$ we obtain:

$$\frac{s}{\propto} = (Y_t - Y_{t-1})Y_t. \qquad (5)$$

If $(Y_t - Y_{t-1})$ is written as ΔY_t, then:

$$\frac{\Delta Y_t}{Y_t} = \frac{s}{\propto} \qquad (6)$$

The left-hand expression is the percentage change in income; the right-hand side is the ratio of the marginal propensity to save to the accelerator. Since this is deduced from the condition for maintaining equilibrium in each time period, Harrod called the rate of change in income the 'warranted' rate of growth.

If the 'actual' rate of growth exceeds (or is lower than) the warranted rate, income will be raised more (or lowered more) than is appropriate for maintaining equilibrium, causing a cumulative deviation from the equilibrium path.

Equation (6) determines the warranted rate of growth. The actual rate of growth is determined in the model, by the rate of growth of the LABOUR FORCE and the rate of growth of labour PRODUCTIVITY. Suppose that the labour force is growing at the rate of 1% per year and labour productivity at the rate of 2% per year; the actual (or the 'natural' rate of growth, as Harrod called it) attainable rate of growth of national income and output is thus 3% per year.

If the natural rate of growth exceeds the warranted rate of growth then equation (5) indicates that the economy will experience a cumulative deviation from the warranted rate, income growing at an excessive rate and causing secular expansion. By contrast, if the natural rate falls below that of the warranted rate, then there will be SECULAR STAGNATION.

See DOMAR ECONOMIC GROWTH MODEL, SOLOW ECONOMIC GROWTH MODEL.

Heckscher-Ohlin factor proportions theory, *n.* an explanation of COMPARATIVE ADVANTAGE in INTERNATIONAL TRADE which is based on differences in factor endowments between countries.

Consider a situation in which two countries (A and B) produce two goods (X and Y). Country A, let us assume, possesses an abundance of labour but a scarcity of capital; by contrast, country B possesses an abundance of capital but a shortage of labour. Thus, the cost of labour is low relative to capital in country A, whereas the cost of capital is low relative to labour in country B. The production of good X, let us assume, is capital-intensive; while the production of good Y is labour-intensive.

Given these differences in labour and capital intensities the following hypothesis about the structure of trade suggests itself: Country A has a comparative advantage in the production of good Y because this uses much of its relatively cheap factor (labour). It will specialize in the production of good Y, exporting Y in exchange for imports of X, the good in which it has a comparative disadvantage.

Country B has a comparative advantage in the production of good X because this uses much of its relatively cheap factor (capital). It will specialize in the production of good X, exporting X in exchange for imports of Y, the good in which it has a comparative disadvantage.

The Heckscher-Ohlin theory presents a *static* supply-orientated interpretation of international trade which assumes that production functions are the same in all countries. The theory takes no account of the influence of dynamic technological change on comparative advantage; nor does it consider the effect of DEMAND and PRODUCT DIFFERENTIATION on the pattern of international trade flows.

See GAINS FROM TRADE, THEORY OF INTERNATIONAL TRADE.

hedging, *n.* the process of reducing uncertainty about future market prices by effectively covering a bet by making an offsetting bet. For example, in order to reduce its exposure to losses from exchange-rate movements, a British firm investing overseas may match the investment in a country with an equivalent amount of loans raised locally in that country. Then if an adverse exchange-rate movement reduces the £ sterling value of its overseas assets it will simultaneously reduce the £ sterling value of its liabilities. OPTIONS are frequently used as an instrument for hedging. See FUTURES MARKET.

Herfindahl index, *n.* a measure of the degree of SELLER CONCENTRATION in a MARKET that takes into account the total number of firms in the market and their *relative* size distribution (share of total market output). See Fig. 90 on page 224.

heteroscedasticity, *n.* a statistical situation where there is a particular pattern in the residual or error terms after an estimated regression equation has been calculated from sample observations of INDEPENDENT VARIABLES and DEPENDENT VARIABLES. If the estimated regression

	Leading firm's share of market output (%)	5-firm concentration ratio (%)	Market share % per firm of remaining firms	Herfindahl index (H)
Firms	1 2 3 4 5			
Market A	12 12 12 12 12	60	5 8	0.104
Market B	40 5 5 5 5	60	8 5	0.190

Fig. 90. **Herfindahl index**. The Herfindahl index (H) is the sum of the squared firm sizes, all measured as a proportion of total market size. In the Fig., for market A, $H = (0.12)^2 \times 5 + (0.08)^2 \times 5 = 0.104$. If all firms in the market are the same size, then the value of the index is equal to the reciprocal of the number of firms; thus, if there are 10 firms all of the same size, $H = 0.1$. The upper limit of the index is 1, which occurs when there is a monopoly. The fig. shows that market B ($H = 0.190$), with a single dominant firm, is almost twice as concentrated as market A despite the latter having fewer firms. See CONCENTRATION MEASURES.

coefficients are good, unbiased estimates of the true population coefficients of the independent variables, then the residual values should be randomly distributed and have a constant VARIANCE. If they are not then the estimated equation is an inaccurate fit or has missed out other important independent variables which are affecting the dependent variable. Heteroscedastistic error terms occur where the variance of the error term is not constant but grows or declines as the independent variable increases. Compare HOMOSCEDASTICITY. See also REGRESSION ANALYSIS.

hidden price reduction, *n.* an increase in the amount or quality of a product offered at an unchanged PRICE, e.g., an increase in the weight of crisps per packet sold at the same price as before. Compare HIDDEN PRICE RISE.

hidden price rise, *n.* a reduction in the quality or amount of a product offered at an unchanged PRICE, e.g., a reduction in the weight of a bar of chocolate sold at the same price as before. Compare HIDDEN PRICE REDUCTION.

hidden reserve, *n.* the undervaluation of the ASSETS, or overvaluation of the LIABILITIES of a firm in its BALANCE SHEET. For example, the value of a firm's land and buildings may be shown in the balance sheet at HISTORIC COST or original cost, whereas the current market price of those assets may be considerably higher. Thus, if the assets were to be revalued to reflect current market values the difference would be formally recorded in the balance sheet as an addition to capital reserves. See INFLATION ACCOUNTING.

hidden tax, *n.* an INDIRECT TAX that is incorporated into the PRICE of a good or service, but the consumer is not made fully aware of its existence or magnitude; for example, the amount of EXCISE DUTY included in the price of cigarettes and beer is not normally made known to the consumer. VALUE-ADDED TAX, by contrast, is incorporated into the price of a product at specified rates.

hidden unemployment, *n.* a situation in which although people are technically in employment, their PRODUCTIVITY is negligible or zero. This can occur when powerful trade unions are able to operate restrictive labour practices such as OVERMANNING, or where governments employ vast bureaucracies of civil servants.

hire purchase, *n.* a contractual means of purchasing a product on an instalment basis. An initial down-payment is usually required followed by monthly fixed payments (including INTEREST charges) for a specified period. In some countries hire purchase is used as an instrument of MONETARY POLICY, with the monetary authorities specifying minimum down-payments and maximum repayment periods as a means of controlling the level of AGGREGATE DEMAND. See CREDIT, CREDIT CONTROL.

histogram or **bar chart,** *n.* a graphical presentation of a FREQUENCY DISTRIBUTION in which the (absolute and relative) size of each category in a total is portrayed by means of the height of the 'bar' or block representing that category. See Fig. 91 on page 226.

historic cost, *n.* the original cost of purchasing an ASSET (such as an item of machinery). For accountancy purposes, the asset is entered in a firm's BALANCE SHEET at historic cost. However, allowance has to be made for the REPLACEMENT COST of the asset which, because of INFLATION, may well be considerably greater than the original price paid. Thus, DEPRECIATION provisions may be inadequate in a period of rapidly rising prices. See INFLATION ACCOUNTING.

hoarding, *n.* the nonproductive retention of MONEY or PRODUCTS. A certain amount of money is held in currency form to finance day-to-day transactions but this is turned-over on a regular basis. Hoarding involves a deliberate abstention from current spending and investing, and may occur because of an increase in LIQUIDITY PREFERENCE. Hoarding often occurs in less-developed countries where people are unfamiliar with, or suspicious of, using the banking system as a savings repository.

Fig. 91. **Histogram**. The classes (here weekly income groups) are depicted on the horizontal axis, and the class frequencies on the vertical axis. The frequencies associated with the various classes are represented by the areas of the rectangles. For example, the area of the largest rectangle comprises 40% of the total area of the histogram, suggesting that 40% of all workers have an income of £100 or less.

holding company, *n.* a company that controls another company or companies. Ownership may be complete (100%) or partial (ownership of 51% + of the voting shares in the company). Such ownership confers powers to control the policies of subsidiary companies. The holding company will report the accounting results of these subsidiary companies as part of the accounting results for the group of companies.

Holding companies are most frequently used as a means of achieving diversified or conglomerate growth, with the firm operating separate companies in different lines of production activity, but with each company subject to varying degrees of centralized control by the 'parent company'.

See DIVERSIFICATION, CONSOLIDATED ACCOUNTS.

homogeneous products, *n.* any identical goods offered in a market by competing suppliers. Given complete knowledge, buyers will regard the products as perfect substitutes for one another and will have no 'preference' for the products of particular suppliers. Homogeneity results in all suppliers having no ability to charge other than a common price for their products. See PERFECT COMPETITION, PRODUCT DIFFERENTIATION.

homoscedasticity, *n.* a statistical situation where there is no particular pattern in the residual or error terms after an estimated regression equation has been calculated from sample observations of INDEPENDENT VARIABLES and DEPENDENT VARIABLES. Homoscedastic residuals suggest that the estimated regression coefficients are good unbiased estimates of the true population coefficients of the independent variables. Compare HETEROSCEDASTICITY. See REGRESSION ANALYSIS.

horizontal firm, *n.* see FIRM.

horizontal integration, *n.* **1.** the tendency for firms to SPECIALIZE at a particular level in the production and distribution of a product rather than engage in a number of successive stages (VERTICAL INTEGRATION). Also called *lateral integration*. **2.** the MERGER of firms making the same product. From the firm's point of view, expansion through horizontal integration may be advantageous because it enables the firm to reduce its production and distribution costs by securing ECONOMIES OF SCALE, or because it removes or reduces competitive pressures and increases the firm's control over the market.

In terms of its wider impact on the operation of market processes, horizontal integration may, on the one hand, promote greater efficiency in resource use, and reduce market supply costs and prices, or, on the other hand, by reducing competition and increasing the level of SELLER CONCENTRATION in the market, it may result in a less efficient allocation of resources and the danger of monopolistic exploitation.

Thus, horizontal integration may produce, simultaneously, both beneficial and detrimental effects. Under UK MONOPOLY POLICY, horizontal integration by an established monopoly firm, or a proposed merger (TAKEOVER) between two competing firms involving a market share in the product concerned of over 25%, can be referred to the MONOPOLIES AND MERGERS COMMISSION to determine whether or not it operates against the public interest.

See MONOPOLY, OLIGOPOLY, OFFICE OF FAIR TRADING, DIVERSIFICATION.

hot money, *n.* short-term and volatile CAPITAL MOVEMENTS between countries which take place primarily in response to interest rate differentials between financial centres (ARBITRAGE), or in anticipation of likely DEVALUATIONS or DEPRECIATIONS and REVALUATIONS or APPRECIATIONS of foreign currencies (SPECULATION). Speculative hot money flows are especially disruptive to the conduct of 'orderly' exchange rate management and the maintenance of balance-of-payments equilibrium, and are thus frequently subjected to EXCHANGE CONTROL regulation by the authorities. See CAPITAL INFLOW, CAPITAL OUTFLOW.

households, *n.* a group of individuals whose economic decision-making is interrelated. In economic theory households perform two roles. On the one hand, they enter the market place as buyers or CONSUMERS of goods and services produced by firms; on the other hand, they provide FACTOR INPUTS to firms in order to produce those goods and services. The term 'households' is used primarily in macro- (national income) analysis, while the term 'consumers' is used in micro- (supply and demand) analysis. See CIRCULAR FLOW OF NATIONAL INCOME MODEL, PERSONAL SECTOR.

human capital, *n.* the body of human knowledge that contributes 'know how' to productive activity. The knowledge base of a nation is added to by research and disseminated by teaching through general education and vocational training. INVESTMENT in human capital results in new, technically improved, products and production processes which improve ECONOMIC EFFICIENCY, and it can be as significant as physical CAPITAL in promoting ECONOMIC GROWTH. See ECONOMIC DEVELOPMENT.

hyperinflation, *n.* a situation of chronic or runaway rates of INFLATION. Unlike CREEPING INFLATION, which usually has little ill-effect on the functioning of the economy, hyperinflation reflects a situation where people begin to lose confidence in the value of MONEY and revert to BARTER. At this point there is a serious danger of economic collapse accompanied by growing social disorder. Hyperinflation is a rare phenomenon, but when it does occur its causes are as much political as economic; for example, the excessive printing of money to finance government spending (wars, in particular), or an acute shortage of goods and services combined with a large pent-up demand, as in periods immediately following the ending of a war.

hypermarket, see SUPERMARKET.

hypothesis, *n.* a prediction derived from theoretical analysis that is couched in a form precise enough to be subjected to testing against empirical data. In economics, hypotheses are generated by a process of logical deduction from sets of initial assumptions about the behaviour of consumers, producers, etc., and are generally tested by collecting economic data and using statistical techniques to analyse them. This testing can lead to modification of the economic theory in the light of the new economic data; or to abandonment of that theory in favour of an alternative theory which better explains the facts. See HYPOTHESIS TESTING.

hypothesis testing, *n.* the development and use of statistical criteria to aid in taking decisions about the validity of a HYPOTHESIS in uncertain conditions. In any decision about the validity of a hypothesis, there is a chance of making a correct choice and a risk of making a wrong choice. Hypothesis testing is concerned with evaluating these chances and providing criteria that minimize the likelihood of making wrong decisions.

For example, suppose we wanted to decide whether or not company size determines management remuneration, and formulated the hypothesis that average management remuneration is larger in bigger firms. This hypothesis can be either true or false and will be either accepted or rejected; these options are shown in the matrix below:

	Hypothesis is true	*Hypothesis is false*
Accept Hypothesis	correct decision	error (type 2)
Reject Hypothesis	error (type 1)	correct decision

If the hypothesis is true and we accept it, and if the hypothesis is false and we reject it, our decision will be correct. On the other hand, we could reject the hypothesis when it should be accepted (a *type 1 error*), or we could accept a hypothesis which should be rejected (a *type 2 error*). The risk of making such errors in testing a hypothesis using available sample data can be minimized. To avoid the risk of making a type 2 error, and to establish clear probabilities for the risk of committing a type 1 error, careful formulation of the hypothesis is necessary. Often this involves formulating a *null hypothesis* which assumes the exact opposite of what we want to prove. For example, in place of the earlier hypothesis that average management remuneration is larger in bigger firms, we would formulate the null hypothesis that average management remuneration is the same in large and small companies. Rejection of this null hypothesis is equivalent to acceptance of the original hypothesis. This null hypothesis can then be tested against sample data.

If repeated samples were taken from the population of firms then this sampling distribution can be approximated by a NORMAL DISTRIBUTION which in turn can be used to assess the PROBABILITY of making a type 1 error. This probability of making a type 1 error is called the *level of significance* at which a test of the significance of the null hypothesis will be conducted (customarily 0.01, 0.05 or 0.10). This level of significance is always specified before any test is made. For large samples, the level of significance established will be determined by the probability distribution of the normal distribution; for small samples the level of significance will be based on the T-DISTRIBUTION.

The final step involves the test of significance: average management remuneration is calculated from sample data for small and large firms and compared with expected management remuneration which, according to our null hypothesis, should be the same in both small and big companies. If the difference between what we expect to find (average remuneration the same), and what we get, is so large that it cannot reasonably be attributed to chance, we reject the null hypothesis on which our expectation is based. On the other hand, if the difference between what we expect (average remuneration the same), and what we get, is so small that it reasonably may be attributed to chance, the results are not statistically significant. In the former case we would reject the null hypothesis and accept its mirror image, namely that management remuneration is larger in bigger firms. In the latter case we would reserve judgement on the issue of company size and management remuneration since no clear link is either proved or disproved.

The statistical techniques of hypothesis testing are widely employed in empirical economic research.

I

identification problem, *n*. a particular problem of applying REGRESSION ANALYSIS where it is difficult to identify the precise relationships between VARIABLES because all the variables change simultaneously. For example, the SCATTER DIAGRAMS in Fig. 92 show observations of the prices of a product and the quantities sold. Where the pattern of observations looks like those in Fig. 92a, and we have reason to believe that supply conditions have changed dramatically because of the effect of weather (foodstuffs) or technology, while demand conditions have been relatively stable, then it seems reasonable to assume that the data represents a demand curve (D_2) with changing supply conditions (S_1, S_2, S_3), so that any regression line fitted can be identified as a demand curve. Where the pattern of observations looks like those in Fig. 92b, and we have reason to believe that demand conditions have changed

Fig. 92. **Identification problem.** See main entry.

dramatically because of changes in disposable income or tastes, while supply conditions have been relatively stable, then it seems reasonable to assume that the data represents a supply curve (S_2) with changing demand conditions (D_1, D_2, D_3), so that any regression line fitted can be identified as a supply curve. However, where the pattern of observations looks like those in Fig. 92c, and both supply and demand conditions have been fluctuating dramatically, then it is difficult to identify any clear-cut pattern in the data, for changes in prices and quantities could have been caused by both supply and demand changes.

identity, *n.* a means of portraying arithmetically the enduring equality between two (or more) VARIABLES which are equal by definition. For example, £1 = 100p (or \$1 = 100c), and no matter how many pounds (or dollars) we have, they can always be converted into pennies (or cents) by multiplying by one hundred. Identities are generally given a three-bar 'identity' sign ($\equiv$) to indicate that the value to the left of the three bars is identical to the value to the right of the sign. The QUANTITY THEORY OF MONEY is one of the best known examples of an identity in economics, written as

$$M.V \equiv P.T$$

where M is the money stock, V is the velocity of circulation of money, P is the general price level, and T is the number of transactions undertaken. See EQUATION.

illegal activities, *n.* any activities which because they are prohibited by law are excluded from a country's NATIONAL INCOME ACCOUNTS. Drug smuggling, for example, is illegal and therefore not included as part of legitimate economic activity.

See BLACK ECONOMY, BLACK MARKET.

IMF, see INTERNATIONAL MONETARY FUND.

immiserizing growth, *n.* a situation in which a DEVELOPING COUNTRY's attempt to increase its growth potential through EXPORTS actually results in a retardation of that potential. This is very much an exceptional situation confined only in *theory* to a country whose export speciality (some mineral or agricultural crop) accounts for a preponderant share of world trade in the product. The country needs to export more to earn the foreign exchange to finance the capital imports which it requires to underpin domestic growth. If all its export effort is concentrated on its speciality, this could lead to an 'oversupply' of product resulting in a deterioration of the country's TERMS OF TRADE. As a result the country's foreign exchange earnings will now buy fewer imports and domestic growth potential will be impaired. See ECONOMIC DEVELOPMENT.

imperfect competition, see MONOPOLISTIC COMPETITION.

imperfect market, see MONOPOLISTIC COMPETITION.

implicit cost or **imputed cost,** *n.* the OPPORTUNITY COST to a FIRM of using resources owned by the firm itself to produce its output. For example, if a firm occupies a building that it owns, it foregoes the opportunity of renting it out for some other alternative use. Thus, implicit costs represent the sacrifice of income that could have been earned by renting out (or selling) the firm's resources to others.

To achieve an accurate measure of the total cost of producing goods or services the firm must *impute* a rent to itself based upon the current market rates for renting the property.

See PROFIT, EXPLICIT COST, SHADOW PRICE.

import deposit, *n.* the requirement that importers of a product (see IMPORTS) pay to the government a specified sum of money (calculated as a percentage of the value of the product) on arrival of the product in the domestic market prior to its eventual sale. Import deposits can be employed primarily as a means of assisting in the removal of a BALANCE-OF-PAYMENTS deficit. See BALANCE-OF-PAYMENTS EQUILIBRIUM, IMPORT RESTRICTIONS.

import duty, *n.* a TAX levied by the government on imported products (see IMPORTS). Import duties are used to raise revenue for the government and as a means of protecting domestic industries from foreign competition. See TARIFF, IMPORT RESTRICTIONS, PROTECTIONISM.

import levy, see TARIFF.

Percentage of domestic consumption	
1955	7
1965	9
1975	16
1987	34

Fig. 93. **Import penetration**. The UK import penetration ratio for manufactured goods. Source: *NIESR*, 1978; *Business Monitor*, 1987.

import penetration, *n.* an increase in the proportion of domestic CONSUMPTION accounted for by IMPORTS. In particular cases the displacement of domestic supply by imports may be beneficial in so far as it reflects COMPARATIVE ADVANTAGE (imports cheaper than domestic goods). Widespread import penetration across the economy, however, not matched by an equivalent amount of EXPORTS can result in balance-of-payments difficulties and a fall in domestic income and output levels.

In the case of the UK, import penetration in the manufacturing sector has increased markedly in the period since 1955 as Fig. 93 shows.

import quota, see QUOTA.

import restrictions or **trade barriers,** *n.* the limitation of IMPORTS into a country by a variety of techniques, e.g., TARIFFS, QUOTAS, IMPORT SURCHARGES, IMPORT DEPOSITS, EXPORT RESTRAINT AGREEMENTS and EXCHANGE CONTROLS. The aim of import restrictions is to assist in the removal of a BALANCE OF PAYMENTS deficit and as a means of protecting domestic industries against foreign competition. In general these practices are contrary to the rules of the GENERAL AGREEMENT ON TARIFFS AND TRADE, but GATT has been powerless to stop them in many cases (see, for example, the MULTI-FIBRE ARRANGEMENT.)

See PROTECTIONISM, BALANCE-OF-PAYMENTS EQUILIBRIUM.

imports, *n.* the goods, services and capital assets that are bought from foreign countries. Imports are important in two main respects. (a) Together with EXPORTS they make up a country's BALANCE OF TRADE. Imports must be financed ('paid for' in foreign currency terms) by an equivalent value of exports in order to maintain a payments equilibrium. (b) They represent a 'WITHDRAWAL' from the CIRCULAR FLOW OF NATIONAL INCOME, serving to reduce real income and output. (See PROPENSITY TO IMPORT).

On the one hand imports are seen as beneficial in that they allow a country to enjoy the benefits of INTERNATIONAL TRADE (obtain goods and services at lower prices), but on the other hand, as indicated by (b) above, detrimental because they reduce income and output. It is important to maintain a *balance* between imports and exports. Imports are beneficial provided that they are matched by exports – i.e., 'lost' income on imports is restored by income 'gained' on exports to maintain domestic income and output levels, and, as indicated by (a) above, imports are financed by exports to preserve a BALANCE-OF-PAYMENTS EQUILIBRIUM.

See BALANCE OF PAYMENTS, INTERNAL–EXTERNAL BALANCE MODEL, GAINS FROM TRADE.

import schedule, *n.* a schedule depicting the relationship between NATIONAL INCOME and the proportion of income spent on IMPORTS, as shown in Fig. 94. See AVERAGE PROPENSITY TO IMPORT. The slope of the import schedule equals the MARGINAL PROPENSITY TO IMPORT.

import substitution, *n.* a strategy pursued by a DEVELOPING COUNTRY as

Fig. 94. **Import schedule**. See main entry.

a means of promoting domestic INDUSTRIALIZATION and conserving scarce FOREIGN EXCHANGE resources. By limiting or removing competing IMPORTS through the use of QUOTAS, TARIFFS, etc., the country aims to establish its own manufacturing industries which, initially, can be expanded to cater for the domestic market, and at a later stage develop an EXPORT trade. See INFANT INDUSTRY, ECONOMIC DEVELOPMENT.

import surcharge, *n.* a special TAX levied on IMPORTS (over and above existing TARIFF rates). Import surcharges are employed primarily as a (temporary) means of assisting in the removal of a balance of payments deficit. See IMPORT RESTRICTIONS, BALANCE-OF-PAYMENTS EQUILIBRIUM.

imputed cost, see IMPLICIT COST.

incentive scheme, *n.* any form or system of rewarding an individual which induces increased effort or production. Such systems of reward include piecework payments systems which are geared to an individual's effort and output; bonuses for reaching stipulated levels of production (e.g., in mining); and profit-sharing schemes. See X-INEFFICIENCY, PRODUCTIVITY.

incidence of taxation, *n.* the location of the ultimate bearer (i.e., payer) of a TAX. For example, in the case of personal INCOME TAX it is the individual taxpayer concerned who bears the tax. In other cases, due account must be taken of SHIFTS IN TAX. For example, suppose the tax authorities impose a PAYROLL TAX on firms who treat the tax as an increase in their input costs and put up their prices by an equivalent amount. Then, assuming there is no fall in sales, it is the consumers who bear the full burden of the tax.

See TAXATION, VALUE-ADDED TAX, PRINCIPLES OF TAXATION, LUMP SUM TAXES.

income, *n.* the flow of returns over a period of time derived from the ownership of FACTORS OF PRODUCTION.

The returns to NATURAL RESOURCES, LABOUR and CAPITAL (the factors of production) are RENT, WAGES and INTEREST respectively. It has been argued that there is a fourth factor of production, i.e., 'entrepreneurship', which is rewarded with PROFIT. An ENTREPRENEUR harnesses the other three factors of production to create income for himself.

Care must be taken when using the term 'income' as it takes on different meanings according to the context in which it is used. Recipients of funds from government welfare programmes do not have their income classified as part of NATIONAL INCOME because it is a TRANSFER PAYMENT. However, to the recipient it is income and would be treated as such in the THEORY OF DEMAND where income is considered as a constraint on consumption. See CIRCULAR FLOW OF NATIONAL INCOME MODEL.

income approach to GDP, see NATIONAL INCOME ACCOUNTS.

income-consumption curve, *n.* a line that depicts the relationship between consumer INCOME and the quantity of a product demanded (see DEMAND) on a graph. See Fig. 95. The slope of the income-consumption curve reflects the INCOME-ELASTICITY OF DEMAND, a steeply-sloping curve indicating inelastic demand with small changes in quantity demanded resulting from large changes in income, and vice-versa.

income determination, theory of, see EQUILIBRIUM LEVEL OF NATIONAL INCOME.

income distribution, *n.* the share-out of NATIONAL INCOME between the various FACTOR INPUTS (FUNCTIONAL DISTRIBUTION OF INCOME), or between factor input suppliers and other recipients (PERSONAL DISTRIBUTION OF INCOME).

income effect, *n.* the change in CONSUMERS' real INCOME resulting from a change in product PRICES. A fall in the price of a good normally results in more of it being demanded (See THEORY OF DEMAND). A part of this increase is due to the *real income* effect (i.e., income adjusted for changes in prices to reflect current purchasing power). If a consumer has a money income of, say, £10 and the price of good X is £1, he can buy 10 units of the product; if the price of good X now falls to 50 pence, he can buy the same 10 units for only £5. The consumer now has an 'extra' £5 to spend on buying more of good X and other goods. The income effect, together

Fig. 95. **Income-consumption curve.** (a) An income-consumption curve for a NORMAL PRODUCT where, as income rises, the demand for the product also rises. (b) An income-consumption curve for an INFERIOR PRODUCT where, as income rises, buyers purchase less of the product, generally because they can now afford to buy more expensive alternatives. See INCOME-ELASTICITY OF DEMAND.

with the SUBSTITUTION EFFECT, provides an explanation of why DEMAND CURVES are usually downward sloping.

See CONSUMER EQUILIBRIUM, REVEALED PREFERENCE, PRICE EFFECT.

income-elasticity of demand, *n.* a measure of the degree of responsiveness of DEMAND to a given change in INCOME:

$$\text{income-elasticity of demand} = \frac{\% \text{ change in quantity demanded}}{\% \text{ change in income}}$$

If a given change in income results in a more than proportional change in quantity demanded then demand is said to be *income-elastic*, while if a given change in income results in a less than proportional change in quantity demanded then demand is *income-inelastic*.

Income-elasticity is positive for a NORMAL PRODUCT and negative for an INFERIOR PRODUCT. Products which have an income-elasticity of demand of less than one are called STAPLE PRODUCTS while products with an income-elasticity of more than one are called LUXURY PRODUCTS. See ENGEL'S LAW, INCOME EFFECT, INCOME–CONSUMPTION CURVE, DEMAND CURVE, (SHIFT IN).

income-expenditure model, see EQUILIBRIUM LEVEL OF NATIONAL INCOME.

income per head or **per capita income,** *n.* the NATIONAL INCOME of a country divided by its POPULATION. This gives the average income for every man, woman and child in a country if it were all shared out equally. The distribution of income is not equal and income per head is therefore not necessarily a good indicator of typical living standards.

income redistribution, *n.* a policy concerned with altering the pattern of INCOME DISTRIBUTION in an economy, mainly with social rather than economic objectives in mind. The general aim of such a policy is to achieve a more equitable distribution of income as between the various sections of the community so as to ensure that everybody is provided with some minimum STANDARD OF LIVING. The transfer of income from one section of the community to another is achieved primarily by the use of a PROGRESSIVE TAXATION system and a variety of welfare provisions (subsidised housing, old-age pensions, etc.)

See ABILITY-TO-PAY PRINCIPLE OF TAXATION, REDISTRIBUTION OF INCOME PRINCIPLE OF TAXATION, WEALTH TAX.

incomes policy, see PRICES AND INCOMES POLICY.

income support, *n.* **1.** a means of supplementing the INCOMES of poorer members of the community by means of TRANSFER PAYMENTS such as supplementary benefits, unemployment benefit, etc. See NEGATIVE INCOME TAX, REDISTRIBUTION OF INCOME PRINCIPLE OF TAXATION. **2.** a method of supporting the incomes of certain producers by providing direct payment where market prices are felt to yield insufficient income. See Fig. 96.

income tax, *n.* a DIRECT TAX levied by the government on the INCOME (wages, rent, dividends) received by households in order to raise revenue and as an instrument of FISCAL POLICY. Income tax is usually paid on a progressive scale (see PROGRESSIVE TAX). In the UK, the INLAND REVENUE assesses and collects taxes on behalf of the government for a fiscal year starting 6th April to the following 5th April. Taxes such as CAPITAL GAINS TAX and WEALTH TAX also impinge upon individuals but are quite separate in their scope and calculation.

Changes in income tax rates can be used as part of fiscal policy to regulate the level of AGGREGATE DEMAND, increases in tax serving to reduce DISPOSABLE INCOME available for consumption spending, while decreases in tax increase disposable income. Income taxes can also be used to affect the distribution of incomes in society in line with the government's social policy. See TAXATION, PRINCIPLES OF TAXATION.

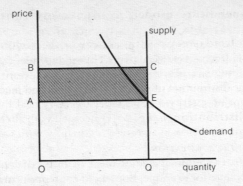

Fig. 96. **Income support**. In many countries income-support systems are used specifically to assist the agricultural sector. In the graph, the equilibrium market price is OA. If this price is considered too low to adequately remunerate farmers the government will set a guaranteed or SHADOW PRICE, say OB, and thus supplement farm incomes by a deficiency payment equal in the aggregate to the shaded area ABCE. Note, in contrast to the PRICE-SUPPORT method, consumers still pay the market-determined price OA and producers sell market-determined output OQ. The UK used the income-support method to assist its agricultural sector prior to joining the EUROPEAN COMMUNITY'S COMMON AGRICULTURAL POLICY scheme in 1973. See AGRICULTURAL POLICY.

income-tax schedules, *n.* the arbitrary classification by the INLAND REVENUE in the UK of various sources of INCOME to facilitate the assessment of TAXATION liability upon an individual. There are 6 schedules lettered A to F. Briefly, the income source of each schedule is:

A: land and property
B: woodlands run as a business
C: INTEREST and DIVIDENDS from public bodies (including government)
D: trades, businesses, professions and vocations, interest received gross
E: WAGES from employment (collected under the PAY-AS-YOU-EARN system – PAYE)
F: company distributions

There are considerable rules and regulations concerning INCOME TAX and the expenses allowable against it.

income velocity of circulation, see QUANTITY THEORY OF MONEY.

incorporation, see COMPANY FORMATION.

increasing returns, see RETURNS TO THE VARIABLE FACTOR INPUT.

independent variable, *n*. a VARIABLE which affects some other variable in a model. For example, the price of a product will influence the demand for it. It is conventional to place the independent variable on the right-hand side of an EQUATION, and to show it on the horizontal axis of a GRAPH. In the example below, price (P) is the independent variable, and quantity demanded (D) the DEPENDENT VARIABLE:

$$D = f(P)$$

See FUNCTIONAL NOTATION.

indexation, *n*. the automatic adjustment of an INCOME payment (e.g., wages) or a value (for example, household contents insurance value) in proportion to changes in a general PRICE INDEX. Indexation is commonly used as a means of countering the effects of persistant price increases (INFLATION). See BASE PERIOD, INDEX-LINKED, INDEX NUMBER.

index-linked, *adj*. (of a VARIABLE) having a value determined in proportion to a specified index. For example, many pension schemes are linked to the retail price index so that as retail prices increase year by year, pensions increase by the same proportion so as to maintain their value in real terms. See BASE PERIOD, INDEXATION, INDEX NUMBER, PRICE INDEX, REAL VALUES.

index number, *n*. a single numerical value that reflects the relative size of a VARIABLE in the period under review compared with its size in some predetermined BASE PERIOD. For example, a retail price index takes the same sample of goods and services in each period and measures the average price of this typical basket of goods and services, showing this average price in the form of a single index number.

The base period of an index is, by convention, given an index number of 100. For the British Retail Price Index, this period is 1974 and subsequent percentage changes commence from that year. In 1986 the Retail Price Index was 386, suggesting that retail prices have increased by 286% on average between 1974 and 1986. Put another way, the same basket of goods in 1986 costs 2.86 times as much as in 1974.

Regardless of whether the index is in terms of price, volume or value, the principle of index numbers remains the same, to exhibit simply and concisely the measured change in a variable from one period to another.

See PRICE INDEX, INDEXATION, INDEX-LINKED.

indicative planning, *n*. a method of controlling the economy that involves the setting of long-term objectives and the mapping-out of programmes of action designed to fulfill these objectives, using techniques such as INPUT–OUTPUT ANALYSIS. Unlike a CENTRALLY-PLANNED ECONOMY indicative planning works through the market (PRICE SYSTEM) rather than replaces it. To this end the planning process specifically brings together both sides of industry (the trade unions and management) and the government.

The only occasion when indicative planning was attempted in the UK was in 1965 when a 'NATIONAL PLAN' was formulated (which set a target economic growth for the UK economy of 3.8% over the period 1964–70), and employed a variety of planning agencies (the NATIONAL ECONOMIC DEVELOPMENT COUNCIL and Economic Development Committees (EDCs) for individual industries) to provide national as well as industry-by-industry coordination. The National Plan itself, however, was abandoned in 1966 after being overtaken by events (a balance of payments crisis resulting in a deflationary package of measures) but the NEDC and the EDCs have continued to function on a less formal basis. By contrast the French have used indicative planning continuously since the 1950s.

See INDUSTRIAL POLICY.

indifference curve, *n.* a curve showing alternative combinations of two products, each of which gives the same UTILITY or satisfaction. See Fig. 97 on page 242. Indifference curves are used (along with BUDGET LINES) to determine a consumer's equilibrium purchases of two products and to analyse the effect of changes in the relative prices of these two products upon quantities demanded (see PRICE EFFECT). See CONSUMER EQUILIBRIUM, INDIFFERENCE MAP.

indifference map, *n.* a collection of ranked INDIFFERENCE CURVES which exhibit graphically an individual's increasing UTILITY, or satisfaction, when moving outwards from the origin, consuming larger quantities of two products. See Fig. 98 on page 243. Indifference curves are an ORDINAL measure and the numbers on the indifference curves in Fig. 98 *do not* indicate an absolute level of utility. Indifference curves never cross because two crossing curves would imply inconsistent or irrational choices between the two products by the consumer (see ECONOMIC MAN).

indirect costs, see OVERHEADS.

indirect investment, *n.* any expenditure on FINANCIAL SECURITIES such as STOCKS and SHARES. This is sometimes referred to as *financial* or *portfolio investment*. See INVESTMENT.

indirect labour, *n.* that part of the labour force in a firm which is not directly concerned with the manufacture of a good or the provision of a service. Indirect-labour cost depends on the amount of remuneration

Fig. 97. **Indifference curve**. A combination of OA units of product X, and OB units of product Y, yields exactly as much satisfaction to the consumer as does the combination of OC units of product X and OD units of product Y.

Indifference curves always slope downwards because, rationally, consumers will always prefer more of both products and so would not be indifferent between two combinations of products where one combination offers more of both. Specifically, they would only give up one product if they receive more of another for it, being indifferent as between combination E, which offers a lot of product X and little of product Y, and combination F which offers less product X and more product Y (see ECONOMIC MAN).

paid to all of those factory employees who are not engaged directly in making products but who provide support services, for example, supervision and clerical work. The wages of such indirect labour are usually counted as part of production OVERHEADS. See DIRECT LABOUR, FIXED COST, STANDARD COST.

indirect materials, *n.* any raw materials which, while they are not incorporated in a product, are nonetheless consumed in the production process, for example, lubricants and moulds for metal castings. The costs of such indirect materials is usually counted as part of production OVERHEADS. See DIRECT MATERIALS, FIXED COST, STANDARD COST.

indirect tax, *n.* a TAX levied by the government on goods and services in order to raise revenue and as an instrument of FISCAL POLICY. Examples of an indirect tax are VALUE ADDED TAX and EXCISE DUTY.

Changes in indirect tax can be used as part of fiscal policy to regulate the level of AGGREGATE DEMAND, increases in tax serving to reduce disposable income available for consumption spending, while decreases

Fig. 98. **Indifference map.** In principle, indifference curves 1, 2, 3, etc., can take the full form indicated in the map, though in practice only the solid-line segment of each curve is relevant, because once the curves become vertical, and the consumer is fully sated with product Y, he will not be prepared to give up extra units of product X to get extra Y; and once the curves become horizontal, and the consumer is fully sated with product X, he will not be prepared to give up extra units of product Y to get extra X. The ridge lines R_1 and R_2 mark the boundaries of the effective segments of the indifference curves.

in tax increase disposable income. Indirect taxes can be used to affect the shape of demand as well as its level, increases in indirect tax serving to discourage consumption of socially disapproved products like cigarettes or alcoholic drinks, while reductions in indirect taxes encourage consumption of socially-approved products like basic foodstuffs or books.

Unlike a DIRECT TAX which varies according to the income of the taxpayer (PROGRESSIVE TAXATION), indirect taxes are regressive, insofar as the same amount is paid by each taxpaying consumer regardless of their income. See TAXATION, REGRESSIVE TAXATION.

indivisibilities, *n.* the minimum physical or technical size limitations on FACTOR INPUTS. For example, a company wants to purchase a machine which can undertake 5,000 operations a day. Due to design and technical difficulties the minimum-size machine available optimally carries out 10,000 operations a day. The machine is indivisible since it cannot be reduced to two optimal half-machines. The AVERAGE COST of each unit of output is consequently greater than it would be if the manufacturer could produce at an output level where the machine was optimally employed.

The manufacturer could achieve ECONOMIES OF SCALE by attaining a large volue of production, but this can give rise to problems of combining large, indivisible inputs with different capacities. For example, if the manufacturer above needs to combine process A machines capable of carrying out 10,000 operations a day and process B machines capable of carrying out 4,000 operations a day then only by producing 20,000 units a day in two process A machines and five process B machines would he be able to use both types of machine in an economically-feasible way. Any other output level would result in a degree of under-utilization of one or other machine.

See PRODUCTION FUNCTION.

induced investment, *n.* the part of an increase, or decrease, in real INVESTMENT which is brought about by a change in the level of NATIONAL INCOME. For example, a rise in national income accompanied by increased consumption spending which puts pressure on existing supply capacity will encourage businesses to invest in new plant and machinery. See ACCELERATOR, INVESTMENT SCHEDULE, AUTONOMOUS INVESTMENT.

Industrial and Commercial Finance Corporation, *n.* see INVESTORS IN INDUSTRY.

industrial classification, *n.* the grouping of economic activities of a similar nature into INDUSTRIES or MARKETS. A system used to group activities in this way in the UK is described as a *standard industrial classification*. Such a classification begins by identifying a wide spectrum of related groups' activities (for example, the 'manufacturing sector'), each group of activities then being subdivided into progressively narrower groups so that the classification can be used with varying amounts of detail for different purposes. Thus, within the manufacturing sector, a broad group such as 'textile manufacture' may be subdivided first into different kinds of textile fabric (wool, cotton, man-made fibres) and these in turn into smaller subdivisions of activity such as spinning, weaving, finishing, etc.

Industrial classifications are used for macroeconomic planning and COMPETITION POLICY purposes, and to obtain statistical information on output and employment. See STRUCTURE OF INDUSTRY, CROSS-ELASTICITY OF DEMAND, MONOPOLY POLICY.

industrial democracy, *n.* the participation of the workforce in the corporate decision-making process alongside management. See WORKER PARTICIPATION, TRADE UNION.

industrial development certificate, *n.* an instrument of REGIONAL POLICY that is used to control the location of firms and industries. In the

UK, industrial development certificates applying to new premises (factories and offices) are used to steer new investment into DEVELOPMENT AREAS and INTERMEDIATE AREAS.

industrial dispute, *n.* a dispute between one or more employers, or organizations of employers, and one or more workers or organizations of workers (TRADE UNIONS), where the dispute relates wholly or mainly to matters of trade. Such matters may comprise terms and/or conditions of employment; the engagement, termination or suspension of employment of workers; the allocation of work between workers; matters of discipline, and so forth.

Serious industrial disputes are often characterized by STRIKE action on the part of workers and/or the LOCK-OUT of workers by management. Industrial disputes may be settled in a number of ways, including voluntary agreement between the parties concerned, or by recourse to an independent arbiter.

See INDUSTRIAL RELATIONS, COLLECTIVE BARGAINING, ARBITRATION, MEDIATION, CONCILIATION.

industrial economics or **industrial organization,** *n.* the branch of economics concerned with the functioning of the PRICE SYSTEM. Industrial economics examines the interrelationships between MARKET STRUCTURE, MARKET CONDUCT and MARKET PERFORMANCE, utilizing the analytical framework of the THEORY OF MARKETS but within an empirical and dynamic setting. See MARKET STRUCTURE-CONDUCT-PERFORMANCE SCHEMA.

industrial estate, *n.* a formally-planned area designated for commercial and industrial use separate from residential accommodation. Industrial estates initially offered low cost work space for light and medium size engineering companies and warehouse distribution facilities. Such estates may be financed privately or by government. In the UK, current attempts to attract high-technology firms into one convenient area, often referred to as *science parks*, situated close to university facilities, follow a similar theme.

industrialization, *n.* the extensive development of organized economic activity for the purpose of manufacture. Industrialization is characterized by the transformation of a primarily agrarian economy into a more specialized, capital-intensive economy. Such a transformation was termed the *Industrial Revolution* in Western Europe and North America during the 18th and 19th centuries. Compare DEINDUSTRIALIZATION. See STRUCTURE OF INDUSTRY, ECONOMIC DEVELOPMENT.

industrial organization, see INDUSTRIAL ECONOMICS.

industrial policy, *n.* a series of measures undertaken by government to promote industrial EFFICIENCY, TECHNOLOGICAL PROGRESSIVENESS and employment opportunities. Industrial policy is implemented both through selective intervention involving the sponsorship and financial support of particular industries, firms and projects, and through across-the-board schemes designed to assist industrial regeneration and expansion.

Examples of selective intervention in British industry include the RATIONALIZATION of declining industries; support for high technology growth industries; support for firms in temporary financial difficulties; support for INVENTIONS and INNOVATION; support for strategic MERGERS.

A number of bodies have been established to sponsor and provide financial assistance in this area, including the National Research and Development Corporation (established 1948), the Industrial Reorganization Corporation (1966–1971), the National Enterprise Board (established 1975), and currently (1986) the British Technology Group, formed through the merger of the National Research and Development Corporation and the National Enterprise Board in 1981.

Examples of more general programmes include support for small business start-ups and development (Small Business Expansion scheme); the adoption of advanced technologies (Micro-Processor Applications Scheme), and vocational training and employment creation (Manpower Services Commission and Youth Opportunities Scheme).

In some countries (most notably the UK), industrial policy has developed on a piecemeal basis and has varied in the degree of enthusiasm accorded to it by the government of the day. In others, for example France, industrial policy has been seen as an arm of INDICATIVE PLANNING and has been applied on a continuous and coordinated basis. See MONOPOLY POLICY, REGIONAL POLICY.

industrial property rights, *n.* the ownership by a business of PATENTS on techniques and products, BRAND NAMES and COPYRIGHTS giving legal entitlement and powers of redress against theft and unauthorized imitation. See MONOPOLY POLICY, PRODUCT DIFFERENTIATION.

industrial relations, *n.* the practice of those processes, forces and institutions through which employers and employees order and regulate their working lives. 'Industrial relations' is an all-embracing term covering all aspects of the employment relationship and its associated institutions and social and economic environment. See TRADE UNION, COLLECTIVE BARGAINING, ARBITRATION, MEDIATION.

Industrial Reorganization Corporation, *n.* a UK organization whose particular role from 1966–71 was to promote and financially assist RATIONALIZATION, MERGERS and industrial projects. See INDUSTRIAL POLICY.

Industrial Revolution, see INDUSTRIALIZATION.

industrial sector, *n.* that part of the economy concerned with the production of INTERMEDIATE PRODUCTS (iron and steel, machinery and equipment, etc.) and FINAL PRODUCTS (washing machines, furniture, etc.) The industrial sector, together with the PRIMARY SECTOR and SERVICE SECTOR form an interlocking chain of economic activities which constitute a modern economy. See STRUCTURE OF INDUSTRY.

industry, *n.* any economic activities classified according to the type of product or service provided: for example, the motor car industry, the insurance industry. Industries are usually defined by reference to their principal products, but there are often problems with respect to how widely or narrowly industry 'boundaries' are drawn. See MARKET, INDUSTRIAL CLASSIFICATION, MARKET STRUCTURE, CROSS-ELASTICITY OF DEMAND.

inelastic, *adj.* relatively unresponsive to change. See PRICE-ELASTICITY OF DEMAND, PRICE-ELASTICITY OF SUPPLY, INCOME-ELASTICITY OF DEMAND, CROSS-ELASTICITY OF DEMAND.

inequality, *n.* a means of portraying arithmetically the relationship between VARIABLES. For example, the inequality: $C \leqslant Y$ suggests that consumption expenditure (C) is less than, or at most, equal to, disposable income (Y). Alternatively, we can write: $Y \geqslant C$, which suggests that disposable income is greater than, or at most, equal to, consumption expenditure. See EQUATION.

infant industry, *n.* a newly-established industry, developed either by private-enterprise interests or set up by the government, often in DEVELOPING COUNTRIES, as part of their INDUSTRIALIZATION programmes. New industries are often subsidized by the government and/or protected from import competition in the hope that in due course they can exploit economies of scale and thus eventually withstand foreign competition.

Infant industries are often cited as a 'legitimate' area for the application of PROTECTIONISM, but policy in this area is often open to abuse. See ECONOMIC DEVELOPMENT.

inferior product, *n.* a good or service for which the INCOME ELASTICITY OF DEMAND is negative; i.e., as income rises, buyers purchase less of the product. Consequently, when the price of such a product falls thereby effectively increasing consumers' real income, then that price cut will have the INCOME EFFECT of tending to decrease the quantity demanded.

This will tend to partially offset the SUBSTITUTION EFFECT of a price cut which causes consumers·to buy more of the product because it is now relatively cheaper. This applies to a very limited range of products. See PRICE EFFECT, NORMAL PRODUCT, INCOME–CONSUMPTION CURVE, ENGEL'S LAW.

inflation, *n.* an increase in the general level of prices in an economy that is sustained over a period of time. The annual increases in prices may be small or gradual (CREEPING INFLATION), or large and accelerating (HYPERINFLATION). The rate of inflation can be measured using, for example, a consumers' PRICE INDEX which shows the annual percentage change in consumer prices. See Fig. 99a. Inflation reduces the PURCHASING POWER of money (see REAL VALUES).

The avoidance of inflation has long been one of the main objectives of MACROECONOMIC POLICY. Inflation is considered to be undesirable because of its adverse effects on income distribution (people on fixed incomes suffer) lending and borrowing (lenders lose, borrowers gain), speculation (diversion of saving away from industry into property and commodity speculation), and international trade competitiveness (exports become relatively more expensive, imports cheaper). Hyperinflation is particularly serious because people lose confidence in the use of money for exchange purposes and the economic system is liable to collapse.

There are two main explanations of why inflation occurs: (a) the presence of excess demand at the full employment level of national output which 'pulls-up' prices (DEMAND–PULL INFLATION); (b) an increase in FACTOR INPUT input costs which 'pushes-up' prices (COST–PUSH INFLATION). An alternative explanation of demand–pull inflation offered by MONETARISM blames excessive creation of money for inflation and prescribes restricting the rate of growth of money to match the growth of potential GNP. Other economists who favour the cost-push explanation argue for PRICES AND INCOMES POLICY as the means to control inflation.

See INFLATIONARY SPIRAL, PURCHASING POWER, PHILLIPS CURVE, EXPECTATIONS–ADJUSTED AUGMENTED PHILLIPS CURVE, ADAPTIVE EXPECTATIONS HYPOTHESIS, QUANTITY THEORY OF MONEY.

inflation accounting, *n.* any adjustments to a firm's accounts to allow for the effects of INFLATION and arrive at a view of the real profitability of the firm. In a period of rising prices when the purchasing power of the money unit is declining, profit calculations based upon the HISTORIC COST of STOCKS and FIXED ASSETS are likely to overstate the real profit position.

	UK	W. Germany	US	Japan
1978	8.3	2.7	7.7	3.8
1979	13.4	4.1	11.3	3.6
1980	18.0	5.5	13.5	8.0
1981	11.9	6.3	10.4	4.9
1982	8.6	5.3	6.1	2.7
1983	4.6	3.3	3.2	1.9
1984	5.0	2.4	4.3	2.2
1985	6.1	2.2	3.5	2.1
1986	3.4	− 0.2	2.0	0.4

(a)

(b)

Fig. 99. **Inflation.** (a) National inflation rates, 1978–1986. Source: OECD *Economic Outlook*, 1987. (b) In the EQUILIBRIUM LEVEL OF NATIONAL INCOME model inflation occurs whenever AGGREGATE DEMAND exceeds full employment aggregate supply (POTENTIAL GROSS NATIONAL PRODUCT): equilibrium national income in the Fig. is OY_2, and if aggregate demand AD_2 exceeds full employment demand AD_1, an INFLATIONARY GAP develops. The traditional prescription for this situation is for the authorities to reduce spending by deflationary FISCAL POLICY and MONETARY POLICY measures – to shift aggregate demand from AD_2 to AD_1.

Various methods of allowing for the effects of inflation on the TRADING AND PROFIT-AND-LOSS ACCOUNT and the BALANCE SHEET have been tried.

One relatively simple method of inflation-adjusting a firm's accounting results is the *current purchasing-power method*. This method uses a PRICE INDEX number to adjust the calculated profit figure from the trading and profit-and-loss account, and to express it in real terms. A more detailed method is the *current cost-accounting method*. This method produces a supplementary current-cost trading and profit-and-loss account and balance sheet. In these current-cost accounts the deduction from revenue for COST-OF-GOODS SOLD is based upon the REPLACEMENT COST of the goods sold (cost-of-sales adjustment); while DEPRECIATION is calculated on the replacement cost of fixed assets used and not on their historic cost (depreciation adjustment). See REVALUATION PROVISION, APPRECIATION (2).

inflation–adjusted PSBR, see PUBLIC–SECTOR BORROWING REQUIREMENT.

inflationary gap, *n*. the excess of total spending (AGGREGATE DEMAND) at the full employment level of national income (POTENTIAL GROSS NATIONAL PRODUCT). As it is not possible to increase output further the excess demand will cause prices to rise, i.e., real output remains the same but the money or NOMINAL VALUE of that output will be inflated. See Fig. 100.

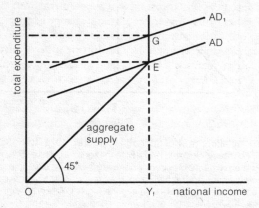

Fig. 100. **Inflationary gap.** The full-employment level of national income/output is reached at output O Y_f, and at this output level the AGGREGATE SUPPLY SCHEDULE becomes vertical. If aggregate demand was at the level indicated by AD the economy would be operating at full employment without inflation (at point E). However if aggregate demand was at a higher level like AD_1 this excess aggregate demand would create an inflationary gap (equal to EG), pulling price upward. See DEMAND-PULL INFLATION.

inflationary spiral or **price–wage spiral,** *n*. a self-sustained increase in the rate of INFLATION brought about by the interaction of rising final prices and rising input costs. For example, an initial sharp increase in the prices of goods and services caused by an increase in raw material costs, can lead to a demand for higher MONEY WAGES by trade unions concerned to protect their members' living standards. If conceded, higher wage costs are soon likely to prompt manufacturers to put up their prices in order to maintain profit margins. The higher prices in turn produce further demand for wage increases, and so on. Once under way, price-cost increases tend to be self-reinforcing, and are exacerbated by EXPECTATIONS of even further increases.

See ADAPTIVE-EXPECTATIONS HYPOTHESIS, EXPECTATIONS-ADJUSTED/ AUGMENTED PHILLIPS CURVE, MONEY ILLUSION, REAL WAGES.

information agreement, *n*. an arrangement under which firms undertake to furnish a central agency, usually their TRADE ASSOCIATION, with data on such things as prices, discounts, conditions of sale, etc. These data are compiled and then circulated to each firm involved in the agreement. Information exchanges can take place either on a post- or prenotification basis. In the former case, information is only made available to other firms after, for example, a change in prices, while in the case of prenotification schemes, firms are notified of proposed price changes etc in advance of a definite commitment being made. It will be readily apparent that such information exchanges, particularly pre-notification exchanges, provide a cloak for COLLUSION between competitors.

In the UK, information agreements covering prices and conditions of sale of goods are required to be registered with the OFFICE OF FAIR TRADING, and can be referred for investigation to the RESTRICTIVE PRACTICES COURT. See MONOPOLY POLICY.

infrastructure or **social overhead capital,** *n*. a nation's roads, railways, housing, hospitals, schools, water supply, etc., accumulated from INVESTMENT, usually by the government or local authorities, in previous periods. It also includes intangible items such as an educated/ trained labour force created by investment in HUMAN CAPITAL.

Infrastructure plays an important role in improving a country's general living standards and in contributing to a higher rate of ECONOMIC GROWTH.

inheritance tax, see WEALTH TAX.

injections, *n*. any expenditures on domestic goods and services originating from outside the household sector. In the basic CIRCULAR FLOW OF NATIONAL INCOME MODEL all spending is done by households (CONSUMPTION expenditure). In the extended circular flow of income model, domestic output is also purchased by businesses, government and overseas buyers. Thus, INVESTMENT, GOVERNMENT EXPENDITURE and EXPORTS, respectively, constitute 'injections' into the income–spending flow. Compare WITHDRAWALS.

injections–withdrawals approach to national income determination, see EQUILIBRIUM LEVEL OF NATIONAL INCOME..

Inland Revenue, *n.* a UK government department that is responsible for assessing individual and corporate TAXATION liabilities (H.M. Inspector of Taxes), and for the collection of taxation monies due (H.M. Collector of Taxes). In the US the Internal Revenue Service performs similar functions.

innovation, *n.* the practical refinement and development of an original INVENTION into a usable technique or product. Innovation is an important means of improving MARKET PERFORMANCE (by, for example, lowering supply costs and enhancing product quality), and in contributing to a faster rate of ECONOMIC GROWTH.

Innovation can be a lengthy and expensive process. For example, the original invention of the Xerox photocopying process was made in 1948, but it took a further 10 years of development work before the first commercial version of the product was put on the market.

See MONOPOLY, TECHNOLOGICAL PROGRESSIVENESS, RESEARCH AND DEVELOPMENT.

inputs, see FACTOR INPUTS.

input–output analysis or **interindustry analysis,** *n.* the study and empirical measurement of the structural interrelationships between PRODUCTION sectors within an economy. The technique was devised by Wassily Leontief (b. 1906) to measure the FACTOR INPUT required by different industries to achieve a given OUTPUT. A particular sector of the economy requires inputs from other sectors, be it raw materials, intermediate goods and services, or labour, in order to produce output. The interdependence between industries, or sectors, is not linear but complex. That is, one sector does not produce, say, coal, for other sectors independent of the requirements of the coal industry for inputs from other sectors. For the mining sector coal is an output. But coal is an input for the electricity industry. By the same token, the coal industry requires inputs (including electricity) in order to produce the coal. The complexity of an economy can be gauged from this simple example.

See VERTICAL INTEGRATION, INDICATIVE PLANNING, GENERAL EQUILIBRIUM ANALYSIS.

inside money, see ENDOGENOUS MONEY.

insider trading, *n.* any transactions in securities such as STOCKS and SHARES by persons having access to privileged (confidential) information not as yet available to the general investing public, and who in consequence stand to gain financially from this knowledge. For example, a person who is employed by a merchant bank and is involved in working out details of a prospective TAKEOVER by a client firm of another firm may himself or through other people arrange to purchase shares in the target firm prior to the public announcement of the takeover. See CITY CODE.

insolvency, *n.* a condition under which an individual or firm's LIABILITIES to CREDITORS exceed ASSETS. The individual or firm is therefore unable to discharge all accumulated liabilities from realizable assets.

Insolvency occurs after a period in which an individual's expenditure has exceeded his income; or a firm's costs have exceeded its sales revenues (LOSSES are made). Frequently an insolvent individual or firm will become bankrupt and arrange for the LIQUIDATION of available assets, the proceeds being distributed amongst creditors. See SHARE CAPITAL, SHAREHOLDER'S CAPITAL EMPLOYED.

	1963	1983
	%	%
Individuals	58	25
Financial institutions		
Pension funds	7	29
Insurance companies	11	22
Investment trust companies	9	6
Unit trusts	1	4
Others	14	14
	100	100

Fig. 101. **Institutional investors**. The ownership of British share capital in 1963 and 1983. Source: *Economist*, July 14, 1984.

institutional investors, *n.* the financial institutions that collect SAVINGS and other deposits and invest (see INVESTMENT) long-term in company STOCKS and SHARES, government BONDS, property and overseas securities. In Britain, the main investing institutions are the INSURANCE COMPANIES, PENSION FUNDS, INVESTMENT TRUST COMPANIES and UNIT TRUSTS. In many other countries the commercial banks are also major long-term investors.

Institutional investors have grown rapidly in Britain and elsewhere since the 1950s, encouraged both by the favourable tax concessions granted by the government to contractual pension and life insurance schemes, and the opportunities which financial institutions provide to pool risks by investing in a variety of financial securities.

Institutional investors now occupy a prominent position in the FINANCIAL SYSTEM and form the primary conduit for channelling personal savings into industrial and commercial investment, displacing direct investment by individual savers. In Britain, as Fig. 101 on page 253 shows, institutional investors now own more than one-half of the ordinary SHARE CAPITAL of British companies.

insurance, *n.* a method of protecting a person or business against the financial consequences of loss of, and damage to, ASSETS through fire, theft, etc (general insurance), and loss of life and limb (life and accident insurance). The term *assurance* is frequently used interchangeably with that of insurance to describe certain kinds of life insurance.

See INSURANCE COMPANY, RISK AND UNCERTAINTY.

insurance company, *n.* a financial institution that provides a range of insurance policies to protect individuals and businesses against the RISK of financial losses in return for regular payments of PREMIUMS. An insurance company operates by pooling risks amongst a large number of contributors. From its past claims record, the company actuary can ascertain the probability of a particular event occurring, for example, a fire, and can assess the average financial loss associated with each event. Using this information he attempts to calculate appropriate premiums for contributors and from the collective pool of premium income to meet outstanding financial claims.

See FINANCIAL SYSTEM, INSTITUTIONAL INVESTORS, RISK AND UNCERTAINTY.

intangible assets, *n.* nonphysical assets such as GOODWILL, PATENTS and TRADEMARKS which have a money value.

intangibles, *n.* costs and benefits usually associated with an INVESTMENT project within the public sector that either cannot be quantified, or which can be quantified but cannot easily be valued in money terms. Examples of the former include the scenic effects of projects such as airport runways in rural areas; examples of the latter might include changes in accident deaths, associated with road building projects which give problems setting a money value per life saved or lost. Such intangibles are important though they cannot easily be incorporated into an investment appraisal. See COST–BENEFIT ANALYSIS.

integration, see HORIZONTAL INTEGRATION, VERTICAL INTEGRATION, DIVERSIFICATION, TRADE INTEGRATION.

interbank clearing rate of interest, *n*. the RATE OF INTEREST at which the COMMERCIAL BANKS in Britain lend short-term funds to one another. The interbank rate of interest influences the BILL-DISCOUNTING RATE at which the CENTRAL BANK is prepared to loan money to the commercial banks. In turn, the interbank rate of interest influences the BASE RATE which is used by commercial banks to calculate rates of interest to be charged to their customers. See also BANK RATE.

intercept, *n*. the point where a straight line on a GRAPH intersects the vertical or horizontal AXIS. See LINEAR EQUATION.

interest, *n*. a payment made by BORROWERS to LENDERS for the use of their money both to finance physical and portfolio INVESTMENT and to finance CONSUMPTION. Interest represents a 'reward' to lenders for foregoing current consumption themselves and for the risk introduced in loaning out money.

In aggregate terms, interest is a source of income and is thus included as a part of NATIONAL INCOME. In the THEORY OF SUPPLY interest is 'a payment for the use of CAPITAL as a FACTOR OF PRODUCTION.

See also RATE OF INTEREST, NATIONAL INCOME ACCOUNTS, MARGINAL EFFICIENCY OF CAPITAL/INVESTMENT, DISCOUNT RATE, COST OF CAPITAL, BASE RATE, BILL DISCOUNTING RATE, BANK RATE, TERM STRUCTURE OF INTEREST RATES, TIME PREFERENCE THEORY, NOMINAL RATE OF INTEREST, EFFECTIVE RATE OF INTEREST.

interest cover, *n*. an accounting measure of the extent to which a firm's earnings cover INTEREST payments due on LOANS; which expresses profit after tax as a ratio of interest due.

interest rate, see RATE OF INTEREST.

interfirm conduct, *n*. an element of MARKET CONDUCT that denotes the ways in which firms interact in the market. Two main patterns of behaviour may be identified:

(a) independent behaviour. Each firm formulates its competitive strategy with respect to price, advertising, etc., unilaterally without considering the actions of other firms. This pattern of behaviour is usually associated with markets consisting of a large number of small suppliers each of which contributes an insignificant proportion of total market supply (see PERFECT COMPETITION; MONOPOLISTIC COMPETITION).

(b) interdependent behaviour. Firms recognize that they are MUTU-ALLY INTERDEPENDENT (i.e., that their own actions directly affect the position of other firms) and thus they explicitly take into account the likely effects of their own competitive strategies on other firms). Interdependency is associated with an OLIGOPOLY, where the bulk of market supply is in the hands of a few large firms, resulting in COLLUSION as a means of coordinating their pricing, production and selling policies.

intermediate area, *n.* a moderately DEPRESSED AREA scheduled under UK REGIONAL POLICY as in need of industrial regeneration. Firms prepared to undertake new investment in such areas may be eligible for REGIONAL SELECTIVE ASSISTANCE. See DEVELOPMENT AREA.

intermediate products, *n.* the goods and services that are used as FACTOR INPUTS by firms in producing other goods or services. For example, steel is an intermediate good which has a variety of end-uses, including motor car bodies, washing machine shells, nuts and bolts, etc.

Intermediate products are not counted as part of gross national product in the NATIONAL INCOME ACCOUNTS where final goods and services are measured.

See FINAL PRODUCTS, VALUE ADDED.

intermediation, *n.* the role of the financial institutions in channelling SAVINGS and other deposits by LENDERS to BORROWERS. Financial intermediaries such as COMMERCIAL BANKS and BUILDING SOCIETIES accept deposits from individuals and businesses and use these funds to make LOANS to creditworthy customers. An intermediary's profit is the difference between rates paid for deposits and rates on loans. See FINANCIAL SYSTEM, DISINTERMEDIATION.

internal balance, *n.* a situation where the economy is operating at FULL EMPLOYMENT and the general level of prices is constant (PRICE STABILITY). The achievement of full employment and price stability are two important macroeconomic objectives of the government. In practice, it is difficult to secure both objectives simultaneously (see PHILLIPS CURVE).

Compare EXTERNAL BALANCE. See also DEMAND MANAGEMENT, INTERNAL-EXTERNAL BALANCE MODEL, MACROECONOMIC POLICY.

internal economies of scale, *n.* the reduction in the individual firm's AVERAGE COSTS of production as OUTPUT increases. Emphasis is often placed on technical economies such as using plant at a greater capacity to reduce unit costs. A larger plant may facilitate a greater division of labour. However, economies within the marketing, managerial and financial spheres may be similarly obtained.

Compare EXTERNAL ECONOMIES OF SCALE. See ECONOMIES OF SCALE, DISECONOMIES OF SCALE.

internal-external balance model, *n.* a theoretical construct that seeks to integrate the achievement of the MACROECONOMIC POLICY objectives

(a)

(b)

Fig. 102. **Internal-external balance model.** (a) See main entry.
(b) Given the ratio of international to domestic prices (P), domestic
demand must be at level X to secure internal balance. If it is not, the
result is unemployment or inflation.

of FULL EMPLOYMENT and PRICE STABILITY (internal balance) and BALANCE-
OF-PAYMENTS EQUILIBRIUM (external balance).

A brief illustration of the model is given in Fig. 102a. The vertical axis
shows the ratio of international prices to domestic prices. This is an index
of the country's foreign competitive position: the higher one moves up
the scale, the larger are exports and the smaller are imports. On the
horizontal axis is domestic real demand, which increases from left to
right. The two curves shown in the figure represent, respectively,

Fig. 102 (continued) **Internal-external balance model**. (c) Given the level of domestic demand (X), the ratio of international to domestic prices must be at level P to secure external balance. If it is not, the result is a surplus or deficit balance of payments.

external balance (EE) and internal balance (DD). The EE curve has a positive slope, indicating that the more unfavourable the international price ratio becomes, the lower domestic real demand must be to maintain balance-of-payments equilibrium. Positions to the left and above the curve represent payments surplus; to the right and below, deficit. The DD curve has a negative slope indicating that the more unfavourable the international price ratio becomes, the higher domestic real demand must be to maintain full employment. Positions to the right and above the curve represent price inflation; to the left and below, unemployment.

Where the EE and DD curves intersect (point A), the country is in general equilibrium. All other positions represent disequilibrium. However, from only a few of these disequilibrium positions can the country attain the two policy objectives of internal and external equilibrium using just a single policy variable – specifically, from only those positions located on the horizontal and vertical dotted lines drawn through the intersection. In situations shown by the horizontal line to the right of point A, for instance, the ratio of international to domestic prices is appropriate, but domestic real demand is too high resulting in both inflation and a balance-of-payments deficit. DEFLATION of demand alone would therefore suffice to realize both goals. In situations shown by the vertical line below point A, domestic real demand is just right, but domestic prices are uncompetitive resulting in both a balance-of-payments deficit and unemployment. A currency DEVALUATION alone would therefore suffice to realize both goals. However, these are special cases. In all other situations both domestic demand and the international price ratio are inappropriate. As a result, the two policy objectives are in conflict, and the separate policy variables must be combined to be effective. In zones 1 and 2, for instance, varying combinations of demand-deflation and currency REVALUATION are required, and in zones 3 and 4, varying combinations of demand-deflation and currency devaluation. In zones 5 and 6, varying combinations of demand REFLATION and currency devaluation are required; and in zones 7 and 8, varying combinations of demand reflation and currency revaluation.

internal financing, *n.* the ability to finance a firm's growth from retained earnings. A company's NET PROFIT can be paid out in DIVIDENDS or retained for internal financing or some mixture of these two. Generally, shareholders look for some immediate income in the form of dividends and some growth in the capital value of their shares (which depends on growth). By paying out more dividends, growth is slowed. Achieving the optimum solution between two conflicting objectives is an important area of study in managerial finance.

See COST OF CAPITAL, RETENTION RATIO, RESERVES.

internalization, *n.* the combining in one firm of two or more related activities, as opposed to these activities being conducted separately in different firms and then being synchronized through arms-length MARKET transactions. Economic theory postulates that a PROFIT-MAXI-MIZING firm will internalize a sequence of activities if the costs of doing so are lower than transacting the same activities through the market.

The most common example of internalization is that of VERTICAL INTEGRATION, where a series of vertically-related activities are combined. Cost advantages accruing through vertical internalization include reduced production costs by linking together successive processes of manufacture (e.g., iron and steel mills, to avoid reheating), and the avoidance of TRANSACTION COSTS incurred in imperfect markets (e.g., monopoly surcharges imposed by input suppliers, unreliable sources of supply, and restrictions on sales outlets).

The concept of internalization is also relevant to HORIZONTAL INTEGRATION by multiplant domestic firms and MULTINATIONAL FIRMS. In the case of multinational firms the establishment of production plants in overseas markets, instead of servicing those markets by direct exporting, occurs because of the transaction costs of market imperfections such as TARIFFS, QUOTAS and exchange rate restrictions and the fact that monopolistic advantages (a patented product, know-how or a unique product) can be better exploited and protected by direct control.

internal rate of return, see DISCOUNTED CASH FLOW.

International Bank for Reconstruction and Development, see WORLD BANK.

international commodity agreement, *n.* an agreement that attempts to stabilize the prices of some internationally-traded COMMODITIES such as cocoa and tin, with the objective of stabilizing foreign exchange earnings and producers' incomes, primarily in the DEVELOPING COUNTRIES. Although international commodity agreements are established to further the interests of producing countries, they may also benefit consumers by removing the uncertainties and inconveniences associated with erratic price movements.

International commodity agreements vary in format but one typical approach involves the establishment of an 'official' price for the commodity, agreed on by member countries, which is then maintained over a period of time by the use of a BUFFER-STOCK mechanism: surplus output is bought in if market supply exceeds demand at the official price and sold off if demand exceeds market supply.

International commodity agreements have been promoted by the UNITED NATIONS CONFERENCE ON TRADE AND DEVELOPMENT as a means of enhancing the economic interests of the developing countries (see NEW INTERNATIONAL ECONOMIC ORDER), but there are often serious difficulties encountered in ensuring their viability. For example, disagreements can occur between member countries on what particular official prices to set arising out of differences in the degree of importance of the commodity to individual members' economies; and often the temptation is to set prices above market-determined rates, which places a financial strain on the buffer stock which may then eventually run out of money.

international competitiveness, *n.* the ability of a country to compete successfully against other countries in INTERNATIONAL TRADE. Countries which are successful will maintain or increase their share of world exports and, by the same token, limit the extent of IMPORT PENETRATION into their domestic economies.

International competitiveness is reflected in two things: (a) price competitiveness; it is important that domestic suppliers are efficient and cost-effective and that governments can control domestic rates of INFLATION and maintain 'realistic' EXCHANGE RATES for their currencies. (b) nonprice competitiveness; it is equally important that domestic suppliers offer export customers attractive new products, improve the quality and performance of their products, meet delivery dates, etc.

international debt, *n.* the money owed to the international community by borrowing countries. In the main, debtor countries consist of DEVELOPING COUNTRIES who have borrowed foreign exchange from advanced countries and private banks to finance their economic development programmes.

As can be seen from Fig. 103 DEBT SERVICING exceeded new lending in 1985. The problem of debt servicing has been especially acute for a number of countries who, in recent years, because of a decline in their foreign exchange earnings, have been forced to renege on, or reschedule their foreign debts. This has reacted adversely on the willingness of lenders to make further LOANS available.

	$ Billions
Total debt outstanding	708
Disbursements, 1985	80
Debt repayments, 1985	102
Capital (50)	
Interest (52)	
Net transfer	− 22

Fig. 103. **International debt.** The long-term debt (in US dollar billions) of 107 developing countries in 1985. Source: World Bank, 1986.

International Development Association, see WORLD BANK.

International Finance Corporation, see WORLD BANK.

international Fisher effect, *n.* a situation where NOMINAL INTEREST RATE differentials between countries reflect anticipated rates of change in the EXCHANGE RATE of their currencies (see FISHER EFFECT).

For example, if British investors anticipate that the US dollar will appreciate by, say, 5% per annum against sterling, then in order to offset the expected change in parity between the two countries, they would be prepared to accept an interest rate approximately 5% per annum less on a dollar-denominated financial security than that which could be expected on an equivalent investment denominated in sterling. From a borrower's viewpoint, when the international Fisher effect holds, the cost of equivalent loans in alternative currencies will be the same, regardless of the rate of interest.

The International Fisher effect can be contrasted with the *domestic Fisher effect* where nominal interest rates reflect the anticipated real rate of interest and the anticipated rate of change in prices (INFLATION). The international equivalent of inflation is therefore changing exchange rates.

International Labour Organization (ILO), *n.* a special agency of the UNITED NATIONS, whose objective is to promote an improvement in living standards and working conditions throughout the world, thereby facilitating social justice as a basis for securing world peace. The ILO was originally founded in 1919 by the Treaty of Versailles and became affiliated to the UN in 1946, shortly after its establishment.

The functions of the ILO encompass all aspects of social and economic conditions affecting employment throughout the world. It promotes national labour standards and work practices, but only in an advisory capacity, as it has no legislative powers. It provides technical assistance in manpower training, social policy and administration, and encourages cooperation between labour groups. The ILO is also concerned with the collection and dissemination of international labour statistics and undertakes research on a variety of labour-related problems.

international liquidity or **international money,** *n.* monetary assets that are generally acceptable as a means of financing INTERNATIONAL TRADE and/or as an INTERNATIONAL RESERVE asset with which to finance BALANCE-OF-PAYMENTS deficits. For example, the US DOLLAR is used as the NUMERAIRE of the oil trade and also serves as an important reserve asset; the SPECIAL DRAWING RIGHT is used only as a reserve asset.

International Monetary Fund (IMF), *n.* a multinational institution set up in 1947 (following the Bretton Woods Conference, 1944) to supervise the operation of a new international monetary regime – the 'ADJUSTABLE-PEG' EXCHANGE RATE SYSTEM. The Fund seeks to maintain co-operative and orderly currency arrangements between member countries with the aim of promoting increased INTERNATIONAL TRADE and BALANCE-OF-PAYMENTS EQUILIBRIUM. The Fund is active in two main areas:

(a) EXCHANGE RATES. Down to 1971 countries established FIXED EXCHANGE-RATES for their currencies which provided pivotal values for concluding trade transactions. A country, provided it first obtained the approval of the Fund, could alter its exchange rate, adjusting the rate upwards (REVALUATION) or downwards (DEVALUATION) to a new fixed level to correct a FUNDAMENTAL DISEQUILIBRIUM in its balance of payments – a situation of either chronic payments surplus or deficit. Since 1971, most of the world's leading currencies have been floating (see FLOATING EXCHANGE-RATE SYSTEM). This has resulted in the Fund losing formal control over exchange rate movements, but member countries are still obligated to abide by certain 'rules of good conduct' laid down by the Fund, avoiding in particular EXCHANGE CONTROLS and BEGGAR-MY-NEIGHBOUR tactics.

(b) INTERNATIONAL LIQUIDITY. The Fund's resources consist of a pool of currencies and INTERNATIONAL RESERVE assets (excluding GOLD) subscribed by its members according to their allocated 'quotas'. Each country pays 75% of its quota in its own currency and 25% in international reserve assets. Countries are given *borrowing* or *drawing rights* with the Fund which they can use, together with their own nationally-held international reserves, to finance a balance-of-payments deficit.

Under the Fund's ordinary drawing-right facilities members with balance of payments difficulties may 'draw' (i.e., purchase foreign currencies from the Fund with their own currencies) up to 125% of their quota. The first 25% (the 'reserve tranche') may be drawn on demand; the remaining 100% is divided up into four 'credit tranches' of 25% each, and drawings here are 'conditional' on members agreeing with the Fund a programme of measures (for example, DEFLATION, DEVALUATION) for removing their payments deficit. Members are required to repay their drawings over a three to five year period.

In 1970 the Fund created a new international reserve asset, the SPECIAL DRAWING RIGHT (SDR) to augment the supply of international liquidity, and it has also provided additional borrowing facilities for its poorer members. See also DOMESTIC CREDIT EXPANSION.

international monetary system, *n.* a system for promoting INTERNATIONAL TRADE and SPECIALIZATION, while at the same time ensuring long-run individual BALANCE-OF-PAYMENTS EQUILIBRIUM. To be effective an international monetary system must be able to: (a) provide a system of EXCHANGE RATES between national currencies, (b) provide an ADJUSTMENT MECHANISM capable of removing payments imbalances, (c) provide a quantum of INTERNATIONAL RESERVES to finance payments deficits. Various international monetary systems have been tried, including the GOLD STANDARD and, currently, the INTERNATIONAL MONETARY FUND system.

See FIXED EXCHANGE-RATE SYSTEM, FLOATING EXCHANGE-RATE SYSTEM, EUROPEAN MONETARY SYSTEM.

international money, see INTERNATIONAL LIQUIDITY, INTERNATIONAL RESERVES.

international reserves or **foreign exchange reserves,** *n.* monetary assets that are used to settle BALANCE-OF-PAYMENTS deficits between countries. International reserves are made up of GOLD, FOREIGN EXCHANGE, INTERNATIONAL MONETARY FUND Drawing Rights, and SPECIAL DRAWING RIGHTS (SDRs). As Fig. 104 shows, gold and foreign exchange (particularly the US dollar) are the most important reserve assets. See EUROPEAN CURRENCY UNIT.

Reserve assets	Percentage of international reserves
Gold	44
Foreign exchange	51
Reserve position in International Monetary Fund	3
Special drawing rights	2

Fig. 104. **International reserves**. International reserves for 1986.

International Securities Regulatory Organization, see STOCK EXCHANGE.

International Standards Organization (SIO), *n.* an international organization established to promote common technical standards in all spheres of operations including science and commerce.

international trade, *n.* the EXCHANGE of goods and services between countries. International trade enables countries to obtain some goods and services more cheaply than they could produce them for themselves (COMPARATIVE ADVANTAGE), or be able to consume goods and services which would otherwise be unobtainable from domestic supply sources (e.g., a scarce raw material or an advanced technology).

The way countries have evolved as political states takes no account of their economic strengths and weaknesses. Through trade, countries can capitalize on their economic strengths, thereby improving their real living standards. However, the benefits of international SPECIALIZATION and trade may not be evenly distributed between countries. The manner in which world trading patterns have developed has not in fact benefited certain DEVELOPING COUNTRIES who have specialized in a narrow range of commodities for which world demand has grown slowly. In addition, protectionist measures (see PROTECTIONISM) imposed by the advanced industrialized countries have also worked against the interests of the developing countries.

See GAINS FROM TRADE, THEORY OF INTERNATIONAL TRADE, FREE TRADE, TRADE INTEGRATION, GENERAL AGREEMENT ON TARIFFS AND TRADE.

interpersonal comparison, see WELFARE ECONOMICS.

interpolate, see EXTRAPOLATE.

intra-industry specialization, *n*. a situation where different firms specialize in particular products within the *same* industry (see SPECIALIZATION). For example, in the textile industry, one firm may specialize in the production of expensive mohair suits, another in cheap casual wear. Specialization enables firms both to exploit ECONOMIES OF SCALE in production, thereby lowering supply costs, and to accommodate consumers' demands for greater product variety. See INTRA-INDUSTRY TRADE.

intra-industry trade, *n*. a situation where firms operating in the *same* industry but in *different* countries SPECIALIZE in particular products and engage in INTERNATIONAL TRADE. For example, in the textile industry a firm in the UK may specialize in the production and EXPORT of expensive mohair suits, while another firm in Taiwan may specialize in the production and export of cheap casual wear. Thus, Britain may export textile products to Taiwan, and by the same token import textiles from Taiwan.

See PREFERENCE-SIMILARITY THEORY (OF INTERNATIONAL TRADE), INTRA-INDUSTRY SPECIALIZATION.

invention, *n*. the creation of new production techniques and processes and new products. Invention is an important aspect of MARKET PERFORMANCE and a contributing factor to ECONOMIC GROWTH. At the level of the individual market, inventions make it possible to lower supply costs and prices to consumers, and to provide consumers with improved products. In a more general way, invention can add to the growth of national income and output by the qualitative improvement of a country's CAPITAL STOCK as investment in new technologies improves PRODUCTIVITY.

See INNOVATION, MONOPOLY, TECHNOLOGICAL PROGRESSIVENESS, RESEARCH AND DEVELOPMENT.

inventory, *n*. the STOCKS of finished goods, WORK-IN-PROGRESS and raw materials held by businesses. See INVENTORY INVESTMENT, INVENTORY COSTS.

inventory analysis, see STOCKHOLDING COSTS.

inventory investment, *n*. the INVESTMENT in raw materials, WORK-IN-PROGRESS, and finished STOCK. In contrast to FIXED INVESTMENT, inventories are constantly being 'turned over' as the production cycle repeats itself, with raw materials being purchased, converted first into work-in-progress, then finished goods, then finally being sold.

The level of inventory investment made by a firm will depend upon its forecasts about future demand and its resulting output plans, and the amount of stock it needs to allow for delivery delays on raw materials and production delays in serving customers, with appropriate buffer stocks to cover unforeseen contingencies. Frequently firms find that actual levels of demand differ from their forecasts, so that demand is less than expected and firms find that stocks of unsold goods build up (unintended inventory investment); or that demand exceeds expectations so that stocks run down (unintended inventory disinvestment). The cost of inventory investment includes order and delivery costs, deterioration and obsolescence of stock and interest charges on funds invested in stock. Firms seek to minimize these costs by establishing economic order quantities and optimum stockholding levels. See INVENTORY COSTS.

investment, *n.* **1.** expenditure on the purchase of FINANCIAL SECURITIES such as STOCKS and SHARES. Also called *financial investment.* PORTFOLIO investment is undertaken by persons, firms and financial institutions in the expectation of earning a return in the form of INTEREST or DIVIDENDS, or an appreciation in the capital value of the securities. **2.** capital expenditure on the purchase of physical ASSETS such as plant, machinery and equipment (fixed capital) and STOCKS (working capital), i.e., *physical* or *real investment.* In economic analysis, the term investment relates specifically to physical investment. Physical investment creates *new* assets thereby adding to the country's productive capacity, whereas financial investment only transfers the ownership of *existing* assets from one person or institution to another.

Investment requires that an amount of current CONSUMPTION is foregone (i.e., saved, see SAVINGS) so as to release the resources to finance it. Investment expenditure is a component of AGGREGATE DEMAND and an INJECTION into the CIRCULAR FLOW OF NATIONAL INCOME. In NATIONAL INCOME analysis, investment in the provision of SOCIAL PRODUCTS such as roads, hospitals and schools undertaken by the government is counted as part of GOVERNMENT EXPENDITURE; thus, investment expenditure is normally defined as consisting only of private sector investment spending.

Investment can be split up into gross and net investment: (a) gross investment is the total amount of investment that is undertaken in an economy over a specified time period (usually one year); (b) net investment is gross investment less replacement investment or CAPITAL CONSUMPTION, i.e., investment which is necessary to replace that part of the economy's existing capital stock which is used up in producing this year's output.

The amount of investment undertaken is dependent on a number of factors other than capital consumption considerations. In national income analysis, the MARGINAL EFFICIENCY OF CAPITAL/INVESTMENT and the RATE OF INTEREST are important determinants of the level of investment. The significance of investment lies in the contribution it makes to economic prosperity. Building new factories, adding new machinery and equipment, and investing in new techniques and products enables industry to supply a greater quantity of more sophisticated products and services to the consuming public, while similar investments in the provision of social capital (schools, health, etc.) contribute vitally to the up-grading of general living standards. Compare DISINVESTMENT. See also ECONOMIC GROWTH, CAPITAL ACCUMULATION, CAPITAL DEEPENING, CAPITAL GOODS, CAPITAL STOCK, CAPITAL WIDENING.

investment bank, *n.* a bank whose particular function is the provision of long-term equity and loan finance for industrial companies. See EUROPEAN INVESTMENT BANK.

investment cycle, see ACCELERATOR.

investment incentives, *n.* inducements offered by the government or local authorities to encourage capital INVESTMENT by the PRIVATE SECTOR either generally or in a specific area. Government inducements may take the form of capital grants towards the cost of equipment or tax reliefs on any profits earned. Local authority inducements usually take the form of rate reductions or exemptions and organizing the local infra structure for the convenience of potential investors. The rationale for such incentives depends primarily upon the government's objectives. It may want to reduce UNEMPLOYMENT, in which case investment through the MULTIPLIER effect will help, or it may want to give certain DEVELOPMENT AREAS additional help in tackling local problems of unemployment or urban renewal. See REGIONAL POLICY.

investment schedule, *n.* a schedule that depicts the relationship between INVESTMENT and the level of NATIONAL INCOME. The investment schedule is usually drawn with a positive slope as in Fig. 105 on page 268 for two reasons: (a) as national income and output rises, a greater amount (in absolute terms) of REPLACEMENT INVESTMENT is required to maintain the economy's existing capital stock, viz.:

	£	£
national income	1,000	2,000
capital stock	100	200
replacement investment (assumed to be 10%)	<u>10</u>	<u>20</u>

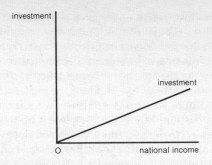

Fig. 105. **Investment schedule**. See main entry.

(b) increases in national income will bring about a greater amount of INDUCED INVESTMENT. Rising demand puts pressure on existing capacity and raises profitability thereby encouraging businesses to invest more. See ACCELERATOR, EQUILIBRIUM LEVEL OF NATIONAL INCOME.

investment trust company, *n.* a financial institution whose capital is subscribed by shareholders and which specializes in long-term investments in stocks and shares and government securities. See FINANCIAL SYSTEM, INSTITUTIONAL INVESTORS.

Investors in Industry, *n.* a holding company for a number of UK institutions which provide loan and equity finance to industry and commerce. The two main divisions of Investors in Industry, the Finance Corporation for Industry and the Industrial and Commercial Finance Corporation, were originally established in 1945 by the Bank of England and the main English and Scottish commercial banks to support high risk investments and the development of small firms.

invisible exports and imports, *n.* any services such as banking, insurance and tourism, which cannot be seen and recorded as they cross boundaries between countries. Invisible exports and imports, together with VISIBLE EXPORTS AND IMPORTS make up the CURRENT ACCOUNT of a country's BALANCE OF PAYMENTS.

invisible hand, *n.* a term devised by Adam SMITH to denote the way in which the market mechanism (PRICE SYSTEM) is capable of coordinating the independent decisions of buyers and sellers without anyone being consciously involved in the process. As the automatic equilibrating mechanism of the competitive market, Smith held that the 'invisible hand' maximizes individual welfare and economic efficiency. See PRIVATE–ENTERPRISE ECONOMY.

invoice, *n.* a document sent by a supplier to a customer that itemizes the products supplied to the customer, their prices, and the total amount of money owed by the customer for these products. An invoice is usually sent after the products have been shipped with their associated DELIVERY NOTE, and serves to inform the customer that payment is required.

See STATEMENT OF ACCOUNT.

involuntary saving, see FORCED SAVING.

irredeemable financial security or **undated security,** *n.* a financial security such as a PREFERENCE SHARE or CONSOL that is issued for an indefinite period of time and is never repayable.

irregular variations, see TIME–SERIES ANALYSIS.

I.S. (investment–saving) schedule, *n.* a schedule displaying the combinations of levels of NATIONAL INCOME and RATE OF INTEREST where the equilibrium condition for the real economy (INVESTMENT = SAVINGS) holds (see EQUILIBRIUM LEVEL OF NATIONAL INCOME).

As shown in Fig. 106, the I.S. schedule is downward–sloping: a lower rate of interest stimulates a higher volume of investment (see MARGINAL EFFICIENCY OF CAPITAL/INVESTMENT) which in turn generates a higher level of output and income through a MULTIPLIER process. However, a higher volume of investment requires a higher volume of saving to keep the real economy in equilibrium (S = I). A higher volume of saving will only be forthcoming at a higher level of income; therefore a lower rate of interest requires a higher equilibrium level of income.

The I.S. schedule interacts with the L.M. SCHEDULE in determining a general equilibrium position for the economy as a whole.

Fig. 106. **I.S. (investment saving) schedule**. See main entry.

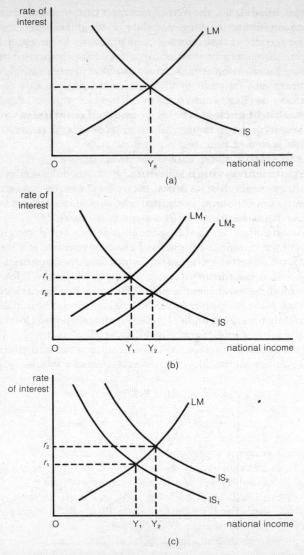

Fig. 107. **I.S./L.M. model.** (a) The general equilibrium position. (b) The effect of a shift in the L.M. schedule. (c). The effect of a shift in the I.S. schedule.

I.S./L.M. model, *n.* a theoretical construct that integrates the real, I.S. (investment-saving), and the monetary, L.M. (demand for, and supply of money), sides of the economy simultaneously to present a determinate general equilibrium position for the economy as a whole.

In the model, SAVING is a function of the level of NATIONAL INCOME and INVESTMENT is a function of the RATE OF INTEREST and the MARGINAL EFFICIENCY OF CAPITAL/INVESTMENT. The I.S. SCHEDULE shows the combinations of levels of national income and rates of interest where the equilibrium condition for the real economy $I = S$ holds (see EQUILIBRIUM LEVEL OF NATIONAL INCOME).

The demand for money L is a function of the level of national income (TRANSACTIONS DEMAND) and the rate of interest (SPECULATIVE DEMAND). The MONEY SUPPLY, M, is given exogenously. The L.M. SCHEDULE shows the combinations of levels of national income and rates of interest where the equilibrium condition for the monetary economy $L = M$ holds (see RATE OF INTEREST).

As shown in Fig. 107a, the I.S. schedule interacts with the L.M. schedule to determine a general equilibrium position, Y_e, for the economy as a whole.

The I.S./L.M. model can be used to illustrate how FISCAL POLICY and MONETARY POLICY can be employed to alter the level of national income. If the authorities wish to increase national income they can, for example, increase the money supply. The increase in the money supply lowers the RATE OF INTEREST. The fall in the rate of interest, in turn, increases the volume of investment (see MARGINAL EFFICIENCY OF CAPITAL/INVESTMENT) which then, via MULTIPLIER effects serves to increase the level of national income. In terms of the I.S./L.M. model depicted in Fig. 107b, the increase in the money supply shifts the L.M. schedule from LM_1 to LM_2, lowering the interest rates from r_1 to r_2 and bringing about an increase in national income from Y_1 to Y_2.

Alternatively, the authorities could increase national income by, for example, increasing government investment, this increase in investment serving to raise the level of national income via multiplier effects. In terms of the I.S./L.M. model depicted in Fig. 107c, the increase in investment shifts the I.S. schedule from IS_1 to IS_2 bringing about an increase in national income from Y_1 to Y_2.

See also MONEY-SUPPLY/SPENDING LINKAGES.

isocost line, *n.* a line showing combinations of FACTOR INPUTS that can be purchased for the same total money outlay. See ISOQUANT CURVE.

isoquant curve, *n.* a curve that shows the varying combinations of FACTORS OF PRODUCTION such as labour and capital which can be used to produce a given quantity of a product with a given state of technology (where FACTOR INPUTS can be substituted for one another in the production process). See Fig. 108.

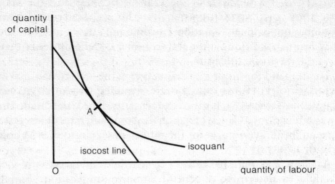

Fig. 108. **Isoquant curve.** The isoquant curve and isocost line.

If the isoquant in Fig. 108 reflects 100 units of production per period, then anywhere along that curve it is possible to determine the combination of factors required to produce 100 units. The slope of the isoquant reflects the 'substitutability' of one factor for the other in the production process (see MARGINAL RATE OF TECHNICAL SUBSTITUTION).

Isoquants slope downward to the right because the two inputs can be substituted for one another in the production process. The isoquants are convex to the origin, because although the inputs can be substituted for one another, they are not perfect substitutes, so that the MRTS of X for Y declines as we move down any equal product curve from left to right.

Isoquants bear a marked similarity with INDIFFERENCE CURVES: combinations of two commodities yielding equal satisfaction to the consumer. But while there is no way of measuring satisfaction in physical units (so that we can only talk of 'higher' or 'lower' indifference curves), we can measure physical output and say by how much production is greater on one equal–product contour than on another.

The ISOCOST LINE shows the combinations of the two factor inputs which can be purchased for the same total money outlay. Its slope reflects the *relative prices* of the two factors of production. Point A, where the isoquant is tangential to the isocost line, shows the least-cost combination of inputs for producing 100 units of input. See PROCESS RAY, PRODUCTION FUNCTION, COST FUNCTION.

isoquant map, *n.* a collection of ranked ISOQUANT CURVES that exhibits, graphically, a producer's increasing output per period when moving outward from the origin using larger quantities of two FACTOR INPUTS, as in Fig. 109a on page 274. Isoquant curves are a cardinal measure and the numbers on the isoquant curves in Fig. 109a indicate the absolute level of output per period. Isoquant curves never cross because two crossing curves would imply inconsistent or irrational choices between the two factor inputs by the producer (see ECONOMIC MAN).

Although it is often possible to substitute factor inputs in the production process, such substitution cannot continue indefinitely. Some minimum amount of both factors is required if production is to be maintained at a given level: for example, in order to produce 300 units in Fig. 109a at least VL of X is required, and at least UT of Y. For at point T the isoquant is horizontal, indicating that at T the MARGINAL RATE OF TECHNICAL SUBSTITUTION of X for Y is zero. Similarly at point L the isoquant is vertical, showing that beyond this point the substitution of Y for X would result in a decrease in output (indicated by the fact that the isoquant sheers away from the Y axis).

The ridge lines in Fig, 109a delineate those portions of the isoquants from which the firm will make its choice of resource combinations. The top one joins all points at which isoquants become vertical, while the bottom one is the locus of all points at which isoquants become horizontal. The typical relations that will obtain betweeen one isoquant and another can be shown by taking a cross-section of the production 'contour' map along the line MN. As we move up this line from M, we can read of the outputs that will be produced by increasing quantities of input Y, when used with the firm's plant and the given quantity OM of input X.

Not only does output increase as we move along MN but the rate at which output rises follows a general pattern. In Fig. 109b, at output BB_1 an increase in input Y promises larger than proportional increases in output; at output DD_1 small percentage increases in the use of Y promise equal percentage changes in output; at output FF_1 increases in factor Y promise less than proportional increases in output. This pattern is recognizable as the 'law of variable factor proportions' (see RETURNS TO THE VARIABLE-FACTOR INPUT).

The same pattern would be recognizable if we traced the behaviour of

ISOQUANT MAP

Fig. 109. **Isoquant map**. See main entry.

output along a line such as OK. Here the distances between successive isoquants reduce as we move towards K, until point P is reached. After this point, the distance between successive isoquants becomes progressively larger. Along the line OK, increasing quantities of the two variable factors X and Y are being combined with the firm's fixed plant and equipment.

The MARGINAL PHYSICAL PRODUCT curve for input Y shown in Fig. 109c is derived from the total product curve in Fig. 109b. As the amount of factor Y used increases from OA_1 to OD_1, its marginal physical product is rising. Then, for further increases in the use of factor Y, its marginal physical product is falling, becoming negative if more than OF_1 of Y is applied.

issued share capital, *n.* the amount of its AUTHORIZED SHARE CAPITAL that a JOINT-STOCK COMPANY has issued to SHAREHOLDERS in order to raise CAPITAL.

issuing house, *n.* a financial institution (often a part of a MERCHANT BANK) that arranges and underwrites the issue of new STOCKS and SHARES on behalf of corporate clients on the STOCK EXCHANGE.

J

J-curve effect, *n.* the tendency for a country's BALANCE–OF–PAYMENTS deficit to initially worsen following a DEVALUATION of its currency before then moving into surplus. This is because the full adjustment of trade volumes to devaluation involves a time lag: there is an immediate fall in export prices and a rise in import prices so that current exports earn less foreign exchange and current imports absorb more foreign exchange thereby increasing the size of the payment deficit (the downturn of the J-curve). Over time, however, the lower export prices will increase overseas demand and export earnings will rise, while higher import prices will reduce domestic demand for imports, leading to an improvement in the balance of payments (the upturn of the J-curve). See BALANCE–OF–PAYMENTS EQUILIBRIUM.

Jevons, William Stanley (1835–82), English scientist and philosopher who developed UTILITY theory in his book *The Theory of Political Economy* (1871). Jevons rejected the idea that the value of a good depends upon the labour needed to produce it, and argued instead that value depends upon the individual consumer's subjective evaluation of the utility of a good. He suggested that goods are valuable only if they provide utility and that labour and other factors of production become valuable when they are used to produce these goods. Specifically, he showed that a consumer will increase purchases of goods until the MARGINAL UTILITY gained from the last pennyworth of one good equals the marginal quality of the last pennyworth of every other good.

Jevons was also particularly interested in linking statistical analysis with theoretical analysis in economics, and he developed statistical series on production in Britain over a long period to try and determine the cause of BUSINESS CYCLES.

jobber, *n.* a dealer who acts as a principal in buying and selling STOCKS and SHARES directly on the STOCK EXCHANGE. A jobber usually specializes in a small group of securities (for example, the shares of companies in a particular industry) and holds blocs of these securities. He makes his income out of the difference between the price at which he is prepared to buy shares and the (higher) price at which he sells. The jobber marks his buying and selling prices upward or downward depending upon whether his bloc of securities is falling or increasing. For example, if there is a heavy public demand for a particular security then as the jobber sells some of his holdings of that security he will mark up his price for that security to reflect its increasing scarcity. In this way the jobber plays an important part in making a market for a security. See MARKET MAKER.

In the UK the distinction between the function of jobbers and STOCKBROKERS (agents who act on behalf of clients) was ended in 1986.

joint costs, *n.* the COSTS involved in producing several products which are in JOINT SUPPLY, for example, petrol, diesel, tar, etc. produced from a common oil-refining process. Joint costs such as oil-refinery running costs are difficult to allocate precisely between the different products in determining the exact cost of each.

joint demand, see COMPLEMENTARY PRODUCTS.

joint-profit maximization, *n.* the possible situation of the optimization of industry profits by firms who coordinate their price and output policies rather than compete against each other. Joint-profit maximization is typically associated with oligopolistic markets (see OLIGOPOLY) where firms, recognizing their MUTUAL INTERDEPENDENCE operate PRICE LEADERSHIP systems and CARTELS.

joint-stock company, *n.* a form of company in which a number of people contribute funds to finance a FIRM in return for SHARES in the company. Joint-stock companies are able to raise funds by issuing shares to large numbers of SHAREHOLDERS and thus are able to raise more capital to finance their operations than could a sole proprietor or even a partnership. Once a joint-stock company is formed then it becomes a separate legal entity apart from its shareholders, able to enter into contracts with suppliers and customers. Joint-stock companies are managed by the board of directors appointed by shareholders. The directors must report on the progress of the company to the shareholders at an ANNUAL GENERAL MEETING where shareholders can in principle vote to remove existing directors if they are dissatisfied with their performance.

The development of joint stock companies was given a considerable boost by the introduction of the principle of LIMITED LIABILITY which limited the maximum loss which a shareholder was liable for in the event of company failure. This protection for shareholders encouraged many more of them to invest in companies.

There are two main forms of joint stock company:

(a) *private company*. Under UK Company Law the maximum number of shareholders in a private company is limited to 50 and the shares the company issues cannot be bought and sold on the STOCK EXCHANGE. Such companies carry the term limited (Ltd) after their name.

(b) *public company*. Under UK Company Law there must be a minimum of 7 shareholders in a public company, but otherwise a company can have an unlimited number of shareholders. Shares in a public company can be bought and sold on the stock exchange and so can be bought by the general public. Such companies carry the term public limited company (Plc) after their name.

Most big firms (OLIGOPOLISTS) are public companies since this is the only practical way of obtaining access to large amounts of capital. Although the shareholders are the owners of a public company very often it is the company's management which effectively controls its affairs. See FIRM, DIVORCE OF OWNERSHIP FROM CONTROL.

joint supply, *n.* a situation where the increase or decrease in PRODUCTION of one good is inextricably linked to a greater or lesser extent with the production of another. An example of joint supply is wool and mutton. An increase in the DEMAND for wool increases the SUPPLY of sheep, which in turn brings about an autonomous shift (increase) in the SUPPLY CURVE of mutton. As a result, if the demand for mutton remains unchanged, the PRICE of mutton will fall. See COMPLEMENTARY PRODUCTS.

joint venture, *n.* a business owned jointly by two independent firms (or by a firm and the government). Joint ventures permit a greater total amount of resources to be employed in the supply of a good or service, and can be especially effective in exploiting complementary resources with one firm, for example, contributing production know-how and the other, market expertise.

K

Keynes, John Maynard (1883–1946), English economist at Cambridge University who offered an explanation of mass UNEMPLOYMENT and suggestions for government policy to cure unemployment in his influential book: *The General Theory of Employment, Interest and Money* (1936). Prior to Keynes, CLASSICAL ECONOMICS had maintained that in a market economy the economic system would spontaneously tend to produce full employment of resources because the exchange mechanism would ensure a correspondence between supply and demand (SAY'S LAW). Consequently the classicists were confident that business recessions would cure themselves, with interest rates falling under the pressure of accumulating savings so encouraging businessmen to borrow and invest more; and with wage rates falling, so reducing production costs and encouraging businessmen to employ more workers. Keynes' concern about the extent and duration of the worldwide interwar DEPRESSION led him to look for other explanations of recession.

Keynes argued that classical political economists were concerned with the relative shares in national output of the different factors of production, rather than the forces which determine the level of general economic activity, so that their theories of value and distribution related only to the special case of full employment. Concentrating upon the economic aggregates of NATIONAL INCOME, CONSUMPTION, SAVINGS and INVESTMENT, Keynes provided a general theory for explaining the level of economic activity. He argued that there is no assurance that savings would accumulate during a depression and depress interest rates, since savings depend on income and with high unemployment incomes are low.

Furthermore, he argued that investment depends primarily on business confidence which would be low during a depression so the investment would be unlikely to rise even if interest rate fell. Finally, he argued that the wage rate would be unlikely to fall much during a depression given its 'stickiness', and even if it did fall, this would merely exacerbate the depression by reducing consumption.

Keynes saw the cause of a depression as reduced AGGREGATE DEMAND, and in the absence of any automatic stimulus to demand he argued that governments must intervene to increase aggregate demand and end depression. He suggested that governments stimulate consumption by putting money into consumers' pockets through tax cuts or directly increase governments' own expenditure to add to aggregate demand. See EQUILIBRIUM LEVEL OF NATIONAL INCOME.

Keynsian economics, *n*. the view held by KEYNES of the way in which the aggregate economy works, subsequently refined and developed by his successors.

Much of what is today called Keynsian economics originated from Keynes' book: *The General Theory of Employment, Interest and Money* (1936). Keynes gave economics a new direction and an explanation of the phenomenon of mass unemployment so prevalent in the 1930s. Economic doctrine before Keynes was based primarily upon what is now termed MICROECONOMICS. Keynes switched from the classical concentration on individual prices and markets and individual demand functions to aggregate analysis, introducing new concepts such as the CONSUMPTION FUNCTION.

The classical economists argued (and were officially supported by the monetary authorities, up to the time of accepting Keynes' arguments) that FULL EMPLOYMENT is the result of a smooth-working PRIVATE-ENTERPRISE ECONOMY. If UNEMPLOYMENT occurred, then WAGES would fall (due to competition in labour markets), to such an extent that unemployed labour would be re-employed (the neoclassical analysis that marginal productivity of labour would now exceed or equal its marginal cost). Keynes introduced the possibility of 'rigid wages' in an attempt to explain what was inconceivable to classical and neoclassical economists, general equilibrium within the economy at less than full employment.

Keynes argued that INCOME depends upon the volume of employment. The relationship between income and CONSUMPTION is defined by the PROPENSITY TO CONSUME.

Therefore, consumption is dependent upon the interrelated functions of income and employment. Anticipated expenditure on consumption and INVESTMENT is termed effective demand and in a situation of equilibrium, equals AGGREGATE SUPPLY. Keynes was of the opinion that in a state of equilibrium, the volume of employment was dependent upon the aggregate-supply function, the propensity to consume, and the amount of investment. The level of employment would therefore increase if either the propensity to consume increased or the level of investment increased, i.e., greater demand for consumer and producer goods leads to an increase in supply. Increasing supply tends to lead to higher levels of employment.

The difficulty of reducing wages, (because of trade union pressure to maintain living standards), means that 'rigidity of wages' may lead to a situation of equilibrium at less than full employment. Where this occurs, the government as a buyer of both consumer and producer goods, can influence the level of AGGREGATE DEMAND in the economy. Aggregate demand may be increased by FISCAL POLICY or MONETARY POLICY. Keynes placed the emphasis on fiscal policy whereby the government spends more on investment projects than it collects from taxes. This is known as DEFICIT FINANCING and stimulates aggregate demand when the economy finds itself in a condition of DEPRESSION. Through the MULTIPLIER effect the stimulus to aggregate demand is a number of times larger than the initial investment. The effect is to move the economy towards a situation of full employment.

Certain Western countries began to question Keynesian economic ideas in the 1970s as they embraced MONETARISM and began to revert to the classical economic idea that government intervention is unnecessary and that markets can ensure prosperity, provided that market rigidities are removed.

See EQUILIBRIUM LEVEL OF NATIONAL INCOME, BUSINESS CYCLES, CIRCULAR FLOW OF NATIONAL INCOME, CLASSICAL ECONOMICS, DEFLATION-ARY GAP, MONEY SUPPLY/SPENDING LINKAGES, QUANTITY THEORY OF MONEY, I.S./L.M. MODEL, SAY'S LAW, INFLATIONARY GAP, SUPPLY–SIDE ECONOMICS.

kinked demand curve, *n.* a curve that explains why the PRICES charged by competing oligopolists (see OLIGOPOLY), once established, tend to be stable. In Fig. 110 on page 282, DD is the DEMAND CURVE if all firms charge the *same* price. Starting from point K, if one firm felt that if it were to charge a higher (unmatched) price than its rivals it would lose sales to these rivals, then its relevant perceived demand curve becomes $D_H K$. On the other hand, the firm may feel that if it were to charge a lower price it would not gain sales from rivals, because rivals would not let this happen – they would match price cuts along DD. Both price increases and decreases are thus seen to be selfdefeating, and this produces a 'kinked demand curve' with prices tending to settle at K. The theory suggests that price K is likely to 'stick' even though costs may change.

It can be seen that there is a sharp step in the marginal revenue curve corresponding to the kink in the demand curve. In consequence, for a

Fig. 110. **Kinked demand curve**. See main entry.

wide range of vertical shifts in the marginal cost curve (between points X and Y) K remains the profit maximizing selling price. See GAME THEORY, MUTUAL INTERDEPENDENCE, PRICE LEADERSHIP.

Kondratief cycle or **long-wave cycle,** *n.* a theoretical long-term cycle ranging from boom to recession over a period of fifty years or so upon which shorter-term BUSINESS CYCLES are superimposed. Based upon statistical observations by Kondratief, explanations for these long waves in economic activity usually rely upon a 'bunching' of significant INNOVATIONS like petrol engines, the motor car, etc., which give an impetus to economic activity for several decades before their impact wanes.

kurtosis, *n.* the sharpness of the peak of a group of numerical observations summarized in a FREQUENCY DISTRIBUTION. Where such a distribution is depicted in the form of a bell-shaped HISTOGRAM or CONTINUOUS DISTRIBUTION, kurtosis reflects the maximum height of the distribution, showing the largest values in the distribution.

L

labour, *n*. the contribution to productive activity made by the workforce both by hand (for example, the assembly of a car) and mentally (for example, devising a stock-control system). Labour is one of the three main FACTORS OF PRODUCTION, the others being NATURAL RESOURCES and CAPITAL. See also ECONOMIC GROWTH, HUMAN CAPITAL.

labour force, *n*. the total number of workers available for employment in an economy. The size of the labour force together with the CAPITAL STOCK determines a country's AGGREGATE SUPPLY potential. See POTENTIAL GROSS NATIONAL PRODUCT, ECONOMIC GROWTH.

labour-intensive firm/industry, *n*. a firm or industry that produces its output of goods or services using proportionately large inputs of LABOUR and relatively small amounts of CAPITAL.

The proportions of labour and capital which a firm uses in production depends mainly on the relative prices of labour and capital inputs and their relative productivities. This in turn depends upon the degree of standardization of the product in so far as fragmented markets where consumers demand product variety are not amenable to the use of large-scale capital-intensive production methods which facilitate ECONOMIES OF SCALE.

Clothing manufacture, plumbing and hairdressing are examples of labour-intensive industries. See BATCH PRODUCTION, CAPITAL-LABOUR RATIO.

labour market, *n*. a FACTOR MARKET that provides for an exchange of work for WAGES. The SUPPLY side of the market is represented by individual workers, or, more commonly, TRADE UNIONS bargaining on a collective basis. The DEMAND side of the market is represented by firms who are requiring labour as a FACTOR INPUT in the production process (see MARGINAL-PHYSICAL PRODUCT, MARGINAL-REVENUE PRODUCT).

The labour market, however, is different from other factor markets in that labour has certain 'peculiarities' that make the application of the usual 'laws' of supply and demand inappropriate. The exchange is never completed within the labour market. The employer purchases only an ability or propensity to work. The employer has then to set the worker to task in a way likely to maximize this propensity, while the worker, who receives in the main a fixed wage, will wish to minimize it. A potential conflict of interests therefore continues even after the act of exchange. Furthermore, work is performed in large groups which produce group norms and social interactions, so the individual buyer and seller may not be the primary relationship in the market. When viewing the labour market as a whole we must allow for it being characterized by powerful institutions, social attitudes, and imperfect and costly information (labour is restricted in the amount of time that it can use to seek out new employments and firms in seeking new workers, while any accumulated HUMAN CAPITAL – skill, training, experience – is illiquid and imperfectly transferable between employments). Finally, all workers do not have similar preferences and the wage must also take account of the utility and disutility of work because labour is the only factor input that has some choice not only in the provision of its inputs but also the area of those inputs.

These are some of the 'peculiarities' which characterize the act of exchange in the labour market and produce a situation in which the wage and employment level is not uniquely determined by the laws of supply and demand. Rather, there is a 'range of indeterminacy' over which rival power blocs within the labour market (trade unions, employers and the government) seek to further their economic objectives by bargaining.

See also COLLECTIVE BARGAINING, SUPPLY-SIDE ECONOMICS, WAGE RATES.

labour theory of value, *n.* a doctrine developed by the classical economists, (particularly Adam SMITH and David RICARDO) that states that the value of a GOOD is determined by the amount of LABOUR input needed to produce that good. Thus, the ratio of the equilibrium prices of two commodities is directly proportional to the ratio of labour required to produce them.

Smith was the first to tentatively suggest a labour theory of value, though he acknowledged that the value of a good must be determined by a number of input costs: RENT, WAGES and PROFIT, even if labour did constitute the greatest part of final value. Ricardo accepted that profits and rent may have to be taken into account but that it did not detract from his main argument of relative values between two goods being fundamentally determined by labour cost. Karl MARX developed Ricardo's ideas, decomposing labour value into three constituent parts.

The three parts are 'constant capital' (the capital used up in production), 'variable capital' (human labour input), and 'surplus value' (the excess value over and above labour and capital used in the production process). Where surplus value exists there is exploitation of the labour input insomuch as they are being paid less than their full input value.

The labour theory of value was replaced towards the end of the 19th century by the MARGINAL-PRODUCTIVITY THEORY OF DISTRIBUTION, which took into account the contribution of all factor inputs into the production process not just labour. See CLASSICAL ECONOMICS.

LAFTA, see LATIN AMERICAN FREE TRADE ASSOCIATION.

lagged relationship, *n.* the relationship between two or more VARIABLES in different time periods. For example, the current value of a variable like consumption expenditure will depend upon income in the previous time period. Time is denoted by the letter t, with $t-1$ being one period back and $t+1$ being one period forward. Such a relationship between income and consumption can be written in the notational form:

$$C_t = f(Y_{t-1})$$

where C_t = consumption in present period, Y_{t-1} = income in the previous period.

See also LEADS AND LAGS, COBWEB THEOREM.

lags, see LEADS AND LAGS.

laissez-faire, *n.* a doctrine of FREE TRADE and competition dating from the time of Adam SMITH to the present day. The implication of the theory is that private enterprise will achieve greater economic growth through human effort than will a CENTRALLY PLANNED ECONOMY where the government is the prime participant, and where human effort is subdued. See also CLASSICAL ECONOMICS, PRIVATE-ENTERPRISE ECONOMY, PRICE SYSTEM.

land, see NATURAL RESOURCES.

last-in-first-out (LIFO), see STOCK VALUATION.

lateral integration, see HORIZONTAL INTEGRATION.

Latin American Free Trade Association (LAFTA), *n.* a regional alliance established in 1960 with the general objective of spurring the INDUSTRIALIZATION of member countries by creating a FREE TRADE AREA. There were seven original members of LAFTA: Argentina, Brazil, Peru, Chile, Mexico, Paraguay and Uruguay, with three other countries joining later: Columbia, Ecuador and Venezuela.

However, because of an initial difference in the level of economic development between the various members and serious nationalistic (sovereignty) differences on policy issues, progress towards trade liberalization has been limited. In 1966, a number of the weaker members (Chile, Colombia, Ecuador, Peru and Bolivia), sought to redress what they considered to be a growing gap between themselves and the more advanced countries of the region (Brazil, Argentina and Mexico) by forming a closer-knit subgroup (the Andean group). See also ECONOMIC DEVELOPMENT.

law of diminishing marginal returns, see DIMINISHING RETURNS.

law of large numbers, *n.* the law that states that large groups tend to behave more uniformly than a single individual. For example, an individual consumer might buy more of a product whose price has risen, whereas most consumers would buy less. See DEMAND CURVE.

law of variable-factor proportions, see RETURNS TO THE VARIABLE-FACTOR INPUT.

leading indicators, *n.* the statistical TIME SERIES that past experience has shown tends to reflect later changes, and which thus can be used to forecast these changes because they precede the changes in a consistent manner and by relatively constant time interval. For example, current birth statistics would provide a firm basis for predicting primary school admissions five or six years ahead. Leading indicators like orders for new machine tools, overtime/short-time working in manufacturing and housebuilding starts are frequently used to forecast cyclical changes in macro-economic variables like GNP. See FORECASTING, TIME-SERIES ANALYSIS.

leads and lags, *n.* **1.** the timing differences that exist between peaks and troughs of leading and lagging indicators, and the overall BUSINESS CYCLE. Thus, in a seven-year business cycle, if the peak of the cycle occurred in the middle year (year four), then a leading indicator, such as starts on new houses, may have peaked in year three. This indicator leads the business cycle by one year. Similarly lagged variables will have peaks or troughs after the business cycle.

2. the time variation from standard payment practice when settling foreign trade debts. The variation from standard practice results from the expectations of traders which may influence the profitability of settling the debt early (lead) or late (lag). The commonest factor which contributes to this practice is expectations of a change in the EXCHANGE RATE. Traders in an importing country have an incentive to postpone settlement to manufacturers in the exporting nation if there is an expectation of a foreseeable devaluation in the rate of exchange of the exporting country's currency. Similarly, if a revaluation (that is, an increase in exchange rate) is in prospect, traders in the debtor nation can be expected to settle early.

See also J–CURVE, LAGGED RELATIONSHIP, LEADING INDICATORS, COBWEB THEOREM.

leakages, see WITHDRAWALS.

learning curve, see EXPERIENCE CURVE.

lease, *n.* a legal contract under which the owner of an ASSET (such as buildings and machinery) grants to someone else the right to use that asset for a specified period of time in return for periodic payments of RENT. See LEASING, LEASEBACK.

leaseback, *n.* an arrangement whereby the owner of an ASSET agrees to sell it to another person or company on condition that the asset can be leased to its original owner for a fixed term at a prearranged RENT. Leaseback is normally undertaken to enable companies with large assets such as property to realise cash for use elsewhere in their business. See LEASE, LEASING.

leasing, *n.* the purchase of an ASSET (mostly buildings, machinery and vehicles) by a leasing company which retains the ownership of the assets, and which then hires out the item for use by clients who pay an agreed RENT. Leasing is a useful source of INVESTMENT in so far as it enables individuals or companies to use assets without having to tie up large amounts of capital. See LEASE, OFF–BALANCE SHEET FINANCING.

least–squares estimation, see REGRESSION ANALYSIS.

ledger, *n.* the accounting records that keep a note of a firm's day-to-day financial transactions with outside parties. For example, the purchases or CREDITORS ledger would show the value of raw materials or services purchased from each supplier, payments made to suppliers for these, and any amounts still owing to suppliers. Similarly, the sales or DEBTORS ledger would show the value of goods or services sold to each customer, amounts they have paid for these, and any amounts still owed by customers. In former times such ledger accounts took the form of bound ledgers in which entries were recorded by hand; nowadays they are generally kept as computer records. See DOUBLE-ENTRY ACCOUNTS.

legal tender, *n.* that part of a country's MONEY SUPPLY which is, in the eyes of the law, totally acceptable in payment for a purchase of a good or service or repayment of a debt. CURRENCY (notes and coins) issued by the government fulfil this requirement. By contrast, a trader is within his legal rights to refuse to accept as payment a cheque drawn against a BANK DEPOSIT.

lender, *n.* a person, firm or institution that makes a LOAN to a BORROWER to enable the borrower to finance CONSUMPTION or INVESTMENT. Lenders frequently require borrowers to offer some COLLATERAL SECURITY, for example, property deeds, which lenders may retain in the event of borrowers failing to repay the loan. See also CREDIT, CREDITOR (ACCOUNTS PAYABLE), FINANCIAL SYSTEM.

lender of last resort, *n.* the rôle of the CENTRAL BANK in making money available to the COMMERCIAL BANKS when the banks are short of funds. When the commercial banks find themselves with fewer liquid assets than they feel it is commercially prudent for them to hold, (that is, when they fall below their RESERVE-ASSET RATIO requirement), then they must improve their liquidity. They can do this either by selling off TREASURY BILLS to the central bank or calling in their short-term loans to the DISCOUNT HOUSES who in turn are then forced to borrow from the central bank. To ensure that commercial banks turn to the central bank for funds only as a last resort, the central bank generally makes funds available at a higher cost than prevailing market interest rates. This penal rate of interest is presently called the BILL-DISCOUNTING RATE OF INTEREST (formerly, minimum lending rate). The discount house must offer collateral such as government bonds as security for the loan.

See FRONT DOOR, BACK DOOR.

level of significance, see HYPOTHESIS TESTING.

leverage, see CAPITAL GEARING.

leveraged bid, see TAKE-OVER BID.

Lewis, Sir W. Arthur (b.1915) West Indian economist who has contributed to the theory of ECONOMIC DEVELOPMENT and whose seminal text is *The Theory of Economic Growth* (1955). He argued that though growth can bring positive benefits in improving living standards in DEVELOPING COUNTRIES, it can also disrupt those countries' cultures especially where growth is too rapid. Lewis has emphasized the importance of economic infrastructure in developing countries, and stressed the need for such social overhead capital as transport networks, communications systems and educational facilities as prerequisites for growth.

liability, *n.* a claim on the resources of an individual or business in respect of monies borrowed. A liability is thus a form of DEBT, for example, a bank overdraft or LOAN, a building society MORTGAGE. See ASSET, BALANCE SHEET.

licence, *n.* **1.** The grant by one FIRM to another firm (*exclusive licence*) or others (*nonexclusive licence*) of the right(s) to manufacture its product, to use its technology or distribution facilities. Similarly, the grant by the government to an authority (for example, a gas corporation) or firm of the rights to supply a particular good or provide a particular service. The granting of a licence in these cases is a CONTRACTUAL arrangement which is entered into usually for a specified period of time, with the licensee usually paying a ROYALTY or FEE for the rights assigned. **2.** a document that shows proof of legal ownership (or entitlement) and compliance with a statutory or private requirement for a payment thereon, for example, a television licence issued by the government or a private fishing licence. Such licences are issued primarily for the purpose of raising revenue. **3.** a document issued as a means of ensuring that premises or persons are 'fit and proper' for the purposes in which they are engaged, for example, a licensed casino, a licensed dealer in securities.

licensed deposit taker, *n.* a COMMERCIAL BANK, SAVINGS BANK, FINANCE HOUSE or other financial institution that is recognized by the Bank of England as being allowed to operate a banking service and which is therefore subject to credit controls.

life-cycle hypothesis, *n.* the hypothesis that states that CONSUMPTION is not dependent solely on current DISPOSABLE INCOME, but it is related to a person's anticipated lifetime earnings. For example, a person may purchase, today, a range of expensive products such as a car, washing machine, etc., on extended CREDIT, expecting that future income rises as he or she moves up a salary scale or obtains increase in basic wage rates to cover interest and repayment charges. This hypothesis is similar to the PERMANENT-INCOME HYPOTHESIS, in that it gives greater breadth to the analysis of SAVING and consumption over and above the simplistic assumption that consumption is solely a function of current income.

limited liability, *n.* a liability that limits the maximum LOSS which a SHAREHOLDER is liable for in the event of company failure to the SHARE CAPITAL which he originally subscribed.

The principle of limited liability limits a shareholder's maximum loss in the event of his company failing to the original share capital which he invested, no further claims by creditors against the shareholder's other assets being permitted. In protecting shareholders in this way many more people were encouraged to invest in companies and JOINT-STOCK COMPANIES grew rapidly. To warn potential creditors that any claims by creditors will be limited in total to the amount of the company's share capital, such companies carry the term: 'Limited' (Ltd.) or 'Public Limited Company' (Plc) after their names.

When a business is subject to *unlimited liability*, as is the case with sole proprietors, unlimited partnerships and unlimited companies then the owners of the business are liable in full for the debts of the business if it fails. This may involve them losing not only the capital that they have put into the business, but also most of their personal assets.

limiting factor, *n.* the critical constraint upon a firm's budgeted activity level. In most circumstances the limiting factor will be the amounts that the company can sell, but in certain cases the limiting factor might be shortage of production capacity, shortages of particular raw materials or the like. Here planning will be aimed at devising a sales programme which generates maximum profit from these limited resources.

See BUDGET, BUDGETING, LINEAR PROGRAMMING.

limit pricing or **entry-forestalling price,** *n.* a pricing strategy employed by established oligopolists (see OLIGOPOLY) in a market to exploit BARRIERS TO ENTRY in order to forestall new entry. A limit-pricing model is shown in Fig. 111, where the barrier to entry is assumed to be ECONOMIES OF SCALE. Established firms produce a total output of OQ_1, which is sold at price OP_1. The MINIMUM EFFICIENT SCALE of output for the entrant to be just as cost-effective as established firms is Q_1Q_2 (equal to OQ). It will be seen that as a result of the addition of this 'extra' output to existing market supply OQ_1, the market price is lowered to OP_2, a price at which entry is unprofitable. Established firms are thus able to set an entry-limiting price of OP_1, thereby securing ABOVE-NORMAL PROFITS of the order AB.

linear equation, *n.* the relationship between two or more VARIABLES which takes the form of a straight line, for example:

$$Y = a + bX$$

where *a* and *b* are constant PARAMETERS, X is the INDEPENDENT VARIABLE and Y is the DEPENDENT VARIABLE. In the graphical representation of the equation, shown in Fig. 112, *a* is the intercept, i.e. the point where the straight line intersects the vertical axis, and *b* gives the slope of the line.

linear programming, *n.* a mathematical technique for utilizing limited resources to meet a desired objective, such as minimizing cost or maximizing profit, where the resource limits are expressed as constraints.

For example, consider a firm making only two products: bookcases and chairs, and trying to decide how many of each to make. The company's output will be limited by the productive resources which it has available, and these are depicted graphically in Fig. 113 on page 293, where quantities of bookcases are represented on the horizontal axis and quantities of chairs on the vertical axis. If the company has only 80 hours

Fig. 111. **Limit pricing.** See main entry.

Fig. 112. **Linear equation.** See main entry.

of machine time available each week, while a bookcase needs 5 hours of machine time to make and a chair 5 hours of machine time, then the maximum output with the available machine would be represented by line XY. Again, if there were only 84 man hours of direct labour hours available, and each bookcase needs 7 hours work while each chair needs 3 hours work, then the maximum output with the available direct labour force would be represented by line RT.

The area OXZT represents all feasible combinations of bookcases and chairs which can be produced with the limited machine hours and man hours available (the *feasible region*).

If each bookcase (b) sold makes a profit of £5, and each chair (c) £4, then in order to maximize profit the firm would seek to maximize output:

$$5b + 4c.$$

For example, in order to earn a profit of £60 the company could produce 12 bookcases or 15 chairs or some combination of the two, as represented by the broken line MT in Fig. 113. Combinations of bookcases and chairs corresponding to larger total profits can be represented by other lines such as LN, which are parallel to MT, but further out from the origin 0. The line LN represents the largest profit which the firm can earn with its available man-hours and machine-hours, since it is the highest broken line which just touches the resource constraints represented by the feasible region OXZT. The firm will therefore settle at point Z producing OV chairs per week and OW bookcases each week in order to maximize its profits from available resources.

Linear programming also provides information about the value of additional resources to a company. For example, it shows how much extra profit could be earned by increasing the amount of machine-hours or man-hours available, and thus indicate the maximum amount which the company should pay for additional units of these resources. These maximum amounts which the company could afford to pay for additional resources without prejudicing profitability are called SHADOW PRICES of the machine-hours and man-hour resources.

Where a company produces more than two outputs, two-dimensional graphical analysis is impossible. However, an optimum combination of outputs can still be calculated using a similar reasoning process through the mathematical approach called the *simplex method*. See PRODUCTION POSSIBILITY BOUNDARY.

Fig. 113. **Linear programming**. See main entry.

liquidation, *n.* the process by which a JOINT-STOCK COMPANY's existence as a legal entity ceases by 'winding up' the company. Such a process can be initiated at the behest of the CREDITORS where the company is insolvent (a compulsory winding up), or by the company directors or SHAREHOLDERS, in which case it is known as a voluntary winding up.

The person appointed liquidator, either by the company directors/shareholders or the creditors, sells off the company's ASSETS for as much as they will realize. The proceeds of the sale are used to discharge any outstanding liabilities to the creditors of the company. If there are insufficient funds to pay all creditors (INSOLVENCY), preferential creditors are paid first (for example, the INLAND REVENUE for tax due), then ordinary creditors pro rata. If there is a surplus after payment of all creditors this is distributed pro rata amongst the shareholders of the company. See also LIMITED LIABILITY, SHAREHOLDERS CAPITAL.

liquidity, *n.* a monetary ASSET (such as CURRENCY) which can be used directly as a means of payment. See MONEY, MONEY-SUPPLY DEFINITIONS, LIQUIDITY PREFERENCE.

liquidity preference, *n.* a preference for holding MONEY instead of investing it. KEYNES identifies three motives for holding money: (a) TRANSACTIONS DEMAND – money held on a day-to-day basis to finance current purchases; (b) PRECAUTIONARY DEMAND – money held to meet unexpected future outlays; (c) SPECULATIVE DEMAND – money held in anticipation of a fall in the price of assets. The amount of money held for these purposes depends on two main factors: the RATE OF INTEREST and the level of NATIONAL INCOME. See MONEY DEMAND SCHEDULE.

liquidity ratio, see RESERVE-ASSET RATIO.

liquidity trap, *n.* a situation where the RATE OF INTEREST is so low that people prefer to hold money (LIQUIDITY PREFERENCE) rather than invest it. At low rates of interest the MONEY DEMAND SCHEDULE becomes infinitely elastic. In these circumstances any attempt by monetary policy to lower interest rates in order to stimulate more INVESTMENT (see MONEY SUPPLY/SPENDING LINKAGES) will be futile, and will simply result in more money being held.

KEYNES argued that in a depressed economy which is experiencing a liquidity trap the only way to stimulate investment is to increase GOVERNMENT EXPENDITURE or reduce TAXES in order to increase AGGREGATE DEMAND and improve business confidence about future prosperity, encouraging them to invest.

listed company, *n.* a public JOINT-STOCK COMPANY whose shares are traded on the main STOCK EXCHANGE. To obtain a full listing on the main stock exchange a company is required to provide comprehensive information about its activities. See QUOTED COMPANY, UNLISTED SECURITIES MARKET.

list price, *n.* the published PRICE of a good or service. The actual price paid by the buyer is often less than this because suppliers are prepared to offer cash and trade DISCOUNTS. Many suppliers specify RECOMMENDED RETAIL PRICES for their products, but again the actual price paid can be much less than that recommended depending upon the strength of retail competition.

L.M. (liquidity-money) schedule, *n.* a schedule that shows the combinations of levels of NATIONAL INCOME and RATES OF INTEREST where the equilibrium condition for the monetary economy $L = M$ holds (see RATE OF INTEREST). See Fig. 114.

The L.M. schedule interacts with the I.S. SCHEDULE in determining a general equilibrium position for the economy as a whole.

See also I.S./L.M. MODEL, SPECULATIVE DEMAND, TRANSACTIONS DEMAND.

loan capital or **debt capital,** *n.* the money employed in a company that has been borrowed from external sources for fixed periods of time by the issue of FIXED-INTEREST FINANCIAL SECURITIES such as DEBENTURES. See SHARE CAPITAL, BALANCE SHEET, CAPITAL GEARING.

loans, *n.* the money advanced by COMMERCIAL BANKS, FINANCE HOUSES, BUILDING SOCIETIES, etc., to business and personal borrowers that is used to finance physical and financial INVESTMENT and purchases of current goods and services.

Fig. 114. **L.M. (liquidity-money) schedule.** The L.M. schedule is upward-sloping: with a given money stock, a higher rate of interest leads to a smaller demand for speculative balances leaving more money available for transaction balances (see MONEY DEMAND SCHEDULE). If these transaction balances are to be demanded, national income will have to be higher (the transaction demand for money is a function of the level of national income). Hence, to ensure that people will willingly take up these balances at a higher rate of interest, a higher level of national income is required.

See CONSUMER CREDIT, BANK LOAN, PUBLIC-SECTOR BORROWING REQUIREMENT, LOAN CAPITAL.

location of industry, *n*. the geographical spread of economic activity within an economy. A multitude of factors influence the location decisions of firms and industries including proximity to raw material supplies, availability of labour, good communications and nearness to markets. Once an industry becomes established in a particular location it tends to act as a focal point for further economic expansion, attracting, directly, the establishment of ancillary trades (component suppliers, back-up services, etc.,) and, indirectly, other firms and industries through EXTERNAL ECONOMIES OF SCALE and regional MULTIPLIER effects. REGIONAL POLICY also has a significant effect on industrial location.

lockout, *n*. an action taken by an employer that involves the exclusion of the workforce from their place of work as part of an INDUSTRIAL DISPUTE. See INDUSTRIAL RELATIONS, STRIKE.

locomotive principle, *n*. the principle that in a world-wide RECESSION, one country, by expanding its AGGREGATE DEMAND, will increase its demand for IMPORTS, stimulating the EXPORTS of other countries and so increasing economic activity in these other countries. In this way one country can act as a locomotive to pull other countries out of recession, at some expense to its balance of payments.

logarithmic function, *n.* a mathematical function that can be expressed in terms of its logarithm, such as $y = \log x$. A logarithm is the index to which a fixed number, the base, must be raised to obtain a given number. It is usual to state which fixed number is being used so that the function can be expressed as:

$$y = \log_a x$$

where x and y are the variables and a is the base number. Common logarithms have a base of 10 whilst natural logarithms have a base of 2.71828 which is written:

$$y = \log_e x.$$

See LOG–LINEAR FUNCTION.

log–linear function, *n.* a mathematical relationship of the form:

$$y = ax^b$$

which, when plotted on a logarithmic GRAPH, appears as a straight line. The relationship can be written:

$$\log y = \log a + b.\log x$$

log y being linearly related to log x. In this instance, x and y are the variables plotted on the horizontal and vertical axes respectively, where *a* and *b* are constants. See EXPONENTIAL FUNCTION, LOGARITHMIC FUNCTION.

Lomé agreements, *n.* the agreements of 1975 and 1979 entered into between the EUROPEAN COMMUNITY and 58 African, Caribbean and Pacific (ACP) countries that provide for TARIFF-free entry into the EC market of a wide range of ACP primary products and manufactures. The agreements also cover the provision of ECONOMIC AID to the ACPs through the EUROPEAN REGIONAL DEVELOPMENT FUND and the EUROPEAN INVESTMENT BANK, and established the Stabex and Minex schemes to stabilize the export earnings of those ACPs especially dependent on volatile agricultural and mineral products.

longitudinal, *adj.* of or relating to SAMPLE observations collected over a number of time periods. For example, we could collect data on changes in the size of sample companies over a number of years and changes in the remuneration of their chief executives over the same time periods, as a basis for investigating the relationship between executive remuneration and company size. Compare CROSS-SECTIONAL.

long run, *n.* an abstract time period (in the THEORY OF SUPPLY) long enough for all FACTOR INPUTS to be varied, but within an existing technological framework (known production methods). Thus, the firm's plant size, which is fixed in the short run, can now be altered to allow for an increased scale of operations.

In the VERY LONG RUN, the technological framework itself changes as a result of new INVENTIONS and knowledge. Compare SHORT RUN. See also ECONOMIES OF SCALE, DISECONOMIES OF SCALE, RETURNS TO SCALE.

long-term capital-employed or **net worth,** *n.* any long-term funds (see FUNDING) employed in a firm. For companies this takes the form of SHAREHOLDERS' CAPITAL-EMPLOYED plus long-term loans such as DEBENTURES.

Lorenz curve, see CONCENTRATION MEASURES.

loss, *n.* the difference that arises when a firm's TOTAL REVENUES are less than TOTAL COSTS. In the SHORT RUN, where firms' total revenues are insufficient to cover VARIABLE COSTS, then they will exit from the market unless they perceive this situation as being temporary. In these circumstances, where firms' total revenues are sufficient to cover variable costs and make some CONTRIBUTION towards FIXED COSTS, then they will continue to produce despite overall losses. In the LONG RUN, however, unless firms' revenues are sufficient to cover both variable and fixed costs, then their overall losses will cause them to exit from the market.

See MARKET EXIT, LOSS MINIMIZATION, TRADING AND PROFIT-AND-LOSS ACCOUNT.

loss-leading, *n* the practice of retailers in selling a particular product at a price below bought-in cost in order to attract customers into the store hoping that they will then be encouraged to make other purchases. This constitutes a form of retailer discrimination against manufacturers, and is usually outlawed by RESTRICTIVE TRADE PRACTICES legislation. See MONOPOLY POLICY, RESALE-PRICE MAINTENANCE.

loss minimization, *n.* the objective of the FIRM in the SHORT RUN when confronted with adverse market conditions which prevent PROFIT MAXIMIZATION. Profit maximization or loss minimization requires the firm to produce at that level of output where MARGINAL COST equals MARGINAL REVENUE. For example, a firm under PERFECT COMPETITION would produce output OQ in Fig. 115 on page 298. However, adverse short-run conditions may mean that at this level of output, price (OP) is

Fig. 115. **Loss minimization**. See main entry.

insufficient to cover average total cost (OC) so that the firm makes losses (equal to area PCXY in Fig. 115). In the short run, the firm will continue to produce this level of output as long as price is sufficient to cover AVERAGE VARIABLE COST (OC$_1$) and make some CONTRIBUTION (equal to area PC$_1$ZY) towards FIXED COSTS, though in the LONG RUN a continuation of this situation of loss-making would force the firm to leave the market.

Ltd. see LIMITED LIABILITY.

lump of labour, *n.* the proposition that there is only so much work to be done in the economy, so if fewer people are needed to produce any given output, UNEMPLOYMENT must rise. It follows that labour-saving technological change will inevitably lead to higher unemployment. The proposition is fallacious for the following reasons: (a) it assumes that the economy is already producing all the products society could possibly want, making no allowance for the fact that labour displaced in one area of the economy can now be redeployed to produce *more* goods and services elsewhere in the economy; (b) technological advance creates its own demand – it leads to higher PRODUCTIVITY and the payment of higher wages thereby increasing purchasing power in the economy which in turn generates more output and employment.

lump-sum taxes, *n.* the taxes that raise revenue for the government without distorting resource allocation patterns. INDIRECT TAXES have a distorting effect because they cause consumers to rearrange their consumption patterns and this rearrangement represents a loss to consumers without any corresponding gain to the government.

Similarly, INCOME TAXES can distort choice patterns in affecting the choice between work and leisure. In practice there are few taxes which do not affect resource allocation other than poll taxes which simply levy a tax per head of population.

See TAXATION, INCIDENCE OF TAXATION, PRINCIPLES OF TAXATION.

luxury product, *n.* any product that has an INCOME-ELASTICITY OF DEMAND greater than one. This means that as incomes rise, proportionately more income is spent on such products. Examples of luxury products include consumer durables like electrical appliances, holidays and entertainment. By contrast, products with an income-elasticity of less than one are referred to as necessary or STAPLE PRODUCTS.

See ENGEL'S LAW, NORMAL PRODUCT, INFERIOR PRODUCT, GIFFEN GOOD.

M

M0, M1, M2, M3, see MONEY SUPPLY.

macroeconomic policy, *n.* the setting of objectives by the government for the economy and the use of control instruments to achieve those objectives. Macroeconomic objectives include: FULL EMPLOYMENT; the avoidance of INFLATION; ECONOMIC GROWTH; and BALANCE–OF–PAYMENTS EQUILIBRIUM. FISCAL POLICY and MONETARY POLICY are the main instruments used to regulate the economy.

See also DEMAND MANAGEMENT, PRICES AND INCOMES POLICY, STABILIZATION POLICY, INTERNAL–EXTERNAL BALANCE MODEL, FIXED TARGETS, OPTIMIZING, BUSINESS CYCLE, EQUILIBRIUM LEVEL OF NATIONAL INCOME, DEFLATIONARY GAP, INFLATIONARY GAP, MEDIUM–TERM FINANCIAL STRATEGY.

macroeconomics, *n.* the branch of economics concerned with the study of aggregate economic activity. Macroeconomic analysis investigates how the economy as a whole 'works', and seeks to identify strategic determinants of the levels of national income and output, employment and prices.

See also CIRCULAR FLOW OF NATIONAL INCOME MODEL, EQUILIBRIUM LEVEL OF NATIONAL INCOME, INTERNAL–EXTERNAL BALANCE MODEL; MACROECONOMIC POLICY, MICROECONOMICS.

mail order, *n.* a form of WHOLESALING/RETAILING operation that is involved in the sale of products to consumers through the post. The mail order firm appoints agents whose task it is to canvass potential customers. Customers are supplied with a catalogue from which they make purchases directly through the post, or through their agent.

Malthus, Thomas (1766–1834) English clergyman whose pessimistic ideas on POPULATION growth were published in his *Essay on the Principle of Population as it Affects the Future Improvement of Society* (1798). Malthus argued that land is finite and that its productivity can, at best, increase only arithmetically (1,2,3,4, etc.); while population increases geometrically (1,2,4,8, etc.), so that the increase in population tends to outrun the increase in food supply. Consequently most people would be condemned to live in misery and poverty with wars, epidemics and famines serving to slow the growth of population.

Malthus's gloomy view of population growth contrasted sharply with the optimistic views about long-term economic development held by his contemporaries and contributed to the belief that economics was the 'dismal science'. Though Malthus did not foresee the dramatic improvements of agricultural techniques which have occurred, nor the tendency for population growth to slow in industrialized countries, his ideas still cause concern, especially in DEVELOPING COUNTRIES. See DEMOGRAPHIC TRANSITION.

managed float, see FLOATING EXCHANGE-RATE SYSTEM.

management accounting, *n.* any accounting activities geared to the preparation of information for managers to help them plan and control a company's operations. Management accounts generally provide more detailed information than financial accounts, for example, breaking down revenues and costs between different products, or factories or departments to provide comparative data and to help reveal profitable and unprofitable activities. Management accounts also tend to provide information about performance more frequently than financial accounts, with monthly or even weekly management accounts rather than annual accounts, to give managers prompt feedback and to enable them to act quickly to check inefficiencies. Management accounts are geared to estimates of future costs and revenues rather than simply reporting past revenues and costs as financial accounts do, so providing valuable management information for preparing accurate estimates and tenders and for use in negotiating price changes. Compare FINANCIAL ACCOUNTING. See also BUDGETING.

management buy-out, *n.* the purchase of a FIRM or division of a firm by its present management. In the former case, the shareholders of the firm may be prepared to accept management's financial terms of purchase because they are better than an outside takeover bidder or merger partner is prepared to offer. In these cases, management buy-outs are often 'defensively' motivated, with the existing management fearing loss of office following a hostile takeover. The sale of a subsidiary or division of a firm to its incumbent management is often undertaken as a means of DISINVESTMENT (2) by the parent firm from a particular line of business rather than resulting from a takeover or merger approach. Again, in the interests of the shareholders of the firm, the financial details of such deals need to be carefully gone into. Management buy-outs are usually financed by outside interests, including VENTURE CAPITAL specialists and banks.

management-utility maximization, *n.* a company objective in the THEORY OF THE FIRM which is used as an alternative to the traditional assumption of PROFIT-MAXIMIZATION. The FIRM is assumed to seek to maximize management's utility or satisfactions, and the managerial preference function comprises three principal components: utility = F (staff, emoluments, investments).

Salaried managers prefer spending company money on these three things (an 'expense preference' for them, as Oliver Williamson puts it) because:

(a) additional staff can lead to managers getting more salary since extra staff generally necessitates more tiers in the organization's hierarchy and so, (given the traditional salary differentials between tiers) will increase the salaries of those at the top of the organization. In addition, extra staff are a source of power, status and prestige and may contribute to job security, insofar as larger departments in a company are less likely to be closed down.

(b) managerial emoluments or 'perks' such as big expense accounts, generous travel budgets and company cars are valued as both (low-taxed) sources of indirect material income and because they boost status and prestige.

(c) discretionary investments over and above those which are strictly economically essential allow managers to pursue 'pet projects' and afford them status, prestige and security through the amount of physical plant and equipment which they control.

See also MANAGERIAL THEORIES OF THE FIRM, DIVORCE OF OWNERSHIP FROM CONTROL.

managerial theories of the firm, *n.* the theories of the FIRM that substitute firm objectives such as SALES-REVENUE MAXIMIZATION and ASSET-GROWTH MAXIMIZATION for the traditional hypothesis of PROFIT MAXIMIZATION. These theories are based on two assumptions: (a) that for large oligopolistic firms there is a DIVORCE OF OWNERSHIP FROM CONTROL which allows the firm's management to set the firm's objectives rather than its shareholders; (b) managers are more interested in sales and assets goals than profit maximization because the size of their salaries and their power and status (managerial utility) are chiefly linked to the size of the firm. Profits are still important but they are seen as contributory to the attainment of some other objective rather than as an end in themselves.

The significance of the managerial theories as an extension of the

THEORY OF THE FIRM lies in their prediction of higher output levels and lower prices in comparison with the profit-maximizing theory.

See MANAGEMENT–UTILITY MAXIMIZATION, BEHAVIOURAL THEORY OF THE FIRM, SATISFICING THEORY.

manpower planning, *n.* the continuing managerial process of identifying the requirement for human resources and implementing a strategy to optimally utilize and develop labour resources in line with strategic objectives. Manpower planning can be undertaken at corporate level, or it may be done at industry or national level. Manpower planning or human-resource planning seeks to identify future manpower requirements and also embodies other personnel management activities, such as recruitment, training, promotion, etc.

marginal analysis, *n.* the examination of the effects of adding one extra unit to, or taking away one unit from, some economic VARIABLE. See also MARGINAL COST, MARGINAL REVENUE, MARGINAL UTILITY, MARGINAL PHYSICAL PRODUCT, MARGINAL REVENUE PRODUCT, MARGINAL PROPENSITY TO CONSUME, MARGINAL PROPENSITY TO SAVE, MARGINAL PROPENSITY TO IMPORT, MARGINAL PROPENSITY TO TAX, MARGINAL RATE OF TAX, MARGINAL RATE OF SUBSTITUTION, MARGINAL RATE OF TRANSFORMATION, MARGINAL-COST PRICING, MARGINAL EFFICIENCY OF CAPITAL/INVESTMENT, DIFFERENTIAL CALCULUS.

Fig. 116. **Marginal cost**. See main entry.

marginal cost, *n.* the extra cost (addition to TOTAL COST) that is incurred in the SHORT RUN in increasing OUTPUT by one unit. Given that FIXED COSTS do not vary with output, marginal costs (MC) are entirely marginal VARIABLE COSTS. MC falls at first (reflecting increasing RETURNS TO THE VARIABLE-FACTOR INPUT – costs increase faster than output), as shown in Fig. 116, but then rises as decreasing returns set in.

MC together with MARGINAL REVENUE determines the level of output at which the firm attains PROFIT MAXIMIZATION.

marginal–cost/average–cost relationship, *n.* the mathematical relationship between MARGINAL COST and AVERAGE COST. See Fig. 117. When average cost (AC) is falling, marginal cost (MC) is always below it; that is, if the cost of an extra unit of output lowers AC, it must itself be less than AC in order to drag the average down. When AC is rising, MC is above it; that is, if an extra unit of output increases AC, its cost must be more than AC in order to pull the average up. The MC curve cuts the AC curve at the minimum point on that curve, as shown in Fig. 117.

Fig. 117. **Marginal-cost/average-cost relationship**. See main entry.

marginal cost pricing, *n.* a pricing principle that argues for setting prices equal to the MARGINAL COST of production and distribution, ignoring whether or not FIXED COSTS are recouped from revenues. The principle has been advocated as a guide to the pricing and output policies of PUBLIC UTILITIES on the grounds that prices which reflect the marginal cost to society of producing an extra unit of output are more socially desirable. The principle is particularly appealing when used for public utilities where marginal costs are effectively zero, such as parks, bridges and museums, because here society can be made better off by lowering the price of these facilities until they are fully used.

However, the marginal-cost-pricing principle deals only with the short-run problem of generating an optimum price and output with existing capacity and ignores the long-run problem of ideal investment in new capacity. See Fig. 118. See also AVERAGE–COST PRICING, TWO–PART TARIFF, MARGINAL–COST/AVERAGE–COST RELATIONSHIP. NATIONALIZATION.

marginal efficiency of capital/investment, *n.* the RATE OF RETURN (PROFITS) expected on an extra pounds worth of INVESTMENT. The

Fig. 118. **Marginal cost pricing.** In decreasing-cost industries where marginal costs are below average total costs, setting a price equal to the marginal cost would result in losses which would have to be met from taxes or other sources (price OP_1); while in increasing-cost industries where marginal costs are greater than average total costs, marginal cost pricing would result in a surplus (price OP_2).

marginal efficiency of investment decreases as the amount of investment increases (see Fig. 119a on page 306). This is because initial investments are concentrated on the 'best' opportunities and yield high rates of return; later investments are less productive and secure progressively lower returns.

The amount of investment undertaken depends not only on expected returns but also on the cost of capital, that is, the RATE OF INTEREST. Investment will be profitable up to the point where the marginal efficiency of investment is equal to the COST OF CAPITAL. In Fig. 119a, at an interest rate of 20% only OX amount of investment is worthwhile. A fall in the interest rate to 10% increases the amount of profitable investment to OY.

It will be readily apparent from Fig. 119a that there is a link between the monetary side of the economy and the real economy: a fall in interest rates will stimulate more investment, which in turn will result in a higher level of national income. (See MONEY SUPPLY/SPENDING LINKAGES).

If expectations change and investors expect to receive better returns from each investment because, for example, of technological progress then at any given rate of interest (such as 20%) more investment will be undertaken than before; that is, the marginal efficiency of investment

MARGINAL FACTOR COST

(a)

(b)

Fig. 119. **Marginal efficiency of capital/investment.** See main entry.

will shift to the right, as shown in Fig. 119b, and investment will increase from OX to OZ.

marginal factor cost (MFC), *n.* the extra cost incurred by a firm in using one more unit of a FACTOR INPUT. Marginal factor cost together with the MARGINAL REVENUE PRODUCT of a factor, indicates to a firm how many factor inputs to employ in order to maximize its profits.

marginal physical product, *n.* the quantity of OUTPUT in the SHORT RUN theory of supply produced by each extra unit of VARIABLE-FACTOR INPUT (in conjunction with a given amount of FIXED-FACTOR INPUT). The

Fig. 120. **Marginal physical product**. See main entry.

marginal physical–product curve, as shown in Fig. 120, rises steeply at first, reflecting increasing returns to the variable-factor input, but then falls as DIMINISHING RETURNS to the variable-factor input set in. See RETURNS TO THE VARIABLE–FACTOR INPUT.

marginal productivity theory of distribution, *n.* a theory of the FUNCTIONAL DISTRIBUTION OF INCOME in which FACTOR INPUTS (labour, etc.) receive a payment for their services (wages, etc.) which is equal to their MARGINAL REVENUE PRODUCT.

marginal propensity to consume (MPC), *n.* the fraction of any change in DISPOSABLE INCOME which is spent on CONSUMPTION:

$$MPC = \frac{\text{change in consumption}}{\text{change in income}}$$

See PROPENSITY TO CONSUME, MULTIPLIER.

marginal propensity to import (MPM), *n.* the fraction of any change in NATIONAL INCOME which is spent on IMPORTS:

$$MPM = \frac{\text{change in imports}}{\text{change in income}}$$

See PROPENSITY TO IMPORT, MULTIPLIER.

marginal propensity to save (MPS), *n.* the fraction of any change in DISPOSABLE INCOME which is saved (see SAVINGS):

$$MPS = \frac{\text{change in savings}}{\text{change in income}}$$

See PROPENSITY TO SAVE, MULTIPLIER.

marginal propensity to tax (MPT), *n.* the fraction of any change in NATIONAL INCOME which is taken in TAXATION:

$$\text{MPT} = \frac{\text{change in tax}}{\text{change in income}}$$

See PROPENSITY TO TAX, MULTIPLIER, MARGINAL RATE OF TAX.

marginal rate of substitution, *n.* a ratio of the MARGINAL UTILITIES of two products. It is measured by the slope of the consumer's INDIFFERENCE CURVE between the two products. In order to maximize his utility, a consumer must equate the ratio of the marginal utilities of the two products to the ratio of their prices (see CONSUMER EQUILIBRIUM).

For an economy, the optimal distribution of national output is achieved when the marginal rate of substitution for all consumers is equal. See PARETO OPTIMALITY.

marginal rate of taxation, *n.* the rate of TAXATION an individual would pay on an incremental unit of INCOME. For example, in a PROGRESSIVE TAXATION structure, if an individual paid tax at 30% up to a limit of £15,000, at which point the rate changed to 40%, the marginal rate of taxation on an income of £15,001 is 40%. The incremental rate of taxation on the last pound earned is 40%. See STANDARD RATE OF TAXATION, AVERAGE RATE OF TAXATION, PROPENSITY TO TAX, PROPORTIONAL TAXATION, REGRESSIVE TAXATION.

marginal rate of technical substitution, *n.* the ratio of the MARGINAL PHYSICAL PRODUCTS of two FACTOR INPUTS in the production process, that is, the amount by which it is possible to reduce factor input X and maintain output by substituting an extra unit of factor input Y. It is measured by the slope of the producer's ISOQUANT CURVE. In order to minimize his production costs a producer must equate the ratio of the marginal physical products of the two factor inputs (shown by the isoquant curve) to the ratio of their factor prices (shown by the ISOCOST LINE). See ISOQUANT MAP.

marginal rate of transformation, *n.* a ratio of the MARGINAL COSTS of producing two products. It is measured by the slope of the PRODUCTION-POSSIBILITY BOUNDARY which indicates the rate at which the production of one product can be replaced by the production of the other as a result of the reallocation of inputs.

For an economy, the optimum composition of national output is achieved when the marginal rate of transformation of the goods produced equals the ratio of their prices. See PARETO OPTIMALITY.

marginal revenue, *n.* the addition to TOTAL REVENUE from the sale of one extra unit of output. Under conditions of PERFECT COMPETITION, the

Fig. 121. **Marginal revenue.** (a) Under PERFECT COMPETITION each extra unit of output sold adds exactly the same amount to total revenue as previous units. (b) Under conditions of imperfect competition (for example, MONOPOLISTIC COMPETITION) the firm faces a downward sloping demand curve and price has to be lowered in order to sell more units. Marginal revenue is less than price: as price is lowered each extra unit sold adds successively smaller amounts than previous units.

firm faces a horizontal DEMAND CURVE at the going market price (marginal revenue = price). See Fig. 121a. Marginal revenue interacts with MARGINAL COST in determining the level of output at which the firm achieves its objective of PROFIT MAXIMIZATION.

See AVERAGE REVENUE, ELASTICITY OF DEMAND, KINKED DEMAND CURVE, MONOPOLY.

marginal revenue product (MRP), *n.* the extra REVENUE obtained from using one more FACTOR INPUT to produce and sell additional units of OUTPUT. The marginal revenue product of a factor is given by the factor's MARGINAL PHYSICAL PRODUCT multiplied by the price of the product.

The marginal revenue product, together with the MARGINAL FACTOR COST, indicates to a firm how many factor inputs to employ in order to maximize its profits. This can be illustrated by reference to the utilization of the labour input under PERFECT COMPETITION market conditions. In a competitive LABOUR MARKET, the equilibrium WAGE RATE and numbers employed (W_e and Q_e, respectively, in Fig. 122a and b), are determined by the intersection of the market demand and supply curves for labour. Because each firm employs only a small fraction of the total labour force it is unable to influence the wage rate. Thus, the wage rate, and hence the marginal cost of labour (MFC), are constant to the firm – each extra worker adds exactly his wage rate to the firm's total factor cost. The firm's MRP declines because although under competitive conditions the product price remains constant, the marginal-physical product falls due to DIMINISHING RETURNS to the labour input.

The firm will maximize its profits by employing additional workers up to the point (Q_e in Fig. 122a), where the last worker's contribution to revenue (MRP), is equal to the going wage rate (MFC).

marginal utility, *n.* the increase in satisfaction (UTILITY) an individual derives from the use or CONSUMPTION of one additional unit of a good or service. Marginal utility is concerned with the utility derived from each incremental unit used or consumed, and is therefore sometimes called *incremental utility.* For example, a person's TOTAL UTILITY (satisfaction) would increase if they purchased, say, an additional pair of shoes. If that person originally had three pairs of shoes, then the incremental unit would be one more pair, making four pairs. The marginal (incremental) utility is positive but *less* than the marginal utility derived from purchasing a third pair of shoes (the increment being from two pairs owned to three pairs owned after the purchase). This is known as DIMINISHING MARGINAL UTILITY.

Marginal utility is not to be confused with total utility. Total utility is the sum total of utility derived from *all* the units used or consumed. Marginal utility is derived only from the *last* unit used or consumed. It is this difference which explains what is known as the value paradox.

firm's use of labour

(a)

labour market

(b)

Fig. 122. **Marginal revenue product**. See main entry.

Water has a high total utility but a low marginal one. Diamonds have a low total utility but a high marginal one. Given the supply function of each this determines price. The low marginal utility good (water) commands a low price whilst the high marginal utility good commands a high price.

Whenever a change in utility occurs, for example, the utility change from owning three to owning four pairs of shoes, the change can be calculated using mathematics. In calculus, such a change is called the first derivative and as we are concerned with utility it is the first derivative of the total UTILITY FUNCTION. The *rate* of change of that change is the second derivative.

See CARDINAL UTILITY, ORDINAL UTILITY, CONSUMER EQUILIBRIUM, PARETO OPTIMALITY, PARADOX OF VALUE.

marginal utility of money, *n.* the increase in satisfaction (UTILITY) an individual derives from spending one incremental unit of MONEY on goods or services.

margin of error, see FORECASTING.

market, *n.* an EXCHANGE mechanism that brings together sellers and buyers of a PRODUCT, FACTOR OF PRODUCTION or FINANCIAL SECURITY.

Economists define a market as a group of products which consumers view as being substitutes for one another (that is, they have a high CROSS-ELASTICITY OF DEMAND). This concept of the market may not correspond exactly with INDUSTRIAL CLASSIFICATIONS which group products in terms of their technical or production characteristics rather than consumer substitutability. For example, glass bottles and metal cans would be regarded by users as substitute packaging materials but are in fact allocated to different industrial classifications (the glass and metal industries, respectively). By contrast, the industrial-classification category of 'steel products', for example, can encompass such diverse users as civil engineers (reinforcing bars), car manufacturers (car bodies) and white-goods manufacturers (washing machine shells). However, in the absence of reliable cross-elasticity of demand data, economists are often forced to fall back on industrial classifications as a best approximation of markets in empirical analysis.

The THEORY OF MARKETS distinguishes between markets according to their structural characteristics, in particular the number of sellers and buyers involved. A number of 'market' situations can be identified, including:

PERFECT COMPETITION	=	many sellers, many buyers
OLIGOPOLY	=	few sellers, many buyers
OLIGOPSONY	=	many sellers, few buyers
BILATERAL OLIGOPOLY	=	few sellers, few buyers
MONOPOLY	=	one seller, many buyers
MONOPSONY	=	many sellers, one buyer
BILATERAL MONOPOLY	=	one seller, one buyer
DUOPOLY	=	two sellers, many buyers
DUOPSONY	=	many sellers, two buyers

Such a classification serves well for theoretical analysis, and there is no need to make 'fine' distinctions relating to the boundaries of the market under consideration. However, from the point of view of applying policy, how widely or narrowly a market is defined depends largely upon the particular issue the policy is concerned with and the degree of precision appropriate for that policy. For example, for macroplanning purposes it may be appropriate to refer broadly to the 'drinks' market or 'food' market. From the point of view of applying MONOPOLY POLICY, however, a disaggregation of such groupings into submarkets is necessary. Thus, the drinks market could be divided as between alcoholic and non-alcoholic drinks, and further divided as between the various types of alcoholic beverage – beer, spirits, wines, etc.

See also LABOUR MARKET, FOREIGN-EXCHANGE MARKET, STOCK EXCHANGE, CAPITAL MARKET, COMMODITY MARKET.

market concentration, see CONCENTRATION MEASURES.

market conduct, *n.* the 'things done' by firms in their capacity as suppliers (and buyers) of final (and intermediate) goods and services. The objectives of firms and the particular policies they adopt with regard to prices, scale of output, product characteristics, etc., together with the effect the presence or otherwise of close competing firms has on the formulation and implementation of those policies, are major facets of market conduct.

In the THEORY OF MARKETS, market conduct interacts with MARKET STRUCTURE in determining MARKET PERFORMANCE, while market structure and performance, in turn, affect market conduct.

See FIRM OBJECTIVES, METHODS OF COMPETITION, INTERFIRM CONDUCT, MARKET STRUCTURE–CONDUCT–PERFORMANCE SCHEMA, PERFECT COMPETITION, MONOPOLISTIC COMPETITION, OLIGOPOLY, MONOPOLY.

market entry, *n.* the entry into a MARKET of a new FIRM or firms. In the THEORY OF MARKETS, entrants are assumed to come into the market by establishing a new plant, thereby adding to the number of competing suppliers in the market. New entry into a market occurs when established firms are earning ABOVE-NORMAL PROFITS. The entry of new firms plays an important role in enlarging the supply capacity of a market and in removing above-normal profits. In practice, new entry also takes place through TAKEOVER of, or MERGER with an established firm.

See CONDITION OF ENTRY, BARRIERS TO ENTRY, POTENTIAL ENTRANT, CONTESTABLE MARKET, PERFECT COMPETITION, MONOPOLISTIC COMPETITION, OLIGOPOLY, MONOPOLY, LIMIT PRICING.

market exit or **exit,** *n.* the withdrawal from a MARKET of a firm or firms. In the THEORY OF MARKETS, a firm will leave a market if it is unable to earn NORMAL PROFITS in the long run. Firm exit plays an important role in removing EXCESS CAPACITY and reducing total market supply. See also LOSS, AVERAGE COST (SHORT-RUN), CONTRIBUTION.

marketing, *n.* the managerial process of determining the requirements of any particular MARKET, that is, the CONSUMER'S needs, real or induced, and satisfying that DEMAND through the related functions of production, distribution, pricing, promotion and after-sales service. See MARKETING MIX, MARKETING RESEARCH.

market maker, *n.* a STOCK EXCHANGE firm which both buys and sells STOCKS, SHARES and BONDS thereby establishing a market for these securities. In the UK this function was formerly undertaken by JOBBERS alone, but since 1986 firms combining the roles of jobber and STOCKBROKER perform the function.

marketing mix, *n.* the range of competitive dimensions along which FIRMS promote their products to customers and potential consumers, including the styling, quality, etc., of the goods and services themselves, their prices, their advertising and promotion, their packaging, their distribution, their selling and their servicing. Management can manipulate all these variables, and if the mix is to be effective each dimension must be developed as one aspect of the total marketing effort. No one dimension should be emphasized in isolation otherwise effort is wasted, for example, pricing decisions should not be divorced from consideration of product and promotion policies.

See METHODS OF COMPETITION, PRODUCT DIFFERENTIATION, PRODUCT MIX.

marketing research, *n.* the systematic collection, assimilation and analysis of facts and opinions to assist managerial decision making in identifying market opportunities for a firm's existing or potential goods and/or services. See TEST MARKET.

market mechanism, see PRICE SYSTEM.

market performance, *n.* the efficiency of MARKETS in utilizing scarce resources to meet consumers' demand for goods and services; that is, how well they have contributed to the optimization of economic welfare.

Five main performance criteria may be identified: (a) PRODUCTIVE EFFICIENCY, (b) DISTRIBUTIVE EFFICIENCY, (c) ALLOCATIVE EFFICIENCY, (d) TECHNOLOGICAL PROGRESSIVENESS, (e) PRODUCT PERFORMANCE. What is being looked for is the ability of a market to produce and distribute its existing products at the lowest possible cost and to charge consumers prices which are consistent with these costs. In a dynamic sense, market performance can also be judged in terms of whether firms introduce new cost-cutting production and distribution techniques, and better products over time.

In the THEORY OF MARKETS, market performance is determined by the interaction of MARKET STRUCTURE and MARKET CONDUCT, while market performance itself has an affect on market structure and conduct.

See also PARETO OPTIMALITY, RESOURCE ALLOCATION, MARKET STRUCTURE-CONDUCT–PERFORMANCE SCHEMA, PERFECT COMPETITION, MONOPOLISTIC COMPETITION, OLIGOPOLY, MONOPOLY.

market power, *n.* the ability of a FIRM to administer within limits the supply price and terms of sale of its product without immediate competitive encroachment. Market power brings with it the particular danger of exploitation of the consumer by the supplier. The exercise of market power is typically associated with an OLIGOPOLY or a MONOPOLY.

See also ADMINISTERED PRICE, MONOPOLY POLICY, SELLER CONCENTRATION, CONDITION OF ENTRY.

market segmentation, *n.* the division of a MARKET into particular subgroups of customers, each with their own buying characteristics, for example, men and women. Firms are thus able to adopt PRODUCT DIFFERENTIATION strategies to cater for the needs of different groups of buyers, enlarging their sales potential. See also PRICE DISCRIMINATION.

market share, *n.* the proportion of total MARKET output or sales accounted for by an individual FIRM. Market-share data is used to measure the degree of SELLER CONCENTRATION in a market. See CONCENTRATION RATIO, CONCENTRATION MEASURES.

market structure, *n.* the way in which a MARKET is organized. The THEORY OF MARKETS focuses especially on those aspects of market structure which have an important influence on the behaviour of firms and buyers and on MARKET PERFORMANCE. Structural features having a major strategic importance in relation to MARKET CONDUCT and performance include: (a) the degree of SELLER CONCENTRATION and BUYER CONCENTRATION as measured by the number of sellers and buyers (whether there are many sellers/buyers in the market, or a few, or only one), and their relative size distribution; (b) the CONDITION OF ENTRY to the market (the extent to which established suppliers have advantages over potential new entrants because of BARRIERS TO ENTRY); (c) the nature of the product supplied (whether it is a HOMOGENEOUS PRODUCT or subject to PRODUCT DIFFERENTIATION).

Market structure, in turn, is affected by market conduct and performance. See VERTICAL INTEGRATION, DIVERSIFICATION, CONCENTRATION MEASURES, MARKET STRUCTURE/CONDUCT–PERFORMANCE SCHEMA.

MARKET STRUCTURE/CONDUCT-PERFORMANCE SCHEMA

Fig. 123. Market structure/conduct-performance schema. See main entry.

market structure/conduct–performance schema, *n.* an analytical framework for investigating the operation of market processes. MARKETS are ultimately judged in terms of their economic performance, that is, how well they have contributed to the achievement of optimal economic efficiency. MARKET PERFORMANCE (see Fig. 123) is determined fundamentally by the interaction of MARKET STRUCTURE and MARKET CONDUCT. The schema attempts to identify those structural and conduct parameters which have a strategic influence on market performance. These relationships have been formalized in the THEORY OF MARKETS.

The schema is useful to public-policy makers (see MONOPOLY POLICY, INDUSTRIAL POLICY) in framing measures designed to improve market performance.

market system, see PRICE SYSTEM.

Marshall, Alfred (1842–1924), English professor of political economy at Cambridge University who depicted precise mathematical relationships between economic variables in his textbook *Principles of Economics*

(1890). Using calculus, Marshall was able to show how value is partly determined by the MARGINAL UTILITY of a good and how the intensity of wants decrease with each unit acquired. Thus, Marshall was able to explain the PARADOX OF VALUE, showing how luxuries like diamonds have a higher price than essentials like water because consumers have few diamonds whilst water is generally plentiful. This analysis enabled Marshall to explain downward-sloping DEMAND CURVES and CONSUMER SURPLUS (the surplus satisfaction derived by a consumer whenever he can buy a good at a lower price than that which he would be prepared to pay rather than go without the good). Marshall also developed the concept of ELASTICITY OF DEMAND.

Marshall argued that the forces of both demand and supply determine value, with demand determining price and output in the short run and, changes in resource inputs and production costs influencing price in the long run. He suggested that supply prices would depend upon production costs and in analysing short-run production cost showed how the marginal product of all resources tends to diminish as variable factor inputs are combined with fixed amounts of other resources (DIMINISHING RETURNS to the variable factor input). In the long run, Marshall suggested that industries would experience reducing costs and prices because of ECONOMIES OF SCALE resulting from greater specialization.

Marshall-Lerner condition, *n.* the PRICE-ELASTICITY OF DEMAND for IMPORTS and EXPORTS condition which must be satisfied if an EXCHANGE-RATE alteration (DEVALUATION or REVALUATION) is to be successful in removing a balance of payments deficit or surplus.

Specifically, the elasticity values for a successful devaluation, for example, are:

demand for imports is price-elastic $(e \geqslant 1)$

demand for exports is price-elastic $(e \geqslant 1)$

How successful the devaluation is thus depends critically on the reaction of import and export volumes to the change in prices implied by the devaluation. If trade volumes are relatively elastic to price changes the devaluation will be successful; that is, an increase in import prices results in a more than proportionate fall in import volume, reducing the total amount of foreign currency required to finance the import bill, while the decrease in export prices results in a more than proportionate increase in export volume, bringing about an increase in total foreign currency earnings on exports.

By contrast, if trade volumes are relatively inelastic to price changes the devaluation will not succeed; that is, an increase in import prices results in a less than proportionate fall in import volume, increasing the total amount of foreign currency required to finance the import bill, while the decrease in export prices results in a less than proportionate increase in export volume, bringing about a fall in total foreign currency earnings on exports.

There are, however, a number of other factors which influence the eventual outcome of a devaluation, in particular the extent to which domestic resources are sufficiently mobile to be switched into export-producing and import-substitution industries.

See DEVALUATION, BALANCE-OF-PAYMENTS EQUILIBRIUM, PRICE-ELASTICITY OF SUPPLY.

Marx, Karl (1818–1883) German philosopher who produced a new theory about historical change based upon conflict between competing groups in his book: *Das Kapital*. The first volume was published in 1867, with the remaining volumes, edited by Friedrich Engels, being published posthumously in 1885 and 1894. Marx argued that at each stage in history one particular class in society would become powerful because of its ownership of the means of production. However, in the meanwhile, another class would be developing whose interests clashed with those of the dominant class. Finally the new class would overturn the old and set itself up as a new dominant group. For example, under feudalism the aristocracy predominated because of their control of the land; then they gave way to the capitalists who gained ascendancy because of their control of capital.

Capitalists were able to drive a hard bargain with workers over wage rates, and the low-paid exploitation of the working class permitted factory owners to accumulate even greater wealth and gain monopoly power. Workers produce goods and services of value, but because they are paid so little, capitalists are able to appropriate much of this value for themselves in the form of high profits. Marx predicted that this exploitation would eventually provoke a revolution in which the 'property-less proletariat' would overthrow the dominant capitalist class and take over the means of production. Initially, under socialism, the nation's productive assets would be acquired and controlled by the State but eventually under COMMUNISM the workers themselves would collectively own the means of production, with goods and services being distributed according to peoples' needs.

See also CENTRALLY-PLANNED ECONOMY, LABOUR THEORY OF VALUE.

mass production, *n.* the manufacture of a PRODUCT in very large quantities using continuous flow capital-intensive methods of production. Mass production is typically found in industries where the product supplied is highly standardized, which enables automated machinery and processes to be substituted for labour. Mass-production industries are usually characterized by high levels of SELLER CONCENTRATION, difficult CONDITIONS OF ENTRY and the exploitation of ECONOMIES OF SCALE which results in low unit costs of supply, Compare BATCH PRODUCTION.

mathematical economics, *n.* the application of mathematical methods to help solve problems in economics.

matrix, *n.* a rectangular array of elements displayed as rows and columns. Matrices may be of any dimension, for example, a matrix which has three rows and two columns. Multiplying rows by columns gives the number of elements in a matrix, which in our example is six. Convention dictates that in all dealings with matrices the row is designated first. See also INPUT–OUTPUT ANALYSIS.

maximum strategy, see GAME THEORY.

mean or **average** or **arithmetic mean,** *n.* a method of representing the centre or middle of a set of n numbers by a single number, i.e., the sum of the n numbers divided by n. For example, if five people had weekly incomes of £100, £100, £150, £250 and £400, then the mean income of the group would be:

$$£\frac{100 + 100 + 150 + 250 + 400}{5} = £\frac{1,000}{5} = £200$$

See also MEDIAN, MODE.

means test, *n.* an examination of the personal and financial circumstances of an individual to assess his or her eligibility for benefits under a country's system of SOCIAL SECURITY. The benefits which are being claimed are not regarded as a universal right, but are assessed under rules and regulations as laid down by legislation and the government department concerned. The payment of the welfare benefit is a right only if an individual is within the limits of income, personal circumstance, etc., for the period of the claim. Many poverty-action groups argue for the abolition of means-tested benefits because of the indignities which an examination of circumstances imposes and because they discourage proud but needy individuals from applying. Others argue for their retention as a means of limiting TRANSFER PAYMENTS and curbing GOVERNMENT EXPENDITURE.

median, *n.* a means of representing the centre or middle of a set of n numbers by a single number, i.e. the value of the middle item when the items are arranged in increasing order of magnitude. For example, if five people had weekly incomes of £100, £100, £150, £250 and £400 then the median income of the group would be £150 (the middle figure). See also MEAN, MODE.

mediation, *n.* a procedure for settling disputes, most notably INDUSTRIAL DISPUTES in which a neutral third party meets with the disputants and endeavours to help them resolve their differences and reach agreement through continued negotiation. In some countries 'conciliation' is distinguished from 'mediation', according to the degree of intervention exercised by the conciliator or mediator in the process of encouraging the parties to settle their differences with a conciliator refraining from advancing, and the mediator expected to advance, proposals of his own for possible settlements. Both forms of intervention leave the bargaining process intact with any resultant settlement being agreed upon by all disputing parties.

In the UK, the ADVISORY, CONCILIATORY AND ARBITRATION SERVICE acts in this capacity.

See also ARBITRATION, COLLECTIVE BARGAINING, INDUSTRIAL RELATIONS.

medium of exchange, *n.* an attribute of MONEY, enabling people to price goods and services and exchange them using money as a common denominator rather than exchanging one good directly for another (as in BARTER).

medium-term financial strategy, *n.* a financial policy introduced by the UK government in 1980 which set out a target range for the growth of the MONEY SUPPLY, and target values for the PUBLIC-SECTOR BORROWING REQUIREMENT expressed as a percentage of GROSS DOMESTIC PRODUCT. The first medium-term financial strategy covered a period of five years ahead, and was revised and extended at annual intervals to provide a set of rolling plans for the economy. The purpose of the medium-term financial strategy was to provide a known firm base for the operation of government MONETARY POLICY, to assist in the control of public expenditure and to influence the public's expectations about future rates of INFLATION.

See also MACROECONOMIC POLICY, MONEY SUPPLY/SPENDING LINKAGES, MONETARISM.

memorandum of association, *n.* a legal document which must be filed with the Register of Companies before a JOINT-STOCK COMPANY can be incorporated, and which governs the external relationship between the company and third parties. The Memorandum must contain certain compulsory clauses stating: (a) the name of the company; (b) the objects of the company; (c) the country in which the company is situated; (d) whether it is limited by shares or other means; (e) the amount and division of share capital; (e) the signature of the subscribers forming the company, each of whom must take at least one share. See ARTICLES OF ASSOCIATION.

mercantilism, *n.* a set of economic ideas and policies which became established in England during the 17th century, accompanying the rise of commercial capitalism. The mercantilists stressed the importance of trade and commerce as the source of the nation's wealth, and advocated policies to increase a nation's wealth and power by encouraging exports and discouraging imports in order to allow the country to amass quantities of GOLD. These protectionist ideas (see PROTECTIONISM) were criticized by later classical economists like Adam SMITH.

merchandizing, see SALES PROMOTION AND MERCHANDIZING.

merchant bank, *n.* a specialist FINANCIAL INSTITUTION that advises client companies on new SHARE issues and *underwrites* such issues (that is, guarantees to buy up any shares which are not sold on the open market). They also advise companies in MERGER and TAKEOVER situations. See STOCK EXCHANGE.

merger or **amalgamation,** *n.* the combining together of two or more firms. Three broad categories of merger may be identified: (a) horizontal mergers between firms that are direct competitors in the same market; (b) vertical mergers between firms which stand in a supplier–customer relationship; (c) conglomerate mergers between firms operating in unrelated markets which are seeking to diversify their activities.

From the firm's point of view a merger may be advantageous because it may enable the firm to reduce production and distribution costs, enable it to expand its existing activities or move into new areas, or remove unwanted competition and increase its market power.

In terms of their wider impact on the operation of market processes, mergers may, on the one hand, promote greater efficiency in resource use, or, on the other hand, by reducing competition, lead to a less efficient allocation of resources.

Usually, any benefit that comes from a merger will depend upon the achievement of greater efficiency in some branch of the enlarged firm's operations. Several important sources of greater efficiency may be distinguished. Horizontal mergers frequently allow firms to secure low cost operation by realizing ECONOMIES OF SCALE in manufacture and distribution, and RATIONALIZATION opportunities. In addition, the combined organization may have access to superior technical know-how and financial resources, previously available to only one of the firms. Vertical mergers may make possible benefits in efficiency of production by making possible more comprehensive production planning, particularly where successive processes are closely linked, and permit economies in stock holding and distribution of goods. Conglomerate mergers may yield economies in overheads (finance, administration and marketing expenditure) and may lead to an important cross-fertilization of ideas and attitudes, particularly where the acquiring company is notably well managed and cost-conscious.

While mergers may result in greater efficiency, thereby enhancing consumer welfare, they may also serve to increase MONOPOLY power. This is most clearly seen in the case of horizontal and vertical mergers. Horizontal mergers *prima facie* increase the level of SELLER CONCENTRATION in the market by reducing the number of independent sources of supply. Where the merging firms are already substantial suppliers this may reduce effective competition and permit the enlarged group more control over the market and discretion over prices. A vertical merger can produce an increase in market power in a variety of ways. If a customer firm, for example, takes over a supplier, and if the supplier is large in relation to other suppliers, other (nonintegrated) customers may find themselves forced to buy from the merged supplier and then sell their products in competition with the merged customer firm. This puts the merged group in a powerful position to discriminate in prices and availability of supplies and so 'squeeze' the profits of other nonintegrated suppliers. Superficially, conglomerate mergers appear to have little relevance to the monopoly power issue, but it is to be noted that the conglomerate may have an opportunity to affect the state of competition in a number of separate markets, by internal transfers of resources, and thus to exercise a larger degree of market power against rival companies than its market share in individual markets would otherwise permit.

In sum, mergers may involve, simultaneously, both benefits and detriments. In the UK, since 1965, mergers which create or extend a firm's market share of a particular product in excess of 25%, or where the value of assets acquired is over £30 million can be referred to the MONOPOLIES AND MERGERS COMMISSION to determine whether or not it is in the public interest.

See also MONOPOLY POLICY, OFFICE OF FAIR TRADING, WILLIAMSON

TRADE–OFF MODEL, HORIZONTAL INTEGRATION, VERTICAL INTEGRATION, DIVERSIFICATION, CITY CODE.

merit goods, see SOCIAL PRODUCTS.

methods of competition, *n.* an element of MARKET CONDUCT that denotes the ways in which firms in a MARKET compete against each other. There are various ways in which firms can compete against each other:

(a) PRICE. Sellers may attempt to secure buyer support by putting their product on offer at a lower price than that of rivals. They must bear in mind, however, that rivals may simply lower their prices also with the result that all firms finish up with lower profits.

(b) Nonprice competition, including (i) *physical*-PRODUCT DIFFERENTI-ATION. Sellers may attempt to differentiate technically similar products by altering their quality and design, and by improving their performance. All these efforts are intended to secure buyer allegiance by causing buyers to regard these products as in some way 'better' than competitive offerings. (ii) *product differentiation via selling techniques.* Competition in selling efforts includes media ADVERTISING, general SALES PROMOTION (free trial offers, money-off coupons), personal sales promotion (repre-sentatives), and the creation of distribution outlets. These activities are directed at stimulating demand by emphasising real and imaginary product attributes relative to competitors. (iii) *New* BRAND *competition.* Given dynamic change (advances in technology, changes in consumer tastes), a firm's existing products stand to become obsolete. A supplier is thus obliged to introduce new brands or redesign existing ones to remain competitive.

(c) *low-cost production* as a means of competition. Though cost-effectiveness is not a direct means of competition, it is an essential way to strengthen the market position of a supplier. The ability to reduce costs opens up the possibility of (unmatched) price cuts, or allows firms to devote greater financial resources to differentiation activity.

See also MONOPOLISTIC COMPETITION, OLIGOPOLY, MARKETING MIX, PRODUCT–CHARACTERISTICS MODEL, PRODUCT LIFE–CYCLE.

M-form (multidivisional-form) organization, *n.* an organiza-tional structure adopted by firms in which the management of a firm is decentralized, with separate groups or divisions of the firm responsible for groups of similar products or serving separate markets. Each group or division will have its own autonomous management team and its own separate marketing, production, etc., functions. With such a structure, the top managers at head office leave the day-to-day running of the divisions to the managers responsible, though they monitor the profitability performance of the divisional managers and generally retain power over the allocation of investment funds to the divisions. Oliver Williamson coined the term 'M-form', and he argued that firms with M-form organizations were less likely to pursue nonprofit goals (MANAGEMENT–UTILITY MAXIMIZING), than firms with U–FORM (UNITARY-FORM) ORGANIZATIONS, because top managers could set clear profit goals for divisions and so suffer little control-loss over their subordinates, compared with U-form firms. Williamson also argued that M-form organizations will gradually increase in popularity as firms grow and shed their U-form structures in favour of M-form structures.

See also MANAGERIAL THEORIES OF THE FIRM, BEHAVIOURAL THEORY OF THE FIRM.

microeconomics, *n.* the branch of economics concerned with the study of the behaviour of CONSUMERS and FIRMS and the determination of the market prices and quantities transacted of FACTOR INPUTS and GOODS and SERVICES. Microeconomic analysis investigates how scarce economic resources are allocated between alternative ends and seeks to identify the strategic determinants of an optimally efficient use of resources.

See also THEORY OF CONSUMER BEHAVIOUR, THEORY OF THE FIRM, THEORY OF MARKETS, THEORY OF DEMAND, THEORY OF SUPPLY, MACROECONOMICS.

middleman, *n.* a trader or firm who provide a service by acting as intermediaries between two parties, frequently producer to consumer or seller to purchaser. Wholesalers may be considered middlemen for they frequently act as distributors from producers to retailers on a COMMISSION or mark-up basis. ESTATE AGENTS or insurance brokers are further examples. See WHOLESALING.

migration, *n.* the movement of people into (immigration) and out of (emigration) a country which serves to increase or decrease the country's POPULATION and labour force. For example, immigration was an important factor in the early colonization of Australia and New Zealand, and the USA and Canada.

Mill, John Stuart (1806–1873) English economist who helped develop CLASSICAL ECONOMIC theory in his book *Principles of Political Economy with some of their Applications to Social Philosophy* (1848). Mill was a social reformer, and though he preferred to see the production and exchange of goods taking place in free markets, he argued that government intervention could improve the material well-being of the people through REDISTRIBUTION OF INCOME. Mill was the first to argue that educational barriers to labour mobility could create noncompeting groups of labour with permanent differences in wage rates between groups. He was also the first to analyse costs where two or more joint products are produced in fixed proportions.

minimax strategy, see GAME THEORY.

Fig. 124. **Minimum efficient scale.** See main entry.

minimum efficient scale, *n.* the point on the firm's long-run AVERAGE COST curve at which ECONOMIES OF SCALE are exhausted and constant returns to scale begin.

In the theory of costs the long-run average cost is conventionally depicted as being U-shaped, with economies of scale serving to reduce average cost as output increases to begin with, but then DISECONOMIES OF SCALE set in and average cost rises as output increases. However, statistical studies suggest that for many industries long-run average cost curves are L-shaped, as shown in Fig. 124.

In industries where the minimum efficient scale is large relative to the total size of the market we would expect to find high degrees of SELLER CONCENTRATION, for the market may only support a few firms of minimum efficient scale size. The potential cost disadvantage to firms seeking to enter a market on a small scale viz-a-viz large established firms can also serve as a BARRIER TO ENTRY in certain industries. See NATURAL MONOPOLY.

minimum lending rate, see BANK RATE.

minimum wage rate, *n.* the minimum rate of pay for LABOUR either decreed by the government or voluntarily agreed between trade unions and employers. Minimum WAGE RATES are designed to ensure that workers are able to enjoy some basic standard of living, although (as

Fig. 125. **Minimum wage rate**. See main entry.

shown in Fig. 125), if wage rates are set much above the 'equilibrium rate', W_e, the effect is to reduce the demand for labour (from Q_e to Q_m). Thus, although those who remain in work (OQ_m) are now better off, those persons who are made unemployed as wages rise (Q_mQ_e) are worse off.

See TRADE UNION, SUPPLY–SIDE ECONOMICS, MARGINAL–REVENUE PRODUCT, PROFIT–RELATED PAY.

minority interest, *n.* that part of a subsidiary company's issued SHARE CAPITAL which is not owned by the HOLDING COMPANY. Where the holding company owns more than 50% of the shares of a subsidiary company then it is able to control that company, but where it owns less than 100% of the shares then the minority interest of other shareholders in the subsidiary company must be recognized. In compiling CONSOLIDATED ACCOUNTS the claims of minority interests in certain group assets located in subsidiary companies must be recognized, and their entitlements to a share in the profits of subsidiary companies must be allowed for.

mixed economy, *n.* a method of organizing the economy to produce goods and services. Under this ECONOMIC SYSTEM some goods and services are supplied by private enterprise, and others, typically basic INFRASTRUCTURE goods and services such as electricity, postal services, water supply, are provided by the State.

The mixed economy is a characteristic feature of most present-day developed and developing countries, 'pure' or totally PRIVATE-ENTERPRISE ECONOMIES and CENTRALLY-PLANNED ECONOMIES being rarely encountered. The precise 'mix' of private enterprise and State activities to be found in particular countries, however, does vary substantially between these two extremes and is very much influenced by the political philosophies of the country concerned. See NATIONALIZATION, PRIVATIZATION.

mobility, *n.* the degree to which a FACTOR OF PRODUCTION is willing or able to move between different locations or uses.

Of the three factors of production i.e., NATURAL RESOURCES (land), LABOUR and CAPITAL, land is geographically immobile, but not necessarily the uses to which it can be put, for example, industry or agriculture. Labour is both geographically and occupationally mobile but is not necessarily willing to move to another location or retrain for another occupation. Capital (in the form of plant and machinery) is frequently relatively immobile because it is difficult to find new uses for specialized plant, and often difficult to change location due to the size and nature of such plant (e.g., electricity-generating machinery). See RESOURCE ALLOCATION.

mode, *n.* a means of representing a set of n numbers by a single number which is the value which occurs most often, that is, the one with the highest frequency. For example, if five people had weekly incomes of £100, £100, £150, £250 and £400 then the modal income would be £100 (the most common income). The mode is useful in that it can be used to represent data grouped in the form of a qualitative FREQUENCY DISTRIBUTION. See also MEAN, MEDIAN.

model, see ECONOMIC MODEL.

monetarism, *n.* a body of analysis relating to the influence of MONEY in the functioning of the economy. The theory emphasizes the importance of the need for a 'balanced' relationship between the amount of money available to finance purchases of goods and services, on the one hand, and the ability of the economy to produce such goods and services, on the other.

The theory provides an explanation of INFLATION centred on excessive increases in the MONEY SUPPLY. Specifically, the monetarists argue that if the government spends more than it receives in taxes, increasing the PUBLIC-SECTOR BORROWING REQUIREMENT to finance the shortfall, then the increase in the money supply which results from financing the increase in the public-sector borrowing requirement will increase the rate of inflation. The 'pure' QUANTITY THEORY OF MONEY ($MV \equiv PT$) suggests that the ultimate cause of inflation is excessive monetary creation (that is, 'too much money chasing too little output') – thus it is seen as a source of DEMAND-PULL INFLATION.

Monetarists suggest that 'cost-push' is not a truly independent theory of inflation – it has to be 'financed' by money supply increases. Suppose, initially a given stock of money and given levels of output and prices. Assume now that costs increase (for example, higher wage rates) and this causes suppliers to put up prices. Monetarists argue that this increase in prices will not turn into an inflationary process (that is, a persistent tendency for prices to rise) unless the money supply is increased. The given stock of money will buy fewer goods at the higher price level and real demand will fall; but if the government increases the money supply then this enables the same volume of goods to be purchased at the higher price level. If this process continues, COST-PUSH INFLATION is validated.

See also MONEY SUPPLY/SPENDING LINKAGES, MONETARY POLICY, MEDIUM-TERM FINANCIAL STRATEGY, CHICAGO SCHOOL.

monetary base control, *n.* the control of the monetary base of the financial system as a means of controlling a nation's MONEY SUPPLY. The monetary base is usually defined as notes and coin in circulation *plus* banks' till money and their operational balances at the central bank (= Mo)' and it is argued that if banks adhere to a well-defined cash reserve ratio then the government, by controlling this narrow monetary base, can control monetary growth.

See MONEY-SUPPLY DEFINITIONS, BANK-DEPOSIT CREATION.

monetary compensatory amounts (MCAs) or **green money,** *n.* the system used by the COMMON AGRICULTURAL POLICY of the EUROPEAN COMMUNITY to convert the common prices agreed for farm products into the national currencies of member countries and to realign prices when the exchange rates of those currencies change.

In brief, every spring the Council of Ministers meets and fixes common prices for individual farm products such as milk, beef, etc., for the coming year. These prices are converted into national currency values on the basis of prevailing EXCHANGE RATES. Should, however, a member alter its exchange rate then the 'common link' is broken and its farm prices will either be more, or less expensive than the other member depending upon whether its exchange rate has fallen or increased. To counter this border taxes and subsidies on food IMPORTS and EXPORTS (monetary compensatory amounts) are deployed. For example, if the exchange rate rises (see APPRECIATION 1) the general effect is to cheapen food imports and make food exports more expensive. To 'compensate' for this movement, that is to ensure 'green money' values and domestic farm incomes remain stable, then food imports are taxed and food exports are subsidized. In contrast, if the exchange rate falls (see DEPRECIATION sense 1) the general effect is to cheapen food exports and make food imports more expensive. To stabilize the situation, food imports are subsidized and food exports are taxed.

monetary economy, *n.* an economy that is characterized by MONEY as a medium of exchange and store of value. This contrasts with a BARTER economy in which a coincidence of wants is essential for trade. It is difficult to perceive in complex modern economies, a farmer giving, say, two sheep for a tractor tyre. Although barter still exists on a small scale most countries are crucially dependent on money transactions as a means of conducting trade.

monetary policy, *n.* a tool of general MACROECONOMIC POLICY under the control of the monetary authorities that seeks to attain government economic objectives by influencing the MONEY SUPPLY and/or RATE OF INTEREST (and therefore credit).

The monetary authorities in the UK consist of the Treasury and the Bank of England (both under the control of government) which attempt to achieve certain objectives such as price stability, decreasing UNEMPLOYMENT or ECONOMIC GROWTH. The means of changing the money supply or rate of interest is by the use of monetary instruments. Such instruments take the form of OPEN MARKET OPERATIONS, SPECIAL DEPOSITS or DIRECTIVES.

One problem in using monetary policy is that the rate of interest cannot be regulated without affecting money supply, and vice versa, so that such changes have to be considered together. For example, if the Central Bank wishes to raise the interest rate, say, from Or_1 to Or_2 in Fig. 126 on page 330, then they can do so by reducing the money supply from OM_1 to OM_2. With the given demand curve for money this would have the effect of raising interest rates as required. However, not all components of the money supply are under the control of government and rising interest rates, can, for example, encourage overseas lenders, swelling the domestic money supply and frustrating the authorities' attempts to restrict money supply.

Monetary policy has received greater emphasis in the late 1970s and 1980s due in large part to the growing influence of FRIEDMAN and the Chicago School, ousting KEYNSIAN ECONOMICS. Monetary policy is generally considered inappropriate for FINE-TUNING as it is too slow to react. Rather, monetary policy is a long-term strategy to be supplemented by FISCAL POLICY.

Fig. 126. **Monetary policy.** See main entry.

See ECONOMIC POLICY, MONEY–DEMAND SCHEDULE, MONEY SUPPLY/SPENDING LINKAGES, MONETARISM, QUANTITY THEORY OF MONEY, MEDIUM-TERM FINANCIAL STRATEGY, BANK-DEPOSIT CREATION.

monetary system, *n.* the policies and instruments employed by a country to regulate its MONEY SUPPLY. The physical form of the money supply (bank notes, coins, etc.), the denomination of the values of monetary units (pounds and pence, etc.), and the total size of the money supply are basic policy issues.

The instruments that can be used to control the money supply include OPEN MARKET OPERATIONS, SPECIAL DEPOSITS, DIRECTIVES and RATES OF INTEREST.

The monetary system also has an external dimension in so far as countries engage in international trade and investment which involves interactive mechanisms such as the EXCHANGE RATE, CONVERTIBILITY and INTERNATIONAL RESERVES.

See also MONETARY POLICY, INTERNATIONAL MONETARY SYSTEM.

monetary unit, *n.* the standard unit of CURRENCY that forms the basis of a country's domestic MONEY SUPPLY. For example, the pound (UK), or franc (France). The monetary units of countries are related to each other for international trade and investment purposes through their EXCHANGE-RATE values. See MONEY.

money, *n.* an ASSET that is generally acceptable as a medium of exchange. Individual goods and services, and other physical assets are 'priced' in terms of money and are exchanged using money as a common denominator rather than one GOOD, etc., being exchanged for another (as in BARTER). The use of money as a means of payment enables an economy to produce more output because it facilitates SPECIALIZATION in production and reduces the time spent by sellers and buyers in arranging exchanges. Other important functions of money are its use as a store of purchasing power (money can be held over a period of time and used to finance future payments) and as a unit of account (money is used to measure and record the value of goods or services, for example, GROSS NATIONAL PRODUCT, over time). See LEGAL TENDER.

money-at-call and short notice, see CALL MONEY.

money-demand schedule, *n.* a schedule that depicts the relationship between the quantity of MONEY demanded, Qd (LIQUIDITY PREFERENCE) and the RATE OF INTEREST (*i*) and the level of NATIONAL INCOME (Y):

$$Qd = f(i, Y)$$

If the rate of interest falls this increases the SPECULATIVE DEMAND FOR MONEY (that is, money held in anticipation of a fall in the price of investment assets such as BONDS). The rate of interest varies inversely with the price of bonds, for example, if the nominal return on a bond is 10p and the price of the bond is £1 then the effective interest rate is 10%; if the price of the bond falls to 50p, the effective interest rate increases to 20%. Consequently the lower the rate of interest is the higher will be the price of bonds. The higher the price of bonds the less likely it is that bond prices will continue to rise and the greater the chances that they will fall. Thus, as shown in Fig. 127a on page 332, the lower the rate of interest the greater is the inducement to hold cash for speculative purposes.

An increase in national income and product increases the TRANSAC-TION-DEMAND FOR MONEY (that is, money held on a day-to-day basis to finance current purchases of goods and services), and shifts the money demand schedule outwards to the right, from mds_1 to mds_2 in Fig. 127b.

The money-demand schedule interacts with the MONEY-SUPPLY SCHEDULE to determine the equilibrium RATE OF INTEREST.

money illusion, *n.* the illusion based on the failure of people to appreciate that a general increase in prices (INFLATION) reduces the real PURCHASING POWER of their income (REAL WAGES). In practice, however, this is unlikely to occur once people have become 'accustomed' to living with inflation, and trade unions negotiate for increases in MONEY WAGES which allow for inflationary EXPECTATIONS. See also ADAPTIVE-EXPECTA-TIONS HYPOTHESIS, INFLATIONARY SPIRAL.

money market, *n.* a MARKET that deals in the short-term lending and borrowing of MONEY. Institutions involved in the money market include

Fig. 127. **Money-demand schedule.** (a) With assumed constant national income. (b) The effect of an increase in national income.

the COMMERCIAL BANKS, DISCOUNT HOUSES, companies and the government. The main financial instruments dealt in are BILLS OF EXCHANGE and TREASURY BILLS. See DISCOUNT MARKET.

money multiplier, see BANK DEPOSIT CREATION.

money supply, *n.* the amount of MONEY in circulation in an economy. The total value of money in circulation depends on how the money supply is defined (that is, what assets are included in its specification). For

Initials		Definition	Amount £bn. end 1986
	'Narrow' money	(Money held predominantly for spending)	
		Bank notes and coin in circulation	13.3
M0		Currency plus banks' till money and operational balances at Bank of England	15.7
M1		M0 plus UK private sector sight bank deposits	75.6
M2		M1 plus UK private sector deposits in banks and building societies	169.4
	'Broad' Money	(Money held for spending and/or as a store of value)	
M3	(formerly Sterling M_3)	M1 plus UK private sector time bank deposits and UK public sector sterling deposits	151.7
$M3_c$	(formerly M_3)	M3 plus UK residents' deposits in other currencies	180.3
M4		M3 plus net building society deposits.	261.4
M5	(formerly Private Sector Liquidity)	M4 plus UK private sector holdings of money market instruments (e.g. Treasury Bills), plus National Savings	276.3

Fig. 128. **Money-supply definitions.** Source: Bank of England *Quarterly Bulletin*, June 1987.

purposes of MONETARY POLICY, the money supply can be defined 'narrowly' or more 'broadly'; narrow definitions (M0, M1 and M2) include only a limited number of monetary assets, while broader definitions (M3, M4 and M5) extend the range of assets included.

Given the number of possible definitions of the money supply, it is not surprising that the monetary authorities not only have difficulty in deciding upon the most appropriate definition for control purposes, but also of ensuring (because, for example, of the potential for asset-

333

switching from one definition to another) that desired target values are achieved. See MONEY–SUPPLY DEFINITIONS.

money-supply definitions, *n.* the definitions of MONEY SUPPLY in terms of their 'narrowness' or 'broadness'. 'Narrow' definitions include only assets possessing ready LIQUIDITY (that is, assets which can be used *directly* to finance a transaction – for example, notes and coins). 'Broad' definitions include other assets which are less liquid but are nonetheless important in underpinning spending (for example, many building society deposits have first to be withdrawn and 'converted' into notes and coins before they can be spent). See Fig. 128 on page 333.

money-supply schedule, *n.* a schedule that depicts the amount of MONEY supplied and the RATE OF INTEREST. In some analyses the MONEY SUPPLY is drawn as a vertical straight line; that is, the money supply is exogenously determined, being put into the economic system 'from outside' by the government (for example, 'narrow' M0 money). However, a significant part of the 'wider' money supply (M3 money), is endogenously determined – for example, bank deposits are 'created' by the banking system and these are highly interest-rate sensitive. Thus, as a general proposition, the higher the rate of interest (the higher the return on loanable funds), the greater the quantity of money supplied (see Fig, 129).

The money-supply schedule interacts with the MONEY–DEMAND SCHEDULE to determine the equilibrium rate of interest. See MONEY SUPPLY/SPENDING LINKAGES.

Fig. 129. **Money-supply schedule**. See main entry.

money-supply/spending linkages, *n.* **1.** the *indirect* link (in the Keynsian view) between MONEY SUPPLY and AGGREGATE DEMAND through the RATE OF INTEREST. In brief, an increase in the money supply (from M to M¹ in Fig. 130a on page 336), brings about a fall in the rate of interest (from r to r^1), which results in an increase in planned INVESTMENT from I to I¹ (Fig. 130b). The rise in investment, in turn, increases aggregate demand and, via the MULTIPLIER effect, raises national income from Y to Y¹ (Fig. 130c). The fall in interest rates can also be shown to increase consumption expenditure (the lower cost of borrowing encourages people to use more loan finance to buy cars, televisions, etc.). See KEYNES, KEYNSIAN ECONOMICS, EQUILIBRIUM LEVEL OF NATIONAL INCOME.

2. the *direct* link (in the monetarist view) between the money supply and the level of aggregate demand. In brief, an increase in the money supply feeds directly into an increase in demand for final goods and services, and not just for investment goods. This proposition is based on the assumption that when households and businesses have more money than they need to hold, they will spend the excess on currently produced goods and services. See also QUANTITY THEORY OF MONEY, MONETARISM, CROWDING-OUT EFFECT.

money wages, *n.* the WAGE RATES expressed in terms of current MONEY values. An increase in the general level of prices which is not matched by an equivalent rise in money wages either because of MONEY ILLUSION on the part of the labour force or because employers refuse to grant money wage increases, will cause REAL WAGES to fall; that is, an unchanged money-wage rate will now buy fewer goods and services at the higher level of prices.

Monopolies and Mergers Commission (MMC), *n.* a commission established in 1948, and responsible, in part, for the implementation of UK MONOPOLY POLICY. The basic task of the Commission is to investigate and report on cases of MONOPOLY, MERGER and ANTI-COMPETITIVE PRACTICES referred to it by the OFFICE OF FAIR TRADING to determine whether or not they operate against the PUBLIC INTEREST.

Under UK monopoly law, a monopoly is defined as a situation where at least one-quarter of a reference good or service is supplied by: (a) one firm (dominant-firm monopoly), or a number of suppliers who restrict competition between themselves (complex monopoly); (b) mergers falling within the scope of the legislation which create or intensify a monopoly situation (defined by the one-quarter market share rule), or where the value of assets taken over exceeds £30 million;

MONEY-SUPPLY/SPENDING LINKAGES

(a)

(b)

(c)

Fig. 130. **Money-supply/spending linkages**. See main entry. (a) Rate of interest. (b) Planned investment. (c) National income.

(c) anticompetitive practices which distort, restrict or eliminate competition in a market.

The criterion of the public interest is used to evaluate monopolies, mergers and anticompetitive practices. The term 'public interest' is not expressly defined in monopoly law, so it has been left to the MMC itself to determine what constitutes offence to the public interest in each case. In monopoly cases the MMC scrutinizes the 'things done' by dominant firms for evidence of the 'abuse' of market power, and invariably condemns predatory pricing policies which result in monopoly profits. Practices such as EXCLUSIVE DEALING, AGGREGATED REBATES, TIE-IN SALES which yield very little in the way of economic benefit and whose main effect is to restrict competition have been invariably condemned by the MMC, especially when employed by a dominant firm to erect barriers to entry and to undermine the market positions of smaller rivals. In merger cases, the MMC is involved in weighing up the possible benefits of the merger (cost savings, etc.) against possible detriment (increased market power), but under present law, can only condemn those mergers which would seriously reduce competition or reduce efficiency.

In all cases the Commission has powers only of recommendation. It can recommend price cuts to deal with the problem of monopoly profits, the discontinuance of offending practices and the prohibition of offending mergers, but it is up to the Office of Fair Trading to implement the recommendations, or otherwise, as it sees fit.

monopolistic competition or **imperfect competition** or **imperfect market,** *n.* a type of MARKET STRUCTURE. A monopolistically-competitive market is one that is characterized by:

(a) *many firms and buyers*, that is, the market is comprised of a large number of independently-acting firms and buyers.

(b) *differentiated products*, that is, the products offered by competing firms are differentiated from each other in one or more respects. These differences may be of a physical nature, involving functional features, or may be purely 'imaginary' in the sense that artificial differences are created through ADVERTISING and SALES PROMOTION (see PRODUCT DIFFERENTIATION).

(c) *free market entry and exit*, that is, there are no BARRIERS TO ENTRY preventing new firms entering the market or obstacles in the way of existing firms leaving the market. (No allowance is made in the 'theory' of monopolistic competition for the fact that product differentiation by establishing strong BRAND LOYALTIES to established firm's products may act as a barrier to entry).

Fig. 131. **Monopolistic competition**. See main entry. (a) Short-run
equilibrium. (b) Long-run equilibrium.

Apart from the product-differentiation aspects, monopolistic competition is very similar structurally to PERFECT COMPETITION.

The analysis of individual firm equilibrium in monopolistic competition can be presented in terms of a 'representative' firm, that is, all firms are assumed to face *identical* cost and demand conditions, and each is a profit maximizer (see PROFIT MAXIMIZATION), from which it is then possible to derive a market-equilibrium position.

The significance of product differentiation is: (a) each firm has a market which is partially distinct from its competitors; that is, each firm faces a downward-sloping demand curve (D in Fig. 131a), although the presence of close-competing substitute products (a high CROSS-ELASTIC-ITY OF DEMAND) will cause this curve to be relatively elastic; (b) the firms' cost structures (MARGINAL COST and AVERAGE COSTS) are raised as a result of incurring differentiation expenditures (SELLING COSTS).

The firm being a profit maximizer will aim to produce at that price (OP) – output (OQ) combination, shown in Fig. 131a, which equates marginal cost (MC) and MARGINAL REVENUE (MR). In the short run this may result in firms securing ABOVE-NORMAL PROFITS.

In the long run, above-normal profits will induce new firms to enter the market and this will have the effect of depressing the demand curve faced by established firms (that is, push the demand curve leftwards, thereby reducing the volume of sales associated with each price level). The process of new entry will continue until the excess profits have been competed away. Fig, 131b shows the long-run equilibrium position of the 'representative' firm. The firm continues to maximize its profits at a price (OP_e) – output (OQ_e) combination where marginal cost equals marginal revenue, but now secures only a NORMAL PROFIT return. This normal profit position for the firm in the long run is similar to the long-run equilibrium position for the firm in perfect competition. But monopolistic competition results in a less efficient MARKET PERFORMANCE when compared to perfect competition. Specifically, monopolistically competitive firms produce lower rates of output and sell these outputs at higher prices than perfectly competitive firms. Since the demand curve is downwards sloping, it is necessarily tangent to the long-run average cost curve (which is higher than the perfectly competitive firms cost curve because of the addition of selling costs) to the left of the latter's minimum point. Firms thus operate a less than optimum scale of plant and as a result there is EXCESS CAPACITY in the market.

monopoly, *n.* a type of MARKET STRUCTURE characterized by: (a) *one firm and many buyers*, that is, a market comprised of a single supplier selling to a multitude of small, independently-acting buyers; (b) *a lack of substitute products*, that is, there are no close substitutes for the monopolist's product (CROSS-ELASTICITY OF DEMAND is zero); (c) *blockaded entry*, that is, BARRIERS TO ENTRY are so severe that is impossible for new firms to enter the market.

In *static monopoly* the monopolist is in a position to set the market price. However, unlike a perfectly competitive producer (see PERFECT COMPETITION), the monopolist's marginal and average revenue curves are not identical. The monopolist faces a downward-sloping demand curve (D in Fig. 132a) and the sale of additional units of his product forces down the price at which all units must be sold. The objective of the monopolist, like that of the competitive firm, is assumed to be PROFIT MAXIMIZATION and he operates with complete knowledge of relevant cost and demand data. Accordingly, the monopolist will aim to produce at that price-output combination which equates MARGINAL COST and MARGINAL REVENUE. Fig. 132a indicates the short-run equilibrium position for the monopolist. The monopolist will supply Q_e output at a price of P_e. At the equilibrium price, the monopolist secures ABOVE-NORMAL PROFITS. Unlike the competitive firm situation, where entry is unfettered, entry barriers in monopoly are assumed to be so great as to preclude new suppliers. There is thus no possibility of additional productive resources entering the industry and in consequence the monopolist will continue to earn above-normal profits over the long-term (until such time that supply and demand conditions radically change.) Market theory predicts that given identical cost and demand conditions, monopoly leads to a higher price and a lower output than does perfect competition.

Equilibrium under perfect competition occurs where supply equates demand. This is illustrated in Fig. 132b in which the competitive supply curve is MC (the sum of all the individual suppliers' marginal cost curves). The competitive output is Q_c and the competitive price is P_c. Since the supply curve is the sum of the marginal cost curves, it follows that in equilibrium, marginal cost equals price. Assume now that this industry is monopolized as a result, say, of one firm taking over all the other suppliers, but that each plant's cost curve is unaffected by this change – that is, there are *no* ECONOMIES OF SCALE or DISECONOMIES OF SCALE arising from the coordinated planning of production by the monopolist. Thus marginal costs will be the same for the monopolist as for the competitive industry, and, hence, their supply curves will be identical. As noted above, the monopolist who seeks to maximize profits will equate cost not to price, but to marginal revenue. In consequence, in equilibrium, the output of the industry falls from Q_c to Q_m and market price rises from P_c to P_m.

The conclusion of competitive optimality, however, rests on a number of assumptions, some of which are highly questionable, in particular the assumption that cost structures are identical for small perfectly-competitive firms and large oligopolistic and monopoly suppliers, while, given its static framework, it ignores important *dynamic* influences, such as TECHNOLOGICAL PROGRESS.

(a)

(b)

(c)

Fig. 132. **Monopoly**. See main entry.

In a static monopoly, a fundamental assumption is that costs of production increase at relatively low output levels. The implication of this is that the firm reaches an equilibrium position at a size of operation which is small relative to the market. Suppose, however, that production in a particular industry is characterized by significant economies of scale. That is, individual firms can continue to lower unit costs by producing much larger quantities. We shall illustrate this by assuming that a perfectly competitive industry is taken over by a monopolist. It is very unlikely in this instance that costs would be unaffected by the change in the scale of operations. Fig. 132c illustrates the case where the reduction in unit costs as a result of the economies of single ownership give rise to greater output and lower price than the original perfect competition situation.

The fall in unit costs as a result of monopolization moves the marginal cost curve of the monopolist (MC_m) to the right of the original supply curve (S_{pc}) so that more is produced (Q_m) at the lower price (P_m). We still make the assumption that marginal costs are rising over the relevant range of output. In the long run, this expectation follows from the proposition that at some size economies of large scale are exhausted and diseconomies of scale set in. The diseconomies are usually associated with the administrative and managerial difficulties that arise in very large complex organizations. However, there is growing evidence to the effect that the long-run average cost curve (and hence MC curve) for many capital-intensive industries is L-shaped. In these industries total demand and individual market shares, not cost considerations, are the factors limiting the size of the firm. The firm may thus grow and find a level of output such that further expansion would be unprofitable. But in doing so it may become so large relative to the market that it attains a degree of power over price. This is not to deny that the monopolist could further increase output and lower price were he not trying to maximize his profit. Such a position would not, however, be the result of a return to perfect competition. What has happened is that the firm, seeking its best profit position, has abandoned the status of an insignificant small competitor. It has not necessarily done so through a systematic attempt to dominate the market. On the contrary, it is the underlying cost conditions of the market that have impelled this growth. In such an industry it is possible that small 'competitive-sized' firms cannot survive. Moreover, to the extent that the unit costs are lower at higher production levels, the large firm is a *technically more efficient* entity.

The case of significant economies of scale, then, may be characterized as one in which atomistic competition becomes technically impossible and under an efficiency criterion, undesirable. The demonstration of competitive optimality implicitly assumes away this kind of complication.

The analysis developed above also neglects dynamic aspects of the market system. According to an influential group of writers, major improvements in consumer welfare occur largely as a result of technological INNOVATIONS, that is the growth of resources and development of new techniques and products over time rather than adjustments to provide maximum output from a given (static) input, and that monopolistic elements function as a precondition and protection of innovating effort. Perfectly competitive firms certainly have the motivation to employ the most efficient known production techniques, since this is necessary to their survival. But their inability to sustain above-normal profits limits both their resources and incentive to develop new technology. By contrast, the pure monopolist, earning above normal profits, will have greater financial resources to promote technical advance but his *incentive* to innovate may be weak given the lack of effective competition. However, technological advance is a means of lowering unit costs and thereby expanding profits; and these profits will not be of a transitory nature, given barriers to entry. Moreover, technical superiority may itself be one of the monopolist's barriers to entry; hence, the monopolist must persist and succeed in the area of technological advance to maintain his dominant position.

One of the most important advocates of the possibility that an industry exhibiting strong monopolistic elements may employ productive techniques superior to those of its competitive counterpart, was SCHUMPETER. To the extent that invention and introduction of new processes and products is centred in the large oligopolistic firm, a comparison of oligopoly/monopoly with perfect competition at a fixed technological position systematically understates the social contribution of the former.

Diagrammatically, the Schumpeterian contention may be illustrated by using Fig. 132c. The competitive market produces Q_{pc} where short-run marginal cost equals price. If this industry were monopolized, the ordinary expectation would be a price rise to $P_m{}^1$ and output decrease to $Q_m{}^1$. However, if the monopolist in such an industry introduces cost-saving innovations, the entire marginal cost curve may fall so that the monopolist may actually produce more (Q_m) at a lower price (P_m) than the original competitive industry, even if the monopolist fully exploits his market power.

It is, of course, possible that society will remain worse off under monopoly, even if the monopoly innovates; the benefits of innovation may not outweigh the costs of monopolistic exploitation.

See also OLIGOPOLY, MONOPOLISTIC COMPETITION, DISCRIMINATING MONOPOLY, MONOPOLY POLICY, CONSUMER SURPLUS, CONCENTRATION MEASURES.

monopoly firm, see DOMINANT FIRM.

monopoly laws, *n.* a body of legislation providing for the control of MONOPOLIES, MERGERS, RESTRICTIVE TRADE AGREEMENTS and ANTI-COMPETITIVE PRACTICES. UK monopoly law is contained in nine main statutes, with the later Acts amending or extending earlier ones: Monopolies and Restrictive Practices (Inquiry and Control) Act, 1948; Restrictive Trade Practices Act, 1956; Resale Prices Act, 1964; Monopolies and Mergers Act, 1965; Restrictive Trade Practices Act, 1968; FAIR TRADING ACT, 1973; Resale Prices Act, 1976; Restrictive Trade Practices Act, 1976; COMPETITION ACT, 1980. See OFFICE OF FAIR TRADING, MONOPOLY POLICY.

monopoly of scale, see DOMINANT FIRM.

monopoly policy, *n.* a policy concerned with promoting the efficient use of economic resources and protecting the interests of consumers. The objective of monopoly policy is to secure an optimal MARKET PERFORM-ANCE: specifically, least-cost supply, 'fair' prices and profit levels, technological advance and product improvement. Monopoly policy covers a number of areas, including the monopolization of a market by a single supplier (DOMINANT FIRM), the creation of monopoly positions by MERGERS and TAKEOVERS, COLLUSION between sellers, and ANTICOMPETITIVE PRACTICES.

Monopoly policy is implemented mainly through the control of MARKET STRUCTURE and MARKET CONDUCT but also, on occasions, through the direct control of market performance itself (by, for example, the stipulation of maximum levels of profit).

There are two basic approaches to the control of market structure and conduct: the nondiscretionary approach and the discretionary approach. The nondiscretionary approach lays down 'acceptable' standards of structure and conduct and prohibits outright any transgression of these standards. Typical ingredients of this latter approach include:

(a) the stipulation of maximum permitted market share limits (say, no more than 20% of the market) in order to limit the degree of SELLER

CONCENTRATION and prevent the emergence of a monopoly supplier. Thus, for example, under this ruling any proposed merger or takeover which would take the combined group's market share above the permitted limit would be automatically prohibited.

(b) the outright prohibition of all forms of 'shared monopoly' (RESTRICTIVE TRADE AGREEMENT) involving price fixing, market sharing, etc.

(c) the outright prohibition of specific practices designed to reduce or eliminate competition, for example, EXCLUSIVE DEALING, REFUSAL TO SUPPLY, etc.

Thus, the nondiscretionary approach attempts to preserve conditions of WORKABLE COMPETITION by a direct attack on the possession and exercise of monopoly power as such.

By contrast, the discretionary approach takes a more pragmatic line, recognizing that often high levels of seller concentration and certain agreements between firms may serve to improve economic efficiency rather than impair it. It is the essence of the discretionary approach that each situation be judged on its own merits rather than be automatically condemned. Thus, under the discretionary approach, mergers, restrictive agreements and specific practices of the kind noted above are evaluated in terms of their possible benefits and detriments. If, on balance, they would appear to be detrimental, then and only then are they prohibited.

The US and the EUROPEAN COMMUNITY by and large operate the nondiscretionary approach; the UK has a history of preferring the discretionary approach.

See PUBLIC INTEREST, WILLIAMSON TRADE–OFF MODEL, OFFICE OF FAIR TRADING, MONOPOLIES AND MERGERS COMMISSION, RESTRICTIVE PRACTICES COURT, HORIZONTAL INTEGRATION, VERTICAL INTEGRATION, DIVERSIFICATION, CONCENTRATION MEASURES.

monopoly profit, *n.* the long-term ABOVE–NORMAL PROFITS accruing to a monopolist. See MONOPOLY.

monopoly tax, *n.* a levy imposed by the government on the ABOVE–NORMAL PROFITS earned by a monopolist. Unlike an order to cut prices or RATE–OF–RETURN REGULATION such a tax does nothing to restore the loss of the CONSUMERS' SURPLUS imposed by the monopoly back to the consumer. The immediate beneficiary is the government itself who may decide to use the tax as a means of raising revenue rather than as an anti-monopoly device. See MONOPOLY POLICY.

monopsony, *n.* a form of BUYER CONCENTRATION, that is, a MARKET situation in which a single buyer confronts many small suppliers. See MONOPOLY, BILATERAL MONOPOLY.

monotonic function, *n.* a function that either increases or decreases continuously along its range. An increasing function cannot decrease below its previous stated value, and vice-versa for a decreasing function. For example, if disposable income has increased in each year over the past 10 years then it may be considered a monotonic function because each year has seen an increase over the previous year without falling below whatever the previous year's disposable income was.

Monte Carlo simulation, see SIMULATION.

moonlighter, *n.* a person who is registered as unemployed and draws unemployment benefit, but who nonetheless takes paid work 'on the side' to supplement his or her income. For example, an out-of-work painter may decorate a friend's house, being paid a sum of money for undertaking the job. This and other BLACK ECONOMY transactions are not officially recorded and hence are not included in a country's NATIONAL-INCOME ACCOUNTS.

moratorium, *n.* the suspension of repayment of DEBT, or INTEREST, for a specified period of time. For example, the freezing of debt repayment obligations extended by advanced country governments and private banks to a developing country which is experiencing acute balance of payments difficulties, or the suspension of debt payments owing to dealers in a commodity market which has suffered a dramatic price collapse. See DEBT SERVICING, INTERNATIONAL DEBT.

mortgage, *n.* the conveyance of an ASSET by a BORROWER (mortgagor) to a LENDER (mortgagee) as security for a LOAN. Upon completion of the obligations imposed by the legal mortgage agreement, the borrower (mortgagor) has the right to have the assets reconveyed from the lender (mortgagee). Unless the borrower (mortgagor) defaults upon the agreement, the lender (mortgagee) does not have the right of possession of the assets so pledged for security.

most-favoured nation clause, *n.* an underlying principle of the GENERAL AGREEMENT ON TARIFFS AND TRADE whereby each country undertakes to apply the same rate of TARIFF to *all* of its trade partners. This general principle of nondiscrimination evolved out of earlier GATT endorsement of bilateral trade treaties whereby if country A negotiated a tariff cut with country B, and subsequently country B negotiated an even more favourable tariff cut with country C, then the tariff rate applying in the second case would also be extended to A.

moving average, see TIME-SERIES ANALYSIS.

multicollinearity, *n.* a statistical situation where a number of INDEPEN-
DENT VARIABLES are highly correlated (see CORRELATION) so that they all
vary together. In such situations it is impossible to disentangle the effect
of any one of these independent variables upon the DEPENDENT VARIABLE
in REGRESSION ANALYSIS.

Multi–Fibre Arrangement (MFA), *n.* a trade pact between some 80
developed and DEVELOPING COUNTRIES which regulates INTERNATIONAL
TRADE in textiles and clothing. Its purpose is to give poor countries
guaranteed and growing access to markets in Europe and North
America, but at the same time to ensure this growth does not disrupt the
older established textile clothing industries of the developed countries.
MFA 1 (1974) established QUOTAS, allowing imports to grow by 6% a
year in real terms. Subsequent extensions of the MFA, MFA 2 (1978) and
MFA 3 (1982) have involved a series of bilateral arrangements
(negotiated on a country-to-country, product-by-product basis) to
restrict imports of particular items, where this causes local market
'disruption'. The MFA now contains upwards of 3,000 quotas for
different countries and different products.
  The MFA is a blatant form of PROTECTIONISM which discriminates
against the interests of the less-developed countries, many of whom are
highly dependent on the textile industries as a leading sector in
promoting their ECONOMIC DEVELOPMENT; it is clearly contrary to the
principles of the GENERAL AGREEMENT ON TARIFFS AND TRADE, but has been
conveniently 'exempted' from that body's rules of good conduct.

multilateral trade, *n.* the INTERNATIONAL TRADE between all countries
engaged in the exporting and importing of goods and services. Compare
BILATERAL TRADE.

multinational firm, *n.* a FIRM that produces and sells in a number of
countries as distinct from a firm which produces in one country and
exports to overseas markets. Direct investment by multinational firms in
the establishment of overseas production units occurs because of the
greater cost-effectiveness and profitability resulting from:
  (a) *firm-specific advantages.* A firm may possess a monopolistic
advantage over its competitors (a patented technology or a unique
product) which can be better exploited and protected by direct control
rather than shared with overseas producers and distributors.
  (b) *locational advantages.* Direct investment enables a firm to reduce
transportation costs and to keep in touch more closely with local market
conditions – changes in consumer tastes, competitors' actions, etc.

(c) *country-specific advantages*. Direct investment enables a firm both to avoid governmental restrictions on market access such as TARIFFS and QUOTAS, and to take advantage of lower labour and other input costs and local investment inducements such as cash grants and tax write-offs.

See also INTERNALIZATION, TRANSFER PRICING.

multiple-correlation coefficient, *n.* a measure of the goodness of fit of an estimated multiple regression equation to the sample observations. See CORRELATION COEFFICIENT, REGRESSION ANALYSIS.

multiple linear regression, see REGRESSION ANALYSIS.

multiplier, *n.* the ratio of an induced change in the EQUILIBRIUM LEVEL OF NATIONAL INCOME to an initial change in the level of spending. The 'multiplier effect' denotes the phenomenon whereby some initial increase (or decrease) in the rate of spending will bring about a more than proportionate increase (or decrease) in national income.

Two important features of the multiplier need to be noted: (a) it is a cumulative process rather than instantaneous effect, and as such is best viewed in terms of a series of successive 'rounds' of additions to income; (b) the value of the multiplier depends on the fraction of extra INCOME that is spent on CONSUMPTION (the MARGINAL PROPENSITY TO CONSUME) (MPC) at each successive round.

For simplicity, let us assume that all income is either consumed or 'withdrawn' as SAVINGS. (That is, the MPC and MARGINAL PROPENSITY TO SAVE (MPS) together = 1.) The value of the multiplier (K) is then given by the formula

$$K = \frac{1}{1 - MPC} \text{ or } \frac{1}{MPS}$$

The larger an increase in consumption from an increment of income, the larger the multiplier. Thus, if MPC is 0.9, MPS is 0.1 and the multiplier value is 10; if MPC is 0.75, MPS is 0.25 and the multiplier value is only 4.

The multiplier effect is illustrated in Fig. 133a and b. With a multiplier value of 4, an initial £500 million of extra spending results in a £2 billion increase in national income, as Fig. 133a shows. In each round a proportion of the additional income created is saved and so leaks from the circular flow, failing to get passed on as additional consumption expenditure in the next round. When the cumulative total of these savings leakages is equal to the initial increase in spending the multiplier process ceases and the economy reaches a new equilibrium.

Fig. 133b demonstrates the multiplier effect in graphical form.

Round	Change in national income (in £ millions)	Change in consumption MPC = 0.75	Change in saving MPS = 0.25
1. Initial Increase in Spending	500	375	125
2.	375	281	94
3.	281	211	70
4.	211	158	53
5.	158	119	39
All later Rounds	475	356	119
Totals	2,000	1,500	500

(a)

(b)

Fig. 133. **Multiplier**. See main entry. (a) The multiplier process.
(b) The multiplier effect of increased spending on national income.

Starting at national income level OY_1, if AGGREGATE DEMAND increases from AD to AD_1, then the initial injection of extra spending AB would serve to increase output and income by Y_1Y_2. This additional income would induce yet more spending (CD) which would in turn increase output and income by Y_2Y_3. This additional income would induce yet more spending (EF) which would in turn increase output and income yet further by $Y_3 Y_4$, and so on. The process ends when the new equilibrium level of income Y_e is reached.

In addition, of course, to the savings 'withdrawal' from the income flow there are also TAXATION and IMPORT withdrawals which further reduce the value of the multiplier. Thus the more sophisticated multiplier is given by the formula:

$$K = \frac{1}{MPS + MPT + MPM}$$

where MPT is the MARGINAL PROPENSITY TO TAX and MPM is the MARGINAL PROPENSITY TO IMPORT. See also CIRCULAR FLOW OF NATIONAL INCOME MODEL, ACCELERATOR.

multiproduct firm, *n.* a FIRM that produces a number of products. Basic economic theory concentrates on the single-product firm to simplify analysis though in practice firms can produce different varieties of the same product (product development) or several different products (DIVERSIFICATION). See PRODUCT–MARKET MATRIX.

mutual interdependence, *n.* a form of INTERFIRM CONDUCT pattern in which some or all of the firms in a market formulate their competitive strategy in the light of anticipated reactions and countermoves of rival firms. The actions of firms both affect and are affected by each other – the situation is circular. A price cut, for example, may appear to be advantageous to one firm considered in isolation, but if this results in other firms cutting their prices also to protect their sales then all firms may suffer reduced profits. Accordingly, firms may seek to avoid price competition, employing such mechanisms as PRICE LEADERSHIP to coordinate their prices. The same mutual interdependency considerations may apply to other areas of competition; for example, if one firm increases its advertising expenditures other firms may follow suit to protect their market shares.

Such interdependency exists in market situations, typically in an oligopolistic market (see OLIGOPOLY), where the leading firms each supply a significant proportion of total market supply.

See also CARTEL, PRICE WAR, DUOPOLY, PRODUCT DIFFERENTIATION, GAME THEORY, KINKED–DEMAND CURVE THEORY, LIMIT PRICING.

N

National Board for Prices and Incomes, *n.* a UK regulatory body which acted to control prices, wages etc. under the government's PRICES AND INCOMES POLICY from 1965–70.

national debt or **government debt,** *n.* the money owed by central government to domestic and foreign lenders. A national debt arises as a result of the government spending more than it receives in taxation and other receipts (BUDGET DEFICIT). This may arise due to, for example, a 'one-off' event (the financing of a war), or reflects the governments commitment to an expansionary FISCAL POLICY.

National debt in the UK is made up of a number of financial instruments primarily short-dated TREASURY BILLS and long-dated BONDS, together with national savings certificates. INTEREST on the national debt is paid out of current budget receipts.

Concern is sometimes expressed at the size of the national debt. In 1986, for example, the UK's national debt stood at £167,000 million compared to current GROSS DOMESTIC PRODUCT of £373,000 million. However, provided that the bulk of the debt is held by domestic residents and institutions there is no cause for alarm. In terms of the CIRCULAR FLOW OF NATIONAL INCOME MODEL, the interest paid on the national debt to domestic lenders is only a TRANSFER PAYMENT and does not represent a net reduction in the real resources of the economy or compromise the ability of the economy to provide goods and services. In 1986 94% of the UK's national debt was held domestically and interest payments accounted for only 11% of total GOVERNMENT EXPENDITURE.

See BUDGET (GOVERNMENT), PUBLIC-SECTOR BORROWING REQUIREMENT.

National Economic Development Council (NEDC), *n.* an organization established in the UK in 1962 in response to concern over the country's poor economic performance compared to other advanced industrial countries. NEDC was created as a form of economic-planning agency, bringing together the government and both sides of industry, management and the trade unions, with a general remit to identify obstacles to the attainment of improved efficiency and growth and to formulate appropriate means of overcoming them. At the 'grass roots' level, NEDC is represented by various subcommittees (Economic Development Committees) each covering a particular industrial sector, with the main NEDC body playing a supportive and coordinating role. See also INDICATIVE PLANNING, NATIONAL PLAN.

National Enterprise Board, *n.* a UK organization that promoted and financially assisted industrial RATIONALIZATION, MERGERS and industrial projects from 1975–81. See also BRITISH TECHNOLOGY GROUP, INDUSTRIAL POLICY.

national income or **factor income,** *n.* the total money income received by households in return for supplying FACTOR INPUTS to businesses over a given period of time. National income is equal to NET NATIONAL PRODUCT, and consists of the total money value of goods and services produced over the given time period (GROSS NATIONAL PRODUCT) less CAPITAL CONSUMPTION. See NATIONAL INCOME ACCOUNTS, CIRCULAR FLOW OF NATIONAL INCOME.

national income accounts, *n.* the national economic statistics that show the state of the economy over a period of time (usually one year). NATIONAL INCOME is the net value of all goods and services (NATIONAL PRODUCT) produced annually in a nation: it provides a useful money measure of economic activity, and by calculating national-income per head of population, serves as a useful indicator of living standards. In this latter use it is possible to compare living standards over time or to make international comparisons of living standards.

National income can be considered in three ways, as Fig. 134 suggests:

(a) the *domestic product/output* of goods and services produced by enterprises within the country. (*value-added approach to GDP*). This total output does not include the value of imported goods and services. To avoid overstating the value of output produced by double-counting both the final output of goods and services and the output of intermediate components and services which are eventually absorbed in final output, only the VALUE ADDED at each stage of the production process is counted. The sum of all the value added by various sections of the economy (agriculture, manufacturing, etc.) is known as the GROSS DOMESTIC PRODUCT; and to arrive at the GROSS NATIONAL PRODUCT it is necessary to add net property income from abroad (defined as net income accruing to a nation's citizens from their ownership of assets abroad).

(b) the total INCOME of residents of the country derived from the current production of goods and services (*income approach to GDP*). Such

Fig. 134. **National income accounts**. See main entry.

incomes are called FACTOR INCOMES because they accrue to factors of production, and they exclude TRANSFER PAYMENTS like sickness or unemployment benefit for which no goods or services are received in return. The sum of all these factor incomes (wages and salaries, incomes of the self-employed, etc.) should exactly match the gross domestic product, since each £1's worth of goods and services produced should simultaneously produce £1 of factor income for their producers. To get from gross domestic factor incomes (= gross domestic product) to gross national factor incomes (= gross national product) it is necessary to add net property income from abroad.

(c) the *total domestic expenditure* by residents of a country on consumption and investment goods (*expenditure approach to GDP*). This includes expenditure on *final* goods and services (excluding expenditure on intermediate products), and includes goods which are unsold and added to stock (inventory investment). However, some domestic expenditure will be channelled to imported goods, while expenditure by nonresidents on goods and services produced by domestic residents will add to the factor incomes of these residents. Thus, to get from total domestic expenditure to total national expenditure (= gross national product) it is necessary to deduct imports and add exports.

All three measures outlined above show the gross money value of goods and services produced – the gross national product. However, in the process of producing these goods and services the nation's capital stock will be subject to wear and tear, and so we must allow for the net money value of goods and services produced (allowing for the depreciation of the capital stock or CAPITAL CONSUMPTION) – the NET NATIONAL PRODUCT. This net national product is called national income.

In practice, data-collection problems mean that the three measures of national income give slightly different figures, necessitating the introduction of a residual error term in the national income accounts which reflects these differences.

national insurance contributions, *n.* the compulsory contributions paid by workers to the government's national insurance scheme; in return for these payments workers receive state pensions, sickness, unemployment and other payments and free or low cost health benefits.

nationalization, *n.* the public ownership of industry. In a CENTRALLY PLANNED ECONOMY most or all of the country's industries are owned by the State, and resources are allocated, and the supply of goods and services determined, in accordance with a NATIONAL PLAN. In a MIXED ECONOMY some industries are owned by the State but the supply of the majority of goods and services is undertaken by PRIVATE-ENTERPRISE industries operating through the MARKET mechanism. The extent of public ownership of industry depends very much on political ideology with centrally planned economy advocates seeking more nationalization, and private-enterprise proponents favouring little or no nationalization. For example, in the UK a Labour government nationalized the iron and steel industry in 1949, having previously nationalized the Bank of England, civil aviation, transport, electricity, coal and gas industries; the iron and steel industry was denationalized by a Conservative government in 1953, but later a large part of the industry was renationalized by a Labour government in 1967. Since 1980 a Conservative government has embarked on a major denationalization programme (see PRIVATIZATION).

The main economic justification for nationalization relies heavily on the NATURAL MONOPOLY argument: the provision of some goods and services can be more efficiently undertaken by a monopoly supplier, because ECONOMIES OF SCALE are so great that only by organizing the industry on a single-supplier basis can full advantage be taken of cost savings. Natural monopolies are particularly likely to arise where the provision of a good or service requires an interlocking supply network as, for example, in gas, electricity and water distribution, and railway and telephone services. In these cases laying down competing pipelines and carriage ways would involve unnecessary duplication of resources and extra expense. Significant production economies of scale are associated with capital-intensive industries such as iron and steel, gas and electricity generation. In other instances, however, the economic case for nationalization is far less convincing: industries or individual firms may be taken over because they are making losses and need to be reorganized, or a political concern with preserving jobs. For example, in the UK, the British Leyland car firm and British Shipbuilders were nationalized in 1975 and 1977, respectively.

A private-enterprise MONOPOLY could, of course, also secure the same efficiency gains in production and distribution as a state monopoly, but the danger exists that it might abuse its position of market power by monopoly pricing. The state monopolist, by contrast, would seek to promote the interests of consumers by charging 'fair' prices. Opponents of nationalization argue, however, that State monopolists are likely to dissipate the cost savings arising from economies of scale by internal inefficiencies (bureaucratic rigidities and control problems giving rise to X-INEFFICIENCY), and the danger is that such inefficiencies could be exacerbated over time by governments subsidizing loss-making activities.

The problem of reconciling supply efficiency with various other economic and social objectives of governments further complicates the picture. For example, the government may force nationalized industries to hold down their prices to help in the control of inflation, but by squeezing the industries' cash flow the longer term effects of this might be to reduce their investment programmes. Many of the nationalized industries are charged with social obligations; for example, they may be required by the government to provide railway, postal and telephone services to remote rural communities even though these are totally uneconomic.

Thus, assessing the relative merits and demerits of nationalization in the round is a difficult matter. From an economic efficiency point of view, under British MONOPOLY POLICY, nationalized industries can be referred for investigation to the MONOPOLIES AND MERGERS COMMISSION to determine whether or not they are operating in the public interest.

See MARGINAL COST PRICING, AVERAGE COST PRICING, TWO–PART TARIFF, PUBLIC UTILITY, RATE–OF–RETURN REGULATION, PRIVATIZATION.

national plan, *n.* a long-term plan for the development of an economy. Such plans usually cover a period of five years or more and attempt to remove bottlenecks to economic development by co-ordinating the growth of different sectors of the economy by making appropriate investment and manpower planning arrangements. National plans are formulated by government agencies in CENTRALLY-PLANNED ECONOMIES, and by collaboration between government, industry and trade unions in MIXED ECONOMIES.

See also INDICATIVE PLANNING, NATIONAL ECONOMIC DEVELOPMENT COUNCIL.

national product, *n.* the total money value of goods and services produced in a country over a given time period (GROSS NATIONAL PRODUCT). Gross national product less CAPITAL CONSUMPTION or depreciation is called NET NATIONAL PRODUCT which is equal to NATIONAL INCOME. See NATIONAL-INCOME ACCOUNTS.

National Research and Development Corporation, *n.* a UK organization that promoted and financially assisted the development and industrial application of INVENTIONS from 1948–81. See INDUSTRIAL POLICY.

natural monopoly, *n.* a situation where ECONOMIES OF SCALE are so significant that costs are only minimized when the entire output of an industry is supplied by a single producer so that supply costs are lower under MONOPOLY than under conditions of PERFECT COMPETITION and OLIGOPOLY. The natural monopoly proposition is the principal justification for the NATIONALIZATION of industries such as electricity, gas and the railways. See MINIMUM EFFICIENT SCALE.

natural rate of economic growth, see HARROD ECONOMIC–GROWTH MODEL.

natural rate of unemployment, see NONACCELERATING INFLATION RATE OF UNEMPLOYMENT.

natural resources, *n.* the contribution to productive activity made by land (for example, a factory site or farm) and basic raw materials such as iron-ore, timber, oil, corn, etc. Natural resources are one of the three main FACTORS OF PRODUCTION, the other two being LABOUR and CAPITAL.

near money, *n.* any easily saleable (liquid) ASSETS that perform the function of MONEY as a STORE OF VALUE, but not that of a universally acceptable MEDIUM OF EXCHANGE. Debate still continues as to what extent liquid assets are money. Clearly, cash is the most liquid of all assets and is universally accepted. The constituent parts of M_3 are defined as money, but short-term bills and fixed interest securities are not. Although easily transformed into cash or bank credit, they are not universally acceptable, but still quite liquid and therefore termed 'near money'. See MONEY–SUPPLY DEFINITIONS.

necessary condition, *n.* a condition that is indispensable for the achievement of an objective. A necessary condition is usually contrasted with *sufficient condition*, which is viewed as the adequacy of a condition to achieve an objective.

For example, an increase in INVESTMENT is a necessary condition in the achievement of higher rates of ECONOMIC GROWTH but it is not a sufficient condition to generate growth in so far as other factors, such as an increase in the LABOUR FORCE, also contribute to raising growth rates.

NEDC, see NATIONAL ECONOMIC DEVELOPMENT COUNCIL.

negative income tax, *n.* a proposed TAX system aimed at linking the TAXATION and SOCIAL-SECURITY BENEFITS systems for low income or no income members of society. This is done by replacing the separate systems for collecting PROGRESSIVE TAXATION and for paying social security benefits, by a single system which links the two together by establishing a common stipulated minimum income level, taxing those above it and giving *tax credits* to those below it.

Proponents of the negative income-tax system point to its advantages in assisting in the removal of the POVERTY TRAP and in making labour markets more flexible.

See SUPPLY–SIDE ECONOMICS.

neoclassical economics, *n.* a school of economic ideas based on the writings of MARSHALL, etc., that superseded CLASSICAL ECONOMIC doctrines towards the end of the 19th century. Frequently referred to as the 'marginal revolution', neoclassical economics involved a shift in emphasis away from classical economic concern with the source of wealth and its division between labour, landowners and capitalists, towards a study of the principles that govern the optimal allocation of scarce resources to given wants. The principles of DIMINISHING MARGINAL UTILITY and STATIC EQUILIBRIUM ANALYSIS were founded in this new school of economic thought.

neoKeynesians, *n.* those economists who tend to support, to a greater or lesser degree, the main thrust of KEYNES' arguments and who have subsequently revised and built upon the theory Keynes propounded.

See DOMAR ECONOMIC–GROWTH MODEL, HARROD ECONOMIC–GROWTH MODEL.

net book value, *n.* the accounting value of a FIXED ASSET in a firm's BALANCE SHEET that represents its original cost less cumulative DEPRECIATION charged to date.

net domestic-fixed-capital formation, see GROSS DOMESTIC-FIXED-CAPITAL FORMATION.

net domestic product, *n.* the money value of a nation's annual output of goods and services, less CAPITAL CONSUMPTION experienced in producing that output. See NATIONAL-INCOME ACCOUNTS.

net national product, *n.* the GROSS NATIONAL PRODUCT less CAPITAL CONSUMPTION or depreciation. It takes into account the fact that a proportion of a country's CAPITAL STOCK is used up in producing this year's output. See NATIONAL-INCOME ACCOUNTS.

net present value, see DISCOUNTED CASH FLOW.

net profit, *n.* the difference between a firm's TOTAL REVENUE and all EXPLICIT COSTS. In accounting terms net profit is the difference between GROSS PROFIT and the costs involved in running a firm. See PROFIT, TRADING AND PROFIT-AND-LOSS ACCOUNT.

net worth, see LONG-TERM CAPITAL-EMPLOYED.

New International Economic Order (NIEO), *n.* an economic and political concept that advocates the need for fundamental changes in the conduct of INTERNATIONAL TRADE and ECONOMIC DEVELOPMENT to redress the economic imbalance between the DEVELOPED COUNTRIES and the DEVELOPING COUNTRIES. The UNITED NATIONS responded to the call of developing countries for such a change by issuing the Declaration and Programme of Action on the Establishment of a New International Economic Order in 1974, which laid down principles and measures designed to improve the relative position of the developing countries. These initiatives have centred on the promotion of schemes such as: (a) INTERNATIONAL COMMODITY AGREEMENTS to support developing countries' primary-produce exports; (b) the negotiation of special trade concessions to enable developing countries' manufactured exports to gain greater access to the markets of the developed countries; (c) the encouragement of a financial and real resource transfer programme of ECONOMIC AID; (d) an increase in economic cooperation between the developing countries.

These aspirations have been pursued primarily through the UNITED NATIONS CONFERENCE ON TRADE AND DEVELOPMENT, but as yet have met with little success.

new-issue market, see CAPITAL MARKET.

newly industrializing country, *n.* a DEVELOPING COUNTRY that has moved away from exclusive reliance on primary economic activities (mineral extraction and agricultural and animal produce) by establishing manufacturing capabilities as a part of a long-term programme of INDUSTRIALIZATION. Brazil, Mexico and Hong Kong are examples of a newly industrializing country. See STRUCTURE OF INDUSTRY, ECONOMIC DEVELOPMENT.

new protectionism, *n.* the use of various devices such as EXPORT RESTRAINT AGREEMENTS, local content requirements and import licensing arrangements which serve to restrict INTERNATIONAL TRADE. See GENERAL AGREEMENT ON TARIFFS AND TRADE, PROTECTIONISM, BEGGAR–MY-NEIGBOUR POLICY.

NIC, see NEWLY INDUSTRIALIZING COUNTRY.

nominal price, *n.* **1.** a PRICE that is minimal in relation to the true worth of a PRODUCT or FACTOR INPUT. There are a number of reasons why a token price may not reflect true market value. Possibly no market exists in which a price can be determined. Alternatively limited amounts of a product may deliberately be priced at much less than the product's true market value, as part of a special sales promotion. **2.** a price of a FINANCIAL SECURITY. See PAR VALUE.

nominal (coupon) rate of interest, *n.* the RATE OF INTEREST payable on the face value of a BOND. For example, a £100 bond with a 5% nominal rate of interest would generate a nominal return of £5 per year. See EFFECTIVE RATE OF INTEREST.

nominal rate of protection, *n.* the actual amount of PROTECTION accorded to domestic suppliers of a final product when a TARIFF is applied to a competing imported final product. For example, assume that initially the same domestic product and imported product are both priced at £100. If an AD VALOREM TAX of 10% is now applied to the imported product its price will increase to £110. This allows domestic VALUE ADDED (and prices) to rise by up to £10 with the domestic product still remaining fully competitive with the imported product. The nominal rate of protection accorded to domestic suppliers is thus 10% of the price of the imports. Compare EFFECTIVE RATE OF PROTECTION.

nominal values, *n.* the measurement of an economic aggregate (for example GROSS DOMESTIC PRODUCT) in terms of current prices. Because of price changes from year to year observations based on current prices can obscure the underlying real trend. See REAL VALUES.

nominee holding, *n.* the SHARES in a JOINT-STOCK COMPANY that are held under the names of a token shareholder on behalf of their ultimate owners. Nominee holdings are used where a person or institution wishes to keep secret the extent of their shareholding in a company, often as a prelude to a TAKEOVER initiative.

nonaccelerating inflation rate of unemployment (NAIRU) or **natural rate of unemployment,** *n*. the underlying level of UNEMPLOYMENT that is consistent with a stable rate of INFLATION. The development of inflationary EXPECTATIONS among wage bargainers and price setters may have caused the nonaccelerating inflation rate of unemployment in the UK to rise over recent decades.

A number of ways of reducing the natural rate of unemployment have been advocated including direct attempts to influence inflationary expectations through PRICES-AND-INCOMES POLICY norms and the use of PROFIT-RELATED WAGE systems.

See PHILLIPS CURVE, EXPECTATIONS-ADJUSTED AUGMENTED PHILLIPS CURVE.

nondiscretionary monopoly policy, *n*. a policy on the control of MONOPOLY that involves the stipulation of 'acceptable' standards of MARKET STRUCTURE and MARKET CONDUCT and which prohibits outright any breach of these standards. See MONOPOLY POLICY.

nonmarketed economic activity, *n*. any economic activity that, although usually legal, is not recorded in the NATIONAL INCOME ACCOUNTS of a nation. The labour and other inputs used in such activities are not paid a cash price for the work done and are therefore unrecorded. Examples of such activities are unpaid cooking and cleaning by housewives and unpaid charity work by voluntary organizations. Such omissions distort international comparisons of gross national income figures not least because rural areas tend to be more self-sustaining whilst urbanized countries tend to purchase what they need rather than making it themselves (e.g., milk, bread, etc.). See BLACK ECONOMY.

nonparametric statistics, *n*. a branch of STATISTICS in which the PARAMETERS of a POPULATION distribution are *not* predetermined. That is, no assumptions have to be made about the shape of the population distribution before the technique can be used. Nonparametric statistical tests can be undertaken on data which is not truly numerical. For instance, on ordinal scale data, tests can be carried out on the ranking of variables. Such tests are sometimes called 'ranking tests'. Compare PARAMETRIC STATISTICS.

nonprice competition, see METHODS OF COMPETITION, PRODUCT DIFFERENTIATION.

nonsystematic risk, *n*. that part of total risk (within the CAPITAL-ASSET-PRICING MODEL) uniquely attributable to the holding of a specific security. Unlike SYSTEMATIC RISK (or market risk), nonsystematic risk is entirely independent of general market variations. Events unique to a particular security may comprise such corporate decisions as dividend policy, changes in capital structure, recruitment of top personnel and so forth. Changes in a firm's share price may be positive or negative depending upon the opinion of investors. The argument is that such nonsystematic variations occur randomly, and therefore if a sufficiently large and well diversified portfolio of shares is held, such variations will cancel each other out, that is, tend towards zero. This means that if investors can eliminate unique risk by diversifying their portfolio, their concern about the riskiness of holding an asset is represented totally by the linear relationship of the BETA COEFFICIENT of systematic risk. The two components of risk, systematic and nonsystematic, are sometimes referred to as *nondiversifiable* and *diversifiable* respectively, for the reasons outlined. See also RANDOM WALK.

normal curve, see NORMAL DISTRIBUTION.

normal distribution, *n.* a special kind of PROBABILITY DISTRIBUTION whose CONTINUOUS DISTRIBUTION (the *normal curve*) has a bell-shaped symmetrical pattern that extends indefinitely at both ends. The normal curve has the special property that it can be defined in terms of its MEAN and STANDARD DEVIATION and once these are known it is possible to calculate the height of the curve (the frequency) corresponding to any given numerical value. As with other continuous distributions, it is also possible to estimate the probability of getting a numerical value between two numbers by the corresponding area under the curve.

The standard normal distribution is a normal distribution whose scale has been changed so that it has a normal curve with a zero mean and unit standard deviation (see Fig. 135 on page 362). This standard normal curve has a total area equal to 1.0, and the probability of getting a particular numerical value which is a given number of standard deviations to the left or right of the mean can be estimated directly from the area under the curve (as in Fig. 135). Where distributions can be approximated by a standard normal curve then about 68% of cases fall within one standard deviation of the mean. 95% of cases fall within two standard deviations of the mean and 99% of cases fall within three standard deviations from the mean.

The normal curve is widely used in the analysis of economic data especially in HYPOTHESIS TESTING.

normal product, *n.* a good or sevice for which the INCOME–ELASTICITY OF DEMAND is positive; that is, as income rises, buyers purchase more of

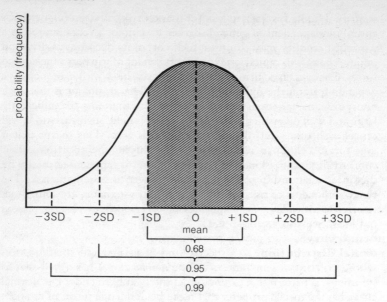

Fig. 135. **Normal distribution**. See main entry.

the product. Consequently, when the price of such a product falls thereby effectively increasing consumers' real income, then that price cut will have the INCOME EFFECT of tending to increase quantity demanded. This will tend to reinforce the SUBSTITUTION EFFECT of a price cut which will cause consumers to buy more of the product because it is now relatively cheaper.

This applies to most products with the exception of INFERIOR PRODUCTS where the income effect is negative. See PRICE EFFECT.

normal profit, *n.* a PROFIT that is just sufficient to ensure that a firm will continue to supply its existing good or service. In the THEORY OF MARKETS, firms' COST curves thus include normal profit as an integral part of supply costs (see ALLOCATIVE EFFICIENCY).

If the level of profit earned in a particular market is too low to generate a return on capital employed comparable to that obtainable in other equally risky markets, then the firm's resources will be transferred to some other use.

See OPPORTUNITY COST, MARKET EXIT, ABOVE–NORMAL PROFIT.

normative economics, *n.* the study of what 'ought to be' in economic theory, rather than what is. For example, the statement that 'people who earn high incomes *ought* to pay more income tax than people who earn low incomes' is a normative statement. Normative statements reflect peoples' subjective value judgements of what is good or bad and depend on ethical considerations such as 'fairness' rather than strict economic rationale. The actual economic effects of a taxation structure which taxes the rich more heavily than the poor (on spending and saving, for example) is a matter for POSITIVE ECONOMICS. See WELFARE ECONOMICS.

null hypothesis, see HYPOTHESIS TESTING.

numeraire, *n.* a monetary unit that is used as the basis for denominating international exchanges in a product or commodity, and financial settlements, on a common basis. For example, the US DOLLAR is used as the numeraire of the oil trade; the SPECIAL DRAWING UNIT is used as the numeraire of the internal financial transactions of the INTERNATIONAL MONETARY FUND and the EUROPEAN CURRENCY UNIT is used to denominate financial transactions within the EUROPEAN MONETARY SYSTEM.

O

OECD, see ORGANIZATION FOR ECONOMIC COOPERATION AND DEVELOPMENT.

off-balance sheet financing, *n.* the payment for use of an ASSET by hiring (LEASING) it rather than buying it. If a company wishes to instal a new £50,000 photocopier it may enter into a lease agreement and agree to pay £12,000 per year over 5 years rather than buy the copier. Each year £12,000 is charged against profits in the company's TRADING AND PROFIT-AND-LOSS ACCOUNT. The copier does not appear in the BALANCE SHEET as a FIXED ASSET because the firm does not own it, but shows up as an annual operating cost which may be offset against PROFIT for TAXATION purposes. Off-balance sheet financing enables a company to make use of expensive assets without having to invest large sums of money to buy them. It also enables a company to keep its LONG-TERM CAPITAL EMPLOYED as small as possible, improving its measured RETURN ON CAPITAL-EMPLOYED.

See LEASE-BACK.

offer curve, see EDGEWORTH BOX.

offer for sale, *n.* a method of raising new SHARE CAPITAL by issuing company shares to the general public at a prearranged fixed price. See OVERSUBSCRIPTION, CAPITAL MARKET.

offer-for-sale by tender, *n.* a method of raising new SHARE CAPITAL by issuing company shares to the general public at a price which is determined by the strength of investment demand for it, subject to a minimum price bid.

See CAPITAL MARKET.

Office of Fair Trading (OFT), *n.* an authority established by the FAIR TRADING ACT, 1973 (FTA) to administer UK MONOPOLY POLICY. The work of the OFT covers six main areas of monopoly control:

(a) MONOPOLIES. The OFT is responsible for the referral of selected good and service monopolies (both private and public sector) to the MONOPOLIES AND MERGERS COMMISSION (MMC) for investigation and report, and the implementation (where appropriate) of the MMC's recommendations. Under the FTA of 1973, a monopoly position is defined as a situation where one firm supplies at least one-quarter of the reference good or service (DOMINANT FIRM monopoly) or where two or more suppliers restrict competition between themselves (COMPLEX MONOPOLY).

(b) MERGERS. The OFT is responsible, in conjunction with Secretary of State for Industry, for the referral of selected mergers to the MMC for investigation and report and the implementation (where appropriate) of the MMC's recommendations. Under the FTA of 1973, mergers which qualify for possible referral are those which create or intensify a monopoly position (defined by the one-quarter market share rule) or where the value of assets taken over exceeds £30 million.

(c) RESTRICTIVE AGREEMENTS. The OFT is responsible for the referral of selected restrictive agreements to the RESTRICTIVE PRACTICES COURT (RPC) for investigation and report, and the implementation (where appropriate) of the recommendations of the Court. The FTA of 1973 provides for the compulsory registration with the OFT of (i) all goods and services agreements which contain restrictions (i.e., anticompetitive provisions) relating to prices charged, terms and conditions, qualities and descriptions, processes, areas and persons to be supplied. (ii) INFORMATION AGREEMENTS (goods only) relating to prices and terms and conditions.

(d) RESALE PRICE MAINTENANCE. The OFT is responsible for monitoring manufacturers' policies towards the retail prices of their products, and can, under the FTA of 1973, refer 'suspected' cases of manufacturers attempting to enforce resale price maintenance to the RPC for investigation. Except in very special circumstances the practice of resale price maintenance in the UK is illegal.

(e) CONSUMER PROTECTION. The OFT is also charged with protecting consumers' interests generally, both by taking action against unscrupulous trade practices such as false descriptions of goods and weights and measures, denial of proper rights of guarantee to cover defective goods etc., and by encouraging groups of suppliers to draw up voluntary codes of 'good' practice.

(f) ANTICOMPETITIVE PRACTICES. The OFT is responsible under the COMPETITION ACT of 1980 for the referral of selected anticompetitive practices to the MMC for investigation and report, and the implementation (where appropriate) of the MMC's recommendations. Anticompetitive practices include such things as EXCLUSIVE DEALING,

REFUSAL TO SUPPLY, TIE-IN SALES, FULL-LINE FORCING, AGGREGATED REBATES, and PRICE-SQUEEZING.

official financing, see BALANCE OF PAYMENTS.

OFT, see OFFICE OF FAIR TRADING.

oligopoly, *n.* a type of MARKET STRUCTURE that is characterized by:

(a) *few firms and many buyers,* that is, the bulk of market supply is in the hands of a relatively few large firms who sell to many small buyers.

(b) *homogenous or differentiated* products, that is, the products offered by suppliers may be identical or, more commonly, differentiated from each other in one or more respects. These differences may be of a physical nature, involving functional features, or may be purely 'imaginary' in the sense that artificial differences are created through ADVERTISING and SALES PROMOTION (see PRODUCT DIFFERENTIATION).

(c) *difficult market entry,* that is, high BARRIERS OF ENTRY which make it difficult for new firms to enter the market.

The primary characteristic associated with the condition of 'fewness' is known as MUTUAL INTERDEPENDENCE. Basically, each firm when deciding upon its price and other market strategies must explicitly take into account the likely reactions and countermoves of its competitors in response to its own moves. A price cut, for example, may appear to be advantageous to one firm considered in isolation, but if this results in other firms cutting their prices also to protect sales then all firms may suffer reduced profits. Accordingly, oligopolists tend to avoid price competition, employing various mechanisms (PRICE LEADERSHIP, CARTELS) to coordinate their prices.

Oligopolists compete against each other using various product-differentiation strategies (advertising and sales promotion, new product launches) because this preserves and enhances profitability – price cuts are easily matched whereas product differentiation is more difficult to duplicate, thereby offering the chance of a more permanent increase in market share; differentiation expands sales at existing prices, or the extra costs involved can be 'passed on' to consumers; differentiation by developing brand loyalty to existing suppliers makes it difficult for new firms to enter the market.

Traditional (static) market theory shows oligopoly to result in a 'MONOPOLY-like' suboptimal MARKET PERFORMANCE: output is restricted to levels below cost minimization; inefficient firms are cushioned by a 'reluctance' to engage in price competition; differentiation competition increases supply costs; prices are set above minimum supply costs yielding oligopolists ABOVE-NORMAL PROFITS which are protected by barriers to entry. As with monopoly, however, this analysis makes no allowance for the contribution that ECONOMIES OF SCALE may make to the reduction of industry costs and prices and the important contribution of oligopolistic competition to INNOVATION and new product development.

See KINKED–DEMAND CURVE, LIMIT–PRICING, PERFECT COMPETITION, MONOPOLISTIC COMPETITION, DUOPOLY, GAME THEORY.

oligopsony, *n.* a form of BUYER CONCENTRATION in a MARKET situation in which a few large buyers confront many small suppliers. See also OLIGOPOLY, BILATERAL OLIGOPOLY, COUNTERVAILING POWER.

OPEC, see ORGANIZATION OF PETROLEUM EXPORTING COUNTRIES.

open economy, *n.* an economy that is heavily dependent on INTERNATIONAL TRADE, EXPORTS and IMPORTS being large in relation to the size of that economy's NATIONAL INCOME. For such economies, analysis of the CIRCULAR FLOW OF NATIONAL INCOME must allow for the influence of exports and imports. Compare CLOSED ECONOMY.

open-market operation, *n.* an instrument of MONETARY POLICY involving the sale or purchase of government TREASURY BILLS and BONDS as a means of controlling the MONEY SUPPLY. If, for example, the monetary authorities wish to *increase* the money supply, then they will buy bonds from the general public. The money paid out to the public will increase their bank balances. As money flows into the banking system the banks' liquidity is increased enabling them to increase their lending. This results in the multiple creation of new bank deposits and, hence, an expansion of the money supply.

See BANK–DEPOSIT CREATION, RESERVE–ASSET RATIO.

operational research, *n.* the study of practical problems to achieve the optimum utilization of available resources for stated objectives. Industry has found many of the mathematical techniques developed particularly applicable to the practical problems which it faces. Techniques such as LINEAR PROGRAMMING, CRITICAL–PATH ANALYSIS and decision theory all help to locate the optimal solution from many possibilities. Operational research has been applied in areas such as PRODUCTION, MARKETING, distribution, finance and inventory control, drawing upon the skills of economists, mathematicians, statisticians, accountants and engineers.

opportunity cost or **economic cost,** *n.* a measure of the economic cost of using scarce resources (FACTOR INPUTS) to produce one particular good or service in terms of the alternatives thereby foregone. To take an example, if more resources are used to produce food fewer resources are then available to provide drinks. Thus, in Fig. 136, the PRODUCTION-

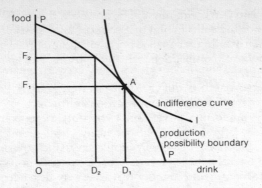

Fig. 136. **Opportunity cost**. See main entry.

POSSIBILITY BOUNDARY (PP) shows the quantity of food and drink which can be produced with society's scarce resources. If society decides to increase production of food from OF_1 to OF_2 then it will have less resources to produce drinks, so that drink production will decline from OD_1 to OD_2. The slope of the production–possibility boundary shows the MARGINAL RATE OF TRANSFORMATION (the ratio between the MARGINAL COST of producing one good and the marginal cost of producing the other). In practice, not all resources can be readily switched from one end use to another (see SUNK COSTS).

In the same way, if a customer with limited income chooses to buy more of one good or service he can only do so by foregoing the consumption of other goods or services. His preference between food and drink are reflected in his INDIFFERENCE CURVE II in Fig. 136. The slope of the indifference curve shows the consumer's MARGINAL RATE OF SUBSTITUTION (how much of one good he is prepared to give up in order to release income which can be used to acquire an extra unit of the other good).

If the indifference curve II is typical of all consumers' preferences between food and drink then society would settle for OF_1 of food and OD_1 of drinks, for only at point A would the opportunity cost of deploying resources (the slope of PP) correspond with the opportunity cost of spending limited income (the slope of II). See also PARETO OPTIMALITY.

optimal factor combination, see DIMINISHING RETURNS.

optimal scale, see PRODUCTIVE EFFICIENCY.

optimizing, *n.* the maximization of society's economic welfare in respect of the macroeconomic objectives of FULL EMPLOYMENT, PRICE STABILITY, ECONOMIC GROWTH and BALANCE-OF-PAYMENTS EQUILIBRIUM.

The essence of this approach can be illustrated, to simplify matters, by reference to the PHILLIPS CURVE 'trade-off' between unemployment (U) and inflation(I). The Phillips curve in Fig. 137 shows that as unemployment falls inflation increases, and vice-versa.

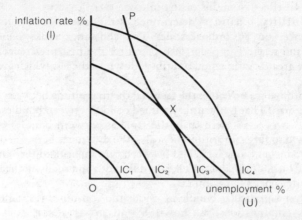

Fig. 137. **Optimizing.** The Phillips curve is drawn as P. The economic welfare of society is represented by a family of INDIFFERENCE CURVES IC_1, IC_2, IC_3, IC_4, each indicating successively higher levels of economic welfare as the origin, O, is approached. The optimum point is at the origin, because here full employment and complete price stability are theoretically simultaneously attained. However, the Phillips curve sets a limit to the combinations of U and I which can be achieved in practice. Given this constraint, the task of the authorities is to select that combination of U and I which maximizes society's economic welfare. This occurs at point X where the Phillips curve is tangential to indifference curve IC_3. See FIXED TARGETS.

optimum, *n.* the best possible outcome within a given set of circumstances. For example, in the theory of CONSUMER EQUILIBRIUM a consumer with a given income and facing set prices for products will adjust the purchases of these products so as to maximize the utility or satisfaction to be derived from spending his limited income. Similarly, in the THEORY OF THE FIRM, a business confronted by a given market price for its product will adjust its output of that product so as to maximize its profits.

See also PROFIT MAXIMIZATION, OPTIMIZING, PARETO OPTIMALITY.

optimum order quantity, see STOCKHOLDING COSTS.

option, *n.* the right to sell (put option) or buy (call option) a COMMODITY (cocoa, tin, etc.) or a financial ASSET (foreign currency, shares) at an agreed price at some future time within a stated period. Options are used primarily in connection with FUTURES MARKETS in commodities and financial assets where prices are liable to fluctuate greatly over time, and can be an effective means of HEDGING or SPECULATING.

ordinal utility, *n.* a UTILITY determined by the ordering of a CONSUMER's preferences on an ordinal scale. The consumer ranks bundles of goods and services in order of preference, the first preference giving him the greatest satisfaction or utility, down to the last which gives him least.

An ordinal scale denotes the fact that the magnitude between ranks is not uniform. That is, the utility gained or lost between bundles ranked one and two, is not necessarily the same as between bundles two and three, and so forth. In arithmetic scales, the difference between one inch and two inches is one inch, and between two inches and three inches is also one inch. Ordinal scales take on different and usually unmeasurable magnitudes between numbers.

Within a particular bundle of goods the consumer is indifferent to various combinations, as shown by an INDIFFERENCE CURVE. The important thing is that rational consumer behaviour must be assumed, meaning that consumers would always choose the bundle with the greater utility rather than the one with lesser utility.

From this concept of ordinal utility are derived INDIFFERENCE MAPS which are frequently used to construct DEMAND CURVES. See also CARDINAL UTILITY, DIMINISHING MARGINAL UTILITY, ECONOMIC MAN.

ordinary least squares, see REGRESSION ANALYSIS.

ordinary shares or **equity,** *n.* a FINANCIAL SECURITY issued to those individuals and institutions who provide long-term finance for JOINT-STOCK COMPANIES. Ordinary SHAREHOLDERS are entitled to any net profits made by their company after all expenses (including interest charges and tax) have been paid and they generally receive some or all of these profits in the form of DIVIDENDS. In the event of the company being wound up they are entitled to any remaining ASSETS of the business after all debts and the claims of PREFERENCE SHAREHOLDERS have been discharged. Ordinary shareholders have voting rights at company ANNUAL GENERAL MEETINGS which depend upon the number of shares which they hold. See also SHARE CAPITAL.

organizational slack, *n.* any organizational resources devoted to the satisfaction of claims by sub-units within the business organization in excess of the resources which these subunits need to complete company tasks. Organizations tend to build up a degree of 'organizational slack' where they operate in less competitive, oligopolistic markets (see OLIGOPOLY), in the form of excess staffing, etc., and this slack provides a pool of emergency resources which the organization can draw upon during bad times. When confronted with a deterioration in the economic environment the organization can exert pressure on subunits within the organization to trim organizational slack and allow the organization to continue to achieve its main goals. Faced with increasing market competition the organization will increasingly be run as a 'tight ship' as slack is trimmed, until in the limiting case of PERFECT COMPETITION organizational slack will be zero and PROFIT MAXIMIZATION becomes the rule.

The concept of organizational slack is a particular feature of the BEHAVIOURAL THEORY OF THE FIRM and is similar in many respects to the concept of X-INEFFICIENCY. See also PRODUCTIVITY.

Organization for Economic Cooperation and Development (OECD), *n.* an organization established in 1961, taking over from the Organization for European Economic Cooperation (OEEC) which was set up in 1948 to assist economic recovery in Europe after the Second World War.

The current membership of the OECD numbers 23 and includes all of the major European countries and the United States, Canada, Australia and Japan. The OECD provides a multinational forum for the discussion of economic affairs of mutual concern, particularly the promotion of economic growth and international trade, and coordinates the provision of ECONOMIC AID to the less developed countries. The OECD is a primary source of international economic data, and regularly publishes comparative statistics.

Organization of Petroleum Exporting Countries (OPEC), *n.* an organization established in 1960 to look after the oil interests of five countries: Iran, Iraq, Kuwait, Saudi Arabia and Venezuela. By 1973 a further eight countries had joined the OPEC ranks: Qatar, Indonesia, Libya, Abu Dhabi, Algeria, Nigeria, Ecuador and Gabon.

1973 was to prove a watershed year for the world economy. Up to this time, since the early 1950s, growth rates in both the advanced and less-developed countries had been accelerating and international trade had increased even more rapidly, stimulated by expansionary policies in the

371

advanced countries and a trade-liberalization programme (see GENERAL AGREEMENT ON TARIFFS AND TRADE). In that year, however, OPEC used its power to wrest the initiative in administering oil prices away from the American oil corporations and the price of oil quadrupled from $2.5 (American dollars) a barrel to over $11.50 a barrel. The effect of this was to produce balance-of-payments deficits in most oil-consuming countries and with it a period of protracted world recession. As the recession bit, oil revenues began to fall, to which OPEC responded by increasing prices sharply again in 1979 from under $15 a barrel to around $28 a barrel.

OPEC is often cited as an example of a successful producers' CARTEL. In a 'classical' cartel market supply is deliberately restrained in order to force prices up by allocating production QUOTAS to each member. Interestingly, in OPEC's case because of political difficulties formal quotas have not been used to cut production until very recently. The main reason it has been able to successfully increase prices in the past has been that the demand for oil is highly price-inelastic. Recently, however, OPEC has been under pressure for two reasons: (a) the total demand for oil has fallen, partly due to the world recession but also due to the fact that its high price has made it economical to substitute alternative forms of energy (coal, in particular) so that oil is now less price inelastic than formerly; (b) the increased profitability of oil production has led to a high rate of investment in new oil fields (the North Sea, in particular) and this has weakened the control of OPEC over world supplies. These factors have led to a dramatic fall in the price of oil (as low as $10 a barrel in 1986) and this has exacerbated the pressures already evident within OPEC itself with different members demanding different responses to the new situation.

organization theory, *n.* a behavioural framework for the analysis of decision-making processes within large complex organizations. Economic analysis frequently considers a FIRM to be a single autonomous decision-making unit seeking to maximize profit. By contrast, organization theory suggests that in large organizations decisions are often decentralized, that decisions are influenced by other than economic motives; and that the decision process is influenced by the company's internal structure, or organization. Nonoptimal or satisficing decisions are the result, rather than profit maximizing.

See PROFIT-MAXIMIZATION, FIRM OBJECTIVES, SATISFICING THEORY, BEHAVIOURAL THEORY OF THE FIRM.

output, *n.* the GOODS and SERVICES that are produced using a combination of FACTOR INPUTS.

output per man-hour, see PRODUCTIVITY.

outside money, see EXOGENOUS MONEY.

overdraft, see BANK LOAN.

overhead cost rate or **recovery rate,** *n.* a means of charging OVERHEADS to products. By relating budgeted overhead costs to budgeted output it is possible to calculate an overhead-rate per unit of product to add to the standard PRIME COST (direct materials cost and direct labour cost) of a product. The addition of overhead-cost rates to the standard prime cost of products serves to establish their total cost, and facilitates their ABSORPTION through selling prices. See BUDGET, STANDARD COST.

overhead costs, see FIXED COSTS.

overhead cost variance, *n.* the difference between the standard overhead cost of a product and its actual overhead cost. Use of OVERHEAD COST RATES for charging OVERHEADS to products will only recover the overheads actually incurred if actual overhead costs correspond with BUDGET and if actual output is the same as budgeted output. If actual expenditure is larger than the budgeted amount, then the standard overhead cost per unit of product will be smaller than actual unit overheads incurred and overheads will be under-recovered in the price set (*expenditure variance*). Again, if actual output turns out to be smaller than planned output, then fixed overheads will remain as under-recovered overheads (*volume variance*). By contrast, over-recovery of overheads occurs when actual overhead costs are less than budget and/or more is produced than planned.

See ABSORPTION, STANDARD COST.

overheads or **indirect costs,** *n.* any COSTS that are not directly associated with a product, that is, all costs other than DIRECT MATERIALS cost and DIRECT LABOUR cost. Production overheads (factory overheads) include the cost of INDIRECT MATERIALS and INDIRECT LABOUR along with other production expenses like factory heat, light and power, and depreciation of plant and machinery. The cost of factory departments such as maintenance, materials stores and the canteen which render services to producing departments are similarly part of production overheads. All SELLING COSTS and DISTRIBUTION COSTS, and all ADMINISTRATION COSTS are also counted as overheads since they cannot be directly related to units of product.

See also FIXED COST, STANDARD COST.

overmanning, *n.* the employment of more LABOUR than is strictly required to efficiently undertake a particular economic activity. This can arise through bad work organization on the part of management, or through trade union-instigated RESTRICTIVE LABOUR PRACTICES.

overseas investment, see FOREIGN INVESTMENT.

oversubscription, *n.* a situation in which the number of SHARES applied for in a new share issue exceeds the numbers to be issued. This requires the ISSUING HOUSE responsible for handling the share issue to devise some formula for allocating the shares. By contrast, *undersubscription* occurs when the number of shares applied for falls short of the number on offer, requiring the issuing house which has underwritten the shares to buy the surplus shares itself. See CAPITAL MARKET.

over-the-counter market, *n.* a MARKET for dealings in company STOCKS and SHARES and certain government securities (for example, local authority bonds) which have not obtained a full STOCK EXCHANGE quotation.

overtime, *n.* the hours of work that are additional to those formally agreed with the labour force as constituting the basic working week. Employers resort to overtime working to meet sudden increases in business activity, viewing overtime by the existing labour force as a more flexible alternative to taking on extra workers. Overtime pay rates can be two to three times basic hourly rates.

overtrading, *n.* a situation where a FIRM expands its production and sales without making sufficient provision for additional funds to finance the extra WORKING CAPITAL needed. Where this happens the firm will run into LIQUIDITY problems and can find itself unable to find the cash to pay suppliers or wages. See also WORKING-CAPITAL RATIO, CURRENT RATIO, CASH FLOW.

P

pac-man defence, see TAKEOVER BID.

paid-up capital, *n.* the proportion of the issued share capital of a JOINT-STOCK COMPANY which has been paid for by the shareholders. Frequently, companies will issue, say, £1 shares but will require subscribing shareholders to pay only, say, 50 pence immediately and the remainder in a number of instalments spread over several months. See CAPITAL MARKET.

Fig. 138. **Paradox of thrift.** The savings schedule rises from S to S₁ but this serves to reduce the equilibrium level of national income from Y to Y₁, and the actual amount saved from S_y to S_y1.

paradox of thrift, *n.* the proposition that there is an inconsistency between the apparently virtuous nature of household SAVINGS and the potentially undesirable consequences of such saving. If most households decide to save a larger proportion of their incomes then they will consume less and this reduced expenditure will lower AGGREGATE DEMAND and so lead to lower levels of output and employment. Thus, an increase in savings will reduce the level of national income.

Thriftiness or saving is beneficial to the economy as it releases resources from the production of consumer goods to be used for producing investment goods. However, if households attempt to save more than businesses plan to invest at a given level of income (i.e., 'withdrawals' exceed 'injections' in the CIRCULAR FLOW OF NATIONAL INCOME MODEL) this will cause the EQUILIBRIUM LEVEL OF NATIONAL INCOME to decline, reducing also the actual amounts saved and invested. See Fig. 138.

paradox of value, *n.* the proposition that the value (PRICE) of a good is determined by its relative scarcity rather than by its usefulness. Water is extremely useful and its TOTAL UTILITY is high but, because it is so abundant, its MARGINAL UTILITY (and hence, price) is low. Diamonds, by contrast, are much less useful than water but their great scarcity makes their marginal utility (and hence, price) high.

parameter or **coefficient,** *n.* the CONSTANT terms in an EQUATION that specify the precise relationship between VARIABLES. Also called *coefficient*. For example, in the LINEAR EQUATION:

$$Y = a + bX$$

the constants *a* and *b* are parameters depicting the relationship between the INDEPENDENT VARIABLE, X and the DEPENDENT VARIABLE, Y. Parameter *a* shows the value which Y will take if X is zero. Parameter *b* shows by how much the dependent variable Y will change as the independent variable X changes. See REGRESSION ANALYSIS.

parametric statistics, *n.* a branch of STATISTICS in which the parameters of a POPULATION distribution are predetermined. That is, there is a particular type of population distribution assumed to be associated with the analysis. Such a technique of statistical inference may assume, for instance, that a sample was drawn from a 'normally' distributed population. Compare NONPARAMETRIC STATISTICS.

Pareto, Vilfredo (1848–1923), Italian engineer who later became professor of economics at Lausanne University. Pareto used the mathematical principles applicable to equilibrium in mechanical systems to construct a general theory of economic equilibrium in his book: *Mannuale di Economica Politica* (1906). Pareto acknowledged that utility was not measurable but argued that a purely ordinal conception of utility (see ORDINAL UTILITY) was sufficient to formulate a theory of choice. This led Pareto to use INDIFFERENCE CURVES to show how an individual's scale of preferences can be represented by an indifference map. Pareto was also known for his ideas on income distribution. See PARETO OPTIMALITY.

Pareto optimality, *n.* the maximization of the economic welfare of the community.

There are three conditions which must hold in order for a Pareto optimum to be attained.

Consider a simplified economy in which there are two goods produced (X and Y) and two consumers (A and B).

(a), *optimal distribution of goods between consumers* requires that:

$$\frac{MU_{XA}}{MU_{YA}} = \frac{MU_{XB}}{MU_{YB}}$$

where MU_{XA} is the MARGINAL UTILITY of good X to consumer A, MU_{YA} is the marginal utility of good Y to consumer A, and so forth. This condition states that the MARGINAL RATE OF SUBSTITUTION between two goods (the ratio of their marginal utilities) must be the same for each consumer. If this were not the case, the consumers could improve their positions by exchanging goods. The consumer who values X highly relative to Y could trade some of his Y to the consumer who values Y highly relative to X. Only when the utility ratios are the same for both consumers is such mutually beneficial trade impossible.

(b), *optimal allocation of inputs in productive uses* where two inputs *i* and *j* are used in the production of goods X and Y. Optimal utilization of inputs requires that the ratio of the MARGINAL PHYSICAL PRODUCTS of *i* and *j* employed in the production of X be the same as the ratio of their marginal physical products in the production of Y. That is:

$$\frac{MP_{iX}}{MP_{jX}} = \frac{MP_{iY}}{MP_{jY}}$$

If this equality is not satisfied, one input is relatively more efficient in the production of one output (and the other input is thus relatively less efficient in the production of the same output). It will thus benefit the community to divert more of the first input into its more efficient use (and to divert the other input from that use). This will permit the community to expand the production of one output at a constant level of resource use. Only when the marginal product ratios are the same can the community not gain by reallocating its inputs among competing uses.

(c) *optimal amounts of output* (illustrated in Fig. 139 on page 378, which depicts a transformation curve that shows the quantities of goods X and Y that can be produced by utilizing fully the resources of the

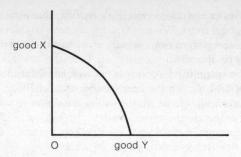

Fig. 139. **Pareto optimality**. The transformation curve or production possibility boundary.

community). The slope of this transformation curve represents the MARGINAL RATE OF TRANSFORMATION, that is, the ratio of the MARGINAL COST of good X to the marginal cost of good Y. Optimal output for any pair of goods, X and Y, requires that the goods be produced in quantities such that:

$$\frac{MU_X}{MC_X} = \frac{MU_Y}{MC_Y}$$

That is, the ratio of marginal cost to marginal utility must be the same for each good, so that the last £'s worth of good X generates the same utility as the last £'s worth of good Y, etc. This condition will be satisfied if the slope of the transformation curve (the marginal cost ratio between X and Y) is equal to the marginal utility ratio between X and Y (the marginal rate of substitution). If the ratios were unequal the community would benefit by producing more of the good that yields the higher marginal utility per unit of marginal cost.

If all these conditions are met, then it would be impossible to improve the welfare of one or more individuals without simultaneously reducing the welfare of another or others. See PRODUCTION POSSIBILITY BOUNDARY, WELFARE ECONOMICS.

Parkinson's law, *n.* an observation by Professor C. Northcote Parkinson suggesting that work expands according to the time available in which to do it. If this observation holds then the inefficiency it creates poses a serious organizational problem for businesses of any significant size. See ORGANIZATION THEORY, X-INEFFICIENCY.

partial-correlation coefficient, *n.* a measure of the strength of relationship between two VARIABLES whilst the influence of other variable(s) is held fixed. Where three (or more) variables are correlated, the relationship between two of them may be influenced in turn by their relationship to the third variable so that the ordinary correlation coefficient between the two can give misleading indications of their precise relationship. The partial-correlation coefficient shows the isolated relationship between the two variables by eliminating the interference of this third variable. Partial-correlation coefficients help us examine economic data on the relationship between variables on a CETERIS PARIBUS (other things being equal) basis.

See CORRELATION COEFFICIENT, DIFFERENTIAL CALCULUS, BETA COEFFICIENTS.

partial derivative, see DIFFERENTIAL CALCULUS.

partial equilibrium analysis, *n.* the analysis of relationships within a particular subsector of an economy (for example, an individual market) that proceeds on the basis that events in this sector have such an insignificant impact on other sectors that feedback effects will be negligible or nonexistent. For example, an increase in the price of carrots is unlikely to have much effect on the general price level so that any possible feedback effects can be safely ignored for purposes of analysing the market for carrots. Thus, in partial equilibrium analysis each subsector is treated as a selfcontained entity. See GENERAL EQUILIBRIUM ANALYSIS.

partnership. see FIRM.

par value, *n.* **1.** the coupon price of a FINANCIAL SECURITY, for example, the initial face value or nominal price of an ORDINARY SHARE (as opposed to its market price). For example, a JOINT-STOCK COMPANY may issue ordinary shares with a par value of, say, 25p though its market price on the STOCK EXCHANGE may be higher or lower than this par value, depending upon current demand and supply for it. **2.** The fixed price of a CURRENCY in terms of other currencies under a FIXED EXCHANGE-RATE SYSTEM.

patent, *n.* the grant of temporary MONOPOLY rights and control over new products, processes and techniques to their INVENTORS by the government. Patent protection is seen as an important means of fostering TECHNOLOGICAL PROGRESS by providing an opportunity for inventors and INNOVATORS to recoup development expenses and secure a profit reward for risk-taking. To minimize the danger of monopolistic exploitation, patents are granted for limited time periods only. See also PATENT OFFICE, INDUSTRIAL PROPERTY RIGHTS.

Patent Office, *n.* a UK government department that administers matters relating to PATENTS, TRADEMARKS and other INDUSTRIAL PROPERTY RIGHTS.

pawnbroker, *n.* a person or firm who makes LOANS taking temporary possession of borrowers' personal ASSETS as security for the loan. Borrowers can reclaim their assets by repaying the loan and interest charges in full, although if they default the pawnbroker is entitled to sell their assets.

pay-as-you-earn (PAYE), *n.* a scheme for collecting INCOME TAX due from the earnings of an individual by deducting the tax owing before an employer pays WAGES or SALARIES. PAYE is *not* a tax, merely a scheme for the collection of tax. See INCOME TAX SCHEDULES.

payback period or **payback method,** *n.* the period it takes for an INVESTMENT to generate sufficient cash to recover in full its original capital outlay. For example, a machine which cost £1,000 and generated a net cash inflow of £250 per year would have a payback period of four years. See also DISCOUNTED CASH FLOW.

payback method, see PAYBACK PERIOD.

Pay Board, *n.* a UK regulatory body which acted to control wages under the government's PRICES AND INCOMES POLICY from 1973 to 1980.

payoff matrix, see GAME THEORY.

payroll tax, *n.* a TAX on a firm's total WAGE bill. The tax may be paid wholly by the firm, or on some shared basis with employees. In so far as such a tax alters the relative price of LABOUR and CAPITAL, it may result in the firm substituting capital for labour. See COST FUNCTION.

penetration price, *n.* a pricing policy that involves charging a comparatively low PRICE for a product in order to secure growing sales and a high market share. This policy will be adopted by a firm where consumers are expected to be price sensitive, that is, demand is price elastic. See also PRODUCT LIFE CYCLE, SKIMMING PRICE.

pension, *n.* any payment made to persons who have retired from paid employment both in the form of a lump sum and regular income. There are two main types of pension scheme: (a) state retirement pensions operated by the government whereby the employee pays NATIONAL INSURANCE CONTRIBUTIONS over his working life and receives TRANSFER PAYMENTS in the form of a state pension after he has retired, thus providing a minimum retirement income for all workers and their dependents. (b) occupational pensions operated by private sector employers whereby the employee and employer make regular contributions to a PENSION FUND or INSURANCE COMPANY scheme. The amount of occupational pension which a worker receives depends upon the size of his regular contributions and the number of years he has contributed. Pensions are paid by pension funds and insurance companies out of the income which they earn by investing contributions in FINANCIAL SECURITIES and property. Occupational pensions provide additional income over and above state retirement pensions.

pension fund, *n.* a financial institution concerned with the management and administration of personal, company and governmental contractual and voluntary retirement schemes. Pension funds collect regular contributions from their working members and make payments to retired beneficiaries. Pension funds specialize in long-term investments in stocks and shares, government securities and property. See also FINANCIAL SYSTEM, INSTITUTIONAL INVESTORS.

per capita income, see INCOME PER HEAD.

percentiles, *n.* the numerical values that divide a group of numerical observations into 100 parts, each containing an equal number of observations. Compare QUARTILES, DECILES.

perfect competition or **atomistic competition,** *n.* a type of MARKET STRUCTURE characterized by: (a) *many firms and buyers*, that is, a large number of independently-acting firms and buyers, each firm and buyer being sufficiently small to be unable to influence the price of the product transacted; (b) *homogeneous products*, that is, the products offered by the competing firms are identical not only in physical attributes but are also regarded as identical by buyers who have no preference between the products of various producers; (c) *free market-entry and exit*, that is, there are no BARRIERS TO ENTRY (hindrances to the entry of new firms) or impediments to the exit of existing sellers; (d) *perfect knowledge* of the market by buyers and sellers.

In a perfectly competitive market, individual sellers have no control over the price at which they sell, the price being determined by aggregate market demand and supply conditions. Each firm produces such a small fraction of total industry output that an increase or decrease in its own output will have no perceptible influence upon total supply and, hence, price. Further, given the infinite CROSS-ELASTICITY OF DEMAND between the homogeneous outputs of the competing sellers, no seller can increase his price above the ruling market price without losing all of his custom. Thus, the demand curve facing the firm will be a horizontal straight line at the ruling market price. In consequence, marginal revenue (MR) equals average revenue (AR). The competitive firm is a *price taker*, accepting price as something completely outside its

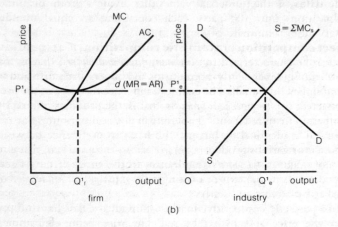

Fig. 140. **Perfect competition**. See main entry. (a) Short-run equilibrium. (b) Long-run equilibrium.

control, and will simply adjust its output independently to the most profitable level at that price; that is, the firm will continue to produce additional units of output so long as price ($= MR = AR$) exceeds marginal cost. When these are equated the firm will maximize profits. Fig. 140a shows the short-run competitive-equilibrium position for a 'representative' firm and the industry.

The individual supply schedules (MCs) of 'x' number of identical firms are summed horizontally to obtain the industry supply curve (SS). Given industry demand (DD), the short-run equilibrium price and output are P_e and Q_e. Taking the equilibrium price as given, the competitive firm establishes its profit maximizing output at the level Q_f ($P = MC$) and, in this case, realizes ABOVE-NORMAL PROFITS ($P_f xyz$).

The long-run equilibrium position can also be ascertained. It is deduced from the assumptions of profit maximization, perfect knowledge and free entry and exit, that unless the returns to the productive resources employed in the industry are at a level that could be derived from alternative uses elsewhere in the economy, there will be resources entering or leaving this industry. In general, outputs will be adjusted to demand until market output is extended (or reduced) and price reduced (or increased) to the point where the average cost of supplying that output is just equal to the price at which that output sells.

If, as in the example above, established sellers are earning above-normal profits then new resources will be attracted into the industry thereby increasing total market supply and reducing market price. This process will continue until the excess profits have been competed away. Fig. 140b shows the long-run competitive equilibrium position for the 'representative' firm and the industry. Given an unchanged industry demand (DD) the long-run equilibrium price and output for the industry are P^1_e and Q^1_e. Given the equilibrium price, the firm establishes its profit maximizing output at the point Q^1_f, where $P = MC$ at the point of minimum long run average cost.

Static market theory shows perfect competition to result in a more efficient MARKET PERFORMANCE than other forms of market organization (see especially the comparison with MONOPOLY). Specifically, market output is optimized at a level equal to minimum supply costs; consumers are charged a price just equal to minimum supply costs, with suppliers receiving a NORMAL PROFIT return. The conclusion of competitive optimality, however, rests on a number of assumptions, some of which are highly questionable, in particular the assumption that cost structures are *identical* for small perfectly competitive firms and large oligopolistic and monopoly suppliers (see OLIGOPOLY, ECONOMIES OF SCALE); while given its static framework it ignores important dynamic influences, such as TECHNOLOGICAL PROGRESS. See also MONOPOLISTIC COMPETITION.

perfect market, see PERFECT COMPETITION.

permanent–income hypothesis, *n.* a hypothesis that suggests a more complex form of relationship between CONSUMPTION and INCOME than that put forward by KEYNES. The permanent income hypothesis advanced by FRIEDMAN argues that both income and consumption are split into two parts, permanent and transitory.

Permanent income depends on a consumer's capital assets, both physical assets and human capital, which determine the ability to earn. The annual figure for permanent income would be the total income a consumer expects to receive divided by a consumer's life expectancy in years. Permanent consumption is similar to permanent income, the relationship being essentially one of proportionality. It would include expenditure on mortgage repayments, heating and lighting and the like.

Transitory income reflects all other factors that occur through chance or accident, such as windfalls or negative transitory income resulting from illness. Transitory consumption is that part of consumption which is not permanent, for example, expenditure on an extra holiday out of a windfall inheritance. Friedman argues that transitory income and transitory consumption are totally unrelated to permanent income and permanent consumption and that both aspects need to be investigated in order to determine the total relationship between consumption and income.

See also KEYNSIAN ECONOMICS, CONSUMPTION FUNCTION, DISPOSABLE INCOME, LIFE-CYCLE HYPOTHESIS.

per se illegality, *n.* the outright prohibition of elements of MARKET CONDUCT (for example, RESTRICTIVE TRADE AGREEMENTS) and MARKET STRUCTURE (for example, MERGERS which would reduce competition) under a NONDISCRETIONARY MONOPOLY POLICY.

Quintile groups of households	Original income %
Bottom fifth	0.3
Second fifth	6.1
Third fifth	17.5
Fourth fifth	27.5
Top fifth	48.6

Fig. 141. **Personal distribution of income.** The personal distribution of original income in the UK, 1984. Original income = income before payment of tax and receipts of state benefits in cash (e.g., pensions) and kind (e.g., health, education) source: *Social Trends*, 1987.

personal distribution of income, *n.* the distribution of NATIONAL INCOME classified according to the size of income received by individuals or households. The size of peoples' incomes differ for a variety of reasons including differences in natural abilities, educational attainments, special skills, and differences in the ownership of WEALTH. The personal distribution of 'original' income is very unequal, as Fig. 141 shows. See also REDISTRIBUTION OF INCOME, PRINCIPLES OF TAXATION, FUNCTIONAL DISTRIBUTION OF INCOME.

personal sector, *n.* that part of the economy concerned with the transactions of HOUSEHOLDS. Households receive INCOME from supplying factor-inputs to other sectors of the economy and influence the workings of the economy through their spending (CONSUMPTION EXPENDITURE on goods and services) and SAVING decisions. The personal sector, together with the CORPORATE SECTOR and FINANCIAL SECTOR constitute the PRIVATE SECTOR. The private sector, PUBLIC (GOVERNMENT) SECTOR and FOREIGN SECTOR make up the national economy. See also CIRCULAR FLOW OF NATIONAL INCOME MODEL.

Fig. 142. **Phillips curve**. See main entry.

Phillips curve, *n.* a curve depicting an empirical observation (based on the work of the British economist A. W. Phillips) of the relationship between the level of UNEMPLOYMENT and the rate of change of MONEY WAGES and, by inference, the rate of change of prices (INFLATION). A fall in unemployment (from A to B in Fig. 142) due to an increase in the level of AGGREGATE DEMAND brings about an acceleration in the rate of increase of money wages (from C to D) reflecting employers' greater willingness to grant wage increases as the demand for their products expands. By contrast, rising unemployment and falling demand leads to a slowing down in the rate of increase of money wages. The 'curve' thus suggests that there is a 'trade-off' between unemployment and DEMAND-PULL INFLATION. However, while there has been strong empirical support of the Phillips curve relationship in the past, in recent years unemployment and inflation have tended to co-exist (see STAGFLATION). This has led to attempts to reformulate the Phillips curve to allow, for example, for the effect of price expectations on money wage increases. See also EXPECTATIONS-ADJUSTED/AUGMENTED PHILLIPS CURVE.

physiocracy, *n.* a school of thought or set of economic ideas based on the writings of QUESNAY and other 18th century French economists and philosophers. The physiocrats felt that land was the single source of income and wealth in society, capable of producing a 'net product'. They also believed in the idea of a 'natural order' in society which harmonized the particular interests of individual citizens with the common interests of society. This made them strong proponents of individual liberty and strong opponents of government intervention in society, other than to protect the individual and his property rights. Adam SMITH was strongly influenced by physiocratic ideas and in his hands the 'natural order' was spelled out in the form of the workings of the market mechanism. See also PRIVATE-ENTERPRISE ECONOMY.

picket, *n.* a person either on STRIKE or supporting that strike, who seeks to prevent other persons from gaining access to a place of work during the course of an INDUSTRIAL DISPUTE. In the UK, picketing one's own place of work is lawful; picketing other people's places of work (*secondary picketing*) is unlawful.

piecework payments, *n.* any WAGE payments made to an individual that are related to the number of goods which he or she produces. In large manufacturing operations this type of wage system has declined in popularity because of the difficulties of determining appropriate piece-rates per unit, but other manufacturers favour the system because of its potential beneficial impact upon worker motivation and PRODUCTIVITY. See also WAGE RATE, X-INEFFICIENCY.

pie chart, *n.* a chart that portrays data in pictorial form, and shows the relative share of each category in a total by means of the relative size of its 'slice' of a circular 'pie'.

Pigou, Arthur Cecil (1877–1959), English student of MARSHALL who succeeded him as professor of political economy at Cambridge University and developed the theory of welfare economics in his book *The Economics of Welfare* (1919). Pigou preferred to accept market prices as indicators of the relative utilities of different goods, but he argued that divergence between private returns and social returns could necessitate taxes and subsidies to achieve an optimal allocation of resources. This distinction between marginal private net product and marginal social net product provided a case for State intervention to increase the efficiency of resource allocation. Pigou thought that interpersonal comparisons have to be made in formulating policy, and he made out a case for a more equitable DISTRIBUTION OF INCOME on the ground of diminishing marginal utility of income. See REAL BALANCE EFFECT.

placing, *n.* a means of raising new SHARE CAPITAL by issuing company shares to a 'selected' group of investors rather than the investing public at large. See CAPITAL MARKET.

planned economy, see CENTRALLY PLANNED ECONOMY.

planning, see CENTRALLY PLANNED ECONOMY, INDICATIVE PLANNING, PLANNING–PROGRAMMING–BUDGETING SYSTEM, CORPORATE PLANNING.

planning–programming–budgeting system, *n.* a framework for the presentation and analysis of information to assist in reaching decisions about resource allocation in the public sector. Planning, programming, budgeting, seeks to establish what a government department is aiming to achieve in terms of: (a) what its objectives are, (b) what activities contribute to these objectives, (c) what resources or inputs contribute to those activities, (c) what the outputs are (what is being achieved). This contrasts with the manner in which governments traditionally account for expenditure in terms of who does the spending (local/central government, which government department, etc.), and how the money is spent (salaries, equipment, etc.). Instead expenditure is classified according to the policy ends which the expenditure is designed to achieve (programme budgets). See also CORPORATE PLANNING, BUDGETING.

plant-and-machinery per employee, *n.* an accounting measure of a firm's degree of mechanization, which expresses the firm's plant and machinery as a ratio of its number of employees. See CAPITAL-LABOUR RATIO, PRODUCTIVITY.

Plc., see LIMITED LIABILITY.

plough back, see RETAINED PROFIT.

point elasticity, *n.* a precise measure of the responsiveness of DEMAND or SUPPLY to changes in PRICE, INCOME, etc. Taking PRICE-ELASTICITY OF DEMAND (E), point elasticity may be defined as:

$$E = (-1) \ \frac{\% \triangle Q}{\% \triangle P}$$

where E = price-elasticity of demand, $\% \triangle Q$ = percentage change in quantity demanded, $\% \triangle P$ = percentage change in price.

Fig. 143. **Point elasticity**. See main entry.

Since the DEMAND CURVE slopes downwards from left to right, the $\triangle Q$ has the opposite sign to $\triangle P$, so (-1) is added to the equation to generate a positive value for the elasticity figure. The numerical value of E signifies the degree of elasticity, that is, it lies between zero and infinity. An example of the measurement of point elasticity is given in Fig. 143.

In order to measure elasticity at a particular price, P, we need to measure the slope of the demand curve at point T where the demand curve is tangential to the straight line LL. The slope of the tangent LL is equal to $\triangle Q/\triangle P$ where the increment in output $(\triangle Q)$ is very small. This gives the formula for point elasticity:

$$E = \frac{\triangle Q}{\triangle P} \times \frac{P}{Q}$$

Where the calculated value of E is greater than 1, demand is described as elastic; where E is less than one, but greater than zero, demand is inelastic. See also ARC ELASTICITY.

poison pill, see TAKEOVER BID.

poll tax, *n.* a TAX that is levied at a fixed rate per head of population. See LUMP-SUM TAXES.

pollution, *n.* the contamination of the environment with dirty or harmful substances. A frequently quoted EXTERNALITY when dealing with industrial production, it can take such forms as smoke from factory chimneys or hazardous chemical waste. It is considered to be a cost of ECONOMIC GROWTH and a negative input into the measure of economic welfare. See also WELFARE ECONOMICS, SOCIAL COSTS.

population, *n.* **1.** the total number of people resident in a country. The size of the population is determined by past and present BIRTH RATES and DEATH RATES, and MIGRATION trends. In most advanced industrial countries, both birth and death rates have declined over the long-run (see DEMOGRAPHIC TRANSITION), which has produced slow-growing populations. See Fig. 144. **2.** all possible observations of a certain phenomenon in statistical analysis, for example, incomes of all people resident in a country. Where it is too time-consuming and expensive to record all possible observations it is necessary to take a SAMPLE, for example, the incomes of 1,000 citizens and generalize about the incomes of all citizens from this sample. See also STATISTICAL INFERENCE.

	Birth rate	Death rate	Total population (millions)
1740	37	36	7
1800	37	25	11
1900	26	17	38
1986	13	12	57

Fig. 144. **Population**. The UK birth and death rates, measured in numbers per 1,000 of the population, from 1740 to 1986.

population census, see CENSUS.

population trap, *n.* a situation in which a country's rate of POPULATION growth is greater than its attainable rate of ECONOMIC GROWTH. As a consequence INCOME PER HEAD declines and the problem of alleviating mass poverty is made worse. To remedy this situation it may be necessary for the government to introduce birth control programmes. This problem is sometimes found in a DEVELOPING COUNTRY. See DEMOGRAPHIC TRANSITION.

porcupine, see TAKEOVER BID.

portfolio, *n.* the collection of FINANCIAL SECURITIES held by an investor. Typically an investor would want to hold a number of different financial securities to spread his RISK, and would seek a mixture of financial securities, some offering high short-term DIVIDEND payments with others offering long-term capital appreciation as their market prices rise significantly. See PORTFOLIO THEORY.

portfolio theory, *n.* the study of the way in which an individual investor may theoretically achieve the maximum expected return from a varied PORTFOLIO of FINANCIAL SECURITIES which has attached to it a given level of RISK. Alternatively, the portfolio may achieve for the investor a minimum amount of risk for a given level of expected return.

Return on a security comprises INTEREST or DIVIDEND, plus or minus any CAPITAL GAIN or loss from holding the security over a given time period. The *expected* return on the collection of securities within the portfolio is the weighted average of the expected returns on the individual INVESTMENTS that comprise the portfolio. However, the important thing is that the risk attaching to a portfolio (its STANDARD DEVIATION) is less than the weighted average risk of each individual investment.

See also CAPITAL ASSET PRICING MODEL, EFFICIENT MARKET HYPOTHESIS, RISK AND UNCERTAINTY.

positive economics, *n.* the study of what 'is' in economic theory, rather than what 'ought to be'. For example, the statement that 'a cut in personal taxes increases consumption spending in the economy', is a factual statement that can be confirmed or refuted by examining the available empirical evidence on the effects of taxation on spending. Positive economics seeks to identify relationships between economic variables, to quantify and measure these relationships, and to make predictions of what will happen if a variable changes. Compare NORMATIVE ECONOMICS.

potential entrant, *n.* a FIRM that is willing and able to enter a MARKET given the right conditions. In the THEORY OF MARKETS, potential entry turns into actual entry into a market when (a) existing firms in the market are earning ABOVE-NORMAL PROFITS, (b) newcomers are able to overcome any BARRIERS TO ENTRY.

'Actual' new entry plays an important regulatory role in a market in removing above-normal profits and in expanding market supply (see, for example, PERFECT COMPETITION). However, the mere 'threat' of potential entry may in itself be sufficient to ensure that existing firms supply the market efficiently and set prices which are consistent with supply costs.

Potential entrants to a market may be newly established firms; firms who currently supply the market with inputs, or who are currently its customers (vertical entry); or firms who currently operate in other markets and which are looking to expand their activities in new directions (diversified entry).

See also CONDITION OF ENTRY, MARKET ENTRY, VERTICAL INTEGRATION, DIVERSIFICATION, CONTESTABLE MARKET.

potential gross national product (GNP), *n.* the maximum level of real OUTPUT an economy is capable of producing at a point in time by fully utilizing all available FACTOR INPUTS. Productive potential depends upon the size of the LABOUR FORCE and the average level of labour

PRODUCTIVITY (that is, output per man). The level of productivity itself is dependent on the current state of technology, the amount of CAPITAL STOCK per worker, and the CAPITAL–OUTPUT RATIO.

Potential GNP interacts with the level of AGGREGATE DEMAND to determine the level of ACTUAL GROSS NATIONAL PRODUCT in an economy. If aggregate demand falls short of potential GNP at any point in time then actual GNP will be equal to aggregate demand leaving a DEFLATIONARY GAP (output gap) between actual and potential GNP. However, at high levels of aggregate demand (in excess of potential GNP), potential GNP sets a ceiling on actual output, any excess of aggregate demand over potential GNP showing up as an INFLATIONARY GAP.

Fig. 145. **Potential gross national product**. The difference between potential GNP and actual GNP.

Potential GNP will tend to grow over time as a result of increases in the labour force and labour productivity. Fig. 145 shows the (hypothetical) path followed by potential GNP over time in the form of a broken line. The rate of growth of actual output (GNP) over time (ECONOMIC GROWTH), shown by the solid line, will depend upon both potential GNP and the rate of growth of aggregate demand. When aggregate demand matches (or exceeds) potential GNP, as at points A and C in the figure, the economy's resources are fully employed and maximum output of goods and services is achieved. When aggregate demand falls short of potential GNP, as at points B and D, some of the economy's resources are left unemployed (see UNEMPLOYMENT) or underemployed. When aggregate demand exactly matches potential GNP, a full employment equilibrium level of aggregate demand exists.

In practice the level and rate of growth of potential GNP are difficult to measure. See also BUSINESS CYCLE.

pound, *n.* the standard CURRENCY unit of the UK and a number of other countries, mainly current and former members of the British Commonwealth. When used in international transactions the UK pound is referred to as STERLING to distinguish it from other country's pounds, such as the Lebanese or Egyptian pound.

poverty trap, *n.* a situation where an unemployed person receiving SOCIAL-SECURITY BENEFITS is not encouraged to seek work because his or her after tax earnings potential in work is *less* than the benefits currently obtained by not working. Given that social security benefits represent the 'bottom line' (that is, the provision of some socially and politically 'acceptable' minimum standard of living) the problem is how to reconcile this with the 'work ethic'. One suggested way is for the government to provide employers with employment subsidies which allow them to pay wages higher than the minimum level of social security, even though the MARGINAL REVENUE PRODUCT of the work undertaken does not warrant it. It will thus be to people's economic advantage to obtain employment, and hopefully in so doing they will acquire work experience and skills which will improve their long-run earnings potential.

Alternatively, the overlap between entitlement to social security benefits (based on one set of income scales) and the threshold level of income at which people start to pay tax (based on a different set of income scales) can be removed by the introduction of a NEGATIVE INCOME TAX. A negative income tax system replaces means-tested social security benefits on the one hand, and PROGRESSIVE TAXES on the other, with a single unitary tax system. Under this unitary tax system people pay taxes when they are in employment and earning more than a stipulated minimum income and receive a tax rebate to bring their income up to the stipulated minimum level when they are either unemployed or earning less than the minimum. See also SUPPLY-SIDE ECONOMICS.

precautionary demand for money, *n.* a demand for money balances to be held for precautionary purposes by individuals and firms to provide a safety net for the uncertainties of everyday life, for example, repairing storm damage to one's home, or a particularly large or unexpected bad debt in the case of a firm. Precautionary and transaction balances are sometimes considered together since they are both a positive function of INCOME (the balances tending to increase as income increases). Compare TRANSACTIONS DEMAND FOR MONEY, SPECULATIVE DEMAND FOR MONEY. See also MONEY DEMAND SCHEDULE, LIQUIDITY PREFERENCE, L.M. SCHEDULE.

predatory pricing, *n.* a pricing policy pursued by a firm (or firms) with the express purpose of harming rival suppliers or exploiting the consumer. Examples of the former include PRICE SQUEEZING and 'selective' price cuts to drive competitors out of the market, while exploitation of the consumer comes about through over pricing by MONOPOLY suppliers and CARTELS. See also MONOPOLY POLICY.

preferred stock, see PREFERENCE SHARE.

preference share or **preferred stock,** *n.* a FINANCIAL SECURITY issued to those individuals and institutions who provide long-term finance for JOINT-STOCK COMPANIES. Preference shares pay a fixed rate of DIVIDEND and are generally given priority over ORDINARY SHARES in receiving dividend. In the event of the company being wound up they also have first claim on any remaining ASSETS of the business after all debts have been discharged. Generally, preference SHAREHOLDERS have no voting rights at company ANNUAL GENERAL MEETINGS. See also SHARE CAPITAL.

preference/similarity theory, *n.* an explanation of INTERNATIONAL TRADE in manufactured products which is based on consumers' demands for product variety, for example, the EXPORT from the UK of cars to, and the import of cars from, West Germany.

The theory postulates that domestic suppliers specialize in the manufacture of the kinds of product demanded by the majority of domestic consumers, but are able to export some of their output to countries where such products appeal to a minority of consumers. By the same token, the minority of domestic consumers have slightly different demands, demands which can be satisfied by imports from those countries where such tastes are those of the majority. Since the kinds of product demanded in a country are determined in large measure by the level of income per head, most exchanges of manufactures take place between countries of a similar industrial structure, each exporting and importing essentially similar products. Through trade the variety of manufactured products available to consumers is extended and the gain from trade derives, not from lower prices as emphasized by the conventional theory of COMPARATIVE ADVANTAGE, but from the choice of being able to consume the precise brand or variety of product demanded.

See also INTRA-INDUSTRY TRADE, THEORY OF INTERNATIONAL TRADE.

premium, *n*. **1.** an addition to the published LIST PRICE of a good or service charged by a supplier to customers. The premium could be charged for express delivery of the product, or could reflect the temporary scarcity of the product. **2.** the sale of new STOCKS and SHARES at an enhanced price. In the UK this involves the issue of a new share at a price above its nominal value. In other countries where shares have no nominal value it involves the sale of new shares above their current market price. **3.** the purchase of a particular company's issued stock or share at a price above the average market price of those of other companies operating in the same area. The price is higher, reflecting investors' optimism about that company's prospects. **4.** a general rise in the prices of all stocks and shares to higher levels in anticipation of an upturn in the economy. **5.** the purchase of a BOND for more than its nominal value. The price which people are prepared to pay for a bond can be more than its nominal value if the nominal rate of interest on that bond exceeds current market interest rates. **6.** the extent to which a foreign currency's market EXCHANGE RATE rises above its 'official' exchange rate under a FIXED EXCHANGE-RATE SYSTEM. **7.** the annual payment made to an INSURANCE COMPANY for an insurance policy.

See also SPECULATIVE DEMAND FOR MONEY.

present value, see DISCOUNTED CASH FLOW.

price, *n*. the money value of a unit of a GOOD, SERVICE, ASSET or FACTOR INPUT. In some markets (for example, see PERFECT COMPETITION), price will be determined entirely by the forces of DEMAND and SUPPLY. By contrast, in other markets (for example, MONOPOLY markets) powerful suppliers have considerable discretion over the price which they charge. In certain circumstances prices may be subjected to governmental PRICE CONTROL or regulated by means of PRICES-AND-INCOMES POLICY. See also EQUILIBRIUM MARKET PRICE, ADMINISTERED PRICE.

Price Commission, *n*. a UK regulatory body which acted to control prices from 1973–80, under the government's PRICES AND INCOMES POLICY.

price competition, *n*. a form of rivalry between suppliers which involves an attempt to win customers by offering a product at a lower PRICE than competitors.

Price competition is especially beneficial to consumers in so far as it results in the establishment of prices which are consistent with the real costs of supplying the product, and serves to improve the RESOURCE ALLOCATION efficiency of the market by eliminating inefficient, high cost suppliers (see PERFECT COMPETITION). From the suppliers' point of view price competition is often something to be resisted because it reduces the profitability of the market, and, where conditions permit (for example, OLIGOPOLY) suppliers may attempt to avoid price competition.

See PRICE LEADERSHIP, PRICE PARALLELISM, COLLUSION, METHODS OF COMPETITION.

price controls, *n.* the specification by the government of minimum and/or maximum PRICES for goods and services. The price may be fixed at a level below the market EQUILIBRIUM PRICE or above it depending on the objective in mind. In the former case, for example, the government may wish to keep the price of some essential good (for example, food) down as a means of assisting poor consumers. In the latter case, the aim may be to ensure that producers receive an adequate return (see PRICE SUPPORT). More generally, price controls may be applied across a wide range of goods and services as part of a PRICES AND INCOMES POLICY aimed at combating INFLATION. See also RATIONING.

price discrimination, *n.* the ability of a supplier to sell the *same* product in a number of separate MARKETS at *different* PRICES. Markets can be separated in a number of ways, including different geographical locations (e.g., domestic and foreign), the nature of the product itself (e.g., original and replacement parts for motor cars) and users' requirements (e.g., industrial and household electricity consumption).

Price discrimination can be both beneficial and detrimental, for example, discriminating prices may be used as a means of ensuring a plant produces at full capacity thereby enabling economies of large-scale production to be attained. On the other hand, price discrimination may be used as a means of enlarging monopoly profits. See DISCRIMINATING MONOPOLIST.

price-earnings ratio, *n.* a ratio used to appraise a quoted public company's profit performance, which expresses the market PRICE of the company's SHARES as a multiple of its PROFIT. For example, if a company's profit amounted to £1 per share and the price of its shares was £10 each on the STOCK EXCHANGE, then its price–earnings ratio would be 10:1. Where a company's prospects are considered by the stock exchange to be good, then it is likely that the company's share price will rise, yielding a higher price–earnings ratio. See EARNINGS PER SHARE.

price effect, *n.* the effect of a change in price upon the quantity demanded of a product. In the THEORY OF DEMAND the price effect can be subdivided into the SUBSTITUTION EFFECT and the INCOME EFFECT. In Fig. 146 on page 396, a consumer has an initial BUDGET LINE XY (which shows the different combinations of the products A and B which he can

Fig. 146. **Price effect**. See main entry.

buy given the relative prices of the two products). I_1 and I_2 are INDIFFERENCE CURVES (which show the alternative combinations of the two products, each of which yields him the same UTILITY or satisfaction). The point (L) where I_2 is tangential to the budget line XY denotes the initial equilibrium position for the consumer, who maximizes his satisfaction by purchasing a combination of O_d of product A and O_e of product B. Assume now that the price of product B increases so that the consumer is now unable to buy as much of product B as before. This new situation is reflected in an inward shift in the budget line from XY to XZ. The consumer will move to a new equilibrium position (point M) where I_1 is tangential to the budget line XZ, purchasing O_f of product A and O_g of product B.

The consumer's real income has been decreased by the rise in the price of product B. However, the movement from L to M and the reduction in the quantity purchased of B, from O_e to O_g, is a result of the combination of an income and substitution effect. To isolate the substitution effect, it is necessary to increase the consumer's income just enough to compensate him for his loss in purchasing power; that is, the budget line is moved to the right parallel to itself until it becomes tangent to his original indifference curve I_2 at point N (Combination N yields the same satisfaction as Combination L).

But the consumer has cut his consumption of product B (whose price has risen relative to product A) and increased his consumption of product A. Hence the movement from L to N, or the decrease in quantity demanded of product B from O_e to O_h is the substitution effect.

The income effect alone is determined by taking the compensating increase in income away from the consumer, that is, we revert back to budget line XZ which cuts indifference curve I_1 at point M yielding the optimal combination of O_f of product A and O_g of product B. The movement from N to M is the income effect and reduces the quantity demanded of product B from O_h to O_g.

For NORMAL PRODUCTS the income effect and the substitution effect reinforce each other so that an increase in price will result in a decrease in quantity demanded. However, in the case of INFERIOR PRODUCTS the income and substitution effects work in opposite directions making it difficult to predict the effect of a change in price on quantity demanded. In extreme cases where a product accounts for a large proportion of household budgets the income effect of a price change may be so large as to swamp the substitution effect so that a decrease in price leads (perversely) to a decrease in quantity demanded. For example, in developing countries where a high proportion of (small) household budgets are spent on foodstuffs such as rice, a fall in the price of rice can lead to a fall in quantity consumed as households' real incomes are increased and they are able to buy more meat and fish in place of rice.

See GIFFEN GOOD, CONSUMER EQUILIBRIUM.

price-elasticity of demand, *n.* a measure of the degree of responsiveness of DEMAND to a given change in PRICE:

$$\text{elasticity of demand} = \frac{\% \text{ change in quantity demanded}}{\% \text{ change in price}}$$

If a change in price results in a more than proportionate change in quantity demanded, then demand is *price-elastic* (Fig. 147a on page 398); if a change in price produces a less than proportionate change in the quantity demanded, then demand is *price-inelastic* (Fig. 147b).

At the extremes, demand can be perfectly price-inelastic, that is, price changes have no effect at all on quantity demanded, which shows up as a straight-line vertical demand curve; or demand can be perfectly price-elastic, that is, any amount will be demanded at the prevailing price, which shows up as a straight-line horizontal demand curve.

TOTAL REVENUE (price times quantity demanded) will be affected by price changes. Where demand is price-elastic a small cut in price will generate a large increase in quantity demanded so that the price cut will serve to increase total revenue (while a price rise serves to reduce total

Fig. 147. **Price-elasticity of demand**. See main entry. (a) Elastic demand. (b) Inelastic demand.

revenue). By contrast, where demand is price–inelastic a large cut in price will generate only a small increase in quantity demanded so that the price cut will serve to reduce total revenue (while a price rise serves to increase total revenue). Where demand has *unitary elasticity* then the percentage price cut will be matched by an exactly offsetting percentage change in quantity demanded so that total revenue remains the same.

It must be stressed, however, that the price-elasticity of demand can vary along the length of a given demand curve. For example, although in Fig. 147a the demand curve as a whole is elastic in configuration, it is more elastic at point X than it is at point Y.

The concept of demand elasticity is useful to firms in setting product prices (including PRICE DISCRIMINATION), and the government in setting rates of indirect taxes such as EXCISE DUTY to raise revenue. See also ARC ELASTICITY, POINT ELASTICITY.

price-elasticity of supply, *n.* a measure of the degree of responsiveness of SUPPLY to a given change in PRICE:

$$\text{elasticity of supply} = \frac{\% \text{ change in quantity supplied}}{\% \text{ change in price}}$$

If a change in price results in a more than proportionate change in quantity supplied then supply is price-elastic (Fig. 148a on page 400); if a change in price produces a less than proportionate change in the quantity supplied, then supply is price-inelastic (Fig. 148b).

At the extremes, supply can be perfectly price-inelastic, that is, price changes have no effect at all on quantity supplied, which shows up as a straight-line vertical supply curve; or supply can be perfectly price-elastic, that is, any amount will be supplied at the prevailing price, which shows up as a straight-line horizontal supply curve.

The degree of responsiveness of supply to changes in price is affected by the time horizon involved. In the SHORT RUN, supply can only be increased in response to an increase in demand/price by working firms' existing plant more intensively, but this usually adds only marginally to total market supply. Thus, in the short run the supply curve tends to be price-inelastic. In the LONG RUN, firms are able to enlarge their supply capacities by building additional plants and by extending existing ones so that supply conditions in the long run tend to be more price-elastic. However, in some cases, for example petrochemicals, the long-run supply responses can be five years or more.

price equilibrium, see EQUILIBRIUM MARKET PRICE.

price fixing, *n.* the establishment of a common PRICE for a good or service by a group of suppliers acting together, as opposed to each supplier setting his own price independently. Price fixing is often a feature of an unregulated OLIGOPOLY market.

See RESTRICTIVE TRADE AGREEMENT, COLLUSION, CARTEL, ADMINISTERED PRICE.

price index, *n.* a weighted average of PRICES of all goods and services produced in the economy measured over time. A commonly used price index is the *Retail Price Index* (*RPI*), which measures the average level of

Fig. 148. **Price-elasticity of supply**. See main entry. (a) Elastic supply.
(b) Inelastic supply.

the prices of goods and services bought by final consumers. Each item in the index is weighted according to its relative importance in total consumers' expenditure. Starting from a selected base year (index value = 100), price changes are then reflected in changes in the index value over time. Thus, if 1970 = 100 and in 1980 the index value stood at 180 this means that retail prices, on average, had risen 80% between the two dates. Price indices can be used to measure the rate of INFLATION and as a GNP DEFLATOR. See also PURCHASING POWER.

price leader, *n.* a FIRM that establishes the market PRICE for a good or service and initiates price changes which are then followed by competing suppliers. Two forms of price leadership have been identified. (a) DOMINANT FIRMS who are able to secure compliance to their prices by smaller rivals because of their powerful positions in the market. (b) *barometric price leaders* whose price changes are accepted by other suppliers because of their recognized adeptness at establishing prices fully reflective of changing market conditions.

Price leader-follower relationships are a typical feature of OLIGOPOLY markets in coordinating price changes, and tend to result in a strong degree of PRICE PARALLELISM. See PRICE LEADERSHIP.

Fig. 149. **Price leadership**. Price leadership by a low-cost firm. See main entry.

price leadership, *n.* a means of coordinating oligopolistic price behaviour (see OLIGOPOLY), allowing firms to secure high profits. One example of price leadership is that of leadership by a DOMINANT FIRM (a *dominant firm-price leader*) possessing cost advantages over his competitors. In Fig. 149, firm A is the low cost supplier with a MARGINAL COST curve MC_A; firm B has higher costs with a marginal cost curve MC_B. The individual demand curve of each firm is dd when they set *identical* prices (that is, it is assumed that total industry sales at each price are divided equally between the two firms); mr is the associated MARGINAL REVENUE curve. Firm A is able to maximize his profits by producing output OQ_A (where $MC_A = mr$) at a price of OP_A. Firm B would like to charge a higher price (OP_B), but the best he can do is to 'accept' the price set by firm A, although this means less than maximum profit. For given firm B's conjecture about the reactions of firm A to any price change by himself, any alternative course of action would mean even less profit. If he were to charge a higher price than P_A he would lose sales to firm A (whose price is unchanged), moving left along a new 'kinked' demand curve segment KP_B; if he were to cut his price below P_A, this would force firm A to undertake matching price cuts, moving right along the demand-curve segment Kd. Firm B could not hope to win such a 'PRICE WAR' because of his higher costs. Thus, firm B's best course of action is to charge the same price as that established by firm A.

price level, *n.* the general level of prices in an economy, as measured by a PRICE INDEX. Price levels in two consecutive time periods are often compared as an indication of INFLATION rates.

price parallelism, *n.* the tendency in an OLIGOPOLY market for suppliers to charge identical PRICES. Parallel prices may come about because suppliers, recognizing their MUTUAL INTERDEPENDENCE, desire to avoid price competition which reduces their profits, or they may come about as a result of deliberate COLLUSION between suppliers to 'fix' prices which maximize their joint profits.

See also PRICE LEADERSHIP, CARTEL.

prices and incomes policy, *n.* a policy concerned with controlling INFLATION by *directly* attempting to halt or slow down the INFLATIONARY SPIRAL of price-wage rises, in contrast to deflationary MONETARY POLICY and FISCAL POLICY which work *indirectly* to achieve the same result. The basic rationale for a prices and incomes policy is that whereas deflationary monetary and fiscal policies can only control inflation by increasing the rate of unemployment, a prices and incomes policy, if applied rigorously, can check inflation *and* maintain high levels of employment.

A prices and incomes policy can be operated on a voluntary or a statutory (compulsory) basis. In the former case, an appeal is made to the collective responsibilities of firms not to increase their prices 'unduly' and for trade unions to 'moderate' their demands for wage increases. The very vagueness of such exhortations, however, is usually given short shrift by vested interests. A statutory policy has more chance of success, certainly in the medium term if it is backed by strong penalties for non-compliance. Typical elements of the statutory approach include: (a) an initial, brief (6 month–1 year) standstill or 'freeze' on all price, wage, dividend, etc., increases; (b) a following period (usually 'phased' to allow for a progressive relaxation of controls) in which either (i) general 'norms' are laid down for permitted price and wages, for example, limiting them to say, 3% per annum, or (ii) more specifically, the establishment of formulas for linking permitted price and wage increases to, for example, in the case of a price rise to nonabsorbable cost increases, and in the case of a wage rise to increases in productivity. This latter approach requires the establishment of some regulatory body (such as the National Board for Prices and Incomes, the Price Commission, the Pay Board, which formerly operated in Britain) to ensure that proposed price and wage increases are indeed justified.

Proponents of a prices and incomes policy see it as a useful way of 'defusing' inflationary expectations, thereby removing the danger of accelerating inflation rates. On the debit side it must be recognized that because such a policy interferes with the operation of market forces it is likely to produce distortions in factor and product markets. See MACROECONOMIC POLICY.

price-squeezing, *n.* a type of RESTRICTIVE TRADE PRACTICE whereby vertically integrated firms (see VERTICAL INTEGRATION) are able to injure nonintegrated competitors. This arises when the integrated firms produce both a raw material and the finished good, while the nonintegrated firms produce only the finished good but have to rely on the integrated firms for their raw material supplies. A 'squeeze' is applied if the integrated firms charge the nonintegrated firms a high price for the raw material and sell the finished product at a price which allows nonintegrated firms only minimal profits or forces losses on them.

Situations can also arise where the integrated firms produce raw materials and finished goods, while the nonintegrated firms produce only the raw material but have to rely on the integrated firms as a market for their raw materials. A 'squeeze' can be applied if the integrated firms pay a low price for the raw material from nonintegrated firms, but a high price for the raw material from integrated firms, allowing the nonintegrated firms only minimal profits or forcing losses on them.

price stability, *n.* the maintenance of an unchanged general level of prices over time in an economy. Price stability, especially the avoidance of rising prices (INFLATION) is one of the main objectives of MACROECONOMIC POLICY.

price support, *n.* a means of supporting the incomes of certain producers by administratively maintaining the PRICES of their products above market price.In many countries, price-support systems are used specifically to assist the agricultural sector by ensuring an adequate level of total farm incomes. In Fig. 150 on page 404, the EQUILIBRIUM MARKET PRICE is OA. If this price is considered too low to adequately remunerate farmers

Fig. 150. **Price support**. See main entry.

the government will set a support price, say OB, at which it is prepared to buy up any unsold output. At the support price of OB, the government is then committed to acquiring the unsold output of CF at a total cost equal to the shaded area CFGH. The main problems with the price support method are that it penalizes consumers and results in wasteful over production. The price support method is used as the basis of the COMMON AGRICULTURAL POLICY of the EC. Compare INCOME SUPPORT. See also AGRICULTURAL POLICY.

price system or **market mechanism,** *n.* a characteristic of an economy in which basic decisions about what to produce, how to produce it and how products (incomes) are to be distributed are determined by the interaction of buyers and sellers in product and factor markets, as indicated in Fig. 151a.

In a PRIVATE-ENTERPRISE ECONOMY, or a MIXED ECONOMY with a significant private sector, the current levels of output and consumption of products are the result of the varied decisions of households and firms being put into operation through the price system as they carry out transactions in markets. The firm is a key element in the market system operating in product markets where it sells products and factor markets where it buys or hires resources. The price system embraces both types of market and broadly operates so as to ensure that resources are allocated in accordance with consumer demand.

For example, suppose initially that carrot and pea prices were such as to equate supply and demand for these products in their respective markets but then there was a change in consumer demand away from

(a)

(b)

	Product markets		Factor markets	
	Pea market	Carrot market	Pea inputs	Carrot inputs
Short Run	D = S	D = S	DF = SF	DF = SF
	D↑	D↓		
	D > S	D < S		
	P↑	P↓		
	Pr↑	Pr↓		
Long Run	market entry	market exit	DF↑	DF↓
	S↑	S↓	DF > SF	DF < SF
	P↓	P↑	Pf↑	Pf↓
	Pr↓	Pr↑		
	D = S	D = S		

Key: D = product demand; S = product supply; P = price of products; Pr = profits of suppliers; Pf = price of factor input; SF = factor supply; DF = factor demand

Fig. 151. **Price system.** See main entry.

carrots and towards peas, as indicated in Fig. 151b. The increased demand for peas, coupled with unchanged pea supply in the short run, would result in an excess demand for peas at the prevailing price and price would rise to ration the scarce peas amongst consumers. The decreased demand for carrots, coupled with unchanged carrot supply in the short run, would initially give rise to an excess market supply at the prevailing price and the price of carrots would fall as suppliers sought to clear unsold stocks.

These changes in prices will affect the profits of carrot and pea suppliers. As demand and prices rise in the pea market, pea growers will experience increased profits, while carrot growers faced with falling demand and prices will find their profits declining. Over the long term pea producers will invest in additional land and machinery and hire more labour to expand supply and new firms will be tempted by high profits to enter the pea market. The resulting expansion in pea supply will force high prices back down to a lower level, leaving firms producing peas making NORMAL PROFITS, at which level there will be no further incentives for new firms to enter the pea market or total supply to expand. By contrast, as demand and prices fall in the carrot market suppliers will find their profits falling and less efficient producers will go out of business as they experience losses, while other producers curtail their carrot output. The resulting decline in carrot supply will continue until carrot supply adjusts to the lower demand and firms left in the carrot market are earning normal profit.

Changes in product markets will have repercussions in factor markets as Fig. 151b indicates. In order to expand pea supply, extra natural, human and capital resources must be drawn into pea production and this can only be achieved by offering them a higher return than they receive elsewhere. The increased demand for peas will result in an increased derived demand for FACTOR INPUTS in pea production and this excess demand for factor inputs in the pea industry will increase the returns to factors employed there. By contrast, the carrot industry will be releasing resources as firms leave the industry, and unemployment of factors of production in the carrot trade will reduce factor returns as the derived demand for them falls. These forces serve to shape the distribution of income between those working in pea and carrot production.

The above example shows how the price system results in a reallocation of resources in response to signals given out by consumers about their changed demand for products which in turn affect the prices of factor inputs. However, autonomous changes in the prices of factor inputs can themselves affect product prices and consumer demand patterns through the price system. For example, assume that carrot production is a relatively labour-intensive process while the growing and picking of peas is highly automated. Consequently, a sharp upward shift in wage rates would affect the two industries differently, the cost and price of carrots rising substantially while peas costs and prices change little. Since carrots are now more expensive while peas are much the same price, consumers will tend to alter their consumption patterns buying less relatively expensive carrots and more relatively cheap peas. Consequently output and employment in the carrot industry will tend to fall while output of peas expands, and a reallocation of resources from carrots to peas might be expected. The process of reallocation may be more direct than this though, for, as firms seek to produce carrots at minimum cost through the most efficient combination of factor inputs, faced then with an increase in wage rates they will alter production methods using less relatively expensive labour inputs and more relatively cheap capital. Increasing wage rates are thus likely to accelerate automation in the carrot industry reducing the demand for labour there.

The price system can provide a sophisticated mechanism for allocating resources in an automatic way. However, it is not necessarily as perfect a resource allocator as it may appear. First, the response of supply within the price system to changes in consumer demand may be very slow and painful, because less efficient firms are not eliminated quickly but linger on making losses. Second, resources are not always as occupationally or geographically mobile as the model implies, especially where workers require significant training to acquire appropriate skills. Third, the price system cannot ensure the provision of certain COLLECTIVE PRODUCTS like defence which are enjoyed in common by all consumers, because no markets for such products exist. Finally, the efficient functioning of the price system depends crucially upon the structural characteristics of product and factor markets. With PERFECT COMPETITION in product and factor markets, the price system might well operate along the lines of the previous example. By contrast, where markets are characterized by MONOPOLY or OLIGOPOLY with high BARRIERS TO ENTRY then firms are not free to enter or leave product markets at will in response to profit opportunities. For example, if our earlier pea market was dominated by a monopoly supplier, then faced with an increase in demand the monopolist may decide not to expand pea supply but exploit the increased demand by raising selling price. Consequently in the long run the monopolist earns above normal profit and no extra factor inputs are devoted to pea production as consumer demand requires. See CENTRALLY PLANNED ECONOMY, THEORY OF MARKETS.

price taker, *n*. a FIRM that sells its output at a fixed PRICE that is determined by market forces (as in PERFECT COMPETITION) or by government-imposed PRICE CONTROLS.

price theory, *n*. an integrative body of MICROECONOMIC theory concerned with the determination of the EQUILIBRIUM MARKET PRICES and quantities transacted of goods and services.

See THEORY OF DEMAND, THEORY OF SUPPLY, THEORY OF MARKETS, THEORY OF CONSUMER BEHAVIOUR, THEORY OF THE FIRM.

price-wage spiral, see INFLATIONARY SPIRAL.

price war, *n*. any competition between rival suppliers centred on aggressive PRICE cutting. Price wars often break out when demand for a product is depressed and there is EXCESS SUPPLY capacity in the market. If FIXED COSTS are a high proportion of total costs, suppliers may be tempted to cut their prices to maintain full capacity working.

Price warfare is beneficial to the consumer and to RESOURCE ALLOCATION within the market in so far as it serves to eliminate inefficient, high cost suppliers. The problem from the suppliers' point of view is that cut throat price competition reduces the profitability of the market and everybody finishes up worse off. For this reason suppliers, particularly OLIGOPOLY suppliers, will normally try to avoid price wars and direct their competitive efforts into PRODUCT-DIFFERENTIATION activities. See METHODS OF COMPETITION.

primary sector, *n*. the part of the economy concerned with the extraction of raw materials and the provision of agricultural crops and animal produce. The primary sector, together with INDUSTRIAL SECTOR and the SERVICE SECTOR form an interlocking chain of economic activities which constitute a modern economy. See STRUCTURE OF INDUSTRY.

prime cost or **direct cost,** *n*. the sum of the DIRECT MATERIALS cost and the DIRECT LABOUR cost of a product. Prime cost tends to vary proportionately with the level of output.

prime rate, *n*. the RATE OF INTEREST charged by COMMERCIAL BANKS for short-term LOANS to their most preferential customers. The prime rate is somewhat lower than other commercial borrowing rates but only applies to what may be called 'blue-chip' companies, generally large companies with the highest credit ratings. See BANK LOAN.

principles of taxation, *n*. the rationale underlying the use of different methods of TAXATION. There are three main principles of taxation:

ABILITY-TO-PAY PRINCIPLE, BENEFITS-RECEIVED PRINCIPLE, REDISTRIBUTION OF INCOME PRINCIPLE.

private company, see JOINT-STOCK COMPANY.

private costs, *n*. the costs (EXPLICIT COSTS and IMPLICIT COSTS) incurred by firms for the use of FACTOR INPUTS in producing their OUTPUTS. Compare SOCIAL COSTS.

private-enterprise economy or **free-market economy** or **capitalism,** *n*. a method of organizing the economy to produce GOODS and SERVICES. Under this ECONOMIC SYSTEM the means of production are privately held by individuals and firms. Economic decision-making is highly decentralized with resources being allocated through a large number of goods and services markets. The MARKET synchronizes the decisions of buyers and sellers and by establishing an EQUILIBRIUM PRICE determines how much of a good will be produced and sold.

See CENTRALLY PLANNED ECONOMY, MIXED ECONOMY, NATIONALIZATION, PRIVATIZATION, PRICE SYSTEM.

private products, *n*. the goods and services that are purchased and paid for by individual consumers for their own personal benefit. Compare SOCIAL PRODUCTS.

private sector, *n*. that part of the economy concerned with the transactions of private individuals, businesses and institutions (the PERSONAL SECTOR, the CORPORATE SECTOR and the FINANCIAL SECTOR, respectively). The private sector together with the PUBLIC SECTOR makes up the domestic economy, and together with the FOREIGN SECTOR make up the national economy.

private time preference, see DISCOUNT RATE.

privatization, *n*. the denationalization of an industry, transferring it from public to private ownership. The extent of State ownership of industry depends very much on political ideology, with CENTRALLY PLANNED ECONOMY proponents seeking more NATIONALIZATION, and PRIVATE-ENTERPRISE ECONOMY advocates favouring little or no nationalization. Thus, in the UK, the wide-ranging programme of privatization embarked upon by a Conservative government since 1980 can be interpreted partly as a political preference for the private enterprise system. Advocates of privatization, however, also espouse the economic virtues of free enterprise over State control. Specifically, they argue that firms left to fend for themselves in a competitive market environment are likely to allocate resources more efficiently and meet changing consumers' demands more effectively than a bureaucratic State monopolist. In this regard it is pertinent to distinguish between industries which can be considered NATURAL MONOPOLIES and those where, in theory, a more fragmented industrial structure could be recreated. In the former category come those industries such as gas and electricity distribution, railway and telephone services where ECONOMIES OF SCALE are so great that only a monopoly supplier is in a position to fully maximize supply efficiency. There could be a serious loss of efficiency through unnecessary duplication of resources if these activities were to be fragmented. The alternative of a private-enterprise MONOPOLY is not appealing either, critics argue, because of the dangers of monopolistic abuse.

In the latter category come industries such as iron and steel, gas and electricity generation, shipbuilding and car manufacture, where because production usually takes place on a multiplant basis, the scope exists for placing each plant under a different ownership interest, thereby creating a more competitive supply situation. However, because these activities are capital-intensive, and, like natural monopolies, are characterized by significant economies of scale, the most that can be hoped for is the creation of a high seller concentration OLIGOPOLY. By contrast, the removal from the public sector of those *individual* firms (as distinct from whole industries) nationalized because they were making losses and needing reorganizing (for example, Ferranti, International Computers, Rolls-Royce, Jaguar, British Leyland, British Shipbuilders) can be more easily justified.

probability, *n.* the likelihood of a particular uncertain event occurring, measured on a scale from 0.0 (such an event is impossible) to 1.0 (such an event is certain to occur). People generally estimate probabilities on the basis of the relative frequency with which an event has occurred in the past under given circumstances, and generalize from this past experience. In some circumstances it is easy to estimate the proportion of occasions on which an event occurs, for example, the probability of getting 'heads' when flipping a balanced coin is 0.5 because with such a coin in the long run we would get 50% 'heads' and 50% 'tails'. In estimating probabilities in business situations though, there may be no or only a few previous experiences which can be used to gauge the relative frequency of an event occurring. See also RISK AND UNCERTAINTY.

probability distribution, *n.* a theoretical FREQUENCY DISTRIBUTION that shows the expected frequency with which a particular event is likely to occur, on average. For example, the PROBABILITY distribution for the likelihood of getting a 'head' when flipping a balanced coin would be:

number of 'heads'	probability
0	0.5
1	0.5

See NORMAL DISTRIBUTION, BINOMIAL DISTRIBUTION.

process ray, *n.* a line depicting the path which a firm can follow in expanding OUTPUT where technical constraints mean that FACTOR INPUTS must be used in fixed proportions in a given production process. Fig. 152 shows the production options open to a firm which has a choice between just three processes A, B and C each of which uses capital and labour in fixed proportions. If this firm wanted to produce, say, 100 units of output per period then it could produce 100 units by settling at point d using process A, or point e using process B, or point f using process C. However, it cannot choose any combination of inputs along the lines joining d, e and f because such intermediate combinations are not technically feasible.

See ISOQUANT CURVE.

Fig. 152. **Process ray.** See main entry.

producer or **supplier,** *n.* the basic producing-supplying unit of economic theory. In economic theory, a producing unit is usually a FIRM though government organizations also produce goods and services.

producer goods, *n.* CAPITAL GOODS and other goods such as fuel and lubricants which are used as FACTOR INPUTS in the production of other products, as opposed to being sold directly to consumers. Compare CONSUMER GOODS.

producers' surplus, *n.* the excess of actual earnings by a producer from a given quantity of output, over and above the amount the producer would be prepared to offer before withdrawing from the market altogether. Alfred MARSHALL considered that such excess earnings occurred over the earnings of the marginal firm in the industry which led to various producers in the industry obtaining ECONOMIC RENTS and QUASI-RENTS in the short run (sometimes quasi-rents are included in the term economic rents). Producers' surplus is directly analogous to CONSUMER'S SURPLUS and is shown in Fig. 153.

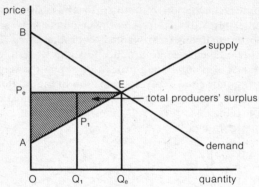

Fig. 153. **Producers' surplus**. See main entry.

At any point along the segment of the supply curve AE the producer would be willing to supply the appropriate quantity and would still receive a greater price OP_e, (the EQUILIBRIUM MARKET PRICE), than he would be prepared to sell at. For example, the producer would be prepared to supply the intra-marginal quantity OQ_1 at a price of OP_1 though in fact he receives the market price OP_e, giving a producers' surplus P_1P_e. The total of all such producers' surpluses is indicated by the shaded area AP_eE. Under conditions of PERFECT COMPETITION the individual producer faces a perfectly horizontal DEMAND CURVE and as long as firms produce a combined output of OQ_e no producers' surplus will accrue. The corollary is that producers must operate in imperfectly competitive markets (MONOPOLISTIC COMPETITION, OLIGOPOLY and MONOPOLY) to achieve producers' surplus. Consumers' surplus is the triangle bounded by P_eBE. Both producer and consumer surplus have implications for ALLOCATIVE EFFICIENCY and WELFARE ECONOMICS.

product, *n.* a generic term covering both GOODS and SERVICES.

product characteristics model, *n.* a THEORY OF CONSUMER BEHAVIOUR that shows how CONSUMERS choose between a number of BRANDS of a product each of which offer particular product characteristics in fixed proportions. For example, consumers buying blackcurrant juice may be looking for two principal product characteristics – flavour and vitamin content. Three brands of blackcurrant juice are available – Brand A, Brand B and Brand C – each of which is differentiated insofar as it places a different emphasis on the two product characteristics. The three brands are represented by the rays in Fig. 154 which show the fixed proportions of product characteristics in each brand. Brand A, for example, has a high vitamin content but has little flavour while Brand C, by contrast, has a lot of flavour but a low vitamin content.

Fig. 154. **Product characteristics model**. See main entry.

Points a, b and c on these rays show how much of each brand of juice can be bought for a given unit of expenditure at the prevailing prices of the three brands. To find the consumer's utility-maximizing brand purchases it is necessary to introduce a set of indifference curves, I_1, I_2 and I_3, showing the consumer's preferences between the two product characteristics. The consumer's final choice will be brand B, as he settles at point b on the highest indifference curve (I_3) consistent with his limited expenditure.

See CONSUMER EQUILIBRIUM, INDIFFERENCE CURVES, PRODUCT DIFFERENTIATION.

product differentiation, *n*. an element of MARKET CONDUCT that denotes the ways in which suppliers attempt to distinguish their own product from those of competitors. Product differentiation is a form of nonprice competition (see MARKET COMPETITION). On the 'supply side' products may be differentiated according to differences in quality, performance, innovatory or novelty features, design, styling and packaging. On the 'demand side', 'imaginary' differences may be cultivated between products by the use of ADVERTISING emphasizing imputed or subjective qualities: 'better than', 'cleaner and whiter than', etc. The more ignorant buyers are of the relative qualities and performance of competing brands, the more susceptible they are likely to be to persuasive advertising.

The purpose of such differentiating activity is to secure an initial demand for the firm's products and, by cultivating BRAND LOYALTIES, to ensure that sales are increased or at least maintained. The significance of product differentiation is that it widens the parameters of competitive action, with firms competing against each other in quality, advertising, etc., rather than on price alone.

Although product differentiation is often referred to as a form of 'market imperfection', this should not be interpreted to mean that heterogeneity is bad. Genuine differences among products, in particular, imply great diversity and more choices for consumers. See also MARKET-MIX, PRODUCT CHARACTERISTICS MODEL, MONOPOLISTIC COMPETITION, OLIGOPOLY, HOMOGENEOUS PRODUCTS, MARKET STRUCTURE.

production, *n.* the act of combining FACTOR INPUTS (labour, capital, etc.) by FIRMS to produce OUTPUTS of goods and services. The relationship between inputs and outputs in physical terms is shown by the PRODUCTION FUNCTION and in cost terms by the COST FUNCTION. See FACTORS OF PRODUCTION.

production census, see CENSUS.

production costs, *n.* the costs of converting FACTOR INPUTS into higher-value OUTPUTS of goods and services. The costs of manufacturing products include costs of raw materials, labour costs, depreciation and maintenance of plant and equipment, and rent, rates, lighting and heating of factory buildings. See also PRODUCTION FUNCTION, COST FUNCTION.

production function, *n.* a function that shows for a given state of technological knowledge the relationship between physical quantities of FACTOR INPUTS and the physical quantities of OUTPUT involved in producing a good or service. Since the quantity of output depends upon the quantities of inputs used, the relationship can be depicted in the form of FUNCTIONAL NOTATION:

$$Q = f(1_1, I_2 \ldots I_n)$$

where Q = output of a product and I_1, I_2, etc., are quantities of the various factor inputs 1, 2 etc., used in producing that output.

It is important to emphasize that factor inputs can be combined in a number of different ways to produce the same amount of output. One method which is technically the most efficient is the one which uses the only small amounts of labour, while another method may employ large quantities of labour and only a little capital. In physical terms, the method which is *technically the most efficient* is the one which uses the fewest inputs. Economists, however, are more concerned with the cost aspects (see COSTS) of the input-output relationship, specifically, the least costly way of producing a given output. See also COST FUNCTION.

production possibility boundary or **transformation curve,** *n.* a method of illustrating the economic problem of SCARCITY. The production possibility boundary shows the maximum amount of goods and services that can be produced by an economy at a given point in time with available resources and technology. Fig. 155 shows a production-possibility boundary for motor cars and hospitals, assuming that all resources are fully employed in the most efficient way. Point A represents the maximum production of motor cars if no hospitals are produced, while point B represents the maximum production of hospitals if no motor cars are produced. At any point along the boundary, such as C, there is a trade-off between the two goods. Motor car production can be expanded *only* by taking resources away from the production of hospitals.

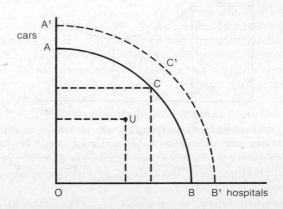

Fig. 155. **Production possibility boundary**. See main entry.

The boundary is curved rather than a straight line because not all resources are equally efficient in production of the two goods. Thus, near point A where a large number of cars are being produced and few hospitals, large numbers of construction workers have been diverted from hospital construction to make cars, and as it is unlikely that they will be as efficient working in engineering as in construction, as we move from point C to point A the production possibility curve flattens. By contrast, near point B where large numbers of hospitals are being built and few cars, large numbers of engineering workers have been diverted from car making to construction work, and since they are likely to be less efficient at the latter than the former, as we move from point C to point B the boundary steepens.

The point labelled U indicates UNEMPLOYMENT. More of both goods can be produced as idle resources are employed up to the limit set by the production possibility boundary. The broken line A¹B¹ shows how the production possibility boundary tends to move outwards over time as a result of long-term ECONOMIC GROWTH which increases POTENTIAL OUTPUT. How far outward the boundary moves and how quickly depends upon the rate of economic growth.

See also OPPORTUNITY COST, LINEAR PROGRAMMING.

Fig. 156. **Productive efficiency**. In the graph, which assumes a long-run AVERAGE COST curve which is U-shaped, plant size OA results in minimum cost. If plant sizes are suboptimal (OB), or if optimal-sized plants (OA) are underutilized because of a shortfall in demand (OX), then actual supply costs will be higher than attainable costs.

productive efficiency, *n.* an aspect of MARKET PERFORMANCE that denotes the efficiency of a market in producing current products at the lowest possible cost in the long run, using existing technology. Productive efficiency is achieved when output is produced in plants of optimal scale and when there is a long-run balance of market supply and demand. See Fig. 156.

See also MINIMUM EFFICIENT SCALE, TECHNOLOGICAL PROGRESSIVENESS, EXCESS CAPACITY, RATIONALIZATION.

productive potential, see POTENTIAL GROSS NATIONAL PRODUCT.

productivity, *n.* the relationship between the OUTPUT of an economic unit and the FACTOR INPUTS which have gone into producing that output. Productivity is usually measured in terms of *output per man-hour* to facilitate interfirm, interindustry, and intercountry comparisons. An increase in productivity occurs when output per man-hour is raised. The main source of productivity increases is the use of more and better CAPITAL STOCK (see CAPITAL WIDENING and CAPITAL DEEPENING).

This important point can be illustrated in the following three stages. (a) Suppose, initially, that the assembly of a motor car is a labour-intensive operation; it takes a team of 10 men working with a minimal amount of capital (spanners and screwdrivers only) one whole day to assemble one car. (b) The firm now invests in hydraulic lifting gear (CAPITAL DEEPENING) and this cuts down considerably the amount of time in aligning parts for assembly, reducing the time it takes to complete the assembly operation to, say, one tenth of a day. The same team of men are now able to assemble 10 cars a day – their productivity has gone up tenfold. (c) The firm introduces a continuous flow assembly line with automatically controlled machines (again, capital deepening), which one man can operate. Output increases to say, 50 cars a day; the productivity of the remaining man has increased from 1 car a day (a one-tenth part of 10 cars) to 50.

Just as importantly, 9 men have been 'released' from the team. Either they too could all be put to work on a similar automated assembly line (capital widening), in which case the total output of the 10 men is now 500 cars per day (10×50), compared to 50 before. Alternatively, they could be redeployed outside the car industry, thereby helping to increase output in other sectors of the economy.

Increased productivity thus makes an important contribution to the achievement of higher rates of ECONOMIC GROWTH.

See also CAPITAL–OUTPUT RATIO, SPECIALIZATION, QUALITY CONTROL, RESTRICTIVE LABOUR PRACTICE, WORK STUDY, X INEFFICIENCY, ORGANIZATIONAL SLACK.

product life-cycle, *n.* the typical sales pattern followed by a product over time as changing consumer tastes and technological INNOVATION cause new products to emerge which supersede existing products. The typical life-cycle followed by a product introduced into a market is depicted in Fig. 157. It consists of four main phases:

(a) product launch, which follows the successful development of a new product and its national launch. When the product is first put on the market sales volume will be low until consumer resistance has been overcome, and at this stage the market is frequently limited to high-income consumers with more adventurous buying habits.

(b) product growth phase, where the product gains market acceptance and sales grow rapidly as the product reaches the mass market. During this phase competitors may begin to enter the field with rival products, so that the distinctiveness of the original product fades.

(c) product maturity, where sales are largely limited to repeat purchases by existing customers, since the majority of potential customers have already made their first purchases. At this stage the market is saturated, so that competitors are unable to benefit from market growth and must compete intensely to maintain or increase their share of the constant market.

(d) product decline, where sales begin to decline as consumer tastes change or superior products are launched. If left to follow this downward trend the product will eventually die as sales fall to low levels, though long before this managers may decide to phase out the product.

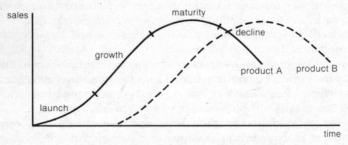

Fig. 157. **Product life-cycle**. See main entry.

Most companies market a number of different products and must formulate a product-range strategy, providing for a regulated process of new product launches, with new products like B in Fig. 157 growing as older products like A reach maturity, so as to maintain an appropriate

PRODUCT MIX of newly-launched products, growth products and mature lines.

A company's pricing policy for a product may be related to the stages of the product's life-cycle. During the launch phase, managers will tend to opt for a high *skimming price* which capitalizes on the new and distinctive nature of the product and the temporary monopoly power which this conveys. In this early stage demand for the product is likely to be less price-elastic (see PRICE-ELASTICITY OF DEMAND), for high prices will not deter high-income pioneer consumers. Furthermore, a high price will reinforce the quality image of the largely untried product as well as recouping research and development and heavy promotion expenditures. During the growth phase managers may change to a low *penetration price*, lowering price to bring the product within reach of the mass of consumers. At this stage demand is likely to be more price-elastic, for the average consumer is more price-conscious than the pioneer consumer. By lowering price the firm can expand sales appreciably, gaining cost-savings from large-scale production and can maintain a large market share in the face of entry by competitors. Once the maturity phase is reached with several similar products firmly established in the market then prices will tend to stay in line with one another, for any attempt by one firm to reduce its price and expand its market-share will provoke retaliation as competitors fight to maintain their market share.

Similarly, other elements of the MARKETING MIX such as advertising and sales promotion need to be adapted to the phases of the product life cycle. See also BOSTON MATRIX, PRODUCT PERFORMANCE.

product life-cycle theory, *n.* a theory that seeks to explain changes in the pattern of INTERNATIONAL TRADE over time, which is based on a dynamic sequence of product INNOVATION and diffusion. Four 'phases' of the cycle can be postulated. (a) To begin with, as new products are introduced, the consuming country is likely to be the producing country because of the close association between innovation and demand. This original producing country – typically an advanced industrial country – becomes an exporter to other high-income countries. (b) Production begins in other leading industrial countries, and the innovating country's exports to these markets are displaced. (c) As these countries' own demand for the product reaches sufficient size to enable producers to take advantage of economies of scale, they too become net exporters, thereby displacing the innovating country's exports in nonproducing countries. (d) Finally, as the technology and product become increasingly standardized to the point where relatively unskilled labour can be used in the production process, DEVELOPING COUNTRIES with lower costs become exporters of the product, further displacing the innovating country's exports. Meanwhile, however, the innovating country has moved on to the production of new products.

See also TECHNOLOGICAL-GAP THEORY, THEORY OF INTERNATIONAL TRADE.

Market

Product		Present	New
	Present	1. market penetration	2. market development
	New	3. product development	4. diversification

Fig. 158. **Product-market matrix**. See main entry.

product-market matrix, *n.* a matrix for analysing the scope for change in a firm's product-market strategy. Fig. 158 shows the matrix, which depicts products on one axis and markets on the other. A firm seeking to achieve profit and growth in changing market conditions has four major strategies available: (a) more effective penetration of existing markets by existing products, increasing the firm's market share; (b) development of new markets for its existing products, capitalizing on the firm's production strengths; (c) development of new products for its existing markets, exploiting the firm's marketing strengths; (d) development of new products for new markets, that is, DIVERSIFICATION. This is generally the highest-risk strategy since it takes the firm furthest from its production and marketing expertise.

See also BOSTON MATRIX, PRODUCT MIX.

product mix, *n.* the mixture of PRODUCTS offered by a FIRM. Since most products tend to follow a typical PRODUCT LIFE-CYCLE it is expedient for companies to maintain an appropriate mix of newly-launched products, growth products and mature lines. In addition, the firm may choose to offer a range of similar products to appeal to different sectors of the market as part of a MARKET-SEGMENTATION strategy. A firm will generally consider its product mix in the context of its broader MARKETING MIX (embracing price, advertising, etc.). See also PRODUCT-MARKET MATRIX.

product performance, *n.* an aspect of MARKET PERFORMANCE that denotes the quality and performance of existing products and firms' record with respect to the development of new products. The

Fig. 159. **Product performance.** An improvement in product quality from OQ_1 to OQ_2 can allow the firm producing the product to charge a higher price to reflect this improvement, increasing price from OP_1 to OP_2. If price is raised less than proportionally with the increase in product quality, as in the Fig., then the consumer receives a net benefit from product improvement.

introduction of new products and the qualitative improvement of existing products may enhance consumer welfare by providing consumers with 'better-value-for-money' in terms of price/quality trade-offs. See Fig. 159.

See also PRODUCT DIFFERENTIATION, TECHNOLOGICAL PROGRESSIVENESS, INVENTION, INNOVATION, RESEARCH AND DEVELOPMENT, PRODUCT LIFE-CYCLE.

profit, *n*. the difference that arises when a firm's TOTAL REVENUE is greater than its TOTAL COSTS. This definition of 'economic profit' differs from that used conventionally by businessmen (*accounting profit*) in that accounting profit only takes into account explicit costs. Economic profit can be viewed in terms of:

(a) the return accruing to enterprise owners (entrepreneurs) after the payment of all EXPLICIT COSTS (payments such as wages to outside factor-input suppliers) and all IMPLICIT COSTS (payments for the use of factor inputs – capital, labour – supplied by the owners themselves).

(b) a residual return to the owner(s) of a firm (an individual ENTREPRENEUR or group of SHAREHOLDERS) for providing capital and for risk-bearing.

(c) the 'reward' to entrepreneurs for organizing productive activity, for innovating new products, etc., and for risk taking.

421

(d) the prime mover of a PRIVATE-ENTERPRISE ECONOMY serving to allocate resources between competing end uses in line with consumer demands.

(e) in aggregate terms, a source of income and thus included as part of NATIONAL INCOME.

See also PROFIT MAXIMIZATION, NORMAL PROFIT, ABOVE-NORMAL PROFIT, RISK AND UNCERTAINTY, NATIONAL-INCOME ACCOUNTS.

profitability, *n.* the PROFIT earned by a firm in relation to the size of the firm, measured in terms of total ASSETS employed, long term capital or number of employees. See RETURN ON CAPITAL-EMPLOYED.

profit-and-loss account, see TRADING AND PROFIT-AND-LOSS ACCOUNT.

profit-and-loss appropriation account, *n.* an account that shows how any NET PROFIT recorded in the TRADING AND PROFIT-AND-LOSS ACCOUNT is divided between TAX payments, DIVIDEND payments and RESERVES.

profit centre, *n.* an organizational subunit given responsibility for minimizing COSTS and maximizing REVENUE within its limited sphere of operations. Profit centres facilitate management control by helping to ascertain a unit's performance and profitability. See also COST CENTRE.

profit margin, *n.* the difference between the SELLING PRICE of a product and its PRODUCTION COST and SELLING COST. The size of the profit margin will depend upon the percentage profit mark-up which a firm adds to costs in determining its selling price. The size of the profit margin is measured by the PROFIT-TO-SALES RATIO. See also FULL-COST PRICING.

profit maximization, *n.* the objective of the firm in the traditional THEORY OF THE FIRM and the THEORY OF MARKETS. Firms seek to establish that price-output combination which yields the maximum amount of profit. The achievement of profit maximization can be depicted in two ways.

(a) Firstly, where TOTAL REVENUE (TR) exceeds TOTAL COST (TC) by the greatest amount. In Fig. 160, this occurs at the output level where the slope of the two curves is identical, and tangents to each curve are consequently parallel as at Q_e. At any output level below Q_e the relevant tangents would be diverging – the TR and TC curves would still be moving further apart and profits would still be rising. At any output level beyond Q_e, on the other hand, the relevant tangents would be converging and the profit surplus of TR over TC would be falling. Thus, Q_e is the optimum point, for here the distance between the total revenue and total cost curves is maximized (equal to AB). The difference

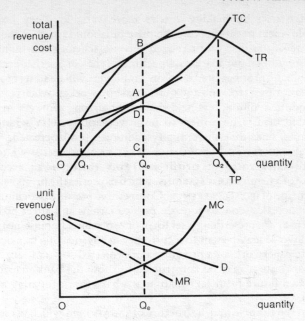

Fig. 160. **Profit maximization**. See main entry.

between the two curves shows up in the total profit curve which becomes positive at output OQ_1, reaches a maximum at output OQ_e (where profit $CD = AB$), and becomes negative beyond output OQ_2.

(b) Secondly, profit maximization can be shown to occur where MARGINAL REVENUE (MR) equals MARGINAL COST (MC) – at output OQ_e in the figure. At all output rates above OQ_e additional units add more to cost than revenue so that total profits are reduced. At all output rates less than OQ_e additional units add more to revenue than cost, thereby expanding total profits. Only where MR = MC are profits maximized.

See also ECONOMIC MAN, FIRM OBJECTIVES.

profit motive, *n.* the objective of a FIRM to ensure that revenue exceeds costs. The term is usually associated with the FIRM OBJECTIVE of PROFIT MAXIMIZATION, but a profit motive would still exist where only satisfactory profits were aimed for. See also PROFIT, SATISFICING THEORY.

profit-related pay, *n.* any payment systems whereby employees receive a proportion of their pay in the form of PROFIT-related payments. Advocates of such schemes suggest that they can help to reduce

UNEMPLOYMENT by making WAGES more variable. They hold that unemployment occurs because the price of labour is stuck at too high a level and argue that profit-related income schemes can build some flexibility into labour markets. Specifically, they argue that because of the automatic profit-related cushion, employers will be slower to lay off workers during a recession and quicker to hire workers when conditions are good. In addition, it is held that profit-sharing workers are better motivated than wage earners to improve PRODUCTIVITY within their companies, since they share in any additional profits created.

See also SUPPLY-SIDE ECONOMICS, WAGE RATE, MINIMUM WAGE RATE.

profit-to-sales ratio or **profit-margins ratio,** *n.* an accounting measure of a firm's PROFIT MARGINS, which expresses the firm's PROFITS as a percentage of its SALES REVENUE. Competitive pressure on selling prices or cost increases serve to squeeze profit margins and affect profits.

pro–forma, *adj.* prescribing a set form or procedure. For instance, a pro-forma invoice may be sent to a customer in advance of a transaction to facilitate paperwork, or a pro–forma or projected SOURCES AND USES OF FUNDS STATEMENT may be constructed to show the bank manager the anticipated future financial situation as a basis for negotiating a short-term LOAN.

progressive taxation, *n.* a structure of TAXATION in which tax is levied at an increasing rate as INCOME rises. The marginal incidence of taxation therefore rises to some pre-determined upper limit, currently 60% in the UK on earned income. For example, a man earning £16,000 with current tax bands as shown in column 1 and the rates of taxation in column 2, would have the tax payable shown in column 3:

Column 1 (£)	Column 2 (%)	Column 3 (£)
0– 2,000	Tax Exempt	NIL
2,001–10,000	30	2,400
10,001–12,000	40	800
12,001–15,000	45	1,350
15,001 +	50	500
	Total	5,050

The increasing rate of taxation is shown in column 2. The greater the individual's earnings, the greater the rate of tax which is levied.

Virtually all western economies exhibit some form of progressive taxation structure as a means of redistributing income from the more affluent members of society to the poorer. This type of ABILITY-TO-PAY

PRINCIPLE is regarded, as far as earned personal incomes are concerned, as the most equitable form of taxation. Compare REGRESSIVE TAXATION, PROPORTIONAL TAXATION. See also INCIDENCE OF TAXATION, REDISTRIBUTION-OF-INCOME PRINCIPLE OF TAXATION.

progress payments, *n.* a contractual arrangement common to large construction projects whereby payment for work done is made at predetermined stages along the route to completion.

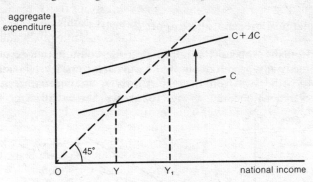

Fig. 161. **Propensity to consume.** The effect of an increase in the propensity to consume on national income. See MULTIPLIER.

propensity to consume, *n.* the proportion of DISPOSABLE INCOME which is spent by households on CONSUMPTION of final goods and services. The average propensity to consume (APC) is given by:

$$\frac{\text{total consumption}}{\text{total income.}}$$

The marginal propensity to consume (MPC) is the fraction of any change in income which is spent:

$$\text{marginal propensity to consume (MPC)} = \frac{\text{change in consumption}}{\text{change in income.}}$$

In the simple CIRCULAR FLOW OF NATIONAL INCOME MODEL all disposable income is either consumed or saved. It follows that the sum of the MPC and the MARGINAL PROPENSITY TO SAVE always adds up to one.

A rise in the propensity to consume increases consumption expenditure for a given income level (increases the consumption injection into the circular flow of national income) and results in an increase in aggregate demand and national income, as Fig. 161 shows.

propensity to import, *n.* the proportion of NATIONAL INCOME which is spent on IMPORTS. The average propensity to import (APM) is given by:

$$\frac{\text{total imports}}{\text{total income.}}$$

The marginal propensity to import (MPM) is the fraction of any change in income spent on imports:

$$\text{marginal propensity to import (MPM)} = \frac{\text{change in imports}}{\text{change in income.}}$$

A rise in the propensity to import decreases consumption expenditure on domestically-produced output for a given income level (increases the imports withdrawal from the CIRCULAR FLOW OF NATIONAL INCOME) and reduces national income, as Fig. 162 shows. See MULTIPLIER.

Fig. 162. **Propensity to import.** The effect of an increase in imports on national income.

propensity to save, *n.* the proportion of DISPOSABLE INCOME which is saved by households (see SAVINGS). The average propensity to save (APS) is given by:

$$\frac{\text{total saving}}{\text{total income.}}$$

The marginal propensity to save (MPS) is the fraction of any change in income which is saved:

$$\text{marginal propensity to save (MPS)} = \frac{\text{change in saving}}{\text{change in income.}}$$

Fig. 163. **Propensity to save**. The effect of an increase in the propensity to save on national income.

In the simple CIRCULAR FLOW OF NATIONAL INCOME MODEL all disposable income is either consumed or saved by households. It follows that the sum of the MARGINAL PROPENSITY TO CONSUME and the MPS add up to one (note that saving is defined as all disposable income which is not spent by consumers regardless of whether savings are placed in banks, hidden under the bed, or whatever).

A rise in the propensity to save decreases consumption expenditure for a given income level (increases the savings withdrawal from the circular flow of national income) resulting in a decrease in aggregate demand and national income, as Fig. 163 shows. See MULTIPLIER.

propensity to tax, *n.* the proportion of NATIONAL INCOME which is taken in TAXATION by government. The average propensity to tax (APT) is given by:

$$\frac{\text{total taxation}}{\text{total income.}}$$

The marginal propensity to tax (MPT) is the fraction of any change in income which is taken in taxation:

$$\text{marginal propensity to tax (MPT)} = \frac{\text{change in taxation}}{\text{change in income.}}$$

Direct taxes reduce total income to (net of tax) DISPOSABLE INCOME. Thereafter a proportion of this disposable income will be spent, and indirect taxes on goods and services bought will reduce still further the proportion of income returned to the business sector as factor returns.

See MULTIPLIER.

427

A rise in the propensity to tax decreases disposable income for a given income level (increases the taxation withdrawal from the CIRCULAR FLOW OF NATIONAL INCOME), decreasing consumption expenditure, which results in a decrease in AGGREGATE DEMAND and NATIONAL INCOME.

property, see ASSET.

proportional taxation, *n.* a structure of TAXATION in which tax is levied at a constant rate as INCOME rises, for example, 10% of each increment of income as income rises. This form of taxation takes the same proportion of tax from a low-income taxpayer as from a high-income taxpayer. Compare PROGRESSIVE TAXATION, REGRESSIVE TAXATION.

protectionism, *n.* a deliberate policy on the part of governments to erect trade barriers such as TARIFFS and QUOTAS in order to protect domestic industries from foreign competition.

While there are arguments for protection especially appealing to sectional interests, protectionism cannot, for the most part, be vindicated as being in the best interests of the national and international community. Take, for example, the often cited contention that tariffs are needed to equalize WAGE RATES between countries. The UK and US textile industries complain that their domestic positions are undermined by foreign suppliers who employ 'cheap labour'. It should be noted, however, that for the economy as a whole high wage rates are the *result*, not the cause of the productive efficiency, other industries successfully meet foreign competition in both domestic and foreign markets despite higher wages. This is because they rank higher in the order of COMPARATIVE ADVANTAGE. Protection of industries which come low in the order of comparative advantage distorts the industrial ranking and leads to inefficient resource utilization. Foreign competition would force contraction of the textile industries, and the resources released from it could then be devoted to products in which the country has a comparative advantage.

Protection might be necessary, it is suggested, in the short term to facilitate an orderly restructuring of industries (particularly where manpower resources are highly localized), but there is the danger that such protection might become permanent in the face of vested interests.

Other arguments for protection, while superficially appealing, can usually be achieved more effectively by alternative means. Thus selective tariffs and quotas may assist in restoring BALANCE-OF-PAYMENTS EQUILIBRIUM, but distort the ordering of industries by comparative advantage. By contrast, aggregate fiscal and monetary policies and exchange-rate adjustments affect all foreign transactions.

There are, however, some seemingly respectable arguments for protection. From the viewpoint of the welfare of the world as a whole the most popular claim made for tariffs, etc., is the so-called INFANT-INDUSTRY argument. Protection can be an effective means of stimulating the development of an industry that is well suited to a country (in terms of potential comparative advantage) but which finds it impossible to get started unless it is protected from imports. Over time, suitably protected, such an industry is able to acquire internal economies of scale (i.e., lower costs through exploiting a larger domestic market) and take advantage of various external economies (a well-trained labour force or the 'learning-by-doing' effect). Eventually the new industry is able to become equally or more efficient than its older competitors. The tariff can then be removed, leaving behind a viable and competitive industry.

Such temporary protection of industries does not conflict with the goal of free traders: maximum specialization on the basis of comparative advantage. It is only through the temporary equalization of competitive conditions that the industry is able to reach that stage of development which allows it to fully realize its potential.

There are problems, however. Industries are frequently selected for protection not on the basis of a favourable comparative advantage but for nationalistic reasons (e.g. diversification of the economy); 'infant industry' becomes a slogan to justify promiscuous protection without regard to merit. The protection afforded may be over-excessive and continued for longer than is strictly necessary.

In some circumstances, tariffs can be employed to improve a country's TERMS OF TRADE by forcing down prices in exporting countries. This applies especially to major importers who are large enough to exercise buying power. It is to be noticed, however, that the gain from lower-priced imports may be offset by two adverse effects of tariffs: their diversion of resources to less productive uses, and the fact that trade partners are likely to retaliate by imposing tariffs of their own.

See also IMPORT RESTRICTIONS, NOMINAL RATE OF PROTECTION, EFFECTIVE RATE OF PROTECTION, BEGGAR-MY-NEIGHBOUR POLICY, GENERAL AGREEMENT ON TARIFFS AND TRADE, MULTI-FIBRE ARRANGEMENT.

provision, *n.* the sums charged in accounting against a firm's profits in anticipation of costs which are likely to arise in the future. The most common general provision made by firms is the provision for doubtful DEBTS which is established in anticipation of some customers not paying what they owe. In addition, a firm may make a specific provision against, say, a damages claim which is presently not yet settled.

Provisions are aimed at trying to ensure that PROFITS are not overstated by making sure that all a firm's costs are charged, even those whose precise amount is not yet certain. See REVALUATION PROVISION.

proxy, *n.* an authorization to a person or firm to act in place of another. During a JOINT-STOCK COMPANY's ANNUAL GENERAL MEETING, for example, a SHAREHOLDER may be unable to attend and vote on items contained in the agenda. The shareholder may therefore give written authorization for someone else to attend and vote at the meeting in his stead. A shareholders proxy is frequently given to the incumbent board of directors to vote with as they think fit, hence the term 'proxy vote'.

PSBR, see PUBLIC-SECTOR BORROWING REQUIREMENT.

PSL$_2$, see MONEY SUPPLY DEFINITIONS.

public company, see JOINT-STOCK COMPANY.

public debt, *n.* the NATIONAL DEBT and other miscellaneous debt for which the government is ultimately accountable. Such miscellaneous debt would include, for example, the accumulated debts of nationalized industries.

public expenditure, see GOVERNMENT EXPENDITURE.

public finance, *n.* the branch of economics concerned with the income and expenditure of public authorities, the relationship of one to the other, and its effect upon the economy in general. When the CLASSICAL ECONOMISTS wrote upon the subject of public finance they concentrated upon the income side, TAXATION. Since the Keynesian era of the 1930s much more emphasis has been given to the expenditure side and the effect FISCAL POLICY has on the economy. Where government income and expenditure in a year are equal, this is known as a BALANCED BUDGET. Where expenditure exceeds income, this is known as a BUDGET DEFICIT and vice versa for a BUDGET SURPLUS.

The government, being the principal actor upon the economic stage, influences virtually every aspect of economic life in a country. Public finance therefore has some difficulty in defining its area of analysis. Government fiscal policy has many objectives including counter-cyclical STABILIZATION POLICY, reducing UNEMPLOYMENT, checking the rate of INFLATION and achieving optimum long-term ECONOMIC GROWTH; as well as the more socioeconomic aspects of taxing individuals in a progressive manner and in a way consistent with encouraging maximum effort of work from its citizens.

See also KEYNESIAN ECONOMICS, PROGRESSIVE TAXATION.

public goods, see SOCIAL PRODUCTS.

public interest, *n.* a 'benchmark' used in the application of MONOPOLY

POLICY (in the UK) to judge whether or not a particular action or policy pursued by a supplier or by a group of suppliers, or a change in the structure of a market, is 'good' or 'bad' in terms of its effects on economic efficiency and the consumer. For example, it is clearly in the public interest if a firm prices its product at a level which yields it only a 'fair' profit return – that is, a profit reward which is just adequate to secure the efficient supply of the product (see NORMAL PROFIT). By the same token, it is clearly against the public interest if a firm profiteers at the expense of the consumer by charging excessive prices (see ABOVE-NORMAL PROFIT). In practice, however, the issue is complicated by difficulties in interpreting data: for example, low profits may reflect a conservative pricing policy or result from the fact that the firm is grossly inefficient. Moreover, there are further complications arising from the fact that particular actions may produce, simultaneously, both beneficial and detrimental effects. In this case a 'trade-off' assessment is required to form a balanced judgement.

See WILLIAMSON 'TRADE-OFF' MODEL.

public ownership, see NATIONALIZATION.

public sector or **government sector,** *n.* that part of the economy concerned with the transactions of the government. Government receives income from TAXATION and other receipts and influences the workings of the economy through its own spending and investment decisions (GOVERNMENT EXPENDITURE) and through its control (via MONETARY POLICY and FISCAL POLICY) of the spending and investment decisions of other sectors of the economy. The public sector, together with the PERSONAL SECTOR, FINANCIAL SECTOR, CORPORATE SECTOR and FOREIGN SECTOR make up the national economy. See CIRCULAR FLOW OF NATIONAL INCOME MODEL.

public-sector borrowing requirement (PSBR), *n.* the excess of GOVERNMENT EXPENDITURE over TAXATION receipts, requiring the government to make good the difference by borrowing money from the banking system (TREASURY BILLS) or from the general public (long-dated BONDS). BUDGET DEFICITS are used as an instrument of FISCAL POLICY as a means of increasing total spending (AGGREGATE DEMAND) in the economy.

The size of the nominal public-sector borrowing requirement (PSBR) depends not only on the government's fundamental spending and taxation plans (its underlying fiscal stance) but also on the level of economic activity and the rate of inflation.

Fluctuations in economic activity lead to movements in the PSBR, for the PSBR tends to increase in a recession as total tax revenues fall and social security payments rise in response to lower incomes and higher unemployment, and to fall in a boom as tax revenues rise and social security payments fall in response to higher incomes and lower unemployment. In order to remove the impact of cyclical fluctuations in economic activity associated with BUSINESS CYCLES upon the PSBR, it is necessary to calculate the *cyclically-adjusted PSBR*. By removing from the PSBR figure the effect of cyclical variations on the budget balance, the cyclically-adjusted PSBR measures what the PSBR would be if economic activity levels were 'on trend'.

INFLATION also has an effect on the nominal PSBR, because since most public sector debt is denominated in nominal terms, its real value falls with the rate of inflation, reducing the real value of the government's liabilities. The real PSBR is defined as the actual PSBR less the erosion by inflation of the real value of the stock of public sector debt (*inflation–adjusted PSBR*). So for a given real PSBR, a higher rate of inflation implies a higher nominal PSBR. When the effects of inflation rates of the 1970s are allowed for, the high nominal PSBR figures (indicating a large fiscal deficit) show a modest real PSBR (indicating a fiscal surplus). The public sector has been adding to its nominal stock of debt at a slower rate than that at which inflation has been eroding the value of past borrowing.

There are three main ways in which a government can finance its borrowing requirement:

(a) by borrowing funds from individuals, firms and financial institutions in the private sector by selling government bonds and bills. This requires high interest rates to make government debt attractive to lenders.

(b) by borrowing funds from overseas lenders by selling government securities. This overseas borrowing has effects on the balance of payments.

(c) by borrowing short-term from the commercial banking system by issuing Treasury bills to them. This has the effect of increasing the banks' reserve assets allowing them in turn to expand their lending.

The first two methods of financing the public-sector borrowing requirement by selling bonds to the nonbank private sector are likely to raise interest rates but because they provide stable (generally long-term) funding for government borrowing they do not affect the MONEY SUPPLY. By contrast, to the extent that the government cannot fund all its borrowing needs from the first two sources it must resort to borrowing from the banking system. This is akin to printing additional money and serves to increase the money supply.

Public-sector borrowing may contribute to 'crowding out' (see CROWDING-OUT EFFECTS) the private sector in two main ways. First by facilitating larger government expenditure it may cause real crowding out as the public sector uses more of the nation's resources, leaving less for private consumption spending and investment and for exports. Second, the additional borrowing by government will tend to raise interest rates thereby causing financial crowding out, as private investment is discouraged by the high interest rates.

Since 1980 the British government has published a MEDIUM-TERM FINANCIAL STRATEGY which lays down targets each year for the public sector borrowing requirement expressed as a percentage of GROSS DOMESTIC PRODUCT.

See MONEY SUPPLY/SPENDING LINKAGES, MONETARISM.

public utility, *n.* an enterprise that provides certain essential goods or services like water, electricity and gas. In some countries such as the US, most of these goods and services are provided by privately-owned (but publicly regulated) companies. In other countries, for instance, the UK, most of these products are provided by publicly-owned corporations (nationalized industries).

See RATE-OF-RETURN REGULATION, MARGINAL-COST PRICING, TWO-PART TARIFF, NATIONALIZATION.

public works, *n.* any expenditure by government on social INFRASTRUCTURE such as roads, houses, hospitals, sewers, etc. Such expenditure was strongly advocated by KEYNES during the DEPRESSION of the 1930s to alleviate the problem of UNEMPLOYMENT and stimulate AGGREGATE DEMAND, via the MULTIPLIER. See KEYNESIAN ECONOMICS, MACRO-ECONOMIC POLICY, GOVERNMENT EXPENDITURE.

pump priming, *n.* any GOVERNMENT EXPENDITURE designed to stimulate AGGREGATE DEMAND and, through the MULTIPLIER effect, create a much larger increase in NATIONAL INCOME. Where an economy finds itself with a DEFLATIONARY GAP, government need not undertake the removal of that gap by itself. Only a small part of the deflationary gap need be removed by the government in order to induce and encourage optimism in the economy. Thereafter additional private sector expenditure will lead towards full employment through increased aggregate demand.

See STABILIZATION POLICY, DEMAND MANAGEMENT.

purchasing power, *n.* the extent to which a given monetary unit can buy goods and services. The greater the amount of goods and services purchased with say, £10, the greater is its purchasing power. Purchasing power is directly linked to the retail PRICE INDEX and can be used to compare the material wealth of an average individual from a previous time period to the present.

See INFLATION, PURCHASING-POWER PARITY THEORY.

purchasing-power parity theory, *n.* a theory of EXCHANGE-RATE determination that postulates that under a FLOATING EXCHANGE-RATE SYSTEM, exchange rates adjust to offset differential rates of INFLATION between countries who are trade partners in such a way as to restore BALANCE-OF-PAYMENTS EQUILIBRIUM. Differential rates of inflation can bring about exchange rate changes in two principal ways. The first relates to the effect of changes of relative prices on import and export demand. As the price of country A's products rise relative to those of country B, demanders of these products tend to substitute away from A and toward B, decreasing the demand for A's currency and increasing the demand for B's currency. This leads to a DEPRECIATION of the bilateral exchange rate of currency A for currency B. Thus, a higher level of domestic prices in country A is 'offset' by a fall in the external value of its currency.

A second way that exchange rates can change in response to differential rates of inflation is through SPECULATION about future exchange rate movements. As prices rise in country A relative to country B, managers of foreign-currency portfolios and speculators anticipate an eventual lowering of the real value of the currency in terms of its purchasing power over tradeable products and tend to substitute away from it in their holdings, again causing a depreciation of currency A.

This theory therefore predicts that differential rates of inflation leads to compensating exchange rate changes. However, it is also possible that exchange-rate changes themselves can lead to differential rates of inflation; if, for example, import demand is highly price-inelastic, an exchange rate depreciation may lead to an increase in domestic inflation. There is thus a problem in respect of causality (see DEPRECIATION entry). see also ASSET-VALUE THEORY.

Q

quality control, *n.* a discipline concerned with improving the quality of goods and services produced. The object of quality control is to prevent faulty components or finished goods from being produced and it uses a variety of devices to help achieve this aim. Techniques of statistical sampling and testing can be used to identify faulty materials and products. Statistical variability limits can be used to ensure, for example, that machines are continuing to hold their tolerances in producing goods. Quality circles can be employed to involve work-groups in the task of quality assurance, by generating discussion about the cause of quality problems and how workers themselves can deal with such problems.

See also PRODUCTIVITY, PRODUCT PERFORMANCE, PRODUCT DIFFERENTIATION.

quantity theory of money, *n.* a theory that posits a direct relationship between the MONEY SUPPLY and the general PRICE LEVEL in an economy.

The basic identity underlying the quantity theory was first developed by Irving Fisher (1867–1947) in 1911. The Fisher equation states that:

$$MV \equiv PT$$

where M is the money stock; V is the VELOCITY OF CIRCULATION of money (the average number of times each £ or $ changes hands in financing transactions during a year); P is the general price level; and T is the number of transactions or the total amount of goods and services supplied.

The above relationship is true by definition because total money expenditure on goods and services (MV) in a period must equal the money value of goods and services produced (PT), and the four terms are defined in such a way that the identity must hold. However, the identity can be converted into a testable equation by assuming that the velocity of circulation of money is constant or changes slowly.

Economists at Cambridge University reformulated the traditional quantity theory of money to emphasize the relationship between the stock of money in an economy (M) and final income (Y). The income velocity of circulation (Cambridge equation) is thus:

$$V = \frac{Y}{M}$$

where V is the average number of times the money stock of an economy changes hands in the purchase of final goods and services. For example, taking Y as gross national product, if a country has a GNP of £5,000m and an average money stock (M) over a year of £1,000m, then V is 5. Velocity cannot be observed directly and is thus determined using Y and M, figures which may be calculated from government statistics.

The term V in the Cambridge equation is not the same as V in Fisher's traditional quantity theory of money. In Fisher's equation, $MV \equiv PT$, rearranged to give:

$$V = \frac{PT}{M}$$

the number of transactions in the period, T, includes *all* transactions for real goods and services plus financial transactions. In the Cambridge equation, PT (where P = average price level) is replaced by Y which contains not *all* transactions, but only those generating final income. This formulation allowed the Cambridge economists to emphasize real income (that is, final goods and services).

The classical economists argued that velocity of circulation was constant because consumers have relatively constant spending habits and so turn over money at a steady rate. This argument converts the identity into an equation that leads to the quantity theory which expresses a relationship between the supply of money and the general price level. If V and T are constant then:

$$M = P \text{ and } \Delta M = \Delta P.$$

The modern exponents of the quantity theory (see MONETARISM) do not necessarily hold that the velocity of circulation is fixed, but they argue that it will change only slowly over time as a result of financial innovations like the spread of bank accounts and cheque payments, and the growing use of credit cards. They also point out that in a fully employed economy there is a maximum amount of goods and services being produced and which therefore can be exchanged, so that the number of transactions, T, is determined by real supply-wide considerations like productivity trends. With V and T fixed or slowly changing, then the price level is determined by the stock of money M. Any increase in the money supply feeds directly into an increase in demand for goods and services (aggregate demand). It follows that if the money supply (M), and hence aggregate demand, increase *over time* faster than the supply capacity of the economy (T), the result will be a rise in the general price level, P (INFLATION). By contrast, Keynesian economists argue that the velocity of circulation is unstable and changes rapidly and may off-set changes in the money stock.

See also MONEY–SUPPLY/SPENDING LINKAGES, MONETARY POLICY.

quartiles, *n.* the numerical values that divide a group of numerical observations into four parts, each containing an equal number of observations. Quartiles are frequently applied to data arranged in decreasing numerical order. Thus, for example, one-quarter of the eight observations below exceed the first quartile (9); while one-half exceed the second quartile (6); and three-quarters exceed the third quartile (3).

Quartiles example: 11,10/8,7/5,4/2,1

Compare DECILES, PERCENTILES.

quasi-rent, *n.* the additional reward to a FACTOR OF PRODUCTION which is in short-term fixed supply, over and above VARIABLE COSTS. In the long-term the reward to the factor of production will equate to TRANSFER EARNINGS. The principle of quasi-rent is illustrated in Fig. 164.

Fig. 164. **Quasi-rent**. See main entry.

In the original situation demand is shown by DD and a given quantity (Q) is produced at price (P). If there is an increase in demand from DD to D_1D_1, quantity cannot be increased in the short term. The supply curve becomes PES. Consequently the excess of demand over supply raises price to P_1 at quantity Q. The section of the supply curve from E to S is vertical and is thus said to be perfectly inelastic.

For exposition, assume a firm covers its average total costs, ATC, (a necessary long-term requirement) at point E.

In the short term the firm need only cover its average variable costs, AVC at point H. The quasi-rent will be the area P_1P_2HG. In the long term the supply curve PL is horizontal (infinitely elastic) and additional productive capacity will be brought to bear to produce quantity Q_1. At this point additional units Q to Q_1 are produced at the same cost per unit, and quasi-rent disappears. Note that fixed costs (the difference between average variable costs and average total cost) are an essential part of long-term costs of production and includes the necessary return for factors of production to be maintained in their present capacity rather than transferred elsewhere (see TRANSFER EARNINGS).

See AVERAGE COST, (SHORT-RUN), MARGINAL COST, ECONOMIC RENT.

Quesnay, Francois (1694–1774), French surgeon whose economic writings helped to lay the basis for the physiocratic school of thought (see PHYSIOCRACY). Quesnay suggested that agriculture was the source of wealth, with the productive class (tenant farmers) creating an economic surplus over and above what they need for their own subsistence. This 'net product' is then available to meet the needs of landowners, and the artisans and merchants. Quesnay wrote *Tableau Économique* (1758), a work designed to show how the net product is produced and circulates between farmers, landlords and merchants, which was, in effect, an INPUT-OUTPUT table.

queueing, *n.* the delays caused to customers waiting for service. Where numerous service channels are provided customers will experience few delays even when many customers arrive simultaneously for service. On the other hand, providing numerous service channels involves large labour costs, as in the case of supermarket checkout staff or telephone operators; or large investment in physical facilities, such as tanker berths or airport runways. Queueing models employing statistical techniques can be used to analyse queues and to balance the cost of resources used to provide service against the cost of the time lost by customers while waiting for service. See also SIMULATION.

quota, *n.* an administrative device to limit (a) output or (b) trade.

(a) Under a producer's CARTEL arrangement each supplier is given a fixed output to produce. Quotas are used by the cartel to establish monopoly prices by ensuring that the total of the firms' output quotas is restricted relative to market demand.

(b) Under a trade quota system, the government directly restricts the volume of permissible IMPORTS to a specified maximum level (the *import quota*) in order to protect domestic industries against foreign competition. As a protectionist device, a quota is much more effective than TARIFFS, especially when import demand is price-inelastic (when import demand is price-inelastic, increasing import prices has little effect on the volume of imports). In these cases the only certain way of limiting imports are physical controls. See also PROTECTIONISM.

quota sample, *n.* a form of STRATIFIED SAMPLE in which the interviewer or sampler selects items himself in proportion to the relative size of each sub-group within the total POPULATION. Quota samples are frequently used in market research, opinion polls and other statistical survey work because they are generally quicker and cheaper than RANDOM SAMPLES.

quoted company, *n.* a public JOINT-STOCK COMPANY whose shares are traded either on the main STOCK EXCHANGE or related secondary markets such as the UNLISTED-SECURITIES MARKET. See LISTED COMPANY.

R

R and D, see RESEARCH AND DEVELOPMENT.

random sample, *n.* a SAMPLE selected by chance in which every item in the POPULATION has an equal chance of being included. Compare QUOTA SAMPLE, STRATIFIED SAMPLE.

random walk, *n.* the statistical requirement that, given the same distribution parameters (MEAN and VARIANCE, for example), successive decisions over time are independent and taken from the same distribution. In terms of SHARE prices, for example, Kendall observed that share prices 'wandered' in a random fashion. The share prices follow a 'random walk' because successive changes in value are independent. This means that the probability of a share price increasing or decreasing in value is equal. This random-walk behaviour of share prices has been incorporated into the CAPITAL-ASSET PRICING MODEL in the form of NONSYSTEMATIC RISK. The EFFICIENT-MARKETS HYPOTHESIS, in its weak form, asserts that investors, because they are in a perfectly competitive market, have taken account of the SYSTEMATIC RISK (the risk concerned with the economy in general) in the share prices. The shocks which occur through non-systematic risk are randomly generated indicating an equal likelihood of increasing or decreasing values which can be eliminated by holding a well-diversified PORTFOLIO.

range, *n.* a measure of variation within a group of numerical observations, that is, the difference between the largest observation and the smallest observation. For example, if five products had prices of £5, £4, £3, £2 and £1, then the range of prices would be £5–£1 = £4. The range provides a quick indication of the variability of a set of data, though it is not a very accurate indication because it considers only the two extreme values in the group and so ignores the dispersion of the remaining observations which lie between the extremes.

See also AVERAGE DEVIATION, STANDARD DEVIATION.

rank correlation coefficient, *n.* a measure of the strength of relationship between pairs of sample observations, based on their ordinal ranking within the sample rather than their precise numerical values. If there were a perfect positive relationship between two variables X and Y ($r = +1$) then the largest value of X should be associated with the largest value of Y; the second-largest value of X should be linked with the second-largest value of Y and so on. Any departure from these rankings would show a weaker relationship between X and Y, reflected in a smaller CORRELATION COEFFICIENT. See also NONPARAMETRIC STATISTICS.

ratchet effect, *n.* an effect directly analogous to an everyday mechanical ratchet, whereby having gone forward one notch the mechanism will not move backwards. The ratchet effect exists in a number of areas within economics, most notably CONSUMPTION, INFLATION and WAGES. With consumption for example, it has been argued that when a household's income falls, that household tries very hard to maintain its consumption at its previous highest level. This means people will utilize their savings or borrow to maintain their previous levels of consumption expenditure. Once income rises again households move forward to attain a higher plateau of consumption. The CONSUMPTION FUNCTION is thus not reversible. See also PERMANENT-INCOME HYPOTHESIS.

rate of exchange, see EXCHANGE RATE.

rate of interest, *n.* the price of LOAN CAPITAL. The cheaper the cost of borrowing money, the more money will be demanded by households and businesses for CONSUMPTION and INVESTMENT purposes respectively. The higher the rate of interest the greater the supply of loanable funds. The 'equilibrium' rate of interest is determined by the intersection of the demand for (D_m), and supply of (S_m), loanable funds – interest rate R in Fig. 165a on page 442. In theory, the monetary authorities can control the rate of interest by changes in the MONEY SUPPLY, and through the rate of interest the level of total spending (aggregate demand) in the economy. If the money supply is increased from S_m to S_m^1 as in Fig. 165b, the effect would be to lower the equilibrium rate of interest from R to R^1.

There is some controversy about the interest sensitivity of the demand for money and supply of money schedules. Keynesians (see KEYNESIAN ECONOMICS) would argue that saving is largely a function of the level of income rather than the rate of interest so that the supply of loanable funds is relatively interest-inelastic. Keynesians also argue that investment plans are primarily determined by businessmens' expectations about future levels of economic activity, with the cost of capital being of secondary importance, so that the demand for loanable funds is also relatively interest inelastic. This means that even quite large changes in interest rates are unlikely to have much effect upon the amounts of

RATE OF INTEREST

(a)

(b)

Fig. 165. **Rate of interest**. See main entry.

money demanded and supplied, and thus upon levels of consumer and investment spending. By contrast, monetarists (see MONETARISM) would argue that both the supply of and demand for loanable funds are relatively interest elastic so that only small changes in interest rates can have a large effect on consumer and investment spending.

See MONEY SUPPLY/SPENDING LINKAGES, EFFECTIVE RATE OF INTEREST, MONEY DEMAND SCHEDULE, MONEY SUPPLY SCHEDULE, MARGINAL EFFICIENCY OF CAPITAL/INVESTMENT, BASE RATE, DISCOUNT RATE.

rate of return, *n.* the PROFITS earned by a business, measured as a percentage of the ASSETS employed in the business.

See NORMAL PROFIT, ABOVE-NORMAL PROFIT, RATE-OF-RETURN REGULATION, RETURN ON CAPITAL-EMPLOYED.

rate-of-return regulation, *n.* the stipulation by the government of maximum permitted levels of PROFIT accruing to a MONOPOLY supplier. Profit regulation is commonly used in the US to control the pricing policies of (privately owned) PUBLIC UTILITIES. In the UK the government also sets financial targets for public utilities (which generally take the form of nationalized industries) requiring them to earn a target rate of return on their investments. See NATIONALIZATION.

rates, *n.* the local property TAXES paid by businesses and households that finance the provision of local services alongside central government taxes.

rational behaviour, see ECONOMIC MAN.

rational-expectations hypothesis, *n.* a HYPOTHESIS that suggests that firms and individuals predict future events without bias and with full access to relevant information at the time the decision is to be made. Only 'new' information will have an effect on EXPECTATIONS or behaviour.

Business expenditure on investment and stocks is affected greatly by the expectations that businessmen have of the future. These expectations, for instance, are major contributory elements in determining the BUSINESS CYCLE. If businessmen operated under conditions of total knowledge, then the business cycle in its present form would cease to exist. Expectations play a major part in wage-bargaining whereby each side (employers and employees) have to anticipate future events such as the rate of inflation. MONEY ILLUSION would not exist and employment would be based on real wages at all times.

From a statistical point of view the hypothesis does not assert that expectations are always accurate. Forecasting errors will occur but such errors will have specific properties of being neither biased nor predictable. Expectations in essence, take the form of a PROBABILITY DISTRIBUTION with a MEAN and a VARIANCE, although it is with the former that the hypothesis is primarily concerned.

The rational-expectation model is perhaps more applicable to markets approaching perfect competition and is rather less successful when applied to modern macroeconomic problems.

See also ECONOMIC MAN.

rationalization, *n.* the reorganization of an industry (or firm) in order

443

to enable it to use its resources more efficiently. Rationalization usually involves the closure of high-cost plants (either through the merging of firms or their exit from the industry) which then allows output to be concentrated in plants of MINIMUM EFFICIENT SCALE and enables a better 'balance' to be achieved between industry supply and demand. See also PRODUCTIVE EFFICIENCY.

Fig. 166. **Rationing**. See main entry.

rationing, *n.* a physical method of allocating a product which is in short supply relative to demand (EXCESS DEMAND). In a free market this situation would not arise – the excess demand would be 'choked off' by an increase in the price of the product (see EQUILIBRIUM PRICE). But if the price is fixed below its equilibrium rate (for example, by the government wishing to hold down the prices of key products such as food) the use of ration tickets provides one practical means of allocating the available supply between consumers on an equitable basis.

In Fig. 166, for example, if the price of a product is fixed by the government at O_r then it is necessary to ration the amount of output which producers are willing to supply, OQ_r, at this price amongst consumers who are demanding the greater amount of OQ_s.

See also BLACK MARKET, PRICE CONTROLS.

real balance effect or **Pigou effect,** *n.* the mechanism by which an increase in the REAL VALUE of MONEY balances leads to an increase in the level of AGGREGATE DEMAND.

Assume wages and prices are perfectly flexible (both upward and downward) in an economy which is at less than full employment. A decrease in wages and prices increases the real value of a household's wealth. Asset wealth (e.g. land, durable goods) decreases in line with other prices so that real wealth in asset terms remains constant. Other wealth is in the form of cash holdings (the obverse being debt, or negative wealth) so that, to the extent that money maintains its original PURCHASING POWER, a decrease in price will increase a household's wealth thus stimulating consumption.

If the Pigou mechanism occurred at the point of full employment, an increase in real money wealth would lead to greater consumer demand. This could not be satisfied because the economy is already operating at full employment. Prices would therefore increase until real money balances were restored to their original level.

The Pigou effect is probably of mainly theoretical interest for trade unions would clearly resist any decrease in nominal wage rates and try to at least maintain *real* wage rates.

real balances, *n.* the real PURCHASING POWER of MONEY balances held. The true value of money lies not in its nominal denomination but in its ability to purchase goods to satisfy wants. If prices and incomes both doubled the real value of money remains constant. See REAL VALUES, REAL BALANCE EFFECT.

real income, see REAL WAGES.

real values, *n.* the measurement of an economic aggregate (for example GROSS DOMESTIC PRODUCT corrected for changes in the PRICE LEVEL over time; that is, expressing the value in terms of constant prices. Thus, Fig. 167 shows that the UK's GDP (real income) declined in real terms between 1980 and 1981, whereas using current, INFLATION-affected prices, GDP is shown to have increased. See GNP DEFLATOR.

UK Gross domestic product

	Constant (1980) prices £ billion	Current prices £ billion
1980	226.9	226.9
1981	224.0	250.0

Fig. 167. **Real values**. See main entry.

real wages or **real income,** *n.* the MONEY WAGE rate (W) divided by the general PRICE LEVEL of products. Notationally this is written W/P. If wages and prices both rise by 10% from an initial index number of, say, 100, the original ratio of W/P is 100/100 = 1, and the new ratio of 110/110 (i.e., 100 plus 10% rise for both W and P) is also 1. An increase in real wages occurs where W rises more quickly than P, or P remains constant.

In the latter instance, a rise in W of 10% would give the ratio 110/100 = 1.1, thus making the wage earner 10% better off because he is capable of purchasing 10% more products with his new wage.

The analysis of real and money wages in relation to employment and output is a continuing central theme within economics although it is generally thought to be real wages which determines the level of employment rather than money wages.

See CLASSICAL ECONOMICS, KEYNESIAN ECONOMICS, MONEY ILLUSION.

recession, *n.* a phase of the BUSINESS CYCLE characterized by a modest downturn in the level of economic activity (ACTUAL GROSS NATIONAL PRODUCT). Real output and investment fall, resulting in rising UNEMPLOYMENT. A recession is usually caused by a fall in AGGREGATE DEMAND, and provided that the authorities evoke expansionary FISCAL POLICY and MONETARY POLICY it can be reversed.

See DEFLATIONARY GAP, DEMAND MANAGEMENT, STABILIZATION POLICY.

reciprocal, *n.* the inverse function of a stated value. Frequently written as a negative exponential such as:

$$Y = ax^{-1}$$

If $a = 3$ and $x = 5$, the equation becomes:

$$Y = 3.\frac{1}{5}$$

Therefore 1/5 is the reciprocal of 5. The numerator becomes 1 and the denominator the value in question, in this case, 5.

recommended retail price, *n.* the practice of manufacturers in indicating a resale PRICE for their products. Unlike RESALE-PRICE MAINTENANCE, the recommended retail price is seen merely as acting as a 'reference point' for retailers in setting their own price. Subject to competitive conditions the actual price paid by consumers is in most cases much less than the recommended price. See LIST PRICE.

recovery, *n.* a phase of the BUSINESS CYCLE characterized by an upturn in the level of economic activity (ACTUAL GROSS NATIONAL PRODUCT). Real output and investment increase and UNEMPLOYMENT falls. A recovery in economic activity is usually dependent on there being an increase in AGGREGATE DEMAND which may come about autonomously or be induced by expansionary FISCAL POLICY and MONETARY POLICY.

See also DEMAND MANAGEMENT, STABILIZATION POLICY.

rectangular hyperbola, *n.* a curve of the mathematical form $Y = a/x$, the area under which is constant at any point along it. The curve is

Fig. 168. **Rectangular hyperbola.** At point a, the area beneath the curve is $OP_1 \times OQ_1$. At point b the area under the curve is $OP_2 \times OQ_2$, and at point c the area under the curve is $OP_3 \times OQ_3$. The area of each rectangle is exactly the same as any other, and each would give the same TOTAL REVENUE (price × quantity).

asymptotic to the axes, that is, the curve approaches but never touches the axes.

For example, a DEMAND CURVE of unitary PRICE–ELASTICITY OF DEMAND (with an elasticity of 1) is a rectangular hyperbola as shown in Fig. 168.

redeemable financial security, *n.* a financial security such as a DEBENTURE or PREFERENCE SHARE which is issued for a fixed period of time and repayable on maturity.

redeployment of labour, *n.* the movement of LABOUR from one firm to another, or from one industry to another, usually made necessary by technical change (the introduction of labour-saving machinery, for example) or by structural change (the decline of an industry, for example). Redeployment often requires a high degree of labour MOBILITY both geographically and in terms of acquiring new job skills. See also RESOURCE ALLOCATION.

rediscounting, *n.* the purchase and sale of BILLS and BONDS between their issue and redemption dates. For example, if a bond with a nominal value of £1,000 redeemable in one year's time is sold initially for £900 (giving a £100 discount on its formal redemption value), then it might be resold or rediscounted for £950 after 6 months. See also DISCOUNT, DISCOUNT MARKET.

redistribution-of-income principle of taxation, *n.* the principle that the TAXATION system, together with the provision of state welfare

447

programmes, should be used to benefit poorer households at the expense of richer households. Fig. 169 shows the extent of income redistribution brought about by taxation and state spending. Thus, the poorest 20% of the population receives only 0.4% of total original income, but after taxation and state benefits they receive 6.9% of total final income. See also PROGRESSIVE TAXATION, ABILITY–TO–PAY PRINCIPLE OF TAXATION.

Quintile groups of households	Original income %	Final income %
Bottom fifth	0.3	7.1
Second fifth	7.1	12.1
Third fifth	17.5	17.5
Fourth fifth	27.5	24.3
Top fifth	48.6	39.0
	100.0	100.0

Fig. 169. **Redistribution-of-income principle of taxation**. The personal distribution of original and final income in the UK, 1984. Final income = original income less taxes paid, plus state spending on education, health, social security benefits. Source: *Social Trends*, 1987.

reducing–balance method, see DEPRECIATION (2).

redundancy, *n.* the loss of jobs by employees brought about by company RATIONALIZATION and reorganization which results from falling demand or PRODUCTIVITY improvement.

reflation, *n.* an increase in the level of NATIONAL INCOME and output. A reflation is often deliberately brought about by the authorities in order to secure FULL EMPLOYMENT and to increase the rate of ECONOMIC GROWTH. Instruments of reflationary policy include fiscal measures (for example, tax cuts) and monetary measures (for example, lower interest rates).

See also FISCAL POLICY, MONETARY POLICY, DEFLATIONARY GAP, DEMAND MANAGEMENT, STABILIZATION POLICY.

refusal to supply, *n.* a type of RESTRICTIVE TRADE PRACTICE whereby a seller deliberately withholds supplies to customers as a means of enforcing EXCLUSIVE DEALING, TIE–IN SALES arrangements, and RESALE PRICE MAINTENANCE. See MONOPOLY POLICY, OFFICE OF FAIR TRADING.

regional development grant, *n.* an instrument of REGIONAL POLICY used in Britain as a means of encouraging new INVESTMENT in DEVELOPMENT AREAS. Such grants are given automatically towards the capital costs of new buildings and works, plant and machinery.

regional policy, *n.* a policy concerned with removing significant imbalances between the regions of an economy in respect of UNEMPLOY-MENT rates and levels of INCOME PER HEAD. The main approach adopted is that of spreading industrial activity around the regions so as to avoid unemployment of labour and capital resources in the DEPRESSED AREAS and undue congestion in the more prosperous ones. A particular emphasis of regional policy is the regeneration of areas which have fallen into industrial decline by encouraging new firms and industries to locate and invest in these areas (the 'inward investment' approach, which involves taking work to the workers). The rationale behind this approach is that the problems of the depressed areas stem largely from overspecialization in industries which have gone into decline (for example, coal mining in South Wales, shipbuilding in North-East England, cotton in Lancashire, etc.), rather than any fundamental economic disadvantage. Accordingly, what is required is a diversifica-tion of the industrial base of such areas so as to provide new employment opportunities, which increases investment-boosting local spending and, via MULTIPLIER effects, increasing income levels.

The 'inward investment' approach to regional policy is implemented in three main ways:

(a) the provision of financial inducements (investment grants, tax relief, rent and rate-free factories, etc.) to firms prepared to locate in designated DEVELOPMENT AREAS.

(b) the use of physical controls on factory and office buildings to prevent firms from locating to any great extent outside these develop-ment areas

(c) investment by the government in INFRASTRUCTURE capital, particularly good road and rail networks and general amenities.

Critics of this approach to regional policy argue that 'forcing' firms to locate in areas which might not suit them and 'subsidizing' their activities might impair economic efficiency. However, there is little evidence to suggest this has been a serious matter.

A possible alternative approach, that of encouraging people to move out of depressed regions (the 'taking the workers to the work' approach) has not found favour because not only does it tend to accentuate the problems of the depressed areas themselves (the loss of skilled workers, reduced local spending and incomes, etc.), but it also creates difficulties for 'receiving' areas, particularly if they are already over-congested with respect to housing, schools, etc.

See also INTERMEDIATE AREA, INDUSTRIAL DEVELOPMENT CERTIFICATE, REGIONAL DEVELOPMENT GRANT, REGIONAL SELECTIVE ASSISTANCE, ENTER-

PRISE ZONE, EUROPEAN REGIONAL DEVELOPMENT FUND, STRUCTURAL UNEMPLOYMENT, DEINDUSTRIALIZATION, LOCATION OF INDUSTRY, FIRM LOCATION.

regional selective assistance, *n.* an instrument of REGIONAL POLICY used in Britain as a means of encouraging new INVESTMENT in DEVELOPMENT AREAS and INTERMEDIATE AREAS. Such grants are allocated on a discretionary basis to cover capital and training costs for projects which meet job-creation criteria.

registered company, *n.* a JOINT-STOCK COMPANY that is registered in the UK with the COMPANY REGISTRAR.

Registrar of Companies, see COMPANY REGISTRAR.

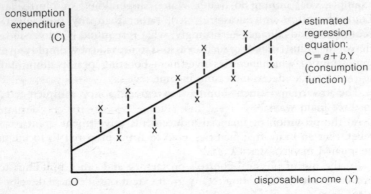

Fig. 170. **Regression analysis.** See main entry.

regression analysis, *n.* a statistical technique for estimating the EQUATION which best fits sets of observations of DEPENDENT VARIABLES and INDEPENDENT VARIABLES, so generating the best estimate of the true underlying relationship between these variables. From this estimated equation it is then possible to predict what the (unknown) dependent variable(s) will be for a given value of the (known) independent variable(s).

Taking the simplest example of a linear equation with just one independent variable and a dependent variable (disposable income and consumption expenditure), the problem is to fit a straight line to a set of data consisting of pairs of observations of income (Y) and consumption (C). Fig. 170 shows such a set of paired observations plotted in graph form, and we need to find the equation of the line which provides the best possible fit to our data, for this line will yield the best predictions of the dependent variable. The line of best fit to the data should be chosen so that the sum of the squares of the vertical deviations (distances) between the points and the line should be a minimum. This method of *ordinary least squares* is applied in most regressions. The *goodness of fit* of the regression line to the sample observations is measured by the CORRELATION COEFFICIENT.

In arithmetic terms the line depicted in Fig. 170 is a linear equation of the form:

$$C = a + bY$$

where the coefficients of the equation, a and b, are estimates (based on single observations) of the true population parameters. These constants, a and b, obtained with the method of ordinary least squares, are called the estimated regression coefficients, and once their numerical values have been determined then they can be used to predict values of the dependent variable (C) from values of the independent variable (Y). For example, if the estimated regression coefficient of a and b were 1,000 and 0.9 respectively then the regression equation would be $C = 1,000 + 0.9$ Y and we could predict that for a disposable income of £10,000, consumer expenditure would be:

$$C = a + bY$$
$$C = 1,000 + 0.9Y$$
$$= 1,000 + 0.9 \ 10,000$$
$$= 10,000$$

The regression coefficient of the slope of the linear regression, b, is particularly important in economics for it shows the change in the dependent variable (here consumption) associated with a unit change in the independent variable (here income). For example, in this case a b value of 0.9 suggests that consumers will spend 90% of any extra disposable income.

The regression equation will not provide an exact prediction of the dependent variable for any given value of the independent variable, because the regression coefficients estimated from sample observations are merely the best estimate of the true population parameters, and are subject to chance variations. Consequently it is possible to construct a CONDITIONAL DISTRIBUTION showing likely values of the dependent variable (C) predicted by the regression equation for a given value of the independent variable (Y). The standard deviation of this conditional distribution gives an indication of the limits between which we would expect consumption expenditure to fall for a given level of disposable income. This is reflected in a statistic called the STANDARD ERROR of the estimate which shows estimated limits within which we could expect C to fall for a given Y with a predetermined probability of say 0.99 or 0.95. For example, if the standard error in the above example for a 0.95 probability were, say, 500, then we could be confident that on 95% of occasions the true consumption figure for an income of £10,000 would lie within the range:

$$£10,000 - 500 \text{ and } £10,000 + 500$$

To acknowledge the imperfections in any estimated regression equation based on a sample in depicting the true underlying relationship in the population as a whole, the regression equation is generally written as:

$$C = a + bY + e$$

with the addition of a *residual* or *error term*, *e*, to reflect the residual effect of chance variations and the effects of other independent variables (such as, say, interest rates on consumer credit) which influence consumption spending but which are not explicitly included in the regression equation.

Where it is felt that more than one independent variable has a significant effect upon the dependent variable, then the technique of *multiple linear regression* will be employed. The technique involves formulating a multiple linear regression equation involving two or more independent variables, such as:

$$C = a + bY + dI + e$$

where I is the interest rate on consumer credit and *d* is an additional regression coefficient attached to this extra independent variable. Estimation of this multiple linear regression equation by the method of ordinary least squares involves fitting a three-dimensional plane or surface to a set of sample observations of consumer spending, disposable income and interest rates in such a way as to minimize the squared deviations of the observations from the plane. In arithmetic terms the sample observations can be used to generate numerical estimates of the three regression coefficients (*a*, *b* and *d*) in the above equation.

Where the underlying relationships between independent and dependent variables are not linear, then techniques of linear regression cannot be applied. However, where relationships are curvilinear, then they can often be transformed into linear relationships by such devices as taking the natural logarithms of the variables, in order to make them amenable to linear regression analysis. See also IDENTIFICATION PROBLEMS.

regressive taxation, *n.* a structure of TAXATION in which tax is levied at a decreasing rate as INCOME rises. This form of taxation takes a greater proportion of tax from the low-income taxpayer than from the high-income taxpayer. Indirect taxes such as value added tax or excise duty become regressive when taken as a proportion of total net income. For example, if an item costs £100 and value added tax is 15%, then £15 in relation to £200 per week net pay $(7\frac{1}{2}\%)$ is greater than £15 to another person earning £600 per week net $(2\frac{1}{2}\%)$. The burden of taxation is therefore proportionately greater on the less affluent members of society and cannot be considered an equitable tax. Compare PROGRESSIVE TAXATION, PROPORTIONAL TAXATION.

See also ABILITY-TO-PAY PRINCIPLE OF TAXATION, INCIDENCE OF TAXATION, REDISTRIBUTION-OF-INCOME PRINCIPLE OF TAXATION.

relative-concentration measure, see CONCENTRATION MEASURES.

relative-income hypothesis, *n.* the HYPOTHESIS that it is not a person's or nation's absolute income which matters but his or its relative income. If this is so, then since all individuals or countries cannot become *relatively* better off, the pursuit of growth for growth's sake becomes futile. See also CONSPICUOUS CONSUMPTION.

relative price, see INDIFFERENCE CURVE, ISOQUANT CURVE.

relativities, *n.* any comparisons between the WAGES or SALARIES of workers in the same firm, the same industry, or between different industries. Such relativities reflect differences in training requirements, skill levels and responsibilities. See also WAGE DIFFERENTIALS.

rent, *n.* the periodic payments made to the owners of ASSETS for the use of their land or other assets as FACTORS OF PRODUCTION. In aggregate terms, rents are a source of income and they are included as a part of NATIONAL INCOME. See also ECONOMIC RENT, QUASI-RENT, NATIONAL-INCOME ACCOUNTS.

replacement cost, *n.* the cost of replacing an ASSET (such as an item of machinery). Unlike HISTORIC COST – the original cost of acquiring an asset – replacement cost makes due allowance for the effects of INFLATION in increasing asset prices over time.

See also REVALUATION PROVISION, INFLATION ACCOUNTING, APPRECIATION (2).

replacement investment, *n.* the INVESTMENT that is undertaken to replace a firm's plant and equipment or an economy's CAPITAL STOCK which has become worn out or obsolete. See CAPITAL CONSUMPTION.

representative firm, *n*. a concept devised by Alfred MARSHALL for use in market analysis. The representative firm is a hypothetical business organization rather than an actual production unit. Because it is an abstract concept, it is not based on a 'typical' business unit of the time and is representative primarily with respect to average costs rather than firm size. Marshall argued that most firms are able to take advantage of INTERNAL ECONOMIES OF SCALE to reduce costs, which in turn leads to growth of individual firms and of the industry itself. In addition, as firms grow larger so EXTERNAL ECONOMIES OF SCALE become increasingly important. The representative firm has middling access to such economies.

Marshall encountered a number of difficulties in his analysis and reverted to one of the most famous analogies in economics, that of a tree representing a firm. Firms grow from seedlings through youth, maturity and finally die, while new firms replace the output of the dying firms. These firms are thus indicative of the supply curve for the whole industry. The industry may therefore be in equilibrium (the forest) but each of the constituent firms (the trees) is not required to be so. The representative firm can therefore be seen as the typical tree in the forest.

See also MONOPOLISTIC COMPETITION.

resale price maintenance (rpm), *n*. a type of RESTRICTIVE TRADE PRACTICE whereby a supplier prescribes the PRICE at which all retailers are to sell the product to final buyers. The main objection to rpm centres on the fact that it restricts or eliminates retail price competition and by prescribing uniform retail margins it serves to cushion inefficient retailers.

The practice of rpm (except in very special circumstances) was made illegal in the UK in 1964 and this led to the rapid expansion of mass retailers such as supermarket chains.

See also MONOPOLY POLICY, OFFICE OF FAIR TRADING, RECOMMENDED RETAIL PRICES.

research and development (R and D), *n*. any scientific investigation leading to the discovery of new techniques and products (INVENTION) and their commercial application (INNOVATION), together with the refinement and improvement of existing technologies and products.

R and D is both an important factor contributing to the competitive strength of the individual firm and, nationally, in promoting a higher rate of ECONOMIC GROWTH.

See TECHNOLOGICAL PROGRESSIVENESS, PRODUCT PERFORMANCE, PRODUCT LIFE-CYCLE.

reserve asset ratio or **liquidity ratio,** *n.* the proportion of a COMMERCIAL BANK's total assets which it keeps in the form of liquid assets to meet day-to-day currency withdrawals by its customers and other financial commitments. In Britain assets held as part of a bank's reserve asset ratio include: TILL MONEY (notes and coins), CALL MONEY (short term deposits with the DISCOUNT MARKET), BALANCES WITH THE BANK OF ENGLAND, and near-mature BILLS OF EXCHANGE and TREASURY BILLS.

The ratio of liquid assets to total assets held can be dictated by reasons of commercial prudence to maintain customers' confidence in the banks' ability to repay their deposits on demand. This is a matter of individual discretion. It is more usually the case, however, that the monetary authorities prescribe mandatory and uniform minimum reserve-asset ratios for the banking sector. This is because the reserve-asset ratio of the banking sector determines the amount of new bank deposits that can be created and, hence, has an important influence on the size of the MONEY SUPPLY.

See also BANK DEPOSIT CREATION, MONETARY POLICY, OPEN MARKET OPERATIONS.

reserves, *n.* **1.** any additional claims of company shareholders which reflect increases in the value of company ASSETS in the BALANCE SHEET. Revenue reserves arise when some after-tax profit is retained in the business to finance the acquisition of extra assets, rather than being paid out as DIVIDENDS. Capital reserves arise when company assets such as buildings are revalued to reflect their increased market value due to inflation. Reserves serve to increase SHAREHOLDERS' CAPITAL EMPLOYED in a company. See also RETAINED PROFITS, CAPITALIZATION ISSUE, RETENTIONS RATIO, APPRECIATION (2), REVALUATION PROVISION, INFLATION ACCOUNTING. **2.** the proportion of a bank's total assets which it keeps in the form of liquid assets. See RESERVE-ASSET RATIO. **3.** monetary assets held by countries to finance balance of payments deficits. See INTERNATIONAL RESERVES.

reserve tranche, see INTERNATIONAL MONETARY FUND.

residual, see REGRESSION ANALYSIS.

residual unemployment, *n.* the UNEMPLOYMENT of certain members of society who cannot locate economically viable employment even in times of full employment. The costs of employing a severely handicapped person, for example, may far outweigh the productivity obtained. Residual unemployment may be reduced in terms of numbers by government subsidies to offset a firm's costs of employment but such unemployment is not easily removed.

resource allocation, *n.* the allocation of an economy's FACTORS OF PRODUCTION between alternative uses in line with patterns of consumer demand (which in turn reflect a given size and distribution of national income). Resources are optimally allocated when the proportions in which factor inputs are combined to produce GOODS and SERVICES reflect their relative costs so as to minimize costs of production, and when the output of goods and services fully reflects the distribution of consumer preferences as between those goods and services. (See PARETO OPTIMALITY.)

More specifically, resources are optimally allocated when in each market the price paid for the good or service fully reflects the *lowest* economic cost of supplying it.

See ALLOCATIVE EFFICIENCY, PRODUCTIVE EFFICIENCY, DISTRIBUTIVE EFFICIENCY, MOBILITY, PRICE SYSTEM, THEORY OF MARKETS.

resources, see FACTORS OF PRODUCTION.

restraint of trade, see RESTRICTIVE TRADE AGREEMENT, RESTRICTIVE TRADE PRACTICE.

restrictive labour practice, *n.* a practice, usually operated by a TRADE UNION in the interests of its members, that has the effect of reducing productive efficiency. For example, a union may insist that a specified number of men work on a particular activity even though this involves employing more men than is strictly required to undertake the activity efficiently (overmanning); different unions operating in the same plant may lay down demarcation rules specifying what tasks their members can work on and what they cannot, which has the effect of limiting job interchangeability; unions may resist the installation of new machinery, especially if this results in job losses. See also PRODUCTIVITY, X-INEFFICIENCY.

Restrictive Practices Court (RPC), *n.* a regulatory body responsible, in part, for the implementation of UK MONOPOLY POLICY. The basic task of the RPC is to investigate and report on cases of RESTRICTIVE TRADE AGREEMENTS, INFORMATION AGREEMENTS and RESALE PRICE MAINTENANCE referred to it by the OFFICE OF FAIR TRADING to determine whether or not they operate against the public interest.

The public interest can be broadly equated with the cause of promoting effective competition in the sense that the legislation in this area contains a presumption that competition is generally preferable to COLLUSION. In the case of restrictive agreements and information agreements all such agreements are presumed to operate *against* the public interest unless the parties to them can prove otherwise by satisfying one or more of eight 'gateways' (that the agreement is beneficial, for example, because it improves efficiency, increases exports, or creates employment), and only then if the benefits, on balance, outweigh any detriments. Agreements found by the Court to be contrary to the public interest are automatically null and void.

Very few agreements have been successfully defended; less than 15 in fact. The vast majority of agreements (over 4,000) registered with the OFT have been abandoned voluntarily without a formal Court trial. Thus, on the surface the attack on collusion between suppliers appears to have been highly successful. However, there is growing evidence to suggest that many agreements have simply been driven underground and are now being operated 'secretly'.

restrictive trade agreement, *n.* a form of COLLUSION between suppliers aimed at removing competition wholly or in part. For the most part such agreements concentrate on fixing common prices and discounts, but may also stipulate production quotas, market-sharing and coordinated capacity adjustments. The main objection to restrictive agreements is that they tend to raise prices above competitive levels and serve to protect inefficient suppliers from the rigours of competition. MONOPOLY POLICY in most countries takes a tough line on restrictive agreements, either prohibiting them outright, or only allowing them to continue in exceptional circumstances.

See also OFFICE OF FAIR TRADING, RESTRICTIVE PRACTICES COURT.

restrictive trade practice, *n.* a means of reducing or eliminating competition between rival suppliers. Examples of restrictive practices include EXCLUSIVE DEALING, REFUSAL TO SUPPLY, PRICE SQUEEZING, TIE-IN SALES, AGGREGATED REBATES, RESALE PRICE MAINTENANCE and LOSS LEADING. As part of MONOPOLY POLICY such practices are either prohibited outright, or allowed to continue only if they can be shown to operate in the 'public interest'.

See also OFFICE OF FAIR TRADING, MONOPOLIES AND MERGERS COMMISSION.

retailing, *n.* the purchasing of products from manufacturers or independent wholesalers, stockholding, physical distribution and the re-selling of products to final consumers. These functions are performed by a variety of retailing organizations ranging from single shops to multiple-branch CHAIN STORES, including SUPERMARKETS, DEPARTMENT

STORES, SPECIALIST SHOPS, DISCOUNT STORES, COOPERATIVES and DO-IT-YOURSELF STORES.

retail price index, see PRICE INDEX.

retained profits or **undistributed profits,** *n.* any after-tax PROFITS that are reinvested (*ploughed back*) in the firm rather than being paid out to the owners of the company in DIVIDENDS. Such retained earnings form a valuable source of capital to be INVESTED in additional FIXED ASSETS and CURRENT ASSETS. They serve to swell the value of the company to the shareholders and increase SHAREHOLDERS' CAPITAL-EMPLOYED by adding to revenue RESERVES. See also RETENTIONS RATIO.

retentions ratio, *n.* an accounting measure of the proportions of PROFIT distributed to shareholders and ploughed back into the business, which expresses DIVIDENDS declared/paid as a percentage of net profit after tax and interest. See also RESERVES, RETAINED PROFITS.

return on capital-employed, *n.* an accounting measure of a firm's PROFITABILITY, which expresses the firm's PROFITS for a time period as a percentage of its period-end capital employed. Generally, profit is taken before deduction of tax and is related to long-term capital employed, though broader comparisons are possible, which relate profit before tax and interest payments to all ASSETS employed, and narrower comparisons which relate after-tax profit to shareholders' capital. A firm's return on capital depends upon its PROFIT-TO-SALES RATIO and its SALES-TO-CAPITAL-EMPLOYED RATIO.

Under MONOPOLY POLICY, return on capital-employed is used to ascertain whether a firm is earning NORMAL PROFIT or ABOVE-NORMAL PROFIT. See also ALLOCATIVE EFFICIENCY, PUBLIC INTEREST.

returns to scale, *n.* the relationship between OUTPUT of a product and the quantities of FACTOR INPUTS used to produce it in the LONG RUN. Where, for example, doubling the quantity of factor inputs used results in a doubling of output then constant 'returns to scale' are experienced. Where ECONOMIES OF SCALE are present a doubling of factor inputs results in a more than proportionate increase in output. By contrast, where DISECONOMIES OF SCALE are encountered a doubling of factor inputs results in a less than proportionate increase in output.

returns to the variable factor input, *n.* the rate of change of OUTPUT within the SHORT RUN theory of supply, resulting from changes in the VARIABLE-FACTOR INPUT in a plant of a given (fixed) size. In the short run, some FACTOR INPUTS are variable but other inputs are fixed. A firm can change its rate of output only by combining more or less of the variable factors with the fixed factors; that is, by changing the proportions in

Fig. 171. **Returns to the variable factor input.** See main entry. (a) The total physical product. (b) The marginal and average physical product.

which the factor inputs are used. As more and more of a variable input is used in conjunction with a given quantity of fixed input:

(a) initially, as Fig. 171a shows, there are *increasing returns* to the variable input: output increases more than proportionately to the increase in the variable input so that the TOTAL PHYSICAL PRODUCT curve rises steadily and both MARGINAL PHYSICAL PRODUCT and AVERAGE PHYSICAL PRODUCT also increase.

(b) CONSTANT RETURNS are then experienced, with the increase in output being exactly proportional to the increase in the variable input (marginal physical product and average physical product being constant).

(c) DIMINISHING RETURNS to the variable input are then experienced (see Fig. 171b), with the increase in output being less than proportional to the increase in the variable input (the total physical product curve flattens out and both marginal physical product and average physical product decrease).

(d) finally, *negative returns* may be experienced with an increase in the variable input bringing about a fall in total output (the total physical product curve turns down and both marginal physical product and average physical product become negative).

revaluation, *n.* an administered increase in the value of one CURRENCY against other currencies under a FIXED EXCHANGE-RATE SYSTEM, as in Fig. 172 on page 460. The objectives of a revaluation are to assist in the removal of a surplus in a country's BALANCE OF PAYMENTS and the excessive accumulation of INTERNATIONAL RESERVES. A revaluation

Fig. 172. **Revaluation.** A revaluation of the pound against the dollar.

makes IMPORTS cheaper and EXPORTS more expensive, thereby encouraging additional imports and lowering export demand.

How successful a revaluation is in removing a payments surplus depends on the reactions of export and import volumes to the change in relative prices, that is, the PRICE-ELASTICITY OF DEMAND for exports and imports. If these values are low, that is, demand is inelastic, trade volumes will not change very much and the revaluation may in fact make the surplus larger. On the other hand, if export and import demand is elastic then the change in trade volumes will operate to remove the surplus. BALANCE-OF-PAYMENTS EQUILIBRIUM will be restored if the sum of export and import elasticities is greater than unity (the MARSHALL-LERNER CONDITION).

See DEVALUATION, EXTERNAL-INTERNAL BALANCE MODEL.

revaluation provision, *n.* an accounting provision made for the increased cost of replacing a FIXED ASSET, over and above its HISTORIC COST. DEPRECIATION charges spread the original cost of a fixed asset over its estimated life, preventing the cost of the asset from being ignored in calculating net profit and so preventing the firm's LONG-TERM CAPITAL EMPLOYED being distributed as DIVIDENDS. However, where the REPLACEMENT COST of a fixed asset is expected to exceed its original cost, a prudent firm may withhold additional profits instead of distributing them, in anticipation of having to pay this additional sum. See INFLATION ACCOUNTING.

revealed preference theory, *n.* an alternative explanation for an individual consumer's downward-sloping DEMAND CURVE, requiring the consumer to reveal what his preferences are in given sets of

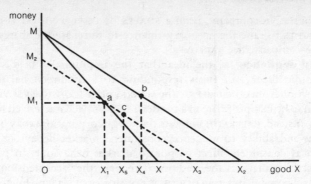

Fig. 173. **Revealed preference theory.** See main entry.

circumstances. The preferences given may be between two or more goods, but where more than two goods exist money is taken to represent all other goods for ease of graphical analysis, as in Fig. 173.

If a consumer decides he prefers a combination of money (OM_1) and good X (OX_1) he will be at point a on the BUDGET LINE (or relative price line) MX. If good X becomes cheaper so more can be had, his *real* income increases and he can move to budget line MX_2. The combination of goods the consumer prefers is now at, say, b.

However, not all the change is due to increasing real income caused by the fall in the price of good X. Some of it is due to the substitution of the now-cheaper good X for others, and this effect is always positive, that is, it is not possible to purchase less of the now-cheaper good X after the change to MX_2, than when on the budget line MX.

If the consumer's new configuration of goods at b is reduced proportionately, by introducing a hypothetical decrease in income in the form of an inward parallel shift of the budget line to position $M_2 X_3$, then the consumer will choose a new position, say, point c; the SUBSTITUTION EFFECT is from X_1 to X_5, while X_5 to X_4 is the INCOME EFFECT.

See CONSUMER EQUILIBRIUM, INDIFFERENCE CURVE, PRICE EFFECT.

revenue, *n.* the money received by a firm from selling its output of GOODS or SERVICES (SALES REVENUE), or money received by government from TAXATION. See AVERAGE REVENUE, MARGINAL REVENUE, TOTAL REVENUE.

reverse takeover, *n.* a situation in which a smaller but dynamic company wishing to expand rapidly, takes over a larger but unprogressive company, issuing SHARES or FIXED-INTEREST FINANCIAL SECURITIES to raise the necessary finance to purchase the shares of the larger company. See TAKEOVER.

revised sequence, *n.* the idea that the traditionally held view in economic theory, of FIRMS responding to a unidirectional flow of instruction from CONSUMERS in the MARKET place (CONSUMER SOVEREIGNTY), may be inappropriate in a modern economy characterized by large firms. Instead, GALBRAITH suggests that large corporations may have the means and ability to influence consumers' market behaviour just as much as consumers affect corporate market behaviour. In perfectly competitive markets the traditional theory (the 'accepted sequence') may still be valid, but in an OLIGOPOLY or MONOPOLY it is no longer valid.

Ricardo, David (1772–1823) English stockbroker who amassed a fortune before retiring early to study economics. In his *Principles of Political Economy and Taxation* (1817), Ricardo argued that the value of products is determined by the amount of labour needed to produce them, and he developed a theory of distribution to explain how this value is shared between major classes in society. Ricardo suggested that however prosperous the economy, wages could never rise above subsistence level. As workers became more prosperous they would have more children and, as these children grew up this additional labour supply would force wages down: an 'iron law of wages'.

Ricardo argued that capitalists would not benefit much from economic progress either, since competition would keep their prices down and wage payments would cut into their profits. He regarded landlords as being the only real beneficiaries from economic progress since with a finite amount of arable land and a growing population to feed, the landlords' rental income would grow and the value of their land would rise. Rising rents would raise the cost of food produced and workers would need larger wages to pay for food, eroding capitalists' profits. Ricardo's theories were used by the emerging industrialists to fight for free trade and an end to high tariffs on imported grain so as to lower food prices and keep wages low. See also ECONOMIC RENT.

ridge lines, see INDIFFERENCE MAP.

rights issue, *n.* the issue by a JOINT-STOCK COMPANY of additional SHARES to existing SHAREHOLDERS at a price which is generally a little below the current market price. Rights are issued to existing shareholders in proportion to their existing shareholdings, and a shareholder can sell his rights if he does not wish to subscribe for extra shares. Compare CAPITALIZATION ISSUE.

risk analysis, *n.* the systematic analysis of the degree of risk attaching to capital projects. Risk reflects the variability of expected future returns from a capital INVESTMENT and as such the statistical technique of PROBABILITY may be applied to assist a decision.

See also CAPITAL BUDGETING, RISK AND UNCERTAINTY, DECISION TREE.

risk and uncertainty, *n.* a situation of potential LOSS of the firm's INVESTMENT resulting from the fact that it is operating in an uncertain business environment. Certain risks are insurable (for example, the risk of fire or theft of the firm's stock), but not the firm's ability to survive and prosper. The firm itself must assume the risks of the market place: if it cannot sell its products it will go bankrupt; if it is successful it will make profits. Thus, risk-taking is to be viewed as an integral part of the process of supplying GOODS and SERVICES and in innovating new products. PROFITS, in part, are a reward for successful risk-taking.

Since managers do not know for certain what the future holds, they are forced to guess what the most likely outcome of any decision will be, effectively assigning a statistical PROBABILITY to the likelihood of future events occurring. All such estimates of the likelihood of future events occurring must, by their very nature, be subjective, though some estimates are likely to be better than others depending upon the amount of information available. Where large amounts of information are available upon which to base estimates of likelihood, so that accurate statistical probabilities can be formulated, we may talk of risk rather than uncertainty. For example, an insurance company dealing with fire insurance policies and claims for large numbers of manufacturers, will be able to compile detailed statistics about numbers of fires and the amount of damage done by each, and can use this information to predict the likelihood of a business experiencing a fire. This detailed statistical information allows the insurance company to charge manufacturers premiums for indemnifying them against fire losses and to make a profit by so doing. By contrast, a single manufacturer would find it very difficult to predict the likelihood of his premises being damaged by fire and the amount of damage, since such an event would tend to be a unique experience for him.

Faced with a possibility of fire, the manufacturer can either choose to bear the risk of losses resulting from a serious fire or can avoid the risk of fire damage by paying an insurance company a premium to bear the risk. Again, the manufacturer can take the risk that the prices of its main raw materials will be much higher next year, or it can contract now through a commodity FUTURES MARKET to buy raw materials supplies for future delivery at a fixed price.

Uncertainty, unlike risk, arises from changes which are difficult to predict or from events whose likelihood cannot be accurately estimated. Unfortunately, many management decisions fall into this category, since they are rarely repetitive and there is little past data available to act as a guide to the future. Such market uncertainty as to the likelihood and extent of losses which might arise in launching a new product, can only be gauged by managers through combining the limited data which is available with their own judgement and experience.

Managers can improve upon their subjective estimates about the future by collecting information from forecasts, market research, feasibility studies, etc., but they need to balance the cost of collecting such information against its value in improving decisions. Where information costs are prohibitive, managers may turn to various RULES OF THUMB like full–cost pricing which give reasonably good (though not optimum) decisions.

The traditional THEORY OF THE FIRM envisaged a firm armed with perfect knowledge about its future costs and revenues, making pricing and output decisions on the basis of a marginal weighting of costs and revenues. This cognitive assumption of perfect knowledge is open to criticism in the light of what appears above.

See ENTREPRENEUR, HEDGING, DECISION TREE, RISK PROFILE, SCHUMPETER.

risk capital, *n.* any business capital subscribed by an individual ENTREPRENEUR or group of ORDINARY SHAREHOLDERS which entails some risk of loss in the event of the enterprise failing. See RISK AND UNCERTAINTY.

risk premium, see RISK PROFILE.

risk profile or **risk premium,** *n.* a depiction of the attitudes towards RISK displayed by decision-makers, based on von Neumann and Morgenstern's concept of the expected UTILITY INDEX. For example, you could ask a businessman how much he would be prepared to pay to play a game of chance offering a 50/50 chance of winning £1 or nothing. If he were neutral in his attitude to risk then he might reply that he would be prepared to pay 50p to play such a game (see point A in Fig. 174). This suggests that the businessman regards 50p as being the certainty equivalent of a 50/50 chance of winning £1 or nothing. Where such a neutral attitude to risk exists the term *expected money value* is used to denote the certainty equivalent of a risk: it is found by taking the money

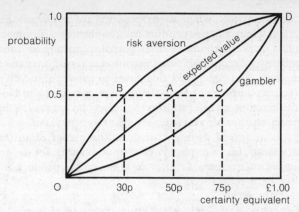

Fig. 174. **Risk profile**. See main entry.

value of each outcome and weighting it by the PROBABILITY of its occurrence (thus, $0.5 \times £1 + 0.5 \times £0 = £0.5$).

However, if the businessman were averse to risk, then when confronted with the same game offering a chance of £1 or nothing, he might be prepared to pay, say, only 30p rather than 50p to play it (see point B in Fig. 174). Here the difference between the 50p certainty equivalent based on the expected value criterion, and the 30p certainty equivalent of the cautious businessman, represents a risk premium (equal to AB in Fig. 174) which the businessman needs to induce him to take the risk. On the other hand, if the businessman were something of a gambler then he might regard the 50/50 chance of £1 or nothing as being the equivalent of, say 75p for certain (point C in Fig. 174). By offering businessmen large numbers of 50/50 chances like the one above it would be possible to construct complete risk profiles such as those shown in Fig. 174.

Attitudes to risk are not merely dependent on the personality of the decision-maker, they are also influenced by the size of the potential gains and losses involved. Where a project risks making a loss which is so large as to endanger the continual existence of the sponsoring company, then managers would tend to adopt a cautious view about the risks involved.

Robinson, Joan (1903–1983) English economist from Cambridge University who helped develop the theory of MONOPOLISTIC COMPETITION in her book *The Economics of Imperfect Competition* (1933). Prior to Robinson's work, economists classified markets into two groups:

PERFECT COMPETITION, where firms' products are perfect substitutes; and MONOPOLY, where a firm's product has no substitutes. Robinson argued that in real markets, goods are often partial substitutes for other goods, and her theory of monopolistic competition analysed price and output in such markets. She concluded that firms in monopolistic competition would restrict output in order to maintain price resulting in a lower level of plant operation than optimum. See also CHAMBERLIN, Edward.

root-mean-square deviation, see STANDARD DEVIATION.

royalty, *n.* an agreed payment made to the owner of an INDUSTRIAL PROPERTY RIGHT, for example a PATENT or COPYRIGHT, for the grant of an exclusive or nonexclusive LICENCE or FRANCHISE to produce and sell for profit the item concerned.

RPI, see PRICE INDEX.

rule of reason, *n.* the individual investigation of elements of MARKET CONDUCT (for example, RESTRICTIVE TRADE AGREEMENTS) and MARKET STRUCTURE (MERGERS) under a DISCRETIONARY MONOPOLY POLICY to determine whether or not their economic effects are, on balance, beneficial or detrimental.

rule of thumb, *n.* a rough-and-ready decision-making aid that provides an acceptably accurate, approximate solution to a problem. Where refined decision-making processes are expensive in terms of information gathering and information processing, then rules of thumb may be justified. For example, COST-PLUS PRICING may be used in practice by firms in the absence of sufficient knowledge about future demand and cost conditions to permit marginal weighting of revenues and costs to achieve an optimum decision. See RISK AND UNCERTAINTY.

S

safety stock, see STOCKHOLDING COSTS.

salary, *n.* a payment made to the employee of an organization. A salary is similar to a WAGE payment in that it is paid for the use of LABOUR as a factor of production. In economic terms, a salary payment differs from a wage payment in two ways: (a) it is not strictly related to the actual number of hours worked by the employee, whereas wage earners are usually paid on an hourly basis; (b) salaries are usually paid monthly, whereas wages are paid weekly.

sale and leaseback, see LEASEBACK.

sales forecasts, see FORECASTING.

sales-per-employee ratio, *n.* an accounting measure of a firm's sales/ size relation, that expresses the firm's SALES REVENUE as a ratio of its size measured in terms of number of employees.

sales promotion and merchandising, *n.* the measures used by firms to increase the sales of their GOODS and SERVICES. ADVERTISING is the most visible form of sales promotion, but a wide variety of other techniques can be used to create and boost sales: money-off packs; free trial samples; coupons offering gifts; product competitions offering prizes; trading stamps; in-store demonstrations; point-of-sale displays, etc.

In the economist's models of imperfect competition, all of these items come under the generic heading of PRODUCT DIFFERENTIATION.

sales revenue, *n.* the income generated from the sale of GOODS and SERVICES. Sales revenue depends upon the volume of a product sold and the price of the product.

sales-revenue maximization, *n.* a company objective in the THEORY OF THE FIRM that is used as an alternative to the traditional assumption of PROFIT MAXIMIZATION. The firm is assumed to seek to maximize sales revenue subject to a minimum profit constraint (determined by the need to pay dividends to shareholders and to finance expansion). In Fig. 175 on page 468, sales revenue is maximized at output level OQ_s. If the firm's minimum profit constraint is at level A, then the sales-revenue maximizing output level of OQ_s will provide sufficient profits. If the

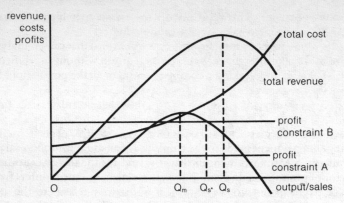

Fig. 175. **Sales revenue maximization**. See main entry.

firm's required profit level is B, however, the sales–revenue maximizing output OQ_s is clearly inadequate. The firm's output would then be lowered to level $OQ_{s\star}$, which is just compatible with the profit constraint. Clearly, the higher the minimum profit figure required, the more important the constraint becomes and the profit-maximizing (OQ_m) and sales–revenue maximizing output levels will be closer together.

See also MANAGERIAL THEORIES OF THE FIRM, FIRM OBJECTIVES, DIVORCE OF OWNERSHIP FROM CONTROL.

sales–revenue variance, *n.* the difference between the budgeted (see BUDGETING) value of SALES and the actual value of sales achieved. This variance can be broken down into two parts: (a) *sales-price variance*, which shows the difference between the predetermined price of a product and the actual price; (b) *sales-volume variance*, which indicates the extent to which sales revenue has been lost because smaller volumes of products were sold than were budgeted for. Both of these are affected by sales mix, and the sales-mix variance shows the effect on revenue of achieving an actual mix of sales different from the product mix anticipated in the sales budget.

sales tax or **turnover tax,** *n.* a form of INDIRECT TAX which is incorporated into the selling price of a product and which is borne by the consumer. Sales taxes include VALUE-ADDED TAX and EXCISE DUTY.

sales–to–capital–employed ratio or **asset–turnover ratio,** *n.* an accounting measure of a firm's ASSET turnover, that expresses the firm's SALES REVENUE as a ratio of its size measured in terms of LONG-TERM

CAPITAL-EMPLOYED. This ratio reveals the extent to which the firm's assets have generated sales over a time period.

sample, *n.* any part of a total group (see POPULATION) that can be analysed in order to make inferences about the total group without the difficulty and expense of undertaking a complete census of all the population. See also RANDOM SAMPLE.

satisficing theory, *n.* a THEORY OF THE FIRM that postulates that firms typically not only seek to secure 'satisfactory' profits rather than maximum profits, as depicted in the traditional theory of the firm, but that other objectives such as increasing sales, market share or the size of the firm may be accorded equal or greater prominence than profits. Organizational theorists suggest that satisficing behaviour is particularly likely to occur in large, hierarchical organizations where concensus decision-making, reconciling the diverse aims of the various subgroups of the organization, tends to be the norm, as opposed to objectives being set by an individual ENTREPRENEUR.

The problem with this approach to firm behaviour is that it is not possible to define unequivocally what is meant by the term 'satisfactory' and hence to construct a *general* theory of the firm. For example, a profit return which is considered to be 'satisfactory' by one firm may be considered too low by some other firm. Thus, the predictive powers of satisficing theory are strictly limited.

See also PROFIT MAXIMIZATION, BEHAVIOURAL THEORY OF THE FIRM, MANAGERIAL THEORIES OF THE FIRM, ORGANIZATIONAL THEORY.

savings, *n.* the proportion of INCOME that is not spent on current CONSUMPTION. Saving is a WITHDRAWAL from the CIRCULAR FLOW OF NATIONAL INCOME MODEL. In the simple circular flow model, all saving is undertaken by households; in the extended model, saving is also undertaken by businesses (retained profits) and the government (budget surplus).

In real terms, saving is important in that it 'finances' physical INVESTMENT. Saving (foregoing current consumption) releases resources which can be devoted to increasing the country's CAPITAL STOCK and hence its capacity to produce a greater quantity of goods over time.

See also SAVINGS SCHEDULE, PARADOX OF THRIFT.

savings bank, *n.* a financial institution that accepts deposits from savers, and which specializes in investments in stocks and shares and government securities. Some of the larger savings banks also offer depositors limited COMMERCIAL-BANKING facilities (for example, the use of a cheque book). See also FINANCIAL SYSTEM.

SAVINGS SCHEDULE

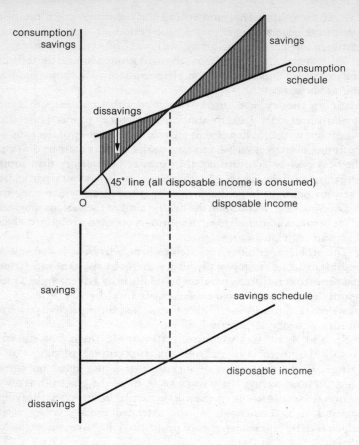

Fig. 176. **Savings schedule**. See main entry.

savings schedule, *n.* a schedule that depicts the relationship between SAVINGS and the level of INCOME. In the simple CIRCULAR FLOW OF NATIONAL INCOME MODEL, all consumption and saving is accounted for by households. At low levels of DISPOSABLE INCOME, households consume more than their current income (see DISSAVINGS). At higher levels of disposable income they consume only a part of their current income and save the rest, as in Fig. 176. Thus, the savings schedule is derived by subtracting the CONSUMPTION SCHEDULE from the 45° line, as shown in the lower part of the Fig. The slope of the savings schedule is equal to the MARGINAL PROPENSITY TO SAVE.

See also LIFE-CYCLE HYPOTHESIS, PERMANENT-INCOME HYPOTHESIS.

Say, Jean Baptiste (1767–1832) French economist who developed Adam SMITH's theory of the market in his *Traité d'économic politique* (1803). Say argued that since every product exchanges for another product, then every product put on the market creates its own demand, and every demand exerted in the market creates its own supply. This statement about interdependence in an exchange economy is often described as SAY'S LAW. The principle has been used to deny the possibility of economic crisis associated with general overproduction of goods and services and to suggest that national economies would automatically function close to full employment.

Say's Law, *n.* the proposition that AGGREGATE SUPPLY creates its own AGGREGATE DEMAND. The very act of producing a given level of national output generates an amount of income (wages, profits, etc.) exactly equal to that output, which if spent is just sufficient to take up the purchases of the whole of the output that has been produced. It follows that, in order to reach the full-employment level at national output, all that needs to be done is to increase aggregate supply.

The key assumptions are that the economic system is 'supply-led' and that all income is spent. In practice, however, some income is 'leaked' into saving, taxation, etc. (see CIRCULAR FLOW OF NATIONAL INCOME MODEL), and there is no automatic guarantee that all of this income will be subsequently 'injected' back as spending. Thus, in contrast to the above proposition, the economic system is 'demand-led', a fall in aggregate demand leading to a multiple contraction of national income and output.

See EQUILIBRIUM LEVEL OF NATIONAL INCOME.

scale economies, see ECONOMIES OF SCALE.

scarcity, *n.* the limited availability of economic resources (the FACTORS OF PRODUCTION) relative to society's unlimited demand for GOODS and SERVICES. See ECONOMICS.

scatter diagram, *n.* a graphical representation of the pairs of values of the INDEPENDENT VARIABLE and DEPENDENT VARIABLE. In order to make sense of such data we need to examine the pattern of the graphed observations, with a view to fitting a line to the graph which adequately represents the relationship between the independent and dependent variable.

Schumpeter, Joseph A. (1883–1950) Austrian economist who developed a theory to explain BUSINESS CYCLES in his book *Capitalism, Socialism and Democracy* (1942). According to Schumpeter, the key to ECONOMIC GROWTH is the innovative (see INNOVATION) ENTREPRENEUR who takes RISKS and introduces new technologies to stimulate economic activity, replacing old technologies by a process of 'creative destruction'. However, because such innovative activity takes place irregularly, spurts of such vigorous production are likely to be followed by both collapse and crisis.

In the longer term, Schumpeter predicted the eventual downfall of capitalism and the rise of socialism. He argued that as capitalist economies become prosperous they will be less driven to innovate, and the innovative entrepreneur will be superseded, as large, slow-growing companies with bureaucratic managements come to predominate. These large companies will resist new technologies which they perceive as threatening and in a climate of growing hostility to capitalism governments will become active in economic affairs.

See also MONOPOLY, PRIVATE-ENTERPRISE ECONOMY.

science park, see INDUSTRIAL ESTATE.

scrip issue, see CAPITALIZATION ISSUE.

seasonal index, see TIME-SERIES ANALYSIS.

seasonal unemployment, see FRICTIONAL UNEMPLOYMENT.

seasonal variation, see TIME-SERIES ANALYSIS.

secondary benefits, *n.* any additional indirect benefits (see COSTS) that stem from the direct primary benefits of an INVESTMENT project. For example, in estimating the benefits of an irrigation project, the increase in grain output resulting from the project would be counted as a primary benefit; while the increased economic activity of grain merchants, millers and bakers handling this extra grain would be counted as a secondary benefit of the project.

See also COST-BENEFIT ANALYSIS.

second-best, *adj.* (of an economy) departing from an optimal pattern of resource allocation (see PARETO OPTIMALITY) because, for example, of MONOPOLY distortions and EXTERNALITIES.

If the production of a product such as a chemical leads to environmental POLLUTION then the marginal SOCIAL COST of producing that output will exceed the marginal PRIVATE COST, and the economy will depart from an optimal pattern of resource allocation. In this 'second-best' situation, the government can improve matters by imposing a 'pollution tax' on offending chemical firms. This will, on the one hand, provide an incentive for the firms to adopt less-polluting production processes and, on the other hand, to the extent that the tax is passed on to chemical buyers, will force buyers to pay the full social costs of the products they consume.

sector, *n.* a part of the economy that has certain common characteristics which enables it to be separated from other parts of the economy for analytical or policy purposes. A broad division may be made, for example, between economic activities undertaken by the state (the PUBLIC SECTOR) and those that are undertaken by private individuals and businesses (the PRIVATE SECTOR). The private sector, in turn, may be subdivided into the PERSONAL SECTOR (private individuals and households), the CORPORATE SECTOR (businesses supplying goods and services) and the FINANCIAL SECTOR (businesses providing financial services).

secular stagnation, *n.* a situation in which the economy remains fixed in a DEPRESSION (a low state of business activity) for long periods of time. Declining rates of population growth, low levels of aggregate demand and a bias towards capital-saving inventions, all mitigate against a revival of investment in capacity-creating investment, prolonging this particular phase of the BUSINESS CYCLE in the absence of positive government stimuli.

Secular stagnation occurs when an economy shows a long-term inclination to withdraw (save) more than it injects (invests). In other words, there is a continual DEFLATIONARY GAP which cannot be remedied by a reduction in the interest rate. If the government maintained a BALANCED BUDGET policy, and achieves BALANCE-OF-PAYMENTS EQUILIBRIUM, then the economy would exhibit a perpetual tendency to operate at an equilibrium-level of national output less than the full-employment level of output. A balanced budget policy merely exacerbates the situation, and government must adopt a policy of BUDGET DEFICIT (sometimes referred to as deficit financing) to increase overall injections to a higher level than overall withdrawals and so return towards full employment. The alternative would be to allow employment to fall to such a level that excess savings were eradicated. See also EQUILIBRIUM LEVEL OF NATIONAL INCOME.

secular trend, *n.* a long-term movement, either upwards or downwards, in some economic variable. For example, Fig. 177 on page 474 shows that the GROSS DOMESTIC PRODUCT (GDP) of the UK has risen steadily in the period since 1976.

Of course, in some years the increase in GDP has been greater than in other years, and there have been a few occasions when GDP has actually

Index numbers 1980 = 100

1976	93.8
1977	96.5
1978	99.8
1979	103.0
1980	100.0
1981	98.3
1982	100.1
1983	103.1
1984	106.4
1985	110.0
1986	113.6

Fig. 177. **Secular trend**. The movement in the UK's gross domestic product, 1976–1986. Source: *Monthly Digest of Statistics*, Central Statistical Office.

fallen, but overall the long-term trend line has been upwards. See also TIME–SERIES ANALYSIS, CYCLICAL FLUCTUATIONS.

securities, see FINANCIAL SECURITY.

Securities and Exchange Commission, the US body that regulates the operations of the New York STOCK EXCHANGE.

Securities and Investments Board, *n*. a UK body set up in 1986 to oversee the functioning of the STOCK EXCHANGE and FUTURES MARKETS, and the activities of UNIT TRUSTS, INSURANCE broking, and financial advisers.

seller concentration or **market concentration,** *n*. an element of MARKET STRUCTURE that denotes the number and size distribution of suppliers in a given MARKET. Market theory predicts that MARKET PERFORMANCE will differ according to whether there are many suppliers in the market each accounting for only a small fraction of total supply (PERFECT COMPETITION), or only a few suppliers, each accounting for a substantial proportion of total supply (OLIGOPOLY), or a single supplier (MONOPOLY). See also CONCENTRATION MEASURES.

seller's market, *n*. a SHORT-RUN market situation in which there is EXCESS DEMAND for goods and services at current prices which forces prices up to the advantage of the seller. Compare BUYER'S MARKET.

selling costs, *n*. the expenditures incurred by suppliers in creating and sustaining a demand for their products. Selling costs include ADVERTISING expenditures; packaging and styling; salaries, commissions and travelling expenses of sales personnel; and the cost of shops and showrooms.

See also PRODUCT DIFFERENTIATION, DISTRIBUTIVE EFFICIENCY, OVERHEADS.

selling price, *n.* the PRICE at which a firm offers a product for sale. Selling price is usually set at a level which covers PRODUCTION and SELLING COSTS and an appropriate PROFIT MARGIN.

semivariable overheads, *n.* any OVERHEADS that are partly fixed and partly variable with respect to output so that they vary roughly with output but not in exact proportion to output. They include such items as electricity and telephone costs which combine a fixed quarterly payment with a charge per unit consumed. In arithmetic terms, semivariable costs (S) can be represented as:

$$S = F + V.Q$$

where F is the fixed cost element, V is variable cost per unit and Q is output.

separation of ownership from control, see DIVORCE OF OWNERSHIP FROM CONTROL.

sequestration, *n.* the holding of part of the ASSETS of parties involved in an INDUSTRIAL DISPUTE or other dispute by a third party (the *sequestrator*) until the dispute is settled. Sequestrators are often appointed by the courts as a means of enforcing fines against TRADE UNIONS who are in breach of employment legislation.

service contract, see EMPLOYMENT CONTRACT.

services, *n.* any intangible economic activities (hairdressing, catering, insurance, banking, etc.), that contribute directly (see FINAL PRODUCTS) or indirectly (see INTERMEDIATE PRODUCTS) to the satisfaction of human wants. Services are an important component of GROSS NATIONAL PRODUCT.

service sector, *n.* that part of the economy concerned with the provision of a wide variety of personal and business services: hairdressing and tourism, transportation and retailing, banking and insurance, etc. The service sector, together with the PRIMARY SECTOR and INDUSTRIAL SECTOR form an interlocking chain of economic activities which constitute a modern economy. See STRUCTURE OF INDUSTRY.

shadow price, *n.* the imputed PRICE or VALUE of a good or service where such a price or value cannot be accurately determined due to the absence of an ordinary price-determined market, or to gross distortions in any markets which exist. To impute a price or value is to make the best estimate possible of what that price or value would be if a normal market existed.

WELFARE ECONOMICS attempts to equate the price of a product to its marginal social cost. The marginal social cost of a product is the summation of all costs associated with it. For instance, the true cost of electricity is not just the capital, labour and inputs of raw material, it is the additional cost of disposing adequately of the waste products such as smoke and dirt, and even the decrease in aesthetic appeal of the area in which the power station is situated. No values are given for these costs because there exists no markets to price them. Shadow prices for such items are frequently estimated in COST-BENEFIT ANALYSIS.

A different use of shadow pricing is when intra-firm trading occurs. The inputs of company division B may be the outputs of company division A. The products in which the two company divisions trade may not have an equivalent market price because no open market for them exists (for example, intermediate components or managerial services). The transactions are given shadow prices, usually based on estimated costs plus a return on the capital involved. Such an estimate of market prices is used frequently in CENTRALLY PLANNED ECONOMIES such as the eastern bloc countries.

A particular application of shadow-pricing can be found in LINEAR PROGRAMMING where the solution to a problem yields hypothetical prices for scarce factor inputs, showing how much additional profit would result from an extra unit of each fully-used resource.

share, *n.* a FINANCIAL SECURITY issued by a JOINT-STOCK COMPANY as a means of raising long-term capital. The SHAREHOLDERS of a company are its legal owners and are entitled to a share in its profits. Shares are traded on the STOCK EXCHANGE. There are two broad kinds of shares: PREFERENCE SHARES and ORDINARY SHARES. See also SHARE CAPITAL, CAPITAL GEARING.

share capital, *n.* the money employed in a JOINT-STOCK COMPANY that has been subscribed by the SHAREHOLDERS of the company in the form of ORDINARY SHARES (equity) and PREFERENCE SHARES and which will remain as a permanent source of finance as long as the company remains in existence.

See also LOAN CAPITAL, CAPITAL-GEARING, STOCK.

shareholders, *n.* the individuals and institutions who contribute funds to finance a JOINT-STOCK COMPANY in return for SHARES in that company. There are two main types of shareholder: (a) holders of PREFERENCE SHARES who are entitled to a fixed DIVIDEND from a company's PROFITS (before ordinary shareholders receive anything), and who have first claim on any remaining assets of the business after all debts have been discharged; (b) holders of ORDINARY SHARES who are entitled to a dividend from a company's profits after all other outlays have been met, and who are entitled to any remaining ASSETS of the business in the event of the company being wound up.

shareholders' capital-employed, *n.* SHARE CAPITAL originally invested by SHAREHOLDERS plus any RESERVES which arise, for example, as retained profits are ploughed back into the company.

share premium, *n.* the proceeds from issuing SHARES at a price higher than their NOMINAL VALUE or present market value. Such proceeds are added to a JOINT-STOCK COMPANY's revenue RESERVES.

share price index, *n.* an index number of the average prices of a sample of company SHARES which is used as an indicator of general share price movements. In the UK the *Financial Times All-Share Index* records day-to-day movements in the average price of all company shares listed on the London STOCK EXCHANGE. In the US share price movements are monitored by the *Dow-Jones Index*. See PRICE INDEX.

share register, *n.* a list of SHAREHOLDERS maintained by a JOINT-STOCK COMPANY that records all company shareholders and the number of SHARES which they hold. As shares are bought and sold on the STOCK EXCHANGE, the register must be constantly amended so as to maintain an up-to-date list of shareholders' DIVIDEND and voting entitlement.

shark repellants, see TAKEOVER BID.

shell company, *n.* a company that is not actively trading but which is still listed on the STOCK EXCHANGE. Such a company can be purchased in a REVERSE TAKEOVER by a company wishing to obtain a stock-exchange listing.

shift in tax, *n.* the redirection of a TAX away from its nominal bearer so that it is ultimately paid for by somebody else. For example, suppose the tax authorities impose a PAYROLL TAX on firms as a means of raising revenue. Firms, however, decide to treat the tax as an increase in their costs of production and so put up their prices by an equivalent amount. Then, assuming there is no fall in sales resulting from the price increase, it is the consumer, not the firms, who finishes up footing the bill. See also INCIDENCE OF TAXATION.

shift system, *n.* a method of organizing work that enables a production unit (a plant) to be run on a more intensive basis. For many plants the 'standard' working day of the labour force is eight hours, but by using a double- or three-shift system the plant can be worked for up to 24 hours.

This enables a firm to make maximum use of its FIXED FACTOR INPUT and lower its unit costs of production accordingly.

See RETURNS TO THE VARIABLE-FACTOR INPUT.

shop steward, *n.* a shop-floor employee who is elected by the local members of a TRADE UNION to represent them in work-place negotiations with management.

short run, *n.* an abstract time period within the THEORY OF SUPPLY in which some FACTOR INPUTS are fixed (FIXED FACTOR INPUTS like plant size), and output can be adjusted only by changing the quantities of VARIABLE FACTOR INPUTS used (for example, raw materials, labour).

In practice, what is defined as the short run can vary greatly from industry to industry. For example, in the petrochemical industry it can take five years or more to commission, build and run-in a new plant so that any expansion of output within this term can only be achieved by increasing the throughput from existing plants. By contrast, in the garment-making industry it may be possible to buy and instal new sewing machines within a few weeks so that in this industry the short-run might be a month or less. Compare LONG RUN. See also RETURNS TO THE VARIABLE-FACTOR INPUT.

SIC (Standard Industrial Classification), see INDUSTRIAL CLASSIFICATIONS.

sickness benefit, *n.* the TRANSFER PAYMENTS in cash or kind made to persons unable to work through illness to provide them with some minimum standard of living until they can return to paid employment. In most countries workers in employment pay NATIONAL-INSURANCE CONTRIBUTIONS to the government in return for sickness benefit rights. See also GOVERNMENT EXPENDITURE, SOCIAL-SECURITY BENEFITS.

significance (tests of), see HYPOTHESIS TESTING.

simple interest, *n.* the INTEREST ON A LOAN that is based only on the original amount of the loan. This means that over time, interest charges grow in a linear fashion. For example, a £100 loan earning simple interest of 10% per annum would accumulate to £110 at the end of the first year and £120 at the end of the second year etc. Compare COMPOUND INTEREST.

simulation or **Monte Carlo simulation,** *n.* a technique for dealing with complex resource allocation problems which cannot be solved exactly by mathematical analysis. The technique involves creating a typical life history of a system which represents the actual problem and its rules of operation. Repeated runs of the simulation, slightly altering the operating rules each time, enables experimentation aimed at discovering methods of improving the performance of the system. Such simulation techniques are frequently employed in examining STOCKHOLDING and QUEUEING problems.

sinking fund, *n.* a fund into which periodic payments are made which, with COMPOUND INTEREST, will ultimately be sufficient to meet a known future capital commitment or discharge a LIABILITY. Such a fund may be used to finance the replacement of FIXED ASSETS at the end of their useful life or to purchase back company loan stock or debentures upon maturity. See also DEPRECIATION (2), LOAN CAPITAL.

skewed distribution, *n.* a group of numerical observations whose FREQUENCY DISTRIBUTION takes the form of a HISTOGRAM, or of CONTINUOUS DISTRIBUTION with two unequally shaped halves with a 'tail' at one end. Compare SYMMETRICAL DISTRIBUTION.

skimming price, *n.* a pricing policy that involves charging a comparatively high PRICE for a product to secure large profit margins. This policy will be adopted by a firm where consumers are not expected to be price sensitive, that is, demand is price-inelastic (see PRICE-ELASTICITY OF DEMAND).

See PRODUCT LIFE CYCLE, PENETRATION PRICE.

slump, see DEPRESSION.

Smith, Adam (1723–1790) Scottish professor of philosophy at Glasgow University, whose writings formed the basis of CLASSICAL ECONOMICS. Smith's most famous book, *An Inquiry into the Nature and Causes of the Wealth of Nations* (1776), stressed the benefits of division of labour, discussed the need for SPECIALIZATION and exchange, and outlined the workings of the market mechanism (PRICE SYSTEM). Smith argued that if producers were free to seek profits by providing goods and services, then the 'invisible hand' of market forces would ensure that the right goods and services were produced. Provided that markets were free of government regulation then in this LAISSEZ FAIRE environment, competition would direct production in ways which would increase public well-being.

In competitive markets, producers would compete to sell more goods, forcing prices down to the lowest level which covered production costs and allowed normal profit to be made. Furthermore, if certain goods were scarce buyers would offer higher prices, drawing more producers into these industries and swelling supply. In this manner production in the market system would be directed by what consumers wanted.

Smith's outline of the market mechanism described the new economic system which was beginning to emerge in the newly-industrializing Western countries.

However, for the system to work Smith acknowledged that two important conditions needed to be met: (a) markets needed to be free of government intervention without the close government regulation of economic activity as had prevailed prior to Smith's day; (b) the self-seeking behaviour of producers could only be harnessed to the common good where competition prevailed, and Smith was deeply suspicious of MONOPOLIES, considering them to be conspiracies against the consumer.

See PRIVATE-ENTERPRISE SYSTEM.

social capital, see INFRASTRUCTURE

social costs, *n.* the COSTS borne by society resulting from the actions of FIRMS. Consider, for example, a river which is used by both a chemical firm to dispose of its waste and by a town as a source of drinking water. Assume that the continuous dumping of waste causes the river to become polluted. The firm incurs PRIVATE COSTS in producing chemicals but pays out nothing for the use of the river or the pollution caused. The town, by contrast, is forced to instal special water treatment plants to counter the pollution. Thus, the extra cost of cleaning up the river is not borne by the firm but by society.

One way to remedy this divergence of private and social costs is to tax the firm an amount equivalent to the costs of treating the pollution. Making the firm pay the *full* costs of supplying chemicals has the merit of encouraging it to look around for the least-costly way of disposing of its waste; that is, instead of dumping its waste in the river it might be cheaper for the firm to invest in a waste disposal plant.

See also EXTERNALITIES, WELFARE ECONOMICS, COST-BENEFIT ANALYSIS.

socialism, *n.* a political doctrine that emphasizes the collective ownership of the means of production, ascribing a large role to the State in the running of the economy with widespread public ownership (NATIONALIZATION) of key industries, though it allows limited scope to market forces. MARX regarded socialism as a transitional stage between the end of a PRIVATE-ENTERPRISE system and the beginnings of COMMUNISM. In practice, the revolutionary, communist form of socialism, which involves abolition of all private property and the curtailment of civil liberties is largely limited to the Eastern bloc countries such as the Soviet Union and China. Elsewhere the main form of economic system is that of the MIXED ECONOMY which combines elements of democratic socialism and the private enterprise tradition. See CENTRALLY-PLANNED ECONOMY.

social overhead capital, see INFRASTRUCTURE.

social products or **merit goods** or **public goods,** *n.* the GOODS and SERVICES that are provided by the State for the benefit of all or most of the populace (education, health, housing, etc.). Unlike PRIVATE PRODUCTS, there is no direct link between the consumption of a social product and payment for it. Social products are paid for out of general taxation and not by individual consumers buying in the market place. See also COLLECTIVE PRODUCTS.

social security benefits, *n.* any benefits provided, on social grounds, to low-income members of society such as the unemployed, retired persons, the disabled, single-parent families, etc. Social security benefits can take the form of money payments (for example, unemployment benefit, pensions, etc.) or payments in kind (for example, clothing coupons, food stamps, etc.).

In certain cases, where the scale of benefit used to determine benefit entitlement overlaps with the PROGRESSIVE-TAXATION system, this can create disincentive to seek employment.

See POVERTY TRAP, NEGATIVE INCOME TAX, SUPPLY-SIDE ECONOMICS.

social time preference, see DISCOUNT RATE.

social welfare function, see WELFARE ECONOMICS.

soft currency, *n.* a foreign CURRENCY that is in weak demand, but in abundant supply on the FOREIGN-EXCHANGE MARKET. Soft currency status is usually associated with an economically weak country which is running a large deficit in its BALANCE OF PAYMENTS; the supply of the currency is high to finance the purchase of imports, but demand for the currency is relatively weak because the amount of it being required for the purchase of exports is much lower. However, under a FLOATING EXCHANGE-RATE SYSTEM, the demand for, and supply of, the currency should be, in theory, brought into balance by a DEPRECIATION (1) in its EXCHANGE-RATE value. Compare HARD CURRENCY.

soft loan, *n.* a LOAN that bears a RATE-OF-INTEREST charge that is substantially below that of the interest rate which is charged normally on a loan for a similar purpose and risk status. Soft loans are often given as a form of ECONOMIC AID TO DEVELOPING COUNTRIES by developed countries and international institutions. See also WORLD BANK.

sole proprietor, see FIRM.

Solow economic-growth model, *n.* a theoretical construct which focuses on the role of technological change in the ECONOMIC GROWTH process.

In the HARROD ECONOMIC-GROWTH MODEL and the DOMAR ECONOMIC GROWTH MODEL, a constant CAPITAL-OUTPUT RATIO is assumed so that there is a linear relationship between increases in the CAPITAL STOCK (through INVESTMENT) and the resulting increase in output. For example, if it requires £3,000 of capital to produce £1,000 of output then the capital–output ratio is one-third, and this is assumed to apply to successive additions to the capital stock. By contrast, the Solow model utilizes a production function in which output is a function of capital *and* labour, with capital being substitutable for labour but with varying degrees of perfection, and which displays DIMINISHING RETURNS. Thus, if capital is increased relative to labour, the resulting increases in output become progressively smaller. On this assumption of a variable capital-output ratio as a country's capital stock increases, diminishing returns set in and produce progressively smaller increments in output. Sustained economic growth thus requires not only CAPITAL-WIDENING but also CAPITAL-DEEPENING investment. Specifically, TECHNOLOGICAL PROGRESSIVENESS (new production techniques, processes and methods, and new products) plays a necessary role in offsetting diminishing returns to capital as the capital stock increases.

sources and uses of funds statement or **funds–flow statement,** *n.*
an accounting statement that shows the sources from which a firm derives its cash and the use to which this cash is put during a trading period. The major source of funds is usually the net cash generated from sales, though this can be added to by cash raised from selling FIXED ASSETS and by raising further LOANS or new SHARE issues. The major applications of funds are the purchase of new fixed assets, repayment of loans and payments of TAXES and DIVIDENDS. When further allowance is made for the cash-flow effect of changes in STOCKS, DEBTORS and CREDITORS, the sources and uses of funds statement shows the net inflow or outflow of cash to the firm.

See TRADING AND PROFIT-AND-LOSS ACCOUNT, WORKING CAPITAL.

special deposit, *n.* an instrument of MONETARY POLICY in the UK, involving the placement of a specified proportion of the banking sector's liquid assets with the Bank of England as a means of controlling the MONEY SUPPLY. Special deposits are excluded from the bank's liquidity or RESERVE-ASSET RATIOS. Thus, if the monetary authorities wish to reduce the money supply they can call for a special deposit. This will lower the liquidity base of the banking sector. As a result banks will be forced to reduce their lending, leading to a multiple contraction of bank deposits and, hence, a fall in the money supply.

The authorities may call for 'supplementary special deposits' (referred to in the UK as the *corset*), from time to time, to counteract sudden increases in banking sector liquidity.

See BANK DEPOSIT CREATION.

Special Drawing Right (SDR), *n.* a monetary asset held by member countries of the INTERNATIONAL MONETARY FUND (IMF) as part of their INTERNATIONAL RESERVES. Unlike other reserve assets such as GOLD, SDRs have no tangible life of their own. They are 'created' by the IMF itself and take the form of book-keeping entries in a special account managed by the Fund. The SDR is valued in terms of a weighted basket of five currencies: US dollar, West German Deutschmark, UK Sterling, French franc, Japanese yen.

specialization, *n.* a form of division of labour whereby each individual and firm concentrates their productive efforts on a single or limited number of activities. If a person specializes in a single task, he or she is likely to be much more efficient than if he attempts to be a jack-of-all trades. The specialist can concentrate on the work he or she is best at doing: familiarity and repetition improves work skills and time is not lost moving from one job to another. For all these reasons, a person's output is greater as a result of specialization.

Similarly, specialization enables an economy to use its scarce resources more efficiently, thereby producing (and consuming) a larger volume of goods and services than would otherwise be the case. This fundamental principle can be illustrated assuming, to simplify matters, a two-person, A and B, and two-product, X and Y, economy. Let us suppose that A has the PRODUCTION-POSSIBILITY BOUNDARY indicated in Fig. 178a on page 484 of 12X or 6Y. Thus, A is twice as efficient at producing X as he is at producing Y (an OPPORTUNITY-COST RATIO of 2X/1Y). Let us assume he chooses to produce (and consume) at point A_{pc} on his production possibility line (6X and 3Y).

B, by contrast, has the production-possibility boundary indicated in Fig. 178b of 12Y or 6X. He is twice as efficient at producing Y as he is at producing X (an opportunity-cost ratio of 2Y/1X). Let us assume he chooses to produce (and consume) at point B_{pc} on his production possibility line (6Y and 3X).

Now, assume that A and B specialize in the production of the product in which they are most efficient. Thus, A specializes totally in the production of X and B totally in the production of Y. Transposing Figs 178a and b onto Fig. 178c we see the establishment of a new production-possibility boundary (and a new opportunity cost ratio of 1X/1Y) for the economy).

Specialization thus results in *production gain*, that is, the economy is now able to produce 12X and 12Y, which is 3 more X and 3 more Y than previously (see Fig. 178d), and *consumption gain*, that is, as a result of specialization *and* exchange, A and B can now consume more of both products. For example, A consumes 8 of the X he produces and exchanges the remaining 4X for 4Y from B (i.e. $1X = 1Y$ from the opportunity cost ratio $1X/1Y$). With specialization and exchange, A is now consuming 2 more X and 1 more Y. By the same token, B consumes 8 of the Y he produces and exchanges 4Y for 4X from A, thereby increasing his consumption by 2Y and 1X.

See also PRODUCTIVITY, COMPARATIVE ADVANTAGE, GAINS FROM TRADE.

Fig. 178. **Specialization.** (a) A's production/consumption possibility boundary before specialization. (b) B's production/consumption possibility boundary before specialization.

(c)

	Production				Consumption			
	Before		After		Before		After	
	X	Y	X	Y	X	Y	X	Y
A	6	3	12	–	6	3	8(+2)	4(+1)
B	3	6	–	12	3	6	4(+1)	8(+2)
Total	9	9	12	12	9	9	12(+3)	12(+3)

(d)

Fig. 178 (continued). **Specialization.** (c) A and B's combined production/consumption possibility boundary after specialization. (d) The production/consumption limits of A and B before and after specialization.

specialist shop, *n.* a retail outlet that specializes in a narrow range of related products; for example, electrical goods and accessories, sweets and confectionery, sportswear stores, bakers, butchers, etc. Specialist shops may be under single-shop ownership or run as a multiple CHAIN-STORE business. See also RETAILING.

specific tax, *n.* a TAX that is levied at a fixed rate per physical unit of output. See AD VALOREM TAX, VALUE–ADDED TAX.

speculation, *n.* the purchase or sale of ASSETS, real or financial, to achieve a CAPITAL GAIN. See ARBITRAGE, SPECULATIVE–DEMAND FOR MONEY, SPECULATOR.

speculative demand for money, *n.* a demand for funds held in highly liquid MONEY form in the hope of taking advantage of bargains in the form of low-priced BONDS or real ASSETS.

Speculative balances are associated with the concept of a 'normal' RATE OF INTEREST. Each individual and institutional holder of speculative balances has their own opinion of what this 'normal' rate is. If the current rate of interest is high, this encourages bond holding but discourages money holding because of: (a) the high OPPORTUNITY COST of holding cash in terms of interest foregone; (b) the negligible risks attached to capital losses, because the interest rate is unlikely to rise even further and so reduce the price of bonds (there being an inverse relationship between the price of bonds and the EFFECTIVE RATE OF INTEREST).

The speculation arises around the future movement of bond prices and when bonds should be bought and sold. When the interest rate is very low and bond prices are high, then: (c) people will want to hold speculative balances because the opportunity cost in terms of interest foregone is small; (d) there will be a general expectation of a rise in the interest rate, with a consequent fall in bond prices, and thus the preference is for cash holding. The effect of such forces is to create an inverse relationship between interest rates and the demand for speculative balances.

Precautionary and transaction balances are functions of the level of money income, whereas speculative demand for money is a function of the rate of interest. Compare PRECAUTIONARY DEMAND FOR MONEY, TRANSACTIONS DEMAND FOR MONEY. See also MONEY–DEMAND SCHEDULE, LIQUIDITY PREFERENCE, L.M. SCHEDULE.

speculator, *n.* a dealer in markets characterized by rapidly changing prices (such as a COMMODITY MARKET or a market from financial securities), who buys and/or sells commodities or securities not because he trades in them, but in the hope of making a short-term gain from movements in the prices of these commodities or securities. For example, in the STOCK EXCHANGE, a speculator may take a 'bullish' view that a particular share price will rise, and gamble on this hunch by buying that share on short-term credit terms at the current price, and reselling it at a higher price after a week or two, using the proceeds from the resale to pay the original seller. On the other hand, the speculator may take a 'bearish' view that a share price will fall, and gamble on this hunch by arranging to sell these shares at the present price (even though he does not own any), using the proceeds from this sale to buy at a lower price the shares which he has promised to deliver a week or two later.

The activities of speculators within a market may be either stabilizing or destabilizing, depending on whether or not they take a collective view about future price movements. For example, if some stock exchange speculators feel that the price of a share is going to rise while other speculators feel that the price of the same share is going to fall, then the former would seek to buy the share, adding to demand for it; while the latter would seek to sell the share, adding to the supply of it; and their efforts would cancel out, having little net effect on the share price. However, if most speculators take the view that a share price will rise then they will all seek to buy it, and thus artificially add to the demand for it and force up its price; while if most speculators take the view that the share price will fall, they will all seek to sell it, artificially adding to its supply and forcing price down.

Whether speculators reduce or accentuate fluctuations in share prices over time depends on whether their collective view about future prices parallels the underlying price changes or moves in opposition to them. For example, if a share price is rising, and speculators take a collective view that it will continue to rise, then they will seek to buy it in the hope of reselling at a higher price, and this buying will accelerate the upward share price movement. On the other hand, if a share price is rising, and speculators take a collective view that it will begin to fall in the immediate future, then they will seek to sell the share in the hope of buying it back later at a lower price, and this selling will slow down the upward share price movement.

Speculators operate in both SPOT MARKETS and FUTURES MARKETS and often make considerable use of OPTIONS in their dealings. For example, a speculator may purchase a share option which entitles him to buy a certain number of a company's shares at a predetermined price at some future date, if he thinks that the share price will increase to more than the predetermined price plus the cost of the option; for then he can gain by exercising the option and immediately reselling the shares at the higher price.

See also ARBITRAGE, HOT MONEY.

spot market, *n.* a market for the purchase and sale of COMMODITIES (tea, rubber, etc.) and financial instruments (FOREIGN EXCHANGE, STOCKS and SHARES) for immediate delivery, as opposed to a FUTURES MARKET which provides for delivery at some future point in time. Spot prices for commodities and financial instruments transacted at different locations are harmonized by ARBITRAGE.

stabilization policy, *n.* the application by government of available macroeconomic tools to regulate the level of AGGREGATE DEMAND in

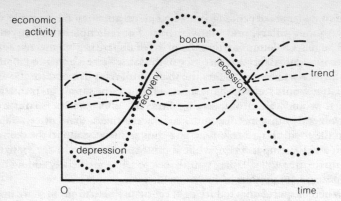

Fig. 179. **Stabilization policy**. See main entry.

order to counter CYCLICAL FLUCTUATIONS in economic activity. Left to its own devices, the economy goes through periods of BOOM and DEPRESSION known as BUSINESS CYCLES (the continuous line in Fig. 179).

During a boom period, employment increases, wages may rise and national income increases more rapidly. During depressed conditions, the reverse is true, with employment falling, wages rising only slowly (if at all) and national income rising only slowly (if at all).

It is one of the functions of government to try and smooth out such fluctuations, which may be very large. The 'best' stabilizing (or counter-cyclical) policy is where the government *exactly* offsets the amplitude of a particular peak or trough of a cycle (the broken line in Fig. 179).

However, two main problems exist: (a) the establishment of the correct magnitude of an INJECTION or WITHDRAWAL into the economy (to counter depressions and booms); (b) the establishment of the correct timing of such an injection or withdrawal. With perfect magnitude and timing the economy would follow the trend line in Fig. 179. If the timing was totally nonsynchronized, then the original cycle (continuous line) would be exacerbated to increase the original fluctuation (assuming magnitude correct), shown as a dotted line in Fig. 179.

Where the magnitude of the injection or withdrawal is inadequate, but the timing is correct, then the original cycle will be counter-weighted but not to the full extent of the original cycle (the dash-dot-dash line in Fig. 179). Clearly, most government action is inaccurate in timing and magnitude due the institutional and behavioural complexities of the economy, the objective being to get as close as possible with the means available and with the least contradiction of objectives.

The macroeconomic tools available fall under the two main headings of MONETARY POLICY and FISCAL POLICY, which also contain AUTOMATIC STABILIZERS. There is still considerable controversy as to exactly how the economy works and the effect monetary or fiscal policy has on assorted variables such as CONSUMPTION, SAVINGS, INVESTMENT, IMPORTS, etc. Combined with sometimes quite considerable inaccuracy of raw data (as published by the government statistical office) this makes for a very difficult task by those economists in government service who try to plan for such changes.

Where the government has not been successful in adequately eradicating such peaks and troughs of the business cycle, it is frequently accused of having stop-go policies (see STOP-GO CYCLE), that is, of making injections into a recovering economy which then 'overheats', and subsequently withdrawing too much at the wrong time, 'braking' too hard.

See CIRCULAR FLOW OF NATIONAL INCOME MODEL, DEMAND MANAGEMENT, DEFLATIONARY GAP, INFLATIONARY GAP, POTENTIAL GNP, MACROECONOMIC POLICY.

stag, *n.* a speculator in fixed-price new SHARE issues who subscribes for large numbers of shares in anticipation of OVERSUBSCRIPTION and a rapid rise in the share price once dealings commence. This enables him to sell his shares for a quick profit.

stagflation, *n.* a situation of depressed levels of real output combined with increases in prices (INFLATION). Stagflation is caused by the dual forces of (a) a deficiency in AGGREGATE DEMAND relative to POTENTIAL GROSS NATIONAL PRODUCT (see DEFLATIONARY-GAP) and (b) rising FACTOR INPUT costs (see COST-PUSH INFLATION).

Stagflation was a particular problem in many countries during the 1970s and early 1980s as a result of the combined effect of cost-push inflationary pressures emanating from the oil price increases of 1973 and 1979, and the deflationary consequences of reduced real purchasing power in the oil-consuming countries which accompanied these increases. This was exacerbated by the development of higher inflationary expectations.

Orthodox FISCAL POLICY and MONETARY POLICY, accustomed to an apparent trade-off between inflation and employment/output (see the PHILLIPS CURVE) was found wanting in the new situation, and many countries turned to alternative approaches; for example, in the UK the embracement of MONETARISM, and in the US SUPPLY-SIDE ECONOMICS.

stagnation, see SECULAR STAGNATION.

standard cost, *n.* an estimated product cost (see COSTS), prepared in advance of production, that shows what a product ought to cost given reasonably efficient working. Such predetermined standard costs are used to provide a basis for price-fixing and as a basis for cost control through VARIANCE ANALYSIS.

See also DIRECT-LABOUR COST VARIANCE, DIRECT-MATERIALS COST VARIANCE, OVERHEAD COST VARIANCE.

standard deviation or **root-mean-square deviation,** *n.* a measure of variation within a group of numerical observations, i.e., the square root of the average of the squared deviations of the observations from the group MEAN. Squaring the deviations eliminates negative signs and concentrates attention on the magnitude of the deviations and not their sign. For example, if five products had prices of £5, £4, £3, £2 and £1 then the mean price is:

$$\pounds\frac{5+4+3+2+1}{5} = \pounds\frac{15}{5} = \pounds3$$

and the distances by which the various prices depart from the mean price are:

		squared deviations:	
£5 − 3 =	£2		$2 \times 2 = 4$
£4 − 3 =	£1		$1 \times 1 = 1$
£3 − 3 =	£0		$0 \times 0 = 0$
£2 − 3 =	− £1		$-1 \times -1 = 1$
£1 − 3 =	− £2		$-2 \times -2 = 4$
	£0		£10

The sum of the squared deviations in the example above is £10 and their average is £10/5 = £2. This figure represents the VARIANCE of the group of observations. In order to compensate for squaring the deviations, the square root of the average is taken, so that in the example above the standard deviation would be $\sqrt{2}$ = £1.41.

Compare AVERAGE DEVIATION, COEFFICIENT OF VARIATION.

standard error, *n.* the error of the MEAN that shows how much SAMPLE means can be expected to vary from sample to sample, if repeated random samples are taken from the same POPULATION and the sample means calculated as an approximation of the true population mean. Standard error can be calculated by means of a formula linking the

STANDARD DEVIATION of the population and sample size. The standard error of the mean decreases as the size of sample is increased, so when the sample size is large, the sample mean becomes a more reliable estimate of the true population mean. See also REGRESSION ANALYSIS.

standard industrial classification, see INDUSTRIAL CLASSIFICATION.

standard of living, *n.* a level of monetary income or measure of consumption. INCOME PER HEAD is also used as a proxy for standard of living. The difficulty lies in assessing those benefits and costs which may improve a person's lifestyle but which have no immediately attributable economic value. For example, two people may have identical salaries but one may live in the country and have splendid scenery, peace and quiet, no traffic jams when driving to work and little pollution. The other person lives in an industrial city which has considerable traffic jams, pollution, noise and crime. Monetary comparisons would suggest a similar standard of living but this may not be the case.

standard rate of taxation, *n.* the basic rate of INCOME TAX, for example, 30 pence per £1 of taxable income. In a PROGRESSIVE-TAXATION system the standard rate of taxation applies only to the initial taxable income band; those with taxable income in excess of the initial band paying a higher MARGINAL RATE OF TAXATION on this additional income.

stand-by arrangement, *n.* an arrangement between the INTER-NATIONAL MONETARY FUND and a member country under which the member country is entitled to borrow up to an agreed amount of foreign currency from the Fund to cover a possible deficit on its BALANCE OF PAYMENTS.

staple product, *n.* any product that has an INCOME-ELASTICITY OF DEMAND less than one. This means that as incomes rise, proportionately less income is spent on such products. Examples of staple products include basic foodstuffs like potatoes and bread. By contrast, products with an income elasticity of more than one are referred to as LUXURY PRODUCTS.

See also ENGEL'S LAW, NORMAL PRODUCT, INFERIOR PRODUCT, GIFFEN GOOD.

statement of account, *n.* a periodic statement sent to a customer by a supplier that sets out both the money value of products supplied to the customer over a monthly or other period, and any amounts still owed by the customer for these products. A statement of account is sent by a supplier some time after an INVOICE has been sent. Compare DELIVERY NOTE.

statements of standard-accounting practice (SSAP), *n.* a series of guideline documents on aspects of the accounting treatment of company finances produced jointly by the main UK professional bodies. The issuing of accounting statements is usually preceded by widespread consultation, including the publication of exposure drafts, before an accounting statement is finalized. Over 20 SSAP's have been issued covering topics like foreign currency translation, accounting for goodwill, and inflation accounting.

state ownership, see NATIONALIZATION.

static analysis, see COMPARATIVE STATIC-EQUILIBRIUM ANALYSIS.

statistical inference, *n.* a process by which we infer conclusions about a statistical POPULATION from which only a SAMPLE has been drawn. For example, if one million Britons holiday in Spain each year, and 200 are asked why they do so, 50% may say because the sun shines continually. From this sample one may infer that 50% of the total population of one million Britons taking a holiday in Spain do so for this reason. However, it is not possible to say with 100% accuracy that this is the case unless the views of all one million were obtained. Nevertheless, it is possible to say with 95% confidence that the estimation of 50% is correct for the whole population.

It is clearly very difficult, expensive and time-consuming to ask *everybody* the reasons for choosing Spain as a holiday destination. The PROBABILITY that the population (the one million holidaymakers) behaves as the sample (the 200 holidaymakers) suggests, can be statistically determined using HYPOTHESIS TESTING.

statistics, *n.* **1.** a branch of mathematics that studies the theory and methods of collecting, tabulating and analysing numerical data. **2.** a grouping of data. Economic analysis makes extensive use of economic data which are subjected to statistical analysis in order to test ECONOMIC THEORIES.

See HYPOTHESIS TESTING.

statute law, *n.* the law laid down by government legislation (in the UK, an Act of Parliament). Examples include the FAIR TRADING ACT, 1973 and the Companies Act, 1983. Once such legislation is on the statute books, it is then up to the courts to interpret and enforce the provisions of this legislation. Compare COMMON LAW.

stepwise regression, *n.* a form of MULTIPLE-REGRESSION ANALYSIS in which INDEPENDENT VARIABLES are added into the regression equation one at a time, and their impact in terms of adding to the explanatory power of the regression equation is noted.

sterling, *n.* the name given to the UK POUND in international dealings to distinguish it from other countries using the pound as the basis of their currencies. Formerly, most countries extensively involved in international trade kept large sterling balances as part of their stock of INTERNATIONAL RESERVES, but nowadays sterling is little used as a reserve asset except by a number of current and former member countries of the British Commonwealth.

sterling area, *n.* a group of countries (predominantly ex-British colonies) whose own national currencies were formerly linked directly to the value of the British POUND, and who hold STERLING as part of their INTERNATIONAL RESERVES.

sterling M₃ (£M₃), see MONEY SUPPLY DEFINITIONS.

stock, *n.* **1.** the part of a firm's ASSETS that are held in the form of raw materials, work-in-progress and finished goods. These are also known as INVENTORIES. Finished goods are held in stock to ensure that goods are available when required by customers. Raw materials and components are held in stock to prevent disruptions to production caused by lack of materials or components and to secure economies from bulk purchasing.

The rate at which firms accumulate and deplete their stocks influences the oscillations in economic activity (see BUSINESS CYCLE). Although the increase and decrease in stocks operates on the same ACCELERATOR principle as capital investment, the decision as to what *level* of stock to hold may not be entirely in the businessman's hands. Involuntary investment may occur when demand turns out to be less than a producer's expectations. See STOCK VALUATION.

2. a FINANCIAL SECURITY issued by a JOINT-STOCK COMPANY or by the government as a means of raising long-term capital. In some countries (for example, the US) stockholders are the equivalent of shareholders and are the owners of the company. In other countries (for example, the UK) stock is a form of repayable, fixed-interest, DEBT and stockholders are creditors of the company not shareholders. Stocks are traded on the STOCK EXCHANGE. See SHARE CAPITAL.

3. a measurement of quantity at one specific point in time. Unlike a FLOW, a stock is not a function of time. The analogy is frequently made between a reservoir holding water, and water entering and leaving the reservoir.

stock appreciation, *n.* the increase in the market value of STOCK held during a specific time period, generally because of INFLATION. Accountants value stock at the lower of either cost or net realizable value in the BALANCE SHEET, not at replacement cost, and when stock is sold, tax is paid on the profits arising. This gives rise to 'phantom profits' and is one

493

reason why British firms were given stock relief in taxation calculations during the inflationary period of the 1970s. Where prices are falling, *stock depreciation* results.

National accounting, as illustrated in the GROSS NATIONAL PRODUCT accounts also has to take the problem of stock appreciation into account. The government statisticians have the difficult task of excluding such monetary appreciation from the final calculation so as to include only *real* stock increases.

See also HISTORIC COST, INFLATION ACCOUNTING, STOCK VALUATION.

stockbroker, *n.* an agent who acts on behalf of individual and company clients, arranging to buy or sell STOCKS and SHARES from JOBBERS (principals who make markets in securities). In most countries, individuals and companies can deal directly with jobbers so that the role of stockbroker and jobber are combined. See STOCK EXCHANGE.

stock control, *n.* the process of controlling STOCKS of finished products, WORK IN PROGRESS and raw materials, in order to minimize STOCKHOLDING COSTS, while maintaining an adequate level of consumer service and appropriate safety stocks to meet contingencies like sudden increases in demand. Stock control requires good forecasts of future consumer demand and production requirements, so that purchasing and production can be planned to avoid carrying excessive stocks with their associated stockholding costs. See also STOCK–TURNOVER RATIO.

stock depreciation, see STOCK APPRECIATION.

stock dividend, *n.* a DIVIDEND payment whereby a SHAREHOLDER is paid a dividend in the form of additional SHARES or STOCKS in the company rather than in cash. See also STOCK SPLITS.

stock exchange, *n.* a MARKET that deals in long-term company securities (STOCKS and SHARES) and government securities (BONDS). Institutions involved in the stock exchange include JOBBERS, STOCKBROKERS and MERCHANT BANKS. The stock exchange performs two principal functions. It provides (a) a primary or new-issue market where new capital for investment and other purposes can be raised by the issue of financial securities; (b) a secondary market for dealings in existing securities which facilitates the easy transferability of securities from sellers to buyers. The stock exchange thus occupies an important position in a country's FINANCIAL SYSTEM by providing a mechanism for converting SAVINGS into physical and portfolio INVESTMENT.

In recent years national stock exchanges such as those based in London, New York and Tokyo have become increasingly interdependent with the growth of MULTINATIONAL FIRMS, and financial institutions and securities firms themselves have become more international in scope. This has led to mounting competitive pressures which has brought about, particularly in the case of the London stock exchange, a number of important changes: the termination of the system of fixed minimum commissions for stockbrokers and the ending of the traditional division between stockbrokers and jobbers (the so-called *big bang*), and the formation of alliances between local securities firms and the international banking and securities groups, so as to provide customers with a more diversified range of financial and investment services.

In recognition of the growth in international securities dealings the London stock exchange was merged with the *International Securities Regulatory Organisation (ISRO)* which represents the big international securities firms. The London stock exchange and ISRO now operate a single investment exchange, for dealings in both domestic and foreign stocks, shares and bonds.

See also CAPITAL MARKET, CITY CODE, SPECULATION, SPECULATOR, FUTURES MARKET, INSTITUTIONAL INVESTORS, UNLISTED-SECURITIES MARKET, OVER-THE-COUNTER MARKET, MARKET MAKER.

stockholding costs or **inventory costs,** *n*. the cost to firms of holding STOCKS of finished products and raw materials in order to provide immediate customer service or to prevent disruptions to production caused by lack of materials. Stockholding costs include costs of warehouse space, insurance, deterioration and obsolescence of stored items and interest on capital tied up in stocks. Such costs are roughly proportional to the value of the stock held, and to contain such costs, stock levels need to be kept low. On the other hand, firms also have costs for ordering and delivering goods for stock such as communicating with suppliers, accounting transactions, transport and unloading and inspecting goods. Many of these ordering and delivery costs will remain the same irrespective of the size of the order.

Since many order and delivery costs are fixed costs, in order to reduce these costs the firm should place large orders at infrequent intervals, and such a policy would have the additional benefit of allowing the firm to earn price discounts for bulk purchase. However if orders are placed at infrequent intervals then stocks, and thus stockholding costs, will be high. It is desirable to strike a balance between these two groups of costs so as to achieve the minimum stock cost, as in Fig. 180 on page 496 which shows the *optimum order quantity* or *economic order quantity* which serves to minimize total stock cost. Order and delivery costs in Fig. 180 decrease as

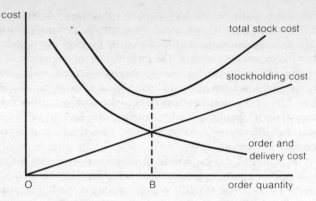

Fig. 180. **Stockholding costs**. See main entry.

larger and less frequent deliveries are made; while larger deliveries at less intervals involve a larger average stock length and thus higher carrying costs. The optimum order quantity OB corresponds to the minimum point on the total stock-cost curve. For simple stockholding situations mathematical formulas can be used to determine the optimum order quantity.

In the simple model above, stock-costs are excluded, implying that replenishment of stock can occur immediately an order is placed, so that once stocks fall to zero an order can be placed and stock replenished. However, there is usually a delay between placing an order and receiving delivery into stock, and a firm needs enough safety stock on hand to cope with expected usage before stock replenishment can be achieved. Where there is some uncertainty about the rate of usage before stock replenishment, or about the lead time before replenishment can occur, then there is the risk of a stock-out unless the firm carries an adequate safety stock. The size of safety stock carried will seek to balance the extra stockholding costs associated with safety stocks on the one hand and the costs of stock-outs on the other hand.

See STOCK-TURNOVER RATIO.

stockpiling, *n.* the act of accumulating STOCKS over and above normal requirements. National and international trade is dependent upon complex and interrelated supply lines from the raw material to the finished good. If at one point along the supply chain a shortage (or bottleneck) can be perceived in advance by firms beyond that point, then those firms will attempt to purchase much greater stocks than their immediate needs warrant. Stockpiling occurs in many areas of economic life, from the government stockpiling food or weapons, to the individual consumer amassing quantities of food in anticipation of a price rise.

stock split, *n.* an increase in the number of SHARES in a JOINT-STOCK COMPANY that does not affect the capitalization of the company. For example, Company X has 10,000 authorized, issued and fully-paid up shares each with a par value of £1; and total SHAREHOLDERS CAPITAL is shown in the BALANCE SHEET at £10,000. The STOCK EXCHANGE values the company at £100,000, making each share worth £10. The company wishes to attract a wider shareholder base by reducing the market PRICE of each share, and so undertakes a two to one stock split, giving existing shareholders two new 50p shares for each share held. The company now has 20,000 authorized, issued and fully paid up shares of 50p nominal value, and capitalization of the company remains unchanged at £10,000. However, now the stock-market price of the shares will be £5, which hopefully will improve the marketability of the shares.

See also SHARE CAPITAL.

stock-turnover ratio, *n.* an accounting measure of a firm's stock-holdings, that expresses the firm's SALES REVENUE as a ratio of its period-end STOCK, to show how many times stocks are turned over in sales during a period's trading.

See also STOCK CONTROL, STOCKHOLDING COSTS.

stock valuation, *n.* the placing of an appropriate money value upon a firm's STOCKS of raw materials, WORK-IN-PROGRESS and finished goods. Where INFLATION causes the price of several different batches of finished-goods stock bought during a trading period to differ, the firm has the problems of deciding: (a) what money value to place upon the period-end physical stock in the BALANCE SHEET; (b) what cost to attach to the units sold in the TRADING AND PROFIT-AND-LOSS ACCOUNT. The second decision has a direct bearing upon the COST-OF-GOODS SOLD and so upon GROSS PROFIT.

Different formulas used to value stock can lead to variations in the balance-sheet value of stock and in the cost of goods sold. For example the *first-in, first-out (FIFO)* method assumes that goods are withdrawn from stock in the order in which they are received so that the cost of goods sold is based on the cost of the oldest goods in stock, while the value of closing stock is based on the prices of the most recent purchases (see Fig. 181 on page 498). By contrast, the *last-in, first-out (LIFO)* method assumes that the most recently purchased goods are (theoretical-

	FIFO			LIFO	
sales (100 × £15)		£1,500	sales (100 × £15)		£1,500
cost of goods sold:			cost of goods sold:		
20 × £10 = £200			100 × £12		£1,200
80 × £12 = £960		£1,160			
100					
profit		£340	profit		£300
closing stock (20 × £12)		£240	closing stock (20 × £10)		£200

Fig. 181. **Stock valuation**. The opening stock is 20 units, costing £10 each; the purchases are 100 units at £12 each; the sales are 100 units at £15 each; the closing stock is 20 units.

ly) withdrawn from stock first so that the cost of goods sold is based on the costs of the most recent purchases, while the value of closing stock is based on the oldest goods available (see Fig. 181). The last-in first-out method gives a higher figure for cost-of-goods sold: one which more closely approximates the replacement cost of goods sold; but it tends to understate the value of period-end stocks.

In the interests of prudence the firm would tend to value stocks at cost or market value, whichever was the lower, to avoid overstating profits.

See also STOCK APPRECIATION, INFLATION ACCOUNTING.

stop-go cycle, *n.* the application by government of available macroeconomic tools to stimulate and then dampen economic activity. Such tools are used in counter-cyclical STABILIZATION POLICY to try and offset the fluctuations in economic activity associated with the BUSINESS CYCLE. Stop-go policies are often referred to in a negative sense, in that government policies of this type during the 1960s and early 1970s, especially, were either ill-timed or involved injections or withrawals of an incorrect magnitude.

Short-term attainment of government economic objectives such as the level of employment and the exchange rate are frequently contradictory to the long-term objectives of, for instance, growth.

See MACROECONOMIC POLICY.

store of value, *n.* an attribute of MONEY, enabling people to hold on to money to finance some *future* purchase of a product or asset without loss of PURCHASING POWER in the interim.

straight-line method, see DEPRECIATION (2).

strategic decisions, *n.* any decisions taken by the most senior management that determine the fundamental long-term objectives of an enterprise and the formulation of overall plans to achieve them.

Decisions of this nature deal with what may be termed the *entrepreneurial functions* of the enterprise, rather than recurrent operational decisions. Strategic decisions are concerned with identifying the strengths and weaknesses of the enterprise in relation to the opportunities and threats in its environment, and formulating programmes of action to exploit these opportunities and deal with potential threats.

See ENTREPRENEUR, CORPORATE PLANNING.

stratified sample, *n*. a SAMPLE that is selected by dividing the total POPULATION into a number of distinct subgroups then selecting a proportionate number of items from each subgroup. See RANDOM SAMPLE.

strike, *n*. a concerted stoppage of work by a group of workers as part of an INDUSTRIAL DISPUTE. See INDUSTRIAL RELATIONS, LOCKOUT, PICKET.

structural unemployment, *n*. the long-term UNEMPLOYMENT caused by the decline of certain industries and changes in production processes. It occurs where changing demand-patterns in an economy dislocate existing production-patterns to the extent that labour becomes redundant. This is a long-term phenomenon requiring the work force to seek other jobs outside the declining industries, possibly in a different part of the country. The problem is one which most governments have had to deal with, for example, the decline in the heavy engineering industries, steel and shipbuilding, in the north of England and in Scotland. Technological change and foreign competition forced the reduction in demand for GOODS associated with those industries, which resulted in mass unemployment of labour. Countering such unemployment requires extensive occupational retraining programmes for the displaced workers, assistance with moving to new areas where jobs are available, and financial inducements to encourage new growth industries to move to regions blighted by concentrations of declining industries.

See FRICTIONAL UNEMPLOYMENT, REGIONAL POLICY, DEINDUSTRIAL-IZATION.

structure of industry, *n*. the productive activities undertaken in an economy classified according to broad groupings of activities by sector, or more narrowly on an industry-to-industry basis.

The three basic sectors of an economy are: (a) the primary sector (raw materials and farming), (b) the industrial or secondary sector (manufactured goods, construction, gas and electricity, etc.), (c) the service sector (retailing, banking, tourism, etc.).

The relative importance of each of these sectors tends to change as the economy expands over time. For example, DEVELOPING COUNTRIES are

	Agriculture		Industry		Manufacturing		Services	
	1960	1984	1960	1984	1960	1984	1960	1984
UK	3	2	43	32	32	18	54	66
US	4	2	38	32	29	21	58	66
Japan	13	4	45	42	34	30	42	54
W. Germany	6	2	53	46	40	35	41	52

Fig. 182. **Structure of industry**. The distribution of gross domestic product in percentages from 1960 to 1984 for the UK, US, Japan and West Germany. Manufacturing percentages are also included in those for industry. Source: *World Development Report*, World Bank.

characterized by very large primary sectors and small industrial and service sectors, whereas DEVELOPED COUNTRIES are characterized by small primary sectors and large industrial and service sectors. Fig. 182 shows that in the most advanced countries there has been a relative decline in the industrial sector, and a corresponding increase in the importance of the service sector.

See INDUSTRIALIZATION, DEINDUSTRIALIZATION, INDUSTRIAL CLASSIFICATIONS, ECONOMIC DEVELOPMENT.

subsidiary company, *n.* a company that is owned by another company (see FIRM). A subsidiary company may continue to trade under its own name, but it is subjected to complete or partial centralized control by the 'parent company'. See also HOLDING COMPANY, CONSOLIDATED ACCOUNTS.

subsidy, *n.* a payment made by the government to either: (a) a FIRM, to enable it to hold or reduce the price of its product to households, thus ensuring that the households maintain their consumption; (b) declining firms and industries, to enable them to remain in business. In the former cases, subsidies are used as an instrument of income redistribution by reducing the price of products such as bread and milk which figure prominently in the budget of lower income groups, or by directly subsidizing incomes.

Subsidies encourage increased output of favoured products, but distort domestic RESOURCE-ALLOCATION processes in general, and can adversely affect international trade (EXPORT SUBSIDIES).

See REDISTRIBUTION-OF-INCOME PRINCIPLE OF TAXATION.

subsistence wage rate, see WAGES-FUND THEORY.

substitute products, *n.* any GOODS or SERVICES that are considered to be economically interchangeable by buyers. For example, if an increase in the price of coffee causes buyers to switch away from it and buy a greater quantity of tea, these two goods can be regarded as substitutes for one another.

The CROSS-ELASTICITY OF DEMAND between two products serves as a measure of the degree of substitutability between them; products which are close substitutes have a high cross-elasticity, while products which are poor substitutes have a low cross-elasticity.

See COMPLEMENTARY PRODUCTS.

substitution effect, *n.* the substitution of one PRODUCT for another resulting from a change in their relative prices. A fall in the price of a product normally results in more of it being demanded. A part of this increase is due to the substitution effect. A lower price for good X, with the prices of other goods remaining unchanged, will increase its relative attractiveness, inducing consumers to substitute good X in place of some of the now relatively more expensive items in their budgets. The substitution effect, together with the INCOME EFFECT, provides an explanation of why DEMAND CURVES are downward sloping.

See CONSUMER EQUILIBRIUM, REVEALED PREFERENCE, PRICE EFFECT.

sufficient condition, see NECESSARY CONDITION.

sunk costs, *n.* any expenditure on durable and specific FACTOR INPUTS such as plant and machinery which cannot be used for other purposes or easily be resold. Such sunk costs have no affect on MARGINAL COSTS and do not influence short-term output decisions. See also OPPORTUNITY COST.

supermarket, *n.* a large self-service retail outlet. Supermarkets may be under single-shop ownership, or run as a multiple CHAIN-STORE business. The larger supermarket chains are able to effect major economies in distribution both on a group basis by being able to obtain favourable discounts and concessions from manufacturers by bulk buying, and at the individual store level by the use of capital-intensive methods of retailing. Initially, supermarkets appeared mainly in the grocery trade but there has been a tendency for them to move into a variety of non-food lines. Similar supermarket-type operations have been established for most other mass-retailed products.

Hypermarkets are an extended form of supermarket, usually located on the outskirts of towns and cities where space is plentiful.

See RETAILING.

super-normal profit, see ABOVE-NORMAL PROFIT.

supplier, see FIRM.

supply, *n.* the amount of a PRODUCT made available for sale by FIRMS. In economic analysis, the total supply of a product is reflected in the SUPPLY CURVE, Compare DEMAND.

supply and demand, see SUPPLY CURVE, DEMAND CURVE.

supply curve, *n.* a line showing the relationship between the PRICE of a good and the quantity supplied per time period. 'Supply' means the total quantity of a good or service which firms are prepared to sell at a given price.

The typical market supply curve slopes upwards from left to right, indicating that as price rises more is supplied. Thus, if price rises from OP_1 to OP_2 in Fig. 183, the quantity supplied will increase from OQ_1 to OQ_2.

Fig. 183. **Supply curve.** See main entry.

Fig. 183 shows the supply curve for the market as a whole. This curve is derived by aggregating the individual supply curves of all of the producers of the good which in turn are derived from the producers' cost curves.

Most supply curves slope upwards because, as the price of the product rises, producers will find it more profitable to manufacture, using their existing production facilities, and because any increase in short-run MARGINAL COSTS associated with increasing output will be covered by the higher price obtained.

The slope of the supply curve reflects the degree of responsiveness of quantity supplied to changes in the product's price. For example, if a large rise in price results in only a small increase in quantity supplied (as would be the case where the supply curve has a steep slope), then supply is said to be price-inelastic (see PRICE-ELASTICITY OF SUPPLY).

The supply curve interacts with the DEMAND CURVE to determine the EQUILIBRIUM MARKET PRICE. See SUPPLY CURVE, (SHIFT IN), SUPPLY FUNCTION.

Fig. 184. **Supply curve, (shift in).** A fall in production costs shifts the supply curve S_1S_1 to S_2S_2, increasing the quantity supplied at price OP from OQ_1 to OQ_2. The magnitude of this shift depends on the sensitivity of product supply to changes in costs.

supply curve, (shift in), *n.* a movement of the SUPPLY CURVE from one position to another (either left or right) as a result of some economic change, other than PRICE.

A given supply curve is always drawn on the CETERIS PARIBUS assumption that all of the other factors affecting supply (costs in particular) are held constant. If any of these change, however, then this will bring about a *shift* in the supply curve. For example, if costs of production fall, the supply curve will shift to the right (see Fig. 184) so that more is now supplied at each price than formerly. See also SUPPLY FUNCTION.

supply elasticity, see PRICE–ELASTICITY OF SUPPLY.

supply function, *n.* a form of notation that links the DEPENDENT VARIABLE, quantity supplied (Q_s), with various INDEPENDENT VARIABLES which determine quantity supplied such as product PRICE (P), prices of factor inputs (P_1 and P_2), the state of technology (T), and business goals (G). The equation states that:

$$Q_s = f(P, P_1, P_2, T, G)$$

Changes in any of these independent variables will affect quantity supplied, and if we wish to investigate the particular effect of any one of these variables upon quantity supplied then we could (conceptually) hold the influence of the other independent variables constant (CETERIS PARIBUS), whilst we focus upon the particular effect of that independent variable.

See also SUPPLY CURVE, SUPPLY CURVE (SHIFTS IN).

supply schedule, *n.* a schedule listing the various PRICES of a PRODUCT and the specific quantities supplied at each of these prices. The information provided by a supply schedule can be used to construct a SUPPLY CURVE showing the price/quantity-supplied relationship in graphical form.

supply-side economics, *n.* the branch of economic analysis concerned with the productive capability of an economy (POTENTIAL GROSS NATIONAL PRODUCT) and with policies which attempt to improve the flexibility of factor markets so as to generate the largest possible output for a given level of AGGREGATE DEMAND. Supply-side economists have examined institutional rigidities in factor markets and the effect of higher factor prices in 'pricing people out of jobs'. This has led them to condemn the activities of trade unions in labour markets on the grounds that trade unions push WAGE RATES up to levels which exceed the MARGINAL-REVENUE PRODUCTIVITY of the workers concerned, thereby restricting potential employment. Such ideas have also led supply-side economists to condemn certain SOCIAL-SECURITY BENEFITS systems and PROGRESSIVE-TAXATION systems for creating a POVERTY TRAP which acts as a disincentive for the unemployed to take lowly-paid jobs.

See also NEGATIVE INCOME TAX, PROFIT-RELATED PAY.

surplus value, *n.* an excess of the receipts of a FACTOR INPUT over its supply PRICE. David RICARDO took the example of rental payments to landlords in possession of superior land. Karl MARX viewed surplus value in terms of labour whereby workers produce more than their own costs. Marx attempted to show that the surplus was due solely to labour when in fact it is the combined productive process which produces the surplus. According to Marx, exploitation of the workers can only be eradicated by paying workers the value of their output rather than their cost. Alfred MARSHALL noted that all factor receipts in excess of factor costs are in the nature of QUASI-RENT in the short run, and where there are no alternative opportunities for a factor, *all* of its reward is a surplus.

See also ECONOMIC RENT, TRANSFER EARNINGS.

symmetrical distribution, *n.* a group of numerical observations whose FREQUENCY DISTRIBUTION takes the form of a bell-shaped HISTOGRAM or of CONTINUOUS DISTRIBUTION with two equally-shaped halves. In a perfectly symmetrical distribution the MEAN will equal the MEDIAN and the MODE. Compare SKEWED DISTRIBUTION.

synergy, see DIVERSIFICATION.

systematic risk, *n*. that part of total risk (within the CAPITAL-ASSET PRICING MODEL) attributable to the holding of a security, or portfolio of securities, which has a definable relationship in respect of variations of all security yields on the stock market. This definable relationship is termed the BETA COEFFICIENT (2). The beta coefficient (β) therefore estimates the degree of responsiveness of a particular security's yield to changes in the level of a specified market index, such as the Financial Times All-Share Index or the Dow-Jones Index. Studies of the measurement of β indicate a linear relationship between the movement of a particular security and the market generally. For instance, if $\beta = 1$, a 10% change in security A is associated with a 10% change in the market generally. The security and the market are said to be perfectly correlated. If $\beta = 0$, the security is said to be risk-free because no matter how much the market moves, the security remains constant (such as TREASURY BILLS). An asset is considered risky if $\beta > 1$. Unlike NONSYSTEMATIC RISK, it is not possible to diversify the risk away because however large the portfolio of shares held, they are all influenced by the market generally to a greater or lesser extent. The two components of risk, systematic and nonsystematic are sometimes referred to as *nondiversifiable* and *diversifiable* for the reasons outlined.

T

table, *n.* a means of presenting statistical data, often summarized in terms of a FREQUENCY DISTRIBUTION.

takeover, *n.* the joining together of two or more FIRMS. Unlike a MERGER, which is usually arranged by mutual agreement between the firms involved, takeovers often involve one firm buying out the other without the full agreement of the acquired firm. For publicly-quoted companies this involves one company buying 50% or more of the voting shares of the other so as to exercise effective control over it, though generally the acquiring company would wish to purchase all the shares of the other company.

Three broad categories of takeover may be identified: (a) horizontal takeovers involving firms that are direct competitors in the same market; (b) vertical takeovers involving firms which stand in a supplier-customer relationship; (c) conglomerate takeovers involving firms operating in unrelated markets which are seeking to diversify their activities.

From the firm's point of view a takeover can be advantageous because it may enable the firm to reduce production and distribution costs, expand its existing activities or move into new areas, or remove troublesome competition and increase its market power. In terms of their wider impact on the operation of market processes, takeovers may, on the one hand, promote greater efficiency in resource use, or, on the other hand, by reducing competition, lead to a less efficient allocation of resources. In sum, they may involve, simultaneously, both benefits and detriments (see MERGER).

In the UK, takeovers which create or extend a firm's market share of a particular product in excess of 25%, or where the value of assets acquired is over £30 million, can be referred to the MONOPOLIES AND MERGERS COMMISSION to determine whether or not they are in the public interest.

See also ASSET STRIPPER, MONOPOLY POLICY, OFFICE OF FAIR TRADING, WILLIAMSON TRADE-OFF MODEL, HORIZONTAL INTEGRATION, VERTICAL INTEGRATION, DIVERSIFICATION, CITY CODE.

takeover bid, *n.* an attempt by one FIRM to TAKEOVER another by acquiring the majority of shares in a public JOINT-STOCK COMPANY. A number of terms are used to describe the various tactics available to the bidding and defending firms, including:

(a) *black knight*; a firm that launches an unwelcome (contested) takeover bid for some other firm.

(b) *golden parachute*; any generous severance terms written into the employment contracts of the directors of a firm that makes it expensive to sack the directors if the firm is taken over.

(c) *greenmail*; a situation in which a firm's shares are being bought up by a (potential) takeover bidder, who is then headed-off from making an actual bid by that firm's directors buying these shares from him at a premium price.

(d) *leveraged bid*; a takeover that is financed primarily by the issue of LOAN CAPITAL (often called *junk bonds*) rather than SHARE CAPITAL which increases the CAPITAL GEARING of the enlarged firm.

(e) *pac-man defence*; a situation in which the firm being bid for itself now makes a bid for the acquiring firm (see REVERSE TAKEOVER).

(f) *poison pill*; a tactic employed in a takeover bid whereby the intended victim firm itself takes over or merges (see MERGER) with some other firm in order to make itself financially or structurally less attractive to the potential acquirer.

(g) *porcupine*; any complex agreements between a firm and its suppliers, customers, or creditors that make it difficult for an acquiring company to integrate this firm with its own business.

(h) *shark repellants*; any measures specifically designed to discourage takeover bidders; for example, altering the company's articles of association to increase the proportion of shareholder votes needed to approve the bid above the usual 50% mark.

(i) *white knight*; the intervention in a takeover bid of a third firm which itself takes over or merges with the intended victim firm to 'rescue' it from its unwelcome suitor.

See CITY CODE.

tangent, *n.* a straight line that just touches, but does not intersect, a curve at a particular point. Tangents are usefully applied in economics to determine the slope, or gradient, of a curve at one particular point along its length. For instance, INDIFFERENCE-CURVE analysis suggests that a rational consumer would seek to maximize his UTILITY by choosing a combination of two products X and Y where his BUDGET LINE is tangential to the highest available indifference curve, for only here do

TANGIBLE ASSETS

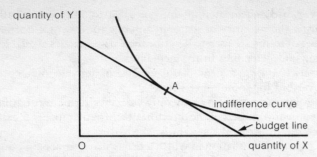

Fig. 185. **Tangent**. Point A is the point of tangency.

the relative prices of the products match their relative utilities. See Fig. 185.

tangible assets, *n.* any physical ASSETS such as plant, machinery, equipment, vehicles and STOCK that have a money value.

tap issue, *n.* the sale and issue of TREASURY BILLS by the Bank of England to government departments and agencies at an unpublished predetermined price. The government departments to which such bills are sold usually have short-term cash surpluses. The three-month Treasury Bills are therefore ideally suited to the purpose and are known as *short taps*. The tap issue, which is not for sale on the open market, derives its name from being constantly available, that is, 'on tap'. There are also longer-dated tap stocks.

See TENDER ISSUE, DISCOUNT MARKET, OPEN MARKET OPERATIONS.

tariff or **import levy,** *n.* a duty (a form of TAX) that is levied on IMPORTS. There are two main types of tariff: (a) ad valorem duty which is levied as a fixed percentage of the value of the good; (b) specific duty which is levied as a fixed sum of money per physical unit of the good.

Tariffs are used to protect domestic industries from foreign competition and to raise revenue for the government.

The economic effects of a tariff are illustrated in Fig. 186. In the Fig., DD and SS are the domestic demand and supply curves of good X. In a closed economy, assuming perfect competition, the domestic price is OP_1. Consider now an open-economy situation with the world price for this particular good being OP_2. Assuming that the country's demand for good X accounts for only a small fraction of total world demand for the good, such that it is unable to affect the terms of trade of the good, then, under conditions of FREE TRADE, the domestic price will also be OP_2. At price OP_2 domestic consumption is O_b, domestic production is

Fig. 186. **Tariff**. See main entry.

O_a, and imports being the difference between the two are equal to ab.

The imposition of a specific tariff, T, will cause the domestic price of imports to rise by the full amount of the duty, to price OP_3 in the Fig. At price OP_3 domestic consumption falls from O_b to O_d, domestic production increases from O_a to O_c and imports are reduced from ab to cd. The area YZLM (import volume cd times tariff per unit OP_2OP_3) represents government revenue from the tariff.

Although producers of the protected good gain by now being able to increase their supply of the good (that is, from O_a to O_c), the overall effect of the tariff is to reduce the productive efficiency of the economy and consumer welfare. The triangle XYZ represents the 'production loss' to the economy. Under conditions of full resource employment production in the tariff-protected industry can only be increased by diverting resources away from other (nonprotected) industries, which rank higher in the order of productive efficiency. Thus, some resources are allocated less efficiently as a result of the tariff. The triangle LMN represents the 'consumption loss' (loss of CONSUMER'S SURPLUS) to society. As a result of the tariff, some buyers are forced to switch to less desirable substitute products while those consumers continuing to buy the good are now forced to pay a price for it which is in excess of the real economic costs of supplying it.

How effective the tariff is as a means of protecting the domestic industry will depend upon the PRICE-ELASTICITY OF DEMAND for the imported good. If import demand is highly price-inelastic, there will be little reduction in the volume of imports. In these cases a more effective means of protection is a QUOTA which places a physical ceiling on the amount of imports permitted.

See also PROTECTIONISM, NOMINAL RATE OF PROTECTION, EFFECTIVE RATE OF PROTECTION.

tax, *n.* a levy imposed by the government on the income of persons and businesses (DIRECT TAX) and on goods and services (INDIRECT TAX). Taxes are used by the government for a variety of purposes, for example, to: (a) raise revenue for the government; (b) alter the distribution of income and wealth; (c) control the level and distribution of spending in the economy; (d) control the volume of imports and exports.

See TAXATION, BUDGET (GOVERNMENT), FISCAL POLICY, PRINCIPLES OF TAXATION.

taxable income, *n.* the amount of an individual's income that is subject to TAXATION once any tax allowances to which the taxpayer is entitled have been deducted.

taxation, *n.* the government receipts from TAXES on household and business income and expenditure. Taxes on income include personal INCOME TAX and CORPORATION TAX; taxes on expenditure include VALUE-ADDED TAX and EXCISE DUTIES. Taxation is a WITHDRAWAL from the CIRCULAR FLOW OF NATIONAL INCOME. Taxes are used to finance GOVERNMENT EXPENDITURE and as instruments of FISCAL POLICY in regulating the level of total spending (AGGREGATE DEMAND) in the economy.

See PRINCIPLES OF TAXATION, PROGRESSIVE TAXATION, REGRESSIVE TAXATION, INCIDENCE OF TAXATION, INLAND REVENUE.

taxation schedule, *n.* a schedule that depicts the relationship between TAXATION receipts and the level of NATIONAL INCOME. Under PROGRESSIVE TAXATION, the schedule has a positive slope, that is tax receipts rise as the level of income rises (see Fig. 187). Likewise, receipts from expenditure taxes will be greater as the level of spending rises.

See also FISCAL DRAG, PROPENSITY TO TAX.

tax avoidance, *n.* any efforts by taxpayers to arrange their financial affairs so as to avoid paying TAX by taking maximum advantage of taxation allowances and reliefs. In this way taxpayers can legally minimize their tax burden. Compare TAX EVASION.

tax base, *n.* the total pool which the tax authorities can tap in levying a TAX. For example, the tax base for INCOME TAX is total taxable income and the tax base for CORPORATION TAX is total taxable profits.

tax burden, *n.* the total amount of TAXATION paid by the citizens of a country in the form of income tax, corporation tax, value-added tax,

Fig. 187. **Taxation schedule**. See main entry.

etc. The total amount of tax as a proportion of GROSS NATIONAL PRODUCT gives some indication of the overall tax burden. See also INCIDENCE OF TAXATION.

tax credit, see NEGATIVE INCOME TAX.

tax evasion, any efforts by taxpayers to evade TAX by various illegal means, such as not declaring all of their income to the tax authorities or falsely claiming reliefs to which they are not entitled. Compare TAX AVOIDANCE.

tax haven, *n.* a country which imposes low rates of personal and corporate TAXES, and which as a consequence tends to attract wealthy individuals and MULTINATIONAL FIRMS seeking to minimize their taxation liabilities.

See also TRANSFER PRICE.

t distribution or **Student's distribution,** *n.* a theoretical sampling distribution which closely approximates the NORMAL DISTRIBUTION. The t distribution is used to establish CONFIDENCE INTERVALS when using small samples to estimate the true population mean. The equation used to calculate the t distribution depends on the size of the sample (n) or, more precisely, the number of DEGREES OF FREEDOM (n–1). When, say, a 95 per cent confidence interval is calculated from a t distribution for a small sample, it will generate wider confidence intervals than would be the case for a 95 per cent confidence interval for a large sample.

The t distribution is frequently used in formulating levels of significance for HYPOTHESIS TESTING.

technical efficiency, *n.* an aspect of PRODUCTION that seeks to identify, in physical terms, the optimal (best possible) combination of FACTOR INPUTS to produce a given level of OUTPUT. See also EFFICIENCY, PRODUCTION FUNCTION.

technological-gap theory, *n*. a theory that seeks to explain changes in the pattern of INTERNATIONAL TRADE over time, which is based on a dynamic sequence of technological and product INNOVATION and diffusion. Technologically advanced countries with a high propensity to innovate (such as the US) are able to achieve trade advantages by being able to offer sophisticated new products on world markets, initially unobtainable from other sources. Over time, however, the technology is diffused and adopted by other countries who are then able to supply the products concerned for themselves. Trade thus increases for the duration of the 'imitation lag'.

See also PRODUCT LIFE–CYCLE THEORY, THEORY OF INTERNATIONAL TRADE.

technological progressiveness, *n*. an aspect of MARKET PERFORMANCE that denotes the extent to which firms develop and introduce new and improved products, production and distribution techniques. Radical INVENTIONS and INNOVATIONS may make it possible to reduce manufacturing and distribution costs, thereby permitting a lowering of the supply price to the consumer. See Fig. 188.

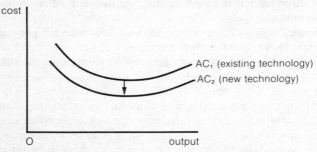

Fig. 188. **Technological progressiveness**. The fall in a firm's long-run average cost curve from AC_1 to AC_2 as a result of technological advance.

In the theory of costs, firms are assumed to operate within existing technological boundaries in both the SHORT RUN and the LONG RUN, but in the VERY LONG RUN, technological progressiveness serves to change the underlying cost conditions. Technological progressiveness in aggregate terms affects a country's rate of ECONOMIC GROWTH.

See also MONOPOLY, PRODUCT PERFORMANCE, RESEARCH AND DEVELOPMENT, SOLOW ECONOMIC–GROWTH MODEL, TECHNOLOGICAL UNEMPLOYMENT, PRODUCTIVITY, AUTOMATION.

technological unemployment, *n.* UNEMPLOYMENT resulting from the AUTOMATION of production activities. Automation serves to improve labour PRODUCTIVITY, reducing the labour needed for making and distributing products, so that some labour may become unemployed. If demand rises as a result of reduced costs and prices of products, labour may not be made unemployed, the same labour force serving to produce a greater output (rather than a reduced labour force producing the same output).

Such unemployment can be particularly problematical at the local level, where industries concentrated in particular regions are affected by dramatic changes in technology. For example, the introduction of numerically controlled machine tools and robot-assembly units has had a specially dramatic effect on engineering employment in the British Midlands area. Government assistance schemes and retraining of labour can alleviate the problem of technological unemployment to some extent, but it is frequently the unskilled workers who first lose their jobs to such progress.

See also UNEMPLOYMENT, STRUCTURAL UNEMPLOYMENT, TECHNOLOGICAL PROGRESSIVENESS.

technology, *n.* the application of scientific and technical knowledge in order to improve products and production processes. See TECHNOLOGICAL PROGRESSIVENESS, PRODUCTIVITY.

tender, *n.* a bid for a product, asset, or financial security by a prospective buyer in competition with others. See also CAPITAL MARKET, TENDER ISSUE.

tender issue, *n.* an issue of TREASURY BILLS by the Bank of England in response to invited TENDERS from DISCOUNT HOUSES and overseas central banks. The discount houses tender for a given quantity of bills, the tender invariably exceeding the quantity of bills on offer, and the Bank of England allots the bills accordingly. COMMERCIAL BANKS, by convention, do not tender directly for Treasury Bills but purchase their requirements on the open market.

See also TAP ISSUE, DISCOUNT MARKET, OPEN MARKET OPERATIONS.

term loan, *n.* a form of BANK LOAN made for a fixed time period at a predetermined RATE OF INTEREST.

terms of trade, *n.* a PRICE INDEX that shows a country's EXPORT prices relative to its IMPORT prices. It is constructed by taking an index of prices received for exports, on the one hand, and an index of prices paid for imports, on the other, and then dividing the first by the second (see Fig.

1976= 100

	1976	1986
Index of export prices	100	150
Index of import prices	100	125
Terms of trade index	100	120

Fig. 189. **Terms of trade**. See main entry.

189). An improvement in a country's terms of trade occurs if its export prices rise at a faster rate than import prices over time.

Superficially, an improvement in a country's terms of trade may be considered to be beneficial: in foreign-exchange terms, a given amount of exports will now finance the purchase of a greater amount of imports, or, put another way, a given amount of imports can now be purchased for a fewer amount of exports. A critical factor in this regard, however, is the PRICE-ELASTICITY OF DEMAND for exports and imports. If, for example, export demand is price-elastic, then price rises (which make the country's exports less competitive in world markets) will result in a more than proportionate fall in export volume, thus lowering foreign exchange receipts and adversely affecting domestic output and employment.

See also BALANCE-OF-PAYMENTS EQUILIBRIUM, DEVALUATION, REVALUATION.

term structure of interest rates, *n.* the relationship between the EFFECTIVE RATE OF INTEREST (yield) on a FINANCIAL SECURITY and the unexpired length of time to its maturity. This relationship is known as *yield to maturity* and can be calculated only for securities which have a fixed rate of interest and specified date of maturity, such as TREASURY BILLS and corporate DEBENTURES. CONSOLS are a notable exception as they do not have a redemption date.

test market, *n.* a MARKET encompassing a moderately large group of CONSUMERS within a limited geographical area, which firms use to market new products as a means of testing consumer response before engaging in full-scale production and mass national marketing of those products. See also PRODUCT DEVELOPMENT, PRODUCT LIFE-CYCLE.

test of significance, see HYPOTHESIS TESTING.

theory of consumer behaviour, *n.* the body of theory concerned with how individual consumers allocate their income in buying GOODS and SERVICES. A basic assumption made by the theory is that consumers seek to maximize the UTILITY or satisfaction to be derived from spending a fixed amount of income. The theory provides an explanation of why DEMAND CURVES slope downward.

See also CONSUMER EQUILIBRIUM, DIMINISHING MARGINAL UTILITY, PRICE EFFECT, INCOME EFFECT, SUBSTITUTION EFFECT, REVEALED PREFERENCE, ECONOMIC MAN.

theory of demand, *n*. the body of theory concerned with the determinants of the market DEMAND for GOODS and SERVICES and the effects of market demand (together with market supply) on the prices and quantities transacted of particular goods and services.

See also DEMAND FUNCTION, DEMAND CURVE, DEMAND CURVE (SHIFTS IN), ELASTICITY OF DEMAND, TOTAL REVENUE, MARGINAL REVENUE, MARGINAL REVENUE PRODUCT, EQUILIBRIUM MARKET PRICE, CONSUMER EQUILIBRIUM, THEORY OF MARKETS, PRICE SYSTEM.

theory of international trade, *n*. the body of theory concerned with the determinants of, and the gains to be obtained from, INTERNATIONAL TRADE and SPECIALIZATION. The theory examines the way in which differences between countries in terms of supply costs and demand structures affect the level, product and area composition of international trade, and the level and distribution of the GAINS FROM TRADE.

See also COMPARATIVE ADVANTAGE, HECKSCHER–OHLIN FACTOR PROPORTIONS THEORY, PREFERENCE SIMILARITY THEORY, PRODUCT LIFE–CYCLE THEORY, TECHNOLOGY GAP THEORY, EDGEWORTH BOX.

theory of markets, *n*. the body of theory concerned with how scarce FACTORS OF PRODUCTION are allocated between the multitude of product MARKETS in the economy. More specifically, the theory of markets is concerned with the determination of the prices and outputs of goods and services and the prices and usage of factors of production.

The 'theory of markets' distinguishes between types of markets by reference to differences in their MARKET STRUCTURE. The main structural distinction is made according to the degree of SELLER CONCENTRATION, that is, the number of suppliers and their relative size distribution. Other structural features emphasized include the character of the product supplied, that is, whether it is a HOMOGENEOUS PRODUCT or differentiated (see PRODUCT DIFFERENTIATION), and the CONDITION OF ENTRY to the market. Given these structural distinctions, the theory examines the way in which market structure interacts with MARKET CONDUCT to produce particular patterns of MARKET PERFORMANCE.

See also PERFECT COMPETITION, MONOPOLISTIC COMPETITION, OLIGOPOLY, MONOPOLY, RESOURCE ALLOCATION, MARKET STRUCTURE–CONDUCT–PERFORMANCE SCHEMA, FACTOR MARKETS, PRICE SYSTEM.

theory of supply, *n.* the body of theory concerned with the determinants of the market SUPPLY of GOODS and SERVICES, and the effects of market supply (together with market demand) on the prices and quantities transacted of particular goods and services.

See also SUPPLY FUNCTION, SUPPLY CURVE, SUPPLY CURVE, (SHIFTS IN), MARGINAL PHYSICAL PRODUCT, COST FUNCTION, MARGINAL REVENUE PRODUCT, DIMINISHING RETURNS, ECONOMIES OF SCALE, ELASTICITY OF SUPPLY, EQUILIBRIUM MARKET PRICE, TOTAL COST, MARGINAL COST, PROFIT MAXIMIZATION, THEORY OF THE FIRM, THEORY OF MARKETS, PRICE SYSTEM.

theory of the firm, *n.* the body of theory concerned with how individual firms combine quantities of FACTOR INPUTS to produce OUTPUTS of goods and services and their pricing and output decisions. A basic assumption of the theory is that the objective of the firm is PROFIT MAXIMIZATION. The theory provides an explanation of why SUPPLY CURVES slope upwards.

See also MARGINAL-PHYSICAL PRODUCT, MARGINAL-REVENUE PRODUCT, COST FUNCTION, MARGINAL COST, MARGINAL REVENUE, FIRM OBJECTIVES, THEORY OF MARKETS, MANAGERIAL THEORIES OF THE FIRM, BEHAVIOURAL THEORIES OF THE FIRM.

third world country, see DEVELOPING COUNTRY.

tie-in sales, *n.* a type of RESTRICTIVE TRADE PRACTICE whereby a supplier requires that the purchaser of product A (the tying good) must also buy his requirements of one or more other products (the tied goods) from the seller of A. Like an EXCLUSIVE DEALING arrangement this may restrict the freedom of the buyer to obtain these goods from rival suppliers and hence limit effective competition. See also MONOPOLY POLICY, OFFICE OF FAIR TRADING.

tight money or **dear money,** *n.* a government policy whereby the CENTRAL BANK is authorized to sell government BONDS on the open market to facilitate a decrease in the MONEY SUPPLY, thereby forcing up RATES OF INTEREST.

See also CHEAP MONEY, KEYNESIAN ECONOMICS, TRANSMISSION MECHANISM, MONETARY POLICY.

till money, *n.* the CURRENCY (notes and coins) held by the COMMERCIAL BANKS to meet the day-to-day cash requirements of their customers. Till money is included as part of the banks' RESERVE ASSET RATIO.

time-deposit account, see DEPOSIT ACCOUNT.

time lag, see LEADS AND LAGS (2).

time-preference theory, *n.* a theory that states that an individual can allocate his expected INCOME stream between two time periods in such a way that the trade-off between present and future CONSUMPTION is optimized.

The concept can be illustrated graphically by using INDIFFERENCE CURVES and BUDGET LINES to determine an individual's preference for present consumption vis-à-vis future consumption. To forego present consumption an individual must expect an increased amount of future consumption.

Fig. 190. **Time-preference theory**. See main entry.

In Fig. 190, the indifference curve II exhibits an individual's trade-off between present and future consumption, along which an individual is 'indifferent' between such combinations.

The diagonal line ab is the budget line. The slope of this line determines the ratio between present and future consumption such that $Oa/Ob = 1 + r$, where r is the individual's rate of interest. Clearly, r will differ between individuals according to their willingness to sacrifice future against present consumption.

The point M in Fig. 190 is where an individual spends all his present income (Od) and is therefore neither a borrower nor a lender. Point N is where an individual optimizes the trade-off between present and future consumption (the indifference curve II) and his budget constraint ab. This is optimized where the budget constraint is tangential to the indifference curve.

The amount an individual borrows or lends is therefore proportionate from point M to point N on the budget line where that individual's indifference curve is tangential to it. See also DISCOUNT RATE.

time series, *n.* any statistical information recorded over successive time periods.

See TIME–SERIES ANALYSIS.

time–series analysis, *n.* the analysis of past statistical data, recorded at successive time intervals, with a view to projecting this experience of the past to predict what will happen in the (uncertain) future. Thus time-series information can be used for FORECASTING purposes.

Fig. 191. **Time-series analysis**. See main entry.

Fig. 191 shows a typical time series. The fluctuations in time-series data, which inevitably show up when such series are plotted on a graph, can be classified into four basic types of variation which act simultaneously to influence the time series. These components of a time series are:

(a) *secular trend*, which shows the relatively smooth, regular movement of the time series over the long term.

(b) *cyclical variation*, which consists of medium–term, regular repeating patterns, generally associated with BUSINESS CYCLES. The recurring upswings and downswings in economic activity are superimposed upon the secular trend.

(c) *seasonal variation*, which consists of short–term, regular repeating patterns, generally associated with different seasons of the year. These seasonal variations are superimposed upon the secular trend and cyclical variations.

(d) *irregular variations*, which are erratic fluctuations in the time series caused by unpredictable, chance events. These irregular variations are superimposed upon the secular trend, cyclical variations and seasonal variations.

Time-series analysis is concerned with isolating the effect of each of these four influences upon a time series with a view to using them to project this past experience into the future. In order to identify the underlying secular trend in a time series, the statistician may use REGRESSION ANALYSIS, fitting a line to the time-series observations by the method of ordinary least squares. Here time would serve as the INDEPENDENT VARIABLE in the estimated regression equation and the observed variable as the DEPENDENT VARIABLE. Alternatively, the statistician may use a moving average to smooth the time series and help identify the underlying trend. For example, he could use a five-period moving average, replacing each consecutive observation by the average (MEAN) of that observation and the two preceding and two succeeding observations.

Exponential smoothing provides yet another technique which can be used to smooth time-series data. It is similar to the moving-average method but gives greater weight to more recent observations in calculating the average. In order to identify the effect of seasonal variations the statistician can construct a measure of seasonal variation (called the *seasonal index*) and use this to deseasonalize the time-series data and show how the time series would look if there were no seasonal fluctuations.

Once the trend has been identified it is possible to EXTRAPOLATE that trend and estimate trend values for time periods beyond the present time period. In Fig. 191, for example, the trend for time periods up to and including time t can be extrapolated to time $t + 1$. Extrapolating thus becomes a method of making predictions or forecasts, though the accuracy of these forecasts will depend critically upon whether underlying forces which affected the time series in the past will continue to operate in the same way in the future.

total cost, *n.* the aggregate sum in the SHORT RUN of a firm's total FIXED COST and total VARIABLE COSTS in producing a particular level of OUTPUT.

The short-run total cost curve in Fig. 192 on page 520 is the sum of the (constant) total fixed costs and the total variable costs. It has an 's' shape because at low levels of output total variable costs rise slowly (because of the influence of increasing RETURNS TO THE VARIABLE-FACTOR INPUT) while at high levels of output total variable costs rise more rapidly (because of the influence of diminishing returns to the variable-factor input).

total cost

total cost

total variable cost

total fixed cost

O   units of output

Fig. 192. **Total cost.** See main entry.

Total cost interacts with TOTAL REVENUE in determining the level of output at which the firm achieves its objective of PROFIT MAXIMIZATION and LOSS MINIMIZATION.

In the THEORY OF MARKETS, a firm will leave a market if in the short run it cannot earn sufficient total revenue to cover its total variable costs. If it can generate enough total revenue to cover total variable costs and make some contribution towards total fixed costs then it will continue to produce in the short run even though it is still making a LOSS. In the LONG RUN, the firm must earn enough total revenue to cover total variable and total fixed costs (including NORMAL PROFIT) or it will leave the market.

see MARGINAL COST.

total domestic expenditure, *n.* the total expenditure by residents of a country on FINAL PRODUCTS (excluding expenditure on INTERMEDIATE PRODUCTS). When expenditure on IMPORTS is deducted from this figure and expenditure by nonresidents on domestically produced goods and services is added, the adjusted expenditure provides an estimate of GROSS NATIONAL PRODUCT. See also NATIONAL-INCOME ACCOUNTS.

total physical product, *n.* the total quantity of OUTPUT produced in the SHORT RUN theory of supply by utilizing various amounts of the VARIABLE-FACTOR INPUT (in conjunction with a given amount of FIXED-FACTOR INPUT). The total physical product curve as shown in Fig. 193 rises steeply at first, reflecting increasing RETURNS TO THE VARIABLE FACTOR-INPUT, but then rises more slowly as diminishing returns to the variable input set in.

total revenue, *n.* the aggregate revenue obtained by a FIRM from the sale of a particular quantity of output, equal to price times quantity. Under conditions of PERFECT COMPETITION, the firm faces a horizontal DEMAND CURVE at the going market price. Each extra unit of output sold

Fig. 193. **Total physical product**. See main entry.

Fig. 194. **Total revenue**. See main entry.

(MARGINAL REVENUE) adds exactly the same amount to total revenue as previous units. Hence, total revenue is a straight upward-sloping line (see Fig. 194a). Under conditions of imperfect competition (for example, MONOPOLISTIC COMPETITION) the firm faces a downward-sloping demand curve and price has to be lowered in order to sell more units. As price is lowered, each extra unit of output sold (marginal revenue) adds successively smaller amounts to total revenue than previous units. Thus, total revenue rises but at a decreasing rate, and eventually falls (see Fig. 194b).

Total revenue interacts with TOTAL COST in determining the level of output at which the firm achieves its objective of PROFIT MAXIMIZATION.

total utility, *n.* the sum total of the satisfaction (UTILITY) an individual derives from the use or CONSUMPTION of a given quantity of goods or

Fig. 195. **Total utility.** The theoretical measurement of total utility derived from three units of product X (say, shoes) is the distance Oa. If four units of product X were used (four pairs of shoes) the total utility is Ob. The marginal utility, however, is the distance ab, being the increase in satisfaction derived from the use or consumption of one additional unit of product X.

services. Whereas MARGINAL UTILITY refers only to the utility derived from the last unit of the good or service used or consumed, total utility refers to the aggregate of the utility so derived. See Fig. 195.

See UTILITY FUNCTION, CARDINAL UTILITY, ORDINAL UTILITY.

trade association, *n.* a central body representing the interests of firms operating in the same line of business. Trade associations compile statistics on industry production, sales, exports, etc., for circulation to member firms, provide a forum for the discussion of trade affairs, and liase with other trade organizations and government departments regarding matters of mutual concern.

trade barrier, see IMPORT RESTRICTIONS.

trade creation, *n.* an increase in INTERNATIONAL TRADE (and economic welfare) that results from the reduction or elimination of trade barriers such as TARIFFS and QUOTAS. Tariff cuts, etc., may be instigated by a single country, by the formation of a CUSTOMS UNION or FREE TRADE AREA, or, more generally, by international negotiation (see GENERAL AGREEMENT ON TARIFFS AND TRADE).

The trade-creating effect of a tariff cut is illustrated in Fig. 196, which, to simplify matters, is confined to one country (A) and one product.

DD and SS are the domestic demand and supply curves for the product in country A. W is the world supply price of the product. Initially country A imposes a tariff on imports of the product raising its price in the home market to W_t. At price W_t domestic production is

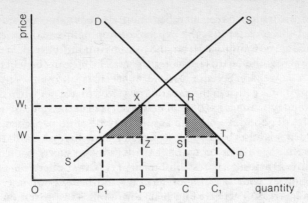

Fig. 196. **Trade creation**. See main entry.

shown by OP, domestic consumption OC, and imports by PC.

The removal of the tariff reduces the price of the product in the home market to W. At price W, imports increase to P_1C_1, domestic production falls to OP_1, and domestic consumption increases to OC_1. The home market obtains an increase in economic welfare from this expansion of trade indicated by the two triangles XYZ and RST. XYZ is the 'production gain' resulting from the reallocation of factor inputs to more efficient uses; RST is the 'consumption gain' resulting from lower prices to consumers.

See also TRADE DIVERSION, GAINS FROM TRADE.

trade credit, *n.* a deferred payment arrangement whereby a supplier allows a customer a certain period of time (typically two to three months) after receiving the products before paying for them.

See also CREDIT, CREDITORS, CREDITORS RATIO, WORKING CAPITAL.

trade cycle, see BUSINESS CYCLE.

trade debt, *n.* a deferred payment arrangement whereby a customer is allowed a certain period of time in which to pay for products after receiving them.

See also DEBT, DEBTORS, DEBTORS-TO-SALES RATIO, WORKING CAPITAL.

trade discount, see DISCOUNT.

trade diversion, *n.* a redirection of INTERNATIONAL TRADE resulting from the formation of a CUSTOMS UNION or FREE TRADE AREA. A customs union/ free trade area involves the removal of trade obstacles such as TARIFFS and QUOTAS on trade between member countries, but the erection, or continuance, of trade barriers against nonmember countries. This serves to increase trade between member countries (see TRADE CREATION), but a part of this increase is at the expense of nonmember countries whose imports are now displaced from the customs union/free trade area. Thus, unlike across–the–board tariff cuts there may be little net benefit to world economic welfare. See also GENERAL AGREEMENT ON TARIFFS AND TRADE.

trade gap, *n.* a deficit in the BALANCE OF TRADE that arises when the value of a country's VISIBLE EXPORTS of goods is less than the value of its VISIBLE IMPORTS of goods. A trade gap as such may be of no particular concern provided it is offset by surpluses generated elsewhere on the BALANCE OF PAYMENTS. See TERMS OF TRADE, BALANCE–OF–PAYMENTS EQUILIBRIUM.

trade integration, *n.* the establishment of FREE TRADE between a number of countries with the aim of securing the benefits of international SPECIALIZATION. There are four main forms of trade integration ranging from a loose association of trade partners to a fully integrated group of nation states:

(a) a FREE TRADE AREA, where members eliminate trade barriers between themselves but each continues to operate its own particular barriers against nonmembers.

(b) a CUSTOMS UNION, where members eliminate trade barriers between themselves and establish uniform barriers against nonmembers, in particular a common external tariff.

(c) a COMMON MARKET, that is, a customs union which also provides for the free movement of labour and capital across national boundaries.

(d) an ECONOMIC UNION, that is, a common market which also provides for the unification of members' general objectives in respect of economic growth, etc., and the harmonization of monetary, fiscal and other policies.

See also GAINS FROM TRADE.

trade investment, *n.* the acquisition of STOCKS and SHARES in one FIRM by another firm. Trade investments may be undertaken for a variety of reasons including: the profitable investment of surplus cash; the protection or advancement of an existing contractual trade relationship by a more direct involvement (for example, a supplier who buys a stake in a customer firm); the provision of a 'launching pad' for a possible future takeover or merger.

trademark, *n.* a word (BRAND NAME) or symbol that is used by a supplier to uniquely distinguish his product from the products offered by other suppliers. See also INDUSTRIAL PROPERTY RIGHTS, PRODUCT DIFFERENTIATION.

trade union, *n.* an organization that represents the economic interests of the LABOUR FORCE. Unions come in a variety of forms, for example:

(a) *in-company union*, a union that represents every grade of labour within a single company. This type of union is common in Japan.

(b) *craft union*, a union that represents a particular group of skilled tradesmen (for example, electricians, plumbers) who may work in many different industries. This type of union is common in the UK.

(c) *industrial union*, a union that represents every grade of labour within a single industry. This type of union is common in Europe.

(d) *general union*, a union that represents a broad spread of employees regardless of occupation or industry. These have become more commonplace in the US and Europe, often as the result of mergers between craft and industrial unions.

The prime objective of a union is to protect and advance the interests of its members by negotiating WAGE RATES and conditions of employment (number of hours worked, grounds for dismissal, etc.). As such, unions have an important influence on the price of labour and supply costs in individual industries, and also, in the broader macroeconomic context, through the impact of wage rate changes on the level of UNEMPLOYMENT and the rate of INFLATION.

Trade unions in the UK are managed by full-time elected officials with assistance from workplace representatives (shop stewards).

See LABOUR MARKET, COLLECTIVE BARGAINING, PHILLIPS CURVE, WORKER PARTICIPATION, INDUSTRIAL RELATIONS, INDUSTRIAL DISPUTE.

Trades Union Congress (TUC), *n.* a UK organization that represents the collective interests of member TRADE UNIONS in dealings with government and employers' organizations, and formulates general trade union policies. Most trade unions are members of the TUC, and vote on policy issues and elect members to the TUC managing council in proportion to their union membership.

trade war, *n.* a situation in which countries engaged in INTERNATIONAL TRADE attempt to reduce competing IMPORTS by the use of TARIFFS, QUOTAS and other import restrictions, and expand their EXPORTS through EXPORT INCENTIVES. Such BEGGAR–MY–NEIGHBOUR MEASURES, bringing with them an escalation of PROTECTIONISM, however, are usually self-defeating, leading to a fall in the total volume of international trade and world income levels.

trading and profit-and-loss account, *n.* an accounting statement that shows a firm's SALES REVENUE generate over a trading period and all the relevant EXPLICIT COSTS experienced in earning that revenue. In the account, the COST-OF-GOODS SOLD is deducted from sales revenue to calculate GROSS PROFIT then the other costs involved are deducted from the gross profit to show any NET PROFIT earned.

trading stamps, *n.* a form of SALES PROMOTION whereby a retailer gives customers stamps with a value related to the value of purchases made, which can then be redeemed with a trading-stamp company for goods or cash.

transaction costs, *n.* the costs incurred in using the MARKET system in buying and selling FACTOR INPUTS and FINAL PRODUCTS. Transaction costs include the costs of locating suppliers or customers and negotiating contracts with them, and the costs associated with imperfect market situations, for example, MONOPOLY surcharges imposed by input suppliers, unreliable sources of supply and restrictions on sales outlets, TARIFFS and QUOTAS.

See also INTERNALIZATION.

transaction demand for money, *n.* a demand for MONEY held to facilitate the synchronization between receipts and expenditures of individuals and firms. Income, especially wages and salaries, is received at discrete intervals, that is, weekly or monthly, whilst expenditure occurs on a much more even basis for smaller items such as lunch or fares. The amount of money an individual desires to hold for such transactions is dependent upon his income.

Firms hold money balances for transactions too, the amount of which is dependent upon the turnover of the firm. Transactions and precautionary balances are sometimes considered together since they are both a positive function of income (the balances held tending to increase as income increases).

Compare PRECAUTIONARY DEMAND FOR MONEY, SPECULATIVE DEMAND FOR MONEY. See also MONEY–DEMAND SCHEDULE, LIQUIDITY PREFERENCE, L.M. SCHEDULE.

transfer earnings, *n.* the return that a FACTOR OF PRODUCTION must earn to prevent its transfer to an alternative use. The earnings that a factor of production receives over and above its transfer earnings is called its ECONOMIC RENT. See also QUASI-RENT.

transfer payments, *n.* any expenditure by the government for which it receives no GOODS or SERVICES in return. In the main, such payments involve the 'transfer' of income from one group of individuals (taxpayers) to other groups of individuals in the form of welfare provisions, for example, UNEMPLOYMENT BENEFIT, SOCIAL-SECURITY BENEFIT, old-age PENSIONS, etc.

Because transfer payments are not made in return for products and services, that is, they do not add to total output, they are not included in the NATIONAL INCOME ACCOUNTS which measure the money value of national output. See also GOVERNMENT EXPENDITURE, WELFARE STATE.

transfer price, *n.* the internal PRICE at which FACTOR INPUTS and PRODUCTS are transacted between the branches or subsidiaries of an integrated firm (see VERTICAL INTEGRATION, HORIZONTAL INTEGRATION). The transfer price may be set by reference to the prices ruling in outside markets for inputs and products (*arms-length pricing*), or it may be administered (see ADMINISTERED PRICE) according to some internal accounting convention (for example, a FULL-COST PRICE).

Transfer pricing gives a firm added discretion in pricing its products, and the danger is that it could well be tempted to employ 'manipulative' transfer pricing to harm competitors (for example, 'price squeeze' a nonintegrated rival firm) and, in the case of a MULTINATIONAL FIRM, to boost its profits (for example, transfer price across national frontiers so that the greater part of the firm's profits are received in a low-taxation economy).

See INTERNALIZATION, TAX HAVEN.

transformation curve, see PRODUCTION–POSSIBILITY BOUNDARY.

transitional unemployment. see FRICTIONAL UNEMPLOYMENT.

transmission mechanism, *n.* the interlinking causal relationship between government exercise of the available tools of FISCAL POLICY and MONETARY POLICY, and the change in the level of economic variables affected by such action. Fiscal policy advocates that a change in government expenditure exerts significant influence on the level of AGGREGATE DEMAND and UNEMPLOYMENT via the RATE OF INTEREST and INVESTMENT. Monetary policy suggests that an increase in MONEY SUPPLY via OPEN-MARKET OPERATIONS directly affects aggregate demand.

See also KEYNESIAN ECONOMICS, MONEY SUPPLY/SPENDING LINKAGES, QUANTITY THEORY OF MONEY.

Treasury, *n.* the UK government department responsible for managing the government's finances, authorizing expenditure plans for various government departments such as Health, Education and Defence, and overseeing the tax-gathering work of the INLAND REVENUE and CUSTOMS AND EXCISE. In addition, the Treasury prepares forecasts of future economic activity levels and advises the Chancellor of the Exchequer on the government's annual Budget.

Treasury Bill, *n.* a FINANCIAL SECURITY issued through the DISCOUNT MARKET by the government as a means of borrowing money for short periods of time (three months). Most Treasury Bills are purchased by the commercial banks and held as part of their RESERVE-ASSET RATIO.

The monetary authorities use Treasury Bills to regulate the liquidity base of the banking system in order to control the MONEY SUPPLY. For example, if the authorities wish to expand the money supply they can issue more Treasury Bills, which increases the liquidity base of the banking system and induces a multiple expansion of bank deposits.

See also BANK-DEPOSIT CREATION PUBLIC-SECTOR BORROWING REQUIREMENT.

Treaty of Rome, *n.* an agreement in 1957 between the six founding countries of the European Economic Community which established the objectives and principles of the EUROPEAN COMMUNITY. These objectives included the promotion of economic prosperity, political unity and cultural exchange. The Treaty provided for the removal of trade restrictions between member countries, free labour and capital mobility, harmonization of tax policies and assistance to poorer regions.

trial balance, *n.* a listing of the balances on a firm's ledger accounts that is prepared prior to the TRADING AND PROFIT-AND-LOSS ACCOUNT and BALANCE SHEET, as an initial check on the arithmetic accuracy of the ledger accounts.

true and fair view, *n.* the opinion formed by an AUDITOR about a JOINT-STOCK COMPANY'S accounts, based upon evidence obtained from auditing the company's LEDGER accounts. The auditor is required to report to a company's shareholders about the accuracy and presentation of a firm's annual report and accounts. After undertaking the appropriate tests, usually on a sample basis, the auditor must be convinced that no material errors or omissions have occurred either in the firm's system of recording accounting transactions, or in their summary and presentation. If he is satisfied that no material irregularities have occurred, he will conclude that the financial statements present a 'true and fair view' for the period (year) under review. If irregularities are noted the accounts may be prefaced with the qualification that 'subject to the following . . . the financial statements audited . . . present a true and fair view'.

See also FINANCIAL ACCOUNTING.

trust, *n.* **1.** ASSETS held and managed by *trustees* on behalf of an individual or group. While these assets are held in trust the beneficiaries have no control over the management of them. In the UK trusts have been used extensively to minimize the effects of income-and-wealth taxes. **2.** (formerly, in the US) a means of organizing CARTELS, provoking the establishment of antitrust (antimonopoly) legislation.

trustee, see TRUST.

turnkey project, *n.* a one-off construction project such as the building of a factory, port, etc., in a country by a foreign FIRM or CONSORTIUM of firms. Turnkey projects involve no further commitment beyond the completion of the project.

turnover tax, see SALES TAX.

two-part tariff, *n.* a pricing method that involves a charge per unit of GOOD or SERVICE consumed, plus a fixed annual or quarterly charge to cover overhead costs. Two-part tariffs can be used by PUBLIC UTILITIES or firms to achieve the benefits of MARGINAL-COST PRICING whilst raising sufficient revenues to cover all outlays (so avoiding a deficit and problems of financing it). Simple two-part tariffs are presently used to charge customers for gas, electricity, telephones, etc., though more sophisticated multipart tariffs can be adopted to reflect the different marginal costs involved in offering products like electricity and transport services at peak and off-peak periods.

See also AVERAGE-COST PRICING, NATIONALIZATION.

two-tier board, *n.* a structure of the BOARD OF DIRECTORS of a company used in certain European countries such as West Germany and Norway which comprises two tiers: (a) a supervisory board on which representatives of workers and managers are represented; (b) a management board which is concerned with the day-to-day running of the business.

The supervisory board is responsible for formulating general policy and the management board with implementing policy. Two-tier boards have gained in popularity in Europe over the past two decades, compared with the UK and US style of unitary boards, and their development has been encouraged by the EUROPEAN COMMUNITY.

type 1 error, see HYPOTHESIS TESTING.

type 2 error, see HYPOTHESIS TESTING.

U

U-form (unitary form) organization, *n.* an organizational structure adopted by FIRMS in which the firm is managed centrally as a single unit specialized along functional lines (marketing, production, finance, personnel). Oliver Williamson coined this term, and argued that firms organized in this fashion are more likely to suffer control-loss and end up pursuing nonprofit management goals (see MANAGEMENT-UTILITY MAXIMIZING), because senior executives responsible for the management functions cannot exert sufficient control over their subordinates selling a wide variety of products in many different markets. Williamson predicts that the U-form organization will gradually decline in popularity as companies grow and adopt the M-FORM (MULTIDIVISIONAL-FORM) ORGANIZATION.

See also MANAGERIAL THEORIES OF THE FIRM, BEHAVIOURAL THEORY OF THE FIRM.

ultra vires, *adj.* (of an action by a JOINT-STOCK COMPANY) exceeding its powers as defined in its MEMORANDUM OF ASSOCIATION. For example, if a company's memorandum authorizes it to trade in the motor car business, and its directors then set up an ice cream business, then they may be regarded as trading 'ultra vires' and the company's contracts with ice cream suppliers and customers may be regarded as void.

uncertainty, see RISK AND UNCERTAINTY.

undated security, see IRREDEEMABLE FINANCIAL SECURITY.

undersubscription, see OVERSUBSCRIPTION.

undistributed profits, see RETAINED PROFITS.

UNCTAD, see UNITED NATIONS CONFERENCE ON TRADE AND DEVELOPMENT.

underdeveloped country, see DEVELOPING COUNTRY.

underwrite, see MERCHANT BANK.

unearned income, see EARNED INCOME.

unemployment, *n.* the nonutilization of LABOUR (and CAPITAL) resources, as a result of which the ACTUAL OUTPUT of the economy is below its POTENTIAL GROSS NATIONAL PRODUCT. Resources lie idle and output is lost. The elimination of unemployment and the achievement of FULL EMPLOYMENT is one of the main objectives of MACROECONOMIC POLICY. The rate of unemployment is measured as the percentage of the total labour force currently without a job (see Fig. 197a).

	UK	W. Germany	Japan	US
1978	6.0	3.5	2.2	6.0
1979	5.1	3.2	2.1	5.8
1980	6.6	3.0	2.0	7.0
1981	9.9	4.4	2.2	7.5
1982	11.4	6.1	2.4	9.5
1983	12.6	8.0	2.6	9.5
1984	13.0	8.5	2.7	7.4
1985	13.1	8.6	2.6	7.1
1986	13.3	8.3	2.8	6.8

(a)

(b)   potential GNP

Fig. 197. **Unemployment.** (a) The annual unemployment percentage rates for the UK, West Germany, Japan and the US. Sources: OECD, NIESR. (b) See main entry.

In the EQUILIBRIUM LEVEL OF NATIONAL INCOME model, unemployment occurs whenever AGGREGATE DEMAND is insufficient to purchase full-employment aggregate supply (potential GNP): equilibrium national income in Fig. 197b is Y_1 compared to the full employment national income of Y_2. The traditional prescription for this situation is for the authorities to boost spending by reflationary FISCAL POLICY and MONETARY POLICY measures – to shift aggregate demand from AD_1 to AD_2.

Supply-side deficiencies (see SUPPLY-SIDE ECONOMICS) may contribute to generalized unemployment if a country is heavily engaged in international trade. An inefficient use of resources and a lack of investment in plant and product modernization may result in a progressive displacement of domestic output by more competitive foreign products (see IMPORT PENETRATION) and a widespread loss of jobs. Although PROTECTIONISM may be used to contain the situation, this is not a truly effective substitute for industrial efficiency.

The three basic forms of unemployment are FRICTIONAL UNEMPLOYMENT, STRUCTURAL UNEMPLOYMENT and CYCLICAL UNEMPLOYMENT.

See also DEFLATIONARY GAP, DEMAND MANAGEMENT, STABILIZATION POLICY, RESIDUAL UNEMPLOYMENT, DISGUISED UNEMPLOYMENT, HIDDEN UNEMPLOYMENT, POVERTY TRAP, DEINDUSTRIALIZATION, TECHNOLOGICAL UNEMPLOYMENT.

unemployment benefit, *n.* the TRANSFER PAYMENTS in cash or kind made to persons in UNEMPLOYMENT to provide them with some minimum standard of living until they can secure new paid employment. In most countries, workers in employment pay NATIONAL-INSURANCE CONTRIBUTIONS to the government in return for unemployment benefit rights. See also GOVERNMENT EXPENDITURE, SOCIAL-SECURITY BENEFITS.

unitary elasticity, see PRICE-ELASTICITY OF DEMAND.

unitary taxation, *n.* a system of TAXATION operated by a country that taxes a foreign-owned MULTINATIONAL FIRM on a proportion of its total world-wide income, rather than on the income which the multinational actually earned within that country. This involves the use of some rule-of-thumb to apportion tax liability: for example, if 10% of the total world ASSETS of a multinational are located in that country, then the country may seek to tax 10% of the multinational's world income, making no allowance for any foreign taxes paid. Countries might adopt unitary taxation to increase their taxation revenues and to counter manipulative TRANSFER PRICING by multinationals, but must bear in mind that such a taxation system is likely to discourage inward investment. Compare DOUBLE TAXATION.

United Nations (UN), *n.* an association of states which have agreed to abide by the principles originally laid down in a charter (the UN Charter). Its main objectives are the maintenance of international peace and security, the upholding of fundamental human rights in all nations and the promotion of social harmonization and progress amongst all nations. The title 'UN' was first used in 1942 when representatives of 26 countries committed their governments to maintain the fight against the

Axis powers. The UN Charter was drawn up by 50 nations and officially created on 24th October 1945. The principal organs of the UN are the General Assembly, a Security Council, an Economic and Social Council, a Trusteeship Council and a Secretariat. There are also many subsidiary organs and affiliated bodies working in accordance with the Charter such as the INTERNATIONAL MONETARY FUND, and FOOD AND AGRICULTURAL ORGANIZATION, the GENERAL AGREEMENT ON TARIFFS AND TRADE, the WORLD BANK, the UNITED NATIONS CONFERENCE ON TRADE AND DEVELOPMENT, the INTERNATIONAL LABOUR OFFICE.

United Nations Conference on Trade and Development (UNCTAD), *n.* a multinational institution established in 1965 to represent the economic interests of the DEVELOPING COUNTRIES and to promote the ideals of the NEW INTERNATIONAL ECONOMIC ORDER. Unctad's main work is undertaken at a series of conferences, held every four years, and has centred on three areas of particular concern to the developing countries:

(a) EXPORTS of manufactures, where it has attempted to negotiate TARIFF and QUOTA-free access to the markets of the developed countries. This is in addition to those concessions obtained through the GENERAL AGREEMENT ON TARIFFS AND TRADE.

(b) exports of commodities, where it has promoted the extension of INTERNATIONAL COMMODITY AGREEMENTS aimed at stabilizing the export prices of primary products as a means of stabilizing developing countries' foreign exchange earnings and producers' incomes.

(c) ECONOMIC AID, where it has attempted to secure a greater volume of financial assistance and technology transfer from the developed countries.

So far, Unctad has achieved very little, mainly because developed countries, particularly in the difficult economic conditions prevailing since the oil price increases of 1973, have not been prepared to support Unctad initiatives to the fullest extent.

unit of account, *n.* an attribute of MONEY that enables people to use money to measure and record the value of GOODS and SERVICES, and financial transactions. A unit of account may take a physical form, for example CURRENCY, or may be an intangible 'book-keeping' asset such as the SPECIAL DRAWING RIGHT and the EUROPEAN CURRENCY UNIT.

unit trust, *n.* a financial institution that sells 'units' to savers (at a price based on a proportion of the underlying value of the trust's assets) and which specializes in long-term investments in STOCKS and SHARES and government securities. See also FINANCIAL SYSTEM, INSTITUTIONAL INVESTORS.

unlimited liability, see LIMITED LIABILITY.

unlisted-securities market, *n.* a MARKET for dealing in company STOCKS and SHARES that have not obtained a full STOCK-EXCHANGE quotation. The unlisted-securities market enables smaller companies to raise new capital without the formalities and expense of obtaining a full listing on the main exchange. An unlisted-securities market was established in the UK in 1980.

upward-sloping demand curve, *n.* a DEMAND CURVE that shows a *direct* rather than an *inverse* relationship between the price of a product and quantity-demanded per period of time, over part or all of its length.

Most demand curves are based on the assumption that consumers are rational in buying products and have full knowledge of price and product characteristics. Where either of these assumptions are modified then the DEMAND FUNCTION can result, not in a normal product as in Fig. 198a on page 535, but in an upward-sloping demand curve as in Fig. 198b.

In Fig. 198a, if price increases from OP_1 to OP_2, quantity demanded *falls* from OQ_1 to OQ_2. In Fig. 198b, if price increases from OP_1 to OP_2, quantity demanded *increases* from OQ_3 to OQ_4. This can be due to: (a) conspicuous consumption (see VEBLEN EFFECT); (b) a real or perceived belief that as price increases, quality improves; (c) or because the product is a GIFFEN GOOD.

See also INCOME EFFECT, ENGELS LAW.

util, *n.* a theoretical measure of UTILITY derived from the CONSUMPTION of a good or service. Early economists believed that the subjective satisfaction (utility) a person enjoyed from, say, taking a Sunday stroll, could be cardinally measured. The unit of such measurement was termed a 'util', and although it was never possible to actually make such measurement, it conveyed limited theoretical meaning to their analyses. Rarely used in modern economics, the term is occasionally used in a more general sense to establish some degree of utility.

See also CARDINAL UTILITY, DIMINISHING MARGINAL UTILITY, ORDINAL UTILITY, TOTAL UTILITY.

utility, *n.* the satisfaction or pleasure that an individual derives from the CONSUMPTION of a GOOD or SERVICE. In the context used by economists utility is not a *property* of a good or service, but the derivation of satisfaction from the *use* of such a good or service. Corn was an example used in the 19th century. Corn has the same property in glut or famine

Fig. 198. **Upward-sloping demand curve**. See main entry.

but its true utility is to the consumer. The consumer's utility will vary according to the state of body and mind. Utility therefore is a condition unique to each individual.

The concept of utility is not contentious, and can be traced back to the attempts of the early Greek philosophers to determine economic value. The problem was more one of measurement. The economists of the early 18th century believed utility could be expressed as an absolute quantity, one, two, etc., known as CARDINAL UTILITY. Measurement between individuals was therefore possible, as indeed was the measurement between different goods as long as they were independent of each other.

Later economists believed that utility measured on such a scale was neither necessary nor indeed possible. Such economists were termed 'ordinalists' because they believed utility could be measured on an ordinal scale, that is, one where only rankings of preference were required, not magnitudes on a numerical scale. Such ORDINAL UTILITY rankings could then be represented on an INDIFFERENCE MAP. An abstract unit of measure was devised to help explain an individual's degree of utility (a UTIL), although such measurement is not strictly required for ordinal rankings. See UTILITY FUNCTION.

utility function, *n.* a mathematical function denoting the quantities of GOODS and SERVICES that constitute an individual's total CONSUMPTION.

Early economists believed that UTILITY depended upon the amount of a particular good in an individual's possession regardless of other goods in that individual's possession. TOTAL UTILITY was therefore additive and could be written:

$$U_t = U_1(x_1) + U_2(x_2) \ldots U_n(x_n) \qquad (1)$$

where U_t = total utility, $U_1 \ldots U_n$ = utility of each good, $x_1 \ldots x_n$ = number of goods denoted x.

The theoretical notion that 'the value of a thing lies in the thing itself' was rejected in favour of a generalized utility function:

$$U_t = U(x_1, x_2 \ldots x_n). \qquad (2)$$

Equation (2) denotes the fact that the total utility derived (U_t) is dependent upon the amounts and relationship of other commodities. This in turn leads into the law of DIMINISHING MARGINAL UTILITY.

See also CARDINAL UTILITY, MARGINAL UTILITY.

utility index, *n.* a means of representing the attitudes towards RISK AND UNCERTAINTY displayed by decision-makers in terms of the MARGINAL UTILITY which they derive from the earnings of risky economic projects. The expected utility index was developed by von Neumann and Morgenstern, and they argued that decisions based on expected utility values will differ from those based on expected money values because of changes in the utility which a decision-maker derives from money. Where each extra pound (dollar) which a decision-maker makes increases his utility by less than the previous pound (dollar) made, then his decreasing marginal-utility of money is likely to affect his attitudes to risk. For if each extra pound (dollar) received adds less to utility than would be lost if he gave up a pound (dollar), he would not bet on a project where the possible money gains equal the possible money losses and each has a probability of 0.5, because the expected utility value of the bet would be negative. Such a decision-maker would be risk-averse. Only where his marginal utility of money is constant would the decision-maker display risk-neutral behaviour; in all other cases the expected money value and the expected utility-value criteria would rank projects differently.

See also RISK PROFILE, DECISION TREE.

utility maximization, see CONSUMER EQUILIBRIUM.

V

value, *n.* the money worth of an ASSET or PRODUCT. Early economists such as Adam SMITH and David RICARDO suggested that the value of an asset or product depended upon the amount of LABOUR needed to produce it, while later economists like Alfred MARSHALL and William JEVONS emphasized that the UTILITY of a product to a consumer determined its value. Nowadays economists accept that both supply and demand factors are important in determining the value of a product.

See also CONSUMER'S SURPLUS, VALUE ADDED, PARADOX OF VALUE.

value added, *n.* the difference between a firm's SALES REVENUE and the cost of its bought-in materials and services. See VALUE-ADDED TAX, VALUE-ADDED PER EMPLOYEE.

value-added approach to GDP, see NATIONAL INCOME ACCOUNTS.

value-added per employee, *n.* an accounting measure of a firm's value-added/size relation, that expresses the firm's VALUE ADDED as a ratio of its size measured in terms of number of employees.

value-added tax (VAT), *n.* an INDIRECT TAX levied by the government on the VALUE ADDED to a good or service. The tax is based on the difference between the value of the output over the value of the inputs used to produce it. The final amount of tax is added on to the selling price of the good and is paid by the buyer. For example, trader B sells output for £10 per unit, the value of his inputs being £8 per unit. Thus, value added is £2 per unit. If VAT is set at 10%, the selling price of the good is £11, with £1 being the amount of tax paid by the final buyer. Trader B would then set off against the £1 VAT output tax collected from the final customer the 80p VAT input tax which he has paid on his £8 of inputs bought, and remit the difference of 20p to the government. In the same way trader A (who supplied trader B with his input for £8 per unit) would have collected 80p VAT-output tax from trader B, against which he will offset any VAT-input tax which he paid on his inputs, and remit the difference to the government. The total of all these sums remitted by traders A, B, etc., to the government will equal the £1 charged on the final sale to the customer.

In the UK, some products are exempted from value-added tax, or zero-rated, while for others VAT is levied at different rates for different groups of product. For example, currently (1986) children's clothing is exempt from VAT, while cars bear a 15% VAT charge.

value judgements, see NORMATIVE ECONOMICS.

variable, *n.* a term that can take a range of numerical values. For example, price, quantity-demanded and quantity-supplied are all variables in so far as each can take a number of different values, and these variables form part of an ECONOMIC MODEL of a MARKET.

See also DEPENDENT VARIABLE, INDEPENDENT VARIABLE, CONSTANT, CONTINUOUS VARIABLE, DISCRETE VARIABLE, ECONOMETRICS, HYPOTHESIS TESTING.

Fig. 199. **Variable costs**. See main entry.

variable costs, *n.* any COSTS that tend to vary directly with the level of output. They represent payments made for the use of VARIABLE FACTOR-INPUTS (raw materials, labour, etc.).

The SHORT-RUN total variable cost curve (TC) in Fig. 199a has an 'S' shape because at low levels of output total variable costs rise slowly (because of the influence of increasing RETURNS TO THE VARIABLE FACTOR-INPUT), while at high levels of output total variable costs rise more rapidly (because of the influence of diminishing returns to the variable input). Average variable costs (AVC in Fig. 199b) fall at first (reflecting increasing returns to the variable input), but then rise (reflecting diminishing returns to the variable input).

In the THEORY OF MARKETS, a firm will leave a market if in the short run it cannot earn sufficient TOTAL REVENUE to cover its total variable cost. If it can generate enough total revenue to cover total variable cost and make some CONTRIBUTION towards total FIXED COST then it will continue to produce in the short run even though it is still making a loss.

See also MARKET EXIT, LOSS MINIMIZATION.

variable factor input, *n.* a FACTOR INPUT to the production process that can be readily varied in the SHORT RUN so as to expand or reduce output within a plant of fixed size. Variable inputs include raw materials, heating and lighting. Variable costs are equal to the quantities of variable inputs used, multiplied by their prices.

See also FIXED FACTOR INPUT, RETURNS TO THE VARIABLE FACTOR INPUT.

variable overheads, *n.* any OVERHEADS that vary proportionately with the level of output of a product, so that variable-overhead cost per unit of output is constant. They include such items as fuel and lubricants, and salespersons' commissions. See also FIXED OVERHEADS, SEMIVARIABLE OVERHEADS.

variable factor proportions (law of), see RETURNS TO THE VARIABLE FACTOR-INPUT.

variance, *n.* **1.** the difference between budgeted and actual results (see BUDGETING), or between STANDARD COSTS/revenues and actual costs/revenues. Variances can be: (a) adverse or negative when actual revenues fall short of budget or standard, or when actual costs exceed budget or standard; (b) favourable or positive when actual revenues exceed budget or standard, or when actual costs are less than budget or standard. **2.** Also called *dispersion*. A measure of variation within a group of numerical observations, that is, the average of the squared deviations of the observations from the group MEAN.

See also STANDARD DEVIATION.

variance analysis, *n.* the analysis of differences between the STANDARD COST (revenue) of a product and its comparable actual cost (revenue) into their constituent parts. Variance analysis highlights matters which are not proceeding to plan, enabling managers to take corrective action to deal with losses or inefficiencies. The main variances are DIRECT-MATERIALS COST VARIANCE, the DIRECT-LABOUR COST VARIANCE, the OVERHEAD–COST VARIANCE and the SALES–REVENUE VARIANCE.

VAT, see VALUE-ADDED TAX.

Veblen, Thorstein Bunde (1857–1929) American economist whose concern about the consequences of the uncontrolled growth of large companies was first expressed in his book *The Theory of the Leisure Class* (1899). Veblen recognized that companies could be useful instruments for organizing production, but was concerned that large companies could be manipulated by managers so that the prosperity of business enterprises need not coincide with the welfare of the community. In the process of developing this thesis, Veblen attacked some of the materialist characteristics of the PRIVATE-ENTERPRISE ECONOMY, which he labelled 'pecuniary emulation', 'conspicuous leisure' and 'CONSPICUOUS CONSUMPTION'.

Veblen was also interested in the process of economic development and suggested that advances in productivity brought about by technology would increase economic depression, exacerbating conflict between workers and management on the one hand, and shareholders and the broader business community on the other. See also VEBLEN EFFECT.

Veblen effect, *n.* a theory of CONSUMPTION that suggests that consumers may have an UPWARD-SLOPING DEMAND CURVE as opposed to a downward-sloping DEMAND CURVE, because they practice CONSPICUOUS CONSUMPTION. A downward-sloping demand curve implies that the quantity demanded of a particular good varies inversely with its price (as price increases, quantity demanded falls). The Veblen effect suggests that quantity demanded of a particular good varies directly with a change in price (as price increases, demand increases).

See also VEBLEN, INCOME EFFECT, ENGELS LAW.

velocity of circulation, *n.* a measure of the average number of times each MONEY unit is used to purchase the year's output of final goods and services (GROSS DOMESTIC PRODUCT). If, for example, the total value of final output is £100 billion and the total MONEY SUPPLY is £10 billion, then, on average, each £1 unit has changed hands 10 times.

There is some controversy between the monetarist proponents of the QUANTITY THEORY OF MONEY and Keynesian economists about the stability of the velocity of circulation of money. Monetarists (see MONETARISM) hold that the velocity of circulation is stable or changes only slowly over time and so argue that there is a direct link between the money supply and the price level, and the rate of growth of money supply and rate of INFLATION. Keynesian economists (see KEYNESIAN ECONOMICS) argue that the velocity of circulation is unstable and that it can change rapidly, offsetting any changes in the money supply.

venture capital, *n.* any SHARE CAPITAL or LOANS subscribed to a firm by financial specialists (for example, the venture-capital arms of the commercial banks and insurance companies), thus enabling the firm to undertake investment in processes and products which because of their novelty are rated as especially high-risk projects, and as such would not normally attract conventional finance.

vertical firm, see FIRM.

vertical integration, *n.* an element of MARKET STRUCTURE in which a firm undertakes a number of successive stages in the supply of a product, as opposed to operating at only one stage (HORIZONTAL INTEGRATION). BACKWARD INTEGRATION occurs when a firm begins producing raw materials which were previously supplied to it by other firms (for example, a camera producer making glass lenses); FORWARD INTEGRATION occurs when a firm undertakes further finishing of a product, final assembly or distribution (for example, an oil company which sells petrol through its own petrol stations).

From the firm's point of view, vertical integration may be advantageous because it enables the firm to reduce its production and distribution costs by linking together successive activities, or because it is vital for it to secure reliable supplies of inputs or distribution outlets in order to remain competitive.

In terms of its wider impact on the operation of market processes, vertical integration may, on the one hand, promote greater efficiency in resource use, or, on the other hand, by limiting competition, lead to a less efficient allocation of resources.

Various efficiency gains may accrue through vertical integration. These include technical economies from combining together successive production processes, for example, the savings made in reheating costs by combining steel furnace operations. Stockholding economies can also arise from the reduction in intermediate contingency and buffer stocks. Vertically integrated firms can eliminate some purchasing and selling expenses in negotiating outside supply and advertising/selling contracts by internalizing these transactions within the firm (see INTERNALIZATION). Managerial economies may accrue by having a single administrative system to handle several production activities, and financial economies may accrue through more advantageous bulk-buying discounts, and by lowering the cost of raising capital. Where firms achieve such efficiency gains through vertical integration, their average costs will tend to fall, thus facilitating a lowering of market prices and an increase in output.

Where a firm *already* dominates one or more vertical stages, vertical integration may lead to various anticompetitive effects. Forward integration can secure a market but it can also foreclose it to competitors; similarly, backward integration can guarantee supply sources but it can also be used to prevent rivals gaining access to those sources. Moreover, if a firm acquires the supplier of a scarce raw material which is used by both itself and by its competitors, then it may be in a position to operate a PRICE SQUEEZE, that is, squeeze the profit margins of its competitors by raising their costs by charging them a higher price for the raw material than the price charged for its own use, while setting a relatively low final product price. Such tactics serve not only to discipline existing competitors, but also act as a BARRIER TO ENTRY to potential new competitors. Denied access to markets or materials or offered access only on disadvantageous terms, potential competitors would need to set up with the same degree of integration as existing firms, and the large initial capital requirements of such large-scale entry can be prohibitive.

Thus, vertical integration may produce, simultaneously, both beneficial or detrimental effects. Under UK MONOPOLY POLICY, vertical integration by an established monopoly firm, or a proposed MERGER between two vertically-related firms (or a TAKEOVER of one by the other) involving assets in excess of £30 million, can be referred to the MONOPOLIES AND MERGERS COMMISSION to determine whether or not it operates against the public interest.

See also TRANSFER PRICE, OFFICE OF FAIR TRADING.

very long run, *n*. an abstract time period in the THEORY OF SUPPLY allowing for the technological framework (known production methods) under which firms operate to change as a result of new INVENTIONS and knowledge. See also SHORT RUN, LONG RUN, INNOVATION, TECHNOLOGICAL PROGRESSIVENESS, RESEARCH AND DEVELOPMENT.

visible exports and imports, *n*. any GOODS such as raw materials and finished manufactures that can be seen and recorded as they cross the boundaries between countries. The net exports/imports of these goods constitute the BALANCE OF TRADE. Visible exports and imports, together with INVISIBLE EXPORTS AND IMPORTS make up the CURRENT ACCOUNT of a country's BALANCE OF PAYMENTS.

voting shares, *n*. the ORDINARY SHARES that allow the SHAREHOLDER to cast a vote for each share held at a company's ANNUAL GENERAL MEETING. See also SHARE CAPITAL.

W

wage differential, *n.* the payment of a different WAGE RATE to different groups of workers. Wage differentials arise from three main factors: (a) differences in interoccupational skills, training and responsibilities (surgeons are paid more than nurses, managers are paid more than labourers); (b) differences in inter-industry growth rates and PRODUCTIVITY levels (high-growth, high-productivity industries pay more than declining or low productivity industries; (c) differences between regions in income per head and local employment levels (prosperous areas in general pay more than depressed areas).

Wage differentials which encourage greater labour MOBILITY between occupations and industries and promote high levels of productivity play an important part in bringing about a more effective use of labour resources. On the other hand, some wage differentials contribute to both economic and social distortions, in particular those that reflect racial or sexual discrimination, and the exploitation of workers by powerful employers ('sweat-shop' labour). By the same token, 'unjustified' wage differentials arising out of the abuse of trade union monopoly power equally mitigate against the best use of labour resources.

wage-price spiral, see INFLATIONARY SPIRAL.

wage rate, *n.* the PRICE of LABOUR. In a competitive market the wage rate is determined by the demand for, and supply of, labour. The demand curve for labour as a factor input is downward-sloping (D in Fig. 200 on page 545), reflecting a fall in the marginal productivity of labour as more labour is used (see MARGINAL-PHYSICAL PRODUCT and MARGINAL-REVENUE PRODUCT). The supply curve (S) for labour is upward-sloping: the higher the wage rate the greater the amount of labour offered. The equilibrium wage rate is W_e where the two lines intersect.

See MINIMUM WAGE RATE, LABOUR MARKET, TRADE UNION, COLLECTIVE BARGAINING, PRICES–AND–INCOMES POLICY.

wage restraint, see PRICES–AND–INCOMES POLICY.

wages, *n.* the payments made to workers for the use of their LABOUR as a FACTOR OF PRODUCTION. In aggregate terms, wages are a source of

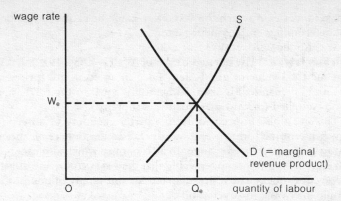

Fig. 200. **Wage rate**. See main entry.

income and are included as a part of NATIONAL INCOME.

See also WAGE RATE, NATIONAL–INCOME ACCOUNTS.

wages drift, see EARNINGS DRIFT.

wages freeze, see PRICES–AND–INCOMES POLICY.

wages-fund theory, *n.* a theory developed by the classical economists (see CLASSICAL ECONOMICS) which states that total WAGES in an economy are limited to the extent of available CAPITAL used for paying wages. Notationally this can be written:

$$W = \frac{C}{L}$$

where W = wages per labour unit, C = capital stock for paying wages, L = wage-earning labour force.

The 'natural' wage rate is the *subsistence-wage rate*. In the short term it is possible for wage-earners to be paid in excess of their 'natural' rate due to short-term fluctuations in demand (the wages fund, C, above) and supply (the LABOUR FORCE, L, above). However, in the longer term, the 'natural' wage rate could only be increased if C increased or L decreased.

The wages-fund theory came under increasing criticism, as people argued that it was difficult to attach a specific portion of capital to wage payments. Rather, it came to be accepted that wage rates depended on the forces of demand and supply in the LABOUR MARKET. The wages-fund theory thus fell into disfavour and was subsequently replaced by labour market theories in which the MARGINAL-REVENUE PRODUCT of labour is the determining employment factor.

See also RICARDO, MARX.

Walras's law, *n.* a law devised by Marie Walras (1834–1910) that states that the total value of goods demanded in an economy (prices times quantities demanded) is always identically equal to the total value of goods supplied (prices times quantities supplied).

This situation can occur only in a barter economy or an economy which uses some form of MONEY for transactions where all money is immediately used for exchange. In an economy which also uses money as a store of value, it is conceivable that the DEMAND for and SUPPLY of money does not equate to the demand for and supply of goods, that is, people may SAVE (or overspend).

The study of such interrelations of markets for goods throughout the economy is termed GENERAL-EQUILIBRIUM ANALYSIS. Walras utilized simultaneous equations to show the effect a change in the demand and supply of one good would have on all other goods in a situation of general equilibrium. See also SAY'S LAW.

wants, *n.* the desire for GOODS and SERVICES. The attempt to satisfy wants forms the basis of all economic activity. Wants are expressed in the market place not by need or desire but by the willingness and ability to actually purchase the good or service in DEMAND. See also ECONOMICS.

wasting asset, *n.* any NATURAL RESOURCES such as coal and oil that have a finite but indeterminate life span depending upon the rate of depletion. See ASSET.

Total marketable wealth		£762 billion %
Most wealthy	1%	21
,, ,,	5%	39
,, ,,	10%	52
,, ,,	25%	75
,, ,,	50%	93

Fig. 201. **Wealth.** The distribution of marketable wealth in the UK, 1984. The total includes land and dwellings (net of mortgage debt), consumer durables, stocks and shares, bank and building society deposits and other financial assets. Source: *Social Trends*, 1987.

wealth, *n.* the stock of net ASSETS owned by individuals or households. In aggregate terms, one widely used measure of the nations' total stock of wealth is that of 'marketable wealth' that is, physical and financial assets which are relatively liquid (see LIQUIDITY). Marketable wealth is not equally distributed in the UK as Fig. 201 shows. In 1982, the richest 5% of the population owned 41% of marketable wealth.

wealth tax, *n*. a TAX levied on a person's private ASSETS when those assets are transferred to the person's beneficiaries. Wealth taxes can be used to redistribute WEALTH within the community as part of governmental policy in INCOME DISTRIBUTION. The UK's wealth tax has taken various forms over the years, notably *estate duties, capital-transfer tax and inheritance tax*.

wear and tear, *n*. the gradual deterioration in the efficiency (and value) of a productive ASSET through constant use. See also DEPRECIATION (2), CAPITAL CONSUMPTION.

weighted average, *n*. a form of arithmetic average, or MEAN, in which each of the items used in a calculation is attached a weight, or importance, to reflect the fact that not all items carry the same importance but may vary relative to each other. Weighted averages are frequently used in price indices to reflect the percentage of a CONSUMER's budget spent on various items to enable a more accurate, or representative, mean price increase to be found. For example, a consumer's STANDARD OF LIVING may be represented hypothetically by three typical purchased goods, A, B and C. Over the time period in question, the three goods have increased in price by 35, 10 and 45 per cent respectively. A consumer, let us assume, spends all of his INCOME on these goods in the proportion 20, 50 and 30 per cent respectively. An unweighted average would give an average mean price increase of:

$$\frac{35 + 10 + 45}{3} = 30\%$$

A weighted average, on the other hand, would give:

$$\frac{\dfrac{20}{100} \times 135 + \dfrac{50}{100} \times 110 + \dfrac{30}{100} \times 145}{\dfrac{20 + 50 + 30}{100}}\%$$

i.e., $(20\% \times 35\%) + (50\% \times 10\%) + (30\% \times 45\%)$.

$$= 7 + 5 + 13.5 = \underline{25.5\%}.$$

The weighted figure is a more representative average mean-price increase because not only have the price increases been taken into account but also the proportion, or weight, of the price increase has been included. Where the denominator is not a percentage but real numbers, the sum of weights is added and becomes the denominator. For example, if the weights attached to three goods were 8, 5 and 2, then the denominator is $8+5+2$, that is, 15.

See also INDEX NUMBER, PRICE INDEX.

welfare criteria, see WELFARE ECONOMICS.

welfare economics, *n.* a normative branch of economics that is concerned with the way economic activity ought to be arranged so as to maximize economic welfare. Welfare economics employs value judgements about what *ought* to be produced, how production *should* be organized, the way income and wealth *ought* to be distributed, both now and in the future. Unfortunately each individual in a community has a unique set of value judgements which are dependent upon his attitudes, religion, philosophy and politics, and the economist has difficulty in aggregating these value judgements in advising policy makers about decisions which affect the allocation of resources (which involves making *interpersonal comparisons* of UTILITY).

Economists have tried for many years to develop criteria for judging economic efficiency to use as a guide in evaluating actual resource deployments. The classical economists treated utility (see CLASSICAL ECONOMICS) as if it was a measurable scale of consumer satisfaction, and the early welfare economists such as PIGOU continued in their vein, so that they were able to talk in terms of changes in the pattern of economic activity either increasing or decreasing economic welfare. However, once economists rejected the idea that utility was measurable then they had to accept that economic welfare is immeasurable, and that any statement about welfare is a value judgement influenced by the preferences and priorities of those making the judgement. This led to a search for *welfare criteria* which avoided making interpersonal comparisons of utility by introducing explicit value judgements as to whether or not welfare has increased.

The simplest criterion was developed by Vilfredo PARETO, who argued that any reallocation of resources involving a change in goods produced and/or their distribution amongst consumers, could be considered an improvement if it made some people better off (in their own estimation) without making anyone else worse off. The Pareto criterion avoids making interpersonal comparisons by dealing only with uncontroversial cases where no one is harmed. However, this makes the criterion inapplicable to the majority of policy proposals which benefit some and harm others, without compensation.

Nicholas Kaldor and John Hicks suggested an alternative criterion (the *compensation principle*), proposing that any economic change or reorganization should be considered beneficial if, after the change, gainers could hypothetically compensate the losers and still be better off. In effect, this criterion subdivides the effects of any change into two parts: (a) efficiency gains/losses, and (b) income-distribution consequences. As long as the gainers evaluate their gains at a higher figure than the value which losers set upon their losses, then this efficiency gain justifies the change, even though (in the absence of actual compensation payments) income redistribution has occurred. Where the gainers from a change fully compensate the losers and still show a net gain this would rate as an improvement under the Pareto criterion.

In addition to developing welfare criteria, economists such as Paul Samuelson have attempted to construct a *social-welfare function* which can offer guidance as to whether one economic configuration is better or worse than another. The social-welfare function can be regarded as a function of the welfare of each consumer. However, in order to construct a social-welfare function it is necessary to take the preferences of each consumer and aggregate them into a community-preference ordering, and some economists, such as Kenneth Arrow, have questioned whether consistent and noncontradictory community orderings are possible. For example, take a community of three people 1, 2 and 3 choosing among three alternative policies A, B and C: individual 1 prefers A to B and B to C hence A to C; individual 2 prefers B to C and C to A hence B to A; individual 3 prefers C to A and A to B hence C to B.

If we now try and aggregate these individually-consistent preferences on the basis of majority rule, we find that: 2 out of 3 prefer A to B; 2 out of 3 prefer B to C; so that logically there should be a social preference for A over C, yet 2 out of 3 prefer C to A.

See also NORMATIVE ECONOMICS, RESOURCE ALLOCATION, UTILITY FUNCTION, CARDINAL UTILITY, ORDINAL UTILITY.

welfare state, *n*. a country that provides comprehensive SOCIAL-SECURITY BENEFITS such as state health services, state retirement pensions, unemployment and sickness benefits, etc. See also TRANSFER PAYMENTS, GOVERNMENT EXPENDITURE.

white knight, see TAKEOVER BID.

wholesaling, *n*. the bulk-purchasing of products from manufacturers in order to hold large quantities of stock for physical distribution, and the reselling of these products (in smaller consignments) to retailers. These functions can be performed either by an independent wholesaler acting as an intermediary between manufacturers and retailers or the functions may be undertaken directly by the larger retailers themselves.

See also INTERNALIZATION, RETAILING.

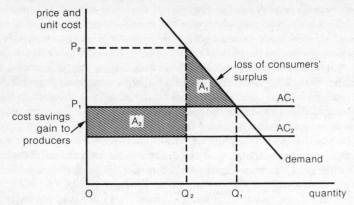

Fig. 202. **Williamson trade-off model**. See main entry.

Williamson trade-off model, *n.* a model devised by Oliver Williamson (b. 1932) for the evaluation of the possible benefits (lower costs) and detriments (higher prices) of a proposed MERGER which can be used in the application of a DISCRETIONARY MONOPOLY POLICY.

Fig. 202 depicts the case of a proposed merger which would introduce market power into a previously competitive market situation. In the premerger market, firms are assumed to produce on identical and constant average-cost curves which are represented in aggregate by AC_1. The competitive price OP_1 is identical with AC_1 (a NORMAL-PROFIT equilibrium) and the competitive output rate is OQ_1. By contrast, the post-merger combine is shown to produce on a lower constant average-cost curve, depicted by AC_2, but to establish a price not merely in excess of AC_2 but in excess of AC_1 (i.e., a price higher than in the competitive case *despite* the availability of ECONOMIES OF SCALE). In such circumstances, a welfare trade-off is required between the loss of CONSUMERS' SURPLUS due to the higher price (the shaded area A_1) and the cost savings gain to the producer (the shaded area A_2). In simple terms, if A_1 exceeds A_2, the merger should be disallowed; if A_2 exceeds A_1, the merger should be allowed to proceed. However, even in the latter case there are problems. Any benefits arising from a merger through cost savings accrue initially to producers. For there to be a benefit to consumers these gains must be passed on – but because of the increase in monopoly power there is no guarantee that they will be.

See also MONOPOLY POLICY, PUBLIC INTEREST.

withdrawals or **leakages,** *n.* that part of NATIONAL INCOME not spent by households on the CONSUMPTION of domestically produced goods and services. In the basic CIRCULAR FLOW OF NATIONAL INCOME MODEL all of the income received by households is spent on current consumption. In the extended circular flow of income model, some of the income received by households is saved, some of it is taxed and some of it is spent on imported goods and services. Thus, SAVINGS, TAXATION and IMPORTS constitute withdrawals or 'leakages' from the income-spending flow. Compare INJECTIONS. See also PROPENSITY TO SAVE, PROPENSITY TO TAXATION, PROPENSITY TO IMPORT.

Standards of Structure
1. A large or an appreciable number of suppliers, none of whom dominates the market, or at least as many as scale economies permit.
2. No artificial barriers to entry.
3. Moderate and price-sensitive quality differentials.

Standards of Conduct
1. Active competition between rival suppliers, avoiding collusive agreements to fix prices, market shares, etc.
2. No use of exclusionary or coercive tactics (exclusive dealings, refusal to supply, tie-in contracts) aimed at harming rival suppliers.
3. Sensitivity towards consumers' demands for product variety.

Standards of Performance
1. Minimization of supply costs.
2. Prices consistent with supply costs, including a 'fair' profit return to suppliers in relation to efficiency, risks, investment and innovation.
3. Avoidance of excessive promotional expenses.
4. The introduction of new technology and new products.

Fig. 203. **Workable competition**. The standards of structure, conduct and performance.

workable competition, *n.* the specification of standards of MARKET STRUCTURE and MARKET CONDUCT that are likely to result in an 'acceptable' MARKET PERFORMANCE. Fig. 203 lists one such classification.

Definitions of workable competition represent an effort to provide more useful guidelines in applying MONOPOLY POLICY to real world markets than can be drawn from the theoretical 'ideal' state of PERFECT COMPETITION. There are, however, important operational difficulties involved in stipulating acceptable norms, for example: what is meant by an 'appreciable' number of firms?; how is it to be established?; what levels of profits are 'fair'?

See also MARKET STRUCTURE–CONDUCT–PERFORMANCE SCHEMA, CONTESTABLE MARKETS, PUBLIC INTEREST, THEORY OF MARKETS, MONOPOLY.

worker participation, *n.* the involvement of employees in the decision-making processes of the FIRM that extends beyond those decisions implicit in the specific content of the jobs that they do. Worker participation most commonly refers to those processes or activities which occur at the workplace: for example, suggestion boxes for workers, job-enrichment schemes such as job rotation, or even the actual devolution of work planning to Works Councils or group supervisors.

The term INDUSTRIAL DEMOCRACY is often used as a synonym for worker participation, but industrial democracy in fact denotes power sharing by the workers with management in corporate decisions decided at higher levels in the organization (that is, up to board of directors level). Whereas worker participation implies the direct involvement of the employee, industrial democracy suggests a system of representation and is thus more consummate with the principle of TRADE UNION representation, joint consultation between managers and worker representations, and worker directors (that is, worker representatives sitting on the board of directors).

Often the more complex systems of worker participation and industrial democracy cannot operate without a management willingness to disclose information on profitability, investment, new technology, working conditions and job prospects to the employee representatives for bargaining purposes.

There is considerable controversy about the effects of the extension of worker participation upon economic efficiency.

At the operational level, worker participation can improve PRODUCTIVITY (output per man) by instilling a greater commitment to, and sense of achievement in, group activities. At the strategic level, major decisions relating to new investment, the introduction of new machinery, etc., may be impaired, it could be argued, by the involvement of too many vested interests when what is required is a more detached longer-term view of the issues involved.

working capital, *n.* an accounting term denoting a firm's short-term CURRENT ASSETS which are turned over fairly quickly in the course of business. They include raw materials, work-in-progress and finished goods STOCKS, DEBTORS and cash, less short-term CURRENT LIABILITIES. Increases in the volume of company trading generally lead to increases in stocks and amounts owed by debtors, and so to an increase in working capital required. Reductions in delays between paying for materials, converting them to products, selling them and getting cash in from customers, will tend to reduce the working capital needed.

See also OVERTRADING, WORKING-CAPITAL RATIO, CASH FLOW, CREDIT CONTROL, SOURCES-AND-USES-OF-FUNDS STATEMENT, STOCK CONTROL, FACTORING.

working-capital ratio, *n.* an accounting measure of a firm's ability to pay its short-term liabilities out of CURRENT ASSETS, which expresses the firm's current assets as a ratio of CURRENT LIABILITIES.

See also CURRENT RATIO, ACID-TEST RATIO, WORKING CAPITAL, CASH FLOW.

work in progress, *n.* any goods that are still in the process of being made up into their final form. Work in progress together with raw materials and STOCKS of finished goods constitute INVENTORY INVESTMENT.

works cost, see FACTORY COST.

work study, *n.* a discipline concerned with determining how LABOUR can be most efficiently employed in relation to other FACTOR INPUTS. Work-study officers examine the time and effort an employee, or group of employees, takes to fulfil a certain task, and then analyse the possibility of rearranging the inputs to achieve a reduction in time or effort whilst maintaining or increasing output. The discipline of work study has two main branches: (a) method study, which is concerned with analysing the methods employed in doing jobs with a view to improving these methods; (b) time study, which seeks to measure the time required to perform jobs.

See also PRODUCTIVITY.

World Bank or **International Bank for Reconstruction and Development,** *n.* a multinational institution set up in 1947 (following the Bretton Woods Conference, 1944) to provide ECONOMIC AID to member countries – mainly DEVELOPING COUNTRIES – to strengthen their economies. The Bank has supported a wide range of long-term investments including infrastructure projects to do with roads, telecommunications and electricity supply, agriculture, industrial projects including the establishment of new industries, as well as social, training and educational programmes.

The Bank's funds come largely from the developed countries, but it also raises money on international capital markets. The Bank operates according to 'business principles' lending at commercial rates of interest only to those governments it feels are capable of servicing and repaying their debts. In 1960, however, it established an affiliate agency, the *International Development Association*, to provide low-interest loans to its poorer members.

Another affiliate of the World Bank is the *International Finance Corporation* which can invest directly in companies by acquiring shares.

XYZ

X-inefficiency, *n.* the 'gap' between the actual and minimum attainable supply costs. See Fig. 204. The traditional THEORY OF SUPPLY assumes that firms always operate on the outer boundary of their attainable cost-curves. In contrast, X-inefficiency postulates that firms typically operate within the outer boundary. This occurs, for example, because of inefficiencies in work organization (RESTRICTIVE LABOUR PRACTICES such as OVERMANNING, demarcation rules) and in the coordination of activities (inefficient deployment and management of resources arising from bureaucratic rigidities). X-inefficiency is likely to be present in large organizations which lack effective competition 'to keep them on their toes' (especially MONOPOLIES).

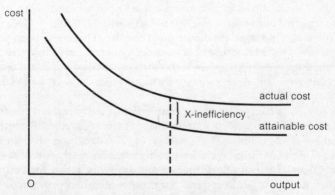

Fig. 204. **X-inefficiency**. See main entry.

See also PRODUCTIVITY, ORGANIZATIONAL SLACK.

yield, see EFFECTIVE RATE OF INTEREST.

yield curve, *n.* a line that traces the relationship between the rates of return on BONDS of different maturities. The slope of the line suggests whether RATES OF INTEREST are tending to rise or fall.

zero-based budgeting, *n.* a management accounting technique that seeks to re-examine and challenge the assumptions underlying a firm's costs. Zero-based BUDGETING involves preparing a budget for each company department from scratch, starting from the basic premise that each department's budget is zero, then justifying every activity and its associated expenditure before it can be included in the budget. This contrasts with conventional budgeting, where departmental budgets are often based on last year's budget suitably updated. The purpose of this process is to identify and remove inefficient or obsolete activities within the firm.

See also X-INEFFICIENCY.

zero-sum game, *n.* a situation in GAME THEORY where game players compete for the given total payoff, so that gains by one player are at the direct expense of the other player(s). For example, where two firms compete against each other in a mature market where total sales are not expanding then each firm can only increase its sales and market share at the expense of its competitor.

Z-scale, *n.* a statistical term for the transformed scale of values applied to observations of a variable with a NORMAL DISTRIBUTION, which have been converted to give them a zero MEAN and unit STANDARD DEVIATION. Use of the Z-scale allows us to convert any set of observations of a variable into standard units with mean $= 0$ and standard deviation $= 1$, regardless of the mean and standard deviation of that set. This conversion permits us to use a single table for the area under a normal curve for purposes of estimating PROBABILITIES and HYPOTHESIS TESTING, and to compare directly sets of observations with different means and standard deviations.

Z-score, *n.* a composite score, summarizing the weighted results of a number of ACCOUNTING RATIOS, that claims to predict a company's likelihood of failure. The concept of Z-scores was developed by applying the statistical technique of discriminant analysis to distinguish the values of various performance-and-liquidity ratios for companies which had gone bankrupt and for those which had prospered. Those accounting ratios which proved to discriminate effectively between failed companies and successful ones were incorporated in a standard formula to calculate an aggregate Z-score. Analysts can calculate Z-scores for particular companies, and use the results to predict whether companies are likely to fail.

APPENDIX: Mathematical Symbols

$\triangle$	change in a variable
∞	infinity
$\geqslant$	more than or equal to
$\leqslant$	less than or equal to
t	current time period
$t-1$	previous time period
$t+1$	next time period
f	function of
r	rate of interest
Σ	[Greek sigma] sum of

COLLINS REFERENCE

COLLINS REFERENCE DICTIONARIES form a new series of paperback subject dictionaries covering a wide variety of academic and general topics, ranging from Biology to Business, and from Maths to Music. Collins Reference Dictionaries fully maintain the reputation of Collins English and bilingual dictionaries for clarity, authority, comprehensiveness and ease-of-use.

For the series, Collins have commissioned expert authors who combine a profound understanding of their subject with great skill and experience in explaining and clarifying difficult terms and concepts. A consistent style and approach is adopted throughout the series with encyclopedic-style explanations following each precise initial definition. Where appropriate, extensive use is made of worked examples, line illustrations, graphs and tables to further aid the reader.

The academic titles are primarily designed to meet the needs of undergraduates, although the dictionaries will also be of considerable value to advanced school students and to people working in related disciplines. The general titles will provide the layman with comprehensive, lively and up-to-date reference works for a wide range of subjects.

Details of some of this exciting new range of dictionaries can be found on the following pages.

COLLINS DICTIONARY OF MATHEMATICS

Ephraim Borowski and Jonathan Borwein

Containing over 4,000 entries and 400 diagrams, this is the only reference work at this level to present this coverage at an accessible price. Covering an enormous range of technical terms from both pure and applied maths, the Dictionary goes beyond basic definitions to provide helpful explanations and examples, geared to the level of student who is liable to be looking up the particular term.

At undergraduate level, the reader will find extensive information on such fields as real and complex analysis, abstract algebra, number theory, metamathematics and the foundations of mathematics, topology, vector calculus, continuum mechanics, differential equations, measure theory, and graph theory. At the advanced school level the subjects covered include set theory, matrices, trigonometry and geometry, calculus, mechanics, statistics, and logic. The biographies of major mathematicians and the discursive explanations of paradoxes also make the Dictionary interesting and informative for the browser, and help to round off what will be an ideal course companion at many levels.

Ephraim Borowski, B.Phil., is a lecturer in philosophy at Glasgow University with a particular interest in logic and the philosophy of mathematics. He is also mathematics consultant to the *Collins English Dictionary*. Dr Jonathan Borwein is a professor of mathematics at Dalhousie University, Nova Scotia.

ISBN 0 00 434347 6

COLLINS DICTIONARY OF ELECTRONICS

Ian R. Sinclair

The *Collins Dictionary of Electronics* is a completely new and up-to-date guide to the science and technology of electronics. Containing over 2,000 entries, from *aberration* to *zero error*, the Dictionary also includes over 100 diagrams, together with lists of symbols used in electronics.

The Dictionary is intended for anyone who needs a source book providing clear, helpful definitions of electronic terms, including advanced school students and those embarking on higher-education courses, as well as technicians and hobbyists. The Dictionary will also prove useful to anyone whose work or study involves the use of electronic devices — which now have become vital tools in areas as diverse as music, archaeology and medicine.

The Dictionary guides the reader through the various fields within electronics such as microprocessor technology, digital electronics, telecommunications, hi-fi, radio, and television. The emphasis throughout is on the practical application of concepts and devices, although the theoretical background is also well covered, and the reader will find entries on such topics as the *superposition theorem*, the *Biot-Savart law*, and the *permeability* and *permittivity of free space*. Where appropriate, the mathematical aspect of a topic is introduced, although this is generally avoided.

Ian R. Sinclair is a professional technical author. He has written many books on computing for Collins, including the *Collins Dictionary of Computing*.

ISBN 0 00 434345 X

COLLINS DICTIONARY OF BIOLOGY

W. G. Hale and J. P. Margham

The *Collins Dictionary of Biology* is a completely new, authoritative and comprehensive guide to the complex discipline of biology. The book is directed primarily to the needs of undergraduates and advanced school students, but will also prove an invaluable source book for anyone with an interest in this wide-ranging and fascinating subject.

The Dictionary has over 5,600 entries ranging from *abdomen* to *zymogen*. There are also 285 diagrams illustrating such features as the generalized structures of animals, genetic organization, parts of plants and animals, etc., plus numerous tables.

All the major fields within biology are covered, including anatomy, biochemistry, ecology, genetics, physiology, evolutionary theory and taxonomy. The entries have been structured to provide more than an isolated definition of the term in question. An entry such as *acquired characters* is thus set in the context of the development of evolutionary theory, while the series of genetic entries guides the reader through such concepts as the basis of *genetic code* and the industrial implications of *genetic engineering*. The Dictionary also includes brief biographies of major biologists.

Professor Hale is Dean of the Faculty of Science and Head of the Department of Biology at Liverpool Polytechnic. Dr Margham is Principal Lecturer and Course Leader for the B.Sc. Honours Applied Biology Degree at Liverpool Polytechnic.

ISBN 0 00 434351 4

COLLINS DICTIONARY OF COMPUTING

Ian R. Sinclair

Aimed primarily at those using microcomputers as a tool – whether it be at university, school or college, or in the home or office – rather than the professional computer expert, the Dictionary will also prove invaluable to anyone whose work is related in any way to computers, be they micro, mini or mainframe.

Far too many computer manuals assume that even the beginner knows the meaning of a vast array of specialized jargon, leaving the user in a state of near despair. Although not a handbook to particular machines, *Collins Dictionary of Computing* contains definitions and explanations of over 2,000 of the terms that the average user is most likely to come across, from *access* to *zero compression*. Written with a clarity and precision that will be welcomed by all computer users, the entries are augmented by nearly 100 diagrams and explanatory captions.

Comprehensive without indulging in unnecessary padding, and of course completely up-to-date, the Dictionary includes such basic terms as *BASIC*, *bit* and *binary*, as well as those strange terms that computer buffs have made peculiarly their own, such as *blow*, *bomb* and *bubble*. Fields covered range through hardware, software, programming, computer logic, data and word processing, languages, systems, and graphics, to those areas of information technology in which computers play such a vital role.

Ian Sinclair, a full-time technical author, has written numerous best-selling computer books for Collins, and is also author of the *Collins Dictionary of Electronics*.

ISBN 0 00 434349 2

COLLINS DICTIONARY OF STATISTICS

Roger Porkess

The *Collins Dictionary of Statistics* is a new and authoritative guide to a subject which has seen a marked increase in its teaching and applications in recent years, in the academic sphere and beyond.

Encyclopedic in treatment after each initial definition, its 426 entries have been selected primarily to cater for the needs of students studying mathematics for university entrance exams, at A level or similar, and for those studying statistics as a service subject in higher education such as scientists and social scientists. However, the Dictionary will also prove to be an invaluable reference guide for the informed layman with a professional interest in the subject.

A comprehensive range of concepts and terms are covered – from *abscissa* to *z-transformation* – including how various statistical measures are calculated and their tests applied. Many of the more advanced topics are dealt with at length and the text contains over 100 graphs and diagrams and numerous worked examples to aid the reader. The Dictionary also contains a useful series of appendices which include full lists of symbols and formulae used, together with the statistical tables required for the tests and techniques described within the book.

Roger Porkess is Head of Mathematics at Denstone College, Uttoxeter and is an experienced A-level examiner. He has written several textbooks, including *Mathematics: a Complete Course for First Examinations*, and the Datalog computing books.

ISBN 0 00 434354 9

COLLINS DICTIONARY OF MUSIC

Sir Jack Westrup and F. L. Harrison
Revised by Conrad Wilson

Collins Dictionary of Music is a concise third edition of the critically acclaimed *Collins Encyclopedia of Music*, and brings that work right up to date with the inclusion of entries on such figures as Jessye Norman, Michael Berkeley, Arvo Pärt, Nigel Osborne, Janet Glover, Philip Glass, Steve Reich and Nigel Kennedy. In addition, existing entries have been updated with, for example, the inclusion of composers' new works, and details of performers' recent careers.

Covering the whole field of Western music, over 6,500 articles describe composers, instruments, compositions, technical terms, performers, musical forms, periods, styles, movements, critics, musicologists, librettists, instrument makers, orchestras, and opera companies.

The essay-length articles on the major composers include a biographical outline and an assessment of their achievements, together with a list of their principal compositions. Extensive articles have also been devoted to such topics as the history of opera, ballet, film music, and music criticism. The numerous articles on musical theory and notation, carefully cross-referenced, are clarified by the use of music examples, and there is also an appendix of signs and symbols.

The late Sir Jack Westrup was Oxford Professor of Music and one of the foremost musical scholars of his day. Frank Harrison has had a distinguished teaching career, his posts having included professorships at Amsterdam, Yale and Princeton. Conrad Wilson, who also revised the second edition, is music critic of *The Scotsman*.

ISBN 0 00 434356 5

COLLINS DICTIONARY OF ART AND ARTISTS

General Editor: Sir David Piper

Collins Dictionary of Art and Artists is the most up-to-date and comprehensive dictionary of art available in paperback. It covers all schools and periods of Western art – from the Ancient Greeks to the present day – in almost 3,000 entries. As well as the giants of painting and sculpture, the Dictionary also includes many fascinating minor figures, and in addition there are entries on groups, movements, writers on art, materials, and techniques.

Contributed by a panel of more than 70 scholars under the General Editorship of Sir David Piper, the entries are succinct, accurate and lively, forming an authoritative guide to all the names and terms the general reader might wish to look up. Entries range in length from a few lines up to 700 words, and although they are concise they do much more than simply list facts. Artists are firmly characterized so as to give the reader a clear idea not only of their work but also of their significance in the history of art. Thousands of works of art are cited, with dates and locations, and the text is enlivened with contemporary anecdotes and quotations.

Sir David Piper is Director of the Ashmolean Museum in Oxford, and one of the most distinguished art historians and critics of his generation. His numerous publications range from the scholarly to the popular, and he has reached a wide audience as one of the presenters of the BBC television series *100 Great Paintings*.

ISBN 0 00 434358 1